An Introduction to Native North America

Second Edition

MARK Q. SUTTON

California State University, Bakersfield

PEARSON

Boston / New York / San Francisco
Mexico City / Montreal / Toronto
London / Madrid / Munich / Paris
Hong Kong / Singapore / Tokyo
Cape Town / Sydney

To my parents, Ray and Jean

Series Editor: *Jennifer Jacobson*
Editorial Assistant: *Amy Holborow*
Production Administrator: *Deborah Brown*
Composition and Prepress Buyer: *Linda Cox*
Manufacturing Buyer: *JoAnne Sweeney*

Cover Administrator: *Joel Gendron*
Editorial-Production Service: *Barbara Gracia*
Copyeditor: *Susanna Brougham*
Text Designer: *Melinda Grosser for* silk
Electronic Composition: *Omegatype Typography, Inc.*

Library of Congress Cataloging-in-Publication Data

Sutton, Mark Q.
    An introduction to native North America / Mark Q. Sutton—2nd ed.
      p.   cm.
    Includes bibliographical references and index.
    ISBN 0-205-38848-5
    1. Indians of North America. 2. Eskimos. 3. Aleuts. I. Title.
E77.S935   2003
970.004'97—dc21

Printed in the United States of America
10 9 8 7 6 5 4 3 2   — 08 07 06 05 04

Contents

6   Native Peoples of the Northwest Coast   123

7   Native Peoples of the Great Basin   151

8 Native Peoples of California 177

9 Native Peoples of the Southwest 202

Preface

The second edition of *An Introduction to Native North America* provides a comprehensive, yet introductory, perspective of the native peoples that inhabit the North American continent. A major reason for producing this second edition was to update Chapter 10, "Native Peoples of the Plains," with materials now available in the recently published volume 13 of the *Handbook of North American Indians,* unavailable when the first edition was written. Thus, the Plains chapter has been substantially revised. In addition, I have added some photographs and a map of language families; I have also expanded and updated other materials, correcting some factual errors. This edition, current through 2002, also incorporates information gathered from my recent visits to a number of groups and reservations.

In response to suggestions from reviewers, I expanded the sections on contemporary native peoples, and included some interactive materials at the end of the regional chapters, in order to provide direction for students to further explore contemporary issues themselves.

The prehistory sections that begin the regional chapters are brief. Though some colleagues suggested that they be expanded to better engage the students, others suggested that they be dropped since most universities offer a separate course on North American prehistory. In the end, I left them as they were (but updated them). This book concerns ethnography, not prehistory, but I do think beginning students would benefit from a basic background in prehistory.

Finally, an Instructor's Manual and Test Bank is available to supplement the second edition. Many reviewers and adopters specifically requested this ancillary.

Acknowledgments

A number of colleagues have taken the time to suggest improvements to the first edition of this book, and I am indebted to them for their efforts. In addition to the excellent comments and suggestions provided by Philip J. Carr, University of

Southern Alabama; Linda B. Eaton, Weber State University; Eileen M. Luna, University of Arizona; and Linda R. Locklear, Palomar College, I benefited from the thoughts of Jill K. Gardner, Brian E. Hemphill, Henry C. Koerper, Krista Moreland, and Richard H. Osborne.

M.Q.S.

I Introduction

///

In 1492, Christopher Columbus sailed west from Spain, looking for a direct and shorter route to the Indies. Instead, he landed on a small island in the Caribbean and encountered a New World occupied by many millions of people belonging to hundreds, perhaps as many as a thousand, different cultures, some of which were as complex as any in the world. Europeans wanted to believe that they had "discovered" a new land, untouched and pristine, a land occupied by wandering, primitive savages who did not "properly" possess the land. They believed it their duty to drag the native populations from their state of savagery into the light of civilization. These beliefs served to justify the conquest of the New World and are still widely held today.

Despite the onslaught of Europeans, native peoples have survived and form a part of the intricate web of contemporary American culture. The native cultures encountered by Europeans were incredibly diverse, ranging from small bands of hunters and gatherers to huge groups with highly complex social and political institutions. This diversity and heritage deserve to be studied and celebrated as part of the collective history of all people. This study will in turn help preserve and contribute to understanding of Native American cultures, increase appreciation of cultural diversity, and combat racism and ethnocentrism. Furthermore, if we look into how native peoples adapted to their environments, we can learn from their successes and failures.

The Geography of North America

Prior to 1492, Europeans thought they knew the geography of the world and the location of its major land masses and bodies of water. The landmasses consisted

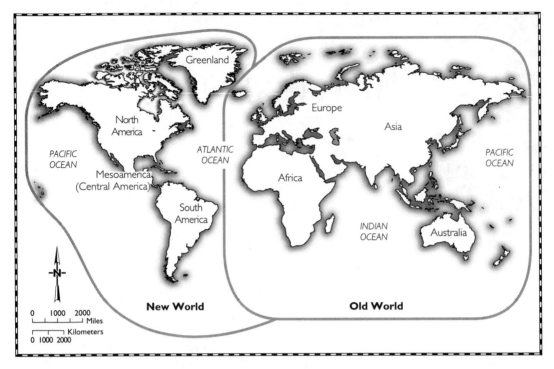

FIGURE 1.1   Simplified map of the world, showing both New and Old Worlds

of Europe, Africa, Asia, and many of the islands of the western Pacific. However, once a huge new landmass full of unfamiliar people had been discovered, it was seen as a "New World," a name that continues to be used today (Fig. 1.1). The world known to the Europeans prior to 1492 was subsequently referred to as the Old World, a term by which it is still known. Today, the New World is also known as the western hemisphere and the Old World as the eastern hemisphere.

The New World is often described as comprising two continents: (1) North America, which extends from the Arctic to Panama, and (2) South America, which runs from Colombia to the southern tip of Chile. However, it is now common for the New World to be thought of as three regions: North, Central, and South America. Many people consider North America to consist of the United States and Canada; Central America to include Mexico and all the countries south to Colombia; and South America to extend from Colombia to the southern tip of Chile. A third way to conceptualize the New World is based on broad cultural distinctions, leading to the specification of three somewhat different regions: North America, Mesoamerica (*meso* meaning "middle"), and South America (Fig. 1.2). According to this frame of reference, the southern boundary of North America is located in northern Mexico. The modern border between the United States and Mexico is not relevant to a definition of past cultures. This frame of reference is used in this book.

After defining the southern boundary of North America, the question arises as to whether to include Greenland to the north. Some researchers include Greenland

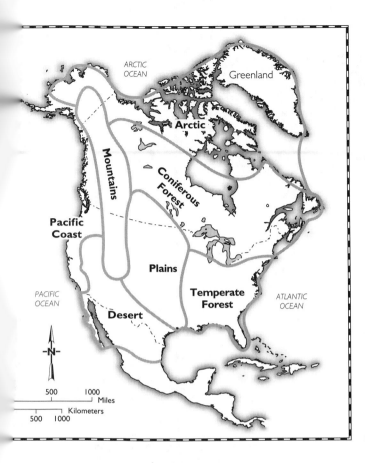

FIGURE 1.3 Major natural areas of North America

Culture Areas

Researchers recognized early on that cultures in similar environments tend to be similar to one another, sharing some aspects of economy, politics, and even language. Large-scale geographic regions where environment and culture were similar were defined in the late 1890s and called culture areas, first in North and South America (Mason 1894), then in other areas of the world. The definition of a culture area is never precise, and there is considerable argument over how many there are, where their boundaries are, which groups should be included in each, and even whether culture areas should be defined at all. Ten culture areas are defined herein, following the *Handbook of North American Indians* (see Fig. 1.4).

Using the culture area concept gives anthropologists the opportunity to compare cultures within broadly similar environments and to determine the extent of influence from cultures outside a particular culture area (diffusion, migrations, etc.). In spite of many weaknesses—such as defining a single area that contains considerable cultural and/or environmental diversity, the use of somewhat arbitrary criteria, the assumption that a static cultural situation exists, and the tendency to equate environment with cause—the culture area concept continues to be useful as a point of comparison and reference. Most anthropologists use this concept,

FIGURE 1.2
divisions of the I

as part of Europe, others as part of North America, while most simply ignore the pro
lem. In this book, Greenland is considered a part of North America, primarily sir
the Eskimo that inhabited much of Arctic North America also lived in Greenland

The geography of North America is complex, and many regions can be defin
within it, based on a number of criteria. For the purposes of this book, seven ge
eral natural areas are defined (Fig. 1.3); these overlap with the culture areas defin
below. In the far north lies the Arctic, a largely treeless region covered with sno
and ice for most of the year, roughly corresponding to the Arctic culture area. 1
the south of the Arctic lies a region containing mountains and a vast, cold, coni
erous forest with thousands of lakes that generally coincides with the Subarct
culture area. Farther south, and east of the Mississippi River, lies an extensive tem
perate forest, much of which has been destroyed over the past 150 years; this regio
is divided into the Northeast and Southeast culture areas. West of the Mississipp
River, an immense region of grasslands called the Plains (both the geographic re
gion and the culture area) extends west to the Rocky Mountains, which run north
to south along much of North America. The Plains is now mostly covered by fields
of corn and wheat. A large desert occupies much of western North America and includes both the Great Basin and Southwest culture areas. Lastly, the Pacific coast
lies along the western boundary of North America and encompasses the Northwest Coast, California, and Plateau culture areas.

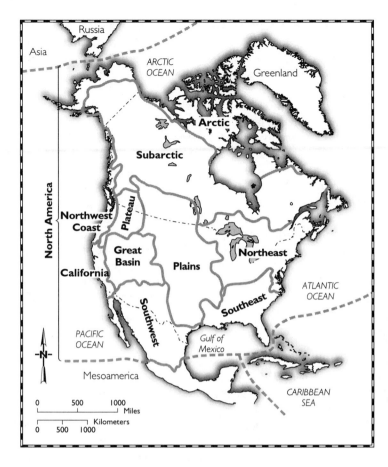

FIGURE 1.4 Culture areas of North America
Adapted from *Handbook of North American Indians,* Vol. 4, *History of Indian-White Relations,* W. E. Washburn, ed., p. ix; copyright © 1988 by the Smithsonian Institution. Used by permission of the publisher.

even if informally, to refer to geographic regions and general culture. Most laypeople also inherently recognize culture areas, having, for example, at least some idea that the native peoples of the Plains are different from those of the Arctic.

Native North Americans

Prior to the arrival of Columbus, all of the people living in North America were native. These included the Eskimo (a term that commonly includes both the Inuit and Aleut) of the Arctic region and the Indians who occupied the continent south of the Arctic. The Eskimo are usually considered to be distinct from Indians, based on their history (they migrated into the New World after the Indians), biology, linguistics, and culture. Nevertheless, they are all Native North Americans.

After 1492, however, immigrants of many ethnicities and cultures flooded the continent, mixing both among themselves and with native peoples. While many full-blooded native peoples still exist, the majority have a mixed biological and cultural heritage (some have even formed new groups, such as the Métis of Canada), complicating their classification (see Snipp 1989). Recently, many more people have claimed Indian ancestry, based on a desire to be Indian, newfound pride in their previously unclaimed ancestry, or changing definitions of what an Indian is.

Today, a good definition of *Native American* is elusive. At least three general defining categories apply: biological, administrative, and mystical (see Snipp 1989). Biological definitions are usually based on some minimum "blood quantum," or percentage of "pure Indian blood" (e.g., one-quarter, one-eighth). Many tribes require a certain percentage of Indian blood to classify a person as a tribal member. Administrative definitions, often based on mystical and biological definitions, are used to serve whatever agency formulated them, such as a government definition of natives for benefit and/or settlement purposes or a tribal definition of members for benefit and/or voting purposes. Mystical definitions may consist of romantic, spiritual, and even fictional views of a people descended from an ancient past. A person can claim to be an Indian if he or she somehow feels like one. All of these definitions are used, sometimes interchangeably. Today, more than two million Americans now identify themselves as Native American.

The People

It seems impossible to find an objective, universally accepted term for the indigenous inhabitants of the Americas (see discussions in Milesuah 1997; Churchill 1999; and Yellow Bird 1999). Some use *Native Americans,* but others have argued that such a category includes Native Hawaiians (although Hawaii is not in North America and Native Hawaiians are technically Polynesian) or even anyone born in North America regardless of their ancestry. The widely used term *Indian* is sometimes considered inappropriate since it is not even a native term, as it was misapplied by Columbus, who thought he was in the East Indies. It is also possible to confuse Indians of the New World with the people of India. In addition, the Aleut and Inuit are not Indians but are still Native Americans, and many prefer to be called Alaska Natives. The terms *Native Peoples* and *Native Nations* suffer from similar problems. Some prefer the term *First People* to refer to indigenous people in general, a term that could include Native Americans. The term *aboriginal* is also used in that same manner. Many Native Americans want to be called by their group name, such as Hopi. For the purposes of this book, the terms *Native American, native peoples, Eskimo* (although Inuit and Aleut will be distinguished), and *Indian* will be used and will apply to those people who were indigenous to North America prior to the European invasion.

In the United States and Canada, Indians are viewed as distinct from the majority, non-Indian population. However, the situation is quite different in Mexico, where Indians form the vast majority of the population. Some 75 percent of Mexicans are of mixed Indian and non-Indian heritage (called mestizo), about 20 percent are full-blooded Indian, and some 5 percent are white, mostly of Spanish heritage (West and Augelli 1989:291). In Mexico, most people identify themselves as Mexican; only those who speak native languages are considered Indios.

Over the course of history, many non-Indians intermarried and had children with Indians. Escaped black slaves sometimes found refuge with native peoples (most Indians were not concerned about skin color). Soon, people of mixed native–black heritage, the Black Indians, came into existence (not limited to North America; see Katz 1997). In North America, Black Indians formed an important part of a number of native groups in the American Southeast, including the Seminole (see Chapter 12).

Political Entities

As with the people themselves, it is difficult to find an accurate term for their political units. The term *tribe* is often employed, but it carries a certain anthropological meaning that does not apply to all groups (see below). *Nation* could be (and often is) used, but that term implies an organization and political autonomy that is not true of all groups. In this book the generic term *group* will be used, and wherever possible, the appropriate political term (e.g., *tribe*).

In the United States, about 700 native groups (Indian and Eskimo) still exist. Of that number, about 556, including some 223 village groups in Alaska, are formally recognized as having a special "government-to-government" relationship with the United States. (For a listing of federally recognized groups, log on to *http://www.doi.gov/bia/tribes/entry.html*). Another 150 native groups have applied for federal recognition. Many other North American groups exist in Canada and northern Mexico.

Population

The native population of North America prior to 1492 has never been accurately determined. It was first thought that there were about 500,000 native people before the arrival of Columbus. This low estimate was made partly to minimize native occupation of the land, further justifying European intrusion. In the early 1900s, however, this view began to change as a result of detailed work on population by researchers from the Bureau of American Ethnology, who estimated that perhaps as many as three million Indians existed in North America before 1492. Today, after much more work, estimates of the native population of North America just prior to the time of Columbus range from about eight million to eighteen million (see Thornton 1987, 1997, Stannard 1992, Ubelaker 1992, and Reddy 1995 for comprehensive discussions of native population figures). After 1492, it has been argued (e.g., Stannard 1992:268), there was a population decline on the order of about 95 percent before the trend was reversed and populations began to recover (see Table 1.1).

Today, the population of Native Americans has increased to between 1.5 and 2.5 million, depending on how it is measured. The criteria for classifying a person as an Indian or a member of a specific group can vary, depending on the group, the census, the political climate, or other factors (see Weaver 2001). Also, people who are Indian but have only recently listed themselves as Indian on the census create an illusion of population increase. Nevertheless, it is clear that native population is increasing rapidly.

TABLE 1.1 Native American Population of the United States[a]

Year	Population	Percent Change	Source
1500	10,000,000+[b]	N/A	estimate
1800	600,000	−94	estimate
1820	471,000	−22	census
1847	383,000	−18	census
1857	313,000	−18	census
1870	278,000	−11	census
1880	244,000	−12	census
1890	228,000	− 7	census
1900	250,000	+10	census
1910	279,000	+12	census
1920	244,000	−13	census
1930	332,000	+36	census
1940	345,000	+ 4	census
1950	357,000	+ 4	census
1960	524,000	+47	census
1970	792,000	+51	census
1980	1,367,000	+73	census
1990	1,900,000	+39	census
2000	2,434,000	+28	census[c]
2050	4,405,000	+81	projected[c]

[a]Compiled from Thornton (1987), Snipp (1989), Reddy (1995:Tables 10, 12, and 18), and 2000 census data.

[b]This estimate of ten million is conservatively in the middle of various modern estimates ranging from eight million to eighteen million (see Thornton [1987, 1997] and Stannard [1992] for comprehensive discussions of native population figures [also see Snipp 1989]).

[c]2000 U.S. census data.

Language

Native North Americans spoke a bewildering array of languages—more than 400, belonging to some sixty-two language families (see Goddard 1996a, 1996b: Table 3, 1996c) (Fig. 1.5). Of those languages, only 209 were still spoken as of 1995, and only forty-six were spoken by children (Goddard 1996b: Table 2). It seems that the others will become extinct very soon. The loss of native languages carries a high price, including the loss of knowledge, philosophy, worldview, and many other aspects of native culture.

Understanding the distribution of languages across North America is important for interpreting relationships between cultures, the transmission of culture and traits, and the interactions between cultures. It is also critical to the reconstruction of group movements over time and has helped cast light on the prehistory of much of North America (see Foster 1996).

Territories and Boundaries

In Europe, nations maintained strict territorial boundaries. The borders defining each country were set and defended by force of arms. Americans still hold this general view regarding territory; thus, we have imposed territorial boundaries on many native groups, even though this may lead to false impressions of how native peoples viewed the land. A glance at the maps in this book will illustrate this point. Each group's territory is bounded by lines, and there are no unassigned areas. In reality, however, many groups did not have a set territory with well-defined and defended borders. In many cases, a group would have a core area and a peripheral area that may have overlapped with the peripheral areas of other groups. Thus it

FIGURE 1.5 General distribution of major language groups in North America
Loosely adapted from *Handbook of North American Indians, Vol. 17, Languages,* Ives Goddard, ed., map in rear pocket; copyright © 1996 by the Smithsonian Institution. Reprinted by permission of the publisher.

is impossible to draw a single, accurate line between the land occupied by any two groups, but this is typically done for the sake of convenience.

In addition, groups have moved about the landscape throughout time, and their territories have changed, just as those of European countries have. When explorers or anthropologists recorded the territory of a group, they defined it as it existed at that point in time (known as the ethnographic present) but may not have reflected past territories. These recorded territories now seem to be set in "anthropological stone," though they reflect only part of a group's historical relationship with the land.

However, some groups did claim specific territories and boundaries, which they frequently defended. In some Northwest Coast groups, clans owned specific areas; some Plains groups had defined hunting territories; and many groups "owned" particular places, such as springs and sacred sites, and others could access to these localities only by their permission. Even if rigid territories were not as important to native peoples as they were to Europeans, native groups certainly had an understanding of geography, as illustrated by Warhus's (1997) book on Native American geography and maps.

Group Names

Each Native American group has always had a name for itself, a name that often translates to something like "The People." However, groups have often been known to the outside world by other names, names that were applied to them by someone else and officially became their name, regardless of the wishes of the groups, assuming they even knew about it. As time passed, many of these names stuck and now even the Indians themselves often use them. In many cases, the new name applied to a group was derogatory. For example, the group known as the Sioux (a Plains group; see Chapter 10) actually encompasses a number of related groups with other names, such as Oglala, Hunkpapa, and Yankton. The word *Sioux* comes from a French translation of a term applied to the general group by their enemies, the Blackfoot, and has something to do with snakes. Although derogatory in origin, this name has been so commonly applied that it is now accepted. Another group, the Creek (in the Southeast; see Chapter 12), got their name from English settlers when the people were describing the locations of their villages, next to creeks.

Archaeologists, not knowing what ancient cultures called themselves, have also given various names to Native American groups. For example, the cultures that lived along the Mississippi River prior to Columbus are called Mississippian; they no doubt called themselves something else, but we do not know the name. Sometimes the names assigned by archaeologists can cause problems. The term *Anasazi*, for example, is used to refer to many of the prehistoric Puebloans who lived in the American Southwest (see Chapter 9). The term originates from a Navajo word that roughly translates to "enemies of our ancestors." However, the current Pueblo groups are not happy with a Navajo word being used to describe their ancestors and prefer the term *Ancestral Puebloans* to *Anasazi*.

As part of their increasing pride and power, many groups are trying to revive their original names and asking that these be used instead of other names. For example, the Nez Perce want to be called Nimiipu ("The People").

The Role of Women

Native North American women, like women in many cultures, are poorly represented in the ethnographic data base; thus, there is little understanding of their roles, power bases, or lives. Part of the problem is that most early anthropologists were men. They were interested only in male activities and talked mostly to men. Some notable exceptions to this general tendency include the work of Anna Gayton in California and Elsie Parsons in the Southwest. Recently, however, a considerable increase has occurred in the anthropological and historical study of women in native cultures (see Boyer and Gayton 1992; Green 1992; Klein and Ackerman 1995; Maltz and Archambault 1995; Purdue 1997; Riley 1997; Sonneborn 1998; Bataille and Lisa 2001).

Western people tend to view the women of many traditional cultures as silent and powerless within their own cultures, as little more than mothers and domestic laborers. This probably reflects the Western view of women up until very recent times. The terms *squaw*, used to refer to average Native American women, and *Indian Princess*, used to refer to royal women (a European concept), are characteristic of this view. It is probably true that women provided much of the food in most traditional societies, but it is not true that women had no power. We just do not fully understand what that power was or how it manifested itself.

In Iroquois society (in the Northeast; see Chapter 11), as an example, males held overt political power, but in reality women generally controlled the men and the political process, exercising much more power than could be seen at first glance. In some cultures, women were the landowners and exerted considerable power; in many others, women led the primary social units and controlled many aspects of their cultures.

Many people assume there are only two genders, men and women, but though there are only two sexes, there are more genders. Gender is a culturally constructed category that defines a given person's role in a specific culture, regardless of sex. Genders include men, women, transvestites, homosexuals, and others. In native North America, this range of genders existed, and individuals of various gender identities often assumed important, high-status roles in their cultures (see Blackwood 1984; Maltz and Archambault 1995; Brown 1997; Jacobs et al. 1997; Lang 1998; Roscoe 1998).

Contemporary Adoptions of Native American Culture

Despite the negative views many people have held about native New World cultures, they have been quick to adopt many skills and products from those cultures (see Weatherford 1988, 1991), especially foodstuffs. Corn (or maize) was first domesticated in Mesoamerica, whereupon it spread to many North American groups and was then adopted by European settlers along the East Coast. Corn is now grown and consumed around the world and currently accounts for about one-third of all of the calories consumed in the United States (in the form of corn kernels, corn on the cob, hominy, grits, tortillas, corn bread, cornstarch, corn syrup, corn-fed pork and beef, etc.). The world is surprisingly dependent on this single plant. Other important native foods adopted by others are beans, squash, peanuts, sunflowers, vanilla, tomatoes, potatoes, and chocolate. In addition to foodstuffs, New World cotton is considered to be of better quality than Old World cotton (Weatherford 1988:43). Native agricultural technology was crucial to the survival of the early colonists, and the Indians taught them how to grow corn. Understanding these ancient agricultural systems may someday be critical to developing sustained agriculture in environments such as rainforests.

A number of other elements from native cultures have also been adopted, including some drugs (e.g., aspirin, cocaine), tobacco (see the Sidelight at the end of Chapter 2), building techniques such as the very efficient pueblo-style architecture of the American Southwest, art (native art is now very popular), various philosophies regarding the supernatural and the environment (e.g., New Age ideas), sports (e.g., lacrosse), and the incorporation of many native terms into the English language (see Cutler 1994).

On the other hand, it has been argued that the native peoples have been exploited for commercial purposes and that elements of native cultures have been appropriated and distorted to suit the needs of the dominant culture, irrespective of the harm done to native peoples (see Meyer and Royer 2001). This is a form of "cultural imperialism," a problem confronted by indigenous people all over the world.

A Brief History of Research on Native North Americans

After Columbus's discovery, Europeans took an immediate and considerable interest in the native peoples of North America. Purposely or not, a great deal of information on native cultures was preserved in the records of the various colonial administrations, mission records, the diaries of explorers and travelers, military registers, census data, various pictorial accounts (drawings, paintings, and photographs), land records, newspaper stories, and many other sources.

By the early nineteenth century, considerable effort was being made to record and classify Indian languages, led by the American Philosophical Society and the American Ethnological Society. Archaeological work in the Mississippi River Valley in the 1830s explored the great complexes of earthen mounds. Many thought that the constructions were too sophisticated to be Indian in origin and so the mounds were thought to be the remains of a pre-Indian (and so *non*-Indian) culture, the so-called Moundbuilders. After several decades of work, it was determined that the mounds had indeed been built by the Indians; thus, they could not be the primitive savages that most people believed at the time. By the 1840s, a number of biographies and histories of Indians were being written.

The formal anthropological study of North American Indians was initiated during the nineteenth century by Lewis H. Morgan, an American social scientist. In the mid–nineteenth century, Morgan began a comprehensive study of the Iroquois in the Northeast (see Chapter 11), publishing the first actual ethnography written about a native group in North America, *League of the Iroquois* (Morgan 1851). This work had a huge impact, both on anthropology (the work set a standard for future work) and on the Iroquois, who became quite famous as a result. Morgan went on to greater accomplishments in anthropology, developing a classification of kinship systems, many of which were named after North American Indian groups. His classifications are still used today.

At about the same time, science grew in importance in Western culture, and many of scientific disciplines familiar to us today were established, including anthropology. Evolutionary theory was formalized, and a significant anthropological theory, known as Unilinear Cultural Evolution, was advanced by a number of anthropologists, but initially by Morgan. This idea proposed that cultures progressively evolve from "savagery" (hunting and gathering), up through "barbarism" (herding and agriculture), and then finally up to "civilization" (conveniently European, the primary criterion being the use of a phonetic alphabet). Thus, by definition, all native North Americans were either savages or barbarians. It is unfortunate that these words were used as classificatory terms, as they were subsequently used to justify the harsh treatment of native peoples.

Beginning in the mid–nineteenth century, a number of museums became involved in the study of Indians. The Smithsonian Institution was established in 1846, and the associated Bureau of Ethnology (later the Bureau of American Ethnology, or BAE) was founded in 1879 (see Judd 1967). The mission of the BAE was to record as much information, as soon as possible, about the native peoples of the United States, as it was believed at that time that all Indians would soon become extinct. Much of the work of the BAE was concentrated in western North America where the Indian cultures were still fairly intact.

Many other museums were also established, including the United States National Museum in Washington, D.C.; the American Museum of Natural History in New York; the Peabody Museum of Archaeology and Ethnology in Cambridge, Massachusetts; the Heye Foundation in New York (recently renamed the National Museum of the American Indian); and the Canadian National Museum. In their early days, many such museums dispatched teams of people simply to collect objects for display, through legitimate collection, theft, or purchase. Too little attention was given to the objects' importance in the context of native cultures (see Cole 1985).

Anthropological work continued, fueled by the view that unspoiled, "primitive" native culture was rapidly disintegrating and that the Indians were becoming extinct. By the late nineteenth century, considerable effort was being expended in conducting "salvage ethnography" before the native peoples disappeared. A leader in this effort was Franz Boas, who is known as "the father of American anthropology." Along with his students (Alfred Kroeber in California being an outstanding example), and later their students, they amassed huge quantities of information, a great deal of which still remains to be analyzed. Much of this effort focused on western North America, as native cultures in the West had survived better than those in the East, where many had been long extinct before any anthropological work could be done.

By the early twentieth century, this information was being gathered, summarized, and published in works such as the two-volume *Handbook of American Indians North of Mexico* (Hodge 1907–1910), the 20-volume work *The North American Indian* (Curtis 1907–1930), and *The Indian Tribes of North America* (Swanton 1953). In 1978, the Smithsonian Institution began publishing a comprehensive 20-volume work, *Handbook of North American Indians*. As of 2002, 12 of the planned 20 volumes had been published. Also, many general texts on Native Americans have been produced (e.g., Leacock and Lurie 1971; Spencer and Jennings 1977; Hodge 1981; Kupferer 1988; Boxberger 1990; Kehoe 1992; Garbarino and Sasso 1994; Trigger and Washburn 1996; King 1999; Nichols 1999; Bonvillain 2001; Oswalt and Neely 2002), as well as a number of encyclopedic treatments (e.g., Furtaw 1993; Davis 1994; Hoxie 1996; Pritzker 1998; Green and Fernandez 1999; Malinowski and Sheets 1998; Klein 2000; Waldman 2000).

Today, a huge literature exists concerning native North America, some of it written from a scholarly viewpoint and some from a popular perspective. New knowledge of native groups continues to emerge and helps to enlighten us all. Recently, more research is being conducted by native peoples themselves, providing a most welcome addition to the literature. Much of this work conveys a distinctly different view of native culture.

The Impact of Anthropology on Native Cultures

The stated goal of anthropology is to gain understanding of other cultures and ultimately of all cultures. In addition, anthropology is motivated by a real desire to record information in order to learn from and "preserve" cultures, not only for the general benefit of everyone but more specifically for the descendants of specific cultures. Most anthropologists share these goals and are sensitive to the interests of native groups. For example, anthropologists mostly support Indian land claims, and some groups have won significant legal victories with the help of anthropologists.

However, anthropologists have impacted native groups in some negative ways. Early anthropological theory formalized the categories of savage, barbarian, and civilized people. Using these classifications, much of the mistreatment of the Indians was justified as necessary to drag the native peoples up to the level of civilization. The boundaries of the territories of most groups were defined by anthropologists, often with relatively little knowledge of the groups; these boundaries are now entrenched in the literature and are thus very difficult to change.

Further, many Indians object to anthropological research as exploitative of Indians, as they feel they have little or no control over the dissemination of the information. They also feel that it is of little practical value to them; after all, many ask, why should Indians participate without some benefit? Some even believe that such research is "imperialistic" in that it fosters white views of Indians (e.g., Deloria 1969). Others have claimed that through their work, anthropologists construct a "reality" of Indian culture that may or may not fit the view of the Indians, and this is sometimes seen as a threat. These issues have become important to anthropologists as they struggle to make anthropology relevant to the Indians and to recognize and rectify any problems their studies may have caused (see Biolsi and Zimmerman 1997; Swidler et al. 1997; also see Deloria 1997).

These criticisms have resulted in a number of changes in the techniques, ethics, and conduct of anthropologists who study Indians. Today, Indian views of themselves and of their past are viewed as far more important to anthropologists than ever before. New laws have been passed to protect native religions and cemeteries, and to require that Indians be consulted concerning projects and activities that affect them. However, while these changes progress, many problems still remain to be resolved.

Popular Views of Native Americans

Soon after Columbus landed in the New World, Europeans formed two basic images of Indians: the good and noble savage and the evil and bloodthirsty savage

Sidelight

THE DOMESTICATED "WILDERNESS"

Most Americans believe that much of North America was a wild and unsettled land prior to the arrival of Europeans, an erroneous view. All people impact their environment, irrespective of their technological complexity. It is simply not true that hunter-gatherers made no impact on the land. While a person with a digging stick may cause less damage than a person with a bulldozer, the digging stick nevertheless affects the environment. In fact, *all* people impact and manage their environment at a minimum of three different levels. Environmental manipulation is active management conducted on a large scale and includes practices such as plowing and water diversion (things agriculturalists do) and burning (things both agriculturalists and hunter-gatherers do). Active resource management takes place on a smaller scale and involves active management of specific plants and animals (things both agriculturalists and hunter-gatherers do). Passive resource management includes practices such as rituals dedicated to the supernatural for weather control (which may be conducted by both agriculturalists and hunter-gatherers). The environment is thus modified and "domesticated"— controlled for the benefit of the people—by all groups, past and present. This is a far cry from an untamed wilderness (see Dolittle 2000).

Many non-Indian management practices often conflict with Native American practices, as they are performed by different groups with different goals. Burning is an excellent example of this. Indians often employed burning to encourage growth of specific plants, to attract game, and to manage fuel (duff) to prevent a catastrophic fire. Current government policy has prevented all burning, thus setting the stage for very hot and catastrophic fires that destroy entire forests. Recently, however, some government agencies have begun to adopt more flexible policies regarding wildfire suppression and prescribed burns. There is much to learn about land and resource management from Native Americans. Intimate knowledge of an area, as many native groups had of their territories, can contribute to management and control.

Europeans also misunderstood the native system of farming in the eastern United States (see discussion in Kehoe 1992:249–251). When planting their crops, the Indians would not totally clear the land but planted various crops around trees, stumps, and rocks. By contrast, Europeans would typically completely clear the land so it could be plowed. Since it was not fully cleared, Europeans saw Indian farmland as "unimproved," weakening any claim the Indians may have had on it. Europeans also failed to recognize the similarities between their methods and the Indians' way of procuring mammals and fish. The Europeans managed their animals in captivity and harvested them at will, and the Indians managed their animals in the wild but still harvested them at will. The Europeans intensively fished some areas during certain times of the year, just as the Indians did. In spite of the similarities in economy and management of the land and resources, the Europeans saw the Indians' land as wild and untamed, and this view served as justification for European conquest.

(see Bordewich 1996; Ellingson 2001). The image of the noble savage reflects the European idea that humans once enjoyed an existence of innocence, naiveté, simplicity, harmony, and contentment. Following this general view, the conservation movement in the United States included Indians among those things to be conserved, and their images were used to convey a sense of loss of the wilderness and closeness to nature. This image is still very popular.

As part of this perspective, today many people see Indians as the first ecologists, living a virtuous life in harmony with the earth (see Grinde and Johansen 1995; Bol 1998). This view is based on a number of assumptions regarding Indians of the past that may or may not be true (see White 1997; but also see Krech 1999). There is no question that some Indian groups made bad ecological decisions, such as over-hunting, overfishing, and overgrazing; however, due to their small populations and less complex technology (at least as compared to the contemporary United States), they did not cause the catastrophic changes in the environment that we see today, such as the destruction of the rainforests, global air pollution, and nuclear accidents.

The second view of Indians, that of warlike, aggressive, and primitive savages, developed from the competition between colonists and Indians for critical re-sources, primarily land. Native practices such as warfare, torture, head-hunting, and slave raiding added to their violent image, in spite of the fact that Europeans of the time were doing exactly the same things. The Indians were viewed as impeding the path of civilization, and when they defended themselves and their lands, they were judged to be primitive and bloodthirsty savages. As savages, Indians were to be feared and either converted to civilization or exterminated. This view flourished as long as conflict between Indians and whites persisted (see Trigger 1985). Later, the notion of the warrior Indian was perpetuated by the press and by phenomena like Buffalo Bill's Wild West, a traveling pageant of the late nineteenth century that depicted Indians in stereotypic activities, including staged attacks on wagon trains.

Once defeated by Euroamericans, Indians were regarded as pitiful and forgot-ten children. No longer a threat to a still expanding America, Indians were roman-ticized and stereotyped by the media in a number of ways, such as gallant warriors, ignorant menial workers, or parasitic poverty-stricken beggars. Each image embod-ied the false notion that native peoples somehow existed in a historical past—liv-ing fossils that had not changed (see Porter 1990:7–11). Today, native cultures have undergone a resurgence. Indians are now admired and emulated by the mainstream public. Nevertheless, past images of Indians persist in the form of sports mascots, names of cars and weapons, and characters in movies and television shows (see Marsden and Nachbar 1988), as well as in the press (see Weston 1996). Perhaps the best images of Indians reveal them simply as *people*; like any other people, they have strengths and weaknesses as well as valuable contributions to make.

A General Prehistory of North America

The prehistory of North America began with the entry of humans into the New World sometime during the late Pleistocene era, a geologic period from about two million to ten thousand years ago, roughly equivalent to the Ice Age. Exactly when this entry occurred is hotly debated. We know relatively little about the early pre-history of North America, but what we do know is briefly considered below. See Fagan (2000) for a discussion of North American archaeology.

The Origin of Native Peoples in the New World

With the "discovery" of Indians by Columbus in 1492, Europeans immediately felt a need to explain where these people came from and how they had arrived in the New World. According to fifteenth-century European Christian tradition, the origin of humanity took place as chronicled in the Bible. The Indians of the New World thus presented a problem: who were these people, where did they come from, and where in the Bible might they find answers to these questions? However, it was first necessary to determine whether the Indians were actually people; if not, their origin did not require explanation or consideration. As silly as this sounds now, it was a real issue then, an issue that could only be resolved by the pope. Therefore, in 1512, the pope declared that the native people of the New World were people, and thus began the attempts by Europeans to explain their origin.

The simplest explanation, and the one held by many native cultures, is that they had always lived in the New World—in fact, they had been created there. This concept is called *in situ* development. All cultures have an origin story (cosmology) within their oral tradition, and though the specific details vary from group to group, none requires a migration of people, which is the basis of all of the Euro-american theories concerning the origins of Native Americans (see Deloria 1995). Many native people still hold to the view of *in situ* development, and anthropologists must take that perspective into account. Summaries of various native cosmologies are included in the case studies in this book.

Early European Ideas on Native American Origins   Most Christian Europeans of the fifteenth and sixteenth centuries (and even today) would not accept the idea that native peoples had been created by non-Christian deities, so some other explanation had to be found. Because it fit with existing Christian belief, the idea that New World native peoples were descendants of one of the Lost Tribes of Israel was appealing. Other popular early ideas, again meshing with existing beliefs, posited that the people had come from the "lost continents" of Atlantis, or Mu, or had somehow crossed the Atlantic Ocean from Egypt. This latter idea seemed logical because pyramids existed in Mexico (they just *had* to be Egyptian), and this hypothesis still has some support, at least to explain influences if not migration.

Other more realistic ideas centered on a migration of people across some land route. Several possibilities were suggested, including a land bridge between northeastern North America and northwestern Europe (across Greenland and Iceland), a land bridge from South America to some unknown location, and a land bridge between Alaska and northeastern Asia, across what is now the Bering Strait. This last idea, first suggested in 1590, forms the basis of the current scientific understanding of Native American origins.

The Bering Land Bridge   Although proposed over 400 years ago, considerable and convincing evidence was required before the idea of a migration across an Arctic land bridge could be accepted. It had been recognized early on that many native peoples looked somewhat physically similar to certain Asian populations and that some connection might exist. Later, archaeological data, including artifacts and skeletal morphology, linked North America and northeastern Asia. More recently, linguistic, blood group, and DNA studies have supported this link. There is little doubt now that native peoples first came into the western hemisphere from northeast Asia. However, the questions of when, how, and why are still debated (see the discussion in Fagan 2000:68–90 for more information).

Asia and North America are separated by a rather narrow body of water called the Bering Strait. On a clear day, from the easternmost tip of Asia, an island can be seen in the Bering Strait; looking east from that island, the westernmost tip of Alaska is visible. Thus, traveling from Asia to North America by boat is relatively simple and could have been done many thousands of years ago (this is how the Eskimo came to North America; see below). However, although this is one method that people could have employed to enter into the western hemisphere, direct evidence of early boats is lacking.

Both the Bering Strait and the Bering Sea to the south are rather shallow, between 150 and 180 feet deep in many places. There is now evidence that, as a result of the vast amount of water that was locked up in glacial ice toward the end of the Pleistocene era, there was a worldwide drop in sea level of about 300 feet. This drop would have eliminated the Bering Sea and exposed a very substantial land bridge, called Beringia (see West 1996), which created a land link between northeast Asia and western Alaska (see Fig. 1.6). As the glaciers expanded, sea lev-

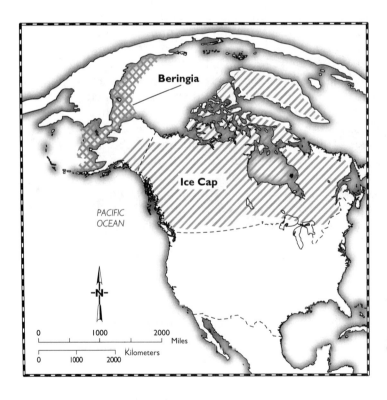

FIGURE 1.6 Northern North America showing the extent of the glaciers and of Beringia ca. 18,000 B.P.
From *Prehistory of North America, Third Edition* by Jesse D. Jennings. Copyright © 1989 by Mayfield Publishing Company. Reprinted by permission of the publisher.

els dropped and exposed Beringia; as the glaciers melted and retreated, sea levels rose again, flooding the land bridge.

The glaciers advanced and retreated a number of times in the last 100,000 years, and there appears to have been a small land bridge between about 60,000 and 35,000 B.P. (B.P. stands for *before present*, essentially "years ago"), although there is currently no solid evidence that people crossed into the New World during this time. The 300-foot drop in sea level commenced about 25,000 B.P., exposing most of Beringia until about 10,000 B.P. This decline in sea level would also have exposed the coastal plains of North America (and coastlines all over the world for that matter), suggesting the possibility that people migrated south along the coast.

As sea levels dropped, the dry land of Beringia would have been colonized by plants and animals. At that time (ca. 20,000 B.P.) the region would have been colder and drier than it is today, and there is reason to believe that no trees existed in Beringia until after about 14,000 B.P.; if so, a lack of firewood could have slowed human colonization. In any case, people crossing Beringia must have been technologically adapted to cold climates, and there is evidence that such cultures were present in northeastern Asia by about 15,000 B.P. Hunter-gatherer groups probably would have crossed Beringia by following game animals or moving along the southern coast to exploit ocean resources. Over hundreds of years, people would have moved further into the interior of North America.

At the height of the last Ice Age (ca. 14,000 B.P.), northeastern Asia, Beringia, and most of Alaska would have been cold but not glaciated, allowing movement of people across the region. At that time, a glacial barrier was present in eastern Alaska, preventing the movement of people into the rest of the western hemisphere. Once the ice began to melt, people could have moved south, following game animals presumably as they did from Asia to Alaska. It is difficult to determine the exact routes and times of the migrations since most of Beringia and the coastal plain, where most of the evidence should be, are now under water.

The Paleoindian Period

Archaeologists are coming to believe that at least four migrations of native people into the New World took place. For the past few decades, it was thought that native people, called Paleoindians, first migrated into the New World about 12,000 years ago. However, increasing evidence points to an earlier date: the first migration may have occurred prior to 14,000 B.P. Several archaeological sites in North America have been dated to between 20,000 and 13,000 B.P., and several others in South America appear to date from earlier than 12,000 B.P.; for example, the Monte Verde site in Chile has been only recently radiocarbon dated to 13,500 B.P. Monte Verde contains a structure foundation, wooden and bone tools, and food residues and is the best-dated early site in South America. It is also possible that the radiocarbon dating conducted so far has yielded results that are too young, meaning that initial colonization may have taken place some 2,000 years earlier (see Fiedel 1999).

Assuming that people walked to South America from North America and that they were living in South America by 13,500 B.P., it seems logical to conclude that people had arrived in North America by at least 14,000 B.P. In addition, some

Sidelight

WEAPONS TECHNOLOGY

Native North American peoples utilized a variety of weapons prior to the introduction of firearms and metal blades by Europeans. Among the most common were the spear, harpoon, atlatl and dart, bow and arrow, and blowgun. Projectile weapons might have had simple wooden tips, tips of stone or bone (e.g., spearpoints or arrowheads), or more complex tips, such as those for bird hunting.

Spears are long, wooden shafts thrown at or thrust into a victim. Such weapons have obvious range limitations but can be quite effective. Thrusting spears were primarily used to dispatch game already immobilized by traps, falls, or mud, and were rarely thrown. Spears were invented in the Old World many hundreds of thousands of years ago and were almost certainly the primary weapon of Paleoindian people. However, they have never completely fallen out of use and are still used by some groups today.

An adaptation of the throwing spear is the harpoon, essentially a throwing spear with a detachable barbed tip, called a head. This type of weapon is used for hunting large fish and sea mammals. A cord is attached to the head and is held by the harpooner. Once the harpoon head enters the body of the animal, it becomes detached from the shaft and remains embedded in the flesh. The harpooner, holding the attached cord, then pulls the animal into the boat or onto shore. This technology is very effective in capturing sea mammals that could otherwise escape or become lost in the water despite being killed by the harpoon.

The atlatl, which comes from a Nahuatl (Aztec) word for "spear-thrower," is a device used to increase the range, accuracy, and efficiency of a thrown spear. The atlatl is handheld and essentially extends the length of the arm, adding power to the throw. The projectile used with an atlatl is called a dart, which looks more like a large arrow than a spear. Like arrows, atlatl darts are long and thin, have feathers on the end (called fletching) to stabilize flight, are often made from several different materials (e.g., a hardwood foreshaft and a cane mainshaft), and can be attached to a variety of tips. As atlatl darts are larger than arrows, they can have larger tips. The end of the dart has a small depression that fits into a hook on the back of the atlatl and is the point of contact between the atlatl and dart.

It takes some time to learn how to use an atlatl, but it can be a very effective weapon and can penetrate even the thick skin of an elephant. The disadvantage of an atlatl is exposure; it is necessary to stand in order to use it and to be situated fairly close to the prey. Atlatls have great antiquity in North America, probably predating 10,000 B.P., and were most likely used in conjunction with the earlier thrusting spears. Atlatls were used into historical times by some groups

evidence suggests that these very early people may not have been the ancestors of the current Indians but rather died out or were absorbed by the next wave of immigrants. The sequences of and relationships between the early migrations into the New World have yet to be worked out.

The best documented—and for many years believed to be the earliest—Paleoindian culture in the New World is called Clovis, named after the town near the archaeological site in New Mexico where it was first identified. Clovis is also the name of the diagnostic artifact, the Clovis point, associated with a number of

in the Southeast (see Chapter 12) and are still used today by some native groups in Australia.

With the bow and arrow, a projectile (the arrow) is propelled by using the energy of a bow rather than the arm. A bow consists of a bow stave and a bowstring. Bow staves are typically made from a single piece of wood but sometimes from bone or horn, often in combination with wood. A bow made from a single piece of material is called a *simple* bow, while a bow made from multiple materials is called a *compound* bow. The bowstring, made from twisted plant fibers or sinew, is attached at each end of the stave. As the bowstring is drawn back, the bow bends and stores energy. The notched end of the arrow is placed against the bowstring; the archer sights down the arrow to the target, then releases the bowstring. The bent bow snaps back to its original position, bringing the bowstring with it and propelling the arrow forward.

Bows and arrows have advantages and disadvantages compared with atlatls. An arrow has less range and striking power than a dart, but arrows are smaller, easier to make and carry, and can be shot faster than darts. A big advantage of the bow and arrow is that they can be used in a sitting, standing, or prone position. Bows and arrows appear to have been invented in the Old World, perhaps in Europe, sometime around 10,000 B.P., perhaps even as early as 15,000 B.P. Bows and arrows were eventually adopted by

peoples in northeastern Asia and ultimately diffused into North America through the Arctic, perhaps as early as 3,000 B.P. By about 1,500 B.P., bow-and-arrow technology had been adopted by most native groups in North America. It was eventually mostly replaced by the much more effective firearms introduced by Europeans.

The blowgun was not typically used in North America, sometimes used in the Southeast, but more commonly used in South America. A blowgun is a hollow tube into which a small projectile, called a dart, is placed. The shooter puts his mouth over one end of the tube and blows as hard as possible, propelling the dart to its target. The dart consists of a small pointed stick with a clump of down on its end; the down seals the dart in the tube, allowing the air pressure to propel it. These darts are too small to seriously injure most animals by themselves, so they are frequently tipped with a poison of some sort.

A variety of other weapons were also used by native groups. These included throwing sticks, bolas (stones tied on the ends of strings; when thrown at animals, the strings wrapped around the animal and immobilized it), clubs, slings, tomahawks, and knives. In addition to such weaponry, many other devices were utilized for hunting animals, such as pits, traps, and nets. Although such weapons technology was primarily used to hunt game animals, in warfare it was quite effective against people as well.

sites. It was seemingly designed for use on a thrusting spear. These points exhibit a unique and sophisticated "fluting" technology found only in North America. Clovis sites date to between about 11,200 and 10,900 B.P., are found all across North America, and are frequently associated with mammoth and mastodon remains. A slightly later culture, called Folsom, also named after an archaeological site in New Mexico containing fluted points, is associated with giant bison remains. These associations gave rise to the notion that Paleoindians were primarily big-game hunters, a notion that is still widely held. However, it seems more likely that

Paleoindians consumed a wide variety of foods that included many of the large Pleistocene megafauna (big animals), such as mammoths, mastodons, giant bison, horses, camels, and sloths. By about 10,000 B.P., a variety of Paleoindian cultures were present all over North America south of the glaciers.

The end of the Pleistocene era marked the beginning of the Holocene era, a geologic period spanning from roughly 10,000 years ago to the present. During the early Holocene the climate became warmer, bringing about the extinction of many species of plants and animals, including the megafauna. Some researchers believe that the demise of some of these animals may have been assisted by human hunters, but evidence for this is not conclusive.

The Archaic Period

The commonly held (if somewhat romantic) view of Paleoindians is that they were big-game hunters, specializing in the exploitation of Ice Age megafauna. At the beginning of the Holocene era, when the climate was becoming warmer and drier and the megafauna became extinct, the Paleoindians adopted a more generalized hunting and gathering economy with a greater emphasis on plant foods. This generalized economy is characteristic of what is commonly referred to as the Archaic period. The name denotes not so much a time period as it does a lifestyle. By definition, the Archaic period follows the Paleoindian period but precedes the advent of agriculture. In some areas the Archaic period persisted until contact with Europeans, while in other areas, where agriculture was introduced, the Archaic era ended earlier. Most Archaic peoples had relatively small populations and either band- or tribe-level political organization, but this was not universally true.

Subsequent Migrations   It appears that the arrival of Paleoindians in North America was followed by several other migrations into North America during the Archaic. About 8,000 years ago, the ancestors of the Eskimo moved from eastern Siberia to occupy western Alaska. Using a new, sophisticated technology for living in such a cold climate, the Paleoeskimo specialized in the hunting of sea mammals and inhabited areas that others would have found too forbidding. Beginning about 4,000 years ago, the early Eskimo began moving east, eventually reaching Greenland, and perhaps even Iceland.

At about the same time, Athapaskan (Na-Dene) people began to move into the Northwest Coast and western Canada, areas that had previously been glaciated. It had taken thousands of years for the region to recover from glaciation, but once habitable it was soon occupied by people. It seems that the eastern portion of the previously glaciated area (in essence, eastern Canada) was occupied at about the same time by Algonquian people moving north from the region that is now the eastern United States.

The Formative Period: Agriculture

A group whose economy specializes in food production is said to be in the Formative period. In many cases, food production takes place through agriculture, but some hunter-gatherer economies became specialized and productive enough to be categorized as Formative, such as those of the Northwest Coast and portions of California. Agriculture developed early in eastern North America with the domestication of a number of native plants, including the sunflower. Corn was first domesticated in Mesoamerica and introduced into North America in about 3,000 B.P. Corn agriculture was adopted by groups in the Southwest and later diffused east into much of eastern North America. When a hunting and gathering group was initially exposed to domesticated plants and animals, such resources would have formed only a minor aspect of their economy, though some eventually became more reliant on crops and decreased their dependency on wild foods. At some threshold, crops would have become the primary food source and the economy "specialized"; at this point the group would be classified as Formative. Like the Archaic period, the Formative period implies certain population sizes and political organizations. Food production can provide a base for a large population, which may then develop complex political organizations, such as a chiefdom. Again, as in the Archaic period, this is not always true.

Mesoamerican Influences on Native North America

The complex cultures of Mesoamerica influenced native North America in a number of ways. However, it is not at all clear how important some of these influences may have been. The first and foremost influence was the diffusion of corn agriculture into North America by about 3,000 years ago. Of course, this had a profound effect on those cultures that adopted agriculture, some of which developed very large populations and extremely complex societies. Corn agriculture became the economic base of most of the cultures in the Southwest and the Mississippi Valley, as well as much of eastern North America.

Other Mesoamerican influences are evident in the presence of large, stadium-like ballcourts in the Southwest, in pyramid-like structures in the Mississippi Valley, and in some of the religious activities and beliefs of Mississippian cultures. Much more research is needed to understand these various influences.

///

2 European Invasion and Conquest

///

The discovery of the New World by Columbus in 1492 was preceded by at least one Asian discovery of the New World some 14,000 years ago. Those intrepid people, all hunter-gatherers, explored and colonized the western hemisphere in a relatively short period of time (see Chapter 1). Europeans had themselves discovered the New World by about 1,000 years ago, and had visited and established colonies in North America hundreds of years before Columbus. However, for various reasons, these contacts were never substantial and the records of such visits were never widely known. Thus, most Europeans had no knowledge of the New World prior to 1492. After Columbus, though, Europeans quickly claimed, conquered, and colonized North America (see Jennings 1993; Allen 1997; and Wilson 1998 for discussions on the discovery and conquest of North America).

The Norse Discovery

The earliest documented contact between Europeans and native peoples of the New World was that of the Vikings from Scandinavia, known as the Norse, about 1,000 years ago. Beginning in 982, the Norse established several colonies in Greenland, considered by many to be technically part of North America but not close enough to be regarded as the first discovery of North America. In 985, a lost Norse ship apparently observed some unknown land west of Greenland. Ten years later, Leif Thorvaldsson, son of Erik Thorvaldsson (or Leif, Erik's son, now commonly known as Leif Eriksson), sailed west to explore this newfound land (hence the name Newfoundland), and in 1004 a small colony was established. That colony lasted only a few years before the survivors moved back to Greenland. Remains of a small Norse settlement were discovered by archaeologists at L'Anse aux Meadows, Newfoundland; they may be those of the colony founded in 1004 (see McGhee 1984; Fitzhugh 1985; Ingstad and Ingstad 2001).

Most Norse contacts in North America were likely with the Eskimo, but were probably never very intense nor sustained for very long; thus, there was no real opportunity for the transmission of disease. There is currently no evidence of any European diseases in North America prior to 1492, or for any major Norse influences on Eskimo culture. In the late fourteenth century, the Eskimo expanded east and south into Greenland, and by about 1400, the Norse had abandoned Greenland, perhaps due to a cooling climate. However, it may be that the Eskimo pushed the Norse out of Greenland; if so, it would be a unique case of Native Americans invading an area occupied by Europeans and supplanting them. It has been argued that the fighting abilities of the northeastern Indians and Eskimo so discouraged the Norse that the European invasion of the New World was delayed by 500 years (McGhee 1984).

Columbus and the Early Exploration of North America

On October 12, 1492, Columbus landed on a small island in the Caribbean, although no one is sure which one. He thought he was in the Indies of Southeast Asia, a region now called the East Indies; the eastern Caribbean islands were subsequently named the West Indies. Thus, Columbus believed that the people he encountered were "Indians." In popular literature, Columbus is usually credited with the discovery of North America. However, when Columbus set out on his voyage, he thought he was going somewhere else; when he got there, he did not know where he was; and when he got back, he did not know where he had been (Brace and Montagu 1977:6).

The Spanish began their conquest of Central and South America while other Europeans rushed to exploit the resources of eastern North America. By 1497, the English were fishing for cod off Newfoundland and there is even a possibility that cod fishing by Basques predated Columbus (Quinn 1974). By the early sixteenth century large numbers of Europeans fished the waters off

Columbus landing in the New World, from a 1728 etching. (CORBIS)

Newfoundland every summer. French Basque whalers were operating off the shores of eastern North America by 1536. The resulting very early contacts were relatively minor and their impact on the native peoples is unknown.

European Colonies in North America

Initially, Europeans reacted to the discovery of the New World by attempting to conquer its people and loot its resources. Only some years later was any thought given to colonization. The Spanish began to explore the southern portion of North America in the early sixteenth century and in 1526 were the first to establish a colony in that region, located in what is now South Carolina.

Partly in response to this Spanish activity, the English founded colonies along the central Atlantic coast. The Roanoke colony was established in 1585, but it soon failed. A second attempt was made at Jamestown beginning in 1607; this colony struggled but survived, marking the beginning of a huge influx of English settlers into eastern North America. Another English colony was established at Popham Beach, Maine, in 1607 but failed the next year.

The French and Dutch also set up colonies in northeastern North America, first as fur-trading centers and later as colonies. The English eventually evicted the Dutch and took over their colonies and territories. The main Dutch colony, New Netherland, was subsequently renamed New York.

Most Europeans held the ethnocentric view that the Indians were either noble savages (idealized, simple children of nature) or primitive, bloodthirsty savages. It was also widely held that Indians had no God-given right to the land and that it was the "white man's burden" to bring civilization to them. Interestingly, most Indians also viewed the Europeans as bloodthirsty savages. In addition, Europeans and Indians often had different concepts about land ownership and use of resources, ideas that dominated many of their dealings (see Washburn 1988 for reviews of the relations between Indians and whites).

A number of European powers competed in the rush to claim portions of North America, including Spain, France, England, and to a lesser extent, Russia, Holland, and Portugal. Holland and Portugal quickly dropped out of the competition, but each of the other powers pursued particular policies and goals in the New World, resulting in different impacts to the native populations.

The Spanish Colonies

The first colonies in the New World were founded by Spain, in Central and South America, and later in what is now the southwestern United States and Florida. These Spanish colonies were government enterprises intended to establish an imperial presence, to control the native populations and economies, and to convert the Indians to Christianity. The procurement of land for settlers was not their goal, as relatively few Spaniards immigrated to the New World. The Spanish were primarily interested in appropriating native riches, particularly gold and silver, and enslaving the Indians to labor in exporting wealth to Spain. First, the natives had to be pacified, which was accomplished through ruthless and brutal campaigns of extermination, so that no doubt was left as to who was in charge (see Stannard 1992 for a gruesomely detailed account). To make matters even worse for the native populations, the spread of diseases introduced by the colonists reduced native numbers by as much as 95 percent in some regions during the first hundred years after the arrival of the Spanish (see Cook 1998).

Once the Indians were pacified, the Spanish introduced policies intended to control and enslave them. The Spanish established a new form of government to maintain political control of the various native cultures. This feudal system, called *encomienda*, entrusted large tracts of land to certain Spaniards; they could demand tribute and services from the resident natives, using military force if necessary. Eventually the Spanish themselves realized that the encomienda system, essentially a form of slavery, concentrated too much power in too few hands, so it was replaced by the *repartimiento* system, which divided the land into smaller units, the (still quite large) haciendas. These haciendas, owned by the elite, required the resident natives to work for the landowner. After the Mexican Revolution of 1910, many haciendas were broken up and the land redistributed to the peasants, either to individuals—who could not sell the land but could pass it on to their heirs—or to collective organizations such as villages.

French and Russian Business Interests

Unlike Spain, France and Russia were not much interested in converting Indians to European religions or in establishing direct control over their populations. The French and the Russians intended to conduct business with the Indians, primarily fur trading. Their policies toward the Indians were designed to ensure the success of the business ventures owned by their respective governments. They had the Indians do the difficult work of resource extraction, mostly of furs. Trading companies then purchased these goods at very low prices, sold them for their real value, and thus made gigantic profits. Neither the French nor the Russians made any concerted effort to colonize North America or to take large tracts of land from the Indians.

English Colonies

The English approached the New World quite differently. They wanted the land for themselves, rather than to exploit Indian labor or native resources. The first English colonies were established to provide living space for landless English citizens, a policy that resulted in large numbers of immigrants. Additionally, the English sent people to the colonies to ease the unemployment problem in England. They also exiled criminals to the colonies, a practice that continued during the colonization of Australia.

Once their colonies grew and became successful, the English began to reap economic benefits in trade and taxes. They considered the native peoples an obstacle, to be pushed out or killed to make way for more colonists. The Dutch had followed the same basic approach before England took over their territory. This pattern of genocide continued after the American Revolution, as the new United States undertook relations with the Indians.

Indian Slavery Among the Colonists

Many Indian groups had long taken other Indians captive, usually during warfare, for the purpose of acquiring hostages or slaves, or for adoption. Europeans eagerly joined in the market for slaves. Immediately upon their arrival in the New World, the Spanish began to export Indian slaves to Spain, but this practice did not last long because Indian population losses were so high. By the mid-sixteenth century, the Spanish, who required a large labor force to operate their new plantations, began to import African slaves to the New World to replace the rapidly disappearing Indians, thus ushering in the era of African slave trade to the New World. The English also joined in the trade of Indian slaves, encouraging an increase in native warfare in the Southeast in order to purchase Indian slaves from their Indian captors. A few Indian slaves were used in the South and some were sent to New England, but most were shipped to the West Indies as plantation labor.

In fact, all of the European colonial powers, but especially the Spanish and the English, used Indians as slaves. Even in the 1850s California, a nonslave territory, Indians declared as vagrants were arrested and essentially sold as slaves on the open market. The legal holding of slaves by Americans was not abolished until the 1860s.

Governmental Policies toward Native Americans

Pre-Revolutionary Policies

By the middle of the eighteenth century, the Spanish had established themselves in southeastern, southwestern, and western North America. The French controlled Canada and the Mississippi drainage (later to be sold to the United States as part of the Louisiana Purchase.) In eastern North America, the English colonies were expanding rapidly and aggressively, bringing the colonists into increasing conflict with the Indians and with the French, the longtime enemies of the British.

The British managed Indian affairs through several departments within their colonial government. In reality, however, the British never had much control over the colonists, who were living in many small and quasi-independent settlements that continually pushed against the Indians for land and resources. Between the early-seventeenth and mid-eighteenth centuries, the British and the local Indians fought many wars, most of them ending with the defeat of the Indians.

Conflicts also emerged between the European powers. The French in Canada allied themselves with the Indians against the British and their colonists to the south (the French wanted to keep the British away from the fur trade, and the English colonists wanted the land controlled by the French and Indians). The battles between them, collectively known as the French and Indian War, ended in 1763 with a British victory, leaving the British in control of Canada and all the land east of the Mississippi, except for Spanish Florida.

In 1763, following an uprising led by the Ottawa chief Pontiac, the British issued a decree limiting settlement west of the existing colonial boundaries. This line, called the Proclamation Line, was to be respected as the limit of English colonization until the government had signed agreements with the Indians. However, settlers ignored the line and streamed west. The 1763 decree implied an acknowledgment of Indian rights (Kelly 1990), as did certain attempts by the English to purchase land rather than to seize it. These somewhat enlightened government policies were largely ignored by the settlers, who wanted more and more land.

U.S. Indian Policies

Control of the lands south of Canada and west of the Mississippi passed to the new United States after 1783. Much has been written about the policies of the U.S. government toward American Indians, and an excellent overview is presented by Kelly (1990; also see Washburn 1973; Dippie 1982; Olsen and Wilson 1984; Prucha 1984; Deloria 1985; Weeks 1990; Hirschfelder and de Montaño 1993:8–35; Iverson 1998). During the late eighteenth century and throughout most of the nineteenth, for a variety of reasons, European Americans generally argued that it was necessary to either civilize or eliminate the Indians. However, the idea of "civilizing" the Indians seems to have served as a rhetorical smoke screen for the real purpose: eliminating the native peoples. Specific incidents reveal a discrepancy between the U.S. government's rhetoric and its actions. For example, even after the Cherokee had become "civilized"—having Americanized their way of life and established a modern state—they were ruthlessly uprooted from the Southeast and marched to Indian Territory in Oklahoma, an event known as the Trail of Tears (see Chapter 12).

Early in its history, the United States considered Indian tribes to be sovereign nations, though not *foreign* nations, and signed more than 400 treaties (by definition, agreements between independent political units) with various Indian peoples (see Prucha 1994 for a history of treaties between Indians and the federal government; also see Wilkins 1997 and http://www.councilfire.com/treaty/index.html for a list of full-text treaties). Many of these agreements were entered into in good faith by the respective governments, only to be broken by aggressive white settlers or, less often, by young Indian men continuing to raid after peace had been declared (see Prucha 1994:17–18; also see Deloria 1969). By the 1830s, Indian groups within the boundaries of the United States were considered to be *dependent* nations. This determination was based on an 1831 Supreme Court decision that denied a Cherokee request for an injunction against their removal; a year later, the government ignored a Supreme Court decision affirming Cherokee sovereignty (see Sherrow 1997). By 1871, most native groups without treaties had been defeated, so treaties were no longer sought. Thus, Indian political units evolved from sovereign to dependent status in relation to the U.S. government, occupying an ambiguous place in the political and cultural life of the United States—and this peculiar state of affairs still exists.

In 1775, the United States created several Indian Commissions, mostly in an effort to obtain Indian military assistance during the Revolutionary War. After the war, some Indians were punished for siding with the British, but there was generally a feeling within the government that the Indians should be treated fairly, perhaps because the U.S. military felt uncertain about its ability to quell potential conflicts (Kelly 1990:28). In 1790, the United States recognized the 1763 Proclamation Line and its provisions in an attempt to control both westward expansion and conflict with native peoples. However, it was virtually impossible to enforce this decision. When settlers continued to venture too far, the U.S. government felt obligated to protect them—it was preferable to fight Indians rather than its own citizens. This population pressure, and competition among European powers for control of the continent, doomed the effort (Horsman 1967).

In 1781, the Indian Department was created to manage native peoples. Its initial placement—within the War Department—provides some clue as to its mission. In 1824, the name of the agency was changed to the Bureau of Indian Affairs (BIA). The BIA became an independent agency in 1834 and was transferred to the newly created Department of the Interior in 1849. Initially, the mission of the BIA was to maintain good relations with sovereign Indian groups, in order to obtain land and promote trade. As the United States grew, however, its goal became the removal of the Indians from all lands east of the Mississippi River, then to their assimilation into American society. More recently, its mission evolved into supporting Indian groups.

The BIA is still the principal federal agency responsible for the welfare of native peoples in the United States and today has four primary responsibilities: (1) education; (2) providing other governmental services to native groups (e.g., law enforcement and health services); (3) management of the 56.2 million acres held in trust for various Indian nations; and (4) fostering Indian self-determination. Not until 1970 was an Indian appointed as the director of the BIA. A history and description of the BIA is provided by Jackson and Galli (1977; also see Porter 1988 and *http://www.doi.gov/bia.html*). In spite of the very checkered history of U.S. Indian policies, the federal government has spent many tens of billions of dollars to help its aboriginal inhabitants, a record no other nation can match.

Manifest Destiny   As European settlers continued to push westward, an idea evolved to justify the displacement of native peoples and the confiscation of their lands. Known as *manifest destiny*, it gave the European Americans a seemingly noble duty: to tame the wild lands of the west and to bring "civilization" to its native inhabitants. The idea gained momentum with the acquisition of the Oregon Territory in 1846 and of California and the American Southwest in 1848. As the Pacific Ocean beckoned, many Americans viewed it as their responsibility, or their "manifest destiny," to conquer and settle the lands west of the Mississippi River.

In the new territories, the West Coast was colonized first, due partly to the California Gold Rush. Two new American population centers, the West Coast and the region east of the Mississippi, were formed, with "Indian Country"—the Plains, Rockies, and Great Basin—lying between them. Many agreements between the government and Indian groups were breached as transportation corridors for wagon trails and railroads between the Mississippi River and California/Oregon were established. These broken treaties created considerable hostility between white settlers and the Indians, setting the stage for the famous Indian Wars of the west (a good history of these conflicts is presented in two volumes by Utley [1967, 1973]; see Brown 1970 for an Indian perspective).

Removal and Reservations   Though the early official U.S. Indian policy might be characterized as one of moderation (still, actual events tell a somewhat different story), after the War of 1812, the policy changed to removal and segregation. Entire cultures were relocated west of the Mississippi River, away from white settlements. This policy was formalized with the Indian Removal Act of 1830. Most of the Indians in the southeastern United States were forced, some at bayonet point, to walk to the Indian Territory established around 1830 in what is now Oklahoma (the word *Oklahoma* is from a Choctaw word meaning "red man"). Thousands of Indians died in these treks. Oklahoma essentially became a large reservation for many disparate groups, most of them separated from their homelands and economic bases. Ironically, oil was later discovered in Oklahoma, much to the dismay of the whites. In 1904, the Indian occupants of the Indian Territory petitioned Congress to admit the territory to the Union as an "Indian State," but their petition was rejected. Oklahoma was admitted to the Union in 1907.

In 1865, it was formally proposed that all Indians be put on reservations to protect them from whites, since neither the government nor the Indians themselves could do so. Over the next few years, a number of reservations were created on the Plains, this time located in the homelands of the affected groups, and a number of large groups moved to these reservations. Other groups were moved to Indian Territory and placed on lands that had been taken away from the Cherokee and Creek as punishment for their support of the Confederacy.

The government attempted to provide for the groups within the various reservations, but many of the politically appointed Indian agents prevented much of the money and supplies from getting to the Indians. Due to this corruption and greed, starvation became a serious concern, so some groups left the reservations to find food. The government perceived these actions as "uprisings," which they often quelled through bloodshed. Other Indians revolted at the poor treatment through raiding and warfare. Finally recognizing the corruption of Indian agents, the government appointed religious organizations—presumed to have higher morals—to administer the reservations and Indian payments through the Board of Indian Commissioners. This also failed, and the plight of the Indians worsened.

The Military Solution   Throughout the history of contact between native peoples and Euroamericans, the Indians almost always fared poorly. Few treaties were honored by the whites. Most of these accords were vague, poorly worded, negotiated with the wrong people, and never ratified by Congress. Virtually all were broken, usually by the whites, who were dealing with expanding populations. The affected native groups often reacted violently, and numerous military confrontations ensued. Many native groups possessed substantial military power and were adept at small-scale warfare. Most groups preferred not to fight but were quite capable if provoked. Small-scale conflict between armed settlers and native groups was a constant feature of the frontier. Large-scale warfare between Indians and the U.S. Army (or with the British prior to 1783) was uncommon and pitched battles were rare. Man for man, the Indians were more than a match for any European or American military force; however, the Indians lacked a sufficient number of modern weapons and were not able to sustain an army in the field for years on end.

Indian military power waned through defeat and population loss. By 1871 no more treaties were negotiated with Indians, and conflict between Indians and whites became an internal affair. In 1867, the United States instituted a "Peace Policy," forming the Indian Peace Commission to try to stop the incessant warfare. To the United States, peace meant the defeat and submission of the Indians, and a central component of the Peace Policy was to impose peace on the native peoples by force if necessary. To accomplish this goal, Gen. William T. Sherman (of Civil War fame) was appointed General of the Army in 1869. Sherman decided that the best way to obtain peace was to exterminate the Indians, although many Americans were opposed to this policy. While the Indians were not exterminated, the ruthless pursuit, defeat, incarceration, and maltreatment of Indians crushed their resistance, thereby achieving "peace."

Assimilation   From the early nineteenth century, many believed that the Indians were on the verge of extinction and that the survivors should be assimilated. Beginning in the 1870s, government policy began to shift from segregating Indians on reservations to attempting to assimilate (i.e., "civilize") Indians into mainstream society. Thought to be a humane solution to the Indian "problem," it was to be accomplished through educating the Indians, converting them to Christianity, and transforming their economies to farming (many Indian economies were already based on farming, but this was ignored).

It was reasoned that if the Indians became civilized, they would no longer require all of the lands of the reservations. Whites generally considered the Indians to have too much land already and proposals were made to parcel out reservation lands to individuals; thus, the Indians could be property owners, like whites. The Dawes Act (or General Allotment Act) of 1887 allowed for the disposition of group-owned Indian reservation land—mostly within actual states, rather than territories such as Arizona and New Mexico. These allotments were made to individual Indians (including women) in 40- to 360-acre parcels, depending on the quality of the land. Some reservation land was exempted due to earlier treaties. Lands that the government considered to be surplus could then be sold to whites, with the money, in theory, being used to help the Indians. The Dawes Act also made citizens of those Indians who received an allotment and moved away from their reservations. (All Indians in the United States were finally granted citizenship and the right to vote in 1924.) Individual ownership of land meant that the owners had to pay property taxes, which most Indians could not afford. Thus, the government held the allotments in trust, tax-exempt and nontransferable, for twenty-five years. Much reservation land was never allotted and remained in tribal hands. Many of these provisions were later changed, resulting in a further loss of Indian lands to whites.

Efforts were also made to educate Indian children. After 1877, schools were established, some on reservations and others as boarding schools. Frequently, Indian children were forcibly removed from their families, taken to boarding schools, and "educated" either to "become" whites (see DeJong 1993) or to serve as domestic help for white families. They were often punished severely if they spoke their native languages or observed their customs. This practice continued until the 1960s, when boarding schools were dropped in favor of local public schools.

The Indian New Deal As the United States gained a New Deal during the presidency of Franklin D. Roosevelt, so did the Indians. Roosevelt appointed a new director of the BIA, John Collier, who initiated sweeping reforms in the BIA and major changes in Indian policy (see Philp 1977), moving away from assimilation and toward cultural pluralism (partly based on a 1928 report that was highly critical of Indian policies). Many of these reforms were passed into law with the Indian Reorganization Act of 1934. With this act, the allotment system was ended and unsold reservation lands were returned to federally recognized tribes. In addition, efforts were made to purchase land to "close up" the allotments and restore the land base. Groups were then allowed to organize tribal governments to manage their own affairs, although to a limited extent. The act also provided for improved education and preferential employment of Indians in the BIA. Collier resigned in 1945 amid accusations of favoritism toward Indians. The Indian Claims Commission was formed in 1946 to resolve the various Indian complaints against the government (see Sutton 1985).

World War II provided an opportunity for many Indians to participate in American society, including work in war industries and in the military. Some 25,000 Indians joined the military and fought overseas. Indians have fought for the United States in every war in its history. Patriotism and the chance to earn battle honors were incentives to join. The movement of Indians to the cities was accelerated by those seeking jobs in war industries and by the return of war veterans, eventually setting the stage for more politically sophisticated Indian activism.

Beginning in the late 1940s, the U.S. government initiated the Termination Policy to end the recognition—including status and rights—of some native groups, to eliminate their reservations, and to move them into white society. After 1958, the government ceased its efforts to terminate tribal governments. In the 1960s and 1970s, the civil rights movement and the war on poverty provided some funding and programs to help many Indians.

The establishment of the National Council on Indian Opportunity and the passage of the American Indian Civil Rights Act, both in 1968, initiated better legal protection (see Pevar 1997 for an outline of Indian legal rights). In 1970, the BIA changed its basic policy from managing Indians to serving them. Beginning in the early 1970s, Indians began to campaign more actively for their rights and a revitalization of their cultures, led in part by the American Indian Movement (AIM). As a result of these efforts, Congress passed the Indian Self-Determination Act (1975, designed to allow tribal governments to administer federal funds provided to them, funds that were subsequently cut in the 1980s), the American Indian Religious Freedom Act (1978, designed to prevent interference in the practice of Native religions), the Indian Gaming Regulatory Act (1988, to allow gaming on Indians lands), and the Native American Graves Protection and Repatriation Act (NAGPRA) (1990, to require the return of skeletal remains and sacred objects). These newfound legal rights allowed a number of groups to sue some states for the loss of their lands, and many have won substantial monetary damages. As a part of self-determination, many groups have established their own school systems, including community colleges.

Today, the government administers some 275 Indian reservations (including reservations, pueblos, and rancherias; see Tiller 1996 for a profile of each) and holds some 56 million acres of land in trust. In 1994, the government issued an executive memorandum directing government agencies to cooperate on a government-to-government basis with federally recognized tribes.

Canadian Indian Policies

As of 2001, there were about 675,000 native people living in Canada. They are organized in some 610 recognized native groups, often called the First Nations, living on 2,240 reserves (equivalent to reservations in the United States). The reserves are held in trust by the Canadian government. Before Canada became an independent nation, its native peoples dealt with the British government. Native peoples in Canada probably endured the Euroamerican invasion better than those in the United States, as Canada had far fewer immigrants and much less development than the United States and the British were a little more sympathetic to their needs. Nonetheless, problems remained. Slavery was not outlawed in Canada until 1834, and Indians were the primary slaves.

In 1867, Canada gained independence (actually dominion status within the British Empire), thereby taking over the responsibility of regulating the native populations. The Office of Indian Affairs was established within the office of the Secretary of State. In 1873, the Office of Indian Affairs was placed in the new Department of the Interior and was renamed the Department of Indian Affairs in 1880. This department was later changed to the Ministry of Indian and Northern Affairs.

Between 1871 and 1921, the Canadian government signed eleven major treaties with native groups, who were moved to reserves where the government was to protect and support them. The Indian Act of 1876 was passed to manage the Indians, although it did not apply to Eskimo groups until after 1939. The act designated Indians as either Status Indians formally recognized with treaty rights, or Non-Status Indians who, for some reason, had lost or given up their status. Another group, the Métis, requested and gained recognition. The Métis are the "third aboriginal group," consisting of the descendants of European fur traders and their Indian (usually Cree) wives (see Slobodin 1981; also see Payment 2001). Over the centuries they had developed their own cultural identity, speaking French or English rather than an Indian language. In 1991, the Métis numbered some 240,000 people in Canada (Payment 2001:675). The Indian Act also denied Indians the right to practice their social and religious customs. To enforce the ban on religious activities, the government confiscated religious paraphernalia from a number of groups, particularly on the Northwest Coast (see Cole 1985). The Indian Act remains the Canadian measure most emblematic of Indian mistreatment.

In 1888, Canada passed a law similar to the U.S. Dawes Act of 1887. The intent of the law was to break up reserve lands through an allotment policy. The Indians had very little power to stop it, but the loss of Indian lands was not as severe as it was in the United States.

An alliance of groups on the Northwest Coast won a small land-claims case against the Canadian government in 1927, which prompted Canada to pass a law forbidding all collective native political action. However, in reevaluating its Indian policies in the 1940s, the Canadian government passed the Indian Act of 1951. In this act, natives were granted citizenship and local voting rights (although they could not vote in national elections until 1960), were allowed to practice their religions, and could pursue claims against the government. Also, Indian groups on reserves, usually called "bands," were expected to establish councils to make decisions that related to the bands. Nevertheless, many of these decisions were subject to approval by the Canadian government.

In 1966, the Department of Indian Affairs and Northern Development was created; in 1969 the Canadian government repealed the Indian Act of 1876 and moved to break up the reserves, in a move similar to the failed U.S. Termination Policy (see above). This caused the politically dormant Canadian native peoples to unite, protest, and make demands, forcing the government both to abandon its termination policy and to repeal the 1927 law against native political activity. The native groups went to court to have their treaty provisions honored and won some victories. In 1974, the government set up the Office of Native Claims. In the past few decades, a number of land claims have been settled with various native groups, resulting in the formation and enlargement of reserves, special rights to land use, and cash payments. Several treaties, known as Comprehensive Land Claim Settlements, have recently been signed with a number of groups (see summary in Bone 1992: Table 10.1; also see Crowe 1991). As a result of one of these agreements, a new Canadian province, called Nunavat, has been created in the eastern part of the current Northwest Territory. Most of the population of the new province is Eskimo, who govern it.

Indian Policies in Northern Mexico

The majority of Mexicans today have some Indian ancestry, but only about 20 percent of the population identify themselves as Indians, or *Indios*. Mexican Indians are less vocal and have less political power than their counterparts in the United States and Canada, partly because Indians in Mexico have even less opportunity for education, employment, and social mobility. Centuries-old customs and traditions have marginalized Mexico's native cultures. Indeed, even after Mexico gained its independence from Spain in 1821, the Mexican government continued the use of the old Spanish system of repartimiento (see above), and the mind-set reflected in this feudal system still exists today in many parts of Mexico.

In the 1850s, to promote market-oriented practices, the Mexican government passed "reform laws" that prohibited communal ownership of land, thus breaking up lands owned by tribes. Much of this land was obtained by non-Indians during that time. The Mexican government also passed laws to abolish the status "Indian" so that only "Mexicans" would be recognized. The laws further stated that anyone could colonize "unoccupied" lands—that is, Indian lands—if one promised to develop them.

A number of groups resisted these policies and led several revolts. The Yaqui (see Chapter 9) have been particularly resistant to the expropriation of their lands by both the Spanish and Mexicans for the past 450 years. The Yaqui led an armed resistance well into the twentieth century, which has gained the Yaqui a good deal of respect in Mexican history. Nevertheless, the Mexican government responded by sending in the army to crush the Yaqui. Many fled the region, and numerous Yaqui now live in Arizona.

After the revolution in 1910, the Mexican government pursued two different and seemingly contradictory policies. The first emphasizes assimilation through government education and economic development programs. The second emphasizes preserving the cultural and artistic heritage of Mexico's Indians. As part of the second policy, the government created the Asuntos Indígenas and the Instituto Nacional Indigenista to help the Indians in their disputes with private firms and government agencies.

Conflict between the government and Indians continues. In southern Mexico, the recent rebellions of Zapotecs in Oaxaca (1980) and of Maya populations in Chiapas (1990) are examples of growing problems. In northern Mexico, non-Indians continue to flood the region, exploitation of the environment remains unregulated, and the Indians continue to lose their lands and culture.

The Cultural and Biological Impacts of European Intrusion

Our knowledge of the consequences of European intrusion on native cultures is growing. First, we now better understand exactly how many native people were affected. Previous estimates of the number of people living in North America in 1492 stood at about 500,000, but it is now thought that eight to twelve million, or as many as eighteen million, lived on this continent. Second, we have gained a broader knowledge of the complex nature of the native cultures that were destroyed or damaged— a catastrophic loss in traditional knowledge and cultural achievement. Together, these impacts on population, land, and culture are astonishing in magnitude. The topic of European impacts on native cultures has been explored at some length, particularly in the past twenty years or so (see Fitzhugh 1985; Ramenofsky 1987; Stannard 1992; Dobyns 1993; Larsen and Milner 1994; Settipane 1995; Baker and Kealhoffer 1996; Cook 1998; Mancall and Merrell 2000; Thornton 2000; Axtell 2001; Larsen et al. 2001).

The population decline suffered by native peoples throughout the New World as a result of European contact and expansion was enormous, perhaps as much as 95 percent in some areas (Stannard 1992:268). Thus, of a total New World population of perhaps approaching 100 million people (probably more than were in Europe at the same time), only some five million survived. In North America, a similar rate of population loss was suffered by the natives; of the approximately eight to twelve million people, only about 375,000 survived into the twentieth century (see Stannard 1992). This type of impact is not confined to the past; native peoples continue to face population declines in many countries, for a variety of reasons.

Sidelight

EUROPEAN DISEASE IN THE NEW WORLD

Diseases introduced into the New World from Europe had a devastating impact on native populations. Contact between native peoples and Europeans resulted in the transmission of European diseases to the natives, but few if any native diseases were transmitted to the Europeans; the exchange seems to have been overwhelmingly one way. Why would this be so?

Humans originally evolved in Africa in relatively small groups, and immunity was evolved over millions of years. Asian populations originally migrated to the New World from northeastern Asia, and these populations were small and separated from diseases developing in the rest of the world. As people first moved into the New World, they carried few diseases. Thus, New World populations were relatively free from contagious and infectious disease.

Disease is the complex of reactions and symptoms exhibited by the host in reaction to being invaded by a parasite. Contagious diseases generally involve small parasites such as viruses and bacteria and are spread from organism to organism mostly through the air or direct contact; infectious diseases involve relatively large parasites, such as worms and flukes. The development of contagious diseases requires a relatively large host population so that the pathogen (virus, bacterium, etc.) can be transmitted, and most pathogens must be transmitted to a new host rapidly before the host (and therefore the pathogen) dies. These "crowd" diseases have developed only relatively recently, since large, settled groups of people are a fairly recent phenomenon. Agriculture, which in many parts of the world displaced the hunting–gathering way of life, is only about 10,000 years old in the Old World and about 8,000 years old in the New World. Thus, only in the past several thousand years, as populations grew and cities

developed based on agriculture, that crowd diseases had a means to emerge.

The other important factor in the development and dispersal of disease is that many human diseases first evolved in animals and then "jumped" to humans. Over the past 10,000 years, farmers have domesticated a wide variety of animals, including pigs, sheep, cows, chickens, dogs, horses, and many others. Large numbers of these animals were kept in close proximity to their human owners, providing ample opportunity for the transmission of disease. Many of the major killer diseases originally arose from animals; the influenza that killed some twenty million people in 1918 may have originated in swine. A similar influenza may have been the first of the New World epidemics (Stannard 1992:68).

Several other factors were also important in the transmission of European diseases. The major population centers in North, Central, and South America were mostly isolated from one another, and travel between them was quite time consuming. Such factors would have prevented the transmission of indigenous disease between these centers. However, in the Old World the extensive trading networks and rapidity and ease of travel between Europe, Asia, and Africa allowed disease to spread quickly. In addition, diseases apparently have an easier time moving east–west rather than north–south, perhaps due to climate and vegetation zones; European diseases dominated North America, whereas African diseases dominated South America.

Finally, humans were not the only ones to suffer from Old World diseases. Animal diseases (e.g., tularemia) brought over with European livestock, pets, and vermin (e.g., rats) may have ravaged native animal populations. Such epidemics would have exacerbated the already grim situation for the native peoples. A good, uncomplicated summary of disease transmission between the Old and New Worlds is provided by Diamond (1992; also see Cockburn 1971 and McNeill 1976).

Most population losses were due to the many diseases inadvertently brought to the New World by the Europeans, including smallpox, measles, influenza, malaria, typhus, bubonic plague, whooping cough, tuberculosis, diphtheria, yellow fever, cholera, and typhoid fever. The population declines associated with these diseases were usually due to multiple factors, including direct disease mortality across the population, greatly increased infant mortality, and a decline in birth rates. In addition, some of the population loss was due to direct action by Europeans (murder, overworking of slaves, failure to provide promised goods, etc.). Malnutrition resulting from imposed economic systems, such as forcing hunter-gatherers to become agriculturalists, lowered immune responses, increased disease, and decreased fertility. The effect of psychological stress on the immune system from the loss of life and culture may have added yet another layer of impact. However, some now believe that several native diseases also hit hard in Mexico in the sixteenth century, killing millions of people (Acuna-Soto et al. 2000).

The huge population decline resulted in loss of culture and knowledge. As the people who knew the ceremonies, songs, stories, technology, and other traditional knowledge died, less and less of this information was passed along to the next generation. After populations had stabilized and began to rebound, much had already been lost. Territory was also lost, making it even more difficult to reconstitute and rebuild cultures.

All of these factors continue to impact native groups. Racism, discrimination, despair, and poor health care are still widespread. Alcoholism is the most serious health problem facing Indians today. In some tribes the rate of alcoholism is as high as 85 percent. (A guide to sources on the current health of Native American populations is provided in Gray 1996.)

The Spanish Mission System

One of the major aspirations of the Spanish in the New World was to convert the masses of "pagan" natives to Christianity. In the late sixteenth century, the Crown had granted exclusive rights to missionize specific regions to the Jesuit and Franciscan orders, and after 1767, the Jesuit territories were given to the Franciscans. While small-scale missionary efforts were undertaken by the French and English throughout North America, the Spanish established mission systems in four major centers of North America: California, the Southwest, the Southeast, and northern Mexico.

In California, missions were established in both Alta and Baja California (see Costello and Hornbeck 1989; Mathes 1989; Crosby 1994). A series of seventeen missions was built in Baja California by Jesuit missionaries, and twenty-one additional missions were established by the Franciscans in Alta California. In the Rio Grande Valley of the Southwest, another system of missions was founded (see Kubler 1940; Spicer 1962; Kessell 1979; Jackson 2000). An extensive mission system was established in La Florida in the southeastern United States (see Thomas 1990; Milanich 1994), where as many as 130 mission localities were founded, although not all were occupied at the same time. The most extensive system was established in northern Mexico (the southern portion of the Southwest), where hundreds of churches were built (Dunne 1948; Polzer 1976; Roca 1979; Polzer et al. 1991; Sheridan et al. 1991; Jackson 1994).

In general, popular beliefs regarding missions and missionaries in the New World are highly romanticized, mythical versions of what people wish they had been: wonderful places where the natives could escape their primitive lives to discover and embrace the superior ways of the Europeans (see Thomas 1991 for a perspective on how this myth developed). This version is still widely taught in schools and remains the "party line" for tourists at many of the surviving missions, some of which are now parks. In truth, many (although not all) missions were little more than concentration camps, where the natives were imprisoned, forced to abandon their culture, and enslaved as labor, although it is true that these judgments are based on today's standards (see Guest 1979, 1983). These practices resulted in severe impacts to the Indians. Entire cultures were wiped out, dying from overwork, disease, and loss of the ability to reproduce. Native peoples were viewed as children, who required stern treatment and discipline if they were to be elevated from their savage or barbarian roots.

Organization of the Missions

Religion was intertwined with colonialism and conquest, and was often seen as the moral force behind the "civilizing" of native populations, and this is still true all over the world. Convinced of the superiority of their culture and religion, missionaries imposed their beliefs and values on native peoples, sometimes by force (this is also still occurring). The intentions of most of the missionaries may have been good, but their methods were often brutal (see Tinker 1993).

Some missionary efforts were made at the actual village or town of a native group, while others were set up in different locations in order to separate the native individuals from their social, economic, and political communities and to concentrate them under Spanish control. This latter style, called *reducción* (or *congregación*), was established by the Spanish in California, the Southwest, and along the Southeast coast.

The missions were religious centers with priests, but military garrisons, or *presidios,* were built nearby to enforce the dictates of the priests. The state used the Church to help establish civil control over regions, while the Church used the state to protect its conversion efforts. The military was also sometimes used to gather new converts and to hunt down those who had escaped.

Missions typically consisted of a church building, housing for the priests, soldiers' quarters (if there was not a separate presidio), workshops, storage structures, animal pens, fields, irrigation works, and where necessary, dormitory-like buildings for the native converts. Buildings were often constructed from adobe (sun-dried mud) bricks, manufactured on site by native labor. Smaller missions, called *asistencias,* were sometimes established away from the major missions, and were often occupied by only a few people.

The Impact of the Missions

The Spanish were determined to subjugate and convert the native populations by pressuring them to settle at the missions so that they could be more easily controlled and their labor used. To do this, it was necessary to break down the traditional political, social, and economic systems of the Indians and remake them in the Spanish mold.

Central to the transformation of native culture was the forced adoption of new belief systems, although it was technically illegal for the Spanish to force someone to convert. Traditional religions were prohibited and replaced by Christianity. Attendance at daily mass was mandatory in some regions. People were baptized, often without even knowing what the ceremony meant. Marriages often had to be approved and performed by the Church. People were also forced to adopt European dress—including clothing of hot, lice-infested wool—foods, customs, and professions such as mason and carpenter.

Native people were usually compelled to learn Spanish, and native languages were often outlawed. In taking control of the native political system, the Spanish often replaced traditional leaders with others who were more cooperative. New laws and rules were instituted to control the movement of people. As they became entrenched, the Spanish then began to dismantle social institutions. Traditional kinship systems were broken up by reorganizing families and forcing children to attend boarding schools.

Economic systems were also changed, sometimes radically. Some groups were forced to adopt European-style agriculture in order to support the Spanish, who produced little. This often meant taking very productive native economies and converting them to less productive systems prone to drought and famine. The often unproductive agriculture required that food be rationed, with much less food given to the Indians than to the Spanish. Famine was a new phenomenon to the Indians and many learned what hunger was for the first time. Occasionally, a few Indians would be permitted to leave the missions to hunt and gather traditional foods. When the Spanish missionaries allowed these occasional excursions, they would hold family members hostage to ensure that the hunter-gatherers would return.

Finally, native people were often forced to live in dirty, overcrowded, unsanitary conditions, quite unlike their native villages. These conditions proved ideal for the spread of contagious disease, and the death toll among the natives, especially children, was staggering. In fact, some missions actually had to be abandoned when all the Indians within the region had died and there was no one left to work. The overcrowded conditions also fostered increased violence.

Native Resistance

Those resisting the Spanish were harshly punished. Many were beaten, some were imprisoned, and others were purposely starved. In some places, the death rate was so high from disease and overwork that the Indians desperately tried to escape. If they had a place to go, they simply ran away. Entire groups retreated into remote regions where the Spanish could not follow.

Other groups revolted violently. Indians at virtually all the missions planned revolts, but most were discovered in advance and thwarted. Large-scale rebellions did take place in La Florida in 1597 and in the Southwest in 1680, but these were so ruthlessly repressed by the Spanish that the Indians did not dare resist further. In California, the Indians at some of the missions revolted in 1824. This uprising was somewhat successful since the mission system was already on the verge of collapse by that time. Indians at several missions on the Colorado River revolted in 1781, eliminated the Spanish from the region, and successfully resisted reconquest until the 1860s.

The Fur Trade

The fur trade was a major economic endeavor undertaken by all of the European powers in North America, particularly by the French, British, and Russians, most intensively in northern North America between 1600 and 1850. Those native groups involved in the fur trade were, in essence, business partners with the European traders. The Indians were largely left on their own to provide furs and little effort was made to directly control them politically or to occupy their lands. Nevertheless, they were directly impacted by European diseases and suffered accordingly.

The French and Dutch initially dominated the early fur trade in northwestern North America, with the Dutch being pushed out by the English at a fairly early date. By the late seventeenth century, the French also controlled the fur trade in the interior of eastern North America, while the British dominated the fur trade in what is now much of eastern Canada and the northeastern United States. The British established the Hudson's Bay Company in 1670. The Hudson's Bay Company became very powerful, expanding across much of North America, and is still in business today, although on a much smaller scale. The French abandoned North America after 1803, leaving virtually all of the trade in central and eastern North America to the British and the Americans. The Russians moved into northwestern North America beginning about 1740 and dominated the fur trade in that region until they were pushed out by the British in the early nineteenth century.

Since its beginning, the fur trade played a dominant role in the economies of native peoples in the Arctic and Subarctic. The trade in furs declined in the 1950s, when the demand for furs decreased, primarily due to pressure from animal-rights groups. Nevertheless, there are still about 100,000 trappers in northern North America, about half of them native people (Bone 1992:213).

The fur trade profoundly altered the native cultures of northern America, mirroring many impacts of Western cultures on indigenous groups around the world. These include changes in political and social structures, economic systems, settlement practices, territoriality, and technology.

To compete in the fur trade, European trading companies vied for partnerships with the various native groups, to form trading blocks against other companies. Competition was keen and frequently violent. Native groups sometimes found themselves at war with former allies and friends. Alliances dissolved and reformed,

Sidelight

NATIVE TOBACCO: THEN AND NOW

Tobacco is a very popular substance that affects the lives of most people on our planet today. Tobacco is sniffed, chewed, and smoked in cigarettes, cigars, and pipes. Those who do not use tobacco are still subject to its effects through secondhand smoke or by having their taxes pay the medical bills for those who do use it. Since its first use, probably hundreds of millions of people worldwide have died of tobacco-related diseases, mostly cancer, and the death toll and associated costs continue to rise.

Tobacco (genus *Nicotiana*) is indigenous to the New World and includes about a dozen species distributed across the hemisphere. These species vary in their nicotine content; a strong tobacco can produce an immediate and almost hallucinogenic response. Native tobacco was used by Indians all across temperate North America, primarily for ceremonial purposes but sometimes for recreation (see Pego et al. 1999). It was smoked in pipes, sometimes chewed (as on the Northwest Coast), and sometimes snorted. Tobacco was cultivated by some native groups, while other groups managed wild tobacco plants, harvesting the leaves on an as-needed basis. Most groups mixed tobacco with either dogwood or sumac to lessen the effect of the nicotine.

Columbus observed natives in the Caribbean smoking "cigars"; in fact, the word *tobacco* comes from a Spanish translation of a native term meaning "cigar." Europeans rapidly adopted and began cultivating tobacco. By the mid–sixteenth century, snuff was being used, and then smoking tobacco in pipes became popular. Tobacco was first thought to be a medicinal aid. By the time people realized it was not, it had already become very popular and accepted in European society.

The primary native tobacco in eastern North America was *N. rustica,* but it was too harsh for the English, so a relatively mild species (*N. tabacum*) was imported from the Caribbean. This species was brought to the Jamestown colony in Virginia by John Rolfe, the husband of Pocahontas (see VIP profile in Chapter 11), who began tobacco farming in the colony. Tobacco farming spread all along the Atlantic coast from the Carolinas to Maryland, and soon the crop became an enormously important export. Farming of *N. tabacum* later spread across the world. Today, China is the largest grower and consumer of tobacco.

---

only to dissolve again as conditions changed. Native leadership fell to those who could manipulate the traders. Some groups were forced to completely restructure their political systems in order to deal with the trading companies.

Traditional economies were substantially affected. Prior to the fur trade, native economies were centered on obtaining resources necessary for the group. Then the economic focus changed from subsistence to trapping. Food and other goods were obtained from trade for furs, rather than directly by the people. After having survived for 15,000 years on their own, native peoples rapidly became dependent on the trading posts for their survival.

Prior to the fur trade, most groups did not own or defend territory. Afterward, specific territories became much more important since traplines had to be set out and monitored. If the traps were raided, the fur would be lost. Thus, traplines and territories were vigorously defended.

Most groups involved in the fur trade had previously moved around the landscape in relatively small groups on a seasonal basis, following game, collecting plants, and/or fishing. But as they became dependent on traded goods, people tended to move closer to the trading posts, creating larger and more permanent villages adjacent to the trading posts. This new living arrangement brought relatively large groups of people into more or less permanent contact with each other. As food came from the traders, the value and prestige of hunters decreased and violence increased. Disputes over territory and/or women escalated, domestic violence became a problem, drinking and associated violence increased, and death rates began to soar. In addition, a number of health problems ensued from nucleation around the trading posts, including those related to poor sanitation, increased disease, poor nutrition from European foods, dental problems due to refined sugars, and alcoholism. People had lived for thousands of years in small, separate groups; they did not do well in large, permanent ones.

Traditional technology was finely tuned to a hunting lifestyle in the north. Then, in the late nineteenth century, the addition of rapid-firing guns and metal traps radically changed native technology and the people became reliant on European tools. This resulted in a loss of native knowledge, skills, and technology. Much later, additional technological changes, such as the use of guns and snowmobiles, increased the efficiency of killing, resulting in the reduction of certain fur species to the point where they could not be hunted profitably. Competing companies sometimes implemented a "scorched stream" policy that resulted in the complete extirpation of certain species from some areas so that other companies could not trap there.

Despite these great pressures, some of the northern North American groups have managed to maintain much of their traditional culture. They survive today partly by trapping, partly by government assistance, and partly by hunting. However, the loss of knowledge and skills over the past few hundred years has made it difficult for native people to return to traditional subsistence hunting, which is now regulated by the government to preserve species. Additional information on the fur trade can be found in Ray (1974), Wishart (1979a), Krech (1981, 1984), and Mackie (1997).

///

3 Native Peoples of the Arctic

///

The Arctic encompasses all of the northern polar regions of the world, including parts of North America, Asia, and Europe. For the purposes of this book, however, only the North American portion of the Arctic (Fig. 3.1) is considered. The natural and cultural Arctic do not precisely match and there is some overlap between some Subarctic groups living in the Arctic environment and vice versa. In this book, the boundaries defined by the Arctic and Subarctic volumes of the *Handbook of North American Indians* (Vols. 5 and 6) are followed. The inhabitants of the Arctic are often collectively referred to by the general term *Eskimo*. Most people have heard of the Eskimo, and even have a basic idea of their adaptation to the Arctic environment; however, the popular understanding masks the substantial diversity and complexity of Eskimo culture (see Fienup-Riordan 1990:1–34). Nevertheless, for the sake of convenience, the term *Eskimo* is used throughout this chapter, with the exception of the case studies.

The term *Eskimo* was first used by Europeans in the late sixteenth century to refer to a specific group in the eastern Arctic, and was subsequently extended to include many other groups. The name was also used by Algonquian Indians in a derogatory sense to mean "eaters of raw flesh" (see Oswalt 1999:5–6). Interestingly, a small portion of the Siberian Arctic is also inhabited by Eskimo (see Fitzhugh and Crowell 1988), who are closely related to the people of the North American Arctic. The Eskimo are biologically distinct from the Indians living to the south. They are relatively recent entrants into North America and retain a number of biological traits traceable to northern Asia, including short and stocky bodies (for conservation of heat in cold climates) and epicanthic eye folds (extension of the skin of the upper eyelid over the edge of the eye) (see Szathmary 1984).

Following the *Handbook of North American Indians*, the native peoples of the Arctic are divided into two groups, the Aleut and the Eskimo. In a very general sense, the

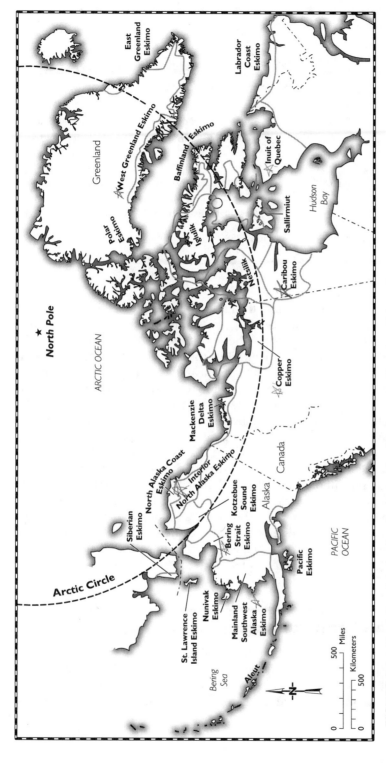

FIGURE 3.1 North American Arctic culture area showing the general location of the various native groups

Adapted from *Handbook of North American Indians, Vol. 5, Arctic*, D. Damas, ed., p. ix; copyright © 1984 by the Smithsonian Institution. Reprinted by permission of the publisher.

45

TABLE 3.1. Linguistic divisions of the Eskimo-Aleut language family and cultural divisions of the North American Eskimo

Language Family	Language Subfamily	General Culture	General Location
Aleut	Aleut	Aleut	Aleutian Islands
Eskimo	Sirenikski	Siberian Eskimo	Far eastern Siberia
	Yup'ik	Western Eskimo	Southwestern and central Alaska, far southeastern Siberia
	Inuit	Northern Eskimo	Northern Alaska and Canada
		Greenland Eskimo	Greenland

Source: Summarized from Woodbury 1984 and Krauss 1988.

Aleut are people of the open ocean and the Eskimo are people of the ice. The Aleut inhabit the Aleutian island chain extending westward from the Alaska Peninsula, while the various Eskimo groups occupy the rest of the North American Arctic. In Alaska, many Eskimo call themselves Yuit, while the Eskimo in Canada and Greenland prefer to call themselves Inuit, both terms meaning roughly "human being."

All North American Arctic groups speak languages of the Eskimo-Aleut language family; so do the Eskimo in extreme northeastern Siberia (see Woodbury 1984; Krauss 1988). The Eskimo-Aleut language is split into two major divisions: Aleut and Eskimo. The Aleut branch consists of one language, Aleut, spoken by people in the far southwestern Arctic, a region that is geographically in the Subarctic but is usually included in the cultural Arctic. The Eskimo branch is divided into three subbranches: Sirenikski, Yup'ik, and Inuit. Sirenikski is a single language spoken by Eskimo groups in far eastern Siberia. Yup'ik languages are spoken by Eskimo groups in southern and central Alaska and a small part of far southeastern Siberia, while the Inuit languages extend from northern Alaska eastward across Canada to Greenland. A very general classification of the North American Arctic people by language, culture, and geography is offered in Table 3.1.

Geography and Environment

The North American Arctic covers about two million square miles (see Chester and Oetzel 1998 for a good overview of the geography of the Arctic). The Arctic is characterized by a cold climate, large bodies of water, icy terrain, and general paucity of vegetation. The land is bounded by the Arctic Ocean to the north, the Bering Strait between Alaska and Asia, and the Bering Sea to the south. The Arctic Ocean has many other named seas, bays, straits, and inlets, as well as many islands, the largest being Greenland. The ocean water is very cold, but fish and sea mammals are abundant.

Four major geographic regions are defined for the Arctic. The Canadian Shield, which consists mostly of exposed granite bedrock with few hills or mountains, encompasses much of the eastern Arctic to Greenland, and much of it is covered with ice. Several large mountain ranges, such as the Brooks Range in northern Alaska, dominate the western Arctic. The Arctic coastal plain stretches from northwestern Alaska east to western Canada. The Aleutian Islands, a series of island chains, run west from southwestern Alaska.

The Arctic receives low levels of solar radiation, about 40 percent less than at the equator, and much of what is received is reflected by snow and ice; thus, the climate is cold year-round. The region receives relatively little precipitation, and even less evaporation, so much of the Arctic can technically be considered a desert. The short but productive summers bring fairly warm weather, and coastal areas are ice-free by early July, although the polar ice pack remains year-round. By September, it begins to cool again and the snow and ice return. Strong winds can blow anytime and can be very dangerous in the winter, so shelter from these winds is essential. One of the major environmental distinctions made by the people who live in the coastal areas of the Arctic is the presence or absence of sea ice in the winter.

The Arctic Circle is the line that divides the nonpolar region of the earth, which has daily cycles of light and dark, from the northern polar region, where there are long periods of unbroken daylight, twilight, or darkness. Above the Arctic Circle, daylight is constant from about April through August, and it is mostly dark between about November and February. These cycles vary somewhat based on ones distance from the North Pole.

The Arctic has low biological activity and a small biomass. Vegetation communities are often divided into Polar Desert (or High Arctic) and tundra (or Low Arctic) (Bone 1992:19). The Polar Desert is permanently frozen and supports a few funguses and plants, mostly lichens. The tundra lies south of the Polar Desert and north of the Subarctic coniferous forest. The subsoil is permanently frozen (called permafrost), but the topsoil thaws during the short summer, creating vast wetlands and bogs (a favorite place for migrating waterfowl) and offering a limited growing season. The tundra supports a low-growing vegetation, such as dwarf willow, alder, and birch trees, as well as low shrubs, some grasses, lichens, mosses, and many flowering plants. The boundary between the Arctic and the Subarctic is often defined as the coniferous forest treeline. The treeline is not a discrete place, but rather a zone wherein the numbers of trees decrease until there are none (see Bone 1992:19). Because there is relatively little vegetation, it follows that the use of plant resources by the Eskimo was quite limited.

A number of land animals live in the Arctic. The most prevalent is the caribou, fairly large reindeerlike animals (up to 400 pounds) that migrate in large herds across vast tracts of the Arctic and Subarctic and graze on the short Arctic vegetation. In various parts of the Arctic are other animals, such as musk ox (except in the far southeastern Arctic), grizzly bears, polar bears, black bears, wolves, wolverines, lynx, many fur-bearing species (e.g., foxes, weasels, and mink), hares and rabbits, and many rodents. Marine mammals in the Arctic waters include nineteen species of whales, eight of seals, two of walrus, two of dolphin, and one of porpoise. Seals were probably considered the most important marine mammal by the Eskimo. Additionally, over a hundred species of birds nest in the Arctic during the summer. Some of these birds, such as ptarmigan, ducks, and geese, were hunted, and their eggs were also eaten. Many fish, including salmon, char, trout, pike, smelt, herring, whitefish, halibut, and cod, were caught and consumed.

A Basic Prehistory of the Arctic

The Arctic has a remarkably complex prehistory. Summaries of what is known of the ancient Arctic are found in Dumond (1984, 1987), Maxwell (1985), McGhee (1996), and Fagan (2000). The information below is abstracted from those sources.

The Paleoindian Period (to ca. 10,000 B.P.)

A large portion of the western Arctic was not covered by ice during the last Ice Age. When Paleoindians crossed Beringia (see discussion in Chapter 1), they entered western Alaska, moving into the North American Arctic. A number of early sites known in the New World suggest an entry by at least 14,000 years ago, and there is some reason to believe that there may have been an even earlier migration into the New World. The technological and economic adaptations of these early people are poorly known. By at least 12,000 years ago, once the ice had melted to some extent, people in the Arctic began to move south to occupy the rest of the New World.

The Archaic Period (ca. 10,000 B.P. to Contact)

The people who remained in the Arctic after others had migrated into the rest of the New World essentially developed a generalized early Archaic, or "Paleo-Arctic," economy. It is possible that these people were the ancestors of the Na-Dene (speakers of Athapaskan languages). By about 7,000 B.P., perhaps even earlier, Na-Dene had begun to move into the Northwest Coast and western Subarctic, possibly from western Alaska. The Aleut occupied the Aleutian Islands by that time, though perhaps earlier.

By at least 4,000 years ago, some of the early Eskimo people moved east and inhabited the previously unoccupied northern portion of the Arctic, where they developed separate cultures from those remaining in the western Arctic. Beginning about 1,000 years ago, western Eskimo people began to move east, replacing those who had colonized those regions 3,000 years earlier, reaching Greenland by about 700 years ago. Thus, all of the people of the North American Arctic east of Alaska moved into that area in fairly recent times and share a common language.

The Contact Period

Sometime after about 1,000 years ago, the Eskimo of the eastern Arctic were first contacted by the Norse moving west from Iceland. Norse contacts were probably brief and never very intense. Thus, there was no real opportunity for the transmission of disease; at least there is no evidence of any Old World diseases prior to 1492, or for any major Norse influences on Eskimo culture. By the late fourteenth century, the Eskimo were expanding east and south into Greenland. By about 1500, the Norse had abandoned Greenland, perhaps due to a cooling climate. It is also possible that the Eskimo pushed the Norse out of Greenland; if so, it is a rare instance of Native Americans invading an area and replacing Europeans.

A Russian naval expedition landed in Alaska in 1732. In 1741, a second one, led by Vitus Bering, was dispatched to the region to claim it for Russia. The Russians contacted the Aleut, some of whom were forced to hunt sea otters for the Russians, an activity that rapidly depleted local sea otter populations. The trade in sea otter pelts expanded rapidly, and the Russian-American Company was established in 1799. The Russians fought—often in violation of imperial law—with the Aleut and Eskimo between 1760 and 1780, and with the Tlingit on the northern Northwest Coast between 1802 and 1804, before finally gaining control of the area. Alaska was purchased by the United States in 1867, and the Russians left the region at that time, although their cultural influences, particularly religion, persist to this day (see Black 1988 for a history of the Russians in Alaska).

After 1840, American whalers became very active in the northern Arctic, where whaling activities reached their peak in about 1900. This intensive hunting depleted whale populations to the point that the Eskimo were struggling to locate them. In addition, the whaling ships commonly stopped at coastal native villages, where the sailors spread venereal diseases. The Americans also distributed rum, which was ultimately detrimental to the Eskimo, as many became dependent on it. The introduction of rifles had a profound effect on the Eskimo as well, both by increasing their reliance on whites for ammunition and by depleting game populations.

For the most part, the governments of both the United States and Canada ignored the native people of the Arctic. There was some effort to build schools, but little other help was provided, and very little was done to control the effects that development in the region (e.g., mining, lumber, fishing, whaling) had on the native groups. The Aleut and Eskimo had to deal with major changes in virtually all aspects of their lives (see discussion of the fur trade in Chapter 2).

The Impact of European Contact

Although contacted in the seventeenth century in the east and in the eighteenth century in the west, most Arctic groups remained largely unaffected by Old World diseases. Most populations were small and dispersed over a vast landscape, impeding the transmission of disease. However, some groups were affected early due to intense contact with the Russians during the mid-to-late eighteenth century. In addition, by the late nineteenth century, many Eskimo were congregated around trading posts and other permanent settlements, ideal places for the spread of disease as well as other problems, such as increased violence. In Alaska, the smallpox epidemic of 1836–1838 was devastating, and epidemics of measles and whooping cough occurred repeatedly. The influenza epidemic of 1918 decimated native populations. The result was huge population losses, upwards of 90 percent in some places.

A Brief History of Ethnographic Research

Contact with, and descriptions of, Arctic peoples began in the eastern Arctic in the sixteenth century and then in the western Arctic in the eighteenth century. However, as of the late nineteenth century, portions of the central Arctic and northern Greenland were still unknown to westerners. Thus, although the existence of the Eskimo has been known for the past 450 years, some groups remained uncontacted until fairly recently. The records of early explorers, ship captains, missionaries, and trading companies are exceedingly useful for descriptions of Aleut and Eskimo cultures.

Serious anthropological work on Arctic cultures began only in the mid–nineteenth century (see Burch 1979; Collins 1984; Hughes 1984). Among the most notable researchers were Hinrich Rink, Franz Boas, E. W. Nelson, and Knud Rasmussen, who himself was part Eskimo. Rasmussen worked with the Greenland Eskimo in the early twentieth century and his work displays "a depth of understanding, sensitivity, and insight that is unequaled in Arctic literature" (Collins 1984:10). In the central Arctic, the work of Diamond Jenness and Kaj Birket-Smith in the early twentieth century is particularly valuable.

Prior to World War II, most anthropological interest in Arctic peoples had focused on their technological adaptations to the Arctic environment. After 1945, when native life began to change rapidly with the encroachment of Western culture and anthropological research interests became much more sophisticated, many other questions were examined, such as those concerned with psychology, ecology, and acculturation. Today, considerable ethnographic work continues to be conducted in the Arctic (e.g., Condon et al. 1996; Burch 1998) and there is still much to learn.

There is a vast literature on Arctic peoples. Perhaps the best overall summaries of Eskimo culture were prepared by Weyer (1932) and Birket-Smith (1936). The Arctic volume (Vol. 5) of the *Handbook of North American Indians*, which was published in 1984 (Damas 1984a), was written mostly in the late 1970s and early 1980s and contains chapters on a wide variety of subjects and groups. More recent treatments of Arctic culture include Fitzhugh and Crowell (1988), Fienup-Riordan (1990); Crowe (1991), Morrison and Germain (1995), Condon et al. (1996), Burch (1998), and Freeman (2000). The summary of Arctic cultures presented below was taken from these sources and discusses groups as they were in approximately the middle of the nineteenth century.

A Broad Portrait of Arctic Groups

The Arctic is a demanding, high-stress environment, and survival requires a very extensive knowledge and understanding of that environment. Arctic peoples have survived by living with the cold, rather than by struggling against it. Eskimo values include self-reliance, cooperation, modesty, sharing with others, and self-control.

There are four basic cultural divisions and adaptations in the Arctic: (1) Aleut; (2) Western Eskimo; (3) Northern Eskimo; and (4) Greenland Eskimo (see Table 3.1). The Aleut, speaking the Aleut language, lived on the relatively warm Aleutian Islands in fairly large, permanent communities. They subsisted almost entirely on fish and sea mammals (see Case Study on the Aleut, below).

The Yup'ik, or Western Eskimo, speaking Yup'ik languages, lived in western Alaska in a sort of Subarctic coastal/forest environment (the Yup'ik remain in their homeland and retain much of their traditional culture today; see Fienup-Riordan 1990). In the winter, the Western Eskimo lived in villages with substantial semi-subterranean houses. In the summer, the families moved about the landscape, living in skin tents. Firewood was abundant and food was usually cooked. The major food resource was salmon, which was dried and stored. Hunting was important, and a variety of animals, including caribou, moose, bears, squirrels, and waterfowl, were exploited. Men hunted and women gathered plants (willow leaves were a favorite) and performed the main household and maintenance chores.

The Northern Eskimo, speaking western Inuit languages, occupied the northern coast of the Arctic from northwestern Alaska to eastern Canada. These were the Eskimo stereotypically familiar to most people (see Case Study on the Inuit of Quebec, below). In northwestern Alaska, the Eskimo lived in permanent villages, but in most other areas, small, highly mobile bands were the rule. People lived in houses of snow or sod in the winter and skin tents in the summer. Dogs and dogsleds were critical for survival. Sea mammal hunting was the major economic focus, seals being the most important game animal, followed by whales and walrus. Other animals were also essential, including the musk ox and fish, and a few groups depended heavily on caribou.

The Greenland Eskimo, speaking the eastern Inuit dialect, inhabited the coasts of Greenland. They lived in large, permanent coastal villages with substantial structures and fairly large populations. Whales and other sea mammals were the major game animals; fish and land mammals were less important.

Dogs were essential to Eskimo life all over the Arctic, performing many tasks. Dogs pulled sleds packed with family belongings. People did not usually ride on the sleds, but walked alongside, often carrying other materials that did not fit on the sleds. In addition, dogs carried loads on their backs, helped in seal hunting by locating breathing holes, assisted in hunting bears by harassing them while the hunter attempted to kill them, and guarded camps from strangers and bears. Dogs could also be eaten in times of famine. Since food was scarce, most Eskimo kept a relatively small number of dogs. They were fed scraps of meat and human feces mixed with oil (it is common around the world to feed human feces to dogs). Grown dogs could usually withstand the cold and stayed outside, but puppies had to be brought inside during particularly harsh weather.

An Inuit family in Greenland, ca. 1950.
(CORBIS/Hulton-Deutsch Collection)

Political Organization

In general, Arctic groups were organized at the band level and had no tribal organizations until fairly recently, when such organizations were imposed on them by the Canadian and U.S. governments. Bands were usually identified by general geographic location by adding the suffix -*miut* (meaning "people of") to the location name. Thus, the name Kuskowagamiut translates to "people of the Kuskokwim River."

Many groups practiced a seasonal round, moving about the landscape throughout the year to exploit different resources. The band would stay together for only part of the year, splitting into smaller units of a few households (or even a single household) for the rest of the year, with the band reassembling the following season. Some other groups were larger and more complex, staying together throughout much of the year, sometimes in permanent villages, although small groups ventured out to perform specific tasks.

Most disputes took place between men, and they usually concerned women. Killing someone over a dispute was usually not acceptable (but probably not rare) as it could lead to retaliation and the initiation of a feud; if a married man was involved, it could deprive a family of its provider as well. However, if someone's behavior endangered the group, swift action would be taken, even if killing the offender was necessary. Most disagreements were resolved through contests, including punching, wrestling, and singing. In a song contest, each individual involved in a dispute would make up a song insulting the other's parentage, hunting abilities, looks, etc. After both had sung their songs, the assembled community would decide whose song was better and therefore who had won the contest. If the dispute was over a woman, she was under no obligation to leave with the winner, but at least the man's need to defend his honor had been fulfilled.

Wife-sharing was not an uncommon custom. The purpose of the practice was to establish and/or cement partnerships between men, or simply to satisfy a desire for sexual variety. Both the husband and wife had to agree to the arrangement, although the wife seems to have had a bit less power in the decision. Such exchange was not considered adultery. It might even create a "kinship" relationship between the two families, who could then ask each other for help in the future.

Most Arctic groups participated in some kind of warfare, usually motivated by revenge. Much of this warfare was supernatural in form and was conducted by shamans. Actual combat was relatively rare. Nevertheless, most males were skilled in warfare and were well armed with bows and arrows, spears, and knives. Many groups used body armor made of wood, bone, and skin. Combat would usually consist of surprise attacks on the enemy by small groups of men, whose goal was to kill everyone in the targeted camp. In the east-central Arctic, the Eskimo were frequently at war with some of the Subarctic groups to the south.

Social Organization

For most Eskimo groups, the primary social unit was the nuclear family, which was also the main economic unit. However, the extended family was not uncommon and formed the main social unit in some groups. The lineage was also important to a few Arctic groups. Most Eskimo employed a bilateral kinship system, similar to that used in most of the United States. The advantage of a bilateral system is that one has twice as many close relatives than in a system where one is related only through the mother or the father (matrilineal or patrilineal).

Most marriages were arranged, often very early in an individual's life. However, some of the arrangements did not work out and some people married whomever they wanted. Females married at about the time they reached puberty, or even before; males tended to marry later, in their late teens. Polygyny was allowed, and in rare cases women could have multiple husbands. Divorce was a simple matter, though rare after the birth of the first child, and women could leave whenever they wished. Divorcees, widows, and widowers remarried as soon as possible, as marriage was necessary in order to constitute an effective labor unit; no one could function as an unmarried person for long in the demanding Arctic environment.

Due to the practice of wife-sharing, a child could be biologically fathered by someone other than the husband of the mother. However, as it was believed that conception could not take place during a wife exchange, the husband was always considered the father and was thus responsible for the child. When a child was born, the husband and one or two midwives would assist, and a shaman might be called if there were serious problems. Afterwards, the mother rested for a few days. If a child was due while the group was traveling, the mother and one or two others might stop to deliver the baby, catching up with the group later.

As in all cultures, children were valued, loved, and cared for. However, infant mortality was very high, and a major cause of infant death was pneumonia. At times, newborns could not be supported without endangering the entire group. In such cases, infanticide might be practiced, but it was always a traumatic decision made by the husband; women were the life-givers and men were the dealers of death. Infanticide of females was more frequent than that of males. Because hunting was very dangerous, resulting in a high adult male mortality rate and thus a constant shortage of males, males were more highly valued and more likely to be kept as infants. If any baby was born during times of famine, it would be killed to preserve the life of the mother. Children were not named until a decision was made whether to keep them, and since one was not believed to be an actual person until one was named, infanticide was not considered murder.

Names were very important, as the name determined the demeanor of the individual as well as the nature of his or her soul. Names were generally passed along through either side of the family; for example, a child might be given the name of a deceased grandparent. Since many Eskimo believed in reincarnation, the child could actually be his or her own grandparent.

An infant was carried by its mother on her back within her parka, and as infants rarely wore clothing, there was skin-on-skin contact with the mother. Without being removed, the infant could be maneuvered to the front of the parka to nurse. Thus, a very close relationship between the mother and child resulted. Strong ties also existed between children and grandparents. Up to the age of five or six, children were allowed to do mostly as they pleased; they ate and slept when they wished, played with other children and puppies, frolicked in the snow, and entertained themselves with various toys, including dolls, models (of boats, sleds, and other things), and wooden tops spun with a sealskin cord. Beginning at an early age, girls were required to start helping their mother with child care, but boys had a bit more freedom. Sex was not hidden or discouraged, and children slept in a common bed with the parents, even while parents were engaging in sexual activities. Most Eskimo people did not keep track of their precise ages, but did know who was older and younger.

In most instances people defecated somewhere outside, but if it was very cold a container was used indoors, to be emptied later. Feces were sometimes saved, mixed with oil, and fed to the dogs. Bathing was not frequent in most areas, but when it did occur, cold water was used. Mothers cleaned their small children with spit instead of water.

Males formed partnerships, or cooperative friendships, with a number of other men. These partnerships varied in intensity, from joking relationships to serious associations for hunting pursuits. These relationships, often cemented with an exchange of wives, were important economically and socially, and a man's partners could be counted on in bad times.

When they were not working, many groups passed the long winter months with constant socializing, including singing, dancing, romancing, acrobatics, and playing games such as tug-of-war, cat's cradle, cup and pin, hoop and pole, tag, and guess who. Many Eskimo enjoyed the blanket toss, where a group holding a walrus skin (later a blanket) tossed a person into the air. In addition to the entertainment involved, tossing a person twenty feet into the air would enable him or her to see game at a greater distance. In portions of the eastern Arctic, houses were often connected by tunnels so that people could pass back and forth without being exposed to the cold weather. A "proper" winter village would have a community dance house where everyone could gather to socialize.

If the elderly became a burden, they might commit suicide for the good of the family. They might have a party to say goodbye or simply walk out into the landscape without telling anyone; at other times, they would be killed (at their request) by others. Everyone recognized that this act was a great and loving sacrifice to assist the group in bad times. Euthanasia was occasionally practiced when an individual was unable to keep up, thereby endangering the group. The dead were rarely buried below ground, as it was extremely difficult to dig graves in the frozen ground. Cremation was also uncommon, as it required a great deal of precious fuel. Instead, the dead were usually placed in rock cairn graves or on platforms, or sometimes just left in the snow, often with their clothing and personal possessions.

Economics

Arctic peoples were organized socially and politically to maximize the individual and communal procurement, distribution, and consumption of food. Eskimo men were the hunters and procured most of the food. However, women played critical economic roles as well; they gathered plants for food or manufacturing material, took care of the children, butchered the animals and distributed the meat, prepared the meals, educated the female children, tanned the skins, made the clothing (which required great skill), and did other tasks (see Guemple 1995). No family could survive without a good hunter and a skilled woman.

Both group and individual hunting were important and food was always shared. Most food came from animals, and this meat was prepared in various ways, such as drying, smoking, boiling, frying, and barbecuing. Few food taboos were practiced. The Eskimo generally ate almost every part of an animal that was possible to eat, including muscle tissue, organs, marrow, fat, and the contents of intestines. One exception was the livers of polar bears, which were not eaten because they made people ill (they contain so much vitamin A that they are actually toxic). The fat (blubber) of sea mammals was an important food, and large quantities were consumed. Interestingly, the Eskimo have a very high metabolism, and in spite of their high fat consumption they have lower average cholesterol today than westerners.

Different species of animals were taken by different groups, depending on the region. In general, a number of sea mammals were hunted, including seals, walrus, and whales. Seals were the most popular and would be captured whenever possible. Groups of hunters would sneak up on seals or walrus lying on the shore or on the ice and harpoon them. Animals in the water would be harpooned from kayaks. In open water, a good kayaker could glide up to an animal unobserved and harpoon it from behind. A float, made from an inflated sealskin, would be attached to the harpoon head to ensure the animal could not escape. Sometimes a team of kayakers might drive a number of animals into an area where other hunters could dispatch them. Walrus are large (about 2,000 pounds), aggressive, and very dangerous to hunt from boats, so hunters would wait until they came on shore to hunt them.

In the winter, when the sea was frozen over, a hunter would locate seals' breathing holes in the ice, often with the help of dogs. A hunter would wait patiently, for hours or even days, until a seal came to the hole to breathe, then harpoon it. When the seal tried to escape, the hunter would hold on to the harpoon line until the seal tired and drowned, or the hunter would dig out the hole enough to drag the seal out and then kill it. The hunter would sometimes need the help of his family and/or dogs to pull the seal out of the water. The wounds of the seal, as well as other sea mammals, were closed by the hunter so that the valuable blood (eaten as food) would not be lost during transport to camp.

Many Eskimo groups also hunted whales. Small species such as beluga and narwhal (the latter found only in the eastern Arctic) were hunted at sea using large, open boats called *umiaks*. Whales were harpooned and a number of sealskin floats were then attached. The hunters would follow the whale until it was exhausted and then kill it. Larger whale species were not hunted; rather, their carcasses were scavenged when they washed up on shore. Umiak owners were rich men, often the heads of households, and were the leaders of whale hunts; upon a successful hunt, they would divide the meat among the crew and then distribute what was left to the rest of the people.

Some groups of Eskimo hunted caribou, which do not occur in large numbers in the Arctic (they live mainly in the south, in the Subarctic). The animals were hunted communally, driven into places where they could be shot with arrows. To assist in driving the caribou, piles of rocks would sometimes be built to resemble humans. Caribou skins were essential to the manufacture of clothing and shelter.

Polar bears inhabited the far northern Arctic and were exceedingly dangerous to hunt. Nevertheless, they were hunted for both skins and meat. Polar bears would sometimes raid Eskimo houses for stored food, increasing the threat of food shortage. Other animals hunted by the Eskimo included musk ox, hares and rabbits, squirrels, and birds, including waterfowl. Fish, both freshwater and ocean species, were also critical resources for some groups. Fish could be obtained during most of the year and were captured from the shore or from kayaks, using weirs, harpoons, nets, and jigging with hooks and lines. The Eskimo did not have the technology to take most ocean fish living in deep water.

Hunters were required to be respectful and thankful to the animals they killed, as the souls of the animals would eventually be reborn and, if they were unhappy about their treatment, would not allow themselves to be killed for food again. Sea mammals and ocean fish were classified as animals of the sea, while caribou, bear, freshwater fish, hares and rabbits, and so on, were considered animals of the land. The two categories could not be mixed in either cooking or storage. Plants never formed a large part of any Eskimo diet, although some groups used more than others.

Hunger was not uncommon and famine was always a threat. Shortages of food occurred on a regular basis, some very short-term and others longer. Short-term shortages were solved by sharing food among successful and unsuccessful hunters and their families, with partners, and with other people in general. Long-term shortages were resolved by storing food for later use. In very cold regions, stockpiles of food would be placed on platforms outside of houses and in stone-covered caches in the landscape. This food would remain frozen and thus preserved for years. In warmer areas, food was dried in the sun and then stored. In times of actual famine, about once per generation, people would eat spare clothing (the skins could be eaten), dogs, and even the dead.

Hunting was a very dangerous activity; bears and walruses killed many hunters, and others died in accidents, such as falling through thin ice or tipping over in their boats. If a person fell into the water, there was little chance of survival; if one was able to get out of the water, there was no way to get dry and stay warm and the individual would freeze very quickly, although it might be possible to roll around in dry snow to absorb enough water to survive. Adult male mortality was so high that there was almost always a shortage of men, despite the practice of female infanticide (see above).

Material Culture and Technology

Eskimo technology was dominated by the use of skins. All clothing was made from skins and fur. Skins of caribou and/or bear were used for bedding and blankets, for containers, as wrapping material for transport, for tents, and for many other items. Skins were also used to cover the frames of boats, and sealskin floats were utilized in sea mammal hunting. Other important materials in Eskimo technology were bone, antler, stone, and wood, and most items were beautifully decorated.

The Eskimo built various types of houses, depending on location, conditions, and length of stay. Strong and warm houses were needed, particularly in the winter. The most well known of these structures is what the Eskimo call a snow house but is referred to by westerners as an *igloo*. In actuality, the Eskimo refer to any dwelling as an igloo, the snow house being just one type. Snow houses were used by the Northern Eskimo in the winter as temporary housing or as quarters for the entire season. Elsewhere, snow houses were not generally used. Some snow houses were quite large and so sturdy that adults could safely stand on their roofs. Many groups constructed large, permanent, semisubterranean dome houses (for use as family dwellings and as men's houses) made from driftwood and whalebones, then covered with sod and insulated with moss. Houses were constructed with a "sunken

An Eskimo family building a snow house (note the kayaks in the background). From an 1870 engraving.
(CORBIS/Bettmann)

living room" and benches on which to sit and sleep. This type of construction kept the coldest air collected at the bottom of the house, making the rest of it warmer. The size of the house was related to how much oil could be spared from the food supply for use in lamps to warm the house; the less available the oil, the smaller the house. In the summer, when the men were hunting or fishing, skin tents, brush shelters, or rock shelters were used.

Two major types of boats were used by the Eskimo, the umiak and the kayak. The umiak is a large, open, walrus-skin boat that could carry a fairly large number of people and material possessions. Umiaks are often called "women's boats" because the women usually rowed them. However, when umiaks were used in whale hunting, they carried an all-male crew.

Kayaks were made in a variety of forms, depending on their intended use. Generally they were small, covered boats, with one or two hatches, used by men in hunting and fishing. Most kayaks were built around a flexible wooden frame, tailor-made to fit the owner. Women would then fashion a sealskin covering for the frame, sewn on so well that it was watertight. The kayak was propelled and controlled by a double-bladed paddle. In use, the kayak became a part of the man, "worn" like a piece of clothing, and was often considered to be a "living being." Boys were trained from infancy to handle a kayak and to withstand wet and cold. Contemporary sport kayaks have borrowed Eskimo technology almost exactly, and today the act of righting a capsized kayak is called the "Eskimo roll."

Sleds were used by many groups and were built of bone and/or wood. The sled runners were made from bone or antler and were covered with a layer of ice to decrease friction on the snow. Frozen fish were sometimes used as sled runners.

The Eskimo's main weapon was the harpoon, which was used to kill most sea mammals. Harpoons were used by hunters in kayaks, but since the hunter was sitting and could not get much weight behind the throw, an atlatl was used to propel the harpoon. Spears were also used. Bows and arrows were not commonly used for hunting from boats, although Eskimo bow technology was sophisticated. The Eskimo employed several disinctive cutting tools. The crescent-shaped woman's knife, the *ulu*, was made from slate or chipped stone (and later from steel), and was used to cut skins for clothing, to butcher animals, and for just about every chore where cutting was required. Men made long-bladed knives from walrus tusk for many of their tasks, such as cutting snow blocks for a snow house.

Bowl-shaped lamps made from stone were essential for light and heat. Moss wicks were placed in the bowl and seal oil was used for fuel. Stone was also used to manufacture drills and other tools. Snow visors, necessary to survive the constant exposure to snow and ice glare, were made of wood, ivory, or antler. The Copper Eskimo in the central Canadian Arctic are known for their cold-hammered native copper tools and ornaments (see Damas 1984; Morrison and Germain 1995; and Condon et al. 1996 for further discussion of the Copper Eskimo). Some other groups also used copper in the same manner.

Probably the most important aspect of Eskimo material culture and technology was their clothing, all made from animal skins. Adequate clothing was vital to daily life, in order to keep warm and dry. Everyone dressed in three major items of clothing: a hooded parka and pants made from caribou hide, and the extremely important *mukluks,* watertight boots made from sealskin. Women wore long pants and short boots; men wore short pants and tall boots. Everyone also wore mittens. Most Eskimo wore several layers of clothing, depending on the weather and temperature. For the inner layer of clothing, the hair side of hides and skins was placed against the body; for the outer layer, the hair side faced away from the body. Most clothing was removed at night and used as pillows, bedding, and/or blankets. Boots would usually stiffen during the night from the cold, and one of the important tasks of an Eskimo wife was to chew her husband's boots first thing in the morning until they were softened enough for him to put them on. When possible, new clothing was made every year.

Most clothing was decorated to some extent. Women went to considerable effort to decorate their clothing, often with patterns of different-colored furs. A woman might have a large wardrobe, with fancy clothing for special occasions. A mother's parka was made large enough so that an infant could be carried on her back inside the parka and maneuvered around her body to nurse.

After puberty, many women would tattoo their faces, arms, and breasts; men rarely had tattoos. Tattooing was accomplished using a bone needle and a mixture of oil and soot. Both sexes wore their hair long, and women often had braids. Men frequently plucked their facial hair; otherwise, ice might form on it and cause frostbite.

Religion

The religious beliefs of Arctic groups were quite complex and primarily concerned with maintaining a relationship with the animals to ensure their continued cooperation in being hunted (see Fienup-Riordan 1988, 1990; Lowenstein 1993). All manner of beings, including humans, animals, and other entities, had souls (sometimes many souls), which determined the nature of the existence of the being the soul inhabited. Many Eskimo believed that humans had three souls; an immortal soul that left the body at death to journey to an afterlife (or to be reincarnated), a soul of breath and warmth that died with the body, and a soul associated with the person's name. Many Eskimo also believed in reincarnation, that the immortal soul would be reborn into a later generation. This included the souls of animals—who, if angry, would not allow themselves to be killed for food. Humans and animals thus shared two major characteristics: they had souls and awareness. These two attributes allowed humans and animals to interact to the benefit of both.

Good and bad spirits inhabited the world and could manifest themselves in any form, including human form. Bad spirits attempted to do harm, but people could be protected by charms or amulets, and also by shamans. A major goal of religious activity was to control evil spirits.

Shamans were the primary religious practitioners, as they had some access to, and control of, the supernatural. They could also cure illnesses or curse others with disease or bad luck. Shamans conducted warfare by putting spells on the enemy. Death was not considered a natural occurrence; when someone died (other than through infanticide or euthanasia), it was reasoned to be the result of the spell of an enemy shaman, and retaliation would follow. Shamans acquired their power through a number of means, generally by seeking a spirit-helper, either during some trial or quest. In other cases, new shamans were initiated by established shamans, who taught the trade to the novice. Both men and women could be shamans but most were men.

Arctic Peoples Today

Until fairly recently, many Eskimo lived in a largely traditional manner, but after World War II, radical change came to the Arctic. Many military bases were opened and employed Eskimo workers. Western material culture became more prevalent, and many Eskimo moved to small towns around bases and regional centers, where they now live in Western-style houses that do not stay as warm as traditional housing.

Traditional subsistence activities, such as whaling (see Freeman et al. 1998), hunting, and fishing, are still very important in the economy and social identity of many Eskimo. Dogsleds are still used, along with snowmobiles ("metal dogsleds"), and many communities are connected by air service. In 1991, there were some 36,000 Eskimo (Reddy 1995: Table 925) and about 2,400 Aleut (Reddy 1995: Table 113). Most Eskimo are now Christian.

In the U.S. portion of the Arctic, all groups have signed the 1971 Alaska Native Claims Settlement Act (ANCSA). At that time, the ANCSA settled land claims by giving native groups title to forty-four million acres, a payment of $962 million and a royalty of $500 million on mineral rights. Thirteen native corporations were established to administer the settlement monies and lands. Native people with at least one-quarter native blood became "shareholders." Many worried that the ANCSA would have a result similar to the Dawes Act and termination policies of the 1950s; however, housing, health care, and education have improved for many people in the Arctic (see Burch 1984).

The Canadian government remains in negotiations to settle other native claims (see Crowe 1991). One agreement resulted in the creation of a new Canadian province, Nunavat, from the eastern part of the Northwest Territory in 1999 (see Rigby et al. 2000). Nunavat is governed by the Eskimo who live there. Many Canadian Eskimo reject the idea of claims settlements, arguing that the land is not for sale.

Greenland won province status from Denmark in 1979 and now governs itself, and the majority of the members of the Greenland legislative assembly are Eskimo. Due to a warming trend in the past 200 years, the seal population in western Greenland has declined considerably and many Eskimo rely on fishing to a much greater degree than in the past. Greenland Eskimo still hunt narwhals from kayaks, but it is illegal for others to do so.

The Eskimo face a number of serious problems today. Alcoholism, with its associated violence and economic impacts, is a huge problem among the Eskimo. There are few jobs in the Arctic, and being dependent on public assistance (welfare) is not an Eskimo value. Teenage pregnancy is also a problem. *Gussak* (white man's food from stores) is very expensive, as much as 400 percent more costly than in other regions, and many people do not like it. The sugar and refined foods have greatly increased dental problems and have even contributed to malnutrition.

ARCTIC ART

Arctic people have an artistic tradition spanning many thousands of years. Much of Arctic art embellished functional manufactured items, which incorporated aspects of everyday life, such as animals and people, generally shown enjoying life. Sculpture was the primary art form and walrus ivory was its most popular medium. Bone was the second most popular material, followed by wood and stone. Difficult to carve, stone was the least used material, although soft soapstone was very popular. Arctic artists were mostly men; more recently, however, Eskimo women have begun creating some outstanding works of art, much of it paintings and drawings, but including some sculpture (see Leroux et al. 1996).

Some art was produced for trade with Europeans in the nineteenth century, but that demand eventually died out. However, after 1948, Canadian and other Western collectors again became interested in Eskimo art. At the same time, tourism in the Arctic began to increase and tourists bought art pieces, again increasing demand (see Blackman and Hall 1988). Much of Arctic art has since become a commodity for sale.

Critics have complained that much contemporary Arctic art is not "true" Eskimo, but is produced for westerners, using Western standards. Others feel that the Eskimo have ingeniously adapted other ideas and materials into their own evolving artistic traditions, just as all other art has evolved over time; it makes it no less Eskimo. General reviews of Eskimo art are presented in Martijn (1964), Graburn (1976, 1978), Fitzhugh (1988), Swinton (1992), Ray (1996), and Hessel (1998).

Nineteenth-century Eskimo sculpture of a hunter and polar bear, carved in ivory. (CORBIS)

Nevertheless, the future looks promising. The Eskimo themselves are working to reinvigorate their culture, and they have regained some measure of control over their territories. Native languages are being taught in schools, and the use of native technologies (clothing, weapons for hunting, dogsleds, etc.) and skills is being encouraged. Some Eskimo families have even returned to a traditional lifestyle, hunting animals and fishing, living in igloos, and traveling by dogsled (which are actually more reliable than snowmobiles).

Learn More About Contemporary Arctic Peoples

The discussion above is only a very brief description of Arctic people today. What else can you discover? Go to the library, and look on the Internet (you can begin with http:/www.ainc-inac.gc.ca./ or http://arcticcircle.uconn.edu/) to learn more about how Arctic groups are managing. Topics you can explore include the following:

1. Chose a particular group or two, and investigate how land claims settlement has affected them economically, politically, and in other ways.
2. Which groups have concluded treaties with either the United States or Canada? Which are in the process? What is the status of the new Canadian province of Nunavut?
3. What traditional practices have been retained by a particular Arctic group? What are the roles of traditional religion, economics, and politics in this Arctic group today?
4. How is having traditional knowledge integral into one's identity as an Inuit?
5. How are Arctic people coping with Western culture? What are the problems faced by Arctic people today?

The Aleut: An Arctic Case Study

The Native American group that inhabited the far western portion of the Alaska Peninsula and the Aleutian Islands, as well as the Pribilof Islands to the north, are the Unangan, often called Aleut by outsiders (see Fig. 3.2). The Aleutians are an island chain extending in an arc some 1,300 miles from southwestern Alaska almost to Asia. A number of Unangan groups lived all across the Aleutians; the term *Aleut* was derived from the name of a specific Unangan group from the Near Islands, and the term has since been applied to all of the Unangan, as well as some of the Eskimo groups to the east (see Clark 1984:195–196). The Aleut numbered about 10,000 people when first contacted by the Russians in 1741. The Aleut are different from the Eskimo in many respects, including language, technology, economy, and the absence of dogs. This case study of the Aleut describes them as they were in about 1740.

Most of the information on the early Aleut was obtained by the Russians in the eighteenth and nineteenth centuries (e.g., Veniaminov 1840). Since that time,

FIGURE 3.2 Location and territory of the Aleut in the western Arctic
Adapted from M. Lantis, "Aleut," in *Handbook of North American Indians, Vol. 5, Arctic,* D. Damas, ed., Fig. 1; copyright © 1984 by the Smithsonian Institution. Reprinted by permission of the publisher.

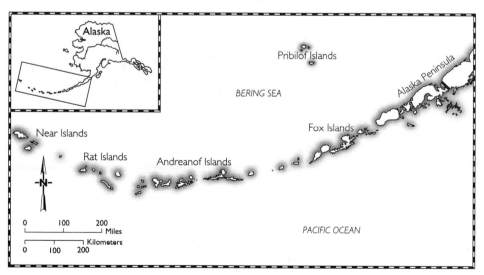

relatively little fieldwork has been conducted among the Aleut, and the information available on them is limited. Important studies and summaries on the Aleut include the work of Jochelson (1933), Collins et al. (1945), Hrdlička (1945), Jones (1976, 1980), Black (1980), Laughlin (1980), Lantis (1984), Black and Liapunova (1988), and Corbett and Swibold (2000), and the information on the Aleut summarized below was synthesized from these sources.

The Natural Environment

The western Alaska Peninsula and the approximately one hundred Aleutian Islands have a generally uniform environment. The Japanese Current passing south of the islands keeps them relatively warm, so there is very little sea ice and no permafrost. On the other hand, the waters of the Bering Sea to the north are colder than those of the Pacific Ocean to the south, and when the two sea temperatures meet along the islands, the weather becomes very stormy, bringing wind, rain, and fog. The islands themselves are very rugged and mountainous, with numerous volcanos. Winter temperatures average about 10°F while the summer can be quite warm, about 70°F. The stormy weather, particularly in the winter, presents a formidable challenge.

An alpine tundra covers most of the islands, and few land plants were exploited by the Aleut, who utilized the ocean almost exclusively, including the shore and open waters. Although cold, the water is never freezing, and the sea supports an immense array of fish, mammals, and other resources. Many of the islands contain streams with salmon and trout. Bird-nesting areas, often on cliffs, were also important to the Aleut, especially to obtain eggs. The mountains were not exploited much by the Aleut, except to obtain sulphur from the rims of volcanos, which was used in making fire.

Language

The Aleut speak the Aleut language of the Aleut division of the Eskimo-Aleut language family. Aleut has three distinct dialects, eastern (or Fox Island), central, and western (or Attuan). The language is very "complex and superbly expressive, and it accommodates beautifully to the entire range of human thought" (Laughlin 1980:107).

A Brief History

The Aleut have occupied the Aleutian island chain for at least 5,000 years, probably even longer. The Aleut were first contacted by the Russian naval expedition led by Vitus Bering in 1741. Russian fur hunters returned to the region in 1745 and began to exploit sea mammal populations. After 1761, the Russians moved into many Aleut villages and attempted to take control of the populations. Between 1763 and 1764, the Eastern Aleut were determined to expel the invaders, destroying four Russian vessels and killing virtually their entire crews. The Russians retaliated in 1766, and the conflict continued until the late 1770s.

Hunting sea otters became a major Russian enterprise. Some Aleut men were paid by the Russian-American Company to hunt otters. In other cases, ambitious Russian administrators took the families of hunters hostage, forcing the men to "ransom" them with sea otter pelts. Hunters that did not produce the desired number of pelts were punished, perhaps by the loss of their families, who would either be killed or taken as slaves. The Russians moved groups of Aleut to the Pribilof and Commander Islands near Siberia to hunt otters, and there many remain today. Other Aleut hunters were taken to Fort Ross, a Russian outpost in northern California, and still others were taken to a Russian outpost in Hawaii.

Beginning in the late eighteenth century, Russian Orthodox missionaries (see Black 1996 for a history of the Russian Orthodox Church in Alaska) entered the Aleutian island region with the goal of converting the Aleut to Christianity. By 1825, only about 1,500 to 2,500 Aleut had survived. Most had died from disease, starvation, exposure from forced labor, and resistance to the Russians (see Okada 1997).

In 1867, the Russians sold Alaska to the United States and the Americans entered the region. The Aleut then came under greater pressure to acculturate. By 1920, the Aleut population numbered about 3,000. Fur seal and sea otter populations eventually crashed, and many Aleut were forced into other economic endeavors. Cod fishing became important in the early twentieth century, with fishing fleets and canneries employing many Aleut, albeit at very low wages. When the cod fishing declined, a number of other industries arose, including other types of fishing, hunting fur seals (again), and even some sheep ranching.

The Aleut were greatly impacted by World War II. When the Japanese invaded the western Aleutian Islands in 1942, the Americans forcibly relocated many Aleut to camps in mainland Alaska. This event was very traumatic to the Aleut, even more so than the earlier Russian invasion, and they suffered considerably from disease and malnutrition. The United States built a number of military bases in the region, many of them on land confiscated from the Aleut. When the Aleut were allowed to return to the islands after the war, they found their homes and churches ransacked and looted by the American military (Madden 1992:56). After the war, the Aleut became heavily dependent on the U.S. military for jobs. In 1990, Congress paid each Aleut $12,000 as restitution (see United States Commission on Wartime Relocation and Internment of Civilians 1982; Madden 1992).

Cosmology

Very little is known of Aleut beliefs about their origin. In one origin tale (summarized from Veniaminov 1840 II:127–128, as cited in Hrdlička 1945:154–155), the earth was barren and lacked people. One day, two hairy, humanlike creatures fell from the sky. They eventually had two offspring that were not hairy, and all people originated from that second pair. The people lived in a warm place in harmony with each other and had no wants or needs. As their population increased, they began to have needs, so they made weapons to hunt animals. As more and more people occupied the land, enmities developed and they turned their weapons against each other. The stronger began to oppress the weaker, who moved away in response and became the other peoples of the earth. The Aleut also believed in a universal creator associated with the east, the sky, light, and water. These beliefs were largely compatible with Christianity, making conversion more acceptable.

Politics and External Relations

The Aleut resided in permanent winter villages consisting of 50 to 200 people, depending on the conditions, living in a number of large houses. Villages were located around bays that had good salmon streams, along with beaches for launching and landing boats. Each group had a fixed territory that included several village locations. If resource availability shifted, the village could move to other locations without disrupting the territory of another group. In the summer, people were more mobile and often lived in smaller camps.

Each house had a headman, and the headman of the largest and/or most powerful house was the village leader. The other headmen served as advisers to the primary leader. The position of head of the house passed from father to son, as did any associated political power. If there was more than one village on an island, they tended to be allied, and a single political leader, usually chosen from among the lesser leaders, led the small confederation. No organization politically united islands.

Most people behaved in an orderly manner according to Aleut custom. Most disputes involved men fighting over women and were resolved by the parties directly involved. One group used public oratory contests (similar to that of the Eskimo, but using speeches rather than singing) to settle disputes. Violent dispute resolution, even murder, occasionally took place, but carried the danger of an expanded conflict among relatives. The rare incorrigible person whose actions continued to threaten the community as a whole could be killed to restore the peace.

Warfare was not uncommon and involved raiding other Aleut who spoke a different dialect or the Eskimo to the east, usually to avenge an insult or to maintain a feud. War expeditions were led by the primary headman of a village. After 1745, the Aleut stopped fighting among themselves to oppose the Russians together. The Aleut were accomplished at warfare, and though technology gave the Russians a marked advantage (the Russians had guns), they still feared the Aleut.

Social Organization

The basic family unit was a patrilocal extended family living in a household. Villages consisted of one or more households, with populations of up to 200 people. Descent was generally patrilineal, and the lineage was the most important kinship unit in society.

The Aleut had three primary social divisions: wealthy, high-status people; commoners; and slaves. The wealthy gained and/or maintained their wealth in a number of ways, including military success, inheritance, the possession of uncommon knowledge, being physically strong, having slaves, or owning boats. To maintain their hold on a political office, the rich were required to share with the commoners in times of need. This relationship between commoners and the elite was a source of some stress in Aleut society. Age seniority was also important. The friendly visitation of people from one village to another was a major social event.

All dressed in their finest clothes and held a public dance inside a large house. Music would be played, both men and women would dance, and wrestling contests were sometimes held.

Slaves were taken by the Aleut in raids. During a raid, enemy men and old people would be killed and women and/or children captured. Women slaves often served as concubines. Children of female slaves could be freed if the father was an Aleut; if not, they would also be slaves.

The division of labor among the Aleut was almost entirely on the basis of sex, although age played a factor as well. In general, men conducted the hunting and warfare and worked wood and bone. Women gathered plants, educated the female children, performed household tasks, and worked with skins and fibers to manufacture clothing, basketry, and matting. Berdaches were a part of Aleut society and such people were readily accepted. Sometimes, young males were purposely raised as females to serve as concubines to men.

Life Cycle

After the birth of a child, the mother had to remain isolated for between twenty and forty days. Unlike the Eskimo, Aleut infants were not constantly carried by the mother within her parka. Instead, the baby was wrapped in a warm blanket and carried in a small cradle. Once they began to walk, they were allowed to do virtually anything they wanted. For boys, the mother's brother served as the primary teacher and mentor, and males were taught to master the kayak as soon as possible. Girls were taught household tasks by their mothers.

Puberty was not specifically celebrated for either sex. At her first menses, a girl was isolated in a special house for forty days, bathed every five days, observed a variety of restrictions and taboos, had all of her joints (ankles, knees, etc.) bound with cord, and learned how to sew and make baskets. During her second menstrual cycle, she was isolated for twenty days. Thereafter, she observed the same restrictions that all menstruating women were required to follow, including frequent washing and various food restrictions and taboos. Unmarried women were isolated from the group for seven days.

A girl usually married as soon as she was proficient at women's work, generally about the time of puberty. As males were expected to be hunters when they married, they generally waited until at least eighteen years of age. One had to marry a person from another village; the ideal marriage was between a male and his mother's brother's daughter, and sister exchange was common. At the time a marriage agreement was reached, an exchange of gifts was made between the two families. The male then had to work for the woman's family for a period of one or two years. Once this obligation had been fulfilled, the couple was married. There was no real ceremony; the couple simply began to live together, often with the wife's family until their first baby was born, and thereafter with the husband's family.

Men could have as many wives as they could support (five being the greatest number reported). Sometimes a second husband would be added to a marriage, the newer male serving as an assistant to the senior husband. A husband might "lend" the sexual favors of his wife to high-ranking guests as a courtesy. A man could engage in legal sexual relations with a fairly large number of women, including his wives, his older brother's wives, his mother's brother's wives, cousins, slaves, and concubines (some of whom were male). Thus, women also had a wide range of sexual partners. Divorce was rather simple; the couple merely split up and moved to separate residences. The male seems to have had greater control over divorce proceedings than the female.

When an individual died, relatives would mourn his or her death, but there was no fear of the dead. Widows and widowers mourned in isolation for forty days, or less than that if the person was lost at sea. People in mourning observed food taboos, did not engage in sex, and did little physical activity. A widow had her joints bound, like a young girl at her first menses.

Burial practices varied by location and by a person's rank and/or occupation. An individual might be buried in a coffin, in a pit, in a cave, or in some cases inside the family home so that the deceased could remain close to the family. The grave goods buried with a person depended on his or her rank. Slaves might be sacrificed at the burials of some important people and corpses were sometimes dismembered. In the eastern Aleutians, certain high-ranking people were mummified; the internal organs were removed, and the body was thoroughly cleaned, dried, stuffed with grass, dressed in fine clothing, wrapped in matting, and then placed in a cave protected from the weather. Many of the possessions of the deceased, even their boats, might be interred with them in the cave. Mummies contained considerable power, and contact with them was considered dangerous. However, whale hunters would seek contact in order to use that power to charm whales.

Economics

Fishing and sea mammal hunting were the two most essential economic activities for the Aleut. Fish, mostly from the ocean, were the primary source of food, and included salmon, herring, cod, and halibut. Ocean fish were obtained using spears, nets, and hooks and lines, usually from boats. Freshwater fish, primarily salmon and trout, were caught using an ingenious trap. A set of two dams would be built across a stream or small river. The first dam was a small one consisting of a rock wall just high enough to protrude out of the water. The second dam was made of wood and extended well out of the water. It was placed about twenty feet upstream from the rock dam. Fish swimming upstream would be able to jump over the rock dam, but not the wooden one; thus, they would become trapped between the two dams, and could easily be collected by women and children under the supervision of an older man.

Sea mammal hunting was the next most important economic activity. Sea lions, seals, sea otters, and some whales were hunted. All but the walrus could be hunted from boats, and all but whales were hunted at their rookeries on shore, where they were speared or clubbed, then taken back to the village in boats. Sea otters were hunted by individuals as well as by groups of men in a minimum of six kayaks. The six boats would travel in a straight line, and when an otter was observed, it would be surrounded by the boats and harpooned when it came up for air. Sea otters were also taken on land when they came ashore. Porpoises were also harpooned from kayaks. Seals were hunted with the aid of seal decoys made from whole, inflated sealskins.

Whaling was not a common activity (see Black 1987); whales that were taken were most often humpbacks, hunted by groups of men in a number of boats. Once a whale was sighted, one or two men in a small kayak would sneak up on the creature and harpoon it, often using poison on the tip of the harpoon. The harpooner would then return to his village and act sick, hoping to magically transfer the sickness to the whale. Meanwhile, other men in kayaks would monitor the whale. If the harpooning was successful, the whale would die in about three days, and the body would be towed to shore. If the hunters lost sight of the dying whale, it might wash ashore at some other location, where those who found it might or might not have identified the harpoon and notified the hunters. Any beached, stranded, or dying whales would be scavenged when encountered.

Researchers disagree as to whether the Aleut whale hunters actually used poison, and if they did, whether it actually affected the animal. The hunters wanted others to believe they had special powers to kill whales, a power sometimes obtained from mummies. Apparently, some kind of mixture of materials was applied to the harpoon heads, and no one ate the flesh near the harpoon entry wound for fear of being poisoned.

A number of birds, including ducks, puffins, geese, ptarmigan, and albatross, were hunted. The Alent used bows and arrows, bolas, and snares to catch them. The eggs of many different birds were collected from their nests. Sea urchins, octopus, and shellfish were collected at low tide and also consumed. Women gathered a few land plants, such as roots and a variety of berries. Kelp, an ocean plant, was also commonly exploited.

Food was usually eaten raw. The damp climate of the Aleutian Islands made storage difficult, and it was not cold enough for long periods to store foods as the Eskimo did. However, some foods were dried and stored in containers made from the stomachs (often called bladders) of seals, which were also used to carry water. Basketry was also used for storage. The Aleut adopted from the Russians the practice of salting meats for storage.

Material Culture and Technology

The most important of the Aleut technologies was their watercraft, and boatmaking was a vital skill. Several types of craft were employed. They built a large, open boat, called a *baidaras*, that was similar to the Eskimo umiak. This boat was between thirty-five and forty-two feet long and was used to transport people and materials. The second major craft was the small kayak, called a *baidarka*, and each able-bodied man owned at least one. Kayaks had either single or double hatches, and though a third hatch was sometimes used, it may have been a postcontact phenomenon. While in the kayak, men wore a gutskin shirt, and the kayak had a drip skirt over the hatch, making the boat watertight and keeping the man dry. Groups of kayakers could ride out storms by lashing themselves together, and the Aleut always carried inflated seal stomach floats as life preservers. Interestingly, the Aleut did not swim.

The interior of an Aleut house, Unalaska Island, 1778. From a drawing by John
Webber in *A Voyage to the Pacific Ocean,* by Capt. James Cook, London 1784.
(Courtesy of Department of Special Collections, Charles E. Young Research Library/UCLA.)

In the winter, the Aleut lived in large, rectangular, semisubterranean houses built with frames of driftwood and/or whalebones and covered with wood, skins, and soil. Multiple entrances were located in the roof, openings that also served as smokeholes, and notched logs were used as ladders. The houses varied greatly in size and could be as large as 200 feet long and 30 feet wide, with a capacity of forty to fifty people. A large extended family might live in such a house, with individual families living in small compartments built along its edges. Benches lined the house and were used for seats and beds, and possessions were stored below them. Secret hiding places were often built into the edges of the house for use if the village was attacked, and some houses had secret exits. When traveling in the summer, caves or small tents were used as shelter.

As clothing was very important, considerable time was spent in its production and maintenance. Aleut clothing needed to be warm and waterproof, especially for the men who worked on and near the water much of the time. Hooded shirts and full-length parkas were commonly used and were typically made from gut, the intestines of sea mammals. Other clothing included parkas made from puffin skins. Although many Aleut often went barefoot, men's boots, made from sea lion flippers and seal esophagi, were both warm and watertight. Women generally wore clothing of seal or sea otter skin. Both sexes carried small pouches for personal items.

Clothing was decorated with bundles of feathers or fur and gut appliqué. Puffin skin clothing was often worn with the feathered side against the body for warmth, and the skin side was highly decorated. Clothing of gut had an iridescent shine. All Aleut clothing was very colorful and elaborately decorated. When hunting, Aleut men wore wooden hats decorated with paint and ivory. The size and shape of the hat denoted the rank of the man (Black 1991). Women had tattoos on their faces and hands, and men had pierced lower lips in which they wore ornaments of ivory and bone. Both sexes wore a variety of jewelry made from bone, shell, and stone.

The bow and arrow was used, but mostly for warfare, as it was not a very practical weapon in a kayak. However, the bow and arrow was used by the far eastern Aleut to hunt large game on the Alaska Peninsula. The Aleut also used wooden helmets, shields, and armor in warfare.

Most animals were hunted from boats using harpoons thrown with an atlatl. Thrusting spears were used to kill exhausted animals. Most tools and utensils were made from wood, including buckets, spoons, and scoops; no pottery was utilized. Small lamps and some bowls were made from carved stone, and ulus (women's knives) were made from chipped stone. Men had various wood and ivory working tools for cutting, drilling, and polishing. The Aleut made very fine basketry and matting from grasses collected and dried for that purpose. Fur would sometimes be woven into mats to create a "carpet." Some iron tools were used, even prior to contact. The iron was obtained from shipwrecks, traded to the Aleut, and cold-hammered into the desired shape.

Religion and Medicine

Relatively little is known of Aleut religion, primarily due to the early disruption of Aleut culture by Russian hunters and traders and to the influences of Russian missionaries. The primary goal of Aleut religious activity was to allow humans to exert control over the universe. The world was comprised of three levels inhabited by various beings: an upper world where there was no night, the earthly world, and a lower world where many of the dead lived. The souls (spirits) of some people and animals could be reincarnated. Many spirits occupied all three worlds. These spirits, including those of the dead, could be either good or bad, and they might roam about or inhabit places, objects, the earth, and/or the air. Some public ceremonies included singing and dancing, but their purpose is not clearly understood. A feast was held in the winter to commemorate the ancestors. Some secret ceremonies were held to enlist supernatural assistance in whale hunting. It was thought that sea otters were reincarnated humans; thus, when hunting sea otters, the Aleut wore their finest clothing, believing that the sea otters would be attracted to the human finery.

Shamans were generally males. A future shaman felt the call of duty when he was a teenager; he then began to learn the extensive knowledge necessary to be successful. A shaman sought to control and use supernatural power to intervene in earthly matters, such as hunting success, control of the weather, foretelling the future, and illness, which originated from evil spirits. Shamans had an extensive knowledge of anatomy, gained through the process of mummifying the dead and from the dissection of the bodies of enemies and slaves. Shamans also knew a great deal about pharmacology and applied that knowledge to treat sickness and injury.

Art, Expression, and Recreation

Most Aleut everyday material culture was superbly crafted and highly decorated. Most art motifs were related to nature, and their art was manifested mostly in stone, bone, ivory, and some wood (see Black 1982). Singing and dancing were important at ceremonies, but few details are known. Games and/or competitions were common and involved tests of skill, strength, and agility. Wrestling was a popular sport, and chess was adopted from the Russians. Storytelling was a major art form of the Aleut, with a great many stories related by both men and women in the evenings.

The Aleut Today

Today, the Aleut have been able to retain much of their culture. The population of the Aleut in 2002 was about 8,000. Most Aleut work for wages in one of the many commercial operations in the region. Nevertheless, traditional marine resources, particularly salmon, still form a major component of the Aleut economy, although overfishing by others continues to be a problem.

The Aleut participated in the Alaska Native Claims Settlement Act (ANCSA) in 1971; the Aleut Corporation was formed in 1972 and holds title to lands, resources, and settlement monies. This corporation will continue to provide the basis for the future economic success of the Aleut.

A cultural revival is taking place among the Aleut. In the town of Unalaska, a museum dedicated to Aleut culture was opened in 1999. The Aleuts also participated in the creation of Native Heritage Culture, an educational institution dedicated to the cultures of native peoples of Alaska, opened in Anchorage in 1999. Each group, including the Aleut, will have both summer and winter houses, museum space, craft workshops, and educational facilities associated with the institution.

The Inuit of Quebec: An Arctic Case Study

The Native American group that inhabited the northern portion of the Quebec-Labrador Peninsula (also called Ungava), including Ungava Bay, the eastern shore of Hudson Bay, and the adjacent islands (Fig. 3.3), are collectively known as the Inuit of Quebec, although they are sometimes called the Labrador Eskimo (they do not recognize the term *Eskimo*). The Quebec Inuit are the people depicted in the classic ethnographic documentary film *Nanook of the North*, made in 1922 by Robert Flaherty (also see Flaherty 1924). The film depicts the culture and lifestyle of the Itivimiut and has become the vehicle by which many people are introduced to the Eskimo. It is estimated that there were about 2,000 Quebec Inuit in 1800, and this case study describes them as they were in about 1850.

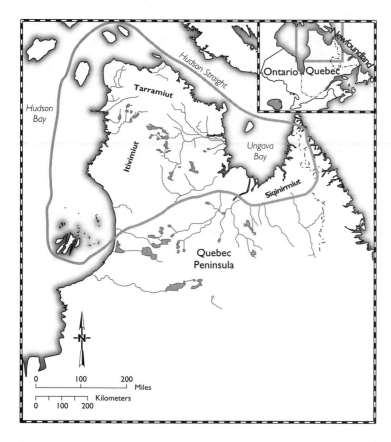

FIGURE 3.3 Location and territory of the Inuit of Quebec in the eastern Arctic showing the general locations of the three major bands
Adapted from B. Saladin d'Anglure "Inuit of Quebec" in *Handbook of North American Indians, Vol. 5, Arctic*, D. Damas, ed., Fig. 1; copyright © 1984 by the Smithsonian Institution. Reprinted by permission of the publisher.

Information on the Quebec Inuit (see Saladin d'Anglure 1984a:506–507) was gathered beginning in the late 1770s by missionaries, but many of these records remain unpublished. Additional information exists in the records of commercial enterprises such as the Hudson's Bay Company. Important descriptions of early Quebec Inuit culture are present in the works of Turner (1888, 1894) and Hawkes (1916). Since World War II, a number of other researchers have worked in the area, and have gathered a great deal of information. Several syntheses of Quebec Inuit culture exist, but the most accessible is that of Saladin d'Anglure (1984a). The information on the Quebec Inuit summarized below was synthesized from these sources.

The Natural Environment

The Quebec Peninsula is encircled by water on three sides. Hudson Bay is to the west, Hudson Strait to the north, and Ungava Bay to the east. The Atlantic Ocean lies to the far east and so was not part of the Quebec Inuit territory. The climate of the peninsula is very cold; snow and ice cover much of the region for most of the year. It becomes warmer during the relatively short summer, and the snow and ice disappear for a brief time.

Three major physiographic areas can be defined within the territory of the Quebec Inuit: the coasts, the islands, and the interior. The coasts are the most productive areas, and the majority of the Quebec Inuit live along them. Marine mammals are abundant, with greater numbers in Hudson Bay than in Ungava Bay. Whales are more abundant in the northern portion of the peninsula. Fish are present all along the coast and at the mouths of rivers. Some land resources are also available, the coast being the optimal place to utilize land and sea resources.

A series of islands lies in eastern and northeastern Hudson Bay, fairly close to the western and northern shores of the peninsula. These islands contain major populations of marine mammals, especially walrus. Birds are also numerous, as are polar bears. However, the islands lack freshwater fish and caribou.

Much of the interior of the peninsula is tundra containing limited vegetation, although there are stands of evergreen forest. A much larger forest lies just to the south of Quebec Inuit territory. The interior encompasses a large number of lakes, rivers, and streams, most of which contain fish. Caribou migrate into the southern interior in the summer and were a major resource to the Quebec Inuit.

Language

The Quebec Inuit speak a western Inuit language of the larger Eskimo-Aleut language family. There are two major dialects of the language, one spoken by the Itivimiut and the other by both the Siqinirmiut and Tarramiut.

A Brief History

The Quebec Inuit were first contacted in 1610 by Europeans looking for a northern passage from Europe to Asia. For the next 150 years, contact between the Quebec Inuit and Europeans was sporadic and not always friendly. In 1750, the Hudson's Bay Company built a trading post on the southern edge of Quebec Inuit territory and began to trade with the Quebec Inuit. European exploration of the region gradually increased, and several other trading posts were established in Quebec Inuit territory during the early-to-mid–nineteenth century. Although involved in the fur trade with the Hudson's Bay Company, the Quebec Inuit remained relatively unaffected by European culture until the mid–nineteenth century.

In 1903, the Canadian government decided to assert control of the region. Various government officials and police were sent into the area. At the same time, an intense competition arose among trading companies in the area, and many new technologies, including metal boats, Western clothing, and guns, were introduced. This competition for the products of the Quebec Inuit altered traditional culture to some extent, but much of their culture remained intact. However, in 1960 the Canadian government greatly increased its presence, essentially ending the traditional lifeways of the Quebec Inuit (see Saladin d'Anglure 1984b).

European diseases did impact the Quebec Inuit, but their dispersed settlements prevented the crowd diseases from taking hold for very long. Interestingly, the dogs also suffered from introduced diseases.

Cosmology

The cosmology of the Quebec Inuit is poorly known, mostly due to the early disruption of native beliefs by missionaries. The following account is summarized from Saladin d'Anglure (1984a:494–496). In mythical times, the earth was covered with water and the first human was created from nothing. This person roamed the waters and eventually found a companion, and the Quebec Inuit came from the union of this couple. Animals already existed, and as humans and animals were very similar, they spoke the same language and could transform into each other as the need arose. This relationship between animals and humans still exists, although it is now invisible to most people and is only accessible by shamans.

Politics and External Relations

The Quebec Inuit did not have a single overall political unit but were organized into about fifty small bands, each of which consisted of two to five families led by a headman. Most researchers designate three major geographic divisions, or regional bands, for the Quebec Inuit, each consisting of a number of local bands. The Siqinirmiut, "people of the sunny side," lived along the southern and western shores of Ungava Bay. The Tarramiut, "people of the shady side," occupied the western shore of Ungava Bay and the northernmost part of the peninsula. The Itivimiut, "people of the other side," lived on the eastern shore of Hudson Bay (see Fig. 3.3).

Most people lived along the coast, where the quantity and diversity of resources were the greatest. Some of the islands were occupied by several local bands, perhaps on a permanent basis. These island bands traded for caribou skins with the coastal bands. It is not clear whether the interior was permanently occupied by the Quebec Inuit, but they did exploit the resources of the interior, at least on a seasonal basis. It is possible that some Quebec Inuit families lived in the interior on a permanent basis, perhaps as a result of being ostracized by coastal groups.

Land was not owned, but ownership of houses, kayaks, personal property, and constructs such as fish weirs was recognized. Umiaks were owned by groups of twenty to thirty people, and their construction and maintenance were the responsibility of the group. Sharing was a major Quebec Inuit value, and the theft of personal belongings was rare. Most conflict among the Quebec Inuit arose from disputes over women. Such conflicts were resolved by way of contests, including song contests. However, in spite of the efforts made to avert actual violence, murders and feuds were not uncommon.

The Quebec Inuit were always at war with the Naskapi, a Subarctic Indian group that inhabited the interior forests of the southern peninsula. If the Naskapi saw a Quebec Inuit family, they would not hesitate to kill and scalp them, taking infants captive. However, much of the warfare was conducted by shamans. It was believed that no death was natural, so it had result from the actions of enemy shamans. Appropriate actions were taken to retaliate through supernatural means.

Social Organization

The basic family unit was the nuclear family, although extended families were not uncommon. Lineages, clans, and moieties were not recognized. The kinship system was very similar to the one used by most Americans today, including parents, aunts, uncles, nieces, nephews, and cousins. Adopted children, stepchildren, and stepparents were all called by the customary kinship term, but with a suffix added to denote the lack of blood ties (as most Americans use the suffix *-in-law*). The midwife was an important person in the kinship system, being the "cultural mother" of an infant.

People could do whatever they pleased as long as they did not interfere with others or endanger the group. People who became difficult were admonished by women. If the pattern of bad behavior continued, the person might be ostracized by the entire group, a very serious consequence since social activities were so important. If the person began to endanger the group, the men of the camp would join together to kill the offender (but this was not considered murder). People guilty of murder were subject to being killed by the relatives of the murdered person.

The division of labor was based on sex, age, competence, and skill. Men generally did the hunting; built houses; used and maintained the boats, sleds, and dogs; and made weapons and tools, including domestic utensils used by women. Women did the domestic chores, took care of infants, processed skins, and manufactured all the clothing, bedding, and tent and boat covers. Women also collected plants and eggs, hunted small game in the vicinity of the camp, helped men prepare for hunting, and distributed the meat. Both sexes contributed to communal efforts in fishing and caribou hunting. Children assisted where they could, helping and learning from those of the same sex.

Life Cycle

A woman was assisted in giving birth by a midwife, who then became the child's "godmother" and participated in its upbringing. Birth spacing was between two and four years, depending on when the last child was weaned. Infants suffered from a high mortality rate, as did mothers giving birth. During times of hardship, infanticide was practiced. Children were named after deceased relatives, and since there was a belief in reincarnation, the soul as well as the name was passed on to the child. Children had to help with the family chores when they were able, but they were allowed to play and enjoy their childhood.

Families lacking a child of one sex might train their children in the roles of both sexes, and it was not infrequent for a person to have skills of the opposite sex. Many children were cross-dressed and given mixed sexual roles until puberty; this was an aspect of the mythic abilities of animals and people to transform themselves. Due to their ability to do both men's and women's work, berdaches were sometimes taken by males as spouses.

Males became men when they killed their first large game. Girls became women at first menses, an event announced to the group so everyone would know a girl was now a woman. At first menses, a woman would receive new, adult clothing, as well as the tattoos necessary to please the spirits and to distinguish her as a woman.

Menstrual blood was viewed as being in opposition to game (food) and as "unproductive," since menstrual blood was not eaten as regular animal blood was.

Many marriages were arranged, and most people were betrothed in infancy. For a first marriage, the betrothal was usually respected, even if the couple did not want to marry; however, subsequent marriages were left much more to the discretion of the individuals involved. A male had to own a kayak to be eligible for marriage and a female had to be able to take care of a household. Polygyny was practiced but was generally limited to good hunters who were able to support a greater number of people. After marriage, the couple generally set up a new household within the husband's band. Divorce was easy; one party just moved out. Remarriages were easy and commonplace; a couple simply moved in together.

When an individual died, provided the body was accessible, the deceased was bound into a fetal position, wrapped in skins, and buried under a pile of rocks. Some of the implements used by the person in life would be buried with the body. Many people died in isolation in the landscape due to accidents or starvation, and so could not be buried.

Economics

The Quebec Inuit derived most of their food and materials from animals. Much of the procurement of animals was done individually, but communal hunting was common. Food was shared on at least three levels. If acquired through a communal effort, the first shares went to the man who killed the animal. Shares would also be given to those who had participated in the hunt and/or located the animal, then to those whose tools (boat, harpoon, etc.) were used in the hunt. Second, those who had shares from the initial distribution, or had obtained the game without help, distributed the meat to their families or others. The third level was the sharing required of an individual who had made his or her first kill. The animal had to be shared with the community, beginning with the eldest members, as part of the ritual involved in the first kill.

Food was prepared in a number of ways, depending on the season, the animal, availability of materials, and taste of the consumer. Foods could be smoked, boiled, fried, or eaten raw. Broth, blood, and water served as beverages.

Adequate food supplies were available in most years, and at times abundant food was available. However, food shortages, even severe shortages, were common. Actual famine, where people died of starvation, was faced at least once in every generation. At those times, cannibalism might be practiced (but was rarely discussed afterward). Famine was often caused by bad weather or loss of vital equipment that prevented a family from moving to their stored supplies.

The most important game animal was the seal. In the summer, seals were harpooned by men in kayaks. In the winter, they were hunted from breathing holes at the edges of the ice pack. The larger bearded seal was also hunted from a kayak.

Walrus, large and dangerous animals, were hunted communally, either by a few men taking a single walrus or by large groups of men attacking a walrus herd that was lying on a beach or swimming in shallow water. Hunters would sneak up on walrus herds and try to harpoon one or two before they could reach deep water. Kayaks were used offshore to try to contain the herd in areas where they could be harpooned. Walrus provided a large quantity of meat, fat, high-quality skin, and greatly desired ivory tusks, which were made into a number of essential tools.

Bowhead and beluga whales were hunted communally. Bowhead whales would be harpooned at sea and, with sealskin floats attached, repeatedly attacked until they died. The dead whale could then be towed to shore and processed. If a bowhead entered a small bay at high tide, the men would block the entrance, trapping the whale. Then at low tide the whale would be stranded and thus easily killed. The same basic techniques were used to obtain belugas, except belugas tended to congregate in larger groups (pods), and entire pods might be trapped and killed in a small bay at low tide. In addition to the meat and fat provided by a beluga, the skin was edible and considered a delicacy.

Caribou were the most important land animal to the Quebec Inuit and were hunted whenever available. However, land and sea animals were not mixed and great care was taken to keep the activities of hunting the two separate. Both the meat and the skins of the caribou were important, and even traded to Quebec Inuit bands on the islands. Each person required two caribou skins each year to make a new set of clothing. Caribou were hunted communally in two ways. First, men, women, and children, shouting and waving pieces of hide, would drive caribou toward hunters hiding behind a stone wall. When the animals were close, the hunters would shoot them with arrows. Caribou were also taken by groups of people as the animals crossed rivers. While swimming the river, the animals were quite vulnerable; once the herd was in the water, men in kayaks would descend on them and spear them. Other hunters (including women and children) would dispatch wounded animals as they waded ashore.

Other land mammals were also hunted. Polar bears were hunted by individual men with the aid of dogs and were killed with a thrusting spear. Foxes were taken in stone traps. Hares would be shot with arrows or caught in snares.

Fishing was very important and could be conducted year-round. Cod and salmon were taken from the ocean; trout and char were taken from freshwater streams and lakes. Women would typically use hook and line while men used a small piece of ivory on a line to lure fish and then a harpoon to kill them.

Char (a large trout) would migrate from lakes to the ocean in early summer and back to the lakes in the late summer. Communal fishing was done at these times, with bands of men, women, and children cooperating in the construction of a fish weir, the harvesting of the fish, and the storage of the fish in caches built of stone. The Quebec Inuit also utilized shellfish and sea urchins in areas that were ice-free.

A variety of birds were hunted. If the birds were in flight, a dart and atlatl or bola were used; if they were on the ground, the bow and arrow or snares were used. The type of arrow tip varied, depending on the animal hunted. Geese, unable to fly during the molt, would sometimes be driven into stone enclosures and then harvested at will. The eggs of birds were collected in the summer.

Plants constituted only a minor aspect of the Quebec Inuit diet. Some plants were collected in the summer and early fall, including a few roots, buds, leaves, and berries from several bushes. In some areas, algae was collected and eaten.

Material Culture and Technology

In the winter, the Quebec Inuit lived in snow houses of varying size, depending on how much oil was available for heating. A semisubterranean house built of stone and covered with sod was used by some groups in the winter. In the summer, tents were used; a large tepee-like tent of sealskin was used for long-term camps, and a smaller, conical tent of seal or caribou skin, supported by a light pole frame, was used in short-term camps. A large snow house or tent was used for community events, including dances, feasts, games, or meetings.

Transportation was quite efficient and included use of kayaks, umiaks, and dogsleds. People did not normally ride on the sleds; instead, they carried additional loads while walking alongside. People often had to help pull the sleds and keep the dogs in order. A kayak and a sled were often used in combination to transport people and material into the interior or along the coast. The man packed the kayak and moved along in the water while the women and children kept pace on shore with the sled.

The Quebec Inuit used two types of kayaks, a large, sturdy kayak (20 to 25 feet long) used for hunting and traveling in the ocean, and a smaller, lighter kayak (12 to 18 feet long) used for freshwater fishing. The smaller kayak had to be light enough to allow it to be transported over land and even carried on sleds. Most people did not know how to swim, and drowning was common. A capsized boat often meant the death of the occupants, either from drowning or from exposure.

Clothing was probably the most important element of technology. People wore multiple layers of pants and hooded parkas, along with boots. Women's parkas had rounded "tails" on them for extra protection when sitting on snow or ice. When in kayaks, men wore waterproof pants and parkas made from seal gut. Pants of polar bear skin were worn only by special men. Skins of different colors, such as that from foxes, hares, and dogs, were used to decorate clothing. The skins of duck and/or fish would also sometimes be used in clothing. Caribou skins obtained in midsummer were made into ceremonial clothing, and those obtained at the end of the summer furnished winter clothing. The families of good hunters could afford to replace their clothing

An Eskimo beginning the process of constructing a snow house in about 1922. Note the use of the walrus-tusk knife. (CORBIS/John Springer Collection)

every year and would have the best materials, whereas poor families would wear clothing made of inferior materials for more than one year.

Women wore necklaces of seal teeth and sewed charms and/or ornaments of ivory or wood onto their parkas. Women also had tattoos on their faces, arms, and breasts, applied to denote adulthood. Hair was worn long by both sexes, but women wore braids and even carried sewing equipment in their hair.

Although the Quebec Inuit had relatively few tools, they made great use of the materials they had. Flint was used to make ulus and drills, and a fire-making kit was made from flint and moss. Lamps and some containers were made from carved stone; others were made from animal stomachs and bladders. Wood was scarce, so many items were made from ivory, bone, and horn. Sewing kits contained needles of bone or ivory and thread of sinew. Sealskins were used for clothing, boots, tents, and boat covers. Many items requiring a great deal of material, such as a boat or a harpoon, were made by highly skilled craftsmen combining many small pieces of material into one large item.

Religion and Medicine

The Quebec Inuit universe is viewed as a rigid sky dome covering the flat earth. Most natural phenomena, such as snowfall, thunder, and wind, are controlled by spirits. Time and space are conceived as being circular; both the past and future are before us and behind us. Individual people and animals are reincarnated from earlier beings and will be reincarnated into future beings. Nothing is stable and everything is in the process of transformation.

A complex series of rules and regulations was necessary to maintain life and order, most of which were related to game animals and human children. Without proper regulation by the humans, game animals would not allow themselves to be reincarnated, transformed, or killed for food and materials. A major spirit was Sedna, the mother of seals, and it was important to maintain a good relationship with her. Regulation of human behavior was necessary to ensure the success of a new baby, from birth through adulthood.

Shamans, people able to transcend the world of ordinary humans and enter the invisible world of spirits and transformation, received their power from a spirit-helper through some act of self-deprivation or sacrifice. They could wage war through the casting of spells, and they were also medical specialists. Most shamans were male, with a few exceptions. The people did suffer from some medical difficulties, including injury, nutritional deficiencies, and some pulmonary problems. Shamans treated them to the best of their abilities. One interesting treatment for an open wound was to bind the lungs of a hare to it to aid in healing. Some shamans gained considerable fame, and their services were sought by many, including neighboring, groups.

Art, Expression, and Recreation

The art of the Quebec Inuit consists mostly of sculpture in stone, bone, ivory, and some wood, and dealt mainly with nature. Music, singing, and dancing were common at communal events. "Drum dancing," during which people acted out a story (often a funny one) to the rhythmic beat of drums, was popular. These drums, similar to large tambourines, were made from dried whale stomachs stretched over wooden frames (some twenty-four inches in diameter), and some had wooden or ivory handles.

The Quebec Inuit played a number of games. Outside games included archery contests, tobogganing, tug-of-war, a ball game played on ice, and the blanket toss, in which a group of people would hold on to a walrus skin and toss a person into the air. This was done at ceremonies and parties, and the person or persons tossed might "dance" while airborne. Other games, including dominoes, cup-and-ball, boxing, and other athletic competitions, were held indoors. Gambling was popular with everyone.

The Quebec Inuit Today

Today, the Quebec Inuit live in about a dozen settlements (see Saladin d'Anglure 1984b). In 1960, the government took over services and began compulsory schooling for children, resulting in the rapid nucleation of settlements. English became the official language, but Inuit is still spoken, is now written, and is becoming the formal written language of the Inuit. Wage labor and government subsidies (welfare) became major sources of income. Hunting fur-bearing animals for the Hudson's Bay Company is still a major part of the economy, but snowmobiles replaced dogsleds and motorboats replaced kayaks.

In 1975, the majority of the Quebec Inuit were partners (with the Cree) in the James Bay and Northern Quebec Agreement, a land settlement that gave the Quebec Inuit a reserve of 5,300 square miles, hunting rights on an additional 54,000 square miles, and $225 million in cash (paid over 20 years). A minority of the Quebec Inuit opposed the agreement, arguing that the land was not for sale and that the Quebec Inuit should adhere to traditional values.

The abuse of alcohol and drugs created serious problems for individuals and contributing to the loss of traditional culture and values. However, in the 1980s the recognition of the loss of culture grew into a movement back to traditional lifestyles, including the readoption of dogsleds, kayaks, traditional clothing, and traditional foods.

Today, the population of the Quebec Inuit is rapidly growing, due primarily to a decrease in infant mortality. However, almost 60 percent of the population is under twenty years old, making the transmission of culture to future generations difficult.

///

4 Native Peoples of the Subarctic

///

The Subarctic culture area is the largest in North America, encompassing most of the northern portion of the continent, most of it covered with an extensive pine forest. Cultures in the Subarctic consisted of small bands of hunter-gatherers that emphasized the hunting of caribou. The Subarctic was home to about thirty major groups of two major language families, Athapaskan and Algonquian (see Fig. 1.5).

Geography and Environment

The Subarctic (Fig. 4.1) is the largest natural region in North America, consisting of some three million square miles (4.5 million square kilometers) stretching from central Alaska across Canada to the Atlantic Ocean (see Gardner 1981). Three major physiographic regions have been defined for the Subarctic: the Canadian Shield and Mackenzie Borderlands, the Cordillera, and the Alaska Plateau.

The eastern two-thirds of the Subarctic lie within the Shield and Mackenzie Borderlands (see Rogers and Smith 1981). The Canadian Shield covers the eastern half of the Subarctic and consists mostly of exposed granite bedrock with few hills or mountains. The Mackenzie Borderlands are essentially the northern extension of the Plains, where it is too cold to support grasslands and bison. The Cordillera (see McClellan and Denniston 1981) is the northern aspect of the main mountain system that runs the length of western North America, generally called the Rocky Mountains in the United States and Canada and the Sierra Madre in Mexico. Finally, the Alaska Plateau (see Hosley 1981) consists of a large region of interior highlands in eastern Alaska and the western Yukon Territory dominated by the Yukon and Kuskokwim rivers. A large number of lakes and regions of muskeg (swamp) are found throughout the Subarctic.

The climate of the Subarctic consists of long, cold winters (e.g., −20°F) and short, warm summers (Bone 1992:19–21). Precipitation is limited, but evapora-

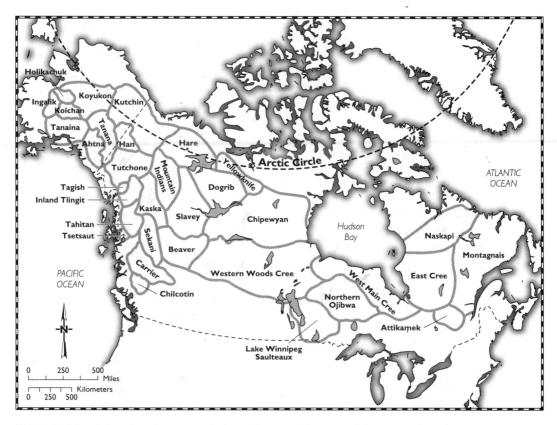

FIGURE 4.1 Subarctic culture area, showing the general location of the various native groups
Adapted from *Handbook of North American Indians, Vol. 6, Subarctic*, J. Helm, ed., p. ix; copyright © 1981 by the Smithsonian Institution. Reprinted by permission of the publisher.

tion rates are low, so there is no shortage of water. Most precipitation falls as snow, which covers the ground for more than six months each year. The deep and un-packed snow, coupled with the rivers and streams that are frozen between about November and May, restricted the movements of prehistoric people and limited their ability to obtain food.

Three major environmental zones characterize the Subarctic. In the north, a zone of tundra with permafrost and low vegetation of lichens and mosses is punctuated with woodland areas containing pine and shrubs. To the south of the tundra zone lies the boreal forest that dominates most of the Subarctic. This large forest consists primarily of conifers, including spruce and pine, though also birch trees. A small region of deciduous forest lies to the south of the boreal forest.

A Basic Prehistory of the Subarctic

At the end of the Pleistocene, the glaciers that had covered the Subarctic region gradually began to melt, retreating north. This glacial retreat exposed scoured land surfaces and created many lake basins. As the ice melted, the tundra and forest zones slowly moved north, as did the caribou. It appears that most of the Subarctic environment could not support human populations until about 7,000 B.P., after the forest had become established in the region. The prehistory of the Subarctic is detailed by Clark (1981), Noble (1981), and Wright (1981). More recent, although brief, general summaries of Subarctic prehistory can be found in Dumond (1987:47–54) and Fagan (2000:158–202).

The Paleoindian Period (to ca. 10,000 B.P.)

The majority of the Subarctic was glaciated during Paleoindian times, and in such areas there are very few sites that date to this period. However, there are a few indications that Paleoindian people exploited the few unglaciated areas, particularly along the coast. The interior of Alaska was not glaciated and thus contains a good record of Paleoindian occupation, including materials that represent the initial migration of humans into the New World (see Fagan 2000:77).

The Archaic Period (ca. 10,000 B.P. to Contact)

As the Subarctic environment became habitable for human colonization, people moved into the region. Along the eastern coast of the Subarctic, sea mammal hunters established themselves as early as 9,000 B.P., an adaptation known as the Maritime Archaic. At about 7,000 B.P., Algonquian groups moved north into the interior eastern Subarctic. At about the same time, people speaking Athapaskan (Na-Dene) languages moved into the interior western Subarctic from the north and west. The Northern Archaic (ca. 7,000 B.P. to contact) generally represents the Athapaskan prehistory of the interior western Subarctic, while the Shield Archaic (also ca. 7,000 B.P. to contact) represents the Algonquian prehistory of the interior eastern Subarctic.

Upon their entry into the Subarctic, prehistoric peoples were organized into small, mobile bands and began to specialize in caribou hunting, although many other animals, such as musk ox, moose, elk, small mammals, waterfowl, and a great variety of fish, were also important resources. This basic adaptation was widespread across the Subarctic and was still followed by groups that were contacted by Europeans.

The Contact Period

Native people in the Subarctic were probably first contacted by the Norse some 1,000 years ago, but the newcomers' stay was brief and probably left no lasting impression on the Indians. After the arrival of Columbus in the New World, French Basque fishermen first contacted Subarctic groups in the east by the early sixteenth century. By the late eighteenth century, all groups in the region had been exposed to Europeans. Interaction between Europeans and the Indians was dominated by the fur trade (see Ray 1974).

In the eastern Subarctic, the French initially governed the trading activities, but after 1670 the British created the Hudson's Bay Company (see Newman 1989), which quickly took control. In the west, the Russians and the North West Company (see Davidson 1967) dominated the trading networks. After the departure of the French and the Russians, the British took control of the trade business in the west. In 1821, the Hudson's Bay Company acquired the North West Company and established a trading monopoly for the entire north. The Indians took full advantage of the demand for fur and adjusted their settlement and subsistence systems to accommodate trapping and trading. Many trading posts were established at places that facilitated the movement of goods by water, and the Indians moved some of their settlements to such places.

Guns were introduced into the region in the late nineteenth century, and the number of animals a hunter could take was thus greatly increased. Game depletion became so severe that it endangered both animal and human populations (see Chapter 2), so the Hudson's Bay Company implemented conservation measures. The Canadian government later established additional hunting regulations to preserve game. As a result, after the early twentieth century, animal populations began to recover, and trapping again became viable. At the same time, many European goods were adopted, including canvas tents, metal canoes, and snowmobiles. Nucleation of settlements around trading posts and government outposts became more common and the Indians became more dependent on Western foods. Today, there are about 100,000 trappers in northern North America, about half of them native people (Bone 1992:213).

In 1885, some Métis, Cree, and other groups united under a Métis leader named Louis Riel and rebelled against the Canadian government (see Beal and Macleod 1984). The Northwest Rebellion of 1885, also known as the Reil Uprising, was suppressed; however, it resulted in some changes in the way that the Métis and Indians were treated by the government. Also in the late nineteenth century several gold rushes occurred in the western Subarctic, and a large number of non-Indians entered the region. This had a considerable impact on both the environment and the Indians, many of whom worked as laborers. The Great Depression of the 1930s severely impacted Subarctic economies, reducing the demand for fur and decreasing opportunities for wage work. After World War II, more non-Indians settled in the region, primarily workers involved in military bases, oil exploration, and mining. Many Indians worked for the government and various companies as laborers.

A number of treaties were signed with Athapaskan groups in the western Subarctic between 1899 and 1921. Because the provisions of most had been misrepresented to the Indians—signatures were forged in some cases—many native groups gave up all rights to their lands with little compensation. These facts have served as the basis for a renegotiation of these treaties in the 1970s and 1980s. In the east, a series of treaties was signed with a number of Algonquian groups (called Treaty One, Treaty Two, etc.).

The Impact of European Contact

The most obvious impacts on native groups in the Subarctic were the changes brought about as a result of the fur trade (see Ray 1974; Krech 1984). Men hunted furs instead of food, settlements coalesced around trading posts, and by 1800 the depletion of fur and game resources from overhunting had forced most groups into a dependent relationship with the trading posts.

Disease also devastated native populations, although isolated groups were somewhat protected. Nevertheless, major smallpox epidemics swept through the eastern Subarctic in 1737 and 1781 and a very large number of Indians died. In the 1930s, tuberculosis became a major problem.

A Brief History of Ethnographic Research

Much of the Subarctic remained isolated from most Europeans until the late nineteenth century, and, as such, few anthropological studies were done until the twentieth century. However, a great deal of ethnographic information was recorded by early explorers, missionaries, and fur companies. Serious anthropological work began in the 1880s, punctuated by a lack of fieldwork during the two world wars (see Burch 1979; Davis 1981; McClellan 1981; Rogers 1981).

The early ethnographic work was mostly descriptive and often sponsored by museums. Major studies were done in the late nineteenth and early twentieth centuries by a number of researchers, notably Frank Speck and Lucien Turner. In the 1920s and 1930s, significant contributions were made by Diamond Jenness and Cornelius Osgood, as well as Regina Flannery (e.g., 1995), whose work on women's issues is particularly notable.

After the 1940s, researchers turned from pure description to working on specific topics and questions, including land tenure, health, ecology, psychology, and ethnohistory. Among the most prominent researchers were Frederica De Laguna, John Honigmann, and Richard Slobodin. Today, people like June Helm and Eleanor Leacock continue to conduct considerable ethnographic work in the region. Although there now exists a substantial amount of information on Subarctic peoples, it remains true that Subarctic cultures are still only "dimly perceived" (Rogers 1981:29).

Summaries of Subarctic culture are found in Helm and Leacock (1971), Nelson (1973), and VanStone (1974). The most recent major synthesis is the Subarctic volume (Vol. 6) of the *Handbook of North American Indians* (Helm 1981), written mostly in the late 1970s. That volume contains chapters on a wide variety of subjects and many groups. The discussion of Subarctic culture presented below was summarized from these sources and characterized the region in about 1850.

A Broad Portrait of Subarctic Groups

Subarctic groups made their primary living by hunting and fishing, with the gathering of plant foods forming a relatively minor component of the economy. They were also heavily involved in the fur trade. Most groups were highly mobile and had low population densities, large territories, simple political systems, and small-scale ceremonial systems. One exception is the Ingalik Indians in Alaska (see Snow

1981), who lived in permanent villages and had more elaborate ceremonies than most Subarctic groups.

Subarctic groups spoke languages of two major families, with Northern Athapaskan (Na-Dene) languages spoken in the west and Algonquian in the east. This distribution may reflect the initial colonization of the region about 7,000 years ago, at which time the Athapaskans began to move south and east from the Alaska region and the Algonquians of the Northeast moved north and west. Some Athapaskan groups eventually moved further south into California, the Southwest, and the southern Plains, and became the linguistic Southern Athapaskans. People remaining in the Subarctic became the Northern Athapaskans (see Krauss and Golla 1981). Most of the Athapaskan groups refer to themselves as Diné.

There are two major branches of the Algonquian languages, Cree and Ojibwa, in the eastern Subarctic (see Rhodes and Todd 1981). Cree was spoken by the Cree, along with the Montagnais and Naskapi, whom some consider to be Cree. Ojibwa was spoken by a number of groups to the south of the Cree, including the Ojibwa (who call themselves Anishinabe) and the Ottawa. Two groups in the Subarctic, the Chipewyan and the Chippewa, have confusingly similar names. The Chipewyan are a Northern Athapaskan group in the north-central Subarctic. *Chippewa* is an old non-Indian name for the Ojibwa or Saulteaux, an Algonquian group in the southern Subarctic. To confuse matters further, the Ojibwa in the United States are still often called Chippewa.

Political Organization

Most Subarctic groups were organized into small, local bands consisting of a few related families. The local band moved frequently within the forest to hunt and to avoid the cold winds. In the summer, a number of local bands might gather into larger groups (a regional band) of several dozen families; however, such groups were but temporary political organizations. Band membership was highly flexible. Families changed local bands at will, and local bands changed regional bands as well. Subarctic groups generally did not have an overarching political organization, although they did recognize the other bands as being related. Europeans assigned "tribal" names to local and regional bands, sometimes to both, resulting in considerable confusion.

Each of the bands, local and regional, had headmen. Appointed because of their experience and physical strength, these leaders had little real power. The headman took charge of important community activities, such as communal hunting and fishing, camp relocation, or other activities. Women rarely had any major authority or significant political power, although they had a great deal of responsibility for camp work and food gathering. During the summer, most of the men would hunt while the women, children, and elderly men would stay in the camp, working.

War was practiced by most groups and was usually based on feuds. War leaders were usually strong and aggressive men. Warfare was frequently conducted by shamans, who placed spells on the enemy. If actual combat occurred, it often involved surprise attacks, during which enemy men were killed and young women were captured. There was little glory associated with war and scalping was not practiced.

Social Organization

The primary social unit was the nuclear family, but extended families were not uncommon. A small number of families would form a local band, and within the band, task groups would perform cooperative work in obtaining resources. These task groups were very important to the functioning of the society.

Throughout the Subarctic, kinship was bilateral with no distinction between mother's and father's side of the family. Kinship recognition did not go beyond two generations, and groups varied in their emphasis on descent and inheritance. There was a tendency toward matrilocality with some groups, as a man often lived with his wife's band during the first year of marriage. In addition, many of the Diné groups employed a system in which a person belonged to one of two major groups of clans, Crow and Wolf, where one's membership depended on the membership of one's mother and was a source of some power for women. Members of these "moieties" assisted each other in times of need.

There were few puberty rites for boys, but first menses was significant for females, who would be isolated from the group, at which time they would observe a number of restrictions and after which they could be sought as wives. In addition to being isolated during menstruation, females were isolated during childbirth, as they were considered to have dangerous powers during both processes. The vision quest was very important throughout the Subarctic, and both boys and girls were encouraged to seek power and a spirit-helper during such an event.

Marriages were usually arranged by one's parents, and polygyny was common. Mates were typically chosen from the local area. Divorce was a simple matter; the husband or wife would merely move elsewhere. Sexual relations before marriage were relatively commonplace, but adultery was not permitted by either sex and could result in the offenders' being beaten. There were few other marriage rules, but a critical rule was the avoidance of incest.

Subarctic groups observed a fairly strict division of labor. Men hunted, fished, and conducted war, while women collected plant resources and did most of the domestic chores. Men made the canoes, but women maintained them. Some groups had berdaches, who were also expected to perform domestic duties. Women carried most of the equipment and materials, as well as the children, during camp relocations. In general, women were treated poorly, and being beaten by one's husband was not uncommon. Thus, women sometimes looked forward to their menstrual cycles, as the isolation provided protection against their husbands and a respite from daily chores. Female infanticide was practiced if a family felt they already had too many female children. It was believed that the soul of the child would simply wait to be born at a more opportune time.

Death was generally believed to be the result of a loss of power, a form of punishment, or witchcraft, perhaps from an enemy shaman. The deceased were mourned and buried in new clothes, along with materials needed for the afterlife, such as tools and food. Individuals could be buried in graves or placed on scaffolds erected in trees.

Music, dancing, and storytelling were very popular and many games were played. After contact, the Indians learned how to make alcoholic beverages, and drinking parties became common social occasions among many groups (see Honigmann 1981a:732–733).

Economics

The people of the Subarctic were primarily hunters and fishers, and a large number of animals were exploited (see Gillespie 1981). Plant collecting, mostly done by women, was also important, but was not the primary source of food. Agriculture was not practiced by any Subarctic groups, and the only domestic animal was the dog. Sharing, reciprocity, and general cooperation were important characteristics of the subsistence system.

The two most important terrestrial animals in Subarctic economies were caribou and moose, used both for food and skins, with most groups relying heavily on one or the other. Caribou are large, reindeer-like animals that migrate along established routes. In about November the animals migrate south into the boreal forests, and around May they move north again into the tundra. Caribou were taken in communal hunts, often with the use of surrounds. They were also driven into water or attacked while crossing a river, where the relatively immobile animals could be speared from shore or canoes. Caribou were also captured with the aid of snares and large nets. If caribou populations were low, groups would increase the hunting of snowshoe hares to compensate. If caribou and hare were scarce during the same year, starvation could result.

Moose was the staple terrestrial game animal for some groups in the boreal forest. Moose are large and dangerous animals that were taken by lone hunters, or small groups of hunters, all year long. Other land animals hunted for food included musk ox, wood bison, elk, deer, bears, beavers, hares, and gophers. Sea mammals were hunted in a few places, and in the far western Subarctic, mountain goats and mountain sheep were important. A number of birds were also hunted, primarily ducks and geese; the eggs of the birds were eaten as well.

As the summers were warm, cold storage throughout the summer was not possible, as it was in the Arctic. Most meat was cut into strips and smoked and/or dried for future use. A "trail mix," called pemmican, was made from a mixture of meat, fat, and berries pounded together, and would keep for months. Some perishables were stored on platforms or wrapped and hung from tree branches. Also, firewood was cut and stockpiled for the winter.

Fish were critical resources for most groups. Popular species included salmon, trout, whitefish, and char (see Gillespie 1981: Table 2). Fish were speared or taken in traps, weirs, and nets. Some groups caught fish from under the ice of frozen lakes with gill nets suspended between two holes in the ice (see Rogers and Smith 1981: Fig. 6).

Various plants resources were utilized for food, manufacturing materials, and medicines, and most such resources were collected during the summer. The most important food plants were various species of berries, followed by fern roots, wild onions, and mushrooms. Birch sap was used as a candy and spruce sap was made into chewing gum.

Material Culture and Technology

A variety of structures were used for shelter, depending on location and circumstances. In the summer, when populations were moving around the landscape, short, conical skin tents were constructed. Hunting parties would sometimes build lean-tos. In the winter, much more substantial houses were built, including semi-subterranean, earth-covered structures.

In the summer, most travel was by foot or in canoes. In the winter, with the extensive snow covering and frozen waters, travel was greatly restricted. However, Subarctic groups used several types of snowshoes, depending on the snow conditions (see Rogers and Smith 1981: Fig. 8), to move around in the winter. The transportation of heavy materials during the winter was accomplished using toboggans, usually pulled by the women. Dogsleds were used by a few groups. Canoes were the primary mode of transportation during the ice-free months, and several types were utilized. In the west, large canoes covered with moose hide might be as long as twenty-four feet. In the eastern Subarctic, birch or spruce bark canoes were common. While these canoes were light and easy to carry, they were fairly fragile and could not transport much.

Well-made, tailored clothing was important in the Subarctic, particularly in the winter. Most clothing was made of tanned caribou or moose hides, but other animal skins were also used. Everyone wore tunics, leggings, and moccasins year-round, as well as coats and blankets in the winter. Ornamentation was limited mostly to decoration on clothing and some tattooing, especially for women.

Other technology included containers made of bark, a few stone tools, and many items made from bone and wood, but no pottery. Native copper was cold-hammered into ornamental objects such as jewelry. Rope, large nets, fencing, snowshoes, and other items were made from babiche, caribou or moose skin cut into long strips and braided together.

Religion

Subarctic groups generally did not believe in supreme or overall deities, only in a general impersonal power (see Honigmann 1981a:718–720). The universe contained power that a person could draw upon and use to accomplish goals, for good or evil. If one did only good things, one's power was strong. If bad things happened, it implied that power had been lost or that someone else was using stronger power in opposition. Everyone had different access to power, resulting in varying talents and abilities.

Spirits, each with different powers, were found in animals, plants, geographic features, and other objects. Some of these spirits were good; some were evil and feared. It was common to seek a spirit-helper in a vision quest at puberty, and spirit-helpers assisted individuals throughout their lives.

It was necessary to thank animals for allowing themselves to be hunted and killed. Animals allowed it because they loved humans, and in return humans were required to reciprocate that love and treat hunted game with great respect. Hunters tried not to kill more animals than they needed and tried to preserve pregnant females and the young. This belief formed a major aspect of the religious belief system of the Subarctic (see Honigmann 1981a:724; Brightman 1993).

All Subarctic groups had shamans, people who had and/or controlled more power than others, and using witchcraft was a major part of being a shaman. Shamans generally carried bags that contained objects inhabited by powerful spirits to help them in their work. Shamans placed spells (both good and bad) on people, protected people from the bad spells of other shamans, and tried to kill enemies with witchcraft. Shamans also cured people, using the sucking cure and some pharmacology. They might also lead caribou hunts. Shamans found to be practicing evil were sometimes killed.

Subarctic Peoples Today

In 2001, there were about 675,000 native people living in Canada, including Indians and Métis people. They are organized into some 610 recognized native groups, often called First Nations, living on 2,240 reserves.

The passage of the Indian Act in 1951 resulted in the expansion of government benefits to many Subarctic groups in Canada. In the 1960s, the Canadian government established a series of schools, health centers, and military installations, and created housing programs for the native people in northern Canada. As a result, new communities were founded and they quickly became major centers. Many native people now live in these towns, and Indians of different tribes often live in the same town. Education is widespread; only small villages lack schools. Most school curricula emphasize European heritages, but some schools are now teaching native languages, and literacy is increasing. Health care is improving and now includes immunization programs. However, new health problems, such as heart disease, obesity, diabetes, tuberculosis, and a variety of other Western ailments, have sprung up (see McCutcheon 1991).

Generally speaking, Subarctic peoples today have managed to maintain their cultural identities and much of their traditional culture while adapting to and using much of Western technology (see Honigmann 1981b). Until fairly recently, many groups still subsisted by hunting and trading; however, this is changing rapidly, as development projects become more common in the region. The construction of all-weather roads and the use of aircraft have greatly increased the human population in the region.

The ongoing development of lumber, oil, minerals, and hydroelectric power has drawn many Indians into wage labor, for which they are paid much less than non-Indians. As they become more and more integrated into mainstream Canadian and American culture and labor, their family structures are becoming more similar to those of typical Western families. While still living in their traditional areas, some groups, particularly those associated with the James Bay project, now reside in modern, Western-style housing with electricity and plumbing, and they shop at grocery stores.

There have been some land-claim settlements in the Subarctic. The western Diné were involved in the Alaska Native Claims Settlement Act (ANCSA) in 1971 and the Cree signed the James Bay Settlement in 1975 (see McCutcheon 1991; Feit

2000). Also, in 1975, some groups banded together and declared a "Diné Nation," with the goal of forming a province within the national Canadian government, as the Inuit have done. In mid-1998, the Nisga (Nishga) tribe (a western Diné group) signed a treaty with the Canadian government.

Learn More About Contemporary Subarctic Peoples

The discussion above is only a very brief description of Subarctic people today. What else can you discover? Go to the library, and look on the Internet (you can begin with http:/www.ainc-inac.gc.ca./) to learn more about how Subarctic groups are managing. Topics you can explore include the following:

1. Chose a particular group or two, and investigate how land claims settlement has affected them. What impact did the James Bay Settlement have on groups that signed the agreement?
2. Do the Algonquian and Athabaskan groups differ from each other? If so, how? Which groups have concluded treaties with Canada?
3. What traditional practices have been retained by these peoples? What are the roles of traditional religion, economics, and politics in Subarctic groups today?
4. What are the problems faced by Subarctic people today?
5. What role do the Métis Indians play in the contemporary Subarctic?

The Western Woods Cree: A Subarctic Case Study

The Native American group that inhabited a large portion of the eastern Subarctic is called the Cree (Fig. 4.2). The general term *Cree* seems to have stemmed from a French derivation of the name of one of the Cree bands. Most Cree call themselves by a term meaning "person" in their particular dialect, the Western Woods Cree term being *nehiyawak*. The Cree have a complex history and are very closely associated linguistically and culturally with the Ojibwa, who have also been called the Chippewa, to the south (see Rogers and Taylor 1981). It was only after the early nineteenth century that the Cree and Ojibwa were recognized as separate cultural entities (see Bishop 1981).

Early anthropologists recognized two major divisions of the Cree: the Plains Cree, who had moved onto the Plains in the 1700s (see Mandelbaum 1940) and the Woods (or Swampy) Cree, who lived in the swampy muskeg forests of the

FIGURE 4.2 Location and territory of the Cree, showing their three major divisions
Adapted from *Handbook of North American Indians, Vol. 6, Subarctic*, J. Helm, ed., p. ix; copyright © 1981 by the Smithsonian Institution. Reprinted by permission of the publisher.

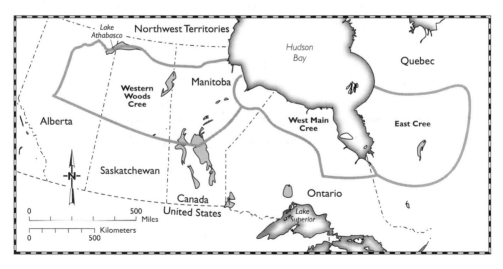

Subarctic. More recently, the Woods Cree have been classified into three major subdivisions: the East Cree, consisting of the East Main Cree (see Preston 1981), although some researchers also include the Montagnais and the Naskapi with the East Cree (see Rogers and Leacock 1981); the West Main Cree (see Honigmann 1981c); and the Western Woods Cree. The long-term interactions between the Cree and the European traders and trappers significantly contributed to the development of the Métis (see Slobodin 1981; also see Payment 2001). This case study describes the Western Woods Cree as they were around 1750. Smith (1981:267) believed that there were approximately 20,000 Western Woods Cree at about that time.

Much of the information accumulated on the Cree in general was obtained in the early twentieth century by Alanson Skinner, John M. Cooper, and Regina Flannery, and after 1950 by John J. Honigmann and Richard J. Preston. Important syntheses on Western Woods Cree culture are presented in Curtis (1928), Fisher (1969), and Smith (1981), and the information on the Western Woods Cree summarized below is from these sources.

The Natural Environment

The territory occupied by the Western Woods Cree lies south and west of the southern extension of Hudson Bay, basically the northern portions of the Canadian provinces of Alberta, Saskatchewan, Manitoba, and Ontario (see Fig. 4.2). Much of the region is relatively flat, with rolling hills, small basins, and a large number of rivers, streams, and lakes. The Cree lived mainly in the forest and did not occupy the coast of Hudson Bay until drawn there by the European trading posts that were built along the coast.

The principal biotic community consisted of the boreal forest, dominated by extensive tracts of black and white spruce, as well as pines, white birch, and aspens. In the low-lying basins, large areas of muskeg (swamp) were present. An extensive variety of fauna inhabited the forest, including moose, caribou, wood bison, elk, hares, and many small mammals. A number of birds were also present, and waterfowl flew over the region in their annual migrations. A great diversity of fish were available in the many bodies of water.

Language

The Cree spoke the Cree language, part of the large Algonquian language family. Algonquian languages were spoken all across the eastern Subarctic and a portion of the Northeast (see Chapter 11). Cree is most closely related to Ojibwa, spoken just to the south, and has two major linguistic divisions, western and eastern. The Western Cree language has six dialects and the Eastern Cree has three.

A Brief History

The Cree were first contacted in the early seventeenth century by the French, although the Western Woods Cree were contacted somewhat later. Soon after contact, the Cree became intimately involved in the fur trade with the French. After

1670, the Hudson's Bay Company entered the region, and the Cree then traded with both the French and the British. Most of the European trading posts were located at river mouths along the shores of Hudson Bay, in order to facilitate transport of goods by ship and to allow access to the interior by canoe.

Until the rebellion of 1885, the Cree generally had friendly relations with the Europeans. Cree trappers served as mentors for the European traders, teaching them and supporting their efforts, and eventually became middlemen for other Indian traders. The Cree fought with the Chipewyan to prevent them from trading with the British, but at the urging of the Hudson's Bay Company, the Cree made peace with the Chipewyan in 1715. By the late eighteenth century, some Cree had moved west and even onto the northern Plains (the Plains Cree; see Mandelbaum 1940).

By 1821, the Hudson's Bay Company had gained control of most of the fur trade in northern North America, prompting the movement of some Cree populations to the trading posts. The depletion of game in eastern Canada may have contributed to the migration of some Cree to the west. The Cree maintained their trading advantage, and by the late nineteenth century they had become the dominant native group in central Canada. Many Western Woods Cree women married European fur traders, and their descendants constitute the Métis, a separate aboriginal group distinct from the Eskimo and Indians and recognized by the Canadian government. A written Cree language was created in 1840, which was perhaps an elaboration of an existing Cree system of symbols used in some rituals.

By the early nineteenth century, as animal populations declined, it became more and more difficult for the Western Woods Cree to support themselves, whereupon poverty became a problem, illness increased, and traditional culture began to break down. The Great Depression hit the Western Woods Cree economy hard, reducing the demand for fur and decreasing the availability of wage work. As late as the early 1940s, many Cree still followed a traditional economic system that included a seasonal round, visiting trading posts for a few weeks in the summer. Some Western Woods Cree bands remained fairly isolated until the mid-to-late twentieth century, preserving much of their traditional culture.

Cosmology

Few Western Woods Cree have discussed their cosmology with anthropologists, so it is known only in brief outline. Far in the past, a woman lived with a dog. The dog turned into a man one night and had sexual intercourse with the woman, who then became pregnant. Thereafter, a giant appeared one day, captured the dog, tore him into many pieces, and threw the pieces about the landscape. The various pieces of the dog became the different animals. The baby became the Cree. The dog, who fathered the people and became all of the animals, was held in very high esteem by the Cree.

Politics and External Relations

The Cree did not have a single tribal identity, although an attempt is now under way to create one. Rather, they identified themselves by their band, and there were many small local bands, each of which functioned as an independent unit during the fall, winter, and spring. The local band consisted of several related families, and had between ten and thirty members. In the summer, several small bands merged into one of many regional bands. A regional band, with between 100 and 200 people, would locate on the shore of a lake where its members could hunt, fish, and gather berries for the summer. Membership in local and regional bands was flexible and depended on a variety of conditions, including availability of game. The bilateral kinship system of the Cree contributed to this flexibility.

The leader or headman of a band, local or regional, was the man who was most experienced, most respected, and/or had supernatural power. If the performance of a headman deteriorated, he would be replaced or the people would change bands to be with a more capable headman. Major duties of the headman included keeping the peace and deciding when and where the band should move to find food. Other decisions were made generally by consensus, but some physically powerful headmen did use force.

The Western Woods Cree had a reputation for being skilled in war, but actual combat was rare. They had mostly hostile relations with the Chipewyan to the northwest (until their peace agreement of 1715) and with the Eskimo groups to the north. The Cree were allied with the Assiniboin against the Sioux on the northern Plains. Men sometimes wore body armor of wood slats and hide and used the bow and arrow as their main weapon. Intertribal warfare intensified after European contact as groups jockeyed for position to profit from the fur trade.

Social Organization

The basic social unit of the Western Woods Cree was the nuclear family, although extended families were not uncommon. Lineages and clans were not recognized. Kinship was reckoned bilaterally, meaning that marriage doubled the number of relatives, greatly increasing the number of people from whom one could expect help. There was little emphasis on descent and inheritance, as political power was not passed along family lines.

The division of labor was based strictly on sex. Men hunted, fished, trapped, engaged in warfare, and manufactured all of the equipment needed for these tasks. Women helped in the procurement of food by doing some fishing, trapping small game near camp, and gathering plant foods. Women also performed domestic duties, set up and disassembled the camps, carried much of the belongings when traveling, cooked, took care of the children, procured firewood, manufactured clothing, and processed meat and hides. Some women, such as widows with no children, frequently participated in hunting activities with the men. During January and February, the weather limited most outside activities and most people stayed inside, processing hides, making or repairing tools or clothing, and telling stories.

It is commonly believed that women were treated very poorly in Cree society and that dogs (important in Cree cosmology) were sometimes treated better than women. But it is important to remember that life was demanding in the Subarctic and women often had a difficult existence. If they were mistreated by the men, they were able to "escape" by feigning menstruation, which required isolation from the men. A discussion of women's roles in Cree society is presented by Flannery (1995).

Cree mother and child
(about 1910).
(CORBIS)

Life Cycle

Little fanfare greeted the birth of a baby. Pregnant women were attended by several experienced women, and the mother gave birth in a kneeling position supported by a wooden pole and the female helpers. Infanticide was practiced, but only as a necessity, as a mother could not care for more than one nursing child at a time. In the case of twins, only one, preferably a male, would be kept.

Infants were wrapped in skin blankets with moss and put in a cradleboard. A baby was given a name within a few months. Most infants nursed until they were about a year old, but some were not weaned until about three years of age. Children were loved and rarely disciplined, and as they grew older they began to help the adults and assume adult roles.

Youths of both sexes went on a vision quest by themselves, without food or water, to seek a spirit-helper from which they would derive power throughout their lives. Upon their return, they did not discuss the vision with others. The relationship between humans and their spirit-helpers was analogous to a contract stating who was expected to do what. A person might sometimes have a symbol of the vision sewn on his or her clothing or carved on tools.

At her first menses, a girl spent four days in a small, isolated hut, either with another girl in the same situation, or with an older woman. The girl observed certain food restrictions and kept herself very busy, so as to ensure an industrious adulthood. After the isolation period was over, the girl kept a low profile in the community for the next month or two. During subsequent menstrual cycles, women were again isolated in the menstrual hut, but rejoined the group immediately upon termination of the cycle. No special puberty ceremony was held for males, but a feast took place when a boy killed his first large animal.

Parents often arranged the marriages of their children, sometimes even before birth, and women often had little choice in the matter. People tended to marry within their local population, and cross-cousin marriage (where a person marries the child of father's sister or mother's brother) was the preferred form. A girl might be "married" by the age of eight or ten and live with her husband, who was older, but the marriage was not consummated until the girl had reached puberty.

Marriage did not involve a special ceremony, merely the acceptance of the gifts that served as the proposal. Afterwards, the couple simply began living together and were considered married. The bride was purchased by the groom's family, who paid as much as possible to increase the status of the bride and thus of the new family. After marriage, the couple lived with or near the bride's family for a period of time, then established their own household. Mothers-in-law and sons-in-law were never allowed to speak directly to each other, communicating only indirectly through others.

Some men had more than one wife, often the sister of the first wife. Two men who were (or wanted to be) close partners might enter into an agreement to exchange wives, a relationship that could also be purchased. This arrangement was perfectly acceptable, although an adulterous woman could be beaten and might even have her nose cut off. Adultery was also cause for divorce. There were few sexual restrictions for those who were unmarried.

People who were ill and knew they were about to die would provide detailed instructions regarding the disposition of their belongings or other directions to the family. The dead were wrapped in skins and placed in a grave, a scaffold in a tree, or under a pile of logs. Personal equipment, including weapons, snowshoes, pipe and tobacco, and food, were placed with the deceased for the journey to the afterlife. If the deceased had a drum or a canoe, these items were placed at or near the grave. Close relatives mourned for up to a year. Mourners cut their hair, wore ragged clothes, and did not wash their faces. Some mourners might blacken their faces and/or smear their hair with white paint. Individuals who were old or helpless would request death in order to reduce the burden on the family. Such people would either be killed or would commit suicide.

Economics

The Western Wood Cree subsisted primarily by hunting and fishing. It was expected that a successful hunter or fisherman would share the catch with others in the band. Moose, a large and dangerous animal, were the primary prey and were taken all year round. They were usually hunted by individuals or small groups of hunters who tracked the moose, even in snow, with the aid of dogs. Moose were killed with bows and arrows from an ambush position, although some pit traps were also employed.

The caribou was the second most important animal. Caribou were hunted communally during their fall and spring migrations. Individual caribou might be caught in snares, but larger numbers were captured with the aid of drive lines and corrals. Other essential game animals included elk, an occasional bison, bears, geese, muskrats, and hares, the last often hunted by women and children using traps and snares. The Cree also trapped a variety of animals for their fur, particularly beaver. Women were responsible for bringing animals back to camp and processing them. Meat was eaten fresh or dried for later use. Some dried meat was mixed with berries and fat and pounded into pemmican.

Fish were the most significant resource in the summer, so the Cree would locate their summer camps at good fishing localities. Few fish were taken in the winter; unlike many Subarctic groups, the Western Woods Cree did not fish under the ice. A large variety of fish were available in the many watercourses and lakes, the most important being whitefish, lake trout, pickerel, pike, and walleye. Men speared fish and both men and women used nets—dip nets at waterfalls and gill nets in lakes. Fish were eaten fresh, smoked and dried, and preserved frozen in caches. Although they were a highly valued resource, fish were generally considered inferior to moose or caribou, but they were a major food item for the dogs.

Plant foods formed a relatively small percentage of the overall Cree diet, but a few plants were extensively utilized, the most important being berries, especially serviceberries. Berries were picked and dried in large quantities, used to make pemmican, and stored in birchbark containers throughout the winter. Other significant plant foods included cattail stalks and roots, and some pine nuts. Many other plants were used for purposes other than food, such as for housing, diaper material, chewing gum, medicines, and firestarters (see Leighton 1985).

Trapping was a critical aspect of the Cree economy. Most trapping activities were conducted at the height of winter, when the furs were best. After the mid–seventeenth century, the Cree economy shifted from subsistence hunting to an emphasis on trapping, the proceeds being used to buy foods from the trading posts. The trapping economy also ultimately resulted in the development of trapping territories owned by families.

Material Culture and Technology

The Cree built several different types of structures. At long-term camps, a large, conical house was built with a frame of log poles tied together in the center. The frame was covered with moose and/or caribou hides or birchbark over a layer of moss. In the winter, houses were constructed in the forest to avoid the wind; in the summer, they were built in the open so that the wind would keep the insects away. Sweathouses, in which men would build a fire, sweat, and be cleansed, were small, domed-shaped structures built with a frame of willow covered with skins. Menstrual huts were small tents placed at the edge of the camp. Small skin or bark tents and/or lean-tos were used when traveling.

During the summer, one could travel either by foot or by canoe. The Cree made fine canoes with birch frames, birchbark coverings, and turpentine caulking. These canoes weighed about eighty pounds and could carry a family and all of their equipment. During the winter, travel by water was impossible and people were forced to walk through the snow. The Cree manufactured snowshoes that allowed them to traverse the deep and unpacked snow. Equipment and materials were transported on toboggans that were up to twelve feet long. The toboggans were usually pulled by people, often women, but dogs were sometimes used.

Basic clothing for both sexes consisted of a tunic of caribou, elk, or moose skin, with detachable sleeves (taken off in the summer), leggings, and moccasins. In addition, women wore skirts of caribou skin. When it was cold, everyone donned a second tunic of caribou or beaver hide, with the hair left on and worn on the inside. In the winter, people also wore a coat or blanket of moose, beaver, or otter skin, with a separate hood, as well as gloves of beaver skin. Blankets and coats of bear and hare skin were also essential apparel. Children's clothing was similar to that of adults. Clothing was made by the women, and much of it was decorated with porcupine quills, moose hair, and paint. After the eighteenth century, European-style clothing became the norm.

Women adorned themselves with brass bracelets and painted their faces red. They would also put animal fat in their hair and wear it parted in the middle and tied behind each ear. Beads or other ornaments were often attached to the hair. Men generally wore their hair long, in one or two ponytails. Many people wore tattoos; men commonly placed them on their faces and arms, while women tattooed their chins.

Most tools were manufactured from wood and bone, with a few items made from stone. Most containers were made of birchbark sewn together with spruce roots and caulked with spruce gum; the Cree did not use pottery. Materials could be boiled in such containers with the aid of hot stones. Axes and knives were fashioned from stone, and bone was used for projectile points, fishhooks, and needles. Most game was caught in snares and traps, and spears and nets were used to harvest fish. Bows were manufactured from birch or willow, and quivers were made from animal skins (e.g., beaver, fox, and otter).

Religion and Medicine

Group ceremonies were lacking, since as most religious activities were at the individual level in association with a person's spirit-helper. A general power possessed by various beings and spirits was called Manitou; Thunder also was a very powerful spirit. There were three categories of persons/spirits: spirit persons, such as an individual's spirit-helper; human persons; and animal persons. Each of these had power and had to be dealt with.

Illness, injury, and death were considered to be the result of evil forces or enemy shamans and required the help of, and treatment by, shamans. Shamans, who were always males, possessed considerable Manitou power; thus, those who frequently dreamed of the supernatural became shamans, as it was apparent that they possessed such power. A novice shaman would be apprenticed to an established shaman until he had learned his trade. Divining the future from the interpretation of cracks on burned animal scapulae was a special talent of shamans.

Shamans employed a variety of techniques to effect cures or to counter spells, including using a spell of their own, the sucking cure, and some pharmacology. A small, special hut was constructed for a shaman to treat a patient. Shamans could place spells on others, causing them harm, but they were also famous for their love potions. In addition, shamans conducted warfare by placing spells on the enemy.

Art, Expression, and Recreation

Artistic expression was rather limited among the Western Woods Cree, but clothing was decorated and individuals made ample use of tattooing. Musicians played drums, made of hide stretched over wooden frames, and the bull-roarer, a device that made a sound as it was twirled in the air. The Cree played a number of games of chance and skill, including the hand game, hoop and pole, dice, and guessing games. Stories told by older people provided great entertainment. Boys played hunting games and girls played with dolls.

The Western Woods Cree Today

Forty-five bands of Western Woods Cree, many with reserves, were recognized by the Canadian government in 1978 (Smith 1981: Table 1), with a combined population of about 35,000. In addition, other Western Woods Cree are not recognized by the government ("nonstatus" Indians). Thus, there are now about 200,000 Cree Indians in Canada, plus many Métis who have Cree ancestry.

Each of the various bands is considered independent by the government. However, in 1971, the Grand Council of the Cree was formed in an attempt to bring all of the various bands under a single political umbrella. This effort continues, and pan-Cree gatherings have been held since 1994. The primary goal of the 1999 gathering was to discuss the idea of organizing a Cree confederacy to unite all of the Cree bands into a single political entity. Interestingly, the East Main Cree, now living in the Canadian province of Quebec, voted against the secession of Quebec.

Most Cree now live in permanent towns associated with government centers or commercial enterprises, most of which have schools and health facilities. Some Cree are employed as wage laborers, but such work is often unavailable. The government provides subsidies to most families, their most reliable source of income. Hunting and trapping are still major components of the Cree economy. During the winter, many men leave for long periods of time to hunt and trap, leaving their families in the towns.

The Cree have been impacted by a variety of large development projects. The largest of these was the James Bay Hydroelectric Project (see McCutcheon 1991). The James Bay project involved the construction of dams and the flooding of river valleys. Many believed that the result would be the loss of hunting for a living, which would compromise Cree self-determination. Nevertheless, the East Main Cree signed the James Bay Agreement in 1975 and became partners in the project (see Niezen 1998). While the agreement did result in some improvement in Cree life (see Salisbury 1986), it seems that the project was not advantageous for them in the long run (Gagné 1994).

In the late 1970s, the government of Alberta built an all-weather road through the territory of the Lubicon Lake Cree, an isolated band of Western Woods Cree (see Smith 1987; Goddard 1991). The government then leased large tracts of Cree land for oil exploration, impacting their ability to earn a living. This action is being fought in the courts and constitutes a major threat to Cree livelihood and independence (see Chapter 13).

Additional information on the Cree can be obtained by visiting *http://www. gcc.ca/*, or *http://fn2.freenet.edmonton.ab.ca/~databank/hpc.html*.

5 Native Peoples of the Plateau

///

The Plateau culture area is located in the north-central portion of Western North America, nestled among four other culture areas (Fig. 5.1). The small size and location of the Plateau ensured that its people would interact with, and be affected by, groups in their neighboring culture areas to a considerable extent. As such, the Plateau culture area is difficult to define (see Walker 1998a). The key resources of the Plateau (salmon, the roots of certain plants, and large mammals) could be viewed as defining characteristics, much as salmon and sea mammals contributed to the lifeways of the Northwest Coast. Other major features of Plateau culture include limited political complexity, broad kinship ties across groups, institutionalized regional trading networks, and settlements along rivers (Walker 1998a:3). The adoption of the horse after 1720 dramatically changed Plateau culture (see below).

Geography and Environment

The Plateau region essentially consists of interior highlands and basins extending from the Great Basin north into southern Canada (see Chatters 1998). It is bounded on the west by the Coast Mountains and the Cascade Range and on the east by the Rocky Mountains, and includes what are now central and northern Idaho, eastern Oregon, eastern Washington, and southern British Columbia. The coastal mountains form a rainshadow that limits rainfall in the interior. The Plateau is drained by numerous rivers, the largest being the Columbia, Fraser, and Snake Rivers. They cut deeply into the highlands and mountains, forming a number of spectacular canyons.

FIGURE 5.1 Plateau culture area, with locations of native groups
Adapted from *Handbook of North American Indians, Vol. 12, Plateau*, D. E. Walker, Jr., ed., p. ix; copyright © 1998 by the Smithsonian Institution. Reprinted by permission of the publisher.

The environment of the Plateau is highly variable and complex. Some researchers view the area as having two divisions—north and south—based on broad differences in language, environment (e.g., Hunn 1990a), and even the different more recent experiences of the Indians; those in the north have dealt with the Canadian government while those in the south have dealt with the U.S. government (Hunn 1990a:361).

The northern Plateau is rather mountainous and is mostly covered by forests of pine and oak. The summers there are warm and the winters can be extremely cold, with considerable snowfall. The mountains on either side of the central region of the Plateau receive substantial rainfall, while the interior has less precipitation. The southern Plateau is not quite as mountainous, and some areas are characterized by extensive lava flows. In the southern Plateau, the winters are cold and the summers are hot. The rainshadow effect of the southern Cascade Range limits rainfall to about six inches a year, making the southern Plateau relatively arid. Much of the southern Plateau is covered by sagebrush and grasslands, and many of the small basins contain marshes.

A variety of animals live in the Plateau, including deer, moose, elk, caribou (in the north), bears, mountain sheep, pronghorn, a few bison, rabbits, rodents, and a number of fur species which were important after contact. For many Plateau groups, the most essential animal resource was salmon, which formed a staple food. Waterfowl and several types of ground-dwelling birds were also commonly exploited. Shellfish, a popular resource, were available in large quantities in several river systems. Insects, particularly grasshoppers, were numerous at times and were most likely consumed.

A great number of plants grow in the Plateau region. Among the most important for the native groups was the variety of tubers, particularly camas, cous, wild carrot, wild onion, and tiger lily. Pine and oak trees produced pine nuts and acorns, which were also used as foodstuffs. People of the Plateau also ate berries, including serviceberries, chokecherries, huckleberries, and currants. Cattail was eaten and used to make matting. Other plants, including willow and hemp, provided materials for basketry, housing, and tools.

A Basic Prehistory of the Plateau

Only a very basic outline of Plateau prehistory is known. The reviews provided by Ames et al. (1998), Chatters and Pokotylo (1998), Pokotylo and Mitchell (1998), and Roll and Hackenberger (1998) are the most current (also see Hayden 1997).

The Paleoindian Period (ca. 14,000 to 10,000 B.P.)

There is relatively little evidence of a Paleoindian occupation of the Plateau region. Such an occupation may be masked by several factors. First, there were several huge floods in the drainage of the Columbia River at the end of the Pleistocene that probably swept away evidence of a Paleoindian occupation in that area. Second, much of the volcanic activity in the southern Plateau occurred in the early Holocene, resulting in many lava flows and ash deposits that probably buried many early sites.

Nevertheless, some Paleoindian material has been found, including several spectacular discoveries of cached material (e.g., the Simon Clovis cache in Idaho and the Wenatchee cache in eastern Washington [Mehringer and Foit 1990]). More recently, several Paleoindian burials have been recovered. The Kennewick burial in Washington appears to possess traits that distinguish it from contemporary Native Americans and has been radiocarbon-dated to approximately 9,400 years ago

(Chatters 1997; also see Chapter 1). The earlier Buhl burial in Idaho is also unusual and may represent an earlier manifestation of Paleoindians (see Green et al. 1998). The recently discovered Hetrick site in Idaho contains evidence of a broad diet during Clovis times.

The Archaic Period (ca. 10,000 B.P. to Contact)

After the Paleoindian Period, Plateau peoples shifted to an Archaic lifestyle. Chatters and Pokotylo (1998) divide the Plateau Archaic into three periods, Early, Middle, and Late. During the Early Period (11,000 to 8,000 B.P.) people lived in small, mobile groups and exploited a variety of resources for subsistence, including salmon, various shellfish, large mammals, and other fish.

By the Middle Period (8,000 to 4,000 B.P.) the climate began to cool slightly, increasing the forest cover and improving conditions for large mammals and tubers. Salmon fishing was clearly important by 6,000 B.P., as were roots.

At the beginning of the Late Period (4,000 B.P. to A.D. 1720) the climate began to cool significantly, producing significant seasonal differences. A shift began from a broadly based hunter-gatherer economy with people living in small, mobile groups, to larger social units that stored food and lived in semipermanent villages. Semisubterranean structures were present by 3,000 years ago, as was the settlement pattern of living in large villages during the winter. Plateau people were by then living on salmon, roots, and large mammals. After about 1,000 years ago, resource use, particularly of salmon, intensified. The reasons for this intensification are unknown but might be related to population expansion and/or pressures from other groups.

Beginning about 700 years ago, it appears that the Northern Paiute and Northern Shoshone began to expand north into the southern Plateau, applying pressure to the Klamath and Nez Perce. This expansion was halted by European contact, but the Northern Paiute and Northern Shoshone remained enemies of the groups on the southern Plateau. Groups on the eastern Plateau, had obtained horses by about 1720, which were later traded to groups on the northern Plateau.

The Contact Period

The Plateau groups and Euroamericans experienced first contact in 1805, when the American expedition led by Lewis and Clark passed through the region. By that time, some Plateau groups had horses and appeared similar to several of the Plains groups that Lewis and Clark had just observed. Almost immediately thereafter, both the British and Americans established trading posts and competed for the fur trade in the region. American traders abandoned the area at the beginning of the war with Britain in 1812, and the British took over sole control of trade on the Plateau. In 1825, the Hudson's Bay Company became the primary trading company.

Missionaries arrived on the Plateau in 1836 and began an attempt to convert the Indians to Christianity. The missionaries treated nonbelievers harshly, and some groups reacted violently, even killing some of the missionaries. Others groups (e.g., the Nez Perce) resented the Christians but did not respond with violence.

After the opening of the Oregon Trail in 1840, the region was flooded with Euroamerican immigrants, who began to occupy Indian lands, bringing new disease into the region. The Indians did their best to accommodate the intruders. In 1846, the United States took control of the Oregon country (essentially the southern Plateau) from the British, who retained the northern Plateau as part of Canada. The Americans immediately began to arrange treaties with the various groups with the intent of "civilizing" them, removing them from the path of white settlement, and putting them on reservations. The U.S. government promised reservations, protection, and peace, and most groups agreed to these terms, signing the Walla Walla Council Treaty of 1855. Immediately after the signing, gold was discovered on some of the reservations. White miners began to confiscate reservation land and ignited the Plateau Indian War, which lasted until 1858.

The Impact of European Contact

European diseases impacted Plateau populations many years before actual contact with Europeans (see Boyd 1998). These diseases were undoubtedly carried onto the Plateau by native traders, who had contacted peoples along the Northwest Coast and Plains regions who had already contracted diseases from Europeans. Smallpox swept through the Plateau a number of times, first in 1775, then again in 1801, 1824, 1853, and 1862. Smallpox, along with various epidemics of malaria, scarlet fever, and measles, killed a very large percentage of the Plateau population, although the exact losses are unknown.

In addition to the near destruction of the population, Plateau groups lost about 90 percent of their original land base. Plateau groups currently retain some lands under the reservation system, but much of that land has been subjected to, and damaged by, development. In addition, Indian access to traditional hunting, fishing, and gathering localities has been restricted (see Lahren 1998).

A Brief History of Ethnographic Research

The earliest information on Plateau groups was gathered by Lewis and Clark in 1805, and their journals (Thwaites 1904) form an invaluable source of data. Other information is available in government exploration records (e.g., Gibbs 1854) and in the diaries and accounts of individual pioneers. Serious anthropological work on Plateau groups was started in the 1890s; since then, a number of ethnographic studies have been completed. Only a few studies were conducted between 1920 and 1960. After 1960, renewed interest in Plateau culture resulted in more research (see Lohse and Sprague 1998 for a history of research on the Plateau).

Summaries of Plateau culture were compiled by Teit (1930), Ray (1938, 1939, 1942), Swanton (1953), Anastasio (1972), and Hunn (1990a, 1990b). The most current and comprehensive synthesis is the Plateau volume (Vol. 12) of the *Handbook of North American Indians* (Walker 1998b), written mostly in the mid-1990s. This work contains chapters on many groups and a wide variety of subjects. The discussion of Plateau culture presented below was summarized from these sources and depicts Plateau groups as they were in the middle of the nineteenth century.

A Broad Portrait of Plateau Groups

Some twenty-four groups lived in the Plateau (see Fig. 5.1), the best known being the Nez Perce, Yakima, Flathead, Klamath, and Modoc. In general, the Plateau supported a relatively low population density, with most groups located near major rivers where salmon could be obtained.

Plateau groups spoke a variety of languages from four major language groups (see Kinkade et al. 1998: Table 1). In the northern Plateau, most groups spoke a language from the Salishan language group, with the exception of one that spoke an Algonquian language and another an Athapaskan language, the latter two being generally related to those spoken in the nearby Subarctic culture area. Groups in the central and southern Plateau spoke languages of the Penutian language group.

Political Organization

Overall, the political organization of Plateau groups was not very complex. The primary political unit was the village, even though many villages would recognize a common relatedness, somewhat akin to a tribe. The principal political leader was the village chief (headman), a position that was sometimes inherited and sometimes elected. Most groups had specialized chiefs, such as war chief or salmon chief, and such persons possessed some authority. A village chief was usually a male, although females were occasionally chiefs, or sometimes co-chiefs along with men. Male chiefs' closest advisers were their wives, and the suitability of the wife to fulfill that role was a major criterion in the selection of a chief. Such women were highly respected by all, not just by other women.

Each village had a council and each adult had the right to voice his or her view on matters of concern. Groups from different villages would often come together to fish or to hunt bison. At those times, an "intervillage council" would be formed to conduct the business of the combined group.

Pacifism seems to have been an important trait, although not all researchers agree with this assessment. Though not uncommon, war was not an important pursuit, and military adventure was not undertaken to gain prestige. A number of Northwest Coast groups raided the Plateau to obtain slaves.

Social Organization

The extended family was the main social unit, but individuals were also important in the society. The eldest members of the family were its leaders. Kinship was bilateral and most groups did not recognize clans. People in one's own generation were usually referred to by the same term. Grandparents were addressed with different terms, depending on both the sex and the side of the family, and grandparents played an important role in raising and educating the children.

Division of labor was based on sex and age. Women gathered the plant foods and materials and performed the domestic chores. Men were the primary political leaders, did the hunting and trading, and participated in warfare. In most Plateau societies, women were respected and enjoyed general equality with men in

Sidelight

THE MODOC WAR

Prior to contact, the Modoc lived in northern California and southern Oregon, on the southern edge of the Plateau (see Ray 1963 for a description of Modoc culture). In 1864, after having been promised a reservation on their ancestral lands, the Modoc were forced to move onto a reservation in southern Oregon. This created a major problem, as the reservation was already occupied by the Klamath. Although they spoke dialects of the same language, the Klamath did not get along well with the Modoc and tensions ran high between the two tribes and government officials.

In 1869, a group of Modoc left the reservation and returned to their ancestral lands. In late 1872, when the government tried to force them to return to the reservation, they fought back under their war leader, Captain Jack (whose real name was Kintpuash), and the Modoc War began (see Quinn 1997 for a detailed history). The Modoc were pursued by U.S. troops and a series of small skirmishes ensued. Finally, in 1873, fifty-three Modoc men and their families, led by Captain Jack, made a stand in a large lava flow, now in Lava Bed National Monument in northern California. The demands of the Modoc were simple—to be allowed to live on a portion of their traditional lands on the Lost River in northern California. The government refused and surrounded the Modoc with troops.

The lava formed numerous natural defensive positions, which were fortified by the Modoc. In this undulating landscape, the defenders could travel from place to place through passages below ground. The hardened lava was extremely rough and sharp and tore up the U.S. soldiers' boots, clothing, and flesh. The Modoc's sandals, made from plant fibers, were easily repaired and were much better suited to the terrain.

On January 17, 1873, a force of some 400 U.S. troops, militia, and Klamath began an assault on the Modoc stronghold. The attack was repulsed, with heavy U.S. casualties, and the troops were forced to retreat. After that defeat, the government initiated peace negotiations. The intent was to imprison the Modoc and then move them to an unspecified reservation away from the Plateau. The Modoc refused; they wanted a reservation in their own homeland. A peace conference was held on April 11, 1873, at which the Modoc again demanded a reservation in their homeland. This was refused, and the Modoc killed several of the white negotiators.

The army launched a second attack on the stronghold on April 13, and while U.S. casualties were again high, they pressed forward against the Modoc. After two days of fighting, the Modoc abandoned the lava beds, escaped the ring of soldiers, and retreated south where they continued a guerrilla campaign against the army. Several small battles were fought over the next few months; during the last one, the Modoc were defeated.

---

economic, domestic, religious, and political spheres (see Ackerman 1995, 1998); however, they had relatively little prestige. Slaves formed the bottom level of Plateau social ranking.

Sometime near puberty, boys and some girls undertook a vision quest to seek and obtain a spirit-helper, although such an event was more important to males. These spirit-helpers were usually an animal likeness and were treated with respect.

Captain Jack and his surviving followers surrendered on June 4, 1873, and the captives became prisoners of war. Despite the surrender, Captain Jack and five of his followers were put on trial, found guilty, and promptly executed as a warning to other Indians who might resist. The night after he was buried, Captain Jack was dug up by grave robbers; his head was removed, embalmed, and put on display in a carnival touring the country. Many other Modoc, even those who did not participate in the war, were killed by vigilantes. The rest were deported to Indian Territory to live on 180 acres. They were finally allowed to return to northern California in 1909.

The Modoc War raised a national debate about treatment of Indians. Public criticism reached the highest levels of government. Under General William Tecumseh Sherman, the army's goal was to punish the Modoc for their resistance and to send a warning to other Indians. However, the Interior Department ruled that the Modoc were a separate but dependent nation, and that their men were prisoners of war and were to be treated as such. The executions of six Modoc proceeded anyway; army leaders argued that the men were executed for the murder of the peace delegates. The treatment of these "murderers" formed a sharp contrast to that of the whites who were held up as heroes after they had murdered some thirty Modoc at a peace conference several years earlier.

This drawn-out and expensive conflict exploded from a fairly small-scale problem: the Modoc wanted to live on a small parcel of land to which they had a reasonable claim and that would have cost the government about $10,000. Instead, the Modoc War cost the government over $500,000 and many dead. In this case and many others, the government went to extraordinary lengths to impose its will on the Indians, irrespective of the merit of the decision.

In 1954, the Modoc War was depicted in a Hollywood movie, *Drum Beat,* starring Alan Ladd, with Charles Bronson as Captain Jack.

Captain Jack (Kintpuash), war leader of the Modoc, 1873.
(CORBIS)

First menses was an important event for females—it signified their entrance into adult society and made them eligible for marriage. During menses, females possessed dangerous power and were feared by men. Menstruating females spent about a week in the menstrual house, isolated from the rest of the group (many women enjoyed this time away from the men). Most chores could not be performed by menstruating women, so they actually enjoyed a respite for a few days each month.

First marriages were arranged by the parents or grandparents, although the bride or groom might elope with someone else if they disliked the arrangement. The first marriage ceremony consisted of an exchange of gifts between the families. Any subsequent marriages were accomplished simply by the couple's moving in together. Divorce was also fairly simple and was accomplished with little ceremony. Most people married someone from another village, sometimes even from a different tribe. The practice of village exogamy cemented alliances between groups, established extensive kinship networks throughout the Plateau, and resulted in considerable multilingualism, which also helped in trade relations. Women would often move to their husband's village after marriage.

The dead were usually buried, although some groups practiced cremation. Mourners generally cut their hair short, dressed in shabby clothing, and were expected to mourn for a year before remarriage. An annual mourning ceremony would take place, where many of the personal effects of the dead were given away. Most, if not all, Plateau groups practiced the levirate and the sororate.

Economics

Plateau peoples were highly mobile and commonly practiced a seasonal round. Most people would live in large, permanent villages during the winter, relying largely on stored food, although some hunting and fishing were conducted. These large villages would usually be located at places where fishing was easy. From spring through fall, these large winter groups would break up into smaller groups that moved about from place to place to fish, hunt, gather roots, or conduct other activities. Much of the food obtained during this time was processed and stored for the winter.

The most important game animals on the Plateau were deer, elk, rabbits, squirrels, some freshwater clams, and salmon (see Hunn et al. 1998). Bison were hunted by some of the eastern Plateau groups after 1720, after horses were obtained. In addition to being hunted, some animals were kept as pets, including young bears, coyotes, wolves, and deer.

Fish were the staple animal food on the Plateau, salmon being the most important (see Hewes 1998). Communal salmon fishing was crucial to Plateau life. In the early summer, people from many tribes would congregate at one or more of the many communal salmon fishing localities. They would construct large wooden traps, called weirs, across streams or rivers. A large number of fish could be captured in this manner. Nets, hooks and lines, and pronged spears were also used to catch fish.

The salmon run usually involved a large number of fish; thus, the fishing conducted by groups on the coast did not significantly diminish the number of fish reaching the interior. Salmon stop eating when they begin their migration, so they get thinner as they move upstream; however, thinner salmon are easier to dry for storage. In addition, salmon do not produce eggs until after the migration begins, so roe was obtained and eaten by Plateau people.

Plant foods—some 135 species—formed a vital component of the diet on the Plateau (see Hunn et al. 1998). Thirty species of plants were eaten for their roots alone. Camas was the most popular of the roots, and special expeditions were made to places where it could be obtained in large quantities. Other significant plants included prickly pear cactus pads and fruit, various small seeds, chokecherries, blueberries, huckleberries, and currants. Plateau groups also used tobacco.

Plateau groups had extensive trade relationships with many surrounding groups, particularly those on the Northwest Coast. Many Plateau people spoke several languages, which facilitated trade transactions. Among the most essential products traded were horses and slaves.

Material Culture and Technology

Plateau winter villages consisted of a number of structures housing extended families, along with at least one sweathouse and a menstrual house. Winter houses were very substantial semisubterranean pithouses, covered with soil for insulation. Most winter villages maintained a large communal ceremonial structure. Summer houses, called longhouses, were lighter structures of matting over wooden frames, but could be quite large, as long as 100 feet. After the mid–eighteenth century, many Plateau groups adopted tepees, which they covered with skins or tule matting. Some winter residences would be dismantled in the spring, and the parts were then used in the construction of the summer houses.

Dugout log canoes were used by most groups, but usually just for transportation and not for fishing. The bow and arrow constituted the primary weapon for hunting and war. Arrowheads, knives, and scrapers were made from fine-grained stone, particularly obsidian, a natural glass that can be honed to a sharp edge. Stone hopper mortars (bottomless baskets glued to stone platforms) and stone pestles were utilized to pound roots and salmon into a flour that could be stored for the winter. Basketry was a well-developed skill, and baskets were used to collect, process, store, and even cook most of the foods eaten. A tradition of ground stone art was also important.

Religion

In most Plateau groups, religion emphasized the relationship between an individual and the supernatural (see Walker and Schuster 1998); thus, most religious practice took place on a personal level. For example, the vision quest was undertaken individually by Plateau youths to find a personal guardian spirit. Puberty ceremonies, during which an individual officially entered the society, are another example. Shamanism was a critical component of Plateau religion. Most shamans focused on curing illness rather than conducting community ceremonies. Shaman used a variety of plants to cure illness, treat injury, and maintain health (see Hunn et al. 1998:534–535, Table 1).

Some large-scale ceremonies were held, mostly to renew ties with the supernatural and with other villages. Such events usually took place in the winter, when everyone was gathered in the winter village. People also celebrated several "first-fruit" ceremonies, dedicated to the first salmon catch of the season, the camas harvest, and others.

Plateau Indians Today

Most Plateau groups have been able to maintain their cultures. The various groups reside on ten reservations in the United States and on 407 reserves (varying in size from 0.5 to 33,000 acres) in Canada (see Lahren 1998). As at many reservations, problems of unemployment, poor health (diabetes is a major cause of death), alcoholism, and substandard services continue to plague Plateau peoples, although the situation appears to be improving. Most Plateau groups are now involved in logging, tourism and recreation, gambling, and other activities that hopefully will contribute to their long-term success.

One major issue still facing Plateau groups, as well as Northwest Coast groups, is fishing rights (see Cohen 1986; Hewes 1998:637–640), most of which were guaranteed by treaty but have since been ignored. The Indians have fought numerous court battles over this issue since the late nineteenth century—most decisions taken in favor of the Indians—and some of them still live along the rivers where their people have fished for millennia. Their greatest victory occurred in 1974, when Indian fishing access rights were affirmed in the *Boldt* decision (reviewed and upheld by the U.S. Supreme Court in 1979). Many whites ignored or resisted this decision, and tensions still run high. In addition, dam construction has limited some fish runs and destroyed traditional fishing localities.

Many Plateau Indians are Christian, speak English, and have adopted many American customs. Native languages are spoken by fewer and fewer people, and preservation of the various cultures has been a major concern. Some people have adopted a contemporary native religion, called Washat, or Seven Drum religion, which incorporates Christian beliefs with aspects of older religious beliefs, including vision questing and shamanistic curing (see Walker and Schuster 1998). This religion has about a dozen congregations and hundreds of followers. Other native religious practices, such as the Sun Dance, the Native American Church, and the Feather Cult, are also practiced by Plateau groups.

Learn More About Contemporary Plateau Peoples

The discussion above provides only a very brief description of Plateau people today. What else can you discover? Go to the library and look on the Internet to learn more about Plateau groups today. Topics you can explore include the following:

1. Chose a particular group or two, and investigate how they have adjusted to European conquest. Look at their tribal land base (e.g., whether they have a reservation), their tribal economy, and the general well-being of the tribal members.
2. What is the status of native fishing rights, particularly after the *Boldt* decision and the refusal of some whites to comply with that decision?
3. What traditional practices have been retained? What are the roles of traditional religion, economics, and politics in Plateau groups today?
4. Other than fishing rights, what problems are faced by Plateau people today?
5. To what degree and to what effect have Plateau tribes adopted gaming?

The Nez Perce: A Plateau Case Study

The Nez Perce (pronounced *nezz purse*) are one of the better-known Plateau groups. They call themselves *Nimípu* (pronounced *nee-mee-poo*), meaning "the people." The name Nez Perce comes from the French for "pierced nose," although the Nez Perce seem never to have pierced their noses. Original Nez Perce territory included portions of Washington, Oregon, and Idaho (Fig. 5.2) and included the central

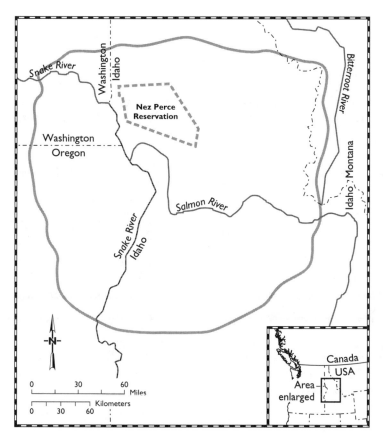

FIGURE 5.2 Location and territory of the Nez Perce in the central Plateau
Adapted from D. E. Walker, Jr., ed., "Nez Perce" in *Handbook of North American Indians*, Vol. 12, *Plateau*, Fig. 1; copyright © 1998 by the Smithsonian Institution. Reprinted by permission of the publisher.

portion of the Bitterroot Mountains, much of the Snake River drainage, and several major valleys, such as the Clearwater Valley. In 1805, there were some 6,000 Nez Perce, living in more than seventy permanent villages. This case study of the Nez Perce describes them as they were in about 1805.

The earliest anthropological work on the Nez Perce was conducted by Spinden (1908), and summaries of Nez Perce culture are presented by Curtis (1911a), Haines (1955), Slickpoo and Walker (1973; the senior author is a Nez Perce), Trafzer (1992), and Walker (1998c). The following discussion is based on these sources. Some excellent photographs of the Nez Perce in about 1900 are presented by Gidley (1979), and a history of one Nez Perce family is presented by Axtell and Aragon (1997).

The Natural Environment

As in much of the Plateau, the climate of Nez Perce territory varies between the mountains and the lower plateau regions. The Columbia and Snake Rivers cross Nez Perce territory and have cut numerous deep canyons throughout the region. Two major valleys, Wallowa and Clearwater, lie in the center of Nez Perce country, but most of the area is mountainous and contains extensive forests of pine and oak.

Language

The Nez Perce people speak Nez Perce, a language belonging to the Sahaptian family of the Penutian language group. While Sahaptian appears to have been limited to the Plateau, people speaking other Penutian languages are located to the south in California. The Nez Perce language has two dialects, upper and lower.

A Brief History

In about 1730, just prior to contact with Europeans, the Nez Perce acquired horses, began to visit the Plains, and adopted many Plains customs, including living in tepees and bison hunting. This transformed Nez Perce society so that at contact, they resembled some of the Plains groups encountered earlier by Europeans. The Nez Perce were first contacted by the American expedition under Lewis and Clark in 1805. Soon afterwards, they were approached by fur traders working for both British and American companies and developed considerable interest in trading for European goods.

The Nez Perce had relatively friendly relations with the British and Americans, trading furs and accepting their presence. However, the foreigners rapidly became an imposition. Christian missionaries entered the area in 1836 and tried to convert the Nez Perce. Then, in 1846, the region was ceded to the United States by Great Britain and the Nez Perce came under American control. American settlers began to flood into Nez Perce territory and friction inevitably arose, although the Nez Perce resisted warfare at that time. Finally, in the early 1850s, the U.S. government began an effort to sign treaties with the Nez Perce that would force them to move onto a reservation.

In 1855, the Nez Perce signed the Walla Walla Council Treaty and received a reservation of about 7,787,000 acres, an area that included much of their original land base. However, gold was discovered on the reservation immediately thereafter and white miners began to encroach on the land. In response to this, in 1863, the government drafted a new treaty that reduced the reservation to about 757,000 acres and coerced some of the Nez Perce to sign it. Most Nez Perce did not sign the treaty and refused to acknowledge it. However, the federal government did recognize it, declaring that many Nez Perce were now living "outside" the new reservation. This treaty is sarcastically known as the Thief Treaty, and even the government later concluded that it was illegal.

In 1873, the federal government attempted to correct some of the reservation boundaries, but in doing so they made an error, returning an area heavily settled by whites rather than the Wallowa Valley where the Wallowa Band of Nez Perce, led by Chief Joseph (see VIP Profile), lived. Local government authorities, including the military commander, tried to correct the error, and many of the white settlers were even willing to move. However, Washington would not relent, and tensions began to rise. The federal government then tried to get Chief Joseph, and all of the other "nonreservation" Nez Perce, to relinquish their land and move within the new reservation boundaries. Thus, in May 1877, threatened with war by the federal government, the Nez Perce were forced to comply and were given thirty days to move.

While moving into the new reservation boundaries, several young Nez Perce men attacked and killed some white men who had earlier abused them; thus began the Nez Perce War. Under pursuit by the U.S. Army, the Nez Perce (men, women, and children), first under Chief Looking Glass, then Chief Joseph, retreated to the north and east. They fled for several months, fighting a number of battles with the army and always managing to escape. The Nez Perce eventually attempted to escape north to Canada, but in October 1877 they were intercepted by a second U.S. force 40 miles short of the Canadian border. A fierce battle ensued. With the exception of a few who made it safely to Canada, the Nez Perce finally surrendered, under the condition that they be allowed to return to the reservation. The army then reneged on the conditions of the surrender, eventually moving the captives to Indian Territory in Oklahoma. In 1885, the survivors were allowed to return to the Plateau, at which time they were sent to the Colville Reservation in Washington and the Nez Perce Reservation in Idaho (see McWhorter 1952, 1983). A Hollywood movie was made about the Nez Perce War, titled *I Will Fight No More Forever*, starring James Whitmore, Sam Elliott, and Ned Romero.

In 1893, through implementation of the Dawes Act of 1887 (see Chapter 2; Greenwald 2002), the Nez Perce lost another 542,000 acres of their reservation to the federal government, who sold it to whites. A Nez Perce tribal government was subsequently formed in 1927. In 1934, the Nez Perce voted against becoming a "federally recognized tribe" under the Indian Reorganization Act (see Chapter 2), but their treaties with the federal government had already established them as a

CHIEF JOSEPH OF THE NEZ PERCE

Chief Joseph was born in 1840, the son of Old Joseph, chief of the Wallowa band of Nez Perce from the Wallowa Valley in northeastern Oregon. He was given the name In-mut-too-yah-lat-lat, which roughly translates to Thunder-Traveling-Over-the-Mountains. The boy was later baptized and named Young Joseph by a white missionary. In 1870, Old Joseph died and Young Joseph inherited the chieftainship of the Wallowa band, thus becoming Chief Joseph.

The role of Chief Joseph as a military strategist and leader in the Nez Perce War of 1877 has been greatly exaggerated. For much of the war, he was the camp chief, the person responsible for setting up and dismantling camp. Looking Glass and others were the war chiefs. Upon the death of Looking Glass during the Battle of Bear Paw, Chief Joseph, more or less by default, briefly became the war chief and primary leader of the tribe during the remainder of the battle. The next day, as the military situation became hopeless, Chief Joseph surrendered the Nez Perce to the U.S. Army. His final words during the proceedings were the famous "I will fight no more forever" (although some historians believe that this speech was never made). Thus, the Battle of Bear Paw ended and the surviving Nez Perce were taken into captivity.

The captives, including Chief Joseph, were moved to Bismarck, North Dakota, then to Fort Leavenworth, Kansas. There they suffered through the cold winter of 1877–1878 with inadequate supplies. In the spring, disease took more lives. Chief Joseph constantly lobbied the military commanders and the BIA officials for better treatment and to be allowed to return to their homeland. In 1878, the authorities moved the Nez Perce to the Quapaw Reservation in Kansas. As the plight of the Nez Perce gained national attention and sympathy, the government, wishing to avoid bad publicity, gave the Nez Perce a reservation in Indian Territory, moving them there in 1880.

With the help of the BIA, Chief Joseph traveled to Washington in 1879 to try to persuade the government to allow the Nez Perce to return to their original reservation. He had meetings with high government officials, including President Hayes, but his pleas had little impact. While in Washington, Chief Joseph made a speech to a large audience and detailed the plight of his people and the injustices they had suffered. This speech was later printed in the *North American Review* (see Chief Joseph 1995 for a reprint of the original text) and was very influential in gaining sympathy for the Nez Perce.

In 1885, under pressure from the public, the government finally allowed the Nez Perce to

///

formal tribe. A more detailed history of the Nez Perce contact and conflict with Euroamerican culture is provided by Josephy (1965).

Cosmology

A number of stories relate the creation of the Nez Perce. Several versions of one such story are consolidated and summarized below. A long time ago, a monster *(Its-welx)* ate all of the people. Coyote learned of this and decided to try to help the people. When he met the monster, Coyote challenged him to a contest in which move onto two reservations, the Colville Reservation near Nesplem in Washington and the Nez Perce Reservation at Lapwai, Idaho. Chief Joseph and some of his followers moved to Colville to be closer to the Wallowa Valley. In 1897, he re-addressed the issue of regaining the Wallowa Valley (pursuant to various treaties) and traveled again to Washington to discuss the matter with President McKinley. During that trip, Chief Joseph went to New York to attend the dedication of Grant's Tomb, probably to gain publicity for the Nez Perce. He returned to the Colville Reservation with vague promises but no action.

Chief Joseph visited the Wallowa Valley in 1899, hoping to spur the BIA into action, but met with refusals from the white residents to sell their land. In 1900, the BIA sent an inspector to discuss the matter with Chief Joseph and the white residents of the Wallowa Valley, at which time it was finally concluded that the Nez Perce should remain at the Colville Reservation. Chief Joseph returned again to the Colville Reservation, having given up hope. He died there in 1904 of what was said to be a broken heart.

The general view that Chief Joseph was a highly skilled war leader is misleading. He was not really a war leader at all and was not chief of all the Nez Perce. He was the leader of one band of Nez Perce who rose to defend his people against the gross injustices inflicted upon them by the United States. However, his eloquent pleas for freedom for his people struck a chord in the hearts of many Americans. This message remains an inspiration to all.

For further details about the life and times of Chief Joseph, see one of the several biographies written about him. These include Howard and McGrath (1941), Scott (1993), and Taylor (1993).

Chief Joseph, Nez Perce leader, in the 1890s. (CORBIS)

each would attempt to inhale the other. Coyote went first, but could not inhale the monster. Next, the monster inhaled Coyote and Coyote went right into his mouth without being chewed and killed. Coyote had taken some stone knives with him and he went to the monster's heart and began to cut it up. The monster tried to get Coyote to leave, but he would not, and Coyote finally cut the monster's heart free, killing him. Coyote then cut up the monster and threw various parts across the landscape. The parts became the tribes that lived near the Nez Perce. When he was finished, Coyote realized that there were no parts of the monster left to make the Nez Perce. So he took some blood of the monster and from that he created the Nez

Perce, making them brave, intelligent, and powerful. The heart of the monster is still present; it is now a hill called Kamiah.

Politics and External Relations

The Nez Perce were organized into a large but unknown number of bands, each of which was essentially independent. There were about seventy permanent villages in Nez Perce territory, usually located along major rivers where the fishing was good. Each village contained several extended families, totaling between 50 and 200 people. Each village had a headman, who often inherited the position, although the appointment had to be confirmed by village members. Several influential persons were charged with assisting the headman. Women were not allowed to speak at village meetings but could communicate their views through their male relatives.

Villages in close proximity were organized into a single band, the chief of the band being from the largest and most influential of the villages. Each band had a war chief, who led the band in times of conflict, and a camp chief, who was responsible for ensuring that the camp was properly organized and each was appointed based on ability. Some bands were allied to form larger, composite bands, some of which also had councils, war chiefs, and camp chiefs. There was no overall tribal chief. Several sodalities existed, including those for shamans and warriors.

The Nez Perce were generally peaceful toward their Plateau neighbors and engaged in trade relations with many, sometimes even traveling as far as the Pacific Coast for trading. The Nez Perce and several of their neighbors, including the Walla Walla, Yakima, and Umatilla, jointly participated in ceremonies, temporarily forming a larger, intertribal political unit.

The Nez Perce were enemies of the Northern Paiute and Northern Shoshone to the south and of the Blackfoot to the east, fighting a constant series of small

Nez Perce and Yakima Indians standing in front of tepees near Astoria, Oregon, in 1922. (CORBIS)

battles with these groups. The Nez Perce were skilled in war, as evidenced by their many successes against the U.S. Army. Among the Nez Perce individual honor was important, and it was considered a dishonor to be wounded in the back by the enemy, as it implied that the warrior was running away and was thus a coward.

Social Organization

The basic social unit of the Nez Perce was the extended family. Each family belonged to one of three classes: wealthy and influential, middle class (which included most people), and slaves captured from other tribes. In addition, men who did the bison hunting formed a special class. Membership in a class depended on one's social position and was hereditary. However, an ambitious or fortunate person could change classes. Kinship was bilateral. Grandparents and grandchildren interacted informally, while parents were treated with much more formality. Siblings and cousins were all considered brothers and sisters, but different kinship terms were used for each.

Division of labor was relatively simple and straightforward; women did the gathering and domestic chores while men hunted, fished, trained horses, and conducted war. Berdaches were present but did not usually marry. The sweathouse was the center of social activity, and frequent bathing and purification rituals brought people together.

Life Cycle

Nez Perce parents typically desired many children; large families were the norm. During the last few months of pregnancy, women stayed in a separate dwelling with other pregnant women. They prepared food and ate apart from the rest of the village. The baby was delivered in a small, separate house with the aid of the mother's mother, a midwife, a female doctor, or older women. Relatives gave food and various gifts, and the infant was placed in a cradleboard until it was ready to walk. The umbilical cord was placed in a small bag and attached to the infant's cradleboard for good luck. Infants were nursed until about the age of two or three; after weaning, the child was cared for by the grandmother. Much of the education of a child also was provided by the grandparents. Nicknames were given to children until they received their formal names sometime around puberty.

Children were given cold and hot baths alternately on an almost daily basis, to help strengthen their minds and bodies. By about the age of six, children contributed significantly to daily chores. Prior to puberty, a child would seek a vision quest during the fall season, and young boys and girls sought their guardian spirit *(wyakin)* and the acquisition of personal power *(somesh)*. If the quest was unsuccessful, additional efforts would be made. Even after a successful vision quest, the individual might later choose to conduct another vision quest to gain more spirit helpers and greater power. Formal names were given to persons who had completed the vision quest, but those names could be changed in response to a significant event in an individual's life.

At her first menses, a young woman was isolated in the menstrual house. She was required to eat separately and could come out of the house only at night. She stayed in the menstrual house for about a week, after which she reentered society, eligible for marriage. During subsequent menstrual cycles, she would continue to use the menstrual house.

Females married young, as soon after puberty as possible. Many marriages were arranged by the family, often to a mate within the same class but from a different village (village exogamy), and some Nez Perce intermarried with other Plateau groups. The marriage ceremony was fairly simple, consisting of several events during which the two families exchanged gifts. Men belonging to the highest class were allowed to have more than one wife, and the second wife could be from a different class. After marriage, the couple often lived with the husband's family. Divorce was relatively uncommon. Age brought respect, power, and wealth.

When a person died, the body was cleaned and dressed in the deceased's finest clothes, wrapped in a blanket, and buried the following day, along with the individual's favorite possessions. Individuals were typically buried in graves overlooking the village. Sometimes a horse belonging to the deceased was killed over the grave and left there. The house and furniture of the deceased were sometimes burned. After the burial, a feast was held, at which time the remaining possessions of the deceased were distributed. Some people had specific wills, sometimes even bequeathing the power of their guardian spirit, and every effort was made to fulfill those wishes. Spouses of the deceased cut their hair short, wore ragged clothing, and were barred from remarriage for one year.

Economics

The Nez Perce were hunters and gatherers who utilized an extensive array of plants and animals. They hunted a large variety of mammals, including deer, elk, moose, mountain sheep, mountain goats, black and grizzly bears, rabbits, and squirrels. Deer and elk were captured by ambush or driven into traps or off cliffs with the aid of fire and/or horses. A variety of birds, such as ducks, geese, and grouse, were also consumed. Meat was eaten fresh; it was also dried and/or smoked to be stored for later consumption. After the Nez Perce obtained horses, they traveled onto the Plains to hunt bison and pronghorn.

Fish were particularly important to the Nez Perce (see Hewes 1998:631–632), including the salmon that ran up the major rivers and streams, along with other species that were variously available during the spring, late summer, and early fall. Fish were caught with harpoons, spears, traps, weirs, or dipping nets, which were lowered from platforms (natural or constructed) or from canoes. Fishing at the large communal traps was directed by specialists who regulated the work and divided the catch. The fish were processed mostly by women, who gutted, dried, and stored the catch in underground pits.

The Nez Perce also used a number of plants for food. The most important was camas. Its bulbs were gathered in July and August; women used wooden digging sticks to harvest the roots. Often villages and bands would gather at the camas grounds to dig roots and to socialize. Camas was prepared by baking the root in a large pit. Another root, cous (or kous, also called biscuitroot because it tastes like a biscuit), was available in the spring. Cous was prepared in a variety of ways and could be stored for a year or more. Wild onions, bitterroot, chokecherries, and huckleberries were also eaten. Some of these berries would be combined with dried meat to form pemmican. Foods were cooked over an open fire, baked in pits, or boiled in baskets to which hot rocks had been added. To ensure that resources would remain available, the Nez Perce would always give thanks to those plants and animals that were taken for food or manufacturing material.

Using a barter system, the Nez Perce traded a variety of materials widely, including bows and baskets. One of their major exports was horses, as they were well-known horse breeders and trainers. Other groups placed orders for specially trained horses, which the Nez Perce would then raise, train, and deliver to the customer.

The Nez Perce followed a predetermined seasonal round. In the winter, they stayed in their villages, depending on stored foods and what resources could be obtained nearby. When spring arrived, they would leave their winter villages to travel to major fishing spots, to gather various fresh plant foods, and to hunt. Special hunting parties visited the Plains during the early summer to hunt bison. In the late summer, they moved back to the main villages to begin salmon fishing. In the fall, they began to gather food to store for the coming winter. Some Nez Perce bands remained on the Plains over the winter, perhaps staying with the Flathead to the north.

Material Culture and Technology

In the permanent villages, the Nez Perce built substantial, semisubterranean, earth-covered structures where extended families lived. Each village had a number of these large structures, as well as at least one sweathouse and one menstrual house. When traveling, the Nez Perce used skin-covered tepees for shelter. They often built long, elliptical tepees that had the appearance of a line of attached tepees, but with a single cover.

Before the introduction of the horse, all transportation was on foot, and people carried all materials on their backs. After the late eighteenth century, however, horses were used for transport, although the travois was not used. The Nez Perce also manufactured dugout canoes and snowshoes.

Nez Perce clothing was usually made from deerskins, well decorated with porcupine quills and beads. Men wore a loincloth, leggings, moccasins, and sometimes long-sleeved shirts. In cold weather, men dressed in robes of bison or elk; these robes were also used as blankets and cushions. Women wore long dresses and moccasins.

Men often wore their hair fairly long, combed straight back or to the side. The hair just above the forehead was cut so it would stand up in the front. Women wore braids, with furs sometimes being woven into the hair. People often painted their faces red, and both sexes wore necklaces, earrings, and bracelets made from bone, elk teeth, and shell.

The bow and arrow was the primary weapon utilized in hunting and war. In combat, men also used small shields and feather bonnets. The bows were made of the strong wood from the yew tree, reinforced with sinew for even greater strength. Other tools were made from bone, horn, wood, and various types of stone.

Religion and Medicine

Fundamental to the Nez Perce religious system was the belief that everything was supernaturally intertwined—the people, the earth, certain geographic locations, and the animals. Power flowed from and through everything, and individuals must control that power with the aid of a guardian spirit, which was obtained during a vision quest. The souls of the dead would journey to an afterlife, but their safe arrival depended on strict adherence to the necessary rituals.

A variety of ceremonies were conducted. Two major first-feast ceremonies were held to celebrate the beginning of the camas and salmon harvests. In the winter, the Guardian Spirit Dance was performed and might last as long as five days. In this dance, individuals would imitate their guardian spirits to summon and control their power. The War Dance was held by men before they went to war and the Scalp Dance was conducted several times a year with allied tribes to celebrate victories. The Nez Perce did not adopt the Ghost Dance.

Shamans (called *tooat*), either men or women, controlled and mitigated evil and healed the sick. This latter function was accomplished by using the sucking cure (sucking foreign objects from a sick person's body), sweats, assorted pharmacology, and good-luck charms. Some shamans were also soothsayers and could locate missing objects and foretell the future.

Art, Expression, and Recreation

Art took various forms, including painting on skins, stone (rock art), and bodies (humans and horses). Clothing was lavishly decorated with porcupine-quill embroidery, and baskets were woven with a variety of artistic designs. Musical instruments included rattles, drums, flutes (used in courtship), and whistles. A number of social dances were held, complete with music and singing. Oral tradition was extensive, and stories were told mostly in the winter. A variety of games were played, including the hand game, hoop-and-pole game, and shinny (played by women). One of the most popular pursuits was horse racing. Wagers were made on the outcome of most games and races.

The Nez Perce Today

In 2002, the Nez Perce population was about 3,300. About half of them live on the Nez Perce Reservation located in west-central Idaho. This reservation consists of about 111,000 acres, including lands privately owned by Nez Perce individuals. Their tribal government was organized in 1948 and is comprised of a nine-member tribal executive committee, the members of which are elected for three-year terms. Other Nez Perce—the descendants of Chief Joseph's band—live on the Colville Reservation in north-central Washington. The tribal Root Festival is held during the first week of May every year, and the Pi-Nee-Was Days celebration is held every August.

The Nez Perce tribe administers many programs dealing with issues such as education, housing, cultural resources, and law enforcement, and is involved in a variety of commercial projects, including a lumber enterprise. In addition, the tribe has opened a casino. One can learn more about the Nez Perce at *http://www.nezperce.org*.

///

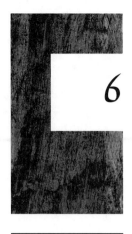

6 Native Peoples of the Northwest Coast

The Northwest Coast culture area (see Suttles 1990a) was home to a number of hunting and gathering cultures that developed very complex social and political organizations, complex economies based on marine resources (particularly salmon and sea mammals), a material culture based on woodworking, and a tradition of distinctive art. Northwest Coast cultures can be divided into three broad regional divisions: northern, central, and southern (see discussion in Suttles 1990a:9–12). The northern group includes the Tlingit, the Tsimshian, and the Haida; the central group includes the Kwakwaka'wakw (Kwakiutl), the Nuxalt (Bella Coola), the Heíltsilk (Bella Bella), the Nuu–chah–nulth (Nootka), and the Coast Salish north of Puget Sound; and the southern group includes the Coast Salish south of Puget Sound, the Chinook, and the coastal tribes south to the California border (some researchers have included several northern California tribes in the Northwest Coast).

Geography and Environment

The Northwest Coast extends along the Pacific coast of North America from southern Alaska over 1,500 miles south to far southern Oregon (Fig. 6.1) (see Suttles 1990b). The region is long and narrow, with little inland territory. High coastal mountains run along the entire length of the Northwest Coast; the coastline is rugged, and many islands lie close to it. The largest is Vancouver Island, located just to the northwest of Seattle and separated from the mainland by the Straits of Georgia and Juan de Fuca. Puget Sound lies directly south of Vancouver Island. The islands and the sinuous coast create many thousands of miles of coastline, much of which was exploited by the Indians of the region.

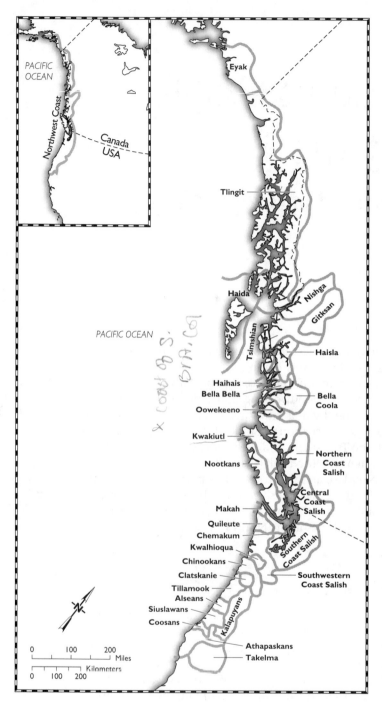

FIGURE 6.1 Northwest Coast culture area, with locations of the native groups Adapted from *Handbook of North American Indians, Vol. 7, Northwest Coast,* W. Suttles, ed., p. ix; copyright © 1990 by the Smithsonian Institution. Reprinted by permission of the publisher.

The climate is wet and relatively mild, with cool summers and wet winters. Rainfall is abundant, although it varies from about 40 inches per year in some places to 130 inches a year in others. The substantial rainfall replenishes a great many rivers and streams, emptying into many bays and estuaries. The largest river in the region is the Columbia, which forms the border between the states of Oregon and Washington.

The ocean environment provided critical resources to the native groups of the Northwest Coast, including a large variety of marine fish, sea mammals, and shellfish. The considerable fluctuation of the ocean tides affected the timing of travel and the collection of coastal resources. Ocean temperature fluctuates greatly by season; off southeastern Alaska, ocean temperatures vary from 43°F in the winter to 59°F in the summer, while off Vancouver Island they vary between 46°F in the winter and 68°F in the summer.

Virtually all of the Northwest Coast is wooded, with a temperate forest of Sitka spruce, western hemlock, and red cedar extending along much of the coast. On the lee side of Vancouver Island and extending inland to the south is a forest made up primarily of Douglas fir and western hemlock. Many species of pine, oak, cedar, and numerous other plants grow in both types of forest. The forests are thick and difficult to travel through, a situation further complicated by the mountain barrier.

On land, the numerous large and small mammals provided food for the native peoples. The critical resource, however, was salmon, which mature in the ocean and then migrate up virtually all of the rivers and streams to spawn. Many aquatic birds also inhabit the region, and these too were hunted.

A Basic Prehistory of the Northwest Coast

The prehistory of the Northwest Coast is poorly known, partly due to the difficulty of working in the wet forest environment. Nine chapters of the Northwest Coast volume of the *Handbook of North American Indians* (Helm 1981) are devoted to prehistory. The most recent syntheses of Northwest Coast prehistory are provided by Matson and Coupland (1995), Moss and Erlandson (1995), and Ames and Maschner (1999).

The Paleoindian Period (ca. 14,000 to 10,000 B.P.)

Evidence of human occupation of the Northwest Coast during the Paleoindian period is sparse. During the Pleistocene, sea levels were lower and most human occupation of the region would have occurred in localities now under water. Several Paleoindian sites are now being investigated on some of the islands along the British Columbia coast (see discussion in Moss and Erlandson 1995:10–13).

The Archaic Period (ca. 10,000 to 6,000 B.P.)

Even after the end of the Pleistocene, relatively little evidence of human occupation of the Northwest Coast exists, although Archaic materials have been found at a few sites. It appears that the formation of the modern forest environments, including colonization of the region by salmon, took place in the early Holocene, and human occupation of the region was probably relatively sparse until the forest became well established. Presumably most of the people occupying the region during the Archaic period lived by hunting sea mammals and fishing.

There is evidence that people, probably speaking Athapaskan (Na-Dene) languages, migrated into the Northwest Coast by about 7,000 B.P., although this may have occurred even earlier. Those groups were the ancestors of the people that live in the region today. It appears that at least some groups depended on salmon as a food source as early as 7,000 B.P.

The Early Pacific Period (ca. 6,000 to 4,000 B.P.)

During this time, the sea reached its modern levels, and local peoples developed an economy based on marine resources, including sea mammals, deep ocean fish, and shellfish, although some hunting of land animals also occurred. Large shell middens were left in many places.

The Middle Pacific Period (ca. 4,000 to 1,500 B.P.)

During the Middle Pacific period, elaborate and complex social and economic systems characteristic of ethnographic times began to emerge. There is some evidence that warfare existed by about 4,500 B.P., and signs of ranked society, such as skull deformation of some individuals and the presence of rank-related artifacts similar to those used in ethnohistoric contexts, were present by about 3,000 B.P. Specialized woodworking tools appear by 2,000 B.P., indicating the manufacture of plank houses and canoes.

The Late Pacific Period (ca. 1,500 B.P. to Contact)

After about 1,500 B.P. some fluctuations in climate and sea levels occurred, perhaps increasing the available resources. Population of the region peaked between 1,200 and 600 B.P., and large, sedentary villages appeared. After 600 B.P. the climate cooled somewhat and population seems to have declined. In addition, warfare intensified and some groups, such as the Tlingit, built forts for protection from their enemies (Moss and Erlandson 1992). The cultural pattern of the Northwest Coast had become well established, as illustrated by the materials recovered from the Ozette site in western Washington (Samuels 1991; also see *www.makah.com* for information on the Ozette site and museum displays).

The Contact Period

People on the Northwest Coast were contacted by Europeans fairly late in time (see Cole and Darling 1990; Suttles 1990c). The first recorded contact was by Russian traders, who encountered the Tlingit in 1741. The Russians built a fort at Sitka in 1799, but it was destroyed by the Tlingit in 1802. In 1804 the Russians returned, defeated the Tlingit, and reestablished the fort, renaming it New Archangel. Eventually the Russians developed a major trade relationship with the Tlingit. Although they had considerable influence on the Tlingit (and on the Eskimo and Aleut to the north;

see Chapter 3), the Russians had relatively little impact on Northwest Coast groups living to the south of the Tlingit (see Black 1988 for a history of Russian America).

The Spanish first entered the region in 1774, partly to counter the Russian movement south. The Spanish established a trading post in Nootka Sound in 1789, entering into an arrangement with the British to share in the fur trade (among the many sea mammals on the Northwest Coast was the sea otter, an animal whose fur was very valuable, sometimes referred to as "soft gold"); however, the Spanish abandoned the region in the 1790s. The famous British captain James Cook visited the region in 1777, and George Vancouver arrived on the Northwest Coast in 1792. The American explorers Meriwether Lewis and William Clark entered the Northwest Coast over land in 1805. The British established an extensive and lucrative trade in sea otter pelts and dominated the fur trade south of Alaska. By 1821 the Hudson's Bay Company had gained control of most of the fur trade along the Northwest Coast (see Vaughan and Holm 1990; Mackie 1997).

Considerable trade also took place between Europeans and the Indians, mostly in furs. Until about 1800, most of the trade with the Europeans south of Russian-controlled territory was conducted from ships that traveled up and down the coast to the native towns, which gave the Indians an advantage in negotiations. After the establishment of permanent trading posts by land-based trading companies (e.g., the American Fur Company) in the early 1810s, however, the Indians were forced to travel to the trading posts, with the advantage shifting to the traders.

Over time, native populations congregated at the trading posts, and some aboriginal political power, which had previously been inherited, went to those who controlled the flow of furs. Warfare to control fur territories and to gain status increased, and raiding for slaves also intensified as groups attempted to strengthen their influence in the trading system. Overhunting ultimately led to the demise of the fur trade by the 1860s.

Beginning in 1840, American settlers entered the region, and when the United States took control of the Oregon Territory (the current states of Washington and Oregon) in 1846, Americans arrived in large numbers and competed with the Indians for land and other resources. Almost immediately, the settlers began to pressure the government to confine the Indians to reservations, and in 1855 the Treaty of Point Elliot, designed to put most Puget Sound groups onto reservations, was signed. Some of the Indians did not sign the treaty, and the small and indecisive Yakima War of 1855–1856 broke out. Little by little, all of the groups in the Oregon Territory were placed on reservations or eliminated.

The Indians living in British-controlled territory (essentially British Columbia) fared better for a short time, but that situation eventually changed, and the British treated the Indians as harshly as the Americans had. In the 1880s, the British used gunboats to destroy Indian towns that were "uncooperative." Reserves were established for some groups but not others. In the 1880s, the Canadian government tried to break up the Indian reserves through a policy of allotment, resulting in an enormous loss of land for the Indians.

Fishing, always a critical activity on the Northwest Coast, became a major commercial enterprise only after about 1865, when the development of canning allowed the fish to reach distant markets without spoiling. By 1920, fish populations began to decline, forcing the closure of many canneries, which resulted in economic depression for many groups. Fishing rights have continued to be an issue in the region (see Parman 1984), and in recent years some Indian groups have regained some of their fishing rights that had been set by treaty.

The Impact of European Contact

European diseases were brought to the Northwest Coast by explorers (see Boyd 1990). Major epidemics swept through the region, including smallpox in 1775, 1801, 1836–1838, 1853, and 1862; malaria in 1830; and measles in 1848. A great many people died and some local groups were wiped out. Trade with Europeans exacerbated the problem as sailors who visited many ports brought with them many different strains of disease, especially venereal diseases.

The fur trade and the introduction of European trade goods caused significant change in social organization, with lower-status people suddenly becoming rich and upsetting the normal social order. Polygyny increased as more men could afford additional wives. The activities of missionaries further impacted religion and social order.

A Brief History of Ethnographic Research

Before anthropologist Franz Boas arrived on the Northwest Coast in 1886, virtually no formal research had been done there and information was limited to the accounts of explorers or traders (see Suttles and Jonaitis 1990). When he arrived, Boas immediately began to study the Kwakiutl, working with other anthropologists and local native people, particularly George Hunt, who made significant contributions to anthropology. Boas worked with the Kwakiutl until his death in 1942. The most detailed studies concerned the Southern Kwakiutl. Many of Boas's students continued his work and also studied other native cultures on the Northwest Coast. Other notable workers include Edward Curtis, who published considerable ethnographic data on Northwest Coast groups in various volumes of his monumental twenty-volume work *The North American Indian,* and Frederica de Laguna, who has done considerable archaeological and ethnographic work in the region since the 1930s.

Europeans have long collected art and artifacts from the Northwest Coast (see Lohse and Sundt 1990). By the mid–nineteenth century, museums, particularly the Smithsonian Institution and the American Museum of Natural History, were seeking collections of objects from the region, believing that the native peoples were about to disappear. The exhibition of Northwest Coast materials and people at the 1893 World's Columbian Exposition (often called the World's Fair) in Chicago created considerable interest in the region and led to a great deal of further study (see Cole 1985; Jacknis 1991).

There now exists a considerable amount of information on Northwest Coast peoples. Summaries of Northwest Coast cultures include Drucker (1955, 1965),

McFeat (1966), Hays (1975), and Woodcock (1977). The most recent major synthesis is Volume 7 of the *Handbook of North American Indians* (Suttles 1990), which contains chapters on many groups and a wide variety of subjects. The discussion of Northwest Coast culture presented below was summarized from these sources.

A Broad Portrait of Northwest Coast Groups

The cultures of the Northwest Coast are distinct in many ways. Northwest Coast groups had complex social and political organizations and large, sedentary populations supported by a subsistence system of fishing, hunting, and gathering (Ames 1994). People lived in large, permanent towns with distinctive architecture. Most material culture involved the working of wood in a characteristic manner and style, and Northwest Coast art has long been, and remains, highly sought after (see this chapter's Sidelight). At the time of contact (ca. 1740), about 200,000 people were living along the Northwest Coast (Boyd 1990:135).

Northwest Coast groups spoke a wide variety of languages (see Thompson and Kinkade 1990: Fig. 1, Table 1), with some forty-five distinct languages belonging to thirteen families. In the north, most groups spoke languages of or related to the Northern Athapaskan (Na-Dene) language family, which was also widespread in the western portion of the Subarctic (see Chapter 4). Penutian and Salishan languages were spoken in the central and southern Northwest Coast. The linguistic diversity of the Northwest Coast was second only to that of California (see Chapter 8).

Political Organization

Most tribes of the Northwest Coast consisted of loose groupings of politically independent bands that recognized a general commonality of language and kinship. However, the primary political unit was the permanent winter town, and people identified themselves by their town. Some towns were allied, and these alliances often constituted "chiefdom-level" political organizations. The social systems (see below) were even more complex.

Each town had a secular leader, a chief, who was the highest-ranking individual (usually male) of the highest-ranking clan in the town. Other clans in the village also had a chief, the highest-ranking individual of that clan. In addition, other leaders for specific purposes, such as warfare, fishing, or sponsoring a ceremony, would emerge as the need arose. Most people who were called chiefs belonged to the nobility, and the title of chief did not necessarily convey a political office.

Warfare was common, but generally small in scale and usually precipitated by a desire for revenge. In some groups, professional military men led raids, sometimes against related towns. Generally, raids involved surprise attacks at dawn, during which the enemy men were killed, women and children were taken as slaves, and the town was looted and burned. The heads of enemy men were often taken as trophies. In combat, the professional military men wore wooden armor (the Tlingit also wore wooden helmets) and employed spears, clubs, and knives as weapons.

Many Northwest Coast groups held slaves (see Donald 1997). Most slaves were obtained from raids, with females preferred. The children of slaves were also considered slaves. Slaves were important symbols of status to their owners and may also have contributed significantly to the economies of the Northwest Coast. Slaves were sometimes killed during a large potlatch.

Towns consisted of one or more rows of plank houses lining a beach above the high-tide line. Houses were usually constructed on pilings to keep them dry, and a boardwalk was often constructed along the front of the town. A beach where canoes could easily land was an important consideration in situating a town, as was the availability of food. Shellfish were concentrated only in certain areas and salmon runs varied depending on the river. The prime location for a town, then, was a sheltered location along a bay with a major river system draining into it. Such localities were sometimes fought over. However, even in the best-placed towns, not all resources were close at hand; thus many groups maintained both summer camps and winter towns in order to draw on different resources at different times of year.

Social Organization

Many Northwest Coast groups were stratified in three classes—nobility (commonly called chiefs), commoners, and slaves—although whether groups in the southern Northwest Coast maintained such a class system is still a matter of debate. There was considerable variety in systems of kinship and descent, the pattern being more matrilineal in the northern area, generally bilateral in the central area, and more patrilineal in the southern area. Families, lineages, and clans existed in most groups, and a few groups had moieties; however, clans were probably the most important social unit. Each clan was originally created by supernatural beings, and each clan had a crest (coat of arms), history, and set of traditions that related to the creator being, the totem of the clan.

A complex series of ranks existed, whereby each person (male or female) occupied an individual rank in the family, each family occupied a rank within the lineage, and each lineage had a rank in the clan. If moieties were present each clan was ranked in the moiety and each moiety was ranked in the town. In addition, if towns were allied in a confederation, each town had a rank in the alliance. Rank was often hereditary, but the system required that the person acquiring a particular rank validate his position by sponsoring a potlatch (see below). The inheritance of property, including titles, rights, and power, was a critical element in maintaining rank.

Most marriages were arranged for economic or political reasons, usually to keep rank within the family, just as wealthy people in the United States tend to stay that way by marrying other wealthy people. Arranging the marriage of a person into a powerful and high-ranking family strengthened the status of a lower-ranking family and broadened their access to resources. Sometimes a man would marry a particular woman so that he could obtain the right to perform songs or dances owned by her father.

The Potlatch

The potlatch was a ceremony of great social and political importance. In this event individuals (male and female) or groups marked important occasions or validated their rank, thereby demonstrating to their guests that they were worthy of possessing it. This was accomplished by feeding, entertaining, and giving gifts to the attendees. The wealthier and higher-ranked people were, the more they could afford to give away; in Northwest Coast society, sharing and giving away wealth made one wealthy—not retaining wealth. On occasion, goods were even purposely destroyed to impress attendees with the wealth of the group. Potlatches also were important religious ceremonies in which origin stories were reenacted and the world was renewed; birth, death, and rebirth were major themes.

Potlatches were held on many occasions, such as the birth of a child, puberty, marriage, a funeral, or the construction of a house. It could also signify the erasing of shame or the changing of power in an alliance. The scale of the event would depend on who was involved, but the concept was the same. It was necessary to have a potlatch to maintain one's rank or to change it. Failure to do so at even a minimum level could result in a loss of rank. Major potlatches were usually held in the winter. Other occasions, such as the naming of a child, might be celebrated in conjunction with a larger potlatch.

A rivalry potlatch was an opportunity for social mobility. In this variation, a lower-ranked individual or group challenged an individual or group of higher rank to a potlatch, the winner claiming the rank. To win, the challenger would have to present a "better" potlatch than that of the challenged. The public determined the winner.

Anyone wishing to have a potlatch, whether an individual or even a whole town, would work to provide materials for the event: food for the guests, gifts for everyone, and the numerous items needed for decoration and display. Persons with particular skills would contribute their specialty—good hunters hunted, skilled fishermen fished, talented weavers wove blankets, expert woodcarvers made masks, boxes, or other goods, and craftworkers collected and strung shells. Sometimes years might be spent in preparation, and vast quantities of materials could be consumed at a large potlatch. It was common to borrow materials to sponsor a potlatch, and the debt was repaid with interest.

Each person attending a potlatch would be fed, entertained, and given gifts, such as shells, blankets, wooden boxes or utensils, strings of redheaded woodpecker scalps (in the south), barrels of fish oil, large obsidian blades (in the south), and even slaves. Other gifts were less tangible, such as the recital of status or the singing of songs owned by the individual or group, or the display of important items owned by the individual or group.

At a large and important potlatch, a group might display its coppers. Coppers were thin sheets of cold-hammered copper obtained from Europeans that were elaborately decorated, each with a name and a history. Coppers were difficult to manufacture and so were very valuable. In an intense rivalry potlatch, an individual might break a copper, or even throw it into the ocean and "drown" it. The rival would have to match the act or risk being shamed.

A typical potlatch was held in the largest structure available to the group holding the event, often a large communal house. The duration of the event depended on the importance of the occasion; some lasted many days. At the beginning of each day, the host, dressed in full regalia, welcomed the guests on the beach as they arrived by canoe. The guests were then seated according to rank. Next, food was served as the host pontificated on the ancestry, history, and rank of the sponsoring group. Gifts were then given away, the best to the highest-ranking people. Each day witnessed at least one major event, such as the performance of dances, dramas, songs, or religious ceremonies. The potlatch ended with a final feast, more oratory, and the presentation of additional gifts.

Many have argued that the potlatch system, with its extensive and conspicuous consumption, was a powerful aspect of the economy. Potlatching created a demand for labor and goods and provided "jobs" for many people. In addition, wealthy people gave gifts of food and goods to poor people at a potlatch, thus providing a sort of welfare system. Others believe that the potlatch system recorded in the late nineteenth century had only recently replaced competition between groups manifested in warfare.

Contact with Europeans changed the potlatch in some ways. The introduction of European trade goods dramatically altered Northwest Coast economies, and Hudson's Bay blankets (perhaps replacing a woven native blanket) became a standard currency at a potlatch. As people died of newly introduced disease, their individual ranks became vacant and their social units, each of which also had rank, became increasingly incapable of defending their ranks. As a result, potlatching seems to have greatly intensified as individuals and social groups attempted to fill the vacuum. Some argue that this escalation took place during the nineteenth and early twentieth centuries, skewing the research of anthropologists then studying the practice; some believe that the potlatch had been less prominent in the past (see Codere 1950; Drucker and Heizer 1967; Jonaitis 1991; also see de Laguna 1988). Whatever the case, it is clear that potlatching was important.

In 1885, the Canadian government banned the potlatch, although the ban was rarely enforced until 1921, when the government bowed to pressure from missionaries. Without potlatches, the demand for goods declined, artisans did not pass on their skills, language and cultural knowledge deteriorated, and morale suffered. In addition, the government confiscated ceremonial potlatch regalia and materials from many groups, an essential part of their culture. The potlatch ban in Canada was removed in 1951, and the practice has revived since that time. Potlatching continued uninterrupted in other areas of the Northwest Coast.

Economics

Northwest Coast groups had very complex economics: They supported large, sedentary populations and complex social and political organizations without agriculture; they were strictly fishers, hunters, and gatherers. Integral to Northwest

Coast economies was the potlatch (see above), where large quantities of goods were consumed and traded.

Land Resources   The natural environment offered a huge variety and quantity of resources. Many hundreds of species of plants were used as food, including many roots and tubers, ferns, numerous kinds of berries and fruits, and some greens, as well as several types of ocean algae. Other plants were used in the manufacture of basketry, cordage, and rope, and, of course, for woodworking. Some tobacco was grown and was chewed with lime, which was made from burning clam shells.

Land animals were less important as resources than those from the ocean, and terrestrial animals declined in abundance and importance in the more northern areas. The most important of the land mammals was the deer, which was more common in the Douglas fir forest in the south. Some mammals, including bears, mountain goats, and hares, were taken for food, while others, such as beaver, mink, and ermine, were taken for their fur. Waterfowl, including ducks, geese, and swans, were important resources at some times and places, depending on migration patterns. Some seabirds were also taken, along with their eggs. The only domestic animal was the dog.

Marine Resources   The marine resources of the Northwest Coast were important to all of the native groups. Marine mammals, including seals, sea lions, sea otters, porpoises, and, occasionally, whales, were commonly exploited. Humpback and California gray whales often entered the various bays to rest and could become quite tame. A few Northwest Coast peoples, such as the Nootka, were fine whalers and could easily harpoon whales in the bays and even on the open ocean. Marine invertebrates, such as mussels, oysters, abalone, clams, other shellfish, crabs, and sea urchins, were important food sources. Many of these species were collected at low tide.

Fish formed the most critical resource in the Northwest Coast. A number of ocean fish were taken from boats, using hook and line and nets. These fish included halibut, sturgeon, flounder, herring, Pacific cod, and smelt. Though less essential, freshwater fish such as trout, sucker, and chub were harvested. The most important fish were of the anadromous species. Taken year-round, they included salmon, sturgeon, steelhead trout, and eulachon. Often referred to as candlefish, eulachon contain so much oil that they actually burn like a candle when dried. A variety of foods were stored in eulachon oil, which was widely used by the Kwakiutl and groups to the north. However, by far the most important of the anadromous fish was salmon.

Salmon   Salmon was the staple food for most Northwest Coast people. Young salmon hatch in fresh water, then swim to the ocean to mature. Maturation takes between two and six years, depending on the species. When mature, the individuals of a species will migrate as a group back to the places where they were born so that they can spawn—hence the term "salmon run." Each river or stream had a salmon run almost every year; in some of the larger streams and rivers separate populations migrated to different places upstream at the same time, making literally millions of fish available for a few weeks each year.

Westerners generally lump the different salmon species into one category, but Northwest Coast people had names for each type and did not even use the word *salmon* in ordinary conversation. Five (perhaps six) major species of salmon (*Oncorhynchus* spp.) were (and still are) present along the Northwest Coast, each with different characteristics. Chinook (or king) salmon are the largest, weighing up to eighty pounds. Chinook salmon run up larger streams and rivers; some rivers have both a spring and a fall run of chinook. Coho (or silver) salmon are smaller, between six and ten pounds, and run far upstream before spawning.

Sockeye are a bit smaller than coho but have the richest meat. Sockeye spawn only in lakes, so they live only in watercourses with lakes. Chum, which weigh between eight and eighteen pounds, spawn only in the lower reaches of rivers. Chum have the leanest meat, are ideal for drying and storing in the damp climate, and constituted the staff of life in winter. Pink salmon, weighing between three and ten pounds, ran in the millions. They do not store well and so their usefulness was limited.

When the salmon began to run, virtually everyone in the town would work to capture, process, and store the fish. Most salmon were taken at strategic spots, usually owned by a clan, on a stream or river where a large weir could be constructed. The fish would be forced into narrow channels of the weir where they could be netted and/or speared in large numbers by the men. Both the chinook and coho salmon could also be taken from the ocean year-round. People used harpoons or trolled from boats with hook and line to capture the fish.

Once they were taken, the fish had to be processed. Women and children gutted the fish, removed the head and backbone for use in soup, and placed the meat on racks to dry. Many salmon along the coast tended to be fatty and were difficult to dry. These fish had to be eaten fresh or smoked and/or stored in candlefish oil. A very large quantity could be caught and processed during the run. Properly processed and stored, fish from a single run could last for years. Roe was also popular but did not generally develop until after the fish were ready to spawn; consequently, coastal people did not have access to much roe.

Although salmon runs involved huge numbers of fish, they did not last long. Of particular concern were the chum runs, since the lives of the people partly depended on how many chum a group could store for the lean season. In some years, the salmon run might be poor and might even occasionally fail. People coped as best they could by monitoring fish populations and even stocking streams. When genuine famine threatened a particular group, they dispersed to live with relatives or to exploit resources in areas they usually did not use.

Material Culture and Technology

Woodworking Northwest Coast technology centered on complex and intricate processes of woodworking. Trees with straight-grained wood were cut down with stone axes and then split into planks with wedges and hammers. The planks would then be trimmed, cut to the desired size, and sanded smooth. Tools made with beaver incisors and flaked stone were used to shape the wood, and pieces of sandstone and dogfish skin were used to sand it. Red cedar was used for house posts, planking for house construction, large totem poles, canoes, masks, and large carvings, while yellow cedar was used for small totem poles, boxes, chests, and canoe paddles. Bows and canoe paddles were made of yew, and hairpins and rattles were made of maple. Woodworking was done by skilled craftsmen, who were usually paid for their services.

Both domestic and community houses were generally large, sometimes as long as sixty feet on one side, and were rectangular or square in shape. They were built with a log frame lined with planks on the sides and roofs. The logs were sometimes carved with the crests of the owners of the house, and both the inside and outside might be elaborately decorated with carvings and paintings. A number of families would occupy a domestic structure, living on raised platforms built along the inside walls. When people moved from the winter town to the summer camp, they would sometimes take along their house planking to put over the frames of the summer residence.

Most travel in the Northwest Coast was by canoe. Canoes came in several sizes and styles (see Suttles 1990a: Fig. 3), from small two-person canoes to large ocean-going vessels that could hold as many as fifty people. The most common size was about thirty-five feet long, but a town might have as many as 200 canoes of various sizes. The canoes were dugouts, carved by master craftsmen from logs of red cedar. After the basic shape of the canoe was hewn from the log, the interior was filled with a mixture of water and urine and boiled to make the sides soft and pliable. The sides were then trimmed and molded into the desired shape, and the canoe was often highly decorated. The canoe was then coated with fish oil to make it waterproof. When finished, it did not appear to be a simple dugout.

A skilled craftsman could fashion a single piece of wood into a four-sided box, called a bentwood box; these had many uses, for example, as drums and storage containers. Boxes, and other wooden items made from planking, might be

An elaborately decorated Tlingit house with a totem pole in front, 1899.
(CORBIS)

sewn together and caulked with shredded wood and pitch to make them watertight. Other craftsmen worked in shell, bone, and ivory. Most Northwest Coast groups also manufactured excellent basketry and matting, made from materials such as cedar bark and spruce root. None of the groups on the Northwest Coast used pottery.

For most of the year, men wore little clothing and women wore skirts or capes of skin or shredded cedar bark. Blankets woven from the inner bark of the yellow cedar or goat hair were worn in the cold; Hudson's Bay blankets were used later. Clothing and costumes for potlatches and other ceremonies were much more elaborate.

Totem Poles   One of the most distinctive features of Northwest Coast material culture is the totem pole (see Stewart 1993). Totem poles were not only significant artistic expressions—they were emblems of rank, usually made and raised by

Sidelight

ART OF THE NORTHWEST COAST

The art of the Northwest Coast is perhaps the most unique and recognizable aspect of the culture area (see Hawthorn 1967; Inverarity 1967; Carlson 1983; Brown 1998; Marshall 1998; Ames and Maschner 1999). Considered by some to be the best in North America, the art was "flamboyant, monumental and complex. It is also deliberately ambiguous" (Marshall 1998:311). Northwest Coast art has a long tradition and has evolved over time.

Much of the art consisted of designs incised or carved or painted on wood, bone, ivory, copper, and stone. Some surfaces were left plain, but most were decorated with hair, feathers, shell, copper, and many colors of paint. Paint was also used to enhance carved surfaces. The designs were often imposed on curved surfaces as well, such as basketry, masks, house poles, and totem poles.

The figures in the artwork depicted animals and supernatural beings, usually those representing clan totems or other beings associated with origin stories. Some figures were done in a naturalistic style, while many others were highly stylized and symbolic representations. Much of the message in the art was in the relationship between figures rather than in the details of the figures themselves. For example, a totem pole would place the highest-ranking figure on top, superior to the others. The message would have been clear, irrespective of the detail of the figures themselves.

For over a hundred years, Northwest Coast artwork has been heavily collected; much of the early art was taken into private collections and museums before its context and meaning could be recorded. Northwest Coast art is still very popular with collectors, and has evolved to suit the tastes of the commercial market. Wood remains the principal medium, but now metal and glass have been added to the sculpting repertoire, as well as painting, silkscreens, clothing, and jewelry. A number of Indians have revived the artistic traditions, and this has been financially rewarding for them.

people of nobility. These poles, some as tall as 50 feet, were made by highly skilled craftsmen using beaver-incisor tools. After the introduction of iron tools, the production of totem poles appears to have increased. The figures carved on a pole displayed family and/or clan symbols (totems) of animals and/or supernatural beings. The poles depicted family history, assumptions of rank, exploits, origin stories, memorials to individuals, or significant events. It was believed that the poles had spirits and connected humans with the supernatural; thus, they were always treated with respect.

There were several types of totem poles. Many were made and raised as part of a potlatch, to celebrate and mark an important occasion. Others served as statements of rank or achievement, as welcome poles at the entrances to towns or houses, or as mortuary poles (grave markers). Some poles were carved and erected in order to shame another person for an

Two totem poles outside a building in Alaska, 1899. (CORBIS)

offense; when the offense was corrected, the pole was removed. Today, some totem poles are carved as tourist attractions and some are even made to sell.

Religion

In general, Northwest Coast peoples believed in the existence and power of numerous supernatural beings rather than a single all-powerful deity. These beings were associated with the creation, status, and privileges of social units, especially clans. All Northwest Coast cultures had ceremonial structures "that featured dramatic representations of supernatural beings, dramatizations of the contact of ancestors with those beings, and the demonstration of supernatural power" (Holm 1990:378). Some have argued that many Northwest Coast groups lacked a consistent system of religious beliefs and that the various ceremonies had essentially become historical pageants (see discussion in Suttles and Jonaitis 1990:84).

Most ceremonies were held in the winter. They consisted of performances held on stages within a large communal house and provided a venue for supernatural

VIP Profile

CHIEF SEATHL

Chief Seathl was a leader of the Suquamish band of the Coast Salish in the Puget Sound region. He was born in 1786. Successful in war, he became a chief at about age twenty and took the family name (title) of Seathl. He had two wives and six children (four of whom died young), and he owned slaves. By 1849, he had become the main chief of the band and encouraged his people to welcome the whites and the trade goods they brought with them. The city of Seattle, founded in Suquamish territory in 1852, was named after the friendly chief. He had established himself as a great orator, and even the whites listened to him with respect.

By 1854, so many whites were coming into the region that many Indians wanted to evict them, by force if necessary. Chief Seathl gave a famous speech (translated into English and printed in a Seattle newspaper) in which he argued for peace, but warned the whites that they must take care of the land or face decline. Based on this speech, Chief Seathl has commonly been viewed as an early environmentalist. He was the first to sign the Treaty of Point Elliot in 1855, which put most of the Indians in the Puget Sound region on reservations. He died in 1866. See Bierwert (1998) for a discussion of Chief Seathl.

beings to interact with humans. Spirits participated with humans in the initiation of people into secret societies, the reaffirmation of ranks and titles, and the reenactment of important events such as the creation of clans. Potlatches, essentially held to confirm rank, also contained many religious rituals.

Other ceremonies were conducted to ensure continued productivity, such as those held at the beginning of the salmon run to secure future salmon runs. Most other ceremonies were associated with individual life-cycle events such as birth, puberty, and death. Certain societies were responsible for conducting specific ceremonies, and new members had to be initiated into those societies.

Northwest Coast Indians Today

Most Northwest Coast groups live on reservations or reserves, although a number of groups were not officially recognized and so have no land base. Numerous land claims are still pending. Many Indians live in poverty, although many work seasonally in the lumber and fishing industries. In 1998, the governments of Canada and British Columbia signed a treaty with the Nisga tribe (or Nishga; see Halpin and Seguin 1990), recognizing their land rights and providing for self-government. It was the first such treaty in British Columbia in over 100 years and took effect in May 2000. Another treaty, this one with the Nuu-chah-nulth, was agreed to in 2001 and is awaiting final approval and implementation. Canada is currently in the process of negotiating treaties with many other native groups.

After the ban on potlatching was lifted by the Canadian government in 1951, Northwest Coast peoples in Canada began to revive the practice, rediscovering their culture and traditions in the process. Today, some groups have re-established the system of ranking and potlatching to affirm certain ranks within the community.

After the decline of commercial fishing in the 1920s, many fishermen were able to make a living in small-scale fishing. Later, commercial fishing revived, and after the 1960s many tribes became much more involved in the industry by building and operating their own processing plants, fish farms, and other facilities. This led to disputes over fishing rights between the Indians and non-Indian fishing companies. Further, the construction of dams has limited some salmon runs and destroyed some traditional fishing localities, which has also had a detrimental impact on Northwest Coast Indians.

Fishing rights continue to be a major issue facing Northwest Coast Indians (see Cohen 1986). The Indians have fought and won many court battles since the late nineteenth century, but with little effect, as such decisions were often ignored by non-Indians. The most significant ruling came in 1974, when Indian fishing rights in Washington state were affirmed in the *Boldt* decision (reviewed and upheld by the U.S. Supreme Court in 1979). Although many non-Indians have ignored or resisted this decision, it is currently being implemented.

In 1998, the Makah tribe in northwestern Washington received permission to resume traditional whale hunting with harpoons and canoes, an activity that has not been performed since the 1930s. The permit limited the Makah to taking five whales per year, but some environmental groups mounted considerable protest to this decision; some used ships to disrupt the hunt. The Makah took their first whale in May 1999. In December 2002, a federal appeals court ordered the Makah to cease whaling pending further environmental review.

A number of efforts, both private and governmental, have been made to restore totem poles and rejuvenate native art traditions. The economic potential for the Indians is considerable. In addition, several replicas of native Northwest Coast towns have been built for tourists.

Learn More About Contemporary Northwest Coast Peoples

The discussion above provides only a very brief description of Northwest Coast people today. What else can you discover? Go to the library and look on the Internet to learn more about Northwest Coast groups today. Topics you can explore include the following:

1. Chose a particular group or two, and investigate how they have adjusted to European conquest. Look at their tribal land base (e.g., whether they have a reservation or reserve), their tribal economy, and the general well-being of their tribal members.

2. What is the status of fishing rights, particularly after the *Boldt* decision and the refusal of some whites to comply with it? How does commercial salmon fishing in the ocean affect tribal economies?
3. What traditional practices have been retained? What are the roles of traditional religion, economics, and politics in Northwest Coast groups today? How important are potlatches in contemporary Northwest Coast society?
4. Other than fishing rights, what problems face Northwest Coast people today?
5. Follow the Makah whaling issue. What are the various arguments, pro and con? What is the current situation?

The Kwakiutl: A Northwest Coast Case Study

The Kwakiutl inhabited a portion of the central coast of British Columbia just north of Seattle (Fig. 6.2). They call themselves Kwakwaka'wakw, or those who speak Kwakwala, the Kwakiutl language. Kwakiutl identity was (and still is) tied to the sea because of their reliance on fishing and sea mammal hunting. Individual groups formed independent social and political units but were united by the common language, as well as participation in the general economic and potlatch system. There were about 8,000 Kwakiutl in 1830 (see Codere 1990: Table 1), and this case study describes them as they were at about that time.

Most of the information on the Kwakiutl was obtained in the late nineteenth and early twentieth centuries by Franz Boas, George Hunt, and Edward Curtis. As

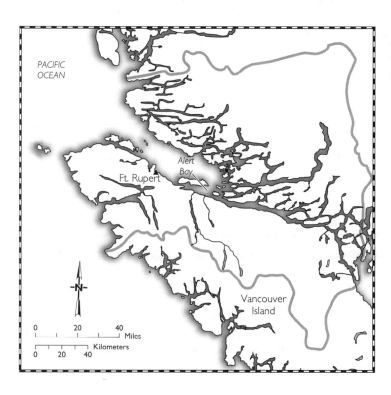

FIGURE 6.2 Location and territory of the Kwakiutl along the coast of British Columbia
Adapted from H. Codere, "Kwakiutl: Traditional Culture" in *Handbook of North American Indians, Vol. 7, Northwest Coast,* W. Suttles, ed., Fig. 1; copyright © 1990 by the Smithsonian Institution. Reprinted by permission of the publisher.

most of the data on the Kwakiutl were obtained from those living at Fort Rupert on northern Vancouver Island, the anthropological view is skewed toward that one group and may not accurately reflect the Kwakiutl as a whole. Important syntheses on Kwakiutl culture are presented by Boas (e.g., 1897, 1909, 1921), Curtis (1915), Ford (1941), Codere (1950, 1990), Boas and Codere (1966), Kirk (1986), Walens (1992), and Galois (1994). The information on the Kwakiutl summarized below is from those sources.

The Natural Environment

The Kwakiutl lived along the central coast of British Columbia, occupying a section of the mainland coast, numerous small islands, and the northern and eastern portions of Vancouver Island. The coastline is very irregular, with many inlets, islands, and fjords. The terrain is rugged, with high mountains, thick forests, many rivers and streams, and narrow beaches. Although the climate is mild, it is very wet, and the rainy season extends from October through April.

There are two basic biotic communities, forest and sea. The forest consists mostly of cedar, spruce, and hemlock trees with a dense undergrowth of ferns. Many animals important to the Kwakiutl, including deer, bears, elk, and mountain goats, lived in the forest. Numerous plants from the forest also were utilized by the Kwakiutl. The rivers and streams that ran through the forest to the sea were the primary sources of salmon, the most essential of the fish taken by the Kwakiutl.

The sea was the main source of food, avenue of travel, and foundation of identity for the Kwakiutl. Marine mammals, such as seals, sea lions, sea otters, porpoises, and whales, were very abundant. Many species of fish, including salmon, were taken from the sea, as were a number of invertebrates, including shellfish, crabs, and octopuses.

Language

The Kwakiutl spoke the Kwakwala language, part of the Wakashan language family. It is related to Nootka, spoken by people living on the southern portion of Vancouver Island. Kwakwala had three major dialects, all mutually intelligible.

A Brief History

The Kwakiutl had their first contact with Europeans in 1786, when a British trading ship visited the region. In 1792, the Kwakiutl were visited by American, Spanish, and British ships, the latter captained by George Vancouver. The Kwakiutl had learned about trading with the Europeans from the Nuu-chah-nulth and were eager to participate. The British wanted sea otter pelts, and the Kwakiutl wanted metal utensils and tools and cloth. When ships arrived at towns, many people would paddle out in canoes to the ships to welcome them. The British established a good trading relationship with the Kwakiutl, and the Kwakiutl visited a number of trading posts. However, it was not until 1849 that a trading post was established in Kwakiutl territory, at Fort Rupert on Vancouver Island. Four Kwakiutl groups moved their winter towns to Fort Rupert, establishing the largest of the Kwakiutl settlements and becoming the center of Kwakiutl culture.

The Kwakiutl then had constant problems with the British, who were trying to establish control over the region. Several native towns, including the one at Fort Rupert, were destroyed by British gunboats and many Kwakiutl were killed. In the 1870s, the center of Kwakiutl culture moved from Fort Rupert to the trading post at Alert Bay, also on Vancouver Island. The British apparently forced many Kwakiutl men into wage labor and some Kwakiutl women into prostitution.

In the 1880s, the Canadian government established reserves for some of the Kwakiutl groups but not others, resulting in a loss of territory to those who were not recognized. Not until just after the turn of the century did the Kwakiutl become a single cultural and political entity. Between 1900 and 1920, the Kwakiutl became very involved in the commercial fishing industry. Being excellent fishermen, they did quite well, using their wages to buy European goods for various purposes, including potlatching (see the general discussion of potlatching, above). However, after 1920, the fishing industry declined and the Kwakiutl fell into hard times. A revival of fishing occurred during World War II, but it never attained the intensity of the early twentieth century.

The Kwakiutl suffered heavily from European diseases. Major epidemics swept through the population in the late eighteenth and early-to-mid nineteenth centuries. Smallpox was the most destructive, but venereal diseases also caused major problems. The Kwakiutl population declined from about 8,000 in 1830, to 2,500 in 1880, to about 1,000 in 1928 (see Codere 1990: Table 1), a loss of about 87 percent.

Cosmology

Kwakiutl cosmology was little concerned with the origin of the universe or the earth. Instead, it centered on the origin of clans and other social units and the transformation of the world and its inhabitants from a state of hunger and immorality to a state of having food and sound morals (see Walens 1981). The culture hero Transformer was responsible for changing the world and creating the Kwakiutl. Much of Kwakiutl ceremony involved ritual feasting, demonstrating that a state of hunger no longer existed.

In mythological times, people, birds, animals, and fish lived in their own worlds—the land, the sky, and the water. All were the same on the inside; they only differed in their outer coverings of fur, feathers, or skin. All were capable of changing their coverings and of living in the other worlds. In addition, in an underworld, ghost beings lived the same life as the earth beings. Each clan was created when one of the supernatural beings took human form and created other humans to form the clan. Clans traced their ancestry back to these beings; obtained power, crests, privileges, songs, and dances from them; and adopted the beings as their totems.

Politics and External Relations

Traditionally, no overall Kwakiutl tribal political organization existed (although one was formed after 1900). There were instead about thirty independent political entities, and each had its own winter town, songs, and traditions. Several winter towns might ally themselves in a confederation. In several instances, such as at Fort Rupert, a number of winter towns moved to the same location and established a larger political unit, considered by some to be a chiefdom.

Each winter town had a secular chief, typically the chief of the highest-ranking clan. Each of the other clans represented at a town also had a chief. Chief positions had formal titles and privileges and were generally passed from father to son. Clans held most of the actual power in a town, with the highest-ranking clan being the most influential. Towns consisted of a number of houses built along a beach facing the water. A walkway of cedar planking would often be built along the front of the houses to allow easy movement between them. Towns would often have a population in the hundreds.

Kwakiutl warfare was common but small in scale, and usually it was waged against other Kwakiutl groups, although some warfare involved other groups. Most warfare was conducted for reasons of revenge or prestige. It has been argued that as potlatching gained in intensity, warfare and other violence decreased, eventually disappearing (Codere 1950). Warfare did decrease as the British took control of the region.

Each Kwakiutl group maintained a small group of professional soldiers, specialists supported by the group as a whole, who led war expeditions and did most of the actual fighting. These men were trained from an early age to be fit, tough, aggressive, merciless, and always ready to fight. Disliked by most people because of their attitude and demeanor, they rarely married. Other men would accompany the soldiers on raids, largely to perform noncombatant duties, such as guarding the canoes, carrying weapons, looting, setting fire to the enemy town, and the like. A typical war expedition might include twenty canoes, carrying some three hundred men, with thirty to forty professional soldiers, preceded by a scouting party in one canoe.

The war expedition would generally approach the enemy town from the sea in war canoes. They would attack at night, sneaking up on the sleeping enemy and entering their houses to kill the men, take the women and children as slaves, and then plunder and burn the town. The heads of slain enemy men were taken as trophies to be displayed on poles back at the home town. If the raiding party was discovered before the actual attack began, they would usually retreat. Most warfare was conducted in the early fall, as the ocean was calm and fog provided cover. If they felt threatened, people from a town might move to a stockaded camp or other defensible location for a time. Upon the return of a successful war expedition, the townspeople would greet them and everyone would retire to a communal house where the soldiers would recount their deeds, list their victims, and distribute loot.

War weapons included lances made of yew wood, whalebone clubs, stone knives, slings to throw round stones, and the bow and arrow. Arrow points were made from bone and were barbed to aggravate the wound. Many soldiers used body armor made of elk hide. The Kwakiutl and other Northwest Coast groups had acquired muskets by the early nineteenth century.

Social Organization

The primary family unit was the lineage (loosely patrilineal), the members of which lived together in a large communal house. Each winter town had from three to seven clans (called *numaym*). Each clan had a crest, rank, and property, including houses, resource localities, and the highly valued rights to perform dances at the winter ceremonials. Each of the various social organizations—families, lineages, clans, and towns—had named and ranked offices (such as clan chief).

The Kwakiutl recognized three social classes: nobles, commoners, and slaves. Most of the population belonged to the commoner class. After 1849, when Fort Rupert was established and the British began to exercise control over the Kwakiutl, slaves were no longer held and the class system became much less important, as anyone, not just nobles, had the chance to amass enough wealth to claim high rank.

Men hunted and fished, carved wood, and fought in wars. Women generally did the domestic chores, weaving, collection of shellfish, and gathering of plant foods and materials. However, there were many exceptions to the sexual division of labor; it was not sharp or rigid. Everyone assisted during the salmon harvest. Women held few formal positions and had relatively low status, but this improved after the abolition of slavery after about 1849, as most of the slaves held by the Kwakiutl were women.

Life Cycle

When a woman became pregnant, she observed a number of rules. She avoided hard work so as to not injure the baby, was the first to open the door of the house each morning (to ensure an easy delivery), slept parallel to the house planking so the baby would not get stuck in the birth canal, and observed certain food restrictions. A midwife helped with birth as the mother straddled a grass-lined pit where the baby landed when born. The infant was then placed in a cradle. Twins were considered a blessing as they were thought to have special powers.

The infant's nasal septum was pierced on the fifth day after birth and the ears were pierced on the ninth day. Female children of high-ranking parents had their heads bound so that they would grow up with flattened foreheads. Although this was a very desirable trait, it was expensive, as it required a professional to perform the procedure and it took many months to complete.

The child was initially given its birthplace as a name. A second name was conferred at about ten months of age. At that time, the infant was formally considered to be a child of the parents but not a member of the overall group. When a boy was between ten and twelve years of age, he was given a third name in a small ceremony where he was obliged to distribute gifts to those who attended.

Young men were initiated into the dancing society dictated by rank and inheritance. Each society had its own house and initiated its members at the beginning of the winter ceremonial period. At about the same time, the young man assumed the rank and responsibilities in his clan by holding a potlatch. Once these ceremonies were completed, the young man was considered a member of the overall group.

At first menses, a girl was confined to her house for four days. She then went through a long purification ritual with the help of her female relatives. When purification was complete, her father sponsored a potlatch to mark the event. The young woman then received a set of new clothes and was given her adult name.

Most people tended to marry outside their clan and town, though no firm rules required this. One usually tried to marry within one's general rank (nobility, commoner, slave), and most marriages of higher-ranked people were arranged to keep rank within the family. Marriage was a way for a man to obtain rank and privileges from the bride's father, including the right to perform dances. The groom and his family paid a bride-price, the amount of which depended on the wealth and status of the families, to the bride's father, partly for the bride but also for the associated rank and privileges that came with her. If a high-ranking man had rights and privileges desired by a young man to further his own status, the young man might "marry" something else from the high-ranking man, such as his arm or his canoe.

In the marriage ceremony the bride-price was presented by the groom and his family to the bride's father, an event that included feasting and oratory. The bride was then lifted and carried to the groom's house. The two families might then "fight" for possession of the bride, with blood often being shed. The next morning, a wedding feast was held for all of the women of the town, with each woman offering advice to the new bride. The couple then lived in the husband's house. If the couple separated, the woman moved back in with her father, and the husband lost the use of his father-in-law's titles and privileges. Both parties were free to remarry.

People feared the ghosts of the dead and took care not to touch corpses. At the death of an individual, unmarried persons of the same sex as the deceased were hired by the family to prepare the body. The body was washed, wrapped in a new blanket, bound in a fetal position, and placed in a small decorated wooden coffin. The coffin was then placed in a canoe pushed out to sea, on the ground near the town, in a cave, or in a tree, where the corpse would often slowly mummify. After disposal of the body, the relatives of the deceased—or the entire town, if the individual was a chief—would publicly mourn by singing songs, eating, and distributing gifts. A totem pole might be raised on the occasion of the death of an important person, and the name of the dead was usually not spoken again. The heir of the deceased would sponsor a potlatch as soon as possible to claim the titles, rights, and privileges due him.

Economics

The Kwakiutl did not practice any agriculture, although some tobacco was grown in a few locations. The only domestic animal was the dog. All food was obtained by hunting and gathering, with fish being the most important resource. Most economic activities ceased during the winter in order to conduct ceremonies, during which time people lived off stored foods.

As with the rest of the Northwest Coast, salmon was the most important fish taken by the Kwakiutl. Relatively small numbers of salmon were taken all year from the sea, but huge numbers were taken when the various species ran up the numerous rivers and streams to spawn, mostly in the fall. The salmon were funneled into weirs, where they were taken with harpoons, gill nets, and dip nets. The fish were dried, smoked, or stored in fish oil. Other fish resources included halibut, eulachon, sturgeon, flounder, herring, cod, and smelt. Roe (eggs) of various fish was considered a delicacy. Fish oil was also used as a condiment.

The Kwakiutl also hunted sea mammals, including seals, sea lions, and some whales. Hunting whales was not a major pursuit, but hunters would take advantage of a beached whale. Other sea mammals were hunted from canoes, with harpoons attached to floats. In addition, women collected mussels, clams, other shellfish, crabs, and sea urchins. Men used spears to hunt octopuses.

Land resources were generally less important than ocean resources, although the Kwakiutl regularly hunted a number of terrestrial animals. Deer, bears, and elk were killed with bows and arrows from ambush, and mountain goats were captured in snares set on mountain trails. Several fur-bearing animals, such as beaver, mink, and ermine, were taken, as were some waterfowl. Plant foods were fairly abundant, and the people used hundreds of species, various berries being the most significant. Several types of ocean algae, which were gathered by women, also served as food.

Material Culture and Technology

The Kwakiutl lived in large, multifamily plank houses built in rows facing the water. The houses were up to a hundred feet long, forty feet wide, and twenty feet high. The fronts were often painted with artistic designs depicting clan totems and histories. The interiors had a large central area for daily activities and ceremonial occasions, with small family apartments lining the sides. Most personal belongings were kept in these apartments. The apartment exteriors were decorated.

Most travel was by canoe. The Kwakiutl made several types, including special war canoes. Most Kwakiutl canoes had high bows and sterns and were highly decorated. Large canoes could carry more than fifty people. Hundreds of canoes of various types and sizes might be found in a single town.

People wore little clothing in the summer; men usually were naked and women generally wore only a small apron of cedar bark. In the winter, most people wore a warm and water-repellent blanket garment made from woven yellow cedar bark or woven mountain goat or dog hair. Most people went barefoot but would wear moccasins in very cold weather. Some high-ranking people wore cloaks of sea otter fur, both as clothing and to denote rank. Special clothing was donned during ceremonies, and costumes enhanced the various dramatic performances. Many people wore hats of basketry or wood, both to keep their heads dry and to indicate rank.

Both men and women had pierced ears, noses, and lips, in which they wore a variety of ornaments made from shell, bone, fur, and copper. Other jewelry, such as necklaces and bracelets, was also popular. Tattooing was rare but many people painted their faces for various occasions, primarily ceremonies. The foreheads of high-status females were flattened in infancy as a sign of beauty and rank.

Men usually wore their hair loose and fairly short, but sometimes it was kept long and covered with grease and red paint. A few men wore beards. Women wore their hair long, arranged in two braids. All groomed their hair frequently with wooden combs to reduce head-lice infestations.

Stone was used for a few tools, including hammers and mortars and pestles for processing berries. Very few items were made from flaked stone. Knives were made from teeth, wood, and shell. A great variety of basketry and netting were manufactured, and considerable matting was made from cedar bark. The Kwakiutl did not use pottery. Weapons included the bow and arrow, spears, harpoons, clubs, and slings.

Religion and Medicine

The Kwakiutl had no belief in a supreme being but did believe that everything—animals, people, trees, totem poles, the sea—had a spirit. All beings—humans, animals, and spirits—were considered essentially the same, all equal partners in behavior, ceremony, and tradition. Much of Kwakiutl ceremony represented the interactions of humans, animals, and spirits and modeled how the universe should function.

Spirits varied in power and abilities. Individuals could pray to these spirits to thank them or even to make requests, such as for luck in fishing or success in war. Raven, Thunderbird, and Killer Whale were three of the most important spirits. The potlatch was an integral part of the ceremonial system.

The ceremonial year was divided into two halves, summer and winter. Summer was the secular time to work and to obtain and store food for the upcoming winter. Few ceremonies were held during the summer, an exception being the First Salmon Ceremony. There, the flesh of the first few fish caught during the salmon run was consumed in a special ceremony. The heads, tails, and spines were returned to the sea to ensure continued abundance of salmon.

Winter was the ceremonial part of the year when supernatural beings visited the town and interacted with humans (see Holm 1990). People's names, songs, and behavior differed during summer and winter, and the secular rank held by men in the summer was changed to its equivalent supernatural rank in the winter. The change was marked by a four-day feast and celebration punctuated by a brief period of mourning for those who had died since the previous winter.

The most important ceremonial event in the winter was the Cedar Bark Dance. This lengthy and elaborate event required considerable preparation, much like a potlatch, and was held in a large dance house with a stage, curtains, dressing rooms, and a central fire pit. Central to the ceremonial was the initiation of novices, mostly male, into the various dancing societies, conducted by the societies according to rank.

Directed by the hereditary leaders of the dancing societies, the rituals were held in semidarkness and included dancing, storytelling, and staged performances of magic, drama, and comedy. Dancers wore elaborate masks and costumes, special effects were produced, and props were maneuvered through trapdoors on the stage. Each performance had four parts: the abduction of the initiate by the spirits; the return of the initiate; the initiate's demonstration of power obtained from the spirit; and the taming of the initiate and his return to normal society.

The initiation of a new member into the Cannibal Society was the most important event of the winter ceremonial. A staged performance depicted human flesh-eating bird monsters capturing the initiate, his attempts to "eat" people by biting members of the audience, his journey into the forest before finally being calmed by the other society members, followed by the final performance and feast on the last day. The ceremonies and initiations of the other dancing societies followed in turn, each according to rank. During the War Dance, the dancer was suspended by his pierced flesh to demonstrate his endurance and worthiness to be a soldier. Women participated in many dances, usually in the last phase where the dancer was tamed and returned to society.

Kwakiutl shamans were ranked by three levels of shamanistic power. The most powerful were able to cause, diagnose, and cure illness, and could cast spells on others. Other shamans were able only to diagnose and cure sickness. The lowest level comprised individuals who had been cured by a shaman and so retained residual power and might then become shamans themselves. To effect treatment, shamans entered trances, employed the sucking cure, and used pharmacological substances. Shamans were generally directed to the profession by a supernatural helper. New shamans were initiated by an established one in a public ceremony. A few shamans gained wealth from their work.

Art, Expression, and Recreation

Like that of most Northwest Coast people, Kwakiutl art was spectacular (see the chapter Sidelight). However, the Kwakiutl did not use totem poles to any great extent. Most art portrayed spirit ancestors, depicted clan histories or rank, or had a ceremonial function.

Kwakiutl music was extensive and varied. It was mostly associated with the various ceremonies, where rattles, clappers, drums, and whistles produced music to which people sang and danced. Most ceremonials involved theater performances of drama and magic.

The Kwakiutl played many games (forty are listed in Boas and Codere 1966:388–400), including cat's cradle, dice, cup and ball, the hoop game, and throwing stones at targets. Canoe races were also very popular.

The Kwakiutl Today

The Kwakiutl have survived to the present time (see Webster 1990), and they continue to be studied by anthropologists (see Wolcott 1967, 1996; Spradley 1972; and Rohner and Bettauer 1986 for studies of the contemporary Kwakiutl). In the late 1990s, there were more than 4,000 Kwakiutl. Few roads have been built in parts of Kwakiutl territory and most travel is by boat or seaplane.

The basic political organization is still the town, and most towns have an elected council. A total of fifteen actual "band" governments are recognized by the Canadian government. Since the lifting of the potlatch ban in 1951, the practice has been revived, but the frequency and scale are much reduced as many titles (ranks) had not been passed on or validated since the early twentieth century. An effort to preserve the Kwakwala language has been made and it is now taught in Kwakiutl schools. Many Kwakiutl converted to Christianity after native religion was banned in the late nineteenth century, but the winter ceremonial is still held and is gaining in popularity.

Canadian government policies were reformed in 1951, and now the government provides some help for education and health. However, common problems among the Kwakiutl are malnutrition, weight gain in middle age, and alcoholism. A leading cause of death is accidental drowning, as it was in precontact times.

The main employers of Kwakiutl people are the fishing and logging industries. Logging is not a very popular job since the Kwakiutl see themselves as sea people, not forest people. Also, logging jobs require extended absences from family, and many men find this undesirable. Some are learning traditional artistic skills, and the production of native art is a rapidly growing and lucrative profession.

///

7 Native Peoples of the Great Basin

///

The Great Basin comprises the large interior depression lying between the Sierra Nevada to the west and the Rocky Mountains to the east and includes much of the western United States. All of the native people in the Great Basin were hunters and gatherers, although a few groups, such as the Southern Paiute and perhaps the Owens Valley Paiute, practiced some small-scale agriculture. The major resource that defines the Great Basin is the pinyon nut, which was a critical food item for many groups. The other characteristic aspect of the Great Basin is the relative recency of Euroamerican contact and prolonged endurance of traditional cultures (see d'Azevedo 1986a).

Many view the Great Basin an arid, sparsely vegetated, inhospitable place. Thus many of the native cultures in the Great Basin are considered "poor hunter-gatherers eking a meager existence from a harsh land." This incorrect and unfortunate misconception can be traced to the encounter between early explorers and the easternmost Western Shoshone, who were living in a very arid region and just getting by at that point in time. This stereotypic view was subsequently expanded to include all Great Basin groups and continues to be perpetuated by many who have never seen the Great Basin or prefer the environment of the eastern United States. It is important to understand that the Indians of the Great Basin were vibrant people well adapted to their environment and were not the destitute people so commonly depicted in much of the literature.

Geography and Environment

The natural Great Basin is a large region of interior drainage and a basin-and-range province that includes most of Nevada, southeastern Oregon, southern Idaho,

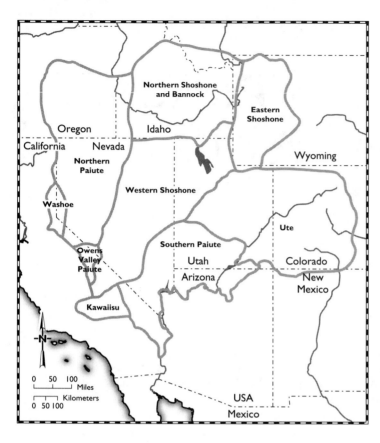

FIGURE 7.1 Great Basin culture area, with the locations of the native groups
Adapted from *Handbook of North American Indians,* Vol. 11, *Great Basin,* W. L. d'Azevedo, ed., p. ix; copyright © 1986 by the Smithsonian Institution. Reprinted by permission of the publisher.

western Utah, and portions of eastern California (see Fig. 7.1). Within this region are two major deserts, the Mojave Desert in the south and the Great Basin Desert in the north. The Mojave Desert occupies much of southeastern California and portions of Arizona and Nevada (see Jaeger 1965; Rowlands et al. 1982). It is a dry desert characterized by hot summers and cold winters. The Great Basin Desert occupies the remainder of the natural Great Basin and is generally wetter and cooler than the Mojave Desert, although its northern regions are arid (see Fowler and Koch 1982). The Great Basin Desert contains many river, lake, and marsh systems, numerous pinyon-covered mountain ranges, and associated valleys.

The Great Basin culture area is defined differently, incorporating all of the territory inhabited by people speaking one of the Numic languages (with the exception of the Comanche on the southern Plains). The culture area covers approximately 400,000 square miles and includes all of the natural Great Basin, in addition to large portions of Wyoming, Colorado, New Mexico, Arizona, and Idaho, including the Snake River Plain (see Fig. 7.1).

The environment of the Great Basin is highly varied and includes alpine zones, forests, rivers, marshes, and very arid regions (see Harper 1986; Mehringer 1986). More than 150 small mountain ranges and an equivalent number of small valleys lie within the Great Basin; hence, the term *basin-and-range province* is commonly used to refer to the region. Elevations range from below sea level in Death Valley to over 12,000 feet in the Toquima Range in central Nevada. At one time a number of the valleys contained rivers terminating in lakes or marshes, several of which were quite extensive.

The climate is generally arid, with warm to very hot summers and cold winters. Precipitation is quite variable, with the southern Great Basin averaging four to six inches per year and the northern Great Basin receiving a few inches more. Many of the mountain ranges receive snowfall every year. The Sierra Nevada and Cascade Mountains create a rainshadow effect along the western edge of the Basin, although the runoff from these mountains produces a great deal of surface water in the region. The western edge of the Rocky Mountains has a similar effect on the eastern edge of the Great Basin.

The Great Basin contains many biotic communities, including alpine zones at high elevations. Many of the mountain ranges are covered with extensive forests of pinyon and juniper, and pinyon nuts were a staple food for the Indians. Pinyon do not grow in abundance north of northern Nevada, and in the Mojave Desert to the south, pinyon and juniper exist only in the higher mountains. Sagebrush and grassland dominate many of the valleys below the pinyon-juniper zone and extend to the north, past the boundaries of the pinyon. In the Mojave Desert, creosote scrub is dominant, with mesquite growing in the bottoms of valleys. In the marshlands, tule, cattail, sedge, and other marsh plants provided major sources of food and material.

Animals available in the Great Basin include deer, mountain sheep, and pronghorn antelope, plus small numbers of bison in the north. Enormous numbers of rabbits, hares, rodents, reptiles, and insects are also present. Beavers inhabited some of the rivers until they were trapped out by Europeans in the early nineteenth century. Waterfowl, particularly geese and ducks, live in large numbers in the marshes along the western and eastern edges of the Basin and were heavily utilized by the people in those areas. In addition, many dozens of species of fish are known throughout the Great Basin (see Sigler and Sigler 1987).

A Basic Prehistory of the Great Basin

The long prehistoric record of the Great Basin grows more complex as our understanding of it deepens. Summaries of Great Basin prehistory by region and topic can be found in the fourteen prehistory chapters in the Great Basin volume of the *Handbook of North American Indians*, (d'Azevedo 1986b). More recent treatments are provided by Grayson (1993), Kelly (1997), Beck and Jones (1997), and Fagan (2000:251–278).

The Paleoindian Period (ca. 12,000 to 10,000 B.P.)

The earliest evidence of occupation of the Great Basin has been found along the shorelines of an extensive system of ancient Pleistocene lakes (see Mehringer 1986: Fig. 1) and dates to about 12,000 B.P. A few researchers believe in a much earlier human occupation of North America in the Great Basin, but most reject that claim.

As in much of North America, the Paleoindians of the Great Basin are thought to have been few in number, very mobile, and specialists in hunting large game, although this is probably too simplistic a view. At the end of the Pleistocene, the climate changed from relatively wet and cool to much warmer and drier, causing most of the lakes to disappear. People were forced to adapt to the changing conditions.

The Archaic Period (ca. 10,000 B.P. to Contact)

As the lakes dried up, many animals abandoned the region, and life became more difficult for the human inhabitants. People were forced to adopt a settlement, subsistence, and technological system compatible with desert conditions. Excavations at Danger Cave in northwestern Utah in the 1950s suggest that people had adopted such a system about 10,000 years ago and that it continued until historical times. This idea—that Great Basin adaptations and cultures had remained essentially unchanged since the Pleistocene—became known as the Desert Culture.

Although the idea of a constant, uniform Desert Culture still persists among some people, a more extensive variation in human occupation of the Great Basin, both by region and through time, seems more likely. The environmental variety, encompassing marshes, rivers, deserts, valleys, and mountains, would almost require variation in adaptation. The idea of the Desert Culture was eventually dropped by most archaeologists in favor of a more general "Desert Archaic" that allowed for regional variations in adaptation.

The Archaic is divided into three major time periods: Early, Middle, and Late. The Early Archaic Period lasted from about 10,000 to 4,000 B.P. With the change in climate and resource availability at the end of the Pleistocene, people either adopted a new lifestyle or moved. By about 4,000 years ago, it was hotter and drier than it is today and humans probably had a difficult time in much of the Great Basin, although the higher elevations probably remained fairly hospitable. Despite the harsh conditions, the Great Basin was never abandoned by people. During this time, people continued a general hunting-and-gathering economy, using the atlatl as their principal weapon.

During the Middle Archaic Period (from about 4,000 to 1,500 B.P.), the climate became cooler and wetter. Some lakes were reestablished, extensive marshlands reappeared, plants and animals returned, and conditions became more pleasant for the human populations. The Late Archaic Period began in about 1,500 B.P., when the climate again turned warmer and drier, much as it is today. At the beginning of the Late Archaic Period, the bow and arrow were introduced into the region from the north, resulting in a marked increase in hunting efficiency.

Many researchers believe that sometime around 1,000 years ago, groups speaking Numic languages expanded across the Basin from a homeland in the southwestern Great Basin. These Numic people had occupied the entire Great Basin and beyond by the time of European contact (see Madsen and Rhode 1994 for a treatment of the "Numic Expansion"), resulting in the distinctive linguistic uniformity of the region. The Late Archaic Period lasted until the hunter-gatherer populations were overwhelmed by American settlers in the late nineteenth century.

Late Farmers

After about 1,600 B.P., groups practicing agriculture began to appear in the eastern and southern Great Basin. In the eastern Great Basin, these farmers, who also hunted and gathered much of their food, are generally known today as the Fremont (see Madsen and Simms 1998). It is not clear where the Fremont originated; perhaps they moved north into the Basin from the Southwest as climatic conditions improved to the point where corn could grow. It is unclear what happened to the Fremont, but they were gone by the time Europeans entered the region. In the southern Great Basin, farmers from the Southwest, called the Virgin Anasazi since they lived along the Virgin River, occupied southern Nevada after about 1,300 B.P. By about 800 B.P., these farmers had also disappeared, and the Southern Paiute entered the region.

The Contact Period

The first European contact with Great Basin groups occurred in the Southwest in the early seventeenth century, when Utes and Southern Paiutes from the Basin began to raid the Spanish and Pueblo groups. The Utes stole horses and traded them to the Northern Shoshone, who then introduced them onto the northern Plains in the late seventeenth century (see Shimkin 1986). One large group of Northern Shoshone, the Comanche, entered the Plains and moved south to Texas (see Chapter 10). However, most Great Basin groups were contacted by Euroamericans relatively late in time, although the basic pattern of contact and conquest resembled that of other areas of North America (see Malouf and Findlay 1986).

Europeans first entered the Great Basin in the late eighteenth century, as the Spanish began to explore the region. The Southern Paiute were contacted by Spanish explorers in 1776, and the Northern Shoshone (the Lemhi Shoshone) encountered Lewis and Clark in 1805. Other parts of the Great Basin were explored in the early nineteenth century, and many groups were contacted intermittently during this time. Prior to 1840, most contact with Great Basin peoples was by Euroamerican trappers and traders.

Until the mid–nineteenth century, Euroamericans knew little about the Great Basin and it was widely believed that the region was impassable. However, in 1843, John Frémont crossed the Basin from east to west and entered California, opening the way for the establishment of immigrant routes to Oregon and California. After that time, immigrants increasingly passed through the Great Basin, and some decided to stay and establish ranches and towns. The Mormons migrated to Utah in the 1840s and founded Salt Lake City in 1847. The Euroamerican intrusion resulted in a major disruption to the native peoples and brought disease to the region. By the 1860s, American ranchers had taken over most of the valleys for cattle ranching, forcing the Indians out of their traditional lands. This loss forced the Indians to adapt, either by working on the ranches and in the towns, or by changing their settlement and subsistence patterns to focus on the mountains and deserts. Eventually, as American settlement expanded, all of the Indians were forced into some association with the Americans.

Remarkably little conflict ensued from these disruptions to native cultures; most groups were too small and poorly armed to put up an effective resistance. In a number of "battles," parties of whites attacked and massacred helpless and unarmed Indians. In one such case in early 1865, a newly formed army unit was assigned garrison duty rather than being sent east to fight in the Civil War. Frustrated over the lack of action and glory, they attacked a peaceful Northern Paiute village near Reno and killed about forty women and children.

However, in a few cases native groups emerged victorious. During the Pyramid Lake War of 1859, the Northern Paiute soundly defeated a militia sent from Reno, after which an armistice was declared. In 1878, the Bannock, along with

VIP Profile

SARAH WINNEMUCCA, NORTHERN PAIUTE LEADER

Sarah Winnemucca, a Northern Paiute from the Reno area of western Nevada, became a strong and passionate advocate for her people in the late nineteenth century, appealing to the American public and all levels of government for fair treatment of native peoples. Sarah was the daughter of Old Winnemucca and the granddaughter of Captain Truckee, both Northern Paiute chiefs. Sarah's native name was Thocmetony, meaning "Shell Flower." She was born in 1844 near Humboldt Lake in west-central Nevada. Sarah had two brothers and three sisters.

In the early 1850s, Sarah moved with her mother to the San Jose area in California for a short time, where she learned to speak Spanish (she also spoke English and Northern Paiute). She returned to the San Jose area in about 1860 and briefly attended a Catholic school before moving back to the Reno area. In 1864 she began to perform on stage in front of white audiences with her father and brothers. They presented a show on Paiute life that included songs, dances, and skits. As her father was the "Chief," Sarah was advertised as an "Indian Princess" and became somewhat of a celebrity.

In 1865, some thirty members of Old Winnemucca's band, including Sarah's mother and two of her sisters, were killed by the U.S. Army in reprisal for the murder of two white miners by other Indians. Many other Northern Paiute were murdered by whites over the next few months. Old Winnemucca and his band, including Sarah, left the area to avoid contact with the whites. The army wanted all the "hostiles" moved onto reservations, so Old Winnemucca surrendered his band at Fort McDermit in 1868. The group was eventually allowed to return to the Pyramid Lake Reservation in Nevada (see Knack and Stewart 1984).

In 1871 Sarah married a white man, Edward Bartlett, but they separated a month later and were divorced in 1876. Old Winnemucca greatly disapproved of the marriage. Sarah became well known to whites in the Pyramid Lake region and was interviewed many times by newspaper reporters. She frequently accompanied her father and brother when they met with officials and politicians to discuss the plight of the Northern Paiute.

Sarah moved to the Malheur Reservation in Oregon in 1874 to serve as an interpreter for the army. In 1876 she married another white man, Joseph Satwaller, but that marriage did not last long either. She served as an interpreter and some Northern Paiute and Northern Shoshone, revolted and began to raid settlers and army installations. Most other Indians in the region remained neutral. The army responded and the Indians were subsequently defeated, thus ending the Bannock War of 1878.

Between 1846 and 1906, thirty-nine formal treaties and agreements were signed with Great Basin groups (see Clemmer and Stewart 1986: Table 1), each one promising peace and friendship, land, the creation of reservations, access to resources, and money. By the late nineteenth century, the government had established some twenty reservations (see Clemmer and Stewart 1986:529–539), and while many groups moved onto them, the government often failed to provide

///

guide for the army during the Bannock War of 1878 and made friends with General Howard, who had been involved in the Nez Perce War of 1877. Her efforts to achieve peace made her a celebrity, and in 1879 she journeyed to San Francisco to be interviewed.

Sarah began to campaign for the rights of her people, making lecture tours around the country, including stops in San Francisco, Boston, and Washington, D.C. In 1881 she married another white man, L. H. Hopkins, and in 1882 her father, then over ninety years old, died. One of his sons, Sarah's brother Natches, then became the chief. Sarah embarked on another speaking tour in the east between 1882 and 1884, and gave some 300 lectures on the plight of the Northern Paiute. While in Boston, she met several women who encouraged her to write a book about her people. That book, *Life Among the Paiutes: Their Wrongs and Claims,* was published in 1883 (Hopkins 1883).

Sarah circulated a petition to give the Northern Paiute a reservation at Fort McDermit. She met with Senator Dawes (of the Dawes Act of 1887) and received his support. Congress considered the matter in 1884, but no reservation was authorized.

In 1885 Sarah founded a school for Paiutes near Lake Pyramid on land owned by her brother

Natches. The school went broke and closed in 1887, but it was one of the first attempts at Indian self-determination in education. Sarah's husband died in 1887 and she moved to her sister's house in Montana, where she died in 1891. Biographies of Sarah Winnemucca have been written by Fowler (1978), Canfield (1983), and Morrison (1990).

Sarah Winnemucca, Northern Paiute, in about 1878.
(Courtesy of the Nevada State Museum photograph collection.)

essential materials that had been promised. In the 1890s, Indian lands were again substantially reduced by the implementation of the allotment policy.

The Impact of European Contact

Probably the greatest impact to native cultures in the Great Basin as the result of European contact was the loss or destruction of habitat and resources, coupled with the considerable alteration of the environment. The loss of the valleys and their rich resource base, along with the destruction of forests for fence posts and firewood and the disruption of game movements caused by fencing, eventually forced many Indians to work for the ranches in order to survive. Indian men cut wood, herded cattle and horses, and built fences—ironically, the very activities that caused the problem. Indian women washed clothes, cooked, and did housekeeping; some were even forced into prostitution. Unable to obtain their traditional foods and paid poorly for their labor, many Indians had to beg and steal food to survive.

The Northern Paiute near Reno relied extensively on the abundant fish that lived in the Pyramid and Winnemucca Lakes, as well as the Truckee River that flows into the lakes. In 1905, the Derby Dam was constructed across the Truckee River, and the water levels in the lakes were drastically reduced. Lake Winnemucca dried up and the level of Pyramid Lake dropped by eighty feet. This resulted in the desiccation of almost the entire region, destroying the Northern Paiute economic base through loss of fish, waterfowl, and marsh resources. This water problem remains an issue today and continues to impact the Northern Paiute and the reservation at Pyramid Lake (see Knack and Stewart 1984).

Through diseases such as malaria, measles, smallpox, and syphilis swept through the Great Basin after 1800, causing many deaths, these crowd diseases were initially less of a problem in the Great Basin than elsewhere due to the dispersed nature of the native populations. However, as people were forced onto reservations or into towns, the incidence of disease increased. From a high of about 40,000 people prior to about 1800, the native population of the Great Basin had fallen to about 12,000 by 1930 (Leland 1986:608).

A Brief History of Ethnographic Research

Many Great Basin Indians were still following a traditional lifestyle when anthropologists initiated serious fieldwork with North American Indians. The Bureau of American Ethnology conducted work in the Great Basin between 1868 and 1880, and a number of other institutions and researchers collected information on various groups in the late nineteenth century. Research on Great Basin Indians continued into the early twentieth century, with a number of people, including Alfred Kroeber and Robert Lowie, conducting significant work.

In the 1930s, Kroeber initiated a systematic survey of cultures and traits in western North America, and much of his work was focused in the Great Basin. Among the people working with Kroeber were Julian Steward and Omer Stewart, both of whom became synonymous with Great Basin ethnography. Other notable researchers working in the Great Basin in the 1930s and 1940s include Isabel T. Kelly, Sven Liljeglad, Willard Z. Park, and Demitri B. Shimkin. Perhaps the most significant contribution to Great Basin ethnography was the work of Julian Steward. In 1938, he published his monumental *Basin-Plateau Aboriginal Sociopolitical Groups,* a volume that became the standard reference for Great Basin cultures and established the field of cultural ecology. Since the 1950s, many other researchers have conducted work in the Great Basin (see D. Fowler 1986).

A considerable amount of information exists about Great Basin peoples. The most well known summaries of Great Basin culture are Steward (1938) and the Great Basin volume (Vol. 11) of the *Handbook of North American Indians* (d'Azevedo 1986b), which is the best and most recent treatment. That volume contains chapters on a wide variety of subjects and many groups. The discussion of Great Basin cultures presented below was summarized from these sources, and the description of the people dates to the mid–nineteenth century.

A Broad Portrait of Great Basin Groups

The Great Basin is characterized by highly mobile, band-level hunter-gatherers with relatively small populations. Leland (1986:609) estimated that only about 40,000 people were living in the Great Basin just prior to contact. Nine major groups occupied the Great Basin: the Washo, Owens Valley Paiute, Northern Paiute, Western Shoshone, Northern Shoshone/Bannock, Eastern Shoshone, Kawaiisu, Southern Paiute, and Ute.

A prominent feature of the Great Basin is its linguistic uniformity. Although the Washo spoke a language of the Hokan family (see d'Azevedo 1986c), related to the Hokan languages in California, all other groups spoke one of six closely related languages of the Numic family of Northern Uto-Aztecan (see Miller 1986). It seems likely that this linguistic uniformity was the result of a recent expansion of these Numic people across the Great Basin.

Political Organization

Most Great Basin groups were organized at the family level. During the fall and winter, as well as other times (e.g., during communal hunts), a number of related families would combine to form a bandlike unit. In the spring, the families in the band would again disperse until the fall.

Scholars have argued whether Great Basin groups had "true" bands, but it is clear that at least some form of band existed. The size of the family and band units varied, depending on a variety of factors, including resource abundance and specific environmental conditions. The names of bands generally reflected particular food resources, such as the *Kucad-ikad-i* (eaters of brine fly larvae), *T-iPatt-ikka* (eaters of pine nuts), or *Watat-ikka* (seed eaters). However, many groups became known by their geographic locality, such as the Reese River Shoshone or the Round Valley Paiute.

Each family and band had a headman, commonly called *degwani* ("talker"). Headmen were given their responsibility by consensus and accepted the duty with honor and pride. The primary responsibility of the headman was to keep track of plant and animal resources so that collection times could be properly scheduled. The headman also gave long speeches and mediated disputes within the group.

Many researchers believe that warfare was relatively unimportant in the Great Basin, although some maintain that it was widely practiced against non–Great Basin groups until the 1850s. It is clear that the Northern and Eastern Shoshone obtained horses in the early eighteenth century and entered the northern Plains, conducting warfare against the Plains groups in that area. In the early nineteenth century, some northern Great Basin groups acquired horses and began raiding neighboring groups (see Layton 1981).

Social Organization

The basic social unit in Great Basin society was the nuclear family, although extended families were common. Most groups figures descent through the male (patrilineal) side. No formal lineages or clans were recognized. Larger social units, loosely defined as bands, formed with the congregation of families during the fall and winter. In some cases, several bands would gather at the same place for the fall pinyon harvest, forming an even larger social unit.

People were expected to marry outside their own band, and potential partners were courted during the fall when bands coalesced. Marriage was an alliance between a man and a woman to form a functional economic unit, as reflected in the strict division of labor. There was no formal ceremony; the couple simply moved in together. After marriage, the wife typically lived with her husband's band, but this was not a firm rule. A few men had more than one wife. Adultery was usually punished by the husband beating his wife and her lover. Divorce was fairly common and uncomplicated; either the husband or the wife merely moved out, the wife returning to her father's band. The economic unit created by a marriage was so important that no one stayed single for long.

Children were desired, although some infanticide was practiced if conditions were difficult. The infant was kept on a cradleboard and was named when it became apparent that the child would survive. At first menses, females were isolated in a menstrual hut located away from the group for a duration of one to four weeks, during which time they observed restrictions in behavior and food. At this time girls were instructed on the various aspects of womanhood, including marriage and childbirth. After first menses, females were eligible for marriage. During subsequent menstrual cycles, women stayed in the menstrual hut for a few days or walked behind the group when traveling. Males had few formal rites of passage.

The division of labor was flexible but was typically based on sex. Men did most of the hunting, although women and children trapped small game when they could. Women and children also helped in the communal drives for pronghorn, hares, and insects. Women gathered and processed most of the plant foods, but men helped with the pinyon harvest. Though headmen were males, women did have a voice in society and could hold high status as a shaman. A discussion of women's roles among the Southern Paiute is provided by Knack (1995).

Economics

Great Basin peoples were hunters and gatherers, and like most hunter-gatherer groups, they procured most of their food by gathering plants. Animals were very important, but the principal defining resource of the Great Basin was pinyon nuts. The Southern Paiute occasionally practiced agriculture, and it is possible that the Owens Valley Paiute did as well. A detailed treatment of Great Basin subsistence systems is presented by C. Fowler (1986; also see Steward 1938; and Wheat 1967).

Pinyon trees, the relatively small pines that grow in much of the Great Basin, produce pine cones containing nuts (technically seeds) that are highly nutritious. Most groups in the Great Basin relied heavily on pinyon nuts for subsistence, although pinyon trees were less common in the northern and southern ends of the region. Not every pinyon grove produced large numbers of cones and nuts, so people had to travel from grove to grove to harvest the pine nuts when they were ready in the early fall. As cones take two years to mature, their progress was monitored; thus, people knew where the good pinyon crops would be located during any given year. Each fall, several groups would coalesce at a single locality to gather pinyon nuts and to socialize.

A Southern Paiute woman grinding seeds on a stone metate in the doorway of a wickiup, 1872. (John K. Hillers/CORBIS)

Pinyon nuts were gathered using two methods, brown coning and green coning. The nuts were often harvested after the cones had turned brown, had opened to expose the nuts, and were about to fall (or had already fallen) onto the ground. People would walk about, gather the cones into large baskets, then sit and shake the nuts out of the cones. The problem with this approach, however, was that birds and rodents also had access to the nuts, reducing the number that the people could gather. If it appeared that the pinyon harvest might be small, people would sometimes gather the green, unopened cones before the animals could get to the nuts. The people would climb into the trees and knock the sap-covered cones off with long, hooked sticks, gather the cones, and then place them into a fire so that the cones would open and the nuts could be removed. In the process, everyone became covered with pine sap, but a larger quantity of nuts could be obtained.

Regardless of the method, women and children did much of the work, although men occasionally helped. The nuts had to be shelled and could be eaten raw but were usually cooked or ground into flour for use in making bread or gruel. Unshelled pinyon nuts could be easily stored for several years.

Many hundreds of other plants served as food resources (see C. Fowler 1986: Table 1). All Great Basin groups harvested the seeds of various grasses, based on what was available in different regions. In the western Great Basin, some groups utilized acorns, and marsh plants were also favored. Roots, such as camas (see Chapter 5 for a more detailed discussion of camas), formed major resources north of the range of pinyon. In the Mojave Desert, agave and mesquite beans were critical foodstuffs. Mesquite beans, which grow on mesquite trees and are similar to green beans, were gathered in the spring, were eaten raw or cooked, or were ground into flour for later use. Mesquite beans could be stored for several years.

Animals formed a major aspect of Great Basin economies. Deer, mountain sheep, and pronghorn were the most popular large mammals, although an occasional bison or elk would be taken. Deer and mountain sheep were usually hunted individually year-round, although some large traps were built to capture small herds. Pronghorn were hunted communally, usually in the fall and winter; the whole group of people would drive fairly large numbers of animals into carefully constructed traps, under the direction of an antelope shaman who charmed the animals into the trap. Once captured, the animals could be killed with arrows at any time the people desired. Pronghorn could be hunted once or twice a year, depending on the population of the herds. A group might hunt pronghorn in a particular location one year and in another the following year, allowing the population to recover between hunts. It was once believed that pronghorn were hunted only every twelve or thirteen years (see Steward 1938:34–36), but it is now reasonably clear that pronghorn could be hunted every year (see Arkush 1995).

Rabbits and hares were also essential resources in most Great Basin economies. Individuals used traps or snares to hunt cottontail rabbits. Hares (or jackrabbits) were usually hunted communally; large numbers were driven into traps and clubbed to death. Hares provided a great deal of meat, and their skins were used for a variety of purposes. Peoples of the southern Great Basin hunted several large reptiles, including the desert tortoise and the chuckwalla.

Insects formed an important, and highly nutritious, food source for Great Basin groups (see Sutton 1988); crickets, grasshoppers, shore flies, caterpillars, and ants were the most commonly exploited. Like other animals, insects appear to have been purposely hunted or gathered, and some were even taken in large communal drives. Some were eaten fresh while others were parched, roasted, dried, ground into flour for bread or soup, or mashed and mixed with other foodstuffs.

In the western and eastern edges of the Great Basin, where marshes were common, waterfowl were heavily utilized. Large numbers of geese and ducks of many species congregated in the marshes. People used decoys made of reed and covered with the skin of a duck or goose to lure the waterfowl to certain spots in the marsh, where they were shot with arrows, grabbed from beneath and drowned, or captured in nets.

In the river and lake systems along the western and eastern edges of the Great Basin, a number of fish species were available, including trout, which was the most popular. Two large fish, the Lahontan cutthroat trout and the cui-ui sucker (both of which can reach up to two feet in length), live in the river and lake systems in west-central Nevada and were heavily exploited by the Northern Paiute in that region. Northern groups favored the salmon of the Snake River, and southern groups made use of many species in the Colorado River.

Material Culture and Technology

Housing varied across the Great Basin, depending on the season and how long people stayed in one place. In the summer, most housing consisted of windbreaks and shades, although some groups constructed wickiups, which are lightly built, dome-shaped structures made from brush. In the winter, some groups built more substantial and sturdy wickiups. Others lived in villages where they maintained large semisubterranean houses. In some places people lived in caves and rock shelters. Most communities also had sweathouses and menstrual huts.

People usually wore little or no clothing. Children almost always wore no clothing, men would wear loincloths or nothing at all, and women dressed in skin aprons that covered both their front and back. In the winter everyone wore woven rabbitskin blankets. Some people wore moccasins of skin or sandals made from yucca fiber. Clothing was sometimes decorated with paint, beads, and ornaments of bone and shell, the latter obtained in trade from California. Some people pierced their ears and others had tattoos. Almost all travel was by foot, but tule rafts were used in marsh areas. Horses were adopted by some groups late in time.

Technology in the Great Basin was based primarily on the use of fiber and wood. Stone was used for grinding implements, projectile points, and a few other tools. Great Basin groups relied very heavily on basketry (see Fowler and Dawson 1986); pottery was rarely used. Baskets were made from a variety of materials and took many forms, including water bottles covered with plant pitch or insect resin to make them watertight, storage containers, trays, traps, bowls, and hats (see Fulkerson 1995). Tule was also used to manufacture many items, including matting, houses, rafts, basketry, decoys, clothing, and cordage (see Wheat 1967; Fowler 1990).

The primary weapons were the bow and arrow and the thrusting spear. Bow staves were made from juniper. People would find a suitable juniper tree and carefully prune and manage the tree so that the trunk grew tall with straight-grained wood. A bow stave blank would then be cut into the trunk and allowed to dry on the tree for a year or so to prevent warping or cracking before being removed. Once the stave was removed, the wound on the tree would eventually heal as another layer of straight-grained wood was regenerated. Additional staves from the same tree could be harvested every few decades. These trees were important resources, were carefully monitored and tended, and were held as family property for many generations. A complete discussion of this practice is found in Wilke (1988).

Religion

Religious concepts in the Great Basin generally focused on subsistence (see Hultkrantz 1986) and involved relatively few ceremonies. Religious activity was mostly individual, and individual power was gained through a spirit-helper that usually appeared during a dream or, less frequently, a vision quest. Most groups believed in a supreme being, called Our Father, but it is possible that this concept arose after contact. Various other supernatural beings were associated with the sky, such as the Sun, Thunder, and Eagle. Spirits existed in many animals and places that were often considered sacred, such as springs, lakes, and mountains. People frequently sought the help and guidance of these spirits, particularly those in the guise of animals.

One of the few major ceremonies was the Round Dance, a world renewal ceremony that took place at the time of major economic events such as the pinyon harvest. At a Round Dance people formed a circle, sang songs, chanted, and danced. As well as being ceremonial in nature, Round Dances were also major social events. The Ute performed the Bear Dance, a ten-day ceremony designed to gain the goodwill of bears, as the dance was thought to influence hunting success and sexual prowess.

Great Basin groups were involved in a number of religious movements, including the Ghost Dance in 1869 and 1889 (see Sidelight). Both episodes of the Ghost Dance in the Great Basin were intended to revitalize native culture. Some Great Basin groups adopted the Sun Dance in the late nineteenth century in an effort to ameliorate poor conditions on the reservations, and the dance is still prac-

Sidelight

THE GHOST DANCE RELIGION

After several epidemics in the late 1860s, a Northern Paiute man named Wodziwob (called Fish Lake Joe by the whites) began to have visions that the dead would be returned to the Northern Paiute. In these visions, special dances and songs were revealed to Wodziwob. In 1869 Wodziwob began to preach that if the Northern Paiute performed these dances and songs during their annual Round Dance (a world renewal ceremony), the dead, along with depleted game, would be restored. Neighboring groups in Nevada, California, and Oregon, suffering terribly at the hands of the whites, eagerly adopted the ceremony in 1870, hoping to improve their situation. However, the dance did not work and conditions actually worsened. Thus, the 1869 Ghost Dance did not last long or spread very far. Wodziwob later argued that he had been fooled by evil spirits.

In the late 1880s, a second Northern Paiute prophet emerged to lead another Ghost Dance. This man, named Wovoka (called Jack Wilson by

the whites), had seen the 1869 version of the Ghost Dance as a boy. Wovoka had become a shaman, like his father before him. He became a ceremonial leader in 1888. In 1889, he became ill and had a vision during which supernatural messengers told him that Northern Paiute and other Indian cultures were valuable, and that they should live in peace and harmony with each other and the whites, should work hard, and should stop fighting. If they did, the vision predicted, they would be reunited with the dead. Because of Wovoka's reputation as a shaman and spiritual leader, many people believed his vision and followed his directions for the performance of a new Ghost Dance ceremony. Further, Wovoka's vision had taken place during a total eclipse of the sun, an occurrence that increased his power in the eyes of many. Wovoka traveled from place to place preaching his message, much of which paralleled Christianity, and a great many people began to participate in the ceremony.

Word of the new prophet spread rapidly, and many California and Great Basin groups took up ticed on some reservations today. In the early twentieth century, the Peyote religion was adopted by a relatively small number of Great Basin Indians (see Stewart 1986, 1987). Peyote, a small cactus with hallucinogenic properties (the leaf pad is chewed), is used both to symbolize and communicate with the supernatural. The Native American Church (see Chapter 13) is a popular religious organization in the Great Basin, as well as in other areas. In the Native American Church, ceremonies consist primarily of prayer assisted by the ingestion of peyote.

Shamans possessed considerable supernatural powers and could cure illness and/or control animals or the weather. Most shamans were males, but female shamans were not unusual. Shamans treated the sick by means of the sucking cure and the use of pharmacology. A shaman might also assist in hunting. For example, an "antelope shaman" led communal pronghorn hunts, charmed the pronghorn, captured their souls, and lured them into the traps.

The death of an individual was often attributed to evil shamans or other forces. Ghosts were feared, and burial rituals were centered on ensuring that ghosts did not

the new religion in 1890. At the same time, Plains groups, desperate from their recent military defeats and the extermination of the bison, became interested in the dance. Many sent delegations to investigate Wovoka, whereupon they enthusiastically returned to their tribes to spread word of the Ghost Dance, although not all Plains groups adopted it. By the time the religion had reached the Plains in the latter part of 1890, it had become exaggerated and militarized to the point that the message was one of restoration to a "prewhite" condition through the death of the whites, return of the bison, and resurrection of the dead. In addition, rumor had it that certain shirts, called Ghost Shirts, had the power to stop bullets. None of this was ever preached by Wovoka; the story simply became enhanced as it was passed along.

The federal government feared the Ghost Dance, not because of concern that the whites might be eliminated, but because the already desperate Indians might be induced to resume hostilities. After all, the Indians reasoned, if Ghost Shirts did repel bullets, they might regain some

military advantage and it might be worth fighting again. Calls for armed resistance increased, and the Indians became very restless. The government arrested important Indian leaders, murdered Sitting Bull, banned the Ghost Dance, and generally increased the already oppressive control of the Indians (see Chapter 10). These actions forced the Ghost Dance "underground," where it continued to be practiced for years. Eventually, the Plains groups understood the true message of Wovoka, which was to live a good life.

Wovoka continued preaching the Ghost Dance until his death in 1932. Others continued the practice, and it still survives among some groups. The Ghost Dance is a classic example of a "revitalization" movement. Some such efforts (e.g., the 1870 version of the Ghost Dance) failed, while others, such as the Longhouse Religion of the Iroquois (see Chapter 11), were successful. Additional information on the Ghost Dance can be found in Du Bois (1939), Stewart (1980), Jorgensen (1986:660–662), and Kehoe (1989).

remain to molest the living. After death, the soul of the deceased would travel along the Milky Way or through an underground passage to the land of the dead, usually located somewhere to the south. Treatment of the deceased varied by group; some employed burial, some cremation, while others placed the deceased in rock crevices.

Great Basin Peoples Today

In 1980, there were some 30,000 Great Basin Indians (Leland 1986:608) and that number continues to increase. Many live on one of the forty-five reservations that now exist (see Clemmer and Stewart 1986), but many more live elsewhere. Many Great Basin groups established formal tribal governments after the passage of the Indian Reorganization Act in 1934 (see Rusco and Rusco 1986:565–571). The government subsequently provided some assistance in improving health care, protecting land from encroachment, and establishing viable economies (see Knack 1986), although the limited land base hindered the development of livestock enterprises. Nevertheless, most Great Basin Indians remained undereducated and unskilled and relied on wage labor and government benefits. Then, in the 1950s, federal recognition of a number of groups was terminated by the government and assistance to those groups ceased, which exacerbated an already bleak situation.

After 1964, the economic situation began to improve. The federal government, through the Bureau of Indian Affairs, began to provide funds for housing, education, roads, community development, vocational training, and employment, and Great Basin Indians saw an increase in their standard of living and life expectancy. However, despite the improvement, the economic situation for most Great Basin people remained substandard compared to that of the people surrounding them (see Knack 1986). Problems with alcohol, drugs, and domestic violence developed and persist to this day. Recently, casinos have been opened on several reservations, resulting in jobs and income for those tribes.

Many important matters remain unresolved for Great Basin peoples (see Johnson 1986), especially issues of land rights and the honoring of treaties and agreements. A number of Great Basin groups have filed claims seeking the return of land and/or compensation for land, and the Indians have won many cases (see Clemmer and Stewart 1986: Tables 4 and 5). Hunting and water rights persist as problems; for example, the Northern Paiute have been fighting to retain sufficient water flow from the Truckee River into Pyramid Lake to maintain their traditional fishery, but the problem remains unresolved.

Grazing is another problem. The government charges the Indians a fee to graze livestock on lands the Indians claim to own, a practice that has resulted in lawsuits. Further, the government has decided that much of the Great Basin is suitable only for grazing; the pinyon-juniper forest has been stripped from large areas and replaced with grasses. The forests are uprooted by a process called chaining, whereby a ship's anchor chain is strung between two large bulldozers and driven across the landscape, ripping up all the trees. Large tracts of forest in the Great Basin have been destroyed in this manner.

Other concerns include jurisdiction of Indian lands, economic development, education, and tribal leadership. In addition, native people strive to have their voices heard and their viewpoints considered in the context of their cultures (see Alley 1986).

Learn More about Contemporary Great Basin Peoples

The discussion above gives only a very brief description of Great Basin people today. What else can you discover? Go to the library and look on the Internet to learn more about Great Basin groups today. Topics you can explore include the following:

1. Chose a particular group or two, and investigate how they have adjusted to European conquest. Look at their tribal land base (e.g., whether they have a reservation), their tribal economy, and the general well-being of the tribal members.
2. What is the status of land rights and treaties with Great Basin groups? How well is the federal government carrying out its responsibilities?
3. What traditional practices have been retained? What are the roles of traditional religion, economics, and politics in Great Basin groups today?
4. What is the role of gaming in contemporary tribal economies in the Great Basin?

The Owens Valley Paiute: A Great Basin Case Study

The Native American group that inhabited the Owens River Valley along the eastern side of the Sierra Nevada is called the Owens Valley Paiute (Fig. 7.2) and sometimes the Eastern Mono. The Owens Valley Paiute differ from other Great Basin groups in that they had a more complex political and social organization and fixed territories, and they practiced irrigation. The Owens Valley Paiute occupied the smallest territory of any Great Basin group but probably had the greatest density of people per square mile in the Great Basin (Thomas 1983:32), with a population of about 2,000 people just prior to contact (Liljeblad and Fowler 1986:415). This case study of the Owens Valley Paiute describes them as they were in about 1850.

The first substantial information on the Owens Valley Paiute was obtained relatively late as Euroamericans entered the region beginning in the late 1850s and early 1860s (see Chalfant 1933; Wilke and Lawton 1976). Major studies of the Owens Valley Paiute were conducted by Julian Steward (1933, 1938) and Harold E. Driver (1937). In addition, Sven Liljeblad, Catherine S. Fowler, and Nancy P. Walter have conducted fieldwork among the Owens Valley Paiute since the 1950s. The most recent syntheses on the Owens Valley Paiute are provided by Busby et al. (1979:161–180) and Liljeblad and Fowler (1986). The following discussion is based on these sources.

The Natural Environment

The Owens Valley is long (approximately eighty miles) and narrow (between four and ten miles), running north and south between the Sierra Nevada on the west and the White and Inyo Mountains on the east. The valley floor is at an elevation of about 4,000 feet, while the mountains on either side reach heights of over 14,000 feet, including Mt. Whitney, the highest point in the continental United States. The Owens Valley receives relatively little rainfall but is well watered by the streams that originate in the Sierra Nevada on the western side of the valley. The winters are cold and the summers are warm to hot.

Three major and distinct environmental zones distinguish the Owens Valley (Thomas 1983:32). First, along the western side of the valley lie the well-watered slopes of the Sierra Nevada, with forests of assorted pines and many streams

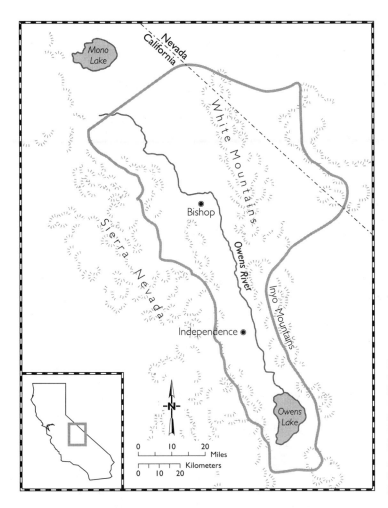

FIGURE 7.2 Location and territory of the Owens Valley Paiute in the western Great Basin
Adapted from S. Liljeblad and C. S. Fowler, "Owens Valley Paiute" in *Handbook of North American Indians, Vol. 11, Great Basin,* W. L. d'Azevedo, ed., Fig. 1; copyright © 1986 by the Smithsonian Institution. Reprinted by permission of the publisher.

flowing from the mountains to the valley floor. Second, the Owens River flows south through the valley floor, fed by the myriad streams from the Sierra Nevada. The Owens River widens at a number of spots, where marshes are formed, and terminates in Owens Lake, located at the southern end of the valley. Finally, the relatively arid White and Inyo Mountains form the eastern edge of the valley and contain more typical Great Basin vegetation, including large tracts of pinyon and juniper. These three zones provide a considerable diversity of plant and animal habitats in close proximity, so that people had easy access to all of them.

Many animals inhabit the Owens Valley and surrounding mountains. They include deer, sheep, some pronghorn antelope, large numbers of rabbits, and a variety of rodents. Several species of fish are present, including the Owens Valley pupfish, native suckers, and minnows. A number of economically important insects are also available in the region.

Language

The Owens Valley Paiute speak dialects of the Mono language. Mono is one of the two languages in the western branch of the Numic language family, Northern Paiute being the other (more northern) branch. Dialect diversity within the Mono language suggests that it has existed for some time, in contrast to Northern Paiute, which is thought to have recently diverged from Mono as its speakers moved to the north (the Numic Expansion; see Madsen and Rhode 1994). The travels of the Owens Valley Paiute to the west for trade resulted in considerable bilingualism among them.

A Brief History

The Owens Valley Paiute were probably not contacted by Europeans until the mid–nineteenth century, although it is possible that the Spanish visited the region prior to that time. In 1855, an expedition led by A. W. von Schmidt entered the area to plot the border between California and Nevada. In 1859, a U.S. military expedition traveled to the valley to look for horse and cattle thieves and to retrieve livestock for ranchers in California (see Wilke and Lawton 1976). The Owens Valley Paiute were found to be guiltless, and the expedition leaders recommended that a large reservation be established in the valley to protect the Indians. This idea was rejected by the government in 1864.

Cattle ranchers began settling in the Owens Valley in 1861, claiming and fencing off the grasslands in the valley bottom. As the Euroamerican population increased, skirmishes escalated over ownership of the irrigated lands, the use of pinyon for firewood, and the loss of game, and the Indians began to steal cattle to replace the game lost to the ranches. In 1862, the army established Camp Independence to quash the Indian resistance. As Euroamerican populations continued to increase, the Owens Valley Paiute became more desperate and several major battles ensued. As a result, the army instituted a scorched-earth policy against the Indians (see Chalfant 1933:146–147) and the Indians were forced to surrender. About 900 Indians were forced to walk several hundred miles to the San Sebastian Reservation north of Los Angeles, and many died along the way. A number of the Owens Valley Paiute eventually returned home, but their land was gone and their resource base had been destroyed. Most settled in camps, towns, or ranches, where they worked as laborers. The government opened an Indian school in 1897, and several very small reservations were established in the valley between 1900 and 1915.

By 1905 Los Angeles had outgrown its water resources and began to look toward the Owens Valley for water. In 1913, Los Angeles started purchasing water rights to irrigated land in the Owens Valley, and by the 1920s the Indians had become openly hostile to the plan. By 1933 the city of Los Angeles owned the vast majority of land and water in the valley, even forcing many of the ranchers to leave. A large aquaduct was built to transport the water to Los Angeles, causing the valley to dry up and Owens Lake to turn into a desert playa. As a result, the Indians were unable to hunt, gather, farm, or even find jobs.

In 1937, an agreement was reached in which several reservations were enlarged, holdings were consolidated, and some water was provided. By the 1940s the federal government began to assist the reservations with housing and irrigation projects.

Cosmology

A number of versions of origin stories were recorded by Steward (1936) among the Owens Valley Paiute. In one version, Coyote (a common hero in oral tradition in western North America) was lured to an island by an attractive girl, and he, being lustful, wanted to have sexual intercourse with her. She lived with her mother and invited Coyote to have sex with her; however, her plan was to kill him. After surviving several attempts on his life, Coyote successfully impregnated the girl and she had many children. The girl instructed Coyote to put all of the children into a basketry jug and told him not to open the jug until he returned home. Nevertheless, Coyote, being curious and indifferent to authority, opened it before he arrived home. When he opened the jug, most of the children escaped and scattered across the landscape, becoming all of the other people on earth. Only one child was left in the jug when Coyote got home, and that child became the Owens Valley Paiute.

Politics and External Relations

The Owens Valley Paiute were organized into seven bands, sometimes called districts, and have been compared to tribelet organizations in California (see Liljeblad and Fowler 1986:414). Bands owned and controlled specific areas for collecting pinyon nuts and seeds, as well as irrigated land bordering one or more of the streams along the western side of the valley. Much of the valley bottom and mountain slopes on the eastern side were community territory.

About thirty small, permanent villages were generally located along the western side of the valley, next to streams. Village populations ranged from about twenty to a hundred people. These settlements were occupied every year by the same families, who cooperated in social, ceremonial, religious, and recreational activities. Some people would live in the village all year long, but most would travel to resource localities between spring and fall, returning to the village in the winter. Each family had a house and each village had a community sweathouse.

Every band had a chief or headman, but that person had limited power and duties and was primarily in charge of irrigation, movement to pinyon-collecting areas, communal hunts, ceremonies, dances, festivals, and the assembly lodge. The chief also could order the execution of a shaman accused of witchcraft. The position of chief was hereditary, usually passed from father to son, but others could become chief by earning the position. The chief had no formal assistants but called upon other people to help him when needed.

The Owens Valley Paiute were not involved in any pattern of warfare with their neighbors. Instead, interaction with groups to the west were highly developed, and the Owens Valley Paiute regularly traded with the Yokuts, Miwok, and Tubatulabal in California. A complex pattern of intermarriage, social relations, and bilateral diffusion of cultural traits developed. To the east, the Panamint Shoshone (the far southern Western Shoshone) came to the Owens Valley to trade salt that they had collected from dry lake basins to the east.

Social Organization

The primary social unit among the Owens Valley Paiute was the nuclear family, which formed a self-sufficient domestic and economic unit. Several unrelated families formed a village unit, and a number of villages formed a band, the largest permanent social unit among the Owens Valley Paiute. Families always shared the resources they collected with their relatives and sometimes with other unrelated families in the village. In addition, like other Great Basin groups, Owens Valley Paiute bands cooperated in communal hunting, some rituals, and certain festive occasions. The kinship system was generally bilateral, and no formal lineage was recognized beyond children, parents, and grandparents. Kin groups did not own land or collecting localities.

The division of labor was based on sex and age. Men did most of the hunting, although everyone participated in communal hunts. Men also conducted most of the trading with neighboring groups and were often gone for many months at a time. Women did the gathering and manufactured many of the items used by the group. Children did not have to assume adult responsibilities until after puberty. Berdaches were common among the Owens Valley Paiute.

Life Cycle

A pregnant woman did not observe food restrictions or other taboos. When it was time to give birth, a woman was placed in a warm pit bed and assisted by a midwife. The baby was bathed and held directly by the mother for the first seven days, after which the infant was kept in a cradle. Children were nursed until about two years of age. A woman would have between eight and ten children, but most died in infancy. Children were generally raised by their mother and grandmother and were taught to be respectful, humble, and clean. Punishment was rarely necessary.

Puberty ceremonies were conducted for children of both sexes. Upon her first menses, a girl was taken by her parents to be bathed in cold water and then steamed with hot water for three days. She then had to carry wood and water baskets. At the end of five days, she bathed again and the ritual ended. An abbreviated version of this ritual was conducted at each subsequent menses. At the age of about fourteen, a boy participated in a hunting ritual that lasted for several days, during which he was awakened early and bathed, ran several miles, and received instructions on nature and animals. He then killed a deer, and with the aid of his grandfather he attempted to obtain supernatural power for hunting. Finally, he was allowed to smoke tobacco for the first time and could sleep in the sweathouse as a man.

Marriage was not allowed between persons related closer than third cousin, making many communities exogamous. Marriage was often designed to unite two families and was sometimes arranged at birth. The ideal marriage arrangement was for the sister of the groom to marry the brother of the bride at the same time, a practice called sister exchange. The marriage ceremony itself was brief and uncomplicated. After marriage, matrilocal residence was typical. Divorce and remarriage were simple procedures and were relatively common. Due to their frequent passage across the Sierra Nevada, men often intermarried with California groups.

When people died, they were buried in simple graves during a funeral ceremony. Singers were hired to perform at the funeral and mourners danced to the songs. The property of the deceased, including his or her house, was burned after the burial. Additional possessions of the deceased were burned at the annual mourning ceremony.

Economics

While the Owens Valley Paiute were strictly hunter-gatherers, they seem to have practiced flood irrigation of some wild plants to increase yields—what some might call incipient agriculture. The irrigation systems were extensive and elaborate and it seems that members of different bands cooperated in their construction (see Lawton et al. 1976; Liljeblad and Fowler 1986:429–430). Irrigated plants included tobacco and grasses that produced seed crops.

Most food was obtained by gathering, and the seeds of the pinyon pine were the most popular. Pinyon nuts were collected from the White and Inyo Mountains on the eastern side of the valley (see description of pinyon harvests, on page 161). Unlike most Great Basin groups, the Owens Valley Paiute also gathered and ate acorns, which they actually preferred to pine nuts when available. Acorn meat was ground in mortars, leached with water to remove the bitter tannic acid, and then boiled and eaten as mush or made into cakes. Small seeds were very important, and a large variety were collected. Numerous varieties of bulbs were also collected from the low-lying areas of the valley floor. Some of these areas were purposely flooded to encourage the growth of the bulb-producing plants, which were then gathered communally.

Hunting was important but was practiced almost casually; some men liked to hunt, while others did not. Individuals hunted deer, but bands would organize communal hunts for deer and other animals, including sheep, pronghorn antelope (rarely), and rabbits, the latter being the most commonly consumed animal. Hunters used snares to capture rabbits and rodents; they used bows and arrows to hunt rabbits as well as certain birds, including waterfowl. Communal hunting of waterfowl, practiced in other areas of the Great Basin, was not done in the Owens Valley.

The fish in the Owens River system were relatively small and formed only a minor part of the diet. Some fish were speared, but most, particularly the small Owens Valley pupfish, were collected by damming and poisoning a stream. The stunned fish would float to the surface, where they were scooped into a basket. They were then dried for later consumption.

In addition to the vertebrate animals, the Owens Valley Paiute made use of a number of insects. Of prime importance were the caterpillars of the Pandora moth that live in yellow pine trees (see Fowler and Walter 1985). When the caterpillars, called *piagi*, are ready to pupate in midsummer, they descend the tree trunks to burrow into the soil. Whole families of Indians would move to the yellow pine forest to harvest piagi. Trenches would be excavated around the trees to capture the caterpillars as they came to the ground. The caterpillars were then collected from the trench, eviscerated, immediately cooked or sun dried, then stored in baskets. It was not uncommon for a family to gather a ton or more of piagi, which was consumed as well as traded to other groups.

Another major insect food was the brine flies that inhabited Owens Lake. The flies lay their eggs in the water, which then develop into larvae and pupae. These materials, mixed with algae, wash up onto the shore of the lake and dry out. The Owens Valley Paiute gathered the resulting product, called *kutsavi*, in huge quantities and stored it for winter.

Material Culture and Technology

The Owens Valley Paiute used a number of different structures, depending on when, where, and for how long they were needed. As many as seven distinct types of dwellings may have been built, the most substantial of which were the semisubterranean communal houses at the permanent villages. These log structures were covered with soil and were constructed, owned, and maintained by the chief. They were used for a variety of purposes, including residences for old and single men and as gathering places to gossip and tell stories; however, they were not used for ritual or ceremonial activities.

Permanent family homes were smaller semisubterranean structures measuring up to twenty feet across. Built with a log frame and covered with soil, they had an entrance in the top that also served as a smokehole. Temporary housing was less substantial and consisted of cone-shaped houses built of tule, wood, or brush, lean-tos built against a tree in the forest, or simple shades used in the summer. Open dance grounds were made for the Round Dance, the mourning ceremony, and other activities.

The Owens Valley Paiute wore relatively little clothing, and children wore nothing most of the time. Women dressed in knee-length skirts and men wore shirts, all made from deerskin. Individuals made their own clothes. In cold weather everyone donned blankets woven from rabbit skins. Sometimes men wore moccasins and women wore sandals and socks woven of sagebrush and bark, especially for protection against snow. No tattooing was practiced, but people painted their faces for ceremonies.

The Owens Valley Paiute made an extensive array of baskets but used only a small amount of pottery. Baskets included large, coarsely woven burden baskets, finely woven seed baskets, seed beaters and winnowing trays, parching trays, storage baskets, and water bottles. The water bottles, which were small, canteenlike baskets, were waterproofed with pine pitch or insect resin. One unusual basket, made only by the Owens Valley Paiute and a few other groups, was a finely made, narrow-necked, flat-shouldered "treasure basket" sometimes decorated with feathers and used to carry shell money.

Pottery was made by a few women who sold or traded it for shell money, baskets, or food. The pottery forms mimicked the shapes of baskets. Many pottery vessels had pointed bottoms and may have been stuck in the ground and ringed with fire for boiling food, replacing the technique of boiling in baskets by adding hot stones to the food.

Stone was used to make a variety of tools, including manos, metates, mortars, and pestles for grinding seeds, acorns, and pine nuts. These large, heavy tools were not carried from place to place, but were left cached at the various living sites. Stone was also used to manufacture cutting tools and arrow points, although some arrows had wooden points. Other tools were manufactured from wood, such as bows made from juniper. Women used digging sticks made of mahogany to dig roots and bulbs. Digging sticks often had a notch or attachment that allowed workers to apply pressure from the foot, making the task much easier.

Religion and Medicine

The Owens Valley Paiute believed in various spirits and supernatural powers. Wolf was viewed as a good spirit, while Coyote was usually seen as harmful, mostly through carelessness and stupidity. Young people listened to stories about Coyote and learned not to repeat the mistakes Coyote made. Men would often seek supernatural assistance in hunting.

Bands or large villages held certain ceremonies, called fandangos after contact, such the Round Dance, conducted each fall. This celebration included considerable singing, dancing, gambling, and other festivities. The pine nut festival was also held in the fall and lasted six days. Other group ceremonies preceded communal activities such as hunts or irrigation projects. The annual mourning ceremony, also known as the Cry, held for those who had died during the previous year, was attended by people from all of the Owens Valley Paiute bands. The one-year mourning period observed by the spouse of the deceased was publicly ended at this ceremony, during which the faces of the mourners were washed for the first time since the death.

The Owens Valley Paiute had two types of shamans, both of which could be either male or female. Individuals became shamans on their own; it was not an inherited profession. The first type of shaman was an "herb doctor," who cured physical conditions such as broken bones and wounds and assisted during childbirth. These skills were obtained through instruction from other shamans and practice.

The second type of shaman was the "spirit doctor," a person who had gained supernatural power through dreaming. A major function of the spirit doctor was to cure illness through supernatural means. Interestingly, spirit doctors did not lead communal hunts as they did in the rest of the Great Basin. Spirit doctors could use their power for evil purposes, but faced severe penalty, even execution, if they were believed to be practicing witchcraft.

Art, Expression, and Recreation

The Owens Valley Paiute used a variety of musical instruments, including flutes, rattles, and bullroarers, although drums were not used. Songs were sung (often by professional singers) at many events, including dances, funerals, and mourning ceremonies. Singing and chanting were an important part of some shamanistic activities as well.

The Owens Valley Paiute played many games, including the hand game, dice, and hoop-and-pole. Athletic events, such as wrestling and racing, were also popular. People often gambled on the outcome of these games.

The Owens Valley Paiute Today

The diversion of water from the Owens Valley to Los Angeles radically changed the valley and its inhabitants, and many people were forced to move to Los Angeles and other California locations to seek employment. In 2002, the Indian population of the Owens Valley was more than 2,000, including many Northern Paiutes and Shoshones.

Beginning in the 1970s, life on the reservations began to improve. There are four reservations in the valley, each with a separate elected council. Each is also affiliated with a larger organization, the Owens Valley Paiute-Shoshone Band of Indians, which administers grants and programs for the valley as a whole. Several of the reservations have opened casinos.

The reservations are striving to maintain their language and culture, and they sponsor a variety of events, including exhibits, dances, and rodeos. An annual pow-wow is held by the Bishop Reservation, where there is now a museum and cultural center. The Owens Valley Paiute continue to gather pine nuts and caterpillars and, at the request of the Indians, the U.S. Forest Service no longer sprays the pine forest to halt moth infestation.

―――///―――

8 Native Peoples of California

///

People have always been attracted to California. The climate is generally mild; food and water abound. This view, widely held by Americans today, was also held by the Indians of California. People have moved into the region for many millennia, resulting in an intricate mosaic of native cultures and a very complex and diverse culture area. California is also the most populous region in North America, now as well as in the past.

At the time of initial European contact (ca. 1542), at least 300,000 Indians were living in California (Cook 1971, 1976, 1978), and perhaps as many as 700,000 or more (Stannard 1992:23–24; Thornton 2000:29). Many of the cultures were large and complex, others less so. All California Indians were hunters and gatherers, although a few groups in southeastern California adopted small-scale agriculture very late in time. Natural resources were abundant and the Indians had developed efficient methods for obtaining them. An enormous diversity of languages flourished there (one of the most diverse regions on earth), divided into twenty-three language families with about one hundred languages and innumerable dialects (Kroeber 1925; Shipley 1978; Hinton 1994). At least sixty different cultures are recognized by anthropologists (see Heizer 1978a), although perhaps twice that many could be defined, depending on how groups are classified.

Native culture in California has several distinct characteristics. Perhaps the most recognized is the widespread use of acorns as a staple food. Second, many California groups had dense and sedentary populations, a relatively uncommon situation among hunter-gatherers (many people think of hunter-gatherers as consisting largely of small, mobile groups). Third, California Indians typically used shell beads as money in complex market and barter economies. Lastly, California is known for the quality of its basketry, some of which is the finest in the world (for a good summary see Bibby 1996).

Geography and Environment

The California culture area does not share the physical boundaries of the modern political state of California (Fig. 8.1). The northern portion of the Mexican state of Baja California (*baja* means "lower") is part of the California culture area, and so many researchers refer to the U.S. state of California as Alta (or upper) California. The California culture area (henceforth called California) encompasses four geographic regions: (1) the North Coast Range, (2) the Sierra Nevada and Cascade Mountains, (3) the Central Valley, which includes the Sacramento and San Joaquin Valleys, and (4) southern California, encompassing the Channel Islands and northern Baja California (in modern Mexico). The Owens Valley and the eastern portion of the Mojave Desert fall within the Great Basin (see Chapter 7), while the Colorado River and the eastern Colorado Desert are included in the Southwest (see Chapter 9).

The climate of most of California can be classified as Mediterranean, meaning it has mild summers and winters. Annual rainfall varies from about fifteen inches in the south to forty inches in the north and perhaps as much as seventy inches in the mountains. Temperatures vary by elevation, but consistently cold temperatures are uncommon except in the mountains.

A Basic Prehistory of California

People first occupied the Central Valley of California at least 12,000 years ago and have lived there continuously ever since. Though many have claimed that humans occupied California in earlier times, no such claim has survived serious scientific scrutiny. Comprehensive treatments of California archaeology are provided by Chartkoff and Chartkoff (1984) and Moratto (1984).

The Paleoindian Period (ca. 12,000 B.P. to 10,000 B.P.)

The earliest people of California were Paleoindians (Clovis people; see Chapter 1) who arrived during the latter part of the Pleistocene (ice ages), between about 12,000 and 10,000 years ago. At this time the climate was much wetter, and lakes, rivers, and marshes were common. Clovis hunter-gatherers lived along several large lakes, apparently exploiting plants and animals along the shorelines, including large game such as mammoths, giant bison, and camels. Early cultural materials have also been found on San Miguel Island and in the San Jose area. More Clovis material (mostly spear points) is known in the deserts to the east, where large lakes also existed at that time.

The Archaic Period (ca. 10,000 B.P. to Contact)

At the beginning of the Holocene, the climate of California became warmer and drier, though with some fluctuations. Due to these climatic changes, many of the

FIGURE 8.1   Map of the California culture area, with the locations of the native groups
Adapted from *Handbook of North American Indians*, Vol. 8, *California*, R. F. Heizer, ed., p. ix; copyright © 1978 by the Smithsonian Institution. Reprinted by permission of the publisher.

large Pleistocene animals became extinct. At the same time, people appear to have adopted a more generalized hunting-and-gathering subsistence economy. Since agriculture was never significantly adopted in California, all of California's post-Pleistocene prehistory until European contact is Archaic.

Little is known about the period between about 10,000 and 3,500 years ago in the region of the North Coast Range, but people there probably practiced a general hunting-and-gathering economy. By around 2,200 years ago, salmon fishers were established on the coast and presumably were the ancestors of the ethnographic Wiyot and Yurok. Farther south along the coast, salmon were less important as a resource than sea mammals and acorns. After about 2,000 years ago, more general hunting-and-gathering cultures existed inland.

Even less is known about the prehistory of the Cascade Mountains and the Sierra Nevada. Though some evidence indicates that early peoples lived in the mountains, the major occupation of the region commenced about 3,500 years ago, probably with the beginning of acorn exploitation. Cultures became larger and increasingly complex until about 1,500 years ago, when populations began to decline, perhaps due to climatic changes. By about 500 years ago, new populations had entered the region and prospered until European contact.

In the Central Valley, very little is known about the Early Archaic, and the period between 10,000 and 6,000 years ago has largely remained unexplored. However, later times are better documented. During the Early Period (ca. 6,000 to 4,000 years ago), people were living along rivers, presumably adapted to riverine and valley resources (but apparently not acorns). The beginning of acorn use defines the Middle Period (ca. 4,000 to 2,000 years ago), although its introduction varied from place to place. During the Late Period (ca. 2,000 years ago to European contact), people intensified fishing and hunting activities, as well as acorn use. The bow and arrow were not introduced until about 1,500 years ago.

In southern California, there is evidence for human occupation from at least 10,000 years ago. It is believed that the ancestors of the Chumash had lived in the Santa Barbara area since about 9,000 years ago (see the chapter Case Study). Early on, people depended on marine shellfish and small seeds, but by about 5,000 years ago acorns seem to have become more important. Cultural complexity appears to have grown over time, perhaps as populations increased. There is good reason to believe that about 2,000 years ago, people from the Mojave Desert (in the Great Basin culture area) moved south into most of southern California, possibly replacing the prior inhabitants, and evolving into the ethnographic groups residing there today.

The Contact Period

Initial European contact in California occurred in 1542, when Juan Cabrillo explored the coast of Baja and Alta California (see Thomas 1989, Gutiérrez and Orsi 1998, and Lightfoot and Simons 1998 for information on European contact in Alta California). Sporadic visits by other European explorers followed. Beginning in 1697, Jesuit missionaries established a series of seventeen missions in Baja California (see Mathes 1989; Crosby 1994). The Spaniards expelled the Jesuits in 1767, and beginning in 1769 the Spanish, under Father Junípero Serra, established the mission system in Alta California, which eventually totaled twenty-one missions. The first was founded in San Diego in 1769 and the last at Sonoma in 1823 (see

Costello and Hornbeck 1989). The founding of the missions was prompted by fear of British and Russian expansion into California. These religious establishments also included a small military contingent. The mission system had a significant impact on California peoples (see Chapter 2).

Beginning in 1803, Russian fur traders, primarily Aleuts under Russian command, began hunting marine mammals along the northern coast of California. In 1811 the Russians established a base at Bodega Bay but moved north to Fort Ross in 1812, founding a major colony of Aleuts and Russians among the Pomo (see Farris 1989). The Russians abandoned Fort Ross in 1842.

After 1824, California became a province of the new Republic of Mexico, and the Mexican government made changes that affected California Indians, including the secularization of the missions, a move that effectively ended the mission system. In 1848, Alta California formally became part of the United States, and the gold rush began the following year. During the 1850s and 1860s, numerous Americans moved to California, and the remaining native peoples were moved onto reservations or assimilated, died of disease, or were murdered.

The Impact of European Contact

Early contact with Europeans, and later with American settlers, had a devastating impact on California Indians. Disease—primarily smallpox, measles, and malaria—spread to dense, settled populations, with horrific consequences. In fact, disease may have greatly impacted native groups long before actual contact with Europeans, with pathogens traveling far and wide as a result of routine trading activities (see Walker et al. 1989; Preston 2002). By around 1906 the original population of about 300,000 (or more) people had been reduced to about 20,000, a decline of over 90 percent (see Cook 1978; Reddy 1995: Tables 23 and 39).

The native populations of California also suffered from forced relocation to some of the missions (see Costa and Costa 1987 and Jackson and Castillo 1995 for discussions of the impact of the missions on native Californians), from military incursions by the Spaniards and Mexicans, and from loss of territory. In spite of these difficulties, some groups did resist and managed to retain their political independence (see Phillips 1993).

Though the Spanish forced California Indians to live and work at the missions, and later, the Mexicans made others work at ranchos, neither of these impacts matched the magnitude of changes to come once California became a territory of the United States, in 1848. With the advent of the gold rush, large numbers of determined settlers overwhelmed the native populations, taking their land, resources, and lives in an aggressive program of land alteration. The new settlers and miners tore up the hills looking for gold and reorganized the landscape to accommodate agriculture. Rivers were rerouted and dammed, forests were cut down, grasslands were overgrazed or plowed, and cities were built (see Castillo 1978; Hurtado 1988; Phillips 1993). Many Indians were arrested, as "vagrants" and sold as "craft apprentices," meaning slaves. Vigilantes killed entire native groups, and in some areas, a bounty was paid for Indian heads.

A Brief History of Ethnographic Research

Anthropological work among California Indians is extensive and varied, and the list of important researchers in California ethnography is long and distinguished (see Heizer 1978b for a detailed history). The earliest systematic work among California Indians was that of Stephen Powers (1877), who provided valuable descriptions of a number of groups. Just after the turn of the century, Alfred Kroeber of the University of California at Berkeley began a lifelong program of research into California Indians, and in 1925 he published his classic *Handbook of the Indians of California*. Kroeber also published hundreds of other books and articles on California Indians, and many of his students went on to conduct significant work on the same subject, though they erroneously assumed that the Indians were about to become extinct.

One early anthropologist of particular note was J. P. Harrington, who worked for the Bureau of American Ethnology (now part of the Smithsonian Institution) and conducted extensive fieldwork among Indians throughout western North America between about 1907 and 1961. Harrington was primarily a linguist but gathered information on all aspects of native culture. He published relatively little of his work, sending his notes and samples back to Washington. In the 1980s, the Smithsonian transferred all of Harrington's notes (some 700,000 pages) to microfilm, providing an invaluable resource for researchers.

Summaries of California culture include Powers (1877), Kroeber (1925), Heizer and Whipple (1971), and various papers published in special journal issues, such as *American Indian Quarterly* (Vol. 13, No. 4, 1989) and *California History* (Vol. 71, No. 3, 1992) (also see Vane and Bean 1990). The most comprehensive synthesis of California Indian culture is the California volume (Vol. 8) of the *Handbook of North American Indians* (Heizer 1978a), written mostly in the late 1960s and early 1970s but not published until 1978. Today, relatively little ethnographic work is being done in California, although there are some notable exceptions. Many Indian groups still live in California, and there remains much to be learned from and about them. Information is beginning to be published by the Indians themselves, both in newsletters (e.g., *News from Native California*) and books (e.g., Lee 1998). The summary below describes California groups as they were in the early nineteenth century.

A Broad Portrait of California Indians

A hallmark of California Indians is their great diversity of groups and languages and complexity of culture. It is therefore very difficult to make broad statements about them. The reader must remember that the basic description offered below is very general. Some sixty different California groups are now recognized (Fig. 8.1).

Political Organization

Most California groups were politically organized into tribes, with formal leaders (chiefs) and relatively large populations living in permanent or semipermanent villages. The position of chief was usually acquired through kinship affiliation, with other factors also considered. Although rare, a small number of California Indian groups were organized into bands, groups usually defined as having small populations, living in nonpermanent camps and "governed" by informal leaders.

Several groups had chiefdom organizations, which are larger and more complex than tribes. Chiefdoms consist of large, permanent populations that include craft specialists, leaders responsible for certain activities, and complex economies. The presence of chiefdoms among hunter-gatherers is one of the interesting aspects of California. A good example of a chiefdom in California is the Chumash (see Case Study).

Warfare was common in California, but usually on a small scale. Though actual battles with numerous combatants were sometimes fought, most armed conflict concerned small groups of men bent on revenge; acquiring territory was not usually the goal of warfare. Two warring groups might cooperate in a communal hunt at another time.

Social Organization

The lineage was the major social unit in many California groups. Lineages often were further organized into clans, and moieties were common in the southern part of California. All of these social units were kinship-based and often formed the basis of political and/or religious entities, such as dual chiefs in some groups that had moieties. In some groups that lacked moieties, a nonkinship-based dual organization was frequently present. Wealth and kinship were often related, with people's rank often dependent on the rank of their parents. Complex social stratification was common and many groups maintained a class structure. There was no set pattern of lineality, although patrilineal groups were the most common.

Most groups celebrated the onset of puberty for both sexes. Boys tended to receive more elaborate ceremonies than girls. Some involved initiation rites that included the use of hallucinogens and/or the seeking of supernatural helpers. There is some evidence that rock paintings were an important part of puberty ceremonies.

Most people were married soon after puberty, typically to a spouse of comparable social status. Social units were often exogamous, and polygyny was usually acceptable, but only among chiefs and the wealthy. Divorce and remarriage were common, so long as they did not interfere with the social, economic, or political needs of the group.

When a person died, he or she was either cremated (common in southern California) or buried. Burial usually took place in formal cemeteries, and sometimes with great ritual. Close relatives would cut their hair and the name of the deceased would never be spoken again. Mourning ceremonies, usually held once a year, were common. All of the dead from the preceding year or so would be mourned in a large-scale event that included feasting and rituals.

Economics

California native cultures featured complex economic systems, including extensive trade, market and barter exchange systems, and the widespread use of money.

California Indians hunted and gathered wild foods (agriculture was adopted by only a few groups late in time). Probably the most important single food resource was acorns; in fact, acorn exploitation is usually considered a major distinguishing feature of the California culture area. Acorns are the nut from the oak tree, many species of which grow in California. They are plentiful, very nutritious, and easy to store. Acorns were collected in the fall, stored in granaries, and processed daily as needed. The nut would be removed from the shell, pounded to a powder in a mortar, leached with water to remove the bitter tannic acid, and made into a mush or bread. It would then be eaten alone or with other foods. Women did most of the work of acorn collection and preparation. Some anthropologists believe that acorns were so plentiful that the Indians never had the incentive or need to adopt agriculture (see Martin 1996).

California Indians used an extensive array of other plant foods, including pine nuts, many grass seeds, roots, and berries. Various animals, both large and small, were also exploited, such as deer, rabbits, rodents (rats and mice), and insects (e.g., caterpillars and grasshoppers). Other essential animals included tule elk and pronghorn antelope in the Central Valley, sea mammals (seals and sea lions) and shellfish on the coast, and salmon and other fish (both marine species on the coast and freshwater species throughout California).

Material Culture and Technology

California material culture tended to be relatively complex. Stone was used to make tools such as grinding implements, arrow points, and knives. Bone was fashioned into tools such as needles and scrapers. Clothing, sacks, tent covers, and other items were made from animal skins. Plants (wood, bark, leaves) were utilized to make a wide array of tools and facilities, including houses, boats, bows, rope, basketry, and digging sticks.

California peoples had a highly developed art of basketry; the Pomo were particularly well versed in it. Crafted to suit a remarkable variety of tasks, the basket forms included trays, bowls, storage containers, hats, traps, cages, seed beaters, hoppers (for stone mortars), fans, sieves, cradles, game pieces, and scoops. Some types of baskets could hold water, and soups and mush were cooked in them by dropping heated rocks into the substance to be cooked and stirring the rocks in the basket with a looped stick.

Religion

The primary religious systems in California centered on various ceremonial cycles, the World Renewal and Toloache ceremonies and the Kuksu cult being the major ones. Other cults, ceremonies, and rituals (e.g., mourning ceremonies, solstice rites) were also common. Most religious systems did not emphasize a single supreme being but involved an array of supernatural beings and powers. Many animals were powerful supernatural entities, Coyote being a prominent character in the oral traditions of numerous groups.

ISHI: "THE LAST WILD INDIAN IN NORTH AMERICA"

The story of Ishi is a classic in California anthropology. He survived the onslaught of American settlers and lived hidden in the hills with his family for many years. He finally surrendered to authorities in 1911 and became famous, only to die of tuberculosis in 1916. The story of Ishi has been told in a number of books (see Kroeber 1971; Heizer and Kroeber 1979) and presented in several films, including _The Last of His Tribe,_ starring Graham Greene as Ishi and Jon Voight as A. L. Kroeber. Ishi was not his real name, of which he never spoke. Kroeber gave him the name Ishi, meaning "man" in the Yana language.

Ishi was born in the mountains of northeastern California in about 1861. He was a Yahi, one of the Yana tribes (see Fig. 8.1). Beginning during the gold rush, prospectors and ranchers increasingly penetrated Yahi territory, bringing disease and death. As ranching expanded, the whites (civilian and military) became more and more annoyed by the occasional presence of the Indians, so they attempted to eradicate them. A series of massacres ensued and the Yahi were thought to be exterminated. But a small group of Yahi, including Ishi, survived and lived undetected for several decades in the foothills, always careful to avoid the whites.

In November 1908, the camp of the small group of Yahi was accidentally discovered by a party of surveyors. The Yahi fled their camp and the surveyors stole their food and tools. Deprived of the material that they had saved up for the winter, all but Ishi eventually died. Ishi lived alone for the next three years, finally surrendering himself to American authorities.

Ishi came down from the hills and turned himself over to the sheriff at Oroville in August 1911, and the event made national news. The sheriff did not know what to do with the "wild Indian," so he locked him in a cell and called the Anthropology Museum of the University of California (then in San Francisco; it later moved to Berkeley). Thomas Waterman, who worked at the museum, went to Oroville to bring Ishi back to San Francisco. Ishi was taken to the museum, but no one there could communicate with him because they did not know the Yana languages. A translator was finally located, and Ishi learned some English. He met and became friends with Kroeber and lived at the museum for the rest of his life.

Ishi became a very popular attraction at the museum, providing demonstrations of his knowledge of flintknapping, toolmaking, and so on, for Sunday visitors. He became a living museum exhibit. Ishi would attend various events in the city and was always a big celebrity. When asked what most impressed him about American culture—whether it be the buildings, ships, or airplanes—Ishi unexpectedly replied that it was the people; he had never seen so many people in all his life. He also thought that matches were the most wondrous thing he had ever seen. On one occasion, Kroeber and Waterman took Ishi back to Yahi territory, at which time he showed them where he had lived and hunted, and how the Yahi lived. A great deal about Yahi culture was learned from Ishi.

Ishi contracted tuberculosis and died in March 1916. Kroeber was not present when Ishi died and was unable to prevent an autopsy, a procedure that violated Ishi's religious beliefs. Ishi's remains were cremated. However, during the autopsy, Ishi's brain was removed, placed in a jar, and shipped to the Smithsonian Institution (not an uncommon practice for those times). The brain was rediscovered in 1999 and was returned in 2000, to be buried with Ishi. In the end, Ishi was a teacher, not only of Yahi culture, but of human dignity.

Ishi
(Courtesy of California History Section, California State Library,
Stellman Collection.)

The World Renewal ceremonies were conducted mainly in northwestern California and were related to a similar system on the Northwest Coast. Priests (usually male) performed a ceremonial cycle that maintained world order, health, and resource productivity, while at the same time seeking to prevent disasters. Toloache ceremonies were conducted south of the San Francisco Bay area. These rites involved the use of the hallucinogenic drug found in the datura (or toloache) plant to facilitate contact with the supernatural world. This drug is very powerful and dangerous (sometimes fatal), even if used properly. Male initiates and by shamans experienced visions during such ceremonies.

The Kuksu cult (or series of related cults) was practiced by groups in the San Francisco Bay area and the northern portion of the Central Valley. Its primary goal was to re-create the original sacred and pure state of the world and to return the living to that world. This was accomplished through a series of secret ceremonies led by persons (usually men) initiated and instructed in the secret society.

In 1870, the Ghost Dance religion, a postcontact revitalization movement (see Sidelight in Chapter 7), swept through much of northern California, as well as other parts of the United States. The Ghost Dance was an attempt to regain native dignity and pride, a movement back to traditional values and practices. A second wave of the Ghost Dance arose in 1890.

California Indians Today

Today there are perhaps some 80,000 California Indians; individuals of many other tribes also currently reside in California. There are 112 federally recognized tribes in the state of California (including some Great Basin and Southwestern groups) that are living on reservations or rancherías (small reservations) totaling nearly 600,000 acres. Some forty other groups are not recognized by the federal government and are scattered throughout the state, although some members of the unrecognized groups also live on various reservations and rancherías.

Many California Indians are politically active and take pride in their heritage. The state of California has established the Native American Heritage Commission to help native peoples deal with critical issues. Several guides to California Indian locales, events, reservations, and rancherías are presented by Eargle (1986, 1992). A number of groups have developed business ventures on their reservations, such as casinos or tax-free tobacco stores, a considerable source of revenue. In early 1998 the state of California signed an agreement with twenty tribes to allow the operation of their casinos, excluding video poker. An initiative to allow expanded gaming in Indian casinos was passed by California voters in November 1998.

Learn More About Contemporary California Peoples

The discussion above provides only a very brief description of California people today. What else can you discover? Go to the library (you could start with *News from Native California*) and look on the Internet (you could begin with *http://www. mip.berkeley.edu/cilc/bibs/toc/html*) to learn more about California groups today. Topics you can explore include the following:

1. Chose a particular group or two, and investigate how they have adjusted to European conquest. Look at their tribal land base (e.g., whether they have a reservation), their tribal economy, and the general well-being of the tribal members.
2. Many small California tribes are attempting to gain federal recognition. What is the motivation for doing so? What is the status of their efforts? What are they doing about land rights?
3. What traditional practices have been retained? What are the roles of traditional religion, economics, and politics in California groups today?
4. What is the role of gaming in contemporary tribal economies in California? In what ways have California Indians "led the nation" in gaming issues?

The Yokuts:
A California Case Study

The Indians who inhabited the San Joaquin Valley during ethnographic times are known as the Yokuts (Fig. 8.2). There were over forty independent Yokuts groups (sometimes called tribelets), each having a distinct name, dialect, and territory. However, for purposes of definition, most researchers separate the Yokuts into three major geographical divisions: Foothill, Northern Valley, and Southern Valley Yokuts. This case study of the Yokuts describes them as they were in about 1850.

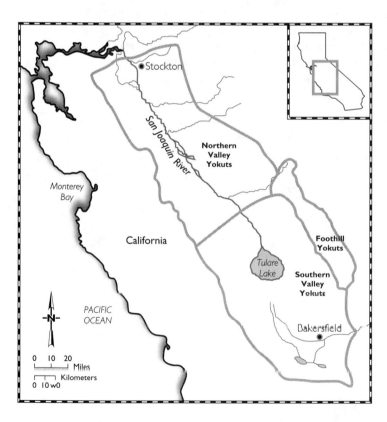

FIGURE 8.2 Location and territory of the Yokuts in central California
Adapted from W. J. Wallace, "Southern Valley Yokuts," and "Northern Valley Yokuts" in *Handbook of North American Indians, Vol. 8, California*, R. F. Heizer, ed., Fig. 1; copyright © 1978 by the Smithsonian Institution. Reprinted by permission of the publisher.

The Yokuts have been studied by several ethnographers, including Powers (1877), Kroeber (1925), Gayton (1948), Latta (1977), Silverstein (1978), Spier (1978), and Wallace (1978a, 1978b). The following discussion of the Yokuts was synthesized from these sources.

The Natural Environment

The San Joaquin Valley forms the southern half of the great valley of central California and is bounded on the east, west, and south by mountains. The valley is drained by the Kern and San Joaquin Rivers, which flow north into San Francisco Bay. The climate of the San Joaquin Valley is hot, with dry summers and mild, semi-arid winters; the average yearly precipitation is about seven inches.

Prior to contact, the San Joaquin Valley contained a network of lakes, rivers, streams, and sloughs fed by water from the Sierra Nevada to the east. As a result, the environment was highly diverse and productive, including grasslands, fresh-water marshes, rivers and streams, and open lakes. Each area contained diverse plant and animal species, and the Yokuts utilized these resources for food, construction materials, firewood, and tool manufacture. However, beginning in the 1860s, the rivers were diverted and channeled for agricultural purposes, causing the lakes and marshes to dry up and turning the San Joaquin Valley into a vast farm-land where little of the original environment survives today.

Some of the Yokuts groups occupied the foothills of the southern Sierra Nevada. The foothills are higher and cooler than the valley and are traversed by several major rivers. These foothills contained extensive stands of a variety of oak species, from which the Yokuts obtained acorns, the staple food of many California groups. Deer and many other resources were also available in foothill areas.

Like all people, the Yokuts managed their environment, through both active and passive means. An important active management technique was burning, which was intended to improve forage for deer, keep stands of grasses pure, and eliminate underbrush for ease in traveling and hunting. People also tended and pruned individual plants to improve production. The Yokuts also practiced passive management of their environment through religious ceremonies designed to ensure the continuation of favorable conditions.

Language

The Yokuts language is part of the Penutian family of languages spoken through-out central California. Each Yokuts tribelet spoke a different dialect of Yokuts, making the language very complex and diverse. Such linguistic diversity is a major characteristic of the California culture area.

A Brief History

It is unclear how long the Yokuts have lived in the San Joaquin Valley, but archae-ological evidence suggests that it must have been for at least several thousand years. The first recorded European contact with the Yokuts took place in 1772 as Spanish troops searched the southern San Joaquin Valley for renegade soldiers. While traveling across a vast expanse of plains, rivers, and lakes, they discovered the Yokuts village of Tulamniu. The Spanish named the largest lake in the region Buena Vista ("beautiful view"). In 1776, Father Garcés spent several weeks in the San Joaquin Valley, apparently interacting well with the Yokuts. Subsequent Spanish expeditions were sent to round up Yokuts for transport to the missions or to recapture any who had escaped from the missions.

Beginning in 1846, when California was seized from Mexico by the United States, Yokuts territory began to be overrun by settlers, and Indian lands passed into American hands. Many of the surviving Yokuts were forced, along with other Indian peoples, onto several reservations. These reservations failed to prosper, and many of the Indians who remained on them were moved to the Tule River Reservation just outside Porterville in 1859. Other Yokuts remained on the Santa Rosa Ranchería near Lemoore. After 1859 the Yokuts played virtually no role in the development of the San Joaquin Valley, except as laborers for American farmers and ranchers.

Cosmology

In general, the Yokuts have only a vague origin tale. When the earth was young, it was covered with water. Animal beings who acted like people inhabited the world, and Eagle was their leader. Eagle directed various birds to dive into the water to get mud to form the earth. Humans then came into being.

Politics and External Relations

Each of the forty or so Yokuts groups was independent, although a general relationship with the other groups was recognized. Each group lived in several large villages of about 350 people. Villages had two hereditary chiefs, usually male, one from each moiety. The most important chief was from the Eagle lineage; he had many responsibilities, including setting the dates of ceremonies, settling disputes and authorizing executions, playing host to visitors, arranging trading expeditions, and helping the poor.

The relations between the Yokuts and their neighbors were generally friendly (Powers 1877:381; Kroeber 1925:497). However, some conflict existed with groups to the west, and occasional hostilities broke out between the Yokuts and the Mono groups in the Sierra Nevada foothills. Small-scale battles were fought, with heads of victims sometimes taken and displayed. No ceremonies related to battle were conducted, either before or after such actions. When conflicts did occur, local groups would band together against common foes. No formal war leaders were known, and a war chief could be anyone who desired the title at the time.

The Yokuts maintained an elaborate year-round trade system, with trails leading to many other locales (Latta 1977:310–314). The primary trade articles from the southern San Joaquin Valley were deer, elk, and pronghorn hides, steatite (a soft, easily carved stone), salt from saltgrass, and fish. Obsidian, a natural volcanic glass, was obtained from the east and could be exchanged for almost anything.

Traders possessing obsidian would exchange it for hides, steatite, asphaltum (natural tar), and other items found in the valley; they would also transport it to the coast, where it was traded for shells and other goods.

Social Organization

The basic social unit was typically the nuclear family. Families were organized into exogamous lineages, clans, and moieties. Lineages were patrilineal and the children inherited their father's totem. Members of opposite moieties acted reciprocally during mourning rites and first-fruit (spring) ceremonies and formed teams for competitive games.

The division of labor was by sex and age. Men generally did the hunting, fishing, and manufacturing of nets and tools. Women typically gathered plant foods and did the cooking, housekeeping, and child care. Children helped the women as best they could, with male children being tutored in men's work as they grew older. Berdaches were accepted in Yokuts society and had important responsibilities.

Life Cycle

A Yokuts child was born with the aid of a midwife; the husband was not present. If the birth was difficult, a shaman would commonly assist. To protect the new baby, both the mother and father practiced food taboos and refrained from unnecessary activities, including sexual intercourse, for two to four weeks. No particular puberty rites were practiced for males. However, females were confined to a menstrual hut for the duration of their first menses. During this time they were not allowed to eat meat or salt or drink cold water.

Both girls and boys married soon after puberty. Gifts (such as shell money or food) were given to the family of the potential bride by the family of the groom. If gifts were given in return by the bride's family, the marriage was approved. Polygyny was permitted but was rare and mostly limited to chiefs. Immediately after marriage, the couple lived with or near the parents of the wife. After about a year, they moved to be near the father of the husband, and a mother-in-law taboo—rules about contact between mothers-in-law and sons-in-law—came into effect. Divorce was a simple matter and could be based on a number of reasons, including infidelity, laziness, and infertility.

The dead were buried in a cemetery, although people of special status were sometimes cremated. An annual mourning ceremony was conducted (see below), during which close female relatives cut their hair and observed food (meat and salt) taboos. The name of the deceased was never again repeated.

Economics

The Northern and Southern Valley Yokuts practiced a subsistence system that emphasized fishing, fowling, and the collection of shellfish, roots, and seeds. Although acorns were the staple of most native California groups, they were locally available only to the Foothill Yokuts; the valley groups obtained acorns through trade. Other plant foods included tule, cattail, grassnuts, and seeds of many types. Using seed-beaters and collecting baskets, Yokuts women could accumulate vast quantities of seeds within a relatively short time.

Fish constituted a major portion of the Yokuts diet. A variety of species were consumed, including perch, suckers, minnows (including some large species), trout, salmon, and sturgeon. People used nets, baskets, hooks, and gorges to catch fish; they also drove them into corrals in shallow water and poisoned them (Latta 1977:89; Wallace 1978a:450; Gayton 1948:14). Fish could be cooked, dried, or ground into meal.

Mammals, primarily tule elk, deer, pronghorn, and rabbits, were another source of food. Deer would be hunted in the foothills; other animals lived on the valley floor and could be hunted communally. Sometimes another tribe would assist in a communal hunt. A fairly large number of people would line up across a designated area and drive the animals toward a trap or to a group of hunters who would then ambush the animals. A good rabbit drive might result in the capture of 200 rabbits; fifteen to twenty pronghorn would not be an unusual catch. These animals also could be shot from blinds or trapped with nooses, snares, or other devices.

Various types of waterfowl, including ducks and geese, were also essential food resources. These birds could be lured with decoys and snared or shot with arrows from blinds. Freshwater mussels and various insects were also eaten, as were dogs, on occasion.

Material Culture and Technology

The Yokuts typically built two types of dwellings. Single-family dwellings consisted of oval-shaped huts covered with tule mats and usually situated in a single row in the village. Larger communal structures, also covered with tule mats, could house as many as ten families. In the communal dwellings, separate sections containing a fireplace and outside door were occupied by individual families.

Tule, a type of bulrush, was critical in the manufacture of baskets and mats and was also bundled together to make boats. Basket weaving was the predominant technological skill (see Bates and Lee 1993) and produced useful items such as conical burden baskets, flat winnowing trays, seed beaters, and necked water bottles. Knives, scraping tools, and projectile points were made from stone, usually imported from other areas. Wooden and stone mortars and stone pestles were also secured in trade. Marine shells were obtained in their natural state from coastal peoples and manufactured into items such as disks, beads, cylinders, and pendants for personal adornment, and for use as money. Transportation was either by foot or boat. Yokuts merchants traveled widely, visiting the coast to the west, the deserts to the east, and other valley areas to the north.

The Yokuts wore little clothing. Men wore deerskin loincloths or no clothes at all. Women wore skirts made from reeds or the skins of ducks or rabbits. In severely cold weather, a rabbitskin blanket would provide warmth. People mostly walked barefoot, using moccasins only in very rocky conditions. Women occasionally wore basketry hats. Both sexes wore their hair long. An interesting story relates how California Indians and Europeans viewed clothing differently. In the early nineteenth century, a European explorer entered the southern San Joaquin Valley during the winter. It was cold, and the explorer was dressed in pants, shoes, shirt, and jacket to keep warm. He encountered a Yokuts man dressed only in a loincloth. The explorer was astonished and asked the Indian why he wore so little. The Yokuts man replied by asking the explorer why he wore no clothing on his face. Somewhat confused, the explorer replied that he needed no clothing on his face, to which the Yokuts man replied, "I am all face!"

Religion and Medicine

Yokuts religion consisted of a series of outdoor ceremonies. The major one was the annual mourning rite, a six-day event conducted in the summer or fall and attended by perhaps thousands of people, including many from other tribes. After numerous ritual events, the ceremony concluded with feasting, festivities, and gambling. Less impressive were the first-fruit rites, observed when each crop of ripening seeds or berries was ready to be gathered. The moieties, one responsible for seeds and the other for berries, were obligated to perform these ceremonies. Under supervision, young adults of both sexes ingested hallucinogenic drugs as a way to obtain visions and to foresee the future.

Shamans (usually males) possessed extensive supernatural power, and supernatural helpers assisted them in conducting ceremonies. Shamans could use their power for good or evil and were often feared. They were also responsible for treating the very sick (minor illness was treated at home). Typically, treatment consisted of making a diagnosis on the first day; upon consultation with the supernatural helper, the shaman would effect a cure on the second day. The sucking cure—the removal of foreign objects from the body of a patient by the shaman's sucking it out with his or her mouth—was often employed. Consistent failure of a shaman to cure illness, or use of power for evil, could result in his or her execution.

Art, Expression, and Recreation

Designs woven into baskets constituted the main artistic expression of the Yokuts. Some tattooing was done, mostly by women who adorned their chins, and earlobes and nasal septa were often pierced for the purpose of wearing ornaments of wood, bone, or shell. The Yokuts also produced some paintings on rock.

Amusement consisted of storytelling, music, and singing. The Yokuts made music with rattles, whistles, and flutes. They smoked or ate tobacco for pleasure or for power. The Yokuts, like many California groups, were obsessed with gambling; both males and females gambled at any opportunity, playing the hand game and using walnut dice. Teams, often from opposite moieties, competed in sports, ball or stick races, and the hoop-and-pole game, and bets were laid on each of these events.

The Yokuts Today

Today, some 3,000 people identify themselves as Yokuts (Reddy 1995: Table 122). Many live on the Tule River Reservation and the Santa Rosa Ranchería (see *http://www.tachi-yokut.com/*). Many other Yokuts live in the region but not on the reservations. Most people on the reservations live in substandard housing and must work elsewhere. However, both the Tule River Reservation and the Santa Rosa Ranchería now have casinos, attracting numerous customers and providing both employment and revenue for the Yokuts community.

The Chumash: A California Case Study

The Chumash occupied an area from San Luis Obispo to Malibu Canyon along the Pacific Coast and inland to the western edge of the San Joaquin Valley (where the Chumash bordered the Yokuts), as well as the islands in the Santa Barbara Channel. The Chumash were divided by territory and language dialect into nine separate groups (see Fig. 8.3). Although estimates vary considerably, the population of the Chumash is known to have been quite high, perhaps as many as 25,000 people living in about 150 permanent villages, sometimes called rancherías. Much of the population was concentrated along the coast.

The name Chumash was originally used by a coastal Chumash group to refer to the Chumash living on the Channel Islands rather than as a descriptive term for the people as a whole. Early researchers called the Chumash the Santa Barbara Indians, a division of what were called the Mission Indians. It is not known what the Chumash called themselves prior to European contact. This case study of the Chumash describes them as they were in about 1770.

Because they were contacted quite early by the Spanish, a wealth of information is available on the Chumash. They have been studied by a number of researchers. Major works include Kroeber (1925), Harrington (1942), Landberg (1965), Grant (1978a, 1978b, 1978c, 1978d), Greenwood (1978), Hudson and Blackburn (a five-volume set published between 1982 and 1987), Johnson (1988), King (1990), Gibson (1991), Glassow (1996), and Holmes and Johnson (1998). The following dis-cussion of the Chumash was synthesized from these sources (also see the Santa Barbara Museum of Natural History website at *www:sbnature. org/chumash/index.htm* for more information).

The Natural Environment

The climate of Chumash territory is generally cool, but the summers can be quite hot. Rainfall averages about fifteen inches a year. Of major importance to the Chumash were the shoreline and ocean habitats. The channel between the islands and

FIGURE 8.3 Location and territory of the Chumash in southern California
Adapted from C. Grant, "Chumash: Introduction" in *Handbook of North American Indians, Vol. 8, California*, R. F. Heizer, ed., Fig. 1; copyright © 1978 by the Smithsonian Institution. Reprinted by permission of the publisher.

the mainland, the ocean shelter provided by the abrupt turn in the coastline (see Fig. 8.3), and its location at the northern edge of the warm Pacific Ocean made the Santa Barbara region home to large numbers of fish and marine mammals. On the coast itself, many species of shellfish comprised important resources for the Chumash. These various habitats and resources made the shore and waters along the Santa Barbara coast and Channel Islands a very productive environment, except during El Niño years.

Away from the ocean, the coastal mountains to the north and east extend right to the shore, providing close access to that region by people on the coast. Numerous small drainages empty into the sea from the mountains. At one time the inland areas were largely covered by an oak woodland in which acorns were abundant; chaparral, coastal sage scrub, and grasslands also were present. A vast number of plants and animals from these areas was exploited by the Chumash. They used a variety of techniques to manage the environment, the most important being the burning of grasslands (see Timbrook et al. 1982 for a good review of Chumash burning) to prevent trees from growing too large, to improve forage, and to increase the production of wild seeds.

Language

The Chumash spoke a number of languages belonging to the Chumashan language group. Chumashan has been classified into three divisions: Northern, Central, and

Island. Northern and Island Chumashan each constituted a single language, with two dialects in each. Central Chumashan consisted of several different languages. People had no difficulty understanding the language spoken in the next village; however, farther from home, the languages became different enough to be unintelligible. Chumashan seems to be a language isolate, although some believe that it is related to the Hokan group. Nevertheless, the language relationships imply that the Chumash had occupied the region for some time.

A Brief History

People have lived in the Santa Barbara area for at least 10,000 years and lived on marine shellfish and small seeds until about 5,000 years ago, when acorns became the primary food resource. Beginning about 3,000 years ago, the people now identified as Chumash experienced a dramatic expansion in population and cultural complexity. By about 800 years ago, craft specialization increased, and populations grew to a density of about ten people per square mile. By the time of European contact in the mid–sixteenth century, the Chumash may have been organized into chiefdoms, with a monetary economy (discussed below), large permanent villages (a few of more than 1,000 people each), extensive craft specialization, intervillage confederacies, and long-distance trade.

Juan Rodríguez Cabrillo, the Spanish explorer, first contacted the Chumash in 1542 during a brief visit as he sailed north. Intermittent contact with Europeans occurred over the next 200 years, but with little apparent impact on the Chumash. With the introduction of the mission system in 1769 (see Chapter 2), the Spanish were in California to stay, and the first mission in the Chumash area was established in 1772. By 1804, four more missions had been built there, the largest (in terms of population) founded in Santa Barbara in 1786 (see Johnson 1989). The missions were located near the coast, in the midst of the highest Chumash population concentrations. Soon a variety of European trade goods (glass beads, metal tools, and foods) were introduced to the Chumash, who quickly came to desire them. The Chumash did not readily accept Christianity, but the Spanish made every effort to convert as many Chumash people as possible, and many native people moved to the missions (see Larson et al. 1994).

At the missions, conditions became crowded and unsanitary. European crowd diseases swept through the Chumash (see Walker et al. 1992), including a devastating measles epidemic in 1806. Many Chumash, particularly children, died. Venereal diseases were also major problems. The precipitous loss of population almost wiped out the Chumash.

Some Spaniards treated the Chumash very harshly, despite the protestation of some of the mission authorities, and several minor Indian revolts occurred. A major uprising took place in 1824, after California had become part of Mexico. It spread to several missions and was later resolved after concessions were made on both sides. While most Chumash returned, the missions in the Chumash region never returned to their prerevolt importance. The missions were secularized in 1834, with much of the land passing into the hands of ranchers. Since many Chumash had been raised in the missions and were unfamiliar with any other way of life, they had little choice but to work for the ranchers; thus, many became isolated from other Chumash and their traditions (see Johnson 1993). The arrival of the Americans after 1848 only made matters worse for the Chumash and the other California Indians (see above).

Cosmology

The Chumash universe was divided into three worlds. The Upper World was the sky and the home of supernatural beings, such as Eagle, Moon, Sun, and Morning Star. The Middle World was the earth, inhabited by people. The Lower World was the home of dangerous beings. Because the supernatural beings lived in the sky, the Chumash placed a considerable emphasis on astronomy for interpreting the cosmos and for linking the Middle World (where humans lived) with the Upper World (the supernatural realm). Astronomical observations formed a major part of both religion and the ceremonial cycle.

There is no recorded Chumash explanation of how the universe and its contents were created, although one story very briefly mentions how humans came to be. Such stories may have been lost over time, but it is also possible that they never existed; perhaps the Chumash did not feel a need to explain the origin of the universe.

Politics and External Relations

The Chumash had a complex political organization classified by many researchers as a chiefdom. There were several confederations of allied villages, and the leaders from each village would meet several times a year to discuss and decide issues of common importance. The presence of craft specialists and at least one craft guild of canoe builders (there may have been more) added to their political complexity.

The chief of a village was called *wot*. The wot attended the confederation meetings, made day-to-day decisions for the village, and dealt with disputes. The next most important authority was the *paxa*, the ceremonial leader of the village. The two officials shared responsibility for many of functions. For example, the wot was responsible for planning fiestas, while the paxa managed the ceremonies at such events. Many people from various villages attended these fiestas to conduct business, socialize, and participate in rituals. Positions of leadership were commonly inherited, sometimes from father to son, but appointments had to be approved by members of the village.

Villages were built on flat ground near important resources, such as a good fishing or hunting locale, or in a place with good natural defenses. Villages consisted of a number of houses grouped together, sometimes in rows, and always included at least one large sweathouse, storage facilities, an athletic (game) field, and a ceremonial site, with a cemetery located nearby. Villages owned communal hunting and gathering areas, but the wot could grant permission for other villages to use them. When away from the main village for special purposes (e.g., hunting), individuals or small groups would live in temporary camps.

The Chumash only rarely practiced warfare. Such conflicts usually took place between confederations and did not involve neighboring groups.

Social Organization

The basis of Chumash social organization was the village, and many believe that Chumash society was stratified. The elite consisted of the wealthy, the political and religious leaders, and the highly skilled (and thus wealthy) specialists. Most people belonged to a middle class, made up of average, hardworking people. The least respected people were unskilled or lazy, or were criminals.

There is some argument about whether the Chumash had matrilineal clans or were bilateral. In most of their territory the Chumash practiced matrilocality, except for chiefs, who practiced patrilocality. In addition, high-ranking families often intermarried to maintain political power. The large sweathouse in each village may have functioned as a "men's house," a place for the men to gather. The large sweathouse was also used for religious activities.

Division of labor among the Chumash was based on sex. Most formal leadership positions were held by men, who also hunted, fished, managed trading activities, and conducted warfare. Women made basketry, prepared meals, and performed domestic chores. With the help of children and old men, women also gathered the various plants needed for food and manufacturing materials. Both sexes participated in the acorn harvest. Each village would have two or three berdaches, who sometimes functioned as undertakers.

Life Cycle

Babies were delivered by the mother, usually alone. At the onset of labor, the woman would dig a shallow hole, build a fire in it to warm the ground, extinguish the fire, and then line the hole with grass. The baby was delivered into this soft, warm place. Immediately after birth, the nose of the infant was broken to produce the flat shape considered attractive.

Ceremonies were held for both sexes upon reaching puberty. Young boys and girls would take *toloache,* a drink made from the hallucinogenic datura plant, under the guidance of a shaman (see Applegate 1975). After ingesting the drink, the youth would experience a vision and acquire a guardian spirit. Girls went through an additional and less formal process at first menses, during which they were secluded and adhered to certain food taboos, such as avoiding meat and salt. Similar restrictions applied during subsequent menses.

Women married soon after puberty, when they were about fifteen years old. Men married at about eighteen years of age. The family of the groom would present gifts to the family of the bride, after which the couple was recognized as being married. While members of a chief's family often married people from distant villages to maintain alliances, most others married someone from the local area. High-status men could have more than one wife. Divorce was frequent and uncomplicated, the leading causes being adultery and the inability to have children.

The Chumash buried their dead in cemeteries located near the main villages. The deceased was bound in a flexed (fetal) position and laid in a grave. A wooden post would be erected to mark the grave; upon it the favorite tools or weapons of the deceased were laid. In coastal towns, whalebones might be used as grave markers.

Economics

The Chumash participated in a complex market system in which money was used to buy and sell items. Shell-bead money was manufactured from certain kinds of marine shells, particularly the *Olivella* shell. Bead money was made by craft specialists and was traded extensively to other groups, becoming a common currency in much of southern California. The Chumash control of the money supply for much of southern California made them quite wealthy, thereby increasing both their political and social complexity.

A relatively high degree of craft specialization and the presence of at least one craft guild set the Chumash apart from most other California groups. Specialists included canoe makers, bow makers, shell-bead makers, merchants, traders, and basket weavers. Whole villages would even specialize in the production of certain items.

The quantity and variety of resources available to the Chumash were impressive. The most critical resources were various fish, primarily sardines, rockfish, surfperch, shark, halibut, and mackerel. Men in canoes obtained these animals, using harpoons, nets, and/or hooks and lines. Marine animals were also essential food sources; these included four species of seals, two species of sea lions, and sea otters. Whales were not hunted, but were butchered and eaten if found stranded on the beach. In addition, people gathered shellfish—especially mussels, clams, and abalone—from shallow water or near the shore (sometimes they would dive for them). Kelp and sea grass were also popular ocean resources. The mainland coastal groups used marine resources to a greater degree than the inland Chumash did. The Island Chumash probably relied upon marine resources almost exclusively.

On land, men hunted deer, rabbits, squirrels, mice, and some birds. Individuals or small groups of men wore deerskin headdresses as a disguise when hunting deer. Animals were taken using bows and arrows, harpoons, snares, pit and deadfall traps, nets, throwing sticks, and clubs.

Plant resources played a significant role in the Chumash economy as well. The most important were the small seeds of the many grasses in the region. Acorns and wild cherry pits were also major foods, but the arsenic in the cherry pits had to be removed before they could be consumed. Pine nuts were important in some areas and were traded to the coast.

Material Culture and Technology

The Chumash built one type of house and two types of sweathouses. Houses were usually fairly large, round, domed dwellings, between fifteen and fifty feet in diameter, and intended for a single family. The chief of a village, being of higher status and required to host meetings, had a larger house. Houses were built with frames of willow or sycamore branches tied together at the top; tule mats were then spread over the frame. A smokehole was left in the top to vent the central fire, and a door was fashioned on one side. Most houses had a nearby acorn granary. Each village had a large sweathouse, a fairly large semisubterranean structure constructed in a manner similar to that of a house but covered with earth. In addition, a number of smaller, individual sweathouses were built in each village.

Rafael Solares, chief of the Santa Ines Chumash group in ceremonial apparel (feathered headdress, bead necklace, cord skirt, and body paint). Photo ((P)NA-CA-CH-132) was taken by Leon de Cessac in 1877 or 1878.
(Courtesy of the Musée de l'Homme, Paris, and the Santa Barbara Museum of Natural History.)

The Chumash moved about on land by foot and carried their goods and belongings themselves. On water, the Chumash employed two types of boats, a small reed boat and a larger plank canoe called a *tomol*. Tomols could be as long as thirty feet, could carry about a thousand pounds, were seaworthy, and were used for fishing, hunting, and traveling to the islands. A tomol was constructed with a number of hand-hewn wooden planks tightly lashed together. Gaps were filled with asphaltum, making the craft waterproof. A tomol was difficult and time consuming to construct, and only persons of high status owned them. The northern coastal Chumash did not use tomols since they lived where the ocean was rougher and the Channel Islands were too far away.

Men usually wore no clothing, but in cold weather they would put on a skin cape. Women wore skirts of either skin or woven plant fibers (including sea grass) and basketry hats. Women adorned themselves with ornaments made of shell or bone, such as hairpins, earrings, necklaces, anklets, bracelets, and decorations sewn on clothing. Both women and men used body paint. Men wore their hair tied up on top of the head and would usually carry a knife in their hair. Women generally wore their hair long.

The Chumash manufactured excellent basketry, some of which could be used as cooking vessels. They also made trays, boxes, bows, throwing sticks, clubs, and digging sticks from different woods. The Chumash are well known for their use of soapstone to make bowls, flat cooking stones, pipes (to smoke tobacco), and ornaments. They made chairs from whale vertebrae and fishhooks from both shell and bone. They decorated many items with inlay made of abalone shell (mother-of-pearl). The Chumash did not use pottery.

Religion and Medicine

The Chumash held various ceremonies, the two most important being the fall harvest ceremony and the winter solstice (when the sun reaches its northernmost point of rising). An organization called the 'antap arranged and integrated ceremonies and celebrations. One joined the 'antap as a child, and parents paid a fee for their children to join. Members would perform many of the ceremonies.

Shamans, usually men, served as intermediaries between humans and the supernatural. A shaman fulfilled many roles, including making astronomical observations and predictions, forecasting weather, guiding persons seeking supernatural power, interpreting dreams, and naming children. Another critical role was curing the sick by using a variety of methods, including the sucking cure and the prescription of medicines. Shamans were powerful people, respected or feared by many. As power was considered neutral, it was up to the shaman whether to use it for good or evil.

Art, Expression, and Recreation

Chumash rock painting was a highly developed art and was important in their religion. One Chumash rock painting "ranks as the finest example of prehistoric rock art in the United States" (Grant 1978b:534). Their art appears to depict the supernatural world and portrays various animals, people, and celestial objects. Other artistic expression can be found in Chumash basketry, stone sculpture, personal ornamentation, clothing decoration, and the extensive use of shell inlay to adorn many items.

Music was diverse, well developed, and integrated into many occasions. Instruments included flutes, whistles, rattles, and the bullroarer, a device that made a great deal of noise when twirled. Interestingly, the Chumash did not use drums. Like most groups, the Chumash played many games, including the hoop-and-pole game, the hand game, other guessing games, dice games (played mostly by women), and races from village to village while kicking a ball. Gambling on the outcomes of these games was common.

The Chumash Today

Today there has been a considerable resurgence of Chumash culture, tradition, and political power. The Chumash are very active in local politics and are consulted in the process of development in the Santa Barbara area. The long decline in Chumash population was finally reversed in the early twentieth century, and now some 5,000 people identify themselves as Chumash. The various Chumash languages are no longer spoken, but there is considerable interest in reviving them and work is progressing to do so.

A number of Chumash communities still exist, although only one, Santa Ynez, is recognized by the federal government. The community at Santa Ynez was formed when the Church gave a group of Chumash a parcel of land for a reservation. The government recognized this landholding group as the Chumash. The Santa Ynez Reservation has established a five-member business council to deal with the federal government and has begun to develop a number of businesses, including a successful casino.

///

9 Native Peoples of the Southwest

///

The Southwest is a geographically large and culturally complex region that includes most of the southwestern United States and northern Mexico (Fig. 9.1). Most of the literature on the Southwest does not encompass the cultures of northern Mexico and is thus confined to the "American Southwest." Others include northern Mexico and apply the term *Greater Southwest.* This chapter follows the latter model, as does the *Handbook of North American Indians,* and the term *Southwest* will be used to refer to the area designated in Figure 9.1 (although the *Handbook* does not include discussions on the native people of Baja California). The Southwest is the best-studied region in North America, due to its spectacular ruins and the many native peoples who continue to practice their traditional ways.

Southwestern cultures are usually divided into Pueblo and non-Pueblo groups (following the organization of the *Handbook*). The Pueblo groups were settled farmers living in permanent towns in a manner familiar to Europeans (thus they were considered less primitive than other Indians). At the time of contact a number of groups located around the Pueblo groups, including the Apache and the Navajo, practiced some farming but were much less settled.

Other settled, but non-Pueblo, farmers lived along the Gila River in Arizona and along both sides of the Colorado River in California and Arizona. Many agricultural groups also lived in northern Mexico and Baja California, but often viewed as occupying the "southern periphery" of the Southwest, these groups appear less spectacular than the Pueblo and are, consequently, less well studied.

The practice of farming is an important defining criterion for the Southwest, as virtually all Southwestern groups employed agriculture to some degree. The primary crops were corn, beans, squash, and cotton, all of which spread to the region from Mesoamerica. Dogs and turkeys were common domesticated animals.

FIGURE 9.1 Southwest culture area, with the locations of the native groups
Adapted from *Handbook of North American Indians, Vol. 9, Southwest.* A. Ortiz, ed., p. ix; and *Vol. 17, Languages,* I. Goddard, ed.; copyright © 1979 and 1996 by the Smithsonian Institution. Reprinted by permission of the publisher.

Geography and Environment

The Southwest comprises four major geographic and environmental regions: the Colorado Plateau, the Sonoran Desert, the mountains, and the major river valleys. The Colorado Plateau lies in the northern Southwest, at elevations above 4,500 feet. The plateau contains many flat-topped mesas; deep canyons, such as the Grand Canyon; and some mountains, several rising to an elevation of 13,000 feet. At the higher elevations, forests of pine, oak, and juniper grow. The plateau is generally cool and has more precipitation than the Sonoran Desert to the south, although much of the area is relatively arid.

The Sonoran Desert lies to the south of the plateau and extends into northern Mexico. Elevations are generally below 3,000 feet, with a few low mountain ranges. The region is quite arid and has very hot summers, often exceeding 120°F. The large saguaro cactus is the most visually striking plant, but mesquite, yucca, and agave are also common. Animals include sheep, deer, rabbits, tortoises, and many rodents.

Several major mountain ranges stretch along the eastern and southern portions of the Southwest. The southern Rocky Mountains run along the northeastern edge, while the Sierra Madre Oriental and Sierra Madre Occidental cover most of northern Mexico. These mountains are relatively well watered and contain forest as well as many animals.

Many rivers drain the Southwest, the major permanent ones being the Rio Grande, Colorado, San Juan, Salt, Gila, Rio Yaqui, and Rio Mayo. Flood-irrigation agriculture is quite practical in these river valleys, and many of the major farming cultures were centered there. In addition, the rivers provided water and other resources, such as fish.

The climate throughout the Southwest consists of hot summers and fairly cold winters. Rainfall varies from region to region. In the far western Southwest, most rain falls in the winter and comes from Pacific storms. In the rest of the Southwest, rain comes during summertime thunderstorms that form from moist air originating in the Gulf of Mexico.

A Basic Prehistory of the Southwest

The prehistory of the Southwest is very complex, and a detailed and fascinating understanding of the region is emerging. The following discussion is a brief and general summary of this very complex subject. Several good general summaries of Southwestern prehistory are available, including McGuire and Schiffer (1982), Cordell (1994, 1997), Plog (1997), and Reid and Whittlesey (1997); also see the prehistory chapters in Volume 9 of the *Handbook of North American Indians* (Ortiz 1979). A summary of the prehistory of the southern portion of the Southwest was provided by Phillips (1989).

The Paleoindian Period (ca. 12,000 to 10,000 B.P.)

A number of well-known Paleoindian sites are located in the Southwest. The most notable are the sites near Clovis and Folsom, New Mexico, among the first Paleoindian sites ever discovered. These sites contained direct evidence of human hunting of mammoths and giant bison. Relatively little else is known about the Paleoindian occupation of the region (see Chapter 1).

The Archaic Period (ca. 10,000 to 2,000 B.P.)

Interestingly, the popularity of the archaeology of Southwestern agricultural groups has resulted in relatively little work being conducted on preagricultural groups.

Thus, we know relatively little about the Archaic (see Huckell 1996 for a review of the Archaic). Generalized hunters and gatherers did occupy the entire region at least as long ago as Paleoindian times, and the various groups are collectively known as the Picosa Culture. However, beginning about 2,000 years ago, or even earlier, domesticated crops and agricultural technologies spread to the Southwest from their ancient roots in Mesoamerica, and many Archaic groups adopted the new crops. The transition from hunting and gathering to farming in this region is called Basketmaker I (see below).

Farmers and Pueblos

After about 2,000 B.P., four main archaeological cultures evolved in the northern Southwest: the Puebloans, the Mogollon, the Hohokam, and the Patayan (see Fig. 9.2). Each was affected by a number of events that took place approximately 500 years ago, including climatic changes, the Spanish invasion from the south, and the Apachean invasion from the north. The actual impacts of these events on pre-historic Southwestern cultures is not fully understood. The late prehistory of much of the rest of the Southwest is poorly understood.

The Puebloans (ca. 2,100 B.P. to present) The ancestral Puebloans, or Anasazi, con-sisted of a number of agricultural groups living on the Colorado Plateau. Anthro-pologists have designated two major time periods for the Puebloans—Basketmaker and Pueblo—each with a number of subdivisions. The early Puebloans, are called

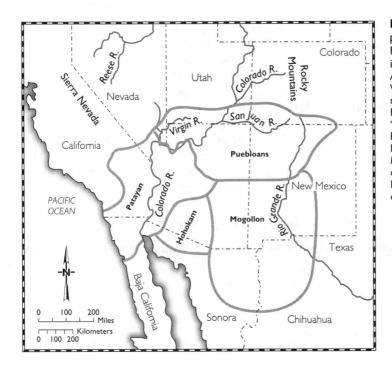

FIGURE 9.2 Location of the prehistoric Puebloan, Mogollon, Hohokam, and Patayan cultures in the Southwest
Adapted from F. Plog, "Prehistory: Western Anasazi," Fig. I; G. J. Gumer-man and E.W. Haury, "Prehistory: Hohokam," Fig. I; A. H. Schroeder, "Prehistory: Hakataya," Fig. I; and P. S. Martin, "Prehistory: Mongollon," Fig. I in *Handbook of North American Indians, Vol. 9, Southwest,* A. Ortiz, ed.; copyright © 1979 by the Smithsonian Institution. Reprinted by permission of the publisher.

Basketmaker I (2,100 to 1,500 B.P.), and they lived in small villages consisting of a few pit houses each. At that time, climatic conditions were not conducive to agriculture. By Basketmaker II and III times (1,500 to 1,300 B.P.), the population was slowly growing, and by the Pueblo I period (1,300 to 1,100 B.P.), the people had adopted above-ground masonry houses and crop storage rooms. The pit house previously used as a dwelling became the kiva, the ceremonial structure widely used by the Pueblo Indians. By Pueblo II times (1,100 to 900 B.P.), climatic conditions for agriculture had improved, Pueblo II populations grew, and village size increased to about ten structures per site. The Pueblo populations were present all over the northern Southwest. Interestingly, there is some evidence of cannibalism during this period.

During the Pueblo III period (900 to 700 B.P.), Puebloan populations grew dramatically and a number of "great" pueblos, dwelling structures with many with hundreds of rooms, were established from southern Colorado to northern Mexico. Pueblo III society was very complex and the people of that period accomplished some remarkable things, such as building the complex at Chaco Canyon (see below). Then, about 700 years ago, a major drought occurred in the Southwest. During Pueblo IV times (700 to 500 B.P.) many of the Puebloan peoples were forced to move and/or consolidate into fewer and smaller pueblos.

The Pueblo V period (500 B.P. to present) is the time of the historic Pueblos. By 500 years ago, Puebloan groups had coalesced into two major groups, the Western and Eastern (or Rio Grande) Pueblos. A great deal of cultural continuity exists between the historic Pueblos and the ancestral Puebloans, and the contemporary Pueblos continue to survive and flourish.

The Chaco Phenomenon (ca. 1,150 to 850 B.P.)   Begun during Pueblo II times, the complex of pueblos at Chaco Canyon had developed into an enormously sophisticated system by the end of the Pueblo III period. It included a great variety of planned settlements, from very small to very large pueblos, a series of towers that facilitated communication over long distances, water-control systems, and an extensive road network that may have been oriented based on astronomical phenomena. Chaco Canyon contained nine major towns, the most famous being Pueblo Bonito, which contained at least four stories and 800 rooms. A number of outlier towns, some eighty kilometers away, were built along the roads. The specific organization and function of the Chaco system are not known, but it may have been the center of a large economic and/or religious organization (e.g., a chiefdom).

The Chaco system collapsed about 850 B.P., perhaps because too many people had stretched the ability of the farms to support them. It is also possible that continuous construction activities had stripped the surrounding countryside of timber. Perhaps warfare, whether conducted locally or elsewhere, was a factor. We do not yet know.

The Mogollon (ca. 1,700 to 500 B.P.)   The Mogollon (pronounced mug-e-OWN) lived in the mountains along the Mogollon Rim in the eastern Southwest and northern Mexico. Unlike the Puebloans, the Mogollon lived in pit houses until after about 900 B.P., when they adopted Puebloan-style architecture. The Mogollon lived in a manner similar to the Puebloans, residing in many large pueblolike towns. They prospered until about 500 B.P. and then apparently disappeared, although many think that the Zuni are descended from the Mogollon. The Apache now occupy most of the Mogollon region.

The Hohokam (ca. 1,800 to 500 B.P.)   The Hohokam lived in the central Sonoran Desert, along the Salt and Gila Rivers (see Crown 1990). The region is hot, with little rainfall, yet the Hohokam developed a very complex culture based on large-scale irrigation, coupled with other farming techniques supplemented by hunting and gathering. They lived in many towns along the rivers, and their material culture reflected some structures and goods of Mesoamerican culture, including stepped pyramids of soil, ballcourts, platform mounds, macaws (kept for feathers), turquoise mosaics, pyrite mirrors, and copper bells.

The early Hohokam lived in small agricultural communities. By 1,225 B.P. the Mesoamerican influence had appeared and construction of the major irrigation projects, truly colossal in scale, had begun. The Hohokam rerouted entire rivers and built hundreds of miles of canals. This remarkable engineering achievement must have been accomplished by thousands of laborers.

By 1,000 B.P. the Hohokam had constructed many hundreds of towns and more than 225 ballcourts. Later the Hohokam began to build planned towns, and some pueblolike settlements appeared. Population pressures from the north may have affected the Hohokam; by about 650 B.P. some sites were fortified. At about the same time, their irrigation system began to deteriorate, and the Hohokam culture had collapsed by about 500 years ago. The O'odham now occupy the region, but it is not clear whether they descend from the Hohokam.

The Patayan (ca. 1,000 to 150 B.P.)   The Patayan, sometimes called Hakataya, developed out of a general Archaic hunting-and-gathering culture in the western portion of the American Southwest. By about 1,000 years ago, Patayan groups along the Colorado and Gila Rivers were practicing agriculture and had developed into the Yuman cultures encountered by Europeans.

The Contact Period

In 1539 a Spanish explorer named Fray Marcos de Niza ventured into the northern Southwest and saw, but did not visit, the pueblo of Zuni. De Niza told stories of great riches there, and so the Spanish mounted a formal expedition to the region in 1540, led by Francisco Vásquez de Coronado. Coronado returned to Mexico City in 1542 and dispelled the myth of great wealth at the pueblos. In the years that followed, several other Spanish expeditions visited the pueblo country but did not stay. In 1598, Juan de Oñate arrived in the Rio Grande Valley with the first Spanish colonists and established the first Spanish settlement at the Tewa pueblo of Yuqueyunque, renaming it San Gabriel. Santa Fe was founded in 1610 and became the Spanish capital of the province. Catholic missions were established at many of the pueblos in the early seventeenth century. The pueblos at Hopi and

Zuni were too far west to be occupied by Spanish troops, but efforts were made to establish missions there.

When resistance was encountered from the Pueblo at Acoma, Oñate burned the town, killed many of the residents, cut off one foot of every male over twenty-five years of age, and enslaved the rest of the population for a period of twenty years. Such actions dissuaded many Pueblos from active resistance, and most Indians dealt pragmatically with the occupation. The Spanish introduced new crops (e.g., wheat, peppers, and tomatoes) and domesticated animals (such as horses, cattle, and sheep) into the region. Many of these commodities would later become very important to the Indians.

By the late seventeenth century the Spanish oppression had become too much for the Indians. Many Pueblos got together and organized a coordinated effort to expel the Spanish—an event known as the Pueblo Revolt of 1680 (see Sando 1979; Knaut 1995). It succeeded; many of the Spanish were killed and the rest driven from the region. After almost one hundred years of Spanish occupation and enslavement, the Pueblos were again free.

However, the Spanish returned in 1692 with a large force of soldiers. They met relatively little resistance as the Pueblo towns either surrendered or were abandoned. By 1696, the reconquest was complete, with most of the people returning to their homes and resubmitting themselves to Spanish rule (see Spicer 1962 and Riley 1999, for history of the Spanish in the Southwest). This submission was superficial, however; the Pueblo people moved much of their culture and religion underground, where it survived into contemporary times. Some Pueblo people sought refuge with the Navajo or the Hopi. One entire Tewa community moved to Hopi, where they established a new town, Hano, next to a Hopi town (see Dozier 1966; Stanislawski 1979).

At about this same time the Jesuits established a series of missions in northern Mexico (see Dunne 1948; Polzer et al. 1991). Very little is known about the details of this system, its impact on the native populations, or their response to it, but it is known that disease was a serious problem. Many native groups in northern Mexico withdrew into relatively inaccessible regions and survived well into the twentieth century (see this chapter's Case Study on the Tarahumara).

During the eighteenth century Spanish power in the New World declined, including Spanish influence over the Pueblos. By the time Mexico took over the region in 1823, outside influence had fallen to the point that the expanding Navajo and Apache

Geronimo, Chiricahua Apache leader, about 1900. (CORBIS/Hulton-Deutsch Collection)

VIP Profile

GERONIMO, APACHE LEADER

Geronimo, a Chiricahua Apache, led his people in their fight to keep their land and remain free. He was known for his ability to outsmart and outfight vastly superior forces of Mexican and American troops and for the poor treatment that he and his people received at the hands of their captors.

Geronimo was born in about 1823 and received the Apache name of Goyahkla. His band moved around in a territory that included portions of both the United States and Mexico. In Sonora in 1850, Mexican militia attacked the Apache, and Goyahkla's mother, wife, and three children were killed. Goyahkla organized and led a successful campaign against the militia in Sonora and at that time was renamed Geronimo.

Geronimo married several more times; one of his wives was a relative of Cochise, the overall leader of the Chiricahua Apache (see Opler 1983). By the 1860s Geronimo was involved in the resistance against the expansion of the United States. In 1863, Mangas Coloradas, then the leader of Geronimo's band, was captured and executed by the Americans, at which time Geronimo became the band leader. Geronimo was captured by the Americans in 1876 and confined at the San Carlos Reservation in Arizona. In 1881 he left the reservation and went to Mexico with a few of his followers. Under the command of General Crook, U.S. troops pursued him, finally capturing him in 1885 and returning him to San Carlos.

That same year, hearing that he was about to be arrested, Geronimo escaped again to Mexico, taking seventeen men and nineteen women and children with him. Both the U.S. and Mexican armies pursued him and he was eventually surrounded by some 5,000 U.S. troops, aided by Apache scouts, under General Miles in Mexico. In September 1886, Geronimo ran out of supplies and negotiated a surrender in which he and his people agreed to return to the reservation. As soon as he was in captivity, the Americans changed the terms.

The government then sent all of the Chiricahua to Florida, where Geronimo and 500 other Apache were imprisoned beginning in 1886. The group was later moved to Alabama in 1887 and 1888. In 1894, Geronimo and the other Chiricahua were allowed to move to the Comanche Reservation in Oklahoma, where Geronimo died in 1909. The Chiricahua were allowed to move back to Arizona in 1913, although some chose to stay in Oklahoma.

Many people, including some army commanders, campaigned for the fair treatment of Geronimo and the Apache, and their case became a major issue in American politics in the late nineteenth century. The resistance of the Apache and Geronimo was admired by many. Additional information on Geronimo can be found in Geronimo (1970), Adams (1971), Davis (1976), Debo (1976), and Lieder and Page (1997).

groups could no longer be contained, they raided the Pueblos and the European settlements. The Spanish, the Mexicans, and some Indians participated in a thriving trade in Indian slaves. In 1848 the northern Southwest came under the jurisdiction of the United States. The Mexican authorities returned to Mexico and the Navajo and Apache expanded further.

By 1860 the United States had gained some control over the region and was involved in conflicts with the Navajo and Apache. When U.S. troops left the Southwest in 1861 to fight the Civil War, the Navajo thought they had won a victory and intensified their raiding against the Pueblos and Euroamerican settlers. The United States responded by waging total war against the Navajo, defeating them in 1864. Most Navajo were imprisoned until 1868, after which they settled on the newly created Navajo Reservation (see this chapter's Case Study on the Navajo).

The Apache resisted the American colonization, but the United States had defeated the last of the Apache groups by 1886. The government established reservations for the various Apache groups in or near their lands in the Southwest. The one exception, the Chiricahua Apache, who had given the government the most trouble, were all imprisoned in Florida in 1886, then moved to Alabama, and then to a reservation near Fort Sill, Oklahoma. In 1913 the Chiricahua were given the option to move to the Mescalero Reservation in Arizona or to stay at Fort Sill. Most returned to Arizona, but some, now called the Fort Sill Apache, stayed in Oklahoma (see Lieder and Page 1997).

The Impact of European Contact

Europeans impacted Southwestern cultures both culturally and biologically. The colonial administrations of Spain, Mexico, and the United States all left their mark (see Spicer 1962). In spite of these influences, many Southwestern groups managed to retain much of their traditional culture.

It has been estimated (Upham 1992:230) that some 90 pueblos with approximately 200,000 people existed in A.D. 1500, with about 132,000 people living in the Eastern Pueblos and about 68,000 in the Western Pueblos (Upham 1992:232). By 1598, European diseases had reduced the eastern populations by at least half (Upham 1992:233; also see Stodder and Martin 1992). Less is known about the impact of disease on the non-Pueblo groups.

A Brief History of Ethnographic Research

The Pueblo people aroused a great deal of interest among early anthropologists, partly because Pueblo culture matched the European ideal of civilization—settled farmers living in permanent towns with architecture somewhat reminiscent of European structures. Another attraction was the relatively intact condition of many of the Pueblo cultures.

The first professional work was conducted in 1879 when Frank Cushing was sent to Zuni by the Bureau of American Ethnology. Cushing learned the Zuni language, participated in Zuni life, and was eventually made a member of the tribe. Alexander Stephen (see Stephen 1936) lived with the Hopi for several years in the early 1880s and was initiated into several of their secret societies. Other important early work was done by Adolph Bandelier and Jesse Fewkes. Beginning in the early twentieth century, anthropological activity increased, with many people, including Pliny Goddard, Elsie C. Parsons, Fred Eggan, and Edward Dozier (himself a Pueblo Indian), conducting research. Interest in and research on Southwestern people continue.

A considerable quantity of information on Southwestern peoples has been gathered. Recent summaries of Southwestern culture include Dozier (1970), Underhill (1991), Sheridan and Parezo (1996), and Griffin-Pierce (2000). Of the two Southwest volumes of the *Handbook of North American Indians*, the first (Vol. 9; Ortiz 1979) is devoted to the Pueblo groups, while the second (Vol. 10; Ortiz 1983) is devoted to non-Pueblo peoples. These volumes contain chapters on a wide variety of subjects and many groups. The discussion of Southwestern cultures presented below was summarized from these sources, and the various groups are described as they were in the late nineteenth century.

A Broad Portrait of Southwestern Pueblo Groups

At the time of contact, the Pueblo people were sedentary farmers who lived in permanent towns (*pueblo* means "town" in Spanish), some of which have been continuously occupied for many hundreds of years. Pueblo people tend to be circumspect, orderly, group-oriented, and conscientious about ceremonial duties.

Many groups have been designated as Pueblo people, though no agreement exists concerning the exact classification of these peoples. Some scholars (e.g., Eggan 1950:2; Dozier 1970:134–176) have divided the Pueblos into two major groups, Western and Eastern (or Rio Grande); though others disagree, this classification is used in this book (see Fig. 9.3).

The Western Pueblos lie to the west of the Rio Grande Valley and include Hopi, Zuni, Acoma, and Laguna peoples. Western Pueblo groups shared similar social and religious traits, including matrilineal clans, matrilocal residence, the importance of women, and the prominence of the kachina cult. Western Pueblo people spoke languages from the Northern Uto-Aztecan (Hopi), Zuni (Zuni), and Western Keresan (Acoma and Laguna) language families. Western Pueblo settlements

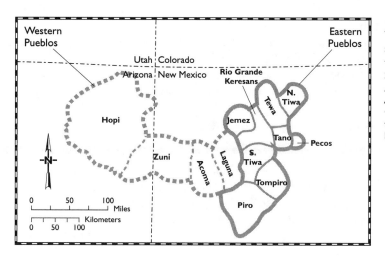

FIGURE 9.3 Location of the Western and Eastern Pueblo areas and the location of contemporary Pueblo groups in the Southwest
Adapted from *Handbook of North American Indians*, Vol. 9, Southwest, A. Ortiz, ed., p. ix; copyright © 1979 by the Smithsonian Institution. Reprinted by permission of the publisher.

tended to consist of multistory, apartment-like complexes built on hills or on top of mesas. The rooms were constructed from stone with wooden beams for floors and roofs. Few doors and no windows existed at ground level; most access was through entrances in the roofs. The roof of one room served as the balcony of the room above. The kivas of the Western Pueblos were either round or rectangular and built below ground. Most walls were covered with mud plaster and then painted, usually white. The large, brightly painted towns on the mesa tops would have been quite a sight, appearing as fortresses to the Europeans. Farmlands were scattered wherever sufficient water allowed for planting.

The Eastern Pueblos are located along the Rio Grande in New Mexico. They tended to have bilateral kinship systems, loose clan structures, a dual social organization with ceremonial moieties to carry out ritual duties, greater emphasis on hunting and warfare ceremonies, and less involvement in kachina cults. The Pueblo groups on the Rio Grande spoke languages either from the Tanoan or Eastern Keresan language families. Many of the Eastern Pueblo settlements were destroyed by the Spanish and never reoccupied, but many are still inhabited, including Jémez, Santa Domingo, Zía, San Felipe, and Santa Ana.

Eastern Pueblo towns tended to be spread out and loosely organized around a central plaza. Houses were generally single-story structures made from adobe bricks. Kivas of the Eastern Pueblos were usually rectangular and built above ground from adobe. Fields were located near the river, where they were flood-irrigated and used year after year.

Political Organization

In all Pueblo groups, politics were so intertwined with social organization and religion that it is difficult to discuss them separately. Each town was an independent political unit but was tied to other towns for ceremonial functions. Every town had a secular chief, usually elected by the religious leaders and installed in the position for life, although one could be removed if incompetent. Secular chiefs fulfilled the routine responsibilities of running the pueblo, but in reality, the religious leaders made all of the important decisions.

War was practiced by all Pueblo groups, mostly for defense. War chiefs did exist and Pueblo groups could often field a formidable force. The Pueblos were raided by the Plains groups to the east, by the Southern Paiute and Ute to the north, and by the Apachean groups moving into the Southwest after about 1500.

Social Organization

Significant differences existed in the social organizations of the Western and Eastern Pueblos. Among the Western Pueblos, matrilineages, matrilineal clans, and other clan groups were central to social organization. Clans held the major ceremonial responsibilities. Women controlled land and inheritance, thereby holding more important rank than women of the Eastern Pueblos.

Among the Eastern Pueblos, kinship and inheritance were bilateral, and both nuclear and extended families formed important social units. Moieties, usually patrilineal, existed but were not very important from a social standpoint. The moieties, such as Winter and Summer, Turquoise and Squash, or Outside and Court, were each responsible for conducting a set of ceremonies. Because there was much communal agricultural work (e.g., irrigation) to do among the Eastern Pueblos, non-kin organizations were more important than they were among the Western Pueblos.

Economics

All of the Pueblos relied almost entirely on agriculture, with corn, beans, squash, and cotton the major crops. Corn was the most important crop, and Pueblo people used dozens of varieties of many colors. Corn was eaten fresh or ground into flour for use in gruel, bread, and tamales. Crops would sometimes fail (or be raided), so everyone kept a supply in special storage structures. All of the Pueblo groups also had domesticated dogs and turkeys.

The agricultural system of the Pueblo people was very complex and flexible, as drought was always a concern. Farmers of the Western Pueblos employed a variety of agricultural techniques (see Hack 1942), including using sand dunes as mulch, following thunderstorms, building check dams to capture flash-flood water and soil, and using springs and seeps. Fields were generally small and spread out over the landscape to take advantage of any available water, a practice that also reduced the risk of crop failure. The Eastern Pueblos along the Rio Grande and its major tributaries utilized the year-round water supply of the river and grew crops in the moist, fertile soil of the river valley. Crops were watered by flood irrigation.

Arrangements for planting began in late winter or early spring. Fields were prepared, fences were built to provide some shelter from the wind for the young plants, and dams and canals were built and repaired. The actual planting of crops took place in May after the danger of frost had passed. When planted, corn was spaced fairly far apart so the plants could better utilize the available moisture. The plants of the second corn crop would be planted in between the individual plants of the first to let half the field lie fallow every year.

Wild resources formed a relatively small component of the Pueblo economy. Numerous plant foods, including pinyon nuts, yucca, small seeds, and berries, were collected, and various other plants were used for medicine or the manufacture of baskets and other items. Many animals were available, including deer, pronghorn antelope, some mountain sheep, fish in the larger watercourses, a few bison in the east, rabbits, rodents, birds (for feathers; eagles were the most valuable and were sometimes captured and kept alive to grow more feathers), some waterfowl along the Rio Grande, and insects.

Material Culture and Technology

Most tools were made from stone or wood. Stone was used to manufacture manos and metates, a technology critical for grinding the all-important corn. Projectile points, knives, axes, and hoes were also made from stone. Containers were fashioned from gourds, basketry, and most important, pottery. All Pueblo groups made very high quality pottery, much of it magnificently decorated.

Cotton was woven into cloth, often dyed, and manufactured into clothing and blankets. Most clothing took the form of short kilts, ponchos, shirts (after contact), pants, and dresses. Deerskin was used for some items, such as moccasins and leggings. Wool became an important material after contact.

Hairstyles were important for all, especially women, as different hairstyles were worn by females at different times in their lives. For example, among the Hopi, prepubescent girls wore their hair straight; postpubescent unmarried girls wore a "butterfly" hairstyle, with large buns on each side of the head. Married women wore their hair in braids. Jewelry was worn, but mostly by men. Paint and other materials were used to decorate the body and face, especially for ceremonies.

Religion

Religious Ceremonies   Religion was the dominant factor in everyday life among all the Pueblo people. It permeated all aspects of political and social organization and of arts and crafts. Religion and the ceremonial cycle emphasized the unity of life. The ceremonial year was divided into two halves, which had added significance among the Eastern Pueblos, who recognized a ceremonial male and female duality.

A common element of Pueblo religion was secret societies, each of which was responsible for the planning and execution of specific ceremonies. Most of these societies were for men only, but a few were for women. Individuals would generally join the society to which their parent belonged. For example, at Hopi, the Snake Society performed the Snake Ceremony and the Flute Society was responsible for the Flute Ceremony. Other societies conducted ceremonies for curing, war, and rain. In the Eastern Pueblos, moieties had added responsibilities for the planning, preparation, and execution of ceremonies.

Most ceremonies commenced in a kiva, a large ceremonial structure owned and maintained by the group responsible for conducting the ceremony. Each kiva had a small hole in the floor, called a sipapu, which was the passage to the Underworld, the place where people originated and many of the Holy People still live. The sipapu was open during ceremonies in order to communicate with the Underworld but was plugged closed at all other times. Preparations for a ceremony would be conducted inside the kiva, followed by secret rituals, and often concluding with a public ceremony ("dance") performed outside in the town plaza. In addition to their ceremonial functions, kivas often served as men's clubs, where men could gather and interact and where ceremonial regalia were stored. Many, but not all, of the ceremonies involved kachinas.

Kachinas   Kachinas are well-known images of the Pueblos (see Adams 1991). Most outsiders view a kachina as just a person dressed up in a costume. However, to the Pueblo people, kachinas are supernatural beings (often ancestors) that manifest themselves in human form. Kachinas wear masks (central to the concept of kachina) that contain the power to transform the wearer into the kachina (see Griffith 1983). Kachinas link Pueblo people to the supernatural world as messengers and mediators, and they perform the vital ceremonies, particularly for curing or to bring rain, that keep nature and the society functioning properly. There are several hundred different kachinas, each of which performs a particular and vital ceremonial function (see papers in Schaafsma 1994). In the past, kachinas lived in the Pueblo towns with the people. Due to a lack of faith among some of the Pueblo people, however, the kachinas became angry and moved away, returning only to perform the necessary ceremonies. The kachinas of the Western Pueblos live in the Third World, entering and leaving through a gateway in the San Francisco Mountains just north of Flagstaff. The kachinas also perform the necessary ceremonies for the inhabitants of the Underworld and so must split their time between the two worlds.

Kachinas were also responsible for a number of social functions. Fierce-looking, giant monster kachinas would visit the homes of children who were misbehaving. The kachina would threaten to carry the child away and eat him or her. Parents would defend the terrified child, who would promise to be good in the future. In addition to kachinas, clowns (a name applied by whites) roamed the town, ridiculing people who had broken rules or customs. The offenders were publically singled out and humiliated, a punishment that the communal-thinking Pueblo peoples found particularly unpleasant. Thus, social order could usually be enforced.

To teach Pueblo children about the kachinas, they were given small likenesses of them (what Westerners would call dolls) made from the root of a cottonwood tree. These "Kachina dolls" are now sold to collectors.

Pueblo Peoples Today

Pueblo peoples have been remarkably resilient in the face of Western culture and pressures to assimilate. The Pueblo population has increased in the past hundred years, and in 1990 there were some 55,000 Pueblo people (Reddy 1995: Table 120). Economic development, health services, and formal education have improved over the past few decades but still lag behind those available to the Pueblo's white neighbors.

Virtually all of the Pueblos have reservations, with those for the Western Pueblos established fairly early. The federal government did not recognize most of the Eastern Pueblos as formal tribes until the 1920s, meaning that many Pueblo lands were taken by whites before they were protected. As a result, the reservations of the eastern groups are generally smaller. Taos Pueblo did not settle their claims until 1970, when they obtained a 48,000-acre reservation.

Many of the Pueblos continue their ceremonial cycles. Due to a desire for privacy and to avoid the exploitation and belittlement of their ceremonies by others, some Pueblos have now closed their religious rites to the public. However, other ceremonies are still open for outsiders to see as long as they behave properly.

Most Pueblo people continue to work as farmers, but increasing numbers have sought their living from wage labor, often away from the reservation. The production of arts and crafts for the tourist and collector markets is big business, and many individual Indians are engaged in this endeavor. Tourism is considerable, and many of the Pueblos receive large numbers of visitors each year. Since the Indians still live in the places being visited, access is restricted in some areas, and some pueblos are closed to the public for certain ceremonies. Nevertheless, visitors are welcome if they respect the Indians and their beliefs. Some of the major tourist destinations include Taos, Acoma, Hopi, and Zuni. Several groups in the Rio Grande Valley have built casinos to take advantage of the tourist trade.

A Broad Portrait of Non-Pueblo Southwestern Groups

By the time of American Annexation in 1848, most of the Southwest was inhabited by many different non-Pueblo peoples, organized here into three broad categories: (1) the Apachean groups, who spoke Southern Athapaskan languages related to languages spoken in the western Subarctic and part of the Northwest Coast; (2) farmers and hunter-gatherers of the Sonoran Desert, who spoke either Yuman or Southern Uto-Aztecan languages; and (3) farmers of northern Mexico, most of whom spoke Southern Uto-Aztecan languages. The non-Pueblo groups in the Southwest are detailed in Volume 10 of the *Handbook of North American Indians* (Ortiz 1983).

The Apachean people moved into the Southwest from the north, beginning in about 1500. They apparently traveled from the Subarctic region south along the eastern flank of the Rockies and into the Southwest, although some groups, such as the Kiowa-Apache and Lipan Apache, moved onto the Plains. The Apacheans were hunter-gatherers organized into a number of different bands having a similar lifestyle. Coincidentally, the Spanish were entering the Southwest from the south at about the same time and encountered the various Apachean bands moving in from the north, including the Mescalero, Jicarilla, Chiricahua, White Mountain Apache, San Carlos Apache, and Navajo, an Apachean group that was later to develop into the largest tribe in the region (see this chapter's Case Study on the Navajo).

Apachean bands were generally small; warfare and raiding were normal parts of their economy. Their arrival in the Southwest had profound effects. The Apachean groups raided their new neighbors, including the Spanish, taking control of much of the land and replacing the prior hunter-gatherer groups in the region.

The farmers and hunter-gatherers of the Sonoran Desert included a number of different groups. To the west, sedentary farmers who spoke Yuman languages, such as the Mojave, Quechan, Cocopa, Maricopa, and Halchidhoma, lived along the lower Colorado and western Gila Rivers in western Arizona and eastern California. These groups had relatively large populations, grew corn and other crops using flood irrigation, exploited fish from the river, and were involved in a pattern of endemic warfare.

Other Yumans included the various Pai groups, including the Yavapai and Hualapi who lived in the northern Sonoran Desert. They were small groups of part-time farmers and hunter-gatherers. The Hualapi practiced some agriculture in the canyon of the Colorado River and hunted and gathered wild resources throughout the rest of the region. One branch of the Hualapi, the Havasupai, today live in the bottom of the Grand Canyon.

Sidelight

THE MYTH OF DON JUAN

Beginning with *The Teachings of Don Juan* (1968), Carlos Castaneda published a series of books about his "anthropological" fieldwork with a Yaqui shaman named don Juan. Castaneda wrote that don Juan introduced him to a "separate reality" in which, with the aid of peyote, people could journey to different worlds and dimensions and gain new understanding. In 1973, Castaneda was granted a Ph.D. in anthropology from UCLA based on his work with don Juan. Castaneda became "one of the godfathers of the New Age movement" and was seen as "addressing the central issues of our time" (*Los Angeles Times*, cited from the back cover of *The Art of Dreaming* [Castaneda 1993]).

It was eventually discovered (see de Mille 1976, 1990) that Castaneda had never actually conducted fieldwork with the Yaqui, that don Juan did not exist, and that all of Castaneda's "data" were fictional. While some at UCLA were greatly embarrassed, nothing was done. Castaneda continued to publish books related to don Juan and Yaqui shamanism until his death in 1998. Most people who buy and read these books do not realize that they are fiction, and the publisher has apparently chosen to ignore that fine detail. While the books are entertaining, they *are* fiction, and it is important for students of Native American cultures and religions to understand this fact.

The O'odham spoke Southern Uto-Aztecan languages, lived in the southern Sonoran Desert, and may be the descendants of the Hohokam. The Akimel O'odham, or "River People" (formerly called the Upper Pima), lived along the eastern Gila River and practiced agriculture, while the Lower Pima lived in northern Mexico. The Tóhono O'odham, or "Desert People" (formerly called the Papago), relied more on hunting and gathering.

The southern Southwest (northern Mexico) was home to many separate groups, mostly Southern Uto-Aztecans, including the Tarahumara (see the Case Study), the Yaqui, and the Mayo. Each of these groups consisted of farmers who depended on hunting and gathering to some extent. Some of the groups adopted sheep and cattle herding after contact. The Yaqui were well known for their fierce military resistance to the Spanish and later the Mexicans. The Yaqui were defeated in the 1880s, and many moved to the United States (see Spicer 1980; Hu-DeHart 1984).

Political Organization

The non-Pueblo groups were politically organized in two basic ways. Most of the part-time farmers and hunter-gatherers were organized into bands, with relatively small populations. The full-time farmers were sedentary, had larger populations, and were organized into tribes. Along the Colorado and Gila Rivers, warfare was common and important.

Social Organization

As with political organization, there was considerable variability in social organization among the various non-Pueblo groups. The full-time farmers often had extended families and exogamous patrilineal clans; several groups had moieties. In those cultures where hunting and gathering formed an important aspect of the economic system, the nuclear family was most important, and many featured patrilineal descent. However, all of the Apachean groups had matrilineal clans and were matrilocal.

Economics

The farming of corn, beans, and squash was the primary economic focus of most people in the Southwest. Those who lived along major rivers, such as the Colorado, Gila, Yaqui, and Mayo, employed flood irrigation, much as the Pueblo people did along the Rio Grande. This method was very productive in most years; however, if the annual floods failed, very difficult times would follow. Groups not located along rivers farmed without irrigation or used water from streams or springs.

Virtually all Southwestern groups grew some crops, but all also depended to some extent on hunting and gathering. Large game animals, including deer, mountain sheep, and bear, were important, but most meat came from rabbits, rodents, and other small animals. Fish were an important resourse in some areas. Plant resources varied greatly from region to region, but most people made use of pinyon, oak, juniper, various cacti, and grass seeds.

Non-Pueblo Peoples Today

Most non-Pueblo groups have survived into contemporary times, although a few were largely destroyed by disease, intertribal warfare, and conquest. In the United States, most groups were forced onto reservations, with the Navajo Reservation eventually becoming the largest in the country. Most of the Apache groups received reservations, but the Yavapai were constantly confused with the Apache and placed on the same reservations with them. Many groups along the lower Colorado River were placed on a reservation on the river and organized themselves into the Colorado River Indian Tribes (CRIT). Virtually all of these groups continue to suffer from poverty and lack of opportunity, although conditions on the various reservations are improving. Most groups are becoming more self-sufficient and managing more of their own affairs.

In northern Mexico, most native groups still live in their traditional homelands, but not on reservations. Thus, they are largely unprotected against encroaching non-Indians and much of their native culture is gradually being assimilated into the larger Mexican culture. The vast majority of these people live as subsistence farmers, with few opportunities, little education, and poor health care.

Learn More About Contemporary Southwestern Peoples

The discussion above provides only a very brief description of Southwestern people today. What else can you discover? Go to the library, and look on the Internet to learn more about Southwestern groups today. Topics you can explore include the following:

1. Chose a particular group or two, and investigate how they have adjusted to European conquest. Look at their tribal land base (e.g., whether they have a reservation), their tribal economy, and the general well-being of the tribal members.
2. What major differences exist between Southwestern groups living in the United States and those living in Mexico? What interaction occurs between the groups and their governments? What are the major issues in tribal/government relations?
3. What traditional practices have been retained? What are the roles of traditional religion, economics, and politics in Southwestern groups today?
4. What kind of relationship exists between Pueblo and non-Pueblo groups?
5. What role does tourism play for Indians in the Southwest?

The Hopi: A Southwestern Case Study

The Hopi are a sedentary agricultural group inhabiting the semiarid region of northeastern Arizona (see Fig. 9.4). *Hopi* roughly translates to "behaving according to Hopi precepts," and a good Hopi follows Hopivotskwani, the Hopi Way, a philosophy in which humans and nature intertwine and cooperate (see Hieb 1979). The Hopi live in twelve major towns, eleven of which are located on the main Hopi Reservation. The other Hopi town, Moenkopi, is located about forty miles to the west within a separate portion of the Hopi Reservation.

The Hopi have successfully maintained much of their traditional culture in the face of intensive pressures to assimilate. This success has made them major tourist attractions for people wanting to see "real Indians." This case study of the Hopi describes them as they were in about 1880.

The Hopi are one of the best-studied native groups in North America. Research began in the late nineteenth century and continues today. A few of the most notable early researchers on the Hopi include Jesse Fewkes, Elsie C. Parsons, and Mischa Titiev. Important syntheses on Hopi culture are present in the works of Curtis (1922), Stephen (1936), Thompson and Joseph (1944), Titiev (1944), Eggan (1950), James (1974), Whiteley (1988, 1998), Rushforth and Upham (1992), Page and Page (1994), Bradfield (1995), and Parezo (1996a). Laird (1977) provided a bibliography with some 3,000 references on the Hopi. In addition, Volume 9 of the *Handbook of North American Indians* (Ortiz 1979) contains nine chapters on Hopi culture. The information on the Hopi summarized below is from these sources.

The Natural Environment

The land of the Hopi, Hopitutskwa, is located on the Colorado Plateau in northeastern Arizona. The current reservation includes only a portion of Hopitutskwa, which was marked by a series of shrines on specific geographic features, some of which have now been destroyed. Most Hopi live in towns located on or near First, Second, and Third Mesas, three narrow rock promontories located along the southern portion of Black Mesa. The mesas rise abruptly hundreds of feet from the valley floor. The towns lie on top and are accessible only by foot (some towns are now located at the foot of the mesas). A number of permanent springs are located at the feet of the mesas, providing water for drinking and agriculture.

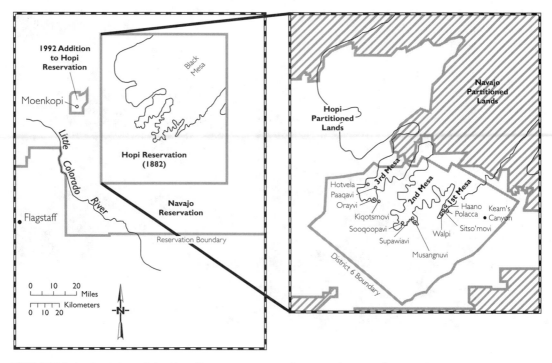

FIGURE 9.4 Location of the Hopi Reservation in northeastern Arizona, showing the Hopi and Navajo partition lands and the location of the various Hopi towns
Adapted from *Rethinking Hopi Ethnography* by Peter Whiteley; copyright © 1998 by the Smithsonian Institution. Used by permission of the publisher.

Three environmental zones are found within the reservation. A desert environment covers about one-half of the area and provides grazing for a few livestock. In addition, many agricultural fields are located in the desert zone (see discussion on agriculture, below). About one-third of the Hopi Reservation has sufficient grasses to graze many livestock. The remainder of the reservation lies in the higher elevations of Black Mesa and contains stands of pinyon and juniper, providing building materials.

Hopitutskwa receives 10 to 13 inches of rain a year, mostly in the summer. There are four distinct seasons; the summer is wet and hot, the fall is cool and dry, the winter is wet and cold, and the spring is cool and dry. Sunshine is abundant at all times. The growing season is about 130 days long, quite sufficient for cultivating corn.

A wide variety of animals are found in Hopitutskwa, including coyotes, foxes, rabbits, rodents, snakes, and eagles. Large mammals were also present in some areas, but most are gone now. Pronghorn antelope lived in the grasslands until they were driven out by livestock. Deer still inhabit the forested upper elevations.

The Hopi town of Walpi, 1913.
(CORBIS)

Language

The Hopi speak the Hopi language, the only branch of the Hopic subfamily of the Northern Uto-Aztecan language family. Northern Uto-Aztecan includes languages spoken in the Great Basin and California, and it is related to the Southern Uto-Aztecan languages spoken by other groups in the Southwest and Mexico. The Hopi language has a number of dialects spoken in different towns, but all are mutually intelligible (see Voegelin et al. 1979).

A Brief History

The Hopi have a fairly long known history (see Spicer 1962; Clemmer 1974; James 1974; Brew 1979; Dockstader 1979), having inhabited the region for at least 1,500 years, perhaps as many as 3,000 years. Several Hopi towns have been occupied for a very long time; Old Orayvi (Oraibi) and Walpi are at least 900 years old and several others are more than 400 years old.

The Hopi were first contacted by the Spanish in 1540. A brief battle was fought and the Hopi were defeated. The victorious Spanish visited several Hopi towns, then left, returning in 1629 to establish Catholic missions at three Hopi towns (Orayvi, Songoopavi [Shungopavi], and Awat'ovi [Awatovi]). The Hopi did not resist, but the missions had little impact since few Spanish stayed on site to enforce missionization and the Hopi were very independent.

The Hopi participated in the Pueblo Revolt of 1680, destroying the missions in the Hopi towns and killing the five priests who lived there. In 1692, the Rio Grande Pueblos were reconquered by the Spanish, who also demanded Hopi allegiance. Most of the Hopi acquiesced in order to avoid conflict, but the Hopi towns were too far away from the Spanish capital at Santa Fe for the Spanish to actually maintain control of the area. Nevertheless, the Hopi moved several of their towns from the valley floor to the tops of the mesas for defensive purposes.

After the 1696 reconquest of the Eastern Pueblos, many refugees came to live at Hopi, but most eventually returned to their towns on the Rio Grande. However, one group, the Tewa, moved to Hopi between 1691 and 1700, establishing the town of Haano (Hano) directly adjacent to the Hopi town of Sitso'movi (Sichomovi) on First Mesa. Haano is still situated on First Mesa and blends into Sitso'movi.

In 1699, some of the people at Awat'ovi decided to adopt Christianity. Other Hopi felt that this was unacceptable—it was not Hopivotskwani—so they killed the pro-Spanish faction at Awat'ovi, and the town was destroyed and abandoned. Several Spanish military expeditions visited the Hopi during the early eighteenth century, but the Hopi were never defeated or occupied. When the Spanish threatened violence, the Hopi either fielded a superior force or claimed loyalty to the Spanish and the threat receded. The Hopi then went about their business.

The Spanish turned over the region to the Mexicans in 1823, but like the Spanish, the Mexicans never established a presence at Hopi and thus made little impact. During this same time (ca. 1600 to 1864), the Hopi were being raided by other Indians, particularly the Navajo, but also the Ute, Southern Paiute, and Comanche. Nevertheless, many individual Hopi and Navajo had friendly trade relations.

After 1848 the Americans occupied the Southwest. At first they had little adverse impact on the Hopi and even made some attempts to control the raiding against the Hopi. However, smallpox swept through the Hopi towns in 1853–1854, killing hundreds of people, and another severe outbreak occurred in 1898. In the mid-1850s a severe drought forced many Hopi to move and live with other Indians and to ask the Americans for food. Little help was forthcoming from the Americans and many Hopi eventually returned home. In the 1870s a group of families from Orayvi made a permanent move to Hopi farming lands in the west to take advantage of the good water in the area, and they founded the town of Moenkopi.

In 1882 the federal government established a 2,500,000-acre reservation for the Hopi, although not all Hopi lands were included. Subsequently, the Navajo Reservation grew to surround the Hopi, and Navajo families began to move onto the Hopi Reservation without Hopi permission. Friction ensued and the Navajo–Hopi Land Dispute began (see Sidelight). In 1992 the Hopi town of Moenkopi was added to the Hopi Reservation.

The government opened schools near the Hopi mesas in 1887. The residents of Orayvi were particularly opposed to the schools, and a number of Orayvi leaders were arrested and imprisoned for refusing to send their children to be educated

Sidelight

THE NAVAJO–HOPI LAND DISPUTE

For about the past hundred years, the Navajo and Hopi have disputed the ownership and use of various lands in northeastern Arizona. With the formal designation of Hopi and Navajo lands by the federal government, the argument grew more intense. Today the Hopi and Navajo are involved in a dispute over control of a major portion of northeastern Arizona, including a large segment of the Hopi Reservation. The Navajo have taken up residence on lands that the Hopi consider their traditional territory.

The Hopi have occupied northeastern Arizona for at least 1,500 years. Within the past several hundred years, the Navajo arrived and occupied a considerable portion of the same region, plus much of northwestern New Mexico. Relations between the Navajo and Hopi were mixed and often tense. In 1864, the U.S. Army forced the Navajo to move to Fort Sumner in New Mexico. In 1868, a formal Navajo reservation was established in northwestern New Mexico and northeastern Arizona, to the east of the Hopi. Over the next few decades, the Navajo Reservation was expanded a number of times, and by 1934 it surrounded the Hopi. This expansion even included one of the main Hopi towns, Moenkopi, although in 1992 Moenkopi and a parcel of surrounding land was added to the Hopi Reservation.

In 1882 the federal government established a 2,500,000-acre reservation for the Hopi, but the wording of the Executive Order included the standard phrase "and other such Indians as the Secretary of the Interior may see fit to settle thereon." Over Hopi protests, the Navajo continued to move onto Hopi lands. By 1936, the government had established an area of 631,000 acres for the exclusive use of the Hopi (called District Six), tacitly acknowledging the Navajo presence on the remainder of the 1882 Hopi Reservation. In 1953 the Hopi filed a case with the Claims Commission about the Navajo presence, but it remained unresolved. The Hopi sued the Navajo in 1961, but the ruling essentially allowed the Navajo to stay on the lands outside of District Six, lands that eventually became known as the Joint Use Area (JUA), to be used by both the Hopi and the Navajo.

The Hopi claim that the Navajo Reservation contains many Hopi sacred sites that should never have been given to the Navajo. The Hopi also argue that even after the Hopi and Navajo reservations were defined, the Navajo continued to encroach on Hopi lands. The Navajo argue that the land is traditionally Navajo and the Hopi were not using it anyway. The Hopi counter that the land has been Hopi for thousands of years, that the Navajo are trespassing, and that Navajo livestock are overgrazing and damaging Hopi land.

This problem became exacerbated when considerable coal and oil reserves were discovered in the JUA. The federal government, no doubt influenced by certain energy companies (specifi-

there. In 1906, differences in opinion on whether the Hopi should cooperate with the Americans led to the splitting of the town of Orayvi, with the Hopi "friendlies" remaining in Orayvi and the "hostiles" founding a new town at Hotvela (Hotevilla), seven miles to the west. Several other small towns were founded during that same time, based on similar disputes (see Whiteley 1988).

A Hopi tribal government was formed in 1935, under the Indian Reorganization Act (see Clemmer 1986). The Tribal Council was formed at that time, although

cally the Peabody Coal Company), decided that the land problem had to be settled so that coal leases could be obtained (see Lacerenza 1988).

In 1974 Congress passed the Navajo–Hopi Land Settlement Act. This law partitioned the JUA between the Navajo and the Hopi (actually accomplished by court order in 1977), ordered a reduction in Navajo livestock (see Wood 1985), and mandated the relocation of those Indians who were suddenly on the wrong side of the line, mostly Navajo who were on Hopi partition lands. Relocation was postponed pending the determination of a detailed plan. Such a plan was finally passed by Congress in 1980 and included giving the Navajo an additional 250,000 acres (and perhaps 150,000 more) for resettlement. The relocation of Navajo families began in early 1981.

Many Navajo have moved but some remain very resistant, feeling that they have a strong tie to the land since many were born there (see Schwarz 1997). Many Navajo view this forced move as a second "Long Walk" (see Kammer 1980; Sills 1986; Lacerenza 1988). Others have argued that the Navajo have always been mobile and never had a problem moving onto Hopi lands, so they should have no problem moving off (see Prucha 1984:1178).

In 1985 some Hopi called for the repeal of the 1974 act partitioning the JUA, arguing that it was done only to facilitate coal leases and demanding the return of the entire Hopi Reservation to the Hopi. In late 1988, several Navajo families filed suit, claiming that the relocation was interfering with their religion and so violated the Religious Freedom Act. This suit was dismissed in early 1989 but was then appealed. The appeal resulted in a ruling that the two parties (the families and the government) should settle their dispute out of court, a process not yet concluded.

Congress made a new effort to settle the issue and passed the Navajo–Hopi Land Dispute Settlement Act of 1996. This law allowed Navajo families in the disputed areas to sign seventy-five-year leases with the Hopi and to live under Hopi jurisdiction. Most families did so, but a few did not. All worried about what would happen when the leases expired. Some families that did not sign leases filed a suit in late 1997 to block the law. The Navajo lost the suit but appealed, lost again, and appealed again to the U.S. Supreme Court. In the meantime, the 26 Navajo families were ordered to sign leases or move by February 1, 2000. Prior to the deadline, however, the two tribes agreed to continue negotiations and so no action was taken on the families. In April 2001, the Supreme Court dismissed the Navajo case; however, the situation "on the ground" remains unchanged.

A great deal has been written on this issue. Among the notable sources are Kammer (1980), Feher-Elston (1988), Parlowe (1988), Clemmer (1991), Benedek (1992), Brugge (1994), and Schwarz (1997).

most Hopi did not really accept the organization until the 1970s, and only then to deal with Bureau of Indian Affairs (BIA) issues, such as coal leases and forced livestock reductions. The Hopi maintained their traditional political organization to deal with town issues. Hopi politics eventually became split into the "progressives," those who supported the Tribal Council and wanted to accept American ways, and the "traditionalists," who wanted to maintain traditional Hopi culture.

Cosmology

To the Hopi, the earth contains four worlds, the surface and three cave worlds below the surface. Taawa, Sun-Father, impregnated Mother Earth and she gave birth to all living things, including people. People lived in the bottom Underworld but it soon became crowded and strenuous, so some of the people were led up through a small opening (i.e., a sipapu) in the ceiling of the cave into the second world, leaving behind as many bad people as possible. The second world also became crowded and arduous, so some of the people were led upward into the third world.

The fourth world was created when two beautiful women (the Hard Substance Women) were transformed by the Sky God into the physical features of the earth. At the same time, many deities were assigned specific duties and powers needed to maintain the earth. Eventually, people were led up into the fourth world, the surface of the earth where people now live; the Bear Clan arrived first, emerging at the Grand Canyon. All people originated this way, including the Euroamericans. Other versions of the Hopi origin story, which vary by town and clan, can be found in Voth (1905).

Politics and External Relations

The Hopi had no formal overall tribal political organization and each Hopi town was largely independent; however, the Hopi did recognize a collective association of all the towns. The culture was bound together not by the towns, but by the ceremonial system that required collective and reciprocal actions on the part of all the Hopi (see Connelly 1979). The failure of a town, clan, or secret society to perform its ritual duties could endanger all the Hopi. The groups were also tied together by kinship.

Each town had a chief (*kikmongwi*), usually a male from the Bear Clan. The town chief had ceremonial authority but little political power and acted more as an adviser than a supervisor. One of the major functions of the town chief was to settle land disputes. It was believed that the Bear Clan was the first to arrive in Hopiland, so the Bear Clan "owned" all the land. Thus, since the chief of each town was a member of the Bear Clan, he owned the land and had the authority to settle land disputes. Land was "lent" to the other clans on the condition that they upheld the ceremonial cycle.

Each town also had a war chief, who was responsible for protecting the town from external forces. In addition, each secret society (see below) had a chief priest (almost always a male) who held considerable ceremonial, and thus political, power. Each of the clans in a town also had chiefs. Clan chiefs were males, usually the brother of the most influential lineage matriarch. Successors to these positions were chosen from the chief's sister's sons, who were trained to assume the responsibilities of the office.

The various chiefs from a town would meet in a council at least once a year. During these meetings, plans for the following year's ceremonies were made, successors to aging leaders were certified, and everyone's role in the society was reaffirmed. Matters of importance to the town were also discussed at the meetings.

When a larger issue faced the Hopi, such as a serious drought, leaders from the various towns might meet to discuss what should be done.

The Hopi did not have codified laws, as proper behavior was encoded into ideology and tradition. Everyone was expected to behave like a Hopi. Most disagreements were settled by the town chief. Minor infractions to the Hopi Way were handled through peer pressure and gossip. More serious offenses were handled by clowns and warrior kachinas, who would embarrass and ridicule, and even whip, the offender in public. The council dealt with behavior detrimental to the group as a whole. Punishment ranged from ostracism to banishment, or even death in some cases.

If the population of a town became too large, sometimes groups of people left to establish a new town. Towns split for other reasons as well, including environmental stress (e.g., Moenkopi), families having too little land (through inheritance problems), the departure of dissatisfied men who had not received their ritual offices, or a serious disagreement between town factions (e.g., Orayvi and Hotvela).

Warfare was not a common element in Hopi society, and they had a reputation for being pacifists. However, the Hopi did have a war chief and war ceremonies and were willing and able to fight if necessary. The Hopi fought against outsiders (e.g., the Navajo, Ute, and Southern Paiute) encroaching on their lands and traditions, and even fought among themselves over philosophical matters, such as cooperation with the Spanish. The Hopi were also quite pragmatic about war, and when confronted with a superior enemy they would pretend to acquiesce to avoid a fight they could not win. As soon as the threat subsided, the Hopi would resume their life unaffected.

Social Organization

Like Hopi political organization, Hopi social organization was inextricably linked to the ceremonial system (see Connelly 1979). The basic social unit was the extended family, called a household. The household consisted of an elder female, her sisters and daughters and their husbands, her granddaughters and their husbands, and any unmarried children. The households were led by the senior female of the group and functioned as matrilineages.

Most anthropologists argue that the Hopi matrilineages were organized into a number of matrilineal clans. The clan head, known as the Clan Mother, was generally the eldest female of the most powerful lineage. The clan Mother held considerable power and prestige. The brother of the Clan Mother was the clan ceremonial leader. Clan meetings were held in the household of the Clan Mother, who was the keeper of the sacred items of the clan. Each clan was associated with a nonhuman supernatural partner, or totem, such as Bear, Cloud, or Reed. Groups of clans formed a series of exogamous phratries, which existed primarily to regulate marriage. However, others have argued that Hopi clans did not function as important social units (see Whiteley 1998:49–79).

The kiva played a central role in Hopi social and ceremonial organization. Kivas were built for ceremonial purposes, and a clan member responsible for a particular ceremony could decide to build and maintain a kiva. Thus, that clan was said to "own" the kiva. If someone from another clan took over the responsibility for the kiva, then that clan became the owner of the kiva. Each kiva had a chief, often the main priest of the ceremony associated with the kiva. The kiva was open most of the time, and men of any clan could go there to talk, weave, smoke, and even sleep. At other times, the kiva was open only to members, during which kiva organization business was conducted. The kivas were also used for initiation rites and by members of the secret societies to prepare and conduct ceremonies.

Labor was cooperative and communal within households. Women hauled water, built houses, made pottery and basketry, performed domestic chores, and ground corn daily. Men did the agricultural work, hunted, herded, gathered the firewood, worked leather, wove cloth and manufactured clothing, and conducted most of the ceremonial activities. Women owned most of the land and buildings while men owned their personal tools, ceremonial regalia, livestock, and fruit trees. Individualism was discouraged; a good Hopi worked with and blended into the group. People who stood out were usually deemed evil or considered to be witches. Sexual activity was not open but was not secret or hidden either, as long as it did not call attention to the individual. Homosexuals and transvestites were accepted members of the culture.

Life Cycle

The life cycle of an individual was viewed as a repetition of the journey of the Hopi through the four worlds. Four phases were recognized: childhood, youth, adulthood, and old age. Passage from one phase to the next was celebrated.

Childhood began at birth and lasted until about five or six years of age. Children were usually born in their mother's house with the assistance of female relatives. The afterbirth was placed in a basket and thrown off the mesa into a special place. The infant was secluded for twenty days, after which a ceremony was held in which the child was named and presented to the supernatural world. The baby spent its first year on a cradleboard. Beginning at about two years of age, Hopi children were taught their reciprocal responsibilities, principally by the females in the household. Considerable time was spent in play, with adult roles defined early and reinforced in play. Children obtained some toys from kachinas—bows and arrows for boys and dolls for girls—and they were allowed to keep small animals as pets.

Discipline was rarely strict, and children were generally allowed to do as they pleased. The mother's brother served as the disciplinarian, while the biological father acted as a friend. Corporal punishment was rare and misbehaving children were usually told to behave "like a Hopi." Problem children were visited by monster kachinas (*So'yoko*), who would appear very fierce and try to persuade the children to behave properly. In some towns, the monster kachinas would threaten to kill and eat misbehaving children, and some carried hooked sticks to capture children and cleavers or saws to dismember them. They entered the home of the child and forcibly dragged him or her screaming and kicking out into the street. Eventually the parents persuaded the monster to release the child with the promise of good behavior in the future. Most children were duly impressed and so began to behave like a Hopi.

The youth phase began at about five or six years of age. At this time, the sexes were separated, the girls remaining in the household with the women and the boys joining the other males in the kivas and fields. Every four years, both males and females were initiated into either the Powamu or Kachina societies during the Powamu Ceremony (see below). They were taken into the kiva and introduced to the ancestor kachinas, thus beginning a reciprocal relationship with the kachinas.

The responsibilities of youths were gradually increased, with more and more expected of them in all aspects of communal society. When a girl turned about ten years old, she participated in a ceremony during which she ground corn for a full day and had her hair fixed in a formal way for the first time. Upon the onset of menses, the girl was required to grind corn for four days. On the fifth day, her hair was washed, and she received a new name. She was also taught to cook, make pottery, and weave baskets. Between the ages of fifteen and twenty, young men were initiated into the culture during the Wuwksim Ceremony (see below) held in November, after which they were expected to join one of the secret societies. Each society had its own secret initiation ceremony in which a boy was reborn as a man. After this final initiation, childish behavior was to vanish and the young man was to follow the Hopi Way. Adolescent females went through a similar ceremony at about the same age.

The onset of adulthood was marked by a series of events, including puberty, initiation rites, marriage, and finally, the birth of a couple's first child. As an adult, each Hopi was expected to follow the Hopi Way and to work for the good of the community. After puberty, youths experienced various covert sexual relations, courted eligible partners, and eventually found a spouse. The first marriage required a major ceremony, lasting weeks or even months (the rites for subsequent marriages were much simpler). First, the bride was required to grind corn at the groom's mother's house for four days, while the groom and his relatives manufactured her wedding apparel. During this time, the bride cooked and cleaned for her new mother-in-law. Once the garment was complete, the bride wore it to return to her mother's house, along with her new husband. The new bride was expected to become pregnant as soon as possible.

Hopi marriages tended to be fairly stable, although either spouse was free to terminate the marriage and adulterous behavior was often the cause. If the couple divorced, each partner retained his or her property and the male returned to his mother's household. Children usually stayed with their mother. Divorcees were free to remarry, but frequent marriages entailed a loss of respect in the community. Only one spouse at a time was allowed.

The old-age phase began as individuals became physically unable to fulfill their responsibilities. They were then expected to select and train a successor to continue their various duties. The Hopi ideal was to live a long life while staying true to the Hopi Way. Although no one kept track of actual age, as people grew older they became more like children in that they became more and more dependent, eventually "going to sleep" and completing the cycle of life. The personal property of the deceased was inherited by his or her relatives.

The dead were buried as quickly as possible, and no formal mourning ceremony was held. The hair was washed and the body wrapped and placed in a grave, upon which some offerings were made. In three or four days, the soul of the person would depart the grave and journey to the Underworld through the sipapu. If the person had been a good Hopi, his or her soul lived in the town and was sustained by the offerings of the living. Those individuals who had not lived according to the Hopi ideal were first purified by fire and then allowed to live in the town. The dead could return and visit in the form of clouds or as kachinas.

Economics

The primary economic system of the Hopi was agriculture, supplemented by some hunting and gathering (see Hack 1942 for the classic description of Hopi agriculture; also see Forde 1931; Kennard 1979; and Bradfield 1995). Corn was the principal crop; the Hopi had twenty-four varieties. Hopi corn was adapted to a number of environmental conditions, including drought, during which the corn developed deep roots and required minimal water. The inventory of corn varieties, each used for specific growing conditions, allowed the Hopi to grow crops where others could not. This native crop diversity is still important, and there is currently an effort to preserve the native crop varieties as a "reservoir" for indigenous crop genetics (see Soleri and Cleveland 1993). The Hopi also grew beans (twenty-three varieties), squash, tomatoes, onions, carrots, melons, peaches, apples, and apricots, as well as cotton. Over the millennia the Hopi developed a very complex agricultural system that made the most of available land and water resources.

People maintained permanent fields in places with reliable water supplies. These included natural reservoirs, streams, and springs where water would be present either year-round or seasonally. Crops would be planted in the moist soil near a spring or at the mouth of a stream. If a stream flooded its banks, crops would be planted along the edge as soon as the water receded, taking advantage of the damp soil. In other cases, water from these sources might be diverted into nearby fields with a small-scale irrigation system.

The Hopi paid very close attention to the changing seasons and to patterns of rainfall. When a thunderstorm was observed during the growing season, farmers immediately planted crops in the moist soil. Some of these fields failed, but others produced good crops. The Hopi also constructed rock dams across small washes to catch runoff from thunderstorms and flash floods. Water would rush down the wash, be slowed or trapped behind the dam, and drop its load of wet soil, instantly forming a ready-made field of wet and fertile soil in which crops were planted. After planting, the farmers would return to tend the growing crops.

In sand dunes, which caught and retained a great deal of rainwater, the Hopi planted a special type of corn. A suitable dune was located and the corn seeds were placed in a hole between ten and fifteen inches deep (ordinary corn is planted three to four inches deep). The sand served as a mulch to retain moisture deep in the dune, and the specially adapted deep roots of the corn could extract sufficient water to grow. Windbreaks were sometimes constructed, either to create a dune or to stabilize an existing dune to protect the plants.

Most fields were small and located at some distance from the main towns. During the agricultural season, most Hopi nuclear families spent the planting and harvesting times at small houses built near the fields. A family might have several fields in different places, so they frequently moved about the landscape. In addition, different crops would be planted and harvested at different times. Daily work in the fields began early and ended before it became too hot. Corn was eaten fresh on the cob, dried and stored on the ear, made into hominy, ground into meal, and made into mush, bread, or *piki*. Other crops were also eaten fresh or cooked and then stored. Corn crops would fail every few years, but the Hopi kept a one- to two-year supply of corn stored for such occasions. In times of drought and crop failure, reliance on wild foods increased.

The Hopi maintained some livestock, including sheep, goats, and some cattle, but in far fewer numbers than the Navajo (see the Case Study on the Navajo). Livestock herds were small and usually owned by men, who sometimes spent considerable time away from their homes to tend the animals. Horses and burros became an important aspect of the economy after the late nineteenth century and were used for transportation, hunting, firewood collection, and pulling wagons.

Before the large-scale introduction of livestock, hunting was fairly important, with pronghorn antelope a major game animal. Deer, mountain sheep, mountain lions, bears, wolves, rabbits, and prairie dogs were also popular. Pronghorn were driven into traps; other animals would be run down and smothered or killed with a club or arrows. Many animals that inhabited Hopi country were driven away by the large numbers of domestic livestock that the Navajo brought into the region. After the introduction of livestock and the depletion of other game, rabbits became the most important hunted animal, usually taken in communal hunts. Eagles were captured live by hand and used in some ceremonies (see Page and Page 1994:193–203). Dogs were also sometimes eaten.

Wild plants provided some food for the Hopi, and some were crucial sources of material for the manufacture of dyes, baskets, and medicines. The Hopi harvested wild tobacco and used a variety of other natural products. They mined soft coal by hand from the deposits on Black Mesa and used it to heat homes and to fire pottery. Salt and pigments were obtained from the Grand Canyon area. In addition, the Hopi traded these materials with many other groups, especially the Zuni, Havasupai, and Navajo.

Material Culture and Technology

Hopi houses were square or rectangular structures of varying sizes and built of stone and wood. Generally, groups of houses would be constructed around a central plaza. A typical house would consist of a block of interconnected rooms used either for living or for storage. A fireplace for heating was built in one of the corners of the primary living area. Interior and exterior walls were covered with mud plaster and painted. The roofs, which were flat, were made from wooden beams and covered with matting and mud. Roofs served as patios or as floors to a second or third story. There were few doors or windows on the lower floor; the entrance to a block of rooms was from the roof. Kivas were built underground, with entrances in their roofs.

Before contact, most transportation was by foot, but by the late nineteenth century horses and wagons were commonly used. All water had to be carried up to the mesa tops in pottery jars from springs at the base of the cliffs.

Clothing was fairly simple and children wore little. Men wove all of the cloth from native cotton (and later wool) and produced all of the clothing. Women wore simple dresses, folded to leave the left shoulder bare and held at the waist by a hand-woven belt. Adult men dressed in a short skirtlike garment, akin to a short kilt. Men also typically wore a headband. Everyone wore yucca-fiber sandals or moccasins, as well as rabbit skin blankets in cold weather. Other important clothing and ritual regalia were manufactured for the various ceremonies.

Men usually wore their hair long. The hairstyles of women indicated their life status, single postpubescent girls wearing their hair in large buns on each side of the head and married women wearing braids. Many adults wore necklaces and earrings of carved shell.

Some tools were made from stone, including manos and metates, hoes, axes, arrow and spear points, and knives. Metal tools became important after contact. Each household had a set of three metates placed in a wooden frame for grinding corn. Wood was used to make digging sticks, shovels, and a variety of other items. Women made pottery, which was widely used for many purposes. In the past, Hopi pottery was highly decorated, but by the late nineteenth century little decoration was applied. In the early twentieth century decoration was revived and persists in contemporary Hopi pottery. Basketry was also popular, made mostly by women.

Religion and Medicine

Information on Hopi religion is limited (but see Frigout 1979), as many of the rites were secret and thus unknown to outsiders. The continuity of life after death was fundamental to Hopi religion. The dead lived on in the Underworld in the same fashion as the living, conducting the same ceremonies (but with a reversed cycle) and having the same obligations. All things, inorganic and organic, living and dead, were interrelated and interdependent through the complex and dynamic universe, a concept that Thompson and Joseph (1944:37) called the "law of universal reciprocity." In the universe, humans were active players and had a choice of how to behave. If humans chose not to fulfill their responsibilities, the universe would not function properly. Thus, much of Hopi ceremonial activity, which had to be done properly, was designed to give something back to the universe that gives to them. The Hopi, as a group and as individuals, adhered to this general philosophy and ethical code of behavior, or the Hopi Way.

Ceremonies were conducted and administered by clans and secret societies. Bringing rain was the primary goal of many ceremonies, but other functions included curing, fertility, and hunting. Conducting successful ceremonies required control of knowledge, behavior, and ritual, and having a "good heart." Kachinas, the spiritual beings that served as messengers and mediators of the supernatural, were integral to Hopi culture and religion (see Fewkes 1903). Upon initiation, young males learned the secrets of the kachinas and joined one of the secret societies.

The Hopi maintained twelve secret societies. Nine were for males and were responsible for conducting major ceremonies. The other three societies were for females and conducted relatively minor ceremonies. Membership in a society was open to any person who met the age and sex requirements, regardless of town or clan affiliation. However, people tended to join the societies to which their relatives belonged. The various secret societies had responsibilities for rain, war, curing, and clowning.

Each society used a kiva in which the members performed rites and stored ritual materials. Most of the preparation and ritual involved in a ceremony were secret, and the kiva was closed when the members of a society were preparing for a ceremony. After the winter solstice, the kachinas traveled from their home in the San Francisco Mountains to the kivas, where they emerged to perform the necessary rites with the aid of the members of the societies. The kachinas returned home after the summer solstice so they could perform the necessary rites for the people of the Underworld.

The annual Hopi ceremonial calendar was divided into two major periods: a cycle wherein kachinas participated in ceremonials, and a cycle in which ceremonials were conducted without kachinas. The Underworld had the same system, but had opposite seasons; when it was winter in Hopiland, it was summer in the Underworld. The ceremonial year began with Powamu, a ceremony designed for the purification of life. It was held in February and marked the arrival of the kachinas in the Hopi towns. Powamu was a nine-day ceremony, with four days of preparation and four days of secret rites in the kivas. On the eighth day the Bean Dance was held to encourage germination and development of both plants and children. On the ninth and last day of Powamu, men who had been initiated during Wuwtsim the year before conducted a public ceremony in which newly sprouted beans were displayed. At the conclusion of Powamu, the monster kachinas visited the homes of misbehaving children.

After Powamu, ceremonies designed to bring rain were conducted. The Hopi asked the supernatural for rain and the kachinas would perform the necessary ceremonies, transmitting the request to the proper supernatural deities. These ceremonies were conducted by a number of societies, and when performed properly, always resulted in rain. The rain ceremonies held in the summer also included running races. In July, the nine-day Niman Ceremony was held to celebrate the return of the kachinas to their home in the San Francisco Mountains and to emphasize the maturation of crops.

The second major round of ceremonies was held without the aid of the kachinas. In mid-August of every year, a ceremony was held to bring the last of the rains to induce maturity for the second corn crop, planted the previous June. Every other year, the nine-day Flute Ceremony was conducted by the Flute Society. In addition to the rain and crop maturation functions, the Flute Ceremony also reenacted the emergence of people into the Fourth World.

The Snake-Antelope Ceremony, conducted jointly by the Snake and Antelope Societies, alternated with the Flute Ceremony (see Forrest 1961). The ceremony lasted nine days, the first four spent in each society's kiva in preparation. The next four days were spent performing secret rites in the kivas and collecting snakes, from gopher snakes to rattlesnakes. On the eighth day the Antelope Society held a race in the morning and a public dance in the afternoon. On the ninth day the Snake Society also held a race in the morning, as well as the Snake Dance in the afternoon. Snake Dance participants performed in costume while holding the snakes

A group of Hopi practice a ceremonial Snake Dance, 1940.
(CORBIS)

in their mouths. The snakes were then released to take the Hopi prayers for rain and crop maturation back to the supernatural world.

After the Flute or Snake-Antelope ceremonies, three ceremonies were performed by the three women's societies, intended to give thanks for the harvest and for the role of women in the society.

In late November, the Wuwtsim ceremony was held, again a nine-day ritual. The first four days were spent in the kiva, preparing and completing the tribal initiation of the young men. At the end of the fourth day all fires were extinguished and a "new fire" was started and distributed to each house and kiva. During the next four days, secret rituals were conducted in the kivas. A public dance was held on the ninth day.

The final and most important ceremony of the cycle was Soyal, a nine-day ceremony held during the winter solstice in late December. For the first four days, preparations were made, followed by four days of secret rites in the kivas, and culminating in a communal rabbit hunt. Soyal was dedicated to the Sun and was designed to reverse the southward movement of the sun in order to bring back the growing season. Almost everyone in the town participated; it was a truly communal ceremony.

If ceremonies and reciprocal responsibilities were not conducted properly, harmful effects would ensue. If the desired outcome of a ceremony (e.g., rain) did not occur, it was because one or more of the participants had performed the ceremony incorrectly, had bad hearts, or were witches. Some individuals might even act against the good of the group; these people were considered witches. Either men or women could be witches, people who were partly controlled by evil power.

Unlike many Pueblo groups, the Hopi did not have medicine societies. Shamans would be asked to supernaturally counter the effects of witchcraft, but it was always possible that the shaman was a witch. Illnesses could also result from bad thoughts or sacrilege. Different doctors worked without supernatural power to cure physical ailments with obvious causes, such as setting broken bones (sometimes called "bonesetters"). Such practitioners employed a variety of plants for medicinal purposes (see Whiting 1939).

Some illnesses were associated with specific secret societies, and if an individual trespassed on the rites of a society, that person could contract the illness controlled by it. Society members were also at risk and had to be careful. The primary priest of the society had the power to cure the illness and so served as a doctor in such situations.

Art, Expression, and Recreation

The artistic skills of the Hopi are reflected in the considerable and intricate ceremonial regalia so essential to Hopi culture. Ceremonial regalia was intricately carved, painted, and adorned with eagle and/or hawk feathers and other materials. Wooden masks and kachina figures were skillfully carved. Designs in woven goods and basketry and decorations on Hopi pottery were elaborate and were also important artistic traditions. The Navajo taught silversmithing to the Hopi in the late nineteenth century, but was a relatively minor art until the 1940s.

Hopi music was extensive and complex. Much of it was associated with ceremonies and consisted of instrumental music, chanting, and singing. Instruments included flutes, copper bells, rattles, and drums. Singing was very common and songs were sung to babies, to lovers, and at many other times. Sometimes young men would sing to women grinding corn, who kept time to the music with their grinding stones.

The Hopi played many games and participated in sports, the most popular being various footraces (often associated with ceremonies; see above). Teams played other competitive games, although there was less emphasis on winning and more on cooperation. These included bow-and-arrow skill contests, ball races (in which a ball was kicked over a race course), and shinny. Other games included dice, guessing games, and cat's cradle.

The Hopi Today

Today the Hopi still live in their towns, still practice their religion, and still follow the philosophy of Hopivotskwani. In 2001 there were about 12,000 Hopi, about 9,000 living on the Hopi Reservation in twelve towns, including Moenkopi, which is located some forty miles west of the other towns. A very few non-Hopi live in Hopi towns, but some areas of the towns are off-limits to non-Hopi, especially the kivas. A number of the towns and houses now have electricity and piped water. Many Hopi live and work off the reservation.

The Hopi Tribal Council, formed in 1935, was not recognized by most Hopi until the mid-1970s, and even today the council has limited power. Over the past few decades, education and health services have improved and the Hopi have diversified their economy, although unemployment remains high. In 1969 the Hopi signed leases with the Peabody Coal Company to strip-mine portions of Black Mesa and agreed to the construction of some coal-powered generating plants. Formal education is now very important, and all Hopi children attend school, some taking classes in the Hopi language. In spite of the changes, the Hopi are trying to remain self-sufficient, a good example being the use of solar energy technology to avoid becoming dependent on the power companies.

The Hopi have maintained their traditional ceremonial system in most towns. For many years non-Hopi have been allowed to attend Hopi ceremonies if they behaved properly. Those few who have caused problems have prompted suggestions that tribal ceremonies be closed to non-Hopi. Photography of most ceremonies was banned in the early twentieth century. In 1921, some whites formed an organization, the Smokis, to parody Indian ceremonies. They conducted a number of Pueblo-like ceremonies, including a Hopi Snake Ceremony, by dressing up and enacting pseudoceremonies. Even a U.S. senator from Arizona, Barry Goldwater, was a member and participated in several dances (see Brinkley-Rogers 1990). Many native people view this organization as an insult and another way to exploit native cultures.

In 1992, the Hopi closed kachina ceremonies to non-Hopi after the publication of a comic book depicting a superhero at a Hopi kachina ceremony, during which the kachina masks were knocked off to reveal human impersonators beneath. Such knowledge was not suitable for young boys who had yet to be initiated into the societies (see discussion in Whiteley 1997:189).

Traditional arts are still important. Some artwork is produced for internal consumption, but much of it is made for tourists and art markets. Kachina dolls are very popular, as are other wooden sculptures (see Laniel-le-François 1989; Teiwes 1989). The silver jewelry industry is growing. Hopi pottery is some of the finest made anywhere. The traditional Hopi practice of elaborately decorating their pottery almost died out in the late nineteenth century; however, it was revived in about 1895 by women who copied the designs from pottery excavated at Hopi archaeological sites. Thus, a tradition in Hopi pottery was reborn on First Mesa, one that continues today and is a huge commercial success.

A new tribal government took over in 1994 and developed a strategic plan, called *Potskwaniat*, a pathway to the future for the Hopi tribe (see Berryhill 1998). It requires that the government behave more like Hopi, with respect and dignity for all people. Many serious issues still face the Hopi. The struggle to maintain their traditional culture is constant and severe. The demands of the energy companies and the federal government to develop the large reserves of coal on the reservation are intense. Perhaps the most emotional issue facing the Hopi is the ongoing Navajo–Hopi land dispute (see Sidelight). Nevertheless, the future looks bright and the Hopi culture will persist. Visit the Hopi tribal Website at http://www. hopi. msn.us/.

The Navajo: A Southwestern Case Study

The Native American group that inhabited much of the northern Southwest (Fig. 9.5) is the Navajo (sometimes spelled Navaho). Today the Navajo have the largest reservation in the United States and the second largest population (behind the Cherokee) of any Indian group in North America. The Navajo were one of the many Apachean groups that moved into the Southwest about 500 years ago. The Navajo adopted various Pueblo, Spanish, and other traits, forming the present Navajo culture.

The current term *Navajo* is thought to have derived from the Tewa word *Návahu'u*, meaning "arroyo with the cultivated fields" (Dutton 1976:5), as the Navajo were doing some farming by the time the Spanish encountered them. The

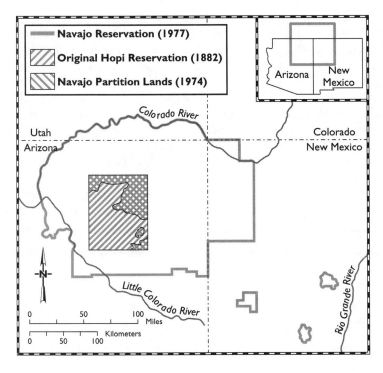

FIGURE 9.5 Location of the Navajo Reservation
Adapted from R. Roessel, "Navajo Arts and Crafts" in *Handbook of North American Indians, Vol. 10, Southwest*, A. Ortiz, ed., Fig. 16; copyright © 1983 by the Smithsonian Institution. Reprinted by permission of the publisher.

Navajo generally call themselves Diné, meaning "people of the surface of the earth," similar to Na-Dene, the term used by their linguistic relatives in the Subarctic. The reservation now occupied by the Navajo in the northern Southwest is called Dinébikéyah, but their traditional homeland, Dinétah, is located partly off the reservation in northern New Mexico. This case study of the Navajo describes them as they were in about 1900.

The Navajo are one of the best known and most studied Indian groups in North America, and studies of their culture continue to this day. One of the earliest anthropological studies of the Navajo was undertaken by Gladys Reichard, beginning in the 1920s. She worked with the Navajo for the remainder of her life and published many important works (e.g., Reichard 1928, 1950). Other important syntheses on Navajo culture are present in the work of Curtis (1907), Kluckhohn and Leighton (1946), Underhill (1956), Shepardson (1963), Downs (1972), Dutton (1976), Iverson (1990), and Parezo (1996b). Volume 10 of the *Handbook of North American Indians* (Ortiz 1983) contains sixteen chapters on Navajo culture. The information on the Navajo summarized below is from the sources above.

The Natural Environment

The Navajo reservation lies mostly in northeastern Arizona but also includes portions of northwestern New Mexico and southeastern Utah. Most of the reservation is located on the Colorado Plateau, a fairly rugged country with mountains, deep canyons, many small mesas, and numerous valleys. Elevations range between 3,000 and 9,000 feet. Many of the landscapes, such as Monument Valley, are familiar to moviegoers, since many westerns have been filmed there.

About half of the reservation consists of high plateau desert. Important plants include yucca, various cacti, and especially grasses for sheep grazing. Summer temperatures in the desert are warm to hot, winters can be quite cold, and rainfall averages between eight and ten inches per year. The remainder of the reservation consists of mountains, mesas, and valleys. Much of this area contains forests of pine and juniper, along with a great many other plants, including cottonwoods, willows, and many grasses. As in the desert, the summers in the forests can be quite warm and the winters very cold. However, rainfall is greater, up to about twenty inches per year. The northern Southwest has about 150 frost-free days, more than adequate for agriculture.

An extensive variety of animals inhabit the region, including many mammals, birds, reptiles, and insects, and the Navajo have a very complex system of classification of the universe and its contents (see Werner et al. 1983). Many of these resources were utilized by the Navajo for food and materials.

Language

The Navajo speak the Navajo language, one very closely related to those spoken by the various other Apachean groups in the Southwest. Together, these languages comprise the southern branch of Athapaskan (or Na-Dene), with the northern branch languages being spoken by groups in the Subarctic and Northwest Coast.

A Brief History

The Navajo entered the Southwest from the north, along with the other Apachean groups, sometime about 500 years ago. They first occupied the area to the north of the Eastern Pueblos. The Navajo were very flexible, adopting some traits from surrounding groups (e.g., the Pueblos and Spanish) and modifying their culture to adapt to the dynamic conditions of their new territory. They raided both the Pueblo and the Spanish, stole horses and sheep from the Spanish, and had started farming and herding sheep by 1630. They took in Pueblo refugees after the Pueblo Revolt of 1680 and learned weaving from them. After 1700 the Navajo came under increasing pressure from the Spanish (to the south), the Ute (to the north), and the Comanche (to the east). To adapt, the Navajo moved west, eventually entering the area occupied by the Hopi and Southern Paiutes.

Raiding was a normal economic activity for the Navajo. Small parties of men would set out to obtain goods, livestock, and slaves, usually by stealth. They raided Pueblo towns as they moved west, then the Spanish, the Mexicans, and eventually the Americans. Slaves were either adopted into the Navajo culture or sold to the Spanish. In turn, some Navajo were captured and enslaved by the Spanish, the Mexicans, and even the Americans (ironically, the U.S. superintendent for indian affairs in New Mexico owned six Navajo slaves [Parezo 1996b:11]).

The Navajo and the Americans signed several treaties soon after the United States took control of the region in 1848. However, several Navajo leaders were murdered by the U.S. Army in 1849, creating considerable mistrust on the part of the Navajo. Navajo raiding continued, partly due to participation in the slave trade and partly to defend their territory from encroaching settlers and miners. Efforts were made to remain at peace with the United States, but the American military authorities were not much interested in friendly relations with the Indians.

By 1860 the continuing problems between the Navajo and the U.S. military resulted in a virtual declaration of war. The army initiated a punitive campaign against the Navajo, who responded in 1861 by attacking Fort Defiance, one of the very few actual Indian attacks against an army fort. In 1862, the new military commander in the territory, General Carleton, planned an attack against the Mescalaro Apache, who were quickly defeated. Carleton then moved against the Navajo in 1863, putting Colonel Christopher (Kit) Carson in command of the combined force of U.S. regular and volunteer troops (including Ute and Pueblo Indians). Carson conducted a scorched-earth campaign in which Navajo crops were burned, settlements destroyed, livestock shot, Navajo males killed, and Navajo women and children captured. The Navajo could not endure such tactics and surrendered in 1864.

Subsequent to the cessation of hostilities, some 9,000 Navajo were rounded up (although several thousand others managed to hide in the hills) and marched south approximately 300 miles to Bosque Redondo (Fort Sumner) on the Pecos River in southern New Mexico, where they were interned along with the recently defeated Mescalero Apache. Bosque Redondo was little more than a large concentration camp characterized by insufficient food, inadequate sanitation and housing, and disease. The situation changed when General Carleton came under criticism for his mistreatment of the Indians and was relieved of command in 1866.

The administrative responsibility for the Navajo was transferred from the army to the Bureau of Indian Affairs (BIA).

In 1868 the government signed a treaty with the Navajo to establish a reservation of 3.5 million acres in northwestern New Mexico and northeastern Arizona and to provide them food and livestock (mostly sheep) for ten years. The Navajo walked back north to their reservation from Fort Sumner.

The Navajo's surrender, forced march to Bosque Redondo in 1864, internment, and subsequent release and march to their reservation in 1868 are known to the Navajo as "the Long Walk," a major turning point in their history. Before 1864, the Navajo were a free and independent group, but after the Long Walk, they were defeated, humiliated, and controlled by the U.S. government. They have not forgotten.

Between 1868 and 1900, the Navajo concentrated on reconstructing their culture and economy (minus the raiding). Sheepherding became the primary economic focus; weaving, silversmithing, and wage labor (especially for the railroad) were also important activities. A number of trading posts were established, binding the Navajo to the surrounding economy. In the late nineteenth century the Navajo saw little reason to send their children to white schools, as their time was better spent raising sheep. The government felt otherwise and forced many Navajo children to attend boarding schools.

During this time the Navajo successfully expanded both their population and territory. As their numbers grew, Navajo families moved onto new land, much of which was then added to the reservation. By 1886, the Navajo Reservation included 11.5 million acres (it now contains some 16 million acres and surrounds the Hopi Reservation). The Navajo tribal government was formally organized by the BIA in 1923 and granted leases to a number of outside companies to exploit the coal, oil, and other resources on the reservation. Though the Navajo did receive royalties on these leases, they were minimal.

With the introduction of livestock onto the reservation after 1868, overgrazing became a problem. Sheep are more destructive grazers than cattle. Cows eat just the exposed grass, leaving the roots to grow again, but sheep will pull out a plant by the roots. By the 1930s, overgrazing by sheep had become such a problem that the government forced the Navajo to significantly reduce their sheep herds and encouraged them to increase the number of cattle. Sheep were sold (at very low prices during the Great Depression) and sometimes even destroyed by the government without compensation to the Navajo. The stock reduction forced many Navajo into other work, including wage labor for whites, and lowered the status of women, who had owned most of the livestock (see Shepardson 1982).

Many Navajo have served in the military, beginning with World War I. The Navajo "Code Talkers" of World War II used their own language in open radio transmissions to communicate with other American units in the Pacific. The language, which at the time was unwritten, was so utterly foreign to the Japanese that they were never able to translate it. The Acoma and Choctaw performed a similar function in World War I, as did the Comanche in France during World War II and a movie, *Windtalkers*, was recently made about the Navajo code talkers.

World War II brought many changes to the Navajo. Prior to the war, most Navajo were fairly isolated on the reservation. During the war, many Navajo served in the military or moved to cities to work in war plants. Others worked for the railroads at remote stations to provide water for the steam locomotives. As a result, the Navajo became integrated into mainstream American society, and many Navajo "communities" still exist in major cities. Additional details of Navajo history are provided in Brugge (1983) and Robert Roessel (1983).

Cosmology

The Navajo believed that there were two types of people: Earth Surface People, ordinary human beings; and Holy People, supernatural and mysterious beings. There are a number of versions of the story telling how the world was created and describing migrations of The People. A common thread, however, is that after the universe was created, the Navajo moved through several worlds (usually between four and five, but sometimes as many as fourteen depending on the version of the story), finally emerging on the present surface of the earth. The following version was summarized mostly from Downs (1972:96–97; also see Gill 1983; Zolbrod 1984; and Parezo 1996b:3–6).

The world was created at "the place where the waters crossed." There were twelve worlds, one lying atop another. Holy People inhabited the lowest of these worlds, but disorder forced them to move up to the next world, then to the next, and so on. Each move resulted in an increase in the knowledge and practices that would ultimately be important to the Earth Surface People (the Navajo). Eventually some of the Holy People arrived on the surface of the earth, only to find it flooded. Then the waters receded and exposed the earth. Among the Holy People were First Man and First Woman, who were the parents of Changing Woman. Changing Woman mated with Sun and gave birth to twin boys. The twins grew up to slay the monsters plaguing the surface of the earth. The bodies of these monsters can still be seen in the landscape as important natural features. Finally, the Earth Surface People (the Navajo) were created and were taught all of the things necessary to live in the world (Dinétah).

The Navajo believed that the Holy People still inhabit the lower worlds as well as the surface of the earth. The Holy People are powerful but not necessarily "good"; in fact, many are "evil." Changing Woman is the only one that is dependable and trustworthy. One of the Holy People, Spider Woman, taught the Navajo the art of weaving.

Politics and External Relations

The Navajo did not traditionally have an overall tribal government (although they do today; see below). The political organization was so fully integrated into the social organization that separate discussion of the two is difficult. The Navajo were organized into a relatively large number of small, autonomous social and political units, sometimes called bands, which may have been the equivalent of the social units called "outfits" or clans (see below). Each band had a male headman who dealt with outsiders, but the females dominated the political process. The family matriarch made most of the family decisions, although the opinion of the male was considered. The family discussed the issues before decisions were made. Although the bands were autonomous, the Navajo recognized a relatedness between the bands, and they often cooperated.

Prior to 1864 the Navajo appear to have had war and peace chiefs. Raiding was conducted most frequently in the winter. In addition to raiding, the Navajo traded with many of their neighbors, including a number of Pueblo groups. Navajo livestock and woven goods were major trade items, as were slaves.

Social Organization

Navajo social (and political) organization (see Witherspoon 1981, 1983) was dominated by their matrilineal relationships, and the bond between mother and child was the closest and strongest relationship in Navajo life. The basic social unit was the nuclear family, organized around the mother and her livestock and fields, and individuals always had the right to live where their mothers lived. When a woman married, she and her husband generally moved to her mother's land, forming a new family unit. If a man divorced, he generally moved back to his mother's land, leaving the children with their mother.

A number of nuclear families related through a matriarch lived in the same immediate vicinity (within shouting distance), effectively forming an extended family unit, also called a residence or homestead unit. Residence units were very mobile, and many had both summer and winter homes. The residence unit would move around to exploit changes in the availability of water, firewood, and grazing. When a residence unit grew too large, it would divide, and a new unit would be formed. The residence unit was the primary social and economic segment of Navajo society.

The outfit was the next-largest social unit (but is becoming less common today), composed of several residence units distributed over a relatively large area. These units worked together on certain endeavors, such as ceremonies. The Navajo also had some sixty matrilineal clans, whose functions were to regulate marriage (they were exogamous) and offer hospitality. In addition, the Navajo recognized age grades, the differing status of young and old people. Despite these kinship ties, the Navajo remained highly individualistic.

Women did the weaving, pottery-making, cooking, butchering, household work, education of female children, hairdressing for both sexes, and (along with the children) the sheepherding. Males herded horses and cattle, did most of the heavy agricultural labor, educated the male children, disciplined all the children, and dealt with outsiders. Men conducted most of the ceremonies and did the silversmithing. Everyone assisted in collecting water and firewood and in planting and harvesting crops.

Women held considerable power in Navajo society, and considerable research has been done on Navajo women (see the special issue on Navajo women in the *American Indian Quarterly*, Vol. 6, Nos. 1–2, 1982; Lamphere 1989; Shepardson 1995). A few females were known to have participated in combat. Berdaches were somewhat venerated as they were thought to possess special powers. Women owned the land and improvements, but individuals of both sexes owned their own personal property, including individual animals, handmade items (e.g., woven articles, silver jewelry), and wages.

Life Cycle

The life cycle of a Navajo person was a "walk" through time over a trail symbolized in ritual (see Reichard 1950:37–49). Each person had a destiny that had to be protected by ceremony, although this destiny could be influenced by an individual's actions. In general, the lifestyle of most Navajo was rather leisurely, with little pressure and no great rush to do things.

During childbirth, the mother was assisted by another woman, and the child was then blessed in a small ceremony. The afterbirth was secretly buried so that witches could not cast a spell on it. The infant spent much of its first few years on a cradleboard and dictated its own feeding and sleeping schedule. Discipline was not severe and corporal punishment was rare.

At a girl's first menses, a four-day puberty ceremony was held in which the girl was required to conduct a number of rituals, such as grinding corn and avoiding certain foods. During this time other females would massage and "sculpt" the young woman's body so that she would be beautiful. When the ceremony was over, the woman was eligible for marriage. When a boy's voice began to change, he was invited into the sweatlodge to spend time with the men. After that, the boy was considered an adult.

Marriage was essentially mandatory, as only married people were considered functioning adults. The adult women of a young man's matrilineage usually selected his wife. The father of the groom made the arrangements with the bride's family, and if they reached an agreement, a bride-price of livestock was given to the bride's family. Economic and political considerations were the most important aspects of mate selection; romantic love had little or nothing to do with it. The wedding was held at the bride's parents' house, and both families attended. After the marriage, the couple usually established a new household near the wife's mother. Some polygyny was practiced, and wealthy males could have two or three wives. However, the wives almost always lived in separate households near their mothers. Divorce was not uncommon but was greatly discouraged, as it meant that the male would lose his economic base (mostly owned by the women) and any prestige related to it.

The Navajo feared the dead, or more specifically, the ghosts of the dead. Ghosts were considered evil, and evil was believed to be contagious; contact with the dead might result in the transmission of evil to the living. Murder was bad since it involved contact with a dead person and a ghost that was evil. The dead were buried as soon as possible, and special power (e.g., a shaman) was needed to touch the dead in order to bury them. Whenever possible, the Navajo got others, such as slaves or whites, to bury their dead for them. Once a person was buried, a four-day mourning ceremony was held, and the hogan (house) and personal property of the deceased were destroyed or buried with them. Some property was inherited, generally from mother to daughter or father to son.

Economics

After contact the Navajo became primarily pastoralists but they also practiced some agriculture and some hunting and gathering. The most important domestic animal was the sheep; wealth was measured by the number of sheep an individual owned. Sheep provided the major source of meat and all of the wool needed for weaving. Sheep were usually kept in pens at the family homestead during the night, driven to pastures for the day, then driven back to the pens for the night, a routine practiced on most days. During the summer, sheep herds might be moved to better pastures far from the homestead, and the herders might be gone for extended periods. Sheep are very easy to control and herd, and almost every capable person took part in herding activities. Dogs were used to help herd the sheep and to guard the herd from packs of wild dogs. Dogs also served to keep the homestead fairly clean by eating garbage and feces.

Other animals, including cattle, were also herded but were much less important than sheep. Horses transported people and materials and contributed to social standing; everyone was expected to own at least one horse. Goats were often kept with the sheep herds and provided a source of milk and cheese. The Navajo also kept some chickens.

A Navajo mother and daughter hoeing cornfields, 1939. (CORBIS)

Each residence unit had one or more agricultural fields, tended by one or more women. Corn was the primary crop, but beans and squash were also grown, along with wheat and oats. Fruit orchards were common and peaches were the most popular fruit.

Hunting was not a very important source of food, although a few small animals, particularly rabbits and rodents, were taken for meat, and the skins of coyotes and bobcats were traded to other groups. Some wild plants were gathered for food, but for the most part plant were used as dyes and medicines.

Material Culture and Technology

The Navajo lived in hogans, which were six- or eight-sided log structures, although some hogans used for ceremonies were round. The front of the hogan always faced east toward the sunrise. Hogans had earth-covered roofs, dirt floors, and a blanket as a door; these structures were warm in the winter and cool in the summer. The Navajo used little interior furniture, and personal belongings were stored in boxes or in between spaces in the logs. People slept on sheepskins laid on the floor. In the summer, when members of the family were tending sheep away from their primary home, they would construct small brush shelters or live in tents.

Small semisubterranean sweatlodges (about ten feet in diameter) were built near residences and were typically used by men once a week. Much of the household work was conducted outdoors under shades, and animals were kept in fenced pens.

After their arrival in the Southwest, the Navajo adopted dress similar to that of the Pueblo people. Men wore cotton kilts, no shirt, and turban-like headgear, while women wore garments made from two blankets joined at the shoulders and held by a sash. After 1868, clothing changed to more Euroamerican styles, and men wore pants, shirts, and felt hats. Women adopted cotton skirts and velvet blouses. Both sexes continued to wear moccasins. Silver jewelry was common and worn by both sexes to advertise wealth and status, and it was bought and sold frequently.

Many tools were made of wood, such as digging sticks, bows, looms, and water troughs. Stone was used to manufacture grinding tools, arrow points, axes, and hoes. The Navajo manufactured some basketry for containers, particularly water canteens, and occasionally used pottery. Equipment related to horses, such as harnesses, was fashioned from leather. After contact, the Navajo rapidly adopted many European goods.

Religion and Medicine

The Navajo had no word for religion, as their supernatural belief system was so integrated into their society that such a distinction was unnecessary. A major study of Navajo religion was conducted by Reichard (1950), and a recent summary was presented by Wyman (1983). In sum, the universe was a single entity in which good and evil coexisted. The Navajo were part of this universe and had to follow its laws to be successful. Religious activity helped keep the universe in a harmonious state, a constant battle since evil disrupted harmony.

Navajo rituals, ceremonies, and chants (songs) formed a very complex system for curing, blessing, and purification, so as to maintain harmony in the universe. A secondary goal of the system was to increase wealth and prosperity by ensuring the well-being of crops and livestock.

The numerous individual ceremonies, called chants or sings, were organized into categories of ceremonies called "Ways." Ceremonies involved singing, music, ritual paraphernalia, and offerings, and had to be conducted properly, as mistakes had adverse consequences. Ways were divided into two main categories, major and minor (see Werner et al. 1983: Tables 20 and 21). The most important of the major Ways was the Holyway, a system of chants used primarily to cure illnesses, real or anticipated. The specific chant selected was based on the origin of the illness. For a major disaster or illness, the complex Yeibeichai ceremony was held. In this nine-day event, masked men, the Yei, performed ceremonies, songs, and dances.

Another major ceremony was the Enemyway, which involved cleansing chants to remove the evil from the ghosts of the dead that may have contaminated a Navajo. During the summer, an individual who wanted to have a curing chant might also sponsor a Squaw Dance, a four-day event attended by many people. Courtship was often conducted near the end of this ceremony (hence the name). Enemyway ceremonies are still occasionally performed for returning veterans. The most important of the other Ways was the Blessingway, which included ceremonies to foster good, bring luck, protect livestock, or bless a new hogan, marriage, or baby.

Many chants involved the practice of drypainting, sometimes called sandpainting (see Parezo 1983; Griffin-Pierce 1992). Drypaintings were made with colored sand and represented events involving Holy People; particular depictions related to specific ceremonies. These renderings, made on the ground, stretched from two to fifteen feet wide. Once finished, the drypainting had completed its function and was destroyed. Today, sandpaintings are made for commercial sale (see Parezo 1983).

Navajo ceremonial specialists, also called singers or chanters, performed the ceremonies. These specialists, usually men, were more than just doctors. They functioned as curers, priests, and shamans. They could learn and use evil songs as well as good ones; those using evil were called witches and were feared (see Kluckhohn 1944). Shamans did use some pharmacological materials for curing, including preparations made from both plants and animals, but most illnesses were dealt with ceremonially.

Since they feared ghosts, the Navajo had little interest in the Ghost Dances of 1870 and 1890, believing that the good segment of the dead person blended back with the universe while the evil part became a ghost. The Native American Church (which used peyote; see Aberle 1983a) did become fairly popular with the Navajo, but many others adopted Christianity.

Art, Expression, and Recreation

The Navajo are well known for their excellent weaving (see Amsden 1934; Reichard 1934; Ruth Roessel 1983; Kaufman and Selser 1985; Bonar 1997), an art practiced primarily by women. Weaving skills were probably learned from the Pueblo refugees taken in by the Navajo after the Pueblo Revolt in 1680, although the Navajo believed that weaving was taught to them by Spider Woman. Woven items, primarily made of wool, included rugs, blankets, clothing, saddle blankets, and sashes. Weaving continues to be an important artistic and economic activity.

The Navajo are also well known for their work in silver. This art may have been learned early on from the Mexicans, but it was greatly developed while the Navajo were incarcerated at Bosque Redondo. Most early Navajo work derived from plain silver coins, but later craftworkers used bulk silver, often adding turquoise as well (see Ruth Roessel 1983). Work in silver continues to be an important artistic and economic activity.

Music was popular and included different categories of traditional songs: casual, sacred, and ceremonial (the latter often called chants). Dancing played a role in some ceremonies. Musical instruments included rattles and drums made from goatskins stretched over the mouth of a pottery vessel full of water or a basket turned upside down. Within the past century, some Christian and Anglo music has become popular among the Navajo (see McAllester and Mitchell 1983).

The Navajo amused themselves in a number of ways; one preferred sport was racing. Horse racing was the most popular, and had high stakes: loser forfeited his horse to the winner. Footraces were also popular. A man would challenge another man to a public footrace and would whip him in jest with yucca leaves if he lost. The participants of these races were generally men, but women also wagered on the outcomes.

The Navajo played a variety of games (see Cliff 1990). Archers would test their skill by throwing a target into the air and shooting at it, with hits counting as points. The hoop-and-pole game involved throwing arrows and/or sticks at a small circular target, much like European darts. Women played shinny. Games of chance, including dice and guessing games, were also common. People commonly gambled on the outcome of games.

The Navajo Today

Today, the Navajo reservation covers some sixteen million acres in four separate tracts. Of the approximately 270,000 Navajo in 2000 (census data), most live on the reservation. The modern tribal government was established in 1923 (see Shepardson 1963, 1983) but was only integrated into internal Navajo politics after about 1945. The government of the Navajo Nation is now very well established (see Iverson 1981, 1983; see the Navajo Nation homepage at *http://www.navajo.org*). The reservation is divided into more than 100 voting regions, called chapters, and nineteen grazing districts. The capital is located in Window Rock, Arizona. The Navajo Nation has its own legal staff, environmental staff, police, health services (see Bergman 1983), and schools, including the four-year Diné College (see Emerson 1983).

The Navajo Nation must deal with many outside interests competing for the considerable mineral wealth within the reservation. The tribal government has had some difficulties. In 1988 the tribal chairman was removed on charges of corruption, an issue that still plagues the Nation. Issues involving the mining of coal and uranium (Brugge et al. 2001), water rights, power plants, pollution, and grazing rights (see Iverson 1981; Aberle 1983b; Tome 1983) continue to occupy the nation. Perhaps the most emotional issue to the Navajo is the land dispute with the Hopi. The loss of land and the forced removal of Navajo families to other lands created considerable distress for many families (see Sidelight on page 224).

The reservation continues to be the center of Navajo life, even for those who do not live there. Pickup trucks have replaced horses and wagons for transportation, but horses are still widely used in herding. Alcohol is prohibited on the reservation, but many Navajos travel to Gallup, New Mexico, on the weekends to drink; some stay there for longer periods, living as "homeless" persons.

Most Navajo living on the reservation are relatively poor, with about half living below the federal poverty level. Most homes lack modern conveniences such as indoor plumbing, electricity, and central heating. However, these numbers are somewhat misleading since many Navajo have chosen not to use these utilities, preferring traditional housing.

The cutbacks in livestock mandated by the federal government beginning in 1933 have forced the Navajo to diversify their economic base. The nation now has interests in coal, gas, oil, timber, and gravel. A new dam built on the San Juan River has increased irrigated agricultural lands. Interestingly, unlike many other native groups, the Navajo Nation has struggled with gaming. In early 1994 the Tribal Council approved the concept, but the council chairman vetoed it. The issue was sent to the voters in 1994 but was rejected (see Henderson and Russell 1997). Recently, however, the Navajo Nation Code was amended to allow gaming, and plans are underway to build a casino near Albuquerque, New Mexico. The production of art for sale to tourists continues to be a major aspect of the Navajo economy. Navajo textiles (see Ruth Roessel 1983; Schiffer 1991), sandpaintings (see Parezo 1983), pottery, and silver work are sold in thousands of shops in the Southwest and around the world.

The Tarahumara: A Southwestern Case Study

The Tarahumara (or Tarahumar, Tarahumare, or Tarahumari) live in the western Sierra Madre in the state of Chihuahua in northern Mexico (Fig. 9.6). Around the time of contact (ca. 1600), the population was about 40,000, occupying an area of about 40,000 square miles. The Tarahumara divide people into two categories: Rarámuri (meaning either "human" or "footrunner"), the name that the Tarahumara apply to themselves and other Indians, and the chabochis, or non-Indians (and so not really human). The Tarahumara generally assign people to one of these two categories based on physical characteristics. There is considerable variation among communities, due to environmental differences and the extent of contact with chabochis. This case study of the Tarahumara describes them as they were in about 1900, but in many respects little has changed in the past hundred years.

A great deal of information on the Tarahumara was recorded by Jesuit and Franciscan priests and Spanish colonial administrators, but most of this material has not been synthesized. Formal anthropological information on the Tarahumara is limited, having only been obtained after about 1890. Major works on the Tarahumara include Lumholtz (1902), Bennett and Zingg (1935), Champion (1962), Pennington (1963, 1983), Fried (1969), Kennedy (1978, 1990), Fontana

(1979), Merrill (1983, 1988), Raat and Janeček (1996), and Sheridan (1996). The information on the Tarahumara summarized below is from these sources.

The Natural Environment

The Tarahumara lived in the western Sierra Madre, commonly called the Sierra Tarahumara. The region is one of mountains and canyons, more rugged on the western side than on the eastern. Many rivers drain the Sierra Tarahumara; the two largest are the Rio Fuerte, flowing west to the Gulf of California, and the Rio Conchos, flowing east to join the Rio Grande. Elevations range between 1,000 and 10,000 feet. Many Tarahumara lived in the upland regions at about 6,000 feet, along the rivers and canyons where arable land could be found, and near extensive forests of pine and oak.

The climate of the upland region was moderate, with relatively cool summers and mild winters, although it froze between October and March, preventing year-round corn agriculture. Rainfall varied, but came mostly in the summer. The bottoms of many of the canyons were hot and almost tropical in climate.

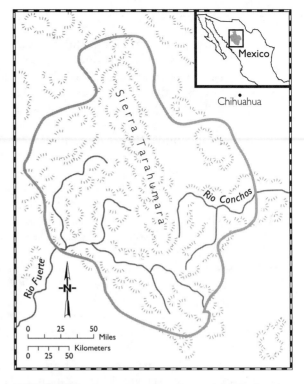

FIGURE 9.6 Location and territory of the Tarahumara in northern Mexico in about 1700
Adapted from C. W. Pennington, "Tarahumara" in *Handbook of North American Indians*, Vol. 10, *Southwest*, A. Ortiz, ed., Fig. 1a; copyright © 1983 by the Smithsonian Institution. Reprinted by permission of the publisher.

The principal biotic communities were forests of oak, mixed pine and oak, and mixed pine and juniper. Agave was also abundant in some areas. A great variety of other plants grew in the Sierra Tarahumara, and the people used many of them for food, manufacturing materials, and medicines. Diverse animals included many large and small mammals, a number of birds (including migrating waterfowl), many species of fish, and a variety of insects. Many animals were hunted for food and fur.

Language

The Tarahumara spoke Tarahumara, a language of the Southern Uto-Aztecan language family (distantly related to Aztec). Most Tarahumara did not speak Spanish, unless it was required for a particular job.

A Brief History

People have inhabited the Sierra Tarahumara for a long time, but very little is actually known of Tarahumara prehistory (see Phillips 1989). The Tarahumara were first contacted by the Spanish in 1607. In 1610, the Jesuits began to enter southern Tarahumara territory, eventually establishing a series of 29 missions and some 60 churches (see Dunne 1948; Polzer et al. 1991). Beginning in the early seventeenth century, the Spanish seized much of the good agricultural land in the valleys and, under the *repartimiento* system (see Chapter 2), forced many Tarahumara to work in the silver mines and the fields of the Spaniards. In 1648, the Tarahumara revolted but were defeated by Spanish troops. They revolted again in 1650 and 1652, and while both these uprisings were suppressed, the missionization of the northern Tarahumara country was delayed until 1678. Two other revolts, in 1690 and 1697, again frustrated the missionization efforts of the Jesuits.

Two smallpox epidemics, in 1693 and 1695, swept through the Tarahumara, but the impact on the population is not well understood. Beginning in the late seventeenth century, many Tarahumara retreated into the mountains to avoid the Spanish. The Jesuits were expelled by the Spanish Crown in 1767 and were replaced by the Franciscans (see Sheridan et al. 1991). The Franciscans took over some of the churches but abandoned others. In 1900 the Jesuits returned, again trying to missionize the Tarahumara (see Roca 1979; Sheridan and Naylor 1979).

The Tarahumara felt the impact of mining, ranching, and lumbering. In the mid–nineteenth century the Mexican government instituted a series of "reform laws" that turned over additional Tarahumara lands to chabochis and sparked several more revolts (in 1876, 1895, and 1898). The construction of a railroad through the Sierra Tarahumara was begun in 1900 and completed in 1961, providing access to formerly isolated areas and increasing migration of non-Indians into the region. This in turn led to greater exploitation of natural resources. Throughout the twentieth century, the Mexican government has tried to assimilate the Tarahumara into Mexican society.

Cosmology

The earth and its inhabitants were the most recent in a series of creations and destructions. Onorùame (God) created the earth, and people originated in a contest between God and his older brother, Riablo (the Devil), as they tried to see who could create human beings first. They each made clay figures and fired them. Onorùame's figures were of a darker color and became the Tarahumara, while the lighter-colored figures of Riablo became the chabochis. Onorùame breathed life into the Tarahumara but had to teach Riablo how to furnish souls. A footrace between the Tarahumara and chabochis was organized, and the wealth of all people was bet on the outcome. The chabochis won, took all the wealth, and left the area. From then on, the Tarahumara were poor and could pay for things only with corn and beer (adapted from Merrill 1988:93–94).

Politics and External Relations

The Tarahumara never comprised a single, unified political entity. In 1900 (and continuing today) two largely separate political systems coexist among the people.

Most Tarahumara were Catholic and lived in towns (pueblos) with churches and a colonial-style town government. The pueblos had formal mayors who organized fiestas, performed marriages, and mediated disputes. Towns also had a police force, a judge, and various other officials.

However, some Tarahumara retained their traditional systems of beliefs, politics, and settlement practices, living in small communities in remote areas. The non-Christian Tarahumara were called *gentils*. Each gentil community consisted of a few contiguous households with a headman and elders. These leaders sometimes congregated to decide issues of regional importance. Although largely independent at the community level, the gentil communities were ultimately connected to the Mexican government.

Both pueblo and gentil communities required a community consensus on any decision. Men had to be thirty-five to fifty years of age to have influence over political decisions; "rich" men, those who owned livestock, had greater political influence. Most crimes were handled within the community. For example, assault, theft, and fighting were punished by elders, who lectured the offenders; the public shame associated with the crime served as part of the punishment. Murder was the worst crime, and those offenders were turned over to Mexican authorities.

Warfare was common prior to contact, both against neighbors, particularly the Tepehuanes to the south, and among themselves. Since contact, however, the Tarahumara have been very peaceful, even earning the reputation for nonviolence among their neighbors. However, this unwarlike attitude did not prevent them from revolting against Spanish and Mexican oppression on several occasions.

Social Organization

The basic Tarahumara social unit was the nuclear family, but extended families were not uncommon, as elderly people would frequently move in with their adult children. Kinship was bilateral, figured equally through both sides of the family (similar to the system commonly used in the United States today). There were no lineage or clan organizations, although a number of sodalities did exist. The town, or small community, formed the hub of the social network. Most things, including land, were owned by individuals, and upon a person's death, the property was passed through kinship lines to other individuals, usually a son or daughter.

Tarahumara families who lived near canyons often would maintain a summer residence and agricultural fields in the uplands, descending into the warmer canyons for the winter. There the families would plant winter crops of corn and tend livestock.

Perhaps the single most important aspect of Tarahumara social organization was the frequent drinking parties (*Tesgüinadas*) at which homemade beer was consumed. These parties were held as a reward for help with labor, at fiestas, at rituals, and for entertainment. The sponsor of the party (generally men) invited friends, relatives, and persons who had assisted him; he would provide all of the beer and food. These beer parties served to establish cooperative and reciprocal relationships and kept families and communities close. A person might attend some 50 beer parties a year.

Though one goal at a beer party was to get drunk, socializing, dancing, and meeting members of the opposite sex were also important. Both sexes tended to be shy and "needed" the drink to work up the courage to have sex, even with their spouses. Many relationships were initiated at beer parties, and many secret liaisons were begun or ended. Lots of joking took place at beer parties, and sexual humor and good-natured insults were traded back and forth.

No strict cultural rules determined the division of labor. Duties reflected differences in ability, physical strength, or preferences. In general, men did heavy labor, house building, woodcutting, firewood collection (oak was preferred), field preparation, fence building, butchering, and herding of cattle. Women and children generally tended the other animals (e.g., goats and sheep). Women also performed domestic chores, including the preparation of corn (the staple food), the manufacture of pottery and wool yarn, the weaving of wool blankets, cooking, laundry, and cleaning. Men helped with these tasks if needed, and any elderly person living with a family would also help. Everyone participated in planting and harvesting activities. Children did a variety of chores as needed. The Tarahumara had a tradition of sharing and helping those in need, although they may have done so partly out of fear of retaliation from witches if they did not share (see Passin 1942). The Tarahumara generally tolerated berdaches but classified them as deviant.

Life Cycle

A woman gave birth in a standing position, assisted by her husband or a female friend. The baby was then washed and put in a blanket, and the placenta and umbilical cord were buried. A "birth fiesta" was held three days later if the baby was male, or four days later if the baby was female. The infant mortality rate was very high, about 50 percent. A family usually desired two or three children. Individuals were given Spanish first names, with surnames indicating the village of birth (e.g., Juan Creel would be a male named Juan from the village of Creel). Children were educated by the parent of the same sex.

Mothers carried their babies in a sling and shared constant contact until babies reached the age of two. As a rule, the children had a great deal of freedom. Misbehaving children were scolded but corporal punishment was rare. Older children served as babysitters. Children's toys reflected their roles in the community; girls had domestic toys (dolls, kitchens, etc.) and gave beer parties for their dolls, while boys cared for herds of toy livestock until they were old enough to care for real animals. Boys spent a great deal of time herding goats until marriage.

Boys began drinking beer at about age fourteen, girls a few years later. Sexual activities began at beer parties, where potential partners felt less shy. Little formal attention was given to puberty; some girls were not even warned of the onset of first menses, which came as a surprise. Catholic children went through confirmation.

Males married in their late teens or early twenties, but girls generally married a bit younger. Some people married for love but others had arranged marriages. When a male found the girl he wanted to marry, usually from his own town, he would tell the mayor. The mayor, in turn, would visit the family of the girl and make the proposal. The family would think it over, and if everyone agreed, the marriage went forward. The brief ceremony was usually held at the girl's parents' house, where the mayor married the couple in front of guests. A fiesta to celebrate the marriage was held at a later date. The Catholic church did not recognize such marriages, and in areas where Catholicism was prevalent a priest was sought to perform the ceremony. The couple would generally live with the wife's parents until they could build their own house.

Marriage was one way to obtain wealth (land and/or livestock), and the wealth of a potential spouse was always a consideration. Men sometimes married older, experienced women, even twenty years their senior, as an ideal wife "knows how to work well." Such unions were looked on as odd but were not prohibited. Polygyny was permitted but was rare. Some men had two wives, but only if the first wife did not object, and the two wives always lived in separate houses. Some men tried to keep the second wife a secret.

A Tarahumara mother and child.
(Photo by R. W. Robinson, 1971, courtesy of the photographer.)

Adultery was not uncommon, as women who became intoxicated at a beer party were more easily seduced. On occasion, consensual wife exchange occurred at beer parties. However, Tarahumara women would not marry or have affairs with chabochis. Divorce was a simple matter; the dissatisfied party could move back to his or her parents' house and so be divorced. A divorced female retained title to any land she owned. It was not uncommon for a Tarahumara to have had two or three spouses in his or her lifetime.

The dead were rapidly buried in cemeteries, but in some areas the bodies were placed in small caves, which were then sealed with rock. The deceased were interred with some of their personal belongings, and their houses were abandoned and burned. The community held a series of "death fiestas," three for a male, four for a female. The first fiesta took place three (for males) or four (for females) days after death, the second three (or four) weeks after death, and the remaining fiestas were held within a year. When the celebrations were completed (the fiestas were considered happy events), the soul of the deceased was safely in heaven. A widow was expected to wait until the fiesta cycle was complete before she remarried. Individual family members, rather than the family as a whole, inherited the property of the deceased.

Economics

The primary subsistence system of the Tarahumara was farming; corn, beans, and squash were the major crops. Corn was planted on the plateaus between April and May and was harvested between October and November. Families who had moved into the canyons for the winter grew an additional corn crop in smaller fields.

Cornfields were tilled using wooden plows pulled by cattle, which had been brought to the region by the Spanish after 1610. The Tarahumara had practiced agriculture before they had draft animals. Once the earth was plowed, people used wooden sticks to plant corn in rows. As the corn grew, they heaped soil on the roots, forming a small hill. Once the corn was hilled, beans and squash were planted between the cornstalks.

Farmers cooperated in the tasks of plowing, weeding, and harvesting. The owner of a field hosted a big beer party for the men who participated in the work. The fields were guarded against pests such as coyotes, foxes, squirrels, crows, and cornworms. Squirrels were trapped and eaten, crows would be shot and hung in the field to scare away other crows, and cornworms were collected from the plants and eaten. Harvested corn was stored in stone or wooden cribs. A variety of other crops, including potatoes, chiles, wheat, mustard greens, some fruits, and tobacco (used in cornhusk cigarettes), were grown in smaller gardens.

Livestock were very important in the Tarahumara economy, and wealth was often measured by the number of animals an individual owned. Surplus corn was also a measure of wealth, as it meant that more beer could be made and so more labor obtained. Goats were the most important animal; they were adaptable to various ecological conditions and provided the most fertilizer, along with some milk and cheese. Cattle were the second most important animal, a source of meat, leather, and plow labor. The Tarahumara also kept horses, burros, sheep (important for wool production), pigs, dogs, turkeys, and chickens. Manure was valued as fertilizer, and animals were kept in fallow fields to deposit manure. Families who did not own any livestock borrowed animals to fertilize their fields. Livestock had to be constantly tended so that they did not break fences and get into the crops. The owner of livestock that damaged someone else's fields was held liable. Dogs were kept as pets and helped to hunt and herd animals, but were not eaten.

The stored corn crop was often exhausted before the next harvest, so people supplemented their food supplies by hunting and gathering, an important activity that continues today. Wild plants gathered for food included the nuts of pine, oak, and walnut trees; the seeds of many other plants (including juniper); many grasses; and the leaves of ash and oak. The hearts of the century plant (*Agave* sp.), or mescal plant, used by the Mexicans to make mescal, were roasted and eaten.

Many animals were hunted, including deer, rabbits, squirrels, mice, birds (e.g., turkeys, quail, and waterfowl), snakes, lizards, fish, and insects (including grasshoppers, cornworms, and grubs). The skins of some animals, including deer, rabbits, jaguars, otters, and foxes, were used for sleeping and sitting mats. Bears were rarely killed, as they were thought to possess the spirits of ancestors.

Hunters would run down deer, turkeys, and rabbits until the animals collapsed from exhaustion. Deer took several days to run down; they were kept on the move until they collapsed and then were beaten to death. Bows and arrows were used to kill other animals, as were pit traps (with wooden stakes at the bottom) and small deadfall traps. People would also throw rocks to kill an animal at close range. Dogs helped track and run down animals.

The Tarahumara caught a variety of fish with hook and line, nets, and/or traps. Also, special plants were ground up and thrown into still water, causing the fish to suffocate and float to the surface for easy capture.

In general, the Tarahumara diet was quite healthy. Meat was usually eaten only at ceremonies, but such activities were frequent. Corn was the primary food and was prepared in a number of ways, mostly as pinole, a flour made by parching the kernels and grinding them several times on a metate. Pinole keeps well for long periods; though it can be prepared in many ways, it was commonly mixed with water and consumed as a beverage. Atole, a cooked corn gruel, was also popular. Corn was eaten in tamales and tortillas and fresh on the ear.

Homemade beer made mostly from corn, took three days to prepare but was good for only about one day; therefore it was necessary to drink all that was made rather quickly. To let any go bad would be considered a waste. The Tarahumara also made several other alcoholic beverages from native plants (e.g., agave), but Mexican liquor was rarely consumed.

Most Tarahumara practiced barter and reciprocity for economic transactions, although there was some use of Mexican money. Some lowland Tarahumara, who were in greater contact with the Mexicans, traveled to mestizo towns to trade with or do wage labor for the Mexicans.

Material Culture and Technology

The Tarahumara lived in simple, rectangular, wooden houses made from hewn boards, with earthen floors, few windows, and wooden roofs, although some houses were made from stone. A winter home in the canyon might consist of a cave or rock shelter, made livable by walling up most of the cave entrance. Crops were stored in carefully constructed wooden or masonry granaries.

Almost all transportation was by foot. Running was, and continues to be, a proud tradition among the Tarahumara, who were renowned for their running skills. (Recently, a Tarahumara team entered a worldwide running contest and won three of the top five spots, with first place going to a 55-year-old man [see Williams 1994].)

Women wore wide, long, brightly colored skirts, long-sleeved blouses, bandanna headbands, and earrings and necklaces made of glass beads, but generally no footgear. Most women wore their hair braided. Men wore loincloths, long-sleeved shirts, sandals, sashes, and headbands. The men also carried small bags in which they kept their important belongings (knife, tobacco, money). Children dressed like adults, but rarely wore footgear.

The Tarahumara used a variety of tools, the metal axe being the most important. Corn was ground on stone metates using a stone mano. Some arrowheads and knives were also made from flaked stone. A number of pottery forms were used, including bowls, spoons, and ollas (large vessels) for storage and cooking. Many items, such as sandals and bags, were manufactured from leather.

Dried gourds formed different kinds of containers, and wood was used for bowls, digging and planting sticks, hoes, plows, and bows. People made baskets in a variety of forms, including storage containers, trays, bowls, and water bottles. Plant fibers provided material for the manufacture of cordage for use in nets, belts, headbands, and rope. Blankets and belts were woven from wool and were often well decorated.

Religion and Medicine

Most Tarahumara practiced a unique brand of Catholicism. The original Tarahumara beliefs (held by the gentils) included three major deities: Father the Sun, Mother the Moon, and their child, Morning Star. Later, these deities were easily transformed into Christian figures (God, Mary, and Jesus) by the Catholics. The traditional Tarahumara universe contained seven levels, the most important being the upper (sky), middle (earth), and lower (the Underworld). Sun and Moon lived in the highest world and created the earth, the Tarahumara, and all other Indians. The Devil lived in the lowest world, created the chabochis, and brought disease and misfortune. The world of the Devil was not the equivalent of the Christian hell; rather, it was heaven for the chabochis.

To the gentils, God and the Devil were not pure good and evil; they represented a balance in the universe, a balance that the Tarahumara sought to maintain. To keep the Tarahumara in the good graces of God, dances, offerings, and good behavior were required. God reciprocated by bringing good fortune. The Tarahumara also made offerings to the Devil, not to secure his assistance but to convince him not to harm them.

Most rituals were performed to maintain or restore balance in individuals or within the community. Many rituals were held to coincide with Catholic holy days, but curing rituals and death ceremonies were conducted whenever necessary. Most rituals involved a fiesta, where dancing, music, eating, and drinking continued for about two days. The fiestas were sponsored and paid for by a person seeking status in the community. The most important and elaborate ritual was held during the Catholic Holy Week.

The Tarahumara believed that all breathing things have souls. People and animals had the same type of soul, but the souls of birds and fish were slightly different. The soul of a human could leave the body while the person was dreaming. The Tarahumara believed in an afterlife, and the souls of the dead (people and animals) were thought to go to heaven if the cycle of fiestas was completed.

Shamans could be either men or women. They were quite powerful, since they could cure illness and communicate with souls through dreaming, and they played major roles in fiestas and all other events. Some shamans were more powerful than others; though peyote was not often used, peyote shamans were the most powerful (see Sidelight on Don Juan). An aspiring shaman felt called to the profession and served an apprenticeship, usually with a relative who was already a shaman. Witches or sorcerers existed (see Passin 1942) and projected evil through dreams or peyote. Witchcraft was the source of most illness and was treated by shamans supernaturally. For other types of illness or injury, shamans used a variety of medicines made from plants and from the grease of various animals.

Art, Expression, and Recreation

Music was important to the Tarahumara and was played at home, at all public occasions, and while tending livestock. The Tarahumara were famous for their violins (adapted from a Spanish design) but also used gourd rattles, flutes, and leather-covered drums. Beer parties formed the major source of entertainment.

The Tarahumara played a number of games. The most popular was a kickball race called *carrera de bola,* in which a wooden ball was kicked over a long predetermined course. The game was often played at beer parties and funerals; the object of the game was to see who could kick a ball over the course in the least amount of time. Footraces were also very popular, and races between individuals and teams (from two to twelve men or women) were common. Racers were often "cured" and protected by shamans, who functioned much like team doctors.

Other games included throwing small disks of stone or pottery into holes in the ground set some distance apart, wrestling, archery contests, and games with bone dice. Gambling on the outcome of sports and games was also customary.

The Tarahumara Today

Although the Tarahumara have lost about 50 percent of their land to European intrusion since contact, they still live in the same basic location and have a population of about 70,000. They continue to have a high infant mortality rate and low life expectancy. The past seventy years have brought a dramatic increase in the chabochi population, greatly intensifying the pressure on the Tarahumara land base. The Tarahumara generally refrain from interaction with the chabochis. Many reside in the hills, away from towns and chabochis; they have thus succeeded in retaining much of their traditional lifestyle. Nevertheless, Tarahumara women sometimes work as domestics in chabochi households, and Tarahumara men will do wage labor. Most families continue to grow or gather most of their own food but now buy some things from stores.

The Tarahumara face an uncertain future; industry and government policy are a challenge to their way of life. The lumber companies are the most recent intruders into the Sierra Tarahumara. Some Tarahumara men work for lumber companies or do road work for the government, and both activities deplete the forests. Drug smugglers are now using the area, placing the Tarahumara in the middle of the drug war.

The state government of Chihuahua has created a Tarahumara Coordinating Commission, and they, along with the Instituto Nacional Indigenista, are trying to "civilize" the Tarahumara. In addition, the government is trying to privatize communal Tarahumara lands to give lumber companies free rein. Only time will tell if the Tarahumara can survive as an independent culture. One bright spot is an increase in tourism, as outsiders pay to visit the area and see traditional Tarahumara. Perhaps this industry will ensure their survival. More information about the Tarahumara can be found at *http://www.tarahumara.org.mx.*

///

10 Native Peoples of the Plains

///

Indians on horseback in feathered headdresses form the popular image of native North Americans. However, this image was typical only of Plains (sometimes called the Great Plains) groups, and only within the past several hundred years. This simplistic view of Plains men is reinforced by the well-known military resistance of the Plains groups and of subsequent public interest (e.g., Hollywood movies) in that aspect of Plains culture. In reality, Plains cultures and peoples were varied and complex.

The precontact population of the Plains was probably rather small, but when horses became available after about 1700, groups on the Plains expanded in population while groups from other regions moved onto the Plains. These factors led to a complicated history and considerable linguistic diversity. Like the other culture areas, the Plains also have a defining characteristic: bison hunting.

Geography and Environment

Broadly defined, the Plains consist of the extensive grasslands that spread across the heartland of North America (see Wedel and Frison 2001). They extend from southern Canada about 1,500 miles south to central Texas, and from the eastern slope of the Rocky Mountains about 1,000 miles east to the Mississippi River Valley (Fig. 10.1). Due to the rainshadow effect of the Rocky Mountains, relatively little on the rain falls on the Plains; water and trees are found only in the river valleys that run east from the Rockies to eventually join with the Mississippi River.

The western portion of the Plains is a vast area of grassland (short grasses with shallow roots) with little surface water and few trees, commonly referred to as the

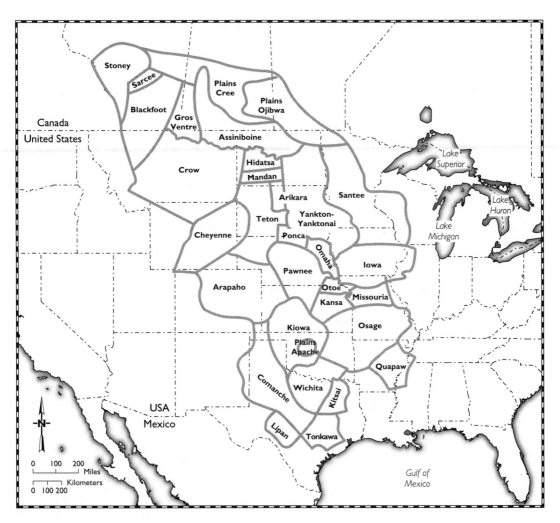

FIGURE 10.1 Map of the Plains culture area showing the locations of the native groups in the early nineteenth century

Adapted from *Handbook of North American Indians, Vol. 13, Plains*, Raymond J. DeMallie, ed., p. ix; copyright © 2001 by the Smithsonian Institution. Reprinted by permission of the publisher.

High Plains (it was called the Great American Desert by American settlers in the early nineteenth century). The High Plains were inhabited by a truly enormous number of bison—estimated to have been about sixty million in 1800—and many pronghorn antelope. Mobile hunter-gatherers on horseback exploited the bison, surviving rather successfully. The eastern part of the Plains consists of a number of widely spaced, broad valleys of the eastern-flowing rivers. This region, generally called the Prairies (or Prairie Plains), is relatively well watered and wooded and contains tall grasses with deep roots. It had fewer bison and was inhabited by settled agriculturalists who occasionally hunted bison. Some researchers have defined the Prairies as a separate culture area set off from the High Plains; however, the people of both regions shared a common tradition of bison hunting, and use of horses, and they engaged in similar patterns of warfare. Following the organization of the Plains volume of the *Handbook of North American Indians* (DeMallie 2001), the Prairies are included in this chapter with the High Plains, but differences between the two areas are noted.

The climate of the Plains is quite variable, with much colder winters in the north and hotter summers in the south. Rainfall is also variable, ranging from less than eight to twenty inches a year, and it is very windy at times. A considerable amount of snow falls on the High Plains, especially in the north. Native agriculture depended on two critical environmental variables: at least eight inches of rain and a hundred frost-free days per year. Corn could not be grown unless these two conditions were met.

A Basic Prehistory of the Plains

The division of the Plains culture area into the High Plains and the Prairies slightly complicates any discussion the prehistory of the Plains (see Wedel 1961; Frison 1978; Wood 1998; also see the eleven chapters on prehistory in the Plains volume of the *Handbook of North American Indians* [DeMallie 2001]). In essence, the Paleoindian and Archaic periods are the same for both regions until about 2,000 years ago, when the Prairie groups adopted corn agriculture.

The Paleoindian Period (ca. 12,000 to 9,000 B.P.)

Considerable evidence, including material from many Clovis sites, indicates that people hunted various Pleistocene megafauna, including the giant bison *(Bison antiquus)*, during the Paleoindian period on the Plains. By about 9,000 B.P., the megafauna had disappeared and the extensive grasslands of the High Plains were established, supporting large populations of the modern species of bison *(Bison bison)*. People adapted to the loss of the large game by exploiting smaller bison and other game. Dogs were present; thus the travois was also present.

The Archaic Period (ca. 9,000 to 2,500 B.P.)

Little is known about the Archaic period on the Plains. Bison continued to be a primary game animal, but people made use of many other resources. By about 6,000 B.P., the Plains had become hotter and drier, bison populations had diminished, and many people may have abandoned the area. Archaeologists have interpreted evidence of large stone rings dating from this period to conclude that tepee structures were in use by about 4,000 years ago; the stone rings apparently formed foundations for the tepees. After about 4,000 B.P., climatic conditions improved and bison populations increased. Group hunting of bison, on foot, reached its peak at about 1,500 B.P. The bow and arrow and ceramics were introduced at about the same time, making hunting and food processing a little easier. Also at this time, bison hides became important commodities in the extensive trade networks that developed on the southern Plains.

Beginning sometime around 1,000 B.P., people speaking Athapaskan languages began to migrate south from southern Canada, along the western edge of the Plains and toward the Southwest. These people, the ancestors of the Apache and Navajo, eventually entered the Southwest about 500 years ago (see Chapter 9), but some (e.g., the Plains Apache) remained on the southern Plains. About 300 years ago, the Northern Shoshone began to enter the northern Plains, pushing back the Black-foot, only to be pushed back into the Great Basin when the Blackfoot acquired guns from the Europeans. At about the same time, the Comanche, a group of Northern Shoshone, entered the northern Plains and moved south to Texas.

The Plains Woodland Period (ca. 2,500 to 1,000 B.P.)

On the Prairies, other events were occurring. Sometime about 2,000 B.P., corn and bean agriculture was introduced onto the Prairies from established farmers to the east. Groups in the river valleys, where soils and water were favorable for farming, adopted the new strategy but still retained bison hunting as their major economic pursuit. Somewhat later, they adopted ceramics and bows and arrows.

The Plains Village Period (ca. 1,000 B.P. to Contact)

By about 1,000 B.P., as populations and agricultural efficiency increased, agricultural settlements were established along the higher terraces of the various rivers (Missouri, Platte, Republican, Arkansas, and Red) that flowed east from the Rocky Mountains. These settlements, consisting of permanent towns with large, multi-family houses, were often fortified with stockades and moats. Beginning about 700 B.P., it appears that a drier climate forced people to alter their agricultural strategies and consolidate their relatively scattered settlements into the major river valleys. There they formed fewer, but larger, towns, permanent towns with bigger houses. Bison remained an important resource.

On the southern Plains, various Plains Village groups were replaced by hunter-gatherers (perhaps the Apachean groups) at about 600 B.P. The Caddo on the south-eastern Plains developed close ties with the Mississippian cultures of the Southeast (see Chapter 12).

The Contact Period

Prior to the arrival of the horse, only small groups of people lived on the High Plains proper. The large distances between water sources and the difficulty of hunting bison on foot limited the number of people who could live there. A person on foot had no hope of running down bison, so the animals had to be driven off cliffs or into arroyos, where those that did not die in the fall or were not crushed by other falling bison could easily be killed. Dogs pulled small travois loaded with the belongings of the people.

Large sedentary agricultural groups had lived in the river valleys of the Prairies for several thousand years. Primarily farmers, they occasionally ventured onto the High Plains on foot to hunt bison. These groups included the Mandan, Hidatsa, and Arikara in the north and the Pawnees, Omaha, and Wichita further south. This pattern of farming and hunting bison on foot was to change dramatically when horses were introduced after about 1700.

The first contact with Plains groups was made by the Spanish on the southern Plains in the late sixteenth century. De Soto crossed the southern Plains in 1540, likely spreading disease. By the time other Europeans visited the Plains, native populations had probably already been impacted by this earlier visit. The groups on the northern Plains (e.g., the Blackfoot) were first contacted by Hudson's Bay Company traders in 1690, and a major trade in furs was established. This trade continued for about 175 years.

Americans first contacted Plains groups in 1804, when the expedition led by Lewis and Clark encountered the agricultural groups (the Mandan, Hidatsa, and Arikara) on the Missouri River. Native peoples with horses were just beginning to enter the High Plains. American contact had relatively little impact until the late 1840s, when settlers began to traverse the Plains to get to California and Oregon. Many Plains groups signed the famous Fort Laramie Treaty of 1851, in which some tribes in the central and southern Plains agreed that the United States could build roads and military posts, and that settlers could move through their territory, in exchange for guarantees of land rights. This general arrangement worked fairly well, since whites at the time had little interest in the Great American Desert, as the sod was too thick to be penetrated by the plows of the time.

In the 1860s, more settlers began to move through Sioux territory on the northern Plains. Under their great leader, Red Cloud, the Sioux resisted, fought, and defeated the U.S. Army, and in 1868, they signed the Fort Laramie Treaty ending the war and creating a large Sioux reservation that included the sacred Black Hills. Other Sioux leaders, including Sitting Bull (see the VIP Profile) and Crazy Horse, refused to sell their lands and did not sign the treaty. That same year, gold was discovered in the Black Hills and miners illegally flooded the area. The Sioux defended their territory and, with the Cheyenne, fought a major war with the United States. Although the Indians won several important victories, such as the famous Battle of the Little Big Horn (see below), they were finally defeated in 1877 and the great Sioux reservation was broken up. Once large steel plows became available and colonization by whites began in earnest after the Civil War, the Plains Prairies were increasingly colonized by white farmers, referred to as "sodbusters." Cattle ranching also became an important aspect of American colonization of the Plains.

The Impact of the Horse on Plains Culture

Ironically, horses first evolved in North America during the Pleistocene. They migrated into Asia across the Bering Land Bridge and subsequently became extinct in

North America. Horses were eventually domesticated in the Old World and then reintroduced into North America by the Spanish, who brought them to the Southwest. There, a number of groups, including the Apache and Ute, stole horses from the Spanish. The Apache had introduced horses onto the southern Plains by the mid–seventeenth century. The Ute traded horses north to the Northern Shoshone, who introduced them onto the northern Plains beginning in about 1690 (see Haines 1938; Secoy 1953). First viewed as pack or food animals (they were initially called "big dogs" or "spirit dogs"), horses rapidly displayed their potential to facilitate travel, hunting, and other tasks and soon they became very highly desired. Although horses could be obtained through breeding and trade, they were most frequently acquired through raiding.

Horses in fact revolutionized Plains culture. Prior to the horse, all travel took place on foot, limiting the distance one could cover in a day. With horses, people could travel much farther and faster, making both water sources and bison much more accessible. Thus, many more people could support themselves on the High Plains as bison hunters. A travois pulled by a horse could carry considerably more than a dog could, so much more material could be transported, including food and large tepees. Life as a bison hunter on the High Plains became much easier.

Horses also radically changed the nature of Plains warfare; in fact, the goal of most warfare became the acquisition of horses. Raiding for horses rapidly evolved into a major activity, with great prestige conferred on men who succeeded. The more horses a man owned, the more prestige he had. At this time, war increased on the Plains as new groups moved onto the High Plans, competing for hunting territories as well as horses. With increased mobility and ease of hunting, the High Plains became a very attractive region. Prairie groups adopted horses and expanded their hunting territories to include the High Plains. Agriculturalist groups moved onto the High Plains and adopted a mobile hunting culture, partly to hunt bison and partly to move away from the expanding American settlements to the east. As more groups moved onto the High Plains, territories and their boundaries underwent many adjustments.

The Impact of European Contact

As in much of North America, the Plains Indians suffered greatly from diseases introduced by Europeans. Plains groups were first contacted by Europeans when the De Soto expedition moved through the southern Plains in 1540. European diseases were likely introduced at that time, as the rich cultures documented by De Soto were gone by the time the next Spaniards arrived (see Perttula 1991). Disease continued to be the major factor in the decline of native populations throughout the nineteenth century. In 1831 a severe smallpox epidemic swept the southern Plains. The U.S. government inoculated central Plains groups against smallpox in 1832, stopping the epidemic. However, groups on the northern Plains were not inoculated and the disease decimated the populations in that region during 1837 and 1838 (see Trimble 1992). Then, in 1849, a severe cholera epidemic ravaged many Plains groups. Disease hit the sedentary Mandan, Hidatsa, and Arikara

VIP Profile

SITTING BULL, HUNKPAPA LEADER

Ta-tan'ka I'-yo-tan-ka, literally translated as "Sitting Bull," is one of the best known North American Indians. He was a leader of the Hunkpapa band of the Lakota Sioux. He was born in 1831 and participated in his first war expedition at age fifteen, when he counted his first coup (see page 269). He counted many coups, was wounded in battle several times, and participated in many battles against other Indians as well as the U.S. Army. The Hunkpapa recognized Sitting Bull as a great soldier and orator, and at thirty-five years of age he was elected Head Chief of the Hunkpapa, continuing his service as a soldier. Sitting Bull did not sign the Fort Laramie Treaty, arguing that the Sioux should not sell their land or be forced onto a reservation.

Although living in peace, Sitting Bull and his band were declared "hostiles" in early 1876, after they failed to report to a U.S. Army fort. Other "hostiles" joined his camp and he was elected War Chief of the combined group. On June 14, 1876, only eleven days before the Battle of the Little Big Horn, Sitting Bull performed a Sun Dance (see page 274) to fulfill an earlier vow made while stealing horses. In a vision during the Sun Dance, he foresaw a great Sioux victory over the whites.

Sitting Bull was with the Hunkpapa at the Battle of the Little Big Horn on June 25, 1876, and although still weak from his Sun Dance, he participated in part of the battle (the famous Crazy Horse led the Indians for most of the battle). Afterward, Sitting Bull led his people to Canada to escape the U.S. Army, living in peace for several years. The army stationed men just below the Canadian border to prevent the Sioux from traveling south to hunt. The Sioux subsequently asked the Canadian government to create a reserve for them, but the request was denied. Unable to hunt, starving, and harassed, Sitting Bull finally agreed to surrender and return to the United States.

In 1881 the Hunkpapa and other Sioux surrendered at Fort Buford, North Dakota. They had been promised pardons and land at the Standing Rock Reservation. Almost immediately, Sitting Bull was arrested and, with his family and a number of other Sioux, was sent to Fort Randall, South Dakota. While there, he was treated fairly well and had many visitors, mostly curious whites. He made many drawings of events in his life, posed for photographs, and signed autographs. In 1883 he was sent to the Standing Rock Reservation as originally promised. There he was treated poorly by the Indian agent, who attempted, and failed, to break his power as chief.

As the plight of the Sioux became known to the public, Sitting Bull became a popular speaker and guest at public events. In 1885 he toured with Buffalo Bill Cody's Wild West show. In accordance with then-popular views, he was cast as

particularly hard, with the Arikara population dropping from about 15,000 in 1700 to only about 400 in 1900.

The other major impact to Plains groups was military conflict with the United States, which included numerous battles. Plains Indians, virtually raised on horseback, were superb light cavalrymen and were easily superior to the best U.S. cavalry. The Indians were, however, overwhelmed by huge U.S. advantages in manpower a villain in shows performed in the United States and as a hero in shows performed in Canada. During that time, Sitting Bull toured a number of cities in the United States and Canada and met with President Cleveland in Washington. After the Wild West tour, he returned to the Standing Rock Reservation, where he continued to press the government to honor its commitments to the Sioux, meeting with numerous government committees, fact finders, and representatives.

In 1890 some of the Sioux became involved in the Ghost Dance. Sitting Bull was asked by the Indian agent to forbid his people to participate in the Ghost Dance, but he was unfamiliar with the ceremony. He asked to investigate the ceremony, but was not allowed to do so. As he knew nothing about it, therefore, he did not feel he had the right to forbid it and so refused the agent's request.

Upon his refusal to forbid the Ghost Dance, more than forty Indian Police (Sioux employed as reservation police) were sent to his home to arrest him. His supporters saw the police coming and gathered around his house. A fight ensued, and Sitting Bull and a number of others were killed. Tensions rose, and many began to fear the renewal of war. This general fear contributed to the massacre at Wounded Knee Creek a few weeks later.

Sitting Bull was buried in a cemetery at Fort Yates in the Standing Rock Reservation. His grave was vandalized a number of times, and in 1953 the body was moved and reburied in Mobridge,

North Dakota. A small granite memorial was later placed at the grave. Additional information on Sitting Bull can be found in Bernotas (1992) and Diessner (1993).

Sitting Bull, Hunkpapa chief and spiritual leader. (CORBIS)

and supplies. The United States could field a full-time military while the Indians had to hunt bison and take care of their families while defending themselves. In the end, however, the destruction of the bison herds by the army in the 1880s finally defeated the Plains Indians.

The most famous battle between Plains Indians and the U.S. Army was the Battle of the Little Big Horn in June 1876. In that battle, the Seventh Cavalry under

The battlefield at Wounded Knee, 1891.
(CORBIS/Bettmann)

Lieutenant Colonel George A. Custer (his rank of general in the Civil War was temporary, but many continue to refer to him by it) was badly defeated by a combined force of Sioux and Cheyenne. For more than a hundred years, this event has been romanticized as a gallant stand of a doomed command, but much more pragmatic analyses of the battle have now been conducted (e.g., Gray 1991; Fox 1993; Michno 1997; Scott et al. 1998; Viola 1999). It seems that Custer's attack was foolish and poorly executed, and his soldiers were killed trying to escape a vastly superior Indian force.

In addition, two of the most infamous events in U.S. military history also took place on the Plains. On November 29, 1864, some 250 peaceful Cheyenne and Arapaho, mostly women and children, were massacred at Sand Creek by Colorado militia trying to earn "glory." Then on December 29, 1890, approximately 150 peaceful Sioux, also including many women and children, were massacred at Wounded Knee Creek, South Dakota, by a U.S. Army force armed with Gatling guns. The army rationalized the attack by stating that the Sioux were hostile Ghost Dancers, but this was not the case. The army later gave medals to many of the soldiers who participated in the murder of so many unarmed people.

A Brief History of Ethnographic Research

As with much of North America, most anthropological work on the Plains was begun only after the confinement of the Indians on reservations. However, considerable information on Plains Indians exists in the records of early explorers, travelers, and missionaries. The artist George Catlin gathered a great deal of information on Plains Indians; he visited many groups in the 1830s. Through his images and descriptions, Catlin (1844) captured the majestic nature of the then-vibrant cultures, just before they were devastated by European diseases.

Serious anthropological study was conducted beginning in the 1880s by James Mooney, George A. Dorsey, and George Grinnell, all of whom worked with Plains Indians who had lived a traditional lifestyle. Other significant work was accomplished in the early twentieth century by Robert Lowie and Clark Wissler. Subsequent researchers have worked with new generations of Plains Indians, and some Indians themselves are providing a new perspective on their own cultures. Useful summaries of Plains culture can be found in Wissler (1948), Lowie (1954), Wedel (1961), Taylor (1994), and Carlson (1998). However, the most comprehensive coverage of all aspects of Plains culture was provided in the recently published Plains volume of the *Handbook of North American Indians* (DeMallie 2001). The discussion presented below was summarized from these sources, and the groups are described as they were in about the mid–nineteenth century.

A Broad Portrait of Plains Groups

There are some thirty-two Plains groups, not including the tribes from the east that were forced to relocate to Indian Territory in Oklahoma by the federal government. Many groups that lived on the High Plains entered the region after acquiring horses, adding considerable linguistic complexity to the Plains; six major language families are present there. The settled agriculturalists on the southern and central Plains spoke languages of either the Caddoan (e.g., the Pawnees and Arikara) or Siouan (e.g., the Mandan and Hidatsa) families, while most of the bison hunters of the northern Plains (e.g., the Blackfoot) spoke Algonquian languages. After about 1800, a number of other Siouan (e.g., the Sioux) and Algonquian (e.g., the Cheyenne) groups entered the Plains from the north and west, as did groups speaking Athapaskan languages (e.g., the Apache). In addition, several Northern Uto-Aztecan groups, including the Northern Shoshone and Comanche, entered the Plains from the northwest.

The northern Plains were occupied by the bison-hunting Blackfoot (composed of three allied groups: Bloods, Blackfoot, and Peigan), Gros Ventres (a French term meaning "Big Bellies"), Crow, and Kiowa, as well as the agricultural Mandan, Hidatsa, and Arikara (see Fig. 10.1). All but the Kiowa, who were pushed south by the expanding Sioux and Cheyenne, remained in the northern Plains.

The Sioux groups had lived as hunters and farmers in the Minnesota region prior to the introduction of the horse. They were pushed out onto the High Plains by the Cree and Ojibwa/Chippewa, who were armed with guns. The Sioux then moved permanently onto the High Plains to pursue mounted bison hunting, seizing lands from other groups on the northern Plains, including the Black Hills, a place that is now a central feature of Sioux identity.

Three major linguistic and geographic divisions characterize the Sioux: (1) the Teton (often called Lakota) living west of the Missouri River, (2) the Yankton/Yanktonai (sometimes called Dakota) living in the eastern halves of North and South Dakota, and (3) the Santee (sometimes also called Dakota) living in southern Minnesota and northern Iowa. Each division is further subdivided into bands, for example, the Hunkpapa and Oglala bands of the Lakota. The various Sioux groups were not usually allied but generally did not fight among themselves. The Sioux now make up the third-largest Indian group in the United States (the Cherokee are the largest), having a combined population of about 108,000 in 2000 (census data).

The Arapaho and Cheyenne (see this chapter's first Case Study) occupied the west central Plains, the Cheyenne having moved into the region after 1800. The Pawnees (see the second Case Study), Omaha, and other agricultural groups lived on the central Prairies. The Kiowa had been pushed into the southwestern Plains by the expanding Cheyenne, where they joined the Plains Apache and the Comanche. The Wichita and other agricultural groups lived in the southern Prairies (the Caddo, sometimes considered a Prairies group, are discussed in Chapter 12).

The Comanche originally formed a division of the Northern Shoshone, a Great Basin group that moved onto the northwestern Plains on foot in the seventeenth century (see Wallace and Hoebel 1952; Hyde 1959). In about 1700, once they had horses, the Comanche split off from the Northern Shoshone somewhere in eastern Idaho and/or western Wyoming. They moved onto the southern Plains in two large bands, the Yamparikas and the Kwqaharis. They were in eastern New Mexico by about 1705, where they began to raid and trade with the Spanish and Pueblo groups. By about 1760 the Comanche began expanding their operations into northern Mexico. A smallpox epidemic (1780–1781) severely affected the Comanche, and it took many years for the population to recover. The Comanche were defeated by the U.S. military in about 1875.

Finally, many eastern, non-Plains groups were pushed onto the Plains by expanding European settlement; these groups included the Sauk, Fox, Kickapoo, Mesquakie, Miami, Illinois, Potawatomi, Delaware, Ottawa, and Shawnee. Other groups, such as the Cherokee, Creek, Choctaw, and Seminole, were forced to resettle onto Indian Territory. All of these groups were forced onto territory claimed by Plains groups, increasing intertribal tension and hostility and making a bad situation even worse.

Political Organization

All of the Plains groups were basically organized into tribes, with chiefs and councils being important political institutions. Most groups had both war chiefs (the young men) and peace chiefs (older and wiser men), the latter holding greater sway in making long-term decisions. On the High Plains, many groups had separate smaller political units (bands) that congregated as tribes in the spring and summer for the communal bison hunts. In the winter, the tribes broke up into their various bands, each led by a headman, spending the winter apart from the other bands.

Prairie groups lived along major rivers (especially the upper Missouri) in large, permanent towns, some of which were fortified. These groups did not break up into bands for the winter and so retained their tribal organization all year. Like the groups on the High Plains, the Prairie groups had chiefs and councils that made decisions for the tribe. When the males were gone from the town for any length of time, strong women could emerge as the de facto leaders of the town or camp until the men returned.

Plains Warfare

One hallmark of Plains culture was extensive warfare. Though much of this pattern seems to have developed after the introduction of the horse (see above), there is considerable evidence that extensive warfare existed before contact (e.g., Bamforth 1994). Warfare was important politically as it maintained relationships, either hostile or friendly, between groups.

The major goals of warfare were to gain prestige, to obtain loot (especially horses), and to avenge an earlier defeat. However, some groups used warfare to gain territory (especially after the introduction of the horse) and to claim and control hunting territories and trade. Although killing simply for the sake of killing was rare, whole enemy populations (not strictly the warriors) were occasionally attacked and killed. Most warfare was conducted by men, but women would occasionally become involved. Males were taught to ride from a very early age and joined military societies as teenagers.

The Plains Indians developed an interesting "point" system of gaining war honors, called *coup*. Coup (French for "touch" or "blow") involved a demonstration of bravery and valor in battle—and living to tell about it—by performing particular deeds that were ranked in value. The most prestigious coup was touching a live enemy, particularly one who was armed. Touching a dead enemy was ranked next in importance; the first man to touch the dead enemy received the highest coup value, the second less, and the third less still. Killing an enemy held some honor, but touching an enemy (alive or dead) was a more valuable coup. Also of value was the rescue of a wounded comrade or the theft of a number of horses; taking even a single horse from the center of an enemy camp was considered extraordinary and received high coup honors. Scalp taking was not particularly important, but scalps were sometimes taken by women and children after a battle.

Men would carry coup sticks into battle, not as weapons, but to touch the enemy. Upon return to their town or village, men would bang their coup sticks against a pole and recount their various feats, called "counting coup." As long as the opposing groups played by the same basic rules, the system prevented large numbers of deaths in battle—other feats were more significant. However, the U.S. Army did not count coup and considered this behavior bizarre and foolish. The goal of the white soldiers was to kill the enemy (the more, the better) and they had no desire to play the coup game. Despite the extensive skill and immense bravery of Plains men, their system of coup counting proved to be a serious disadvantage when fighting the U.S. Army.

Social Organization

The tribes on the High Plains lived a mobile lifestyle, congregating in the summer and splitting into smaller groups in the fall and winter. They tended to live in smaller groups and had somewhat less complex social organizations than Prairie groups did. In contrast, the Prairie tribes lived in permanent towns consisting of many large, earth-covered houses and had a more complex social organization based on clans. Prairie tribes also had many more sodalities than did tribes on the High Plains.

Perhaps the most important aspect of Plains social structure was kinship. The extended family formed the basic social and residential unit, and behavior toward certain people was rigidly dictated based on kinship. Individualism was highly prized, and individual honor, glory, and prestige were actively sought, although cooperation was valued in many matters, such as communal hunting. Great deeds in raiding formed the usual path to glory; however, achievements in diplomacy, trade, and religion also brought honor and prestige. Sharing was valued, and charity to the poor was common; some groups had a "Beggars Dance" where the rich were asked to help the poor. Gifts were given at most occasions, and formal "give-away parties" were sometimes organized for special events.

The other major aspect of Plains society was the non-kin-based associations (called sodalities) based on some common activity or interest. Most of these were fraternal societies for men, often associated with military activities, although some groups also had craft-based societies for women, such as the hide-working society. Most societies were age-graded so that boys joined the lowest-ranked society and moved up as they grew older. Sodalities would often compete in war, hunting, or other endeavors. On rare occasions, when needed, the military societies could also serve as the military and the police for the tribe. Raids were usually carried out by a military society rather than by the tribe as a whole.

Division of labor was relatively strict; men did the hunting and warfare while women performed the domestic tasks. However, some males chose not to become participants in military activities, and berdaches were relatively common among Plains groups. Much less frequently, a female would choose to assume a male role. In some groups (e.g., the Blackfoot), women occasionally accompanied their husbands on raids, helping them steal horses.

In general, women played important roles in Plains societies and worked in hide processing, house building, and other tasks. Women could gain significant status by gaining supernatural power. Women might also be wealthy, owning horses, houses, and other items, much of which they retained if they divorced. The role of women in Plains society is discussed by Weist (1980) and Peters (2000).

Several groups had associations of contraries—men who did everything opposite (e.g., saying yes but meaning no) and to the extreme (extraordinary bravery in battle). Contraries were few in number, lived apart and alone, fought separately from the other members of a war expedition, and never married (all of these being extreme acts). They could return to normal society if another man took their place.

Economics

The primary economic focus of all Plains and Prairie groups was the bison, commonly called the buffalo (see below). On the Prairies, agriculture was also critical, but even the Prairie groups depended on the bison for food and materials. In addition, other mammals, such as pronghorn antelope, deer, elk, and rabbits, were hunted. Some birds were also exploited, such as waterfowl, wild turkey, sage grouse, and quail. Eagles, whose feathers were necessary for ceremonies and decoration, were captured by hand and strangled. Fish and shellfish were taken where available but were not widely used. Some groups also hunted and ate turtles.

In addition to animals, people gathered a number of plants. Food was obtained from many kinds of roots, various berries, and prickly-pear cactus fruits. Other plants were used in manufacturing baskets, cradleboards, utensils, rope, dyes, and many other items. The lodgepole pine held particular importance for Plains groups; its long, straight trunks were used in the construction of tepees and for travois.

The Bison in Plains Culture   The semiannual communal bison hunt was the single most important economic task of the Plains people. In about 1800, approximately sixty million bison roamed the Plains, but this number was reduced to twenty million by 1850, and to less than 1,000 by 1895 (Thornton 1987:52). Since the early twentieth century, efforts have been made to save the bison, and today about 60,000 bison live in various places in the United States.

Bison calves, which weigh about forty pounds at birth, are born in the spring. Calves have light-colored hair, which was valued for children's robes. By the time they are about a year old, young bison weigh about 400 pounds. By two years of age, they begin to grow horns. Bulls (males) typically graze apart from the cows (females).

Bison congregate in great herds in the spring and early summer as the grass grows thick. By late summer, the grass dries out and the bison herds break up into smaller groups for the winter. In the winter, bison move to areas protected from the bitter cold and where snow is shallow enough to allow them to paw through and reach the grass underneath. The establishment of the Oregon Trail along the Platte River in 1845 split the bison habitat, creating separate northern and southern bison herds.

Bison were taken year-round and were hunted by individuals or small groups, although communal bison hunting was much more common. In the spring and summer, when the communal hunts were held, individuals were strictly forbidden to hunt bison to avoid frightening and dispersing the herd. Prior to obtaining horses, Plains people would drive bison either off a cliff or into an arroyo, where they would be killed by the fall or be so badly injured that they were immobilized and could be killed with a spear (these places are called jumps). This practice could kill many more bison than could be used at one time, resulting in some waste. However, this did not impact the huge population of bison. After horses were obtained, bison were located, tracked, surrounded, and driven on horseback into corrals, to jumps, or into waiting groups of other hunters on horseback, who would then ride alongside the animals and shoot them.

Spears or arrows were the preferred weapons; firearms were too noisy (they frightened the bison and attracted enemies) and too difficult to reload on horseback, and ammunition was scarce. The hunter would drive the spear or arrow through the ribs and into the heart when possible; otherwise, the kidneys were targeted. The dead animals were skinned and butchered, and the skins and meat were brought to camp. The meat was cut into strips to dry and the skins were processed according to need (for robes, rawhide, or other items).

The best meat parts (tongue and hump) were eaten first. Most of the other meat was smoked or dried for later consumption, the toughest cuts being dried and pounded into pemmican, a "trail mix" of meat, fat, and berries that would keep for months. Most parts of the animal were used: horns for bowls, scoops, or glue; hides for robes, tepee coverings, and containers; stomach and bladder for containers; bones for many different tools; hooves for rattles; dried dung ("buffalo chips") for fuel; hair for rope; the tail for a flyswatter; and brains for tanning hides (see Taylor 1994: Table IV.1).

The bison were hunted to virtual extinction by whites. Many were shot for skins and tongues, both of which were very popular in Europe. Others were killed for their meat, many to feed railroad construction workers. The meat of females was more tender, so they were killed in greater numbers, reducing reproductive capacity. Other bison were shot for sport from railroad cars. Finally, as part of U.S. tactics in the conflict with the Indians, the army hired hunters to kill as many bison as they could, solely to disrupt the food supply of the Indians. The virtual extinction of the bison coincided with the defeat of the Indians.

Agriculture   For groups in the High Plains, bison hunting was the critical economic activity. On the Prairies, however, agriculture was also a very important aspect of the economy. Corn, beans, and squash were grown where the river valleys had sufficient fertile and watered ground. Fields were located near the towns and were tended for the several months it took for the crops to mature. They would then be harvested, stored, and used throughout the year. After the harvest, Prairie groups conducted summer bison hunts.

Material Culture and Technology

All Plains groups constructed large, conical tepees (a Dakota word) for shelter. Full-time bison hunters used them all year long, while the Prairie groups employed them only during their hunts, living in their permanent earth-covered houses the rest of the year. Tepees were built using a number of twenty- to twenty-five-foot poles and a covering of tanned bison skin. The ends of three or four poles were tied together and then set to form a frame. More poles would be set to lean against the foundational ones until a cone-shaped frame was completed. The already tailored bison-skin covering (made from ten to twenty or more skins, depending on the size of the tepee) would then be attached to the top of one pole and then wrapped around the frame until it was covered. The bottom of the covering was secured by stakes, and the seam was fastened with a piece of bison bone. A fire would be built in the center. Tepees were very efficient and comfortable shelters, simple to put up and take down and easy to transport. The tepee poles would be used to form the legs of a travois, for travel.

The Prairie groups lived in earth-covered houses, which could be sixty feet in diameter, large enough so that the horses could stay inside in very cold weather. A log frame with four vertical posts held up the center; smaller branches lay between the logs, and woven mats covered the branches. Grass-covered earth was then placed on the top of this rugged frame. These sod houses were quite warm and, with proper maintenance, would last for ten to twelve years. On the southern (and warmer) Plains, other groups, such as the Wichita, lived in large thatch houses.

Before the introduction of horses, transportation was by foot. Small skin boats were used to cross rivers. On land, the belongings of the group would be transported on travois pulled by dogs. Once horses became available, the size and capacity of travois were greatly enlarged, and so the quantity of material culture that could be moved from camp to camp increased.

Skin or hides from a variety of animals were used for clothing, tepee coverings, and other items. Hides were stretched on the ground or on wooden frames and processed. First, the excess tissue was scraped from the inside, and the hair might or might not be scraped from the outside to form rawhide. The rawhide could then be tanned to form a soft and pliable skin; deer or bison brains were applied to the skin to accomplish this task. Then, if desired, the skin could be dyed or otherwise decorated.

Clothing was made mostly from tanned deerskins (buckskin), but large bison-skin robes were worn in the winter with the hair on the inside, with the outside often decorated. Paint was used widely to adorn people and horses, and specific patterns denoted men and horses ready for war. Quills and feathers were utilized to decorate clothing, weapons, shields, pipes, and hair. Eagle feathers were awarded to persons (almost always men) who performed great deeds, usually in war. A successful man could accumulate a number of feathers and wear them in a long, flowing bonnet, the stereotypic feathered headdress that most people associate with Indians.

Before the horse, ceramic containers were important, but as hide became more readily available, these rather fragile vessels were replaced by hide containers, called parfleches. The prevalence of hide containers made basketry relatively unimportant to Plains groups. Weapons included the bow and arrow, lances, and clubs of wood and stone. Metal weapons, such as axes, hatchets, and knives, were introduced by Europeans, as were guns.

Religion

All Plains groups viewed the earth as sacred and the bison as the most sacred animal. The specifics of religion practiced by the various groups differed, often greatly. Many beliefs and ceremonies dealt with the bison, to promote reproduction and to thank bison for sacrificing themselves (see Harrod 2000). Astronomical observances were also common and important among Plains groups. The agricultural societies had a formal priesthood and held a number of large-scale ceremonies related to crop production and harvesting.

All groups kept sacred (or medicine) bundles, which consisted of items kept "bundled" together in a parfleche or bag. Some were gifts from supernatural deities, others symbolized fertility, and still others represented war. One of the most important sacred items was the calumet, a ceremonial pipe.

Men often undertook a vision quest to obtain power from supernatural forces. During a quest, the individual remained isolated, without food or water, until visited by a spirit. A shaman might accompany the individual, and sometimes a drug would be used to contact the supernatural. The vision was often a defining moment in a person's life. Among the Blackfoot, women possessed an innate power that made a vision quest unnecessary (Kehoe 1995).

Groups on the High Plains often placed their dead in trees or on scaffolds. The body would be left to decay, after which the bones would be placed in rocky outcrops. Sometimes a body would be buried by covering it with rocks. Prairie groups usually buried their dead in cemeteries.

The Calumet Ceremonial   The Calumet Ceremonial was a Plains ritual intended to bring people together in peace, and the calumet itself was a sacred symbol of peace. The calumet has often been referred to as a "peace pipe," in which tobacco was smoked and passed around to the participants of a meeting. In some groups, the calumet consisted of a solid object, and no tobacco was smoked. The Calumet Ceremonial was used to establish a "kinship" relation between individuals and groups, and was conducted to recognize alliances, ceremonies, or other events. It is not to be confused with smoking tobacco in a regular pipe, a practice common to many groups.

A complete calumet pipe consisted of a stone bowl and wooden stem, both finely decorated. It took about sixty hours to make a pipe bowl, as it had to be shaped, drilled, and polished. The best stone for the manufacture of the bowl was red catlinite (or pipestone)—named after George Catlin, the painter—that originated from a quarry in southwestern Minnesota and was widely traded for pipemaking.

The Sun Dance   The Sun Dance (sometimes called Medicine Lodge) is a world renewal ceremony practiced by many Plains groups, each following the same basic theme but differing in detail (see Liberty 1980; Archambault 2001). A Sun Dance would be undertaken by an individual male (women could not lead a Sun Dance) who wanted either to contribute to the welfare of his tribe or to thank the supernatural for some past favor. Self-sacrifice for the good of the group was the common theme of the ceremony, and the event was calm and cheerful. Most of the tribe would take part in some aspect of the ceremony.

A Sun Dance would be held in the summer, when sufficient bison could be hunted to support a large gathering of people, and lasted about a week. A specialist shaman, with several assistants, would construct the ceremonial site, consisting of one large open-topped enclosure with a tall central pole, sweatlodges, and several other special structures. After the ceremony these structures were left standing to decay naturally. Important meetings would often take place during a Sun Dance, while everyone was together. The dancer was not allowed to ingest any food or

Plains Cree conducting a Sun Dance, ca. 1880.
(CORBIS/Bettmann)

water during the ceremony. He danced around the central pole, from which were hung ritual objects, while spectators drummed or sang special songs. This dancing lasted until the strength of the dancer was gone.

If the dancer so desired, he could engage in self-torture as part of his sacrifice for the group, but he was allowed to back out at any time. A shaman would attach rawhide lines to the top of the pole, pinning the other ends of the lines to the chest of the participant by passing a wooden or bone skewer through his chest muscle and attaching the line to it. The man would then dance around the pole, without water or food, until the pin and line were torn from his chest, sometimes even hanging from the pole by the lines before they tore out. Skewers were sometimes attached to the cheeks rather than the chest. At other times, up to six bison skulls would be attached with thongs to the back muscles of the dancer, who would walk until they tore out (this was popular among the Sioux). The process would cause considerable pain, loss of blood, and visions. The resulting scars would mark the dancer as an important man for the rest of his life.

Plains Indians Today

Most Plains cultures have survived, and like many other Native American groups, their populations are growing and gaining political power (see Iverson 1985 for a series of articles on Plains people in the twentieth century). Many Plains groups have reservations and reserves in the United States or Canada, including the Sioux, who have some twenty-four reservations (see *http://www.state.sd.us/tourism/sioux/sioux.htm*). However, most are isolated from population and transportation centers, making it difficult to attract industry and thus inhibiting economic development. The major reservation enterprises continue to be wheat farming and cattle ranching, with some reintroduction of bison to their former range.

Some attempts have been made to develop Plains reservations. For example, a large dam project was built on the Missouri River to provide water and power for Indian agriculture. However, it actually flooded the best farmland, thus decreasing productivity. Tourism has increased in recent times and has provided some employment. People are attracted to the natural beauty of the Plains and a variety of cultural events, including powwows, ceremonies, and reenactments (e.g., the Little Big Horn battle). A statue of Crazy Horse, a Lakota leader, is currently being carved into a mountain near Mt. Rushmore and is already a tourist attraction.

Huge problems still remain. A decline in mortality and improvement in birth rates have greatly increased the populations of Plains groups. However, the lack of economic opportunity has forced many individuals to move to cities to seek employment. Unemployment, discrimination, alcoholism, suicide, and family violence remain at epidemic levels.

Learn More About Contemporary Plains Peoples

The discussion above provides only a very brief description of Plains people today. What else can you discover? Go to the library, and use the Internet to learn more about Plains groups today. Topics you can explore include the following:

1. Choose a particular group or two, and investigate how they have adjusted to European conquest. Look at their tribal land base (e.g., whether they have a reservation), their tribal economy, and the general well-being of the tribal members.
2. What major differences exist between Plains groups living in the United States and those living in Canada? What kind of interaction takes place between the groups and their governments? What are the major issues in tribal/government relations?
3. What traditional practices have been retained by Plains groups? What are the roles of traditional religion, economics, and politics today? Is the bison still an important animal?
4. What efforts are being made to develop industries on Plains reservations? What problems exist?

The Cheyenne: A Plains Case Study

The Cheyenne inhabited the central portion of the High Plains (Fig. 10.2) and were divided into Northern and Southern groups. Formerly agriculturalists living on the Middle Missouri River, the Cheyenne abandoned agriculture, migrated to the Plains, and adopted mounted bison hunting in the late eighteenth century. The Cheyenne call themselves tsétsEhéstAhese, anglicized to *Tsistsistas,* meaning "those who are from this (group)" (Moore et al. 2001:881). The term *Cheyenne* seems to derive from a Sioux word meaning "red-speakers" or "Indians of alien speech" (cf. Swanton 1953:278). This case study of the Cheyenne describes them as they were in about 1850, when there were approximately 10,000 Cheyenne.

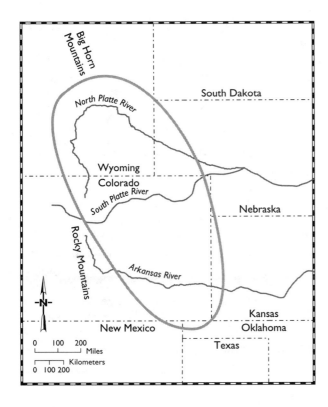

FIGURE 10.2 Location and territory of the Cheyenne in the early nineteenth century
Adapted from *Handbook of North American Indians,* Vol. 13, *Plains,* Raymond J. DeMallie, ed., p. ix;. and from John H. Moore, Margot P. Liberty, and A. Terry Straus, "Cheyenne," in *Handbook of North American Indians,* Vol. 13, *Plains,* Raymond J. DeMallie, ed., p. 863; copyright © 2001 by the Smithsonian Institution. Reprinted by permission of the publisher.

Most information on aboriginal Cheyenne culture was obtained in the late nineteenth and early twentieth centuries. Important syntheses on Cheyenne culture include the work of Dorsey (1905), Mooney (1907), Curtis (1911b, 1930), Grinnell (1923), Hoebel (1960), Berthrong (1963), Powell (1980), Moore (1987, 1996), Hoig (1989), Stands in Timber and Liberty (1998), and Moore et al. (2001). The information on the Cheyenne below was synthesized from those sources.

The Natural Environment

Like much of the High Plains, the climate of Cheyenne territory consists of cold winters, hot summers, and relatively little rain. The grass is short and there are few trees, a perfect habitat for bison. Rivers cut across the region, with water, trees, and other resources available in the river valleys. The valleys also provide shelter from the snow and winds of winter. Here trees provide food for horses when deep snow keeps them from foraging for grass.

Language

The Cheyenne speak an Algonquian language, related to Blackfoot, Arapaho, and a number of groups in eastern North America. The Northern and Southern Cheyenne now speak distinct dialects, but they are mostly mutually intelligible.

A Brief History

Prior to 1700 the Cheyenne lived in Minnesota as hunter-gatherers and appear to have been first contacted by whites (the French) in about 1680. In the eighteenth century they slowly moved onto the High Plains, partly due to pressure from displaced groups (particularly the Sioux) further east, partly to seek trade with the French on the middle Missouri River, and partly lured by the ease of hunting bison on horse back. In the late eighteenth century the Cheyenne had adopted a Prairie lifestyle as bison-hunting farmers situated in large permanent towns. After obtaining a sufficient number of horses in the early nineteenth century, the Cheyenne allied themselves with a closely related group called the Sutaio. By the 1830s the Cheyenne had abandoned agriculture and become full-time bison hunters on the High Plains, absorbing the Sutaio as one of the ten Cheyenne bands.

Some Cheyenne moved south into the region vacated by the Kiowa. Others stayed in South Dakota and Montana, thus creating the split between the Southern and Northern Cheyenne. In 1825 the Cheyenne signed a treaty with the United States in which they acknowledged the United States and agreed to provisions for trade and passage of whites through Cheyenne territory. This general (if uneasy) peace with the United States lasted for several decades. The Cheyenne also signed the Fort Laramie Treaty of 1851.

The Cheyenne suffered a cholera epidemic in 1849, and after 1857 they came into increasing conflict with the U.S. government and encroaching settlers (see

Grinnell 1915 for a military history of the Cheyenne). White settlers were invading Cheyenne territory, resulting in relatively minor hostilities and raiding, although the Cheyenne generally remained at peace with the United States. One of the worst massacres in U.S. history took place in 1864, when peaceful and friendly Cheyenne camping at Sand Creek—and flying both U.S. and white flags at the time—were attacked by Colorado militia looking for glory. Several hundred Cheyenne and some Arapaho were killed, most of them unarmed women and children killed while seeking refuge in the creek bed.

In 1868 the Cheyenne living in the southern portion of their territory were compelled to accept a reservation in Indian Territory, which they were forced to share with their allies, the Arapaho (see Berthrong 1976). Those Cheyenne still in the north took part in the general uprising of 1875–1876 and participated in the Battle of the Little Big Horn. By 1878 the Cheyenne in the north had been defeated and were also forced to move onto the reservation in Oklahoma. However, in the summer of 1878, about 300 Cheyenne left that reservation and fought their way back to their homes in Montana. A good historical novel depicting this saga is *Cheyenne Autumn*, written by Mari Sandoz (1953) and made into a Hollywood movie in 1964. In 1884, the government formally established a separate reservation for the Northern Cheyenne in southern Montana, the Tongue River Reservation (see Svingen 1993 for a history of that reservation), with the Southern Cheyenne remaining in Oklahoma (see Berthrong 1976). Thus, the Cheyenne occupied the High Plains for only about eighty years before being overwhelmed by the U.S. Army.

Both Cheyenne reservations were substantially reduced in the late nineteenth century by whites taking "unallotted" lands (permitted under the Dawes Act of 1887). The Northern Cheyenne tried to raise cattle, but in 1914 the government banned communally owned herds and confiscated many of the cattle. Then, in 1919, the government sold off 12,000 of the Cheyenne's 15,000 horses, ostensibly to improve cattle grazing, without compensation to the Cheyenne. Until 1934 the Cheyenne were basically treated as prisoners in a large internment camp. After 1934, both the Northern and Southern Cheyenne organized themselves under the Indian Reorganization Act into federally recognized tribes (the Southern Cheyenne combined with the Arapaho), gaining federal monies to redevelop their economy and buy back reservation lands lost to allotment.

Cosmology

Most researchers have argued that the Cheyenne did not have an origin story for the earth; it just existed. The Cheyenne were not really interested in explaining the origin of the earth; however, they did have explanations for how the Cheyenne traditions began. Long ago, a woman who had been captured by the Assiniboins taught the Cheyenne about tribal government and gave them the knowledge of the Council of Forty-Four. Earlier, a young man named Sweet Medicine had given the Cheyenne the Sweet Medicine Bundle containing the four Sacred Arrows and instructed them on the ceremonies necessary to maintain the world.

Politics and External Relations

The Cheyenne were originally organized into about ten bands, although others emerged after confinement to reservations. Bands were composed of a number of related families, each with a population between 300 and 400. An exception was the Dog Soldiers, a military society that began to camp together and more or less formed a band. During the early summer, the Cheyenne would operate as a single large group to hunt the huge herds of bison. During the fall and winter, they would break up into their various bands to spend the winter in sheltered areas that had enough food for the horses. Tribal identity was of greater importance than band identity, so the Cheyenne bands did not feud; this was not permitted by the overall tribal government. Each band occupied a particular place in the tribal camp, organized in a circle (the "camp circle"), the same way chiefs were seated within a tepee.

The principal political authority among the Cheyenne tribe was the Council of Forty-Four Peace Chiefs (all males), including four primary "at large" chiefs. The four primary chiefs held more or less equal power, and the other forty chiefs served as "advisers" to the primary chiefs. All council members had at some time participated in warfare and may have even led military societies, but they were also older and seasoned men whose desire for war was tempered by experience. Once elected to the council, a new chief would have to resign his leadership post within his military society. Council members would serve in that capacity for ten years and could not be dismissed for any reason. At the end of his term, a chief could nominate his successor. In addition, the Arrow Keeper, who was the steward of the Sweet Medicine Bundle containing the four Sacred Arrows, held informal political power and was able to influence the behavior of people and settle disputes.

The Cheyenne believe that the Council of Forty-Four, given to them long ago (see above), is the oldest political institution of the tribe and has supernatural authority. The Council was a civil body whose primary functions were the control and regulation of internal Cheyenne affairs. The primary internal concern was the maintenance of law and order (see Llewellyn and Hoebel 1941), the most important issues being the control of intertribal violence and the regulation of the communal bison hunts. Homicide (murder, not warfare) was the most serious crime, since it involved violence of one Cheyenne against another. Suicide, accidental deaths, and abortion were considered homicide. Property theft and adultery were rare. Guilty parties would have to pay compensation to the victims, and murderers, including a mother who aborted her fetus, would be ostracized and might even be exiled. Those who somehow disrupted or threatened the success of the communal bison hunts were summarily punished by beating or loss of property. Council rulings were enforced by the military societies.

Warfare was an essential aspect of Cheyenne culture. Men gained prestige through their courage, deeds, and coup, and most warfare consisted of raiding other groups for horses and glory. War parties could be organized by any man who could persuade a few friends to accompany him on a raid, which was not difficult to do. Larger raids would be undertaken by one of the military societies, with the war chiefs of that society taking the lead. In peacetime, however, the military was subordinate to the civil authority of the Council of Forty-Four, and only the council could authorize warfare on the tribal scale, usually to avenge an earlier defeat. Women could participate in warfare but could not be regular members of the military societies, although some were included as "sisters."

The Cheyenne were allied with the Mandan, Arikara, Arapaho, Sioux, and—after a peace agreement in 1840—the Kiowa and Comanche. The Crow and Pawnees were their greatest enemies, though they were also hostile to the Ute and Shoshone. Eventually, the United States became the greatest enemy of all, and the Cheyenne were the most formidable of the groups fighting it.

A successful war expedition counted coup without casualties. If an expedition was successful, a Scalp Dance was held, supervised by one or more berdaches, who might even have accompanied the men on the raid. During the Scalp Dance, the coups and victories of the raid were celebrated, reaffirming the superiority of the Cheyenne over their enemies. Other events also took place during the Scalp Dance, involving both males and females and including the Courtship, Matchmaking, Round, Slippery, and Galloping Buffalo Bull dances, all intended to encourage courtship and mating.

Social Organization

The basic Cheyenne social unit was the family, usually a relatively small extended family living together in a tepee. Each family had a status relative to the others, depending on the number of horses they owned, how they maintained their households, whether their members behaved well, whether the females were chaste, and so on. Groups of relatives would generally camp together and formed important social units. Political organizations such as the band, the various men's and women's societies, and the Council of Forty-Four were also important social organizations. The Cheyenne did not have clans and recognized both sides of the family equally (a bilateral kinship system).

The division of labor was fairly strict. Men engaged in warfare and hunting, while women did the domestic chores, raised the children, tanned hides, made clothing and tepee covers, set up and dismantled camp, and gathered wild plants. Males dominated Cheyenne society and women were subordinate. However, women could be aggressive and strong-willed (see Michelson 1932; Marriott 1977; Weist 1979; Little Coyote and Giglo 1997), and while they did not have access to official power or authority, they were held in high esteem. The Cheyenne had berdaches, called *hemaneh* ("halfman-halfwoman"), who were highly respected and sometimes served as doctors or second wives.

As with most Plains groups, military societies were critical, and the Cheyenne had at least eight (see Moore et al. 2001: Table 1). Membership was not based on kinship, although a man tended to join his father's society. The societies enforced council decisions, provided a police force, did community service, and conducted most warfare. The Dog Soldiers were the most important and powerful of the Cheyenne military societies. The war chiefs from each of these societies formed the primary group of war chiefs for the tribe as a whole. The Cheyenne also had a contrary society (see Schwartz 1989).

A Southern Cheyenne family in front of their home; note the horse-drawn travois, 1890. (CORBIS)

There were a number of women's societies as well, including the Quilling Society, which specialized in embroidery with porcupine quills. Some women would serve apprenticeships in the society, later to become full members and expert quillers.

Individual Cheyenne were very concerned about what other people thought of them and acted accordingly. Cheyenne values include sharing, reverence for elders, respect for specialized knowledge ("medicine"), following a chosen path (e.g., career or philosophy), modesty, proper behavior, hospitality, and appreciation for the natural order. Self-control, including the repression of sexual urges, was the norm, with virginity and sexual abstinence viewed as a demonstration of self-control. Being a good Cheyenne required adherence to these values, which are still held by the Cheyenne today.

Life Cycle

Grandparents were very indulgent with their grandchildren. Mothers would punish daughters for misdeeds, but the males were rarely punished and had little formal instruction until they began to function as adults. Beating a child was unacceptable behavior, as it was considered violence of one Cheyenne against another.

Children usually received nicknames, sometimes having to do with a particular body feature, such as a long nose. A formal name was not given until about the age of five or six, and new and/or additional names might be conferred if the person changed status, such as becoming a chief or doctor, or performed some heroic act.

There was no real puberty ceremony for boys. A male gained status by performance in war, and later in peace, always with generous and humble behavior. A vision quest to seek personal power could be undertaken at any age. A girl's first menses was an important event and signified that she was now a woman and eligible to marry and a horse was given away at that occasion. After puberty, a woman wore a chastity belt until she was married, and even afterward when her husband was away.

Men married when they had a respectable war record, usually between twenty and twenty-five years old, with women marrying when they were between sixteen and twenty. Courtship was long and arduous, as most Cheyenne were shy with members of the opposite sex. When a man chose the woman he wanted to marry, he asked his family to help arrange the marriage. If they agreed to the match, they would assist him by providing appropriate gifts; if not, he was on his own. Gifts, especially horses, were taken to the family of the girl and left there while her family considered the offer. If the girl and her family (particularly her brother) refused, the gifts were returned. If they agreed, the gifts were distributed among the family. The next day, gifts of equal value were given to the prospective groom's family, and if accepted, the marriage was approved. The bride then moved in with her husband's family for a few days while a new residence was established near the bride's family. Once complete, the new bride and groom moved into their new tepee and the marriage was consummated. Out of respect, men avoided their mothers-in-law

Polygyny was permitted, and about one-third of Cheyenne men had more than one wife. Adultery was rare and was punished by fines. The ideal birth spacing was ten years, partly due to the importance of sexual abstinence, although the actual spacing was about three years. Divorce was simple and could be initiated by either spouse.

When a person died, the funeral took place as soon as possible. Deceased individuals would be dressed in their finest clothing, with some of their personal property accompanying them, and were then typically placed on a scaffold in a tree; however, it was not uncommon for bodies to be placed on the ground or in a crevice with rocks piled over them. If a man was killed in battle, every effort was made to recover his body for proper burial. Much of the property of a deceased person was given away, often to relatives. The entire family mourned; in particular, widows would slash their legs if their husband had died violently, and then were expected to either cut their hair or wail for a long time.

Economics

As with most Plains groups, the essence of Cheyenne economy was bison, used for food, skins, and many other purposes. The main communal bison hunt took place in early summer and involved the entire tribe. In the early fall, a second communal bison hunt was conducted by each band. Bison were hunted on an individual, opportunistic basis at all other times.

The Cheyenne also hunted, in order of importance, pronghorn antelope, deer, elk, mountain sheep, and (unlike most High Plains groups) fish and turtles. Wolves and foxes were sometimes taken for their fur. Dogs were eaten on special occasions and horse meat was also consumed in times of scarcity.

Women also contributed to the food supply. Using a digging stick, they gathered eight to ten kinds of roots, the three most important being the "prairie turnip," Jerusalem artichoke (actually a sunflower), and groundnut. In addition, women collected the fruit of the prickly-pear cactus and chokecherries, the latter ground up with bison meat and fat to make pemmican.

Once the plant foods had been gathered and the meat processed and stored, the Cheyenne were prepared for the winter. Each band lived apart from the others in a river valley, sheltered from the cold. The band might move to another sheltered camp if forage became scarce or if some other opportunity arose.

Material Culture and Technology

The tepee was the primary shelter used by the Cheyenne. Most transportation was by horseback, but usually only by males; women and children were frequently expected to walk. The travois transported most of their possessions.

Clothing was manufactured from tanned elk or deer hides. Women wore short-sleeved dresses and moccasins and men wore loincloths and moccasins. In cold weather men would also wear leggings and long-sleeved shirts, and both sexes would wear bison robes. Clothing was often decorated with porcupine-quill embroidery, made by the women of the Quilling Society. Other personal adornment included decorations (e.g., elk teeth) sewn on dresses, feathers worn in the hair (although one had to earn the right to wear them), some tattooing and body painting, and jewelry.

The primary weapons of the Cheyenne were bows and arrows, lances, coup sticks, shields (very important since some shields were thought to have supernatural power), clubs, axes, knives, and guns. Many weapons would be decorated with feathers and ornaments to imbue them with power. Other tools included those used to butcher animals and process hides. Pemmican and plant foods were processed in stone mortars, and stone hammers were used for grinding, pounding stakes, and breaking up bone to get at the marrow.

Religion and Medicine

The Cheyenne universe consisted of the world above and the world below, separated by the surface of the earth. The Creator (called Maheo) was male, resided in the sky, was spiritual, and provided energy to the world. The world below was essentially female and material. Four major deities lived in the four cardinal directions. The dead (except those who committed suicide) went to live in the sky.

Four major ceremonies were meant to renew the Cheyenne world. Individuals who wished to obtain supernatural intervention usually sponsored these events. The most essential Cheyenne ceremony was the Sacred Arrow Renewal Ceremony, a four-day ritual held annually just before the summer bison hunt. Four Sacred Medicine Arrows—the contents of the sacred Sweet Medicine Bundle and the most sacred possession of the Cheyenne—were held by the tribe; two of the arrows held power over bison and two over people. The four arrows symbolized the existence of the tribe as a whole. The Arrow Keeper was responsible for the care of the Sweet Medicine Bundle. As long as the arrows were cared for and honored, the Cheyenne would thrive.

A Sun Dance was also held every summer, sponsored by individuals as a gift to the group. An annual Animal Dance was conducted to ensure the well-being of the people and human mastery over the animals. During the Animal Dance, men imitated various animals and were "hunted" by members of the Bowstring Society. Women were also involved in the Animal Dance, which was light-hearted compared to the Sacred Arrow Renewal Ceremony. The forth major ceremony, the Sacred Hat, was primarily a Northern Cheyenne ceremony centered on a bundle consisting of a headdress made from bison hide and horn.

The Cheyenne believed that illness derived from both natural and supernatural causes; thus, doctors had to possess not only medical skill but also the ability to control supernatural power. Doctors also used supernatural power for a number of personal rituals, including preparing a man for war. Doctors (or shamans, usually men) were trained through an apprenticeship. A doctor's wife acted as his assistant and also required training. In addition to pharmacology, doctors used songs, rattles, feathers, objects of power, and tobacco to treat their patients (they also treated horses). Doctors were typically paid in horses or other goods. The Cheyenne adopted the Ghost Dance in 1890 but gradually abandoned it.

Art, Expression, and Recreation

Cheyenne life was rich with music and storytelling. Songs were performed at all ceremonies and for entertainment (see Giglio 1994). Various forms of painting were also common. Humans, horses, and tepees were adorned with paint and decorative items. Paintings intended to depict a story or event were worked on skin and on ledger books captured from the U.S. Army.

Games included the hoop-and-pole game, ball games, archery contests, horse racing, and gambling with dice made from bison foot bones. Work parties of women returning from root gathering would sometimes pretend to be a hostile military force, intending to attack the village. The men would respond by "attacking" this enemy, at which time they were met with a hail of sticks and dried bison dung. Those "wounded" or "killed" were out of the game, while those who "survived" could count coup on the enemy, taking as many roots as they wished as booty. This game made the root gathering fun, released some sexual tension, and allowed the women to assert some superiority over the men.

The Cheyenne Today

The population of the Cheyenne has substantially increased over the past eighty years to about 15,000 in 2000 (Moore et al. 2001: Table 2). The Cheyenne continue to uphold traditional values, particularly religious values and ceremonies, and they continue to conduct Sacred Arrow Renewal and Sun Dance ceremonies. In addition, the Native American Church remains important and powwows are still held. The military societies continue to function as a police force at community events, and their members still serve in the military, albeit the U.S. military. What once constituted coup has changed, first to individual acts of bravery (though not necessarily touching an enemy) and then later to simply having served in the military.

The Cheyenne tribal political organization continues to be the Council of Forty-Four, with the Northern and Southern divisions having separate councils (the Southern Cheyenne share their government with the Arapaho on their reservation). One Northern Cheyenne man, Ben Nighthorse Campbell, is a U.S. senator representing Colorado and a member of the Council of Forty-Four for the Northern Cheyenne.

The Southern Cheyenne, along with the Arapaho, continue to live on their reservation in Oklahoma, although many work off the reservation. In the late nineteenth century, two million acres of the reservation were lost to allotment, but the southern Cheyenne have managed to buy back several thousand acres of that land. Most tribal members receive a small amount of oil and mineral royalty money each year. Housing and health care have improved, but the people still struggle with poverty and discrimination (see Hoig 1992).

The Northern Cheyenne continue to live on the Tongue River Reservation in Montana, where they have managed to obtain title to most of the land and have purchased other lands. The principal economic pursuit is raising cattle and running several tribally owned enterprises. Unemployment is at about 30 percent. Although coal was discovered on the reservation, the tribe has decided not to mine it at this time. To encourage education, a tribal college was built on the reservation.

Additional information on the Cheyenne can be found at *http://www. cheyenneandarapaho.org* and *http://www.ncheyenne.net/*.

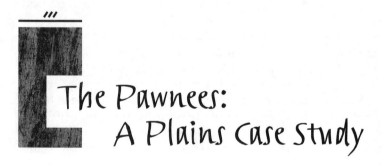

The Pawnees: A Plains Case Study

The Pawnees were farmers and bison hunters of the Prairies. Their primary homeland was south-central Nebraska and northern Kansas, along the Platte, Loup, and Republican Rivers (see Fig. 10.3). They called themselves Chaticks-Si-Chaticks, which means "People of People" but is sometimes translated as "Men of Men". The Pawnees consisted of four major independent groups, often called bands, and did not have a single tribal identity until about 1850 (the identities of the four bands are still maintained). The origin of *Pawnee* is unclear, but it appears to be an

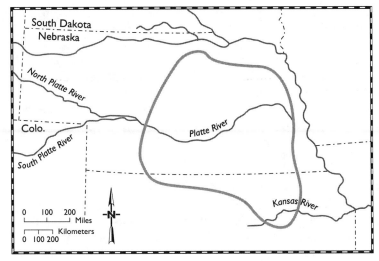

FIGURE 10.3 Location and territory of the Pawnees on the Prairies in about 1830 Adapted from Douglas R. Parks, "Pawnee," in *Handbook of North American Indians, Vol. 13, Plains,* Raymond J. DeMallie, ed., p. 515; copyright © 2001 by the Smithsonian Institution. Reprinted by permission of the publisher.

old name, used to refer to a number of groups on the central Plains. At some point it came to refer only to the Chaticks-Si-Chaticks. The Pawnees almost died out through disease, warfare, and the loss of their resource base (land and bison) as the Sioux and American settlers encroached on their territory. This case study of the Pawnees describes them as they were in about 1830.

Much of what is known of the Pawnees was obtained in the late nineteenth and early twentieth centuries by George Grinnell, Alice C. Fletcher, George A. Dorsey, and James R. Murie (himself a Pawnee; see Parks 1978). Important syntheses on Pawnee culture are contained in the works of Smith (1852), Grinnell (1889), Murie (1914, 1989), Lesser (1933), Hyde (1951), Weltfish (1965), Blaine (1990, 1997), Lacey (1996), and Parks (2001). The information on the Pawnees summarized below is from these sources.

The Natural Environment

The Pawnees lived in a region of rolling parklands, woodlands, lakes, and broad, gently flowing rivers. The largest river in Pawnee territory is the Platte, flowing east through the center of the Pawnee world. The Platte River is wide and shallow, easily crossed, and contains well-watered and accessible farmlands. The river valley also formed a natural route of travel for wagon trains and railroads.

The climate of the central Prairies is one of extremes. In the summer, temperatures can reach over 100°F, with little rainfall. The winters can be very cold, well below 0°F, with considerable snowfall and high winds. Both the bison and the humans sought refuge in sheltered valleys during the winter.

The two major environmental zones are the grasslands and the wooded river valleys. Bison were the primary game animal, living mostly to the west on the High Plains. Many other animals, including deer, elk, pronghorn antelope, wolves, rabbits, and a variety of rodents, lived in the wooded valleys and nearby rolling parkland. In addition, several species of fish inhabited the rivers and a variety of birds were present, including some migrating species of waterfowl.

Like all Plains groups, the Pawnees managed their environment through both ceremony and action. Plants and animals were managed through ceremony, both to thank them for their contribution to Pawnee life and to ensure their continued productivity. Additionally, the Pawnees burned the dry grasslands near their towns to encourage new growth and improved grazing for horses.

Language

The Pawnees spoke one of the Caddoan languages, a linguistic grouping that extends from the northern to the southern Plains. Other Caddoan groups included the Wichita and Caddo to the south and the Arikara to the north. The four major Pawnee bands spoke two main dialects—Skiri (spoken by the Skiri) and South Band, spoken by the three southern groups.

A Brief History

The ancestors of the Pawnees were a diverse people with a complex history. Some may have come to the Plains from the Southwest and others from the Mississippi River area. Pawnee ancestors eventually settled in the valleys of the Platte, Loup, and Republican Rivers, where they developed their distinctive lifestyle.

Archaeological data indicate that the Pawnees were living in the central Plains by at least 1,100 B.P. Between 1,100 and 600 B.P., the people of the central Plains, including the Pawnees, developed their distinctive ceremonial system, including calumet ceremonialism, corn ceremonialism, and medicine-lodge ceremonialism. The regional traits, including the political, social, and economic systems, also developed during this time.

Like all groups on the Plains, the Pawnees took part in a complex series of affiliations with neighboring groups. Different Pawnee bands had both trading and raiding relationships with various groups, and alliances would form and dissolve, depending on the situation. The Apache and tribes to the east sometimes raided the Pawnees and other groups for captives, some of which were sold as slaves. The Skiri were allied with the Arikara and Mandan, and the southern groups were allied with the Wichita. The Pawnees had difficult relations with other groups, their most menacing enemy being the Sioux to the north.

After the horse was introduced onto the northern Plains, a number of groups entered the region and began to compete for resources and territory. In the late nineteenth century the Sioux were expanding and beginning to exert control over groups on the northern Plains, such as the Arikara and Mandan. Later, the Sioux pushed south onto the central Plains and attempted to control that region, which included the Pawnees (see Blaine 1990:98–142). The Sioux killed a great many Pawnees and destroyed their towns. The pressure from the Sioux became so intense that the Pawnees allied themselves with the Americans to fight them, and a number of Pawnee scouts served with the U.S. Army against the Sioux during and after the Civil War. However, the Americans were little interested in protecting the Pawnees, and the Sioux continued to attack them even while the Pawnees were being guarded by U.S. troops on their reservation.

The Pawnees had known of the Americans for some time before their arrival in Pawnee territory, and many initially welcomed them as partners in trade dominated by the Pawnees until the mid–nineteenth century. One very persuasive leader, Knife Chief, was friendly with the Americans. Due to his influence, most Pawnee bands had generally friendly relations with the United States and signed treaties in 1818, 1825, 1833, 1849, and 1857. The Pawnees established a reservation in Nebraska in 1857, and Quaker missionaries began to operate among the Pawnees in 1869.

The Pawnees suffered severely from disease, a loss of access to resources, and incessant attacks by the Sioux, resulting in a considerable loss of population. In the mid-to-late eighteenth century, the Pawnee population may have been as high as 10,000. However, beginning in the early nineteenth century, disease and warfare reduced the population until it stood at less than 700 by 1900. This rapid population decline, coupled with the increasing difficulty in finding bison, forced some Pawnees to move onto the Wichita Reservation in Indian Territory in 1875, where they were obligated to rely on government rations (see Wishart 1979b). In 1875 the Pawnees were provided a small reservation of their own in Oklahoma, where the Pawnees living with the Wichita later moved. In 1938, the Pawnees reorganized their tribe and established their present form of government.

Cosmology

A number of stories relate the creation of the Pawnees, and each town had its own creation story. The various stories reflect the complicated social history of the Pawnees and their diverse origins. Included in these stories, as in all oral traditions, are aspects of history, morality, and general information. The following Skiri story (from Weltfish 1965) is one example.

Heaven existed in an unorganized universe of darkness. Heaven (a male figure, perhaps Tirawahat) first created the cardinal directions: Evening Star (a female deity in the west), Morning Star (a male deity in the east), North Star, and South Star. Then the semicardinal directions were created: Yellow Star in the northwest, Black Star in the northeast, White Star in the southwest, and Red Star in the southeast; each served as a pillar to support the sky over the earth (as the Pawnee house is constructed; see below). Heaven gave the stars the power to create people. Next, the earth was created by two storms, the first to give it structure and the second to endow it with life. Two more storms created trees and underbrush, and two more created watercourses, the first forming the beds of rivers and streams and the second filling them with flowing water. Two more storms created cultivated seeds, in which the seeds were first dropped and then made to grow. The stars then created a man and a woman and sent them to earth where they began to multiply. Thus, the world and the Pawnees came to be.

Politics and External Relations

The Pawnees were grouped into four major political divisions; the Skiri (sometimes called the Wolf Pawnees), the Chawi (Grand Pawnees), the Kitkahahki (Republican Pawnees), and the Pitahawirata (Tappage Pawnees), the latter three sometime collectively referred to as the South Bands. Each band had a number of towns; the Skiri had perhaps as many as nineteen.

Each town had two types of chiefs, hereditary and elected. The hereditary main chief was the caretaker of the town's sacred bundle, an office generally passed from father to son. Other chiefs were elected based on their deeds and wisdom. Most daily decisions in a town were made by the main chief, aided by one or two administrative assistants. The main chief also allocated the agricultural lands owned by the town to individual families. The chief's assistants implemented these decisions. However, most work in a town was accomplished because people realized it was necessary, not because a chief told them to do it.

The towns of each band were organized into a loose confederacy governed by a council consisting of the main chiefs from each town. The council made important decisions for the band, such as the regulation of the bison hunts. The council hierarchy was organized according to the ranks of the chiefs. Others could speak at council meetings, beginning with the most prominent persons. By the 1850s, the Pawnees had also appointed a chief for the tribe as a whole.

Towns varied in population size from 300 to 2,000 people, living in from forty to several hundred earth-covered houses, each with thirty to fifty people. Members of different bands might live in a single town, forming separate communities within the town. If another town was located nearby, the physical boundaries of the two might overlap, but the town identities were kept separate. Most towns were fortified to some extent to protect against raids, and men volunteered to be sentries.

The Pawnees participated in the Plains system of counting coup. The main goal of raiding was to obtain horses and honors; killing people was a secondary goal. Actual combat was not generally sought but sometimes occurred on an opportunistic basis; however, the Pawnees did employ ambushes and undertook many attacks by stealth at night. Donning wolf-skin robes, the Pawnees would disguise themselves as wolves to carry out reconnaissance activities and to sneak into an enemy camp to steal horses. Counting coup on an enemy was accomplished if and when the opportunity presented itself.

Social Organization

The town was the primary social unit. Each town had members, with membership passed from the female line, and men generally married a woman from their own town.

Pawnee society was organized into two classes. The upper class consisted of hereditary chiefs, priests, doctors, town criers, and administrative assistants. About half of the population were commoners who held no hereditary positions. It was difficult to change classes, but an ambitious man might do so. Becoming an elected chief was the pinnacle of status for a commoner. There were also social outcasts, including lazy people, those without a known father, persons accused of witch-craft, and criminals. The social outcasts lived on the outskirts of town and survived by charity or stealing what they needed.

Another outcast group consisted of persons who had survived being scalped. Such individuals were greatly feared, pitied, and highly respected, as it was thought that they were very spiritual and powerful. They were regarded as beyond the law and could do almost anything they wished. If such a person became too greatly feared, the community could decide to execute him or her.

Social status could be gained in different ways. Men might accomplish im-portant deeds in diplomacy or warfare, become a doctor, or a religious leader, or amass wealth, such as horses. Women were valued for their general skills, and some were excellent craftworkers—positions of high status. Women could also become wealthy.

The basic social unit was the extended family, people living together in a house-hold. Membership in a household was highly flexible and could change based on a variety of circumstances, such as marriage, divorce, or the death of a spouse. The house was divided into duplicate north and south halves that alternated in con-ducting the basic functions of the household; thus, everyone shared in the work. For example, two meals were prepared for the members of the household each day, one by each half. The family members themselves assigned the time (morn-ing or evening) at which each half was to perform a task.

Each half of the house contained three women's "stations," divided by age. The young women occupied the western side of the house, conducted minor house-hold duties, and took care of the economically productive young men of the house. The central station was occupied by mature women who did the most of the house-hold work. The eastern station, nearest the door, was occupied by the elder women ("grandmothers"), who provided care for all of the children in the household and general assistance to the mature women. Mothers had a formal relationship with their children, while the "grandmothers" had a much less formal and intimate re-lationship. Kinfolk assisted each other, ensuring that all had what they needed (being called poor was a great insult). It was important for everyone to visit each other and to maintain relationships.

Women did much of the farming during the spring and fall, gathered sub-stantial amounts of raw material (including plants), and made and maintained much of the family's equipment. This work provided a chance for social interac-tions, too. Men did the hunting and took part in warfare, but they would also learn to cook and sew so they could help the women. The Pawnees maintained several men's societies (sodalities), including doctor and military societies. These secular organizations contributed to warfare, hunting, civic work, and other group tasks.

Life Cycle

Children were greatly valued by the Pawnees and were carried on cradleboards until they were weaned. Each child obtained a guardian animal spirit, identified to the child either by a vision or by a doctor associated with that animal. Children were taught to have self-control, think before they acted, be self-sufficient and

Pawnee family at the entrance to their lodge at Loup, Nebraska, 1873.
(CORBIS)

independent, take responsibility, and cooperate for the good of the group. Of course, some Pawnees did not adhere to these ideals, and such individuals became social outcasts.

A child was first given a child's name, such as Ta'-ka ("white") or Ka-tit ("black") for boys and Ki-ri'-ki ("bright eyes") for girls. Adult names were given as an honor for some deed the persons had accomplished. People with multiple honors could have multiple names. A Pawnee never called another Pawnee by a personal name but instead used a kin term, such as *father* or *uncle*.

Young men formed lasting friendships with other young men, but those relationships diminished as they became older. Having little spare time and residing mostly in their own households, women formed far fewer friendships. Parents attempted to prevent relationships between their children and lower-status persons. With some exceptions, everyone participated in the communal hunts. By their mid-teens, males were expected to experience an adventure of some kind—a trading expedition, travel to faraway places, or a raiding expedition.

People were expected to marry within their class and town, both to maintain the strength of the town and to ensure that the sacred bundle never left it, and marriages were often arranged, especially among upper-class families. Polygyny was fairly common among the Pawnees, particularly among the upper class. Females married at about fifteen years of age, and males at about eighteen. Young men would usually marry a capable older woman, while a young girl would marry a mature man (she might be a second wife, the first often being her sister). Once the young woman matured, she might take a younger man as a second husband. Several brothers might share their wives and property in a sort of communal family. Several sisters might set up a similar arrangement. Since a child with an unknown father was considered a social outcast, women would not have sexual intercourse with more than one man during a given menstrual cycle, even if she had more than one husband. After marriage, the man moved in with his wife's family, but he always had a home in his sister's house.

The treatment of the dead varied among the Pawnee bands, depending on the rank of the deceased (see Echo-Hawk 1992). In general, the person was buried within a day or two of death, usually in the community cemetery. The family would hire a priest to prepare the deceased for burial and to conduct the ceremony. The deceased were dressed in their best clothing, sometimes anointed with paint (red ochre mixed with fat), wrapped in matting or a bison robe, and placed in the grave. Sometimes the deceased's favorite horse would be killed to accompany the individual to the afterlife. Friends and family would mourn, cry, and place offerings in and on the grave.

Economics

Like other Prairie groups, the Pawnees divided their economy between agriculture and bison hunting. Corn (called *a-ti'-ra*, "mother") was the most important crop, followed by beans, squash, and pumpkins. In late April or early May, women planted the crops in small family plots, usually along the bank of a river. They cleared the fields with antler rakes, planted using digging sticks, weeded twice with bison scapula hoes, then left the crops to grow on their own. After the spring planting, most Pawnees—literally thousands of men, women, and children—traveled to the High Plains to hunt bison. Those unable to travel remained in the towns as caretakers.

After the summer hunt, the Pawnees returned to their towns in late August or early September to harvest the crops planted in the spring. In November, people departed for the winter bison hunt, returning to the town again in March. Upon return from each hunt, the Pawnees repaired houses, processed and stored foods, renewed or changed social ties, and performed ceremonies. Food was either eaten fresh or preserved by drying and/or smoking, and pemmican was made. Surplus and preserved corn and meat were stored in containers placed in large pits (over ten feet deep) lined with sand and bark. These cache pits would be opened as needed.

Communal bison hunting was a precisely organized effort led by highly experienced men. Individuals were not permitted to go out alone, for fear that they might stampede the herd and thus spoil the hunt. Military societies ensured that overanxious males were controlled. When the time came, groups of hunters would attack the herd in a way that prevented the animals from panicking. Arrows were used to kill the bison when possible, as firearms were too noisy and ammunition was scarce. Once killed, the animals were skinned and butchered, and the skins and meat were processed back in camp.

In addition to the primary agricultural crops and bison, other foods were available. Men would hunt deer, elk, and rabbits all year, and some fish and turtles were also consumed. Women gathered a variety of wild plants, such as berries, wild turnips, and prickly-pear cactus fruits. Men grew tabacco in special fields. Smoking tobacco in a pipe was an important activity during both ceremonial and social occasions.

The Pawnees traded extensively with surrounding groups and, as with other Plains groups, horses formed the typical medium of exchange and gift giving. The trading relationship between the Pawnees and the Americans became critical as the Pawnees became dependent on American manufactured goods and foods.

Material Culture and Technology

The Pawnees spent much of the year living in substantial earth-covered houses. The houses served a dual purpose as residences and as sites for ceremonial activities. A house could be quite large, as much as fifty to sixty feet in diameter and twelve feet high inside, with a smokehole in the top and an entrance at the side, facing east. With proper maintenance, a house would last between ten and fifteen years. Some fifteen to fifty people lived in each. Houses were constructed as a model of the universe and a womb, with the earth on the bottom, the sky on top supported by pillars, and the smokehole as the zenith of the sky. Ceremonies or communal events would be held in chiefs' or priests' houses which were larger and could hold more people. When traveling in the winter, the Pawnees used conical tepees, perhaps as large as eighteen feet in diameter, as shelters. The same tepee covering was used over a smaller, rounded frame for shelter during the summer hunt. Hunting camps, like towns, were organized as a model of the cosmos.

Men usually traveled on horseback, constantly prepared to defend themselves or the group. During hunting expeditions, women and children usually walked beside the travois, and sick or injured people would be transported on it. The Pawnees also used a shallow-draft reed boat for traversing rivers.

The Pawnees paid close attention to clothing and personal appearance, which served as "badges" of rank on formal occasions. Children went mostly naked until the age of six; after that the boys wore a loincloth and the girls wore a skirt. Men would dress in a loincloth, leggings, and moccasins made from deerskin, while women would be clothed in a sleeveless shirt, a skirt, leggings, and moccasins. In cold weather, a bison skin robe would be worn by both sexes. Both men and women wore handkerchiefs on their heads, like turbans. Men often shaved the sides of their heads, leaving a band of short hair on top that ran from the forehead to the back of the neck (the so-called "Mohawk" style), and plucked their facial hair. Women wore their hair long and braided, with one braid on each side.

Both men and women would wear tattoos on their faces, and paint—especially red paint—was freely applied to both the face and chest. Many men wore eagle feathers in their hair, the number depending on their accomplishments in battle. Other items might be worn as decorations or symbols of rank, such as scalps or European trade goods.

The Pawnees' primary weapons were the bow and arrow, club, lance, and shield. Guns were obtained later and became very important. Knives and arrow points were made of stone, and many other implements were manufactured from horn, bone, and wood. Most containers were made from animal skin, as the pottery of prehorse times was too fragile. Hoes were made from the scapulae of bison, dishes were made of wood, and corn was ground with wooden mortars and pestles. A variety of plants were utilized for weaving and for dyes. Many items, such as arrows, pipes, and baskets, were manufactured by specialist craftworkers, who would take orders and receive payment for their products.

Religion and Medicine

The Pawnees did not have a formal, organized religion but conducted a number of activities related to the supernatural. This diversity and flexibility made them willing to accept new ideas, such as Christianity. A fundamental Pawnee belief views the sky and the earth as dual realms—the celestial realm was the charge of priests, while the earthly realm was the responsibility of doctors.

A number of deities lived in the sky, including Tirawahat, the primary deity who created the universe (see Chamberlain 1982, 1992; also see above). Stars were considered the source of power, and nothing could occur on earth without the approval of the heavens. Bundles of sacred objects connected the Pawnees with the heavens. Each town would possess a sacred bundle given to the people by their guardian constellation. In addition, a number of other sacred bundles were held by the Pawnees as a whole; these were given to the people long ago by Tirawahat.

A regular cycle of important ceremonies associated with bundles comprised much of Pawnee religious life; these rituals were conducted by priests (usually males) who served as intermediaries between humans and the supernatural. The ceremonies were intended primarily to maintain balance and harmony in the universe, and many were rehearsed to ensure correctness. Most ceremonies were conducted in a house and always included offerings (of tobacco, corn, and meat), gifts to the priests, singing, and the burning of incense.

The Thunder Ritual of the Evening Star took place in early spring and began the ritual season. The New Fire ceremony was conducted when a war party returned with appropriate trophies (e.g., scalps). Another kind of ceremony took place if a person dreamed that he or she should sponsor one. Possibilities included a human sacrifice (generally of a captive female) to Morning Star, the Young Corn Plant ritual, and the Corn Planting ceremony. This latter event had to be sponsored by a woman.

The Pawnees believed in an afterlife. Upon death, a good Pawnee would journey to the sky to live again with Tirawahat. Bad people did not make such a journey and did not live again. The Pawnees adopted the Ghost Dance in 1892 (see Sidelight in Chapter 7), which resulted in a cultural revival of sorts, rejuvenating some social groups and games.

The earthly realm was quite separate from the celestial one, and the associated religious activities were conducted by doctors (or shamans). Doctors belonged to one of several medicine societies organized by specialty, not unlike Western medical organizations. In addition, prominent doctors belonged to the Medicine Lodge. In the fall, the Medicine Lodge would hold a major ceremony lasting as many as thirty days. Through a series of performances, including dancing, singing, hypnotism, and illusion, the participating doctors would publicly demonstrate their power.

Doctors could be either male or female. There were two basic ways to become a doctor: by being trained by an experienced doctor during an apprenticeship or by supernatural intervention. In the latter case, a human might be brought to a place in the landscape where animals had gathered to hold a ceremony. The animals would then give the chosen novice knowledge and power. The power of doctors was meant to control plants and animals and enemies, and/or to cure illness. Specialists practiced medicine in order to cure illness and treat injury. Illness originated from anxiety or hostility and had to be removed or driven from the body. Pawnee doctors were widely known for their skill in treating injuries, receiving gifts when they were successful.

Art, Expression, and Recreation

The Pawnees had a rich tradition of music and art, much of it associated with the many ceremonies, where oratory, music, singing, and dancing were integral (see Densmore 1929; Weltfish 1965). Many ceremonies contained elements of theater and pageantry. Much of Pawnee material culture, such as robes, tepee covers, weapons, and shields, were artistically decorated. Celestial objects, particularly stars, were very popular symbols in art.

Games were very important to the Pawnees. Males raced horses and played the hoop-and-pole game, with different skill levels for different ages. Both sexes played the hand game. Women played the plum seed game, in which marked plum seeds served as "dice." Gambling was involved in many games. Though popular, gambling became an obsession with a few Pawnees, who became addicted. The Pawnees recognized this social problem and attempted to help the afflicted gamblers.

One of the most common forms of entertainment, which also served to transmit cultural knowledge, was storytelling. Stories were told in most households almost nightly, especially in the winter. People would venture from house to house to hear new stories or to be entertained by master storytellers.

The Pawnees Today

The Pawnee Nation of Oklahoma lists some 2,500 citizens. Between 500 and 800 of them live on their 650-acre reservation near Pawnee, Oklahoma, which they have occupied since 1875. The remainder of the Pawnees are scattered throughout the country, living in places like Oklahoma City and Wichita and working in various professions, including the military.

The current Pawnee tribal government, formed in 1938, consists of two councils. The Chief's Council is composed of elected chiefs from the various bands and considers political issues for the tribe. The Business Council is the more powerful of the two and administers the various tribal business interests, including oil leases, a service station, and land developments. The Pawnees remain heavily dependent on grants and aid from the federal government.

Pawnee women appear to have lost much of the power and prestige they held in the traditional society, perhaps due to a shift of responsibilities for farming from women to men. Some traditional customs are still practiced and the sacred bundles are still important (see Blaine 1983). Ghost Dances are still conducted, the latest performed in 1998, although as a traditional activity rather than an attempt to promote change (as in the original version on the Plains).

More information on the Pawnees can be obtained at *http://www.pawneenation.org.*

———

11 Native Peoples of the Northeast

///

The Indians of the Northeast (Fig. 11.1) were primarily farmers who also depended to some degree on hunting and gathering; however, a few groups in the northeastern portions of the region lived exclusively by hunting and gathering. The primary agricultural crops of the region consisted of the "three sisters"—corn, beans, and squash—and sunflowers. Groups living in the northern part of the Northeast and around the Great Lakes depended less on agriculture and more on hunting, fishing, and gathering.

Northeastern groups spoke languages from three principal language families: Algonquian, Northern Iroquoian, and Siouan. Groups speaking Algonquian languages lived along the Atlantic coast and in the Great Lakes region, while most of the groups speaking Northern Iroquoian languages lived inland and in the northern portion of the Northeast culture area. A few groups speaking Siouan languages lived in the far western portion of the Northeast.

Geography and Environment

The Northeast culture area encompasses the northeastern United States and southeastern Canada. It lies east of the Mississippi River, south of the Subarctic, and generally north of the thirty-fifth parallel (see Fig. 11.1). The Northeast can be divided into three major environmental zones: the Coastal Region, the Saint Lawrence–Lowlands Region, and the Great Lakes–Riverine Region.

The Coastal Region extends along the Atlantic coast from Virginia north to Newfoundland. A broad alluvial plain dominates the coast south of New York. The Appalachian Mountains run along the western side of the Coastal Region, begin-

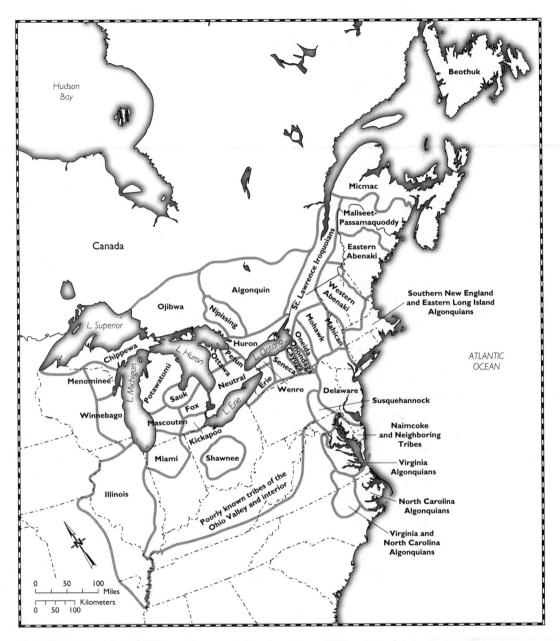

FIGURE 11.1 The Northeast culture area showing the general location of the various native groups
Adapted from *Handbook of North American Indians, Vol. 15, Northeast*, B. E. Trigger, ed., p. xi; copyright © 1978 by the Smithsonian Institution. Reprinted by permission of the publisher.

ning in the northern Southeast culture area and extending north into southern Canada. In their northern reaches, the Appalachians are heavily eroded and not very rugged. Several rivers flow from the mountains east to the sea.

The Saint Lawrence–Lowlands Region is dominated by a large, linear depression running from the Great Lakes northeast to the Gulf of Saint Lawrence. Lakes Erie and Ontario lie to the west, and the Saint Lawrence River flows from the lakes east to the sea. This is a region of thick forests, many rivers and streams, and numerous lakes.

The Great Lakes–Riverine Region is dominated by the three western Great Lakes (Superior, Michigan, and Huron) in the north and the Ohio River Valley in the south. The lake region is fairly flat and includes many rivers, lakes, and islands. Severe weather is not uncommon on the Great Lakes. The Ohio River traverses much of the Northeast, flowing west to join the Mississippi River. The central Appalachians, including some very rugged areas, run along the southern portion of the valley, while the northern portions are relatively flat and heavily forested.

A vast deciduous forest of maple, birch, oak, hickory, elm, and willow extends across much of the Northeast, slowing grading into a coniferous (e.g., pine, fir, spruce) forest on the northern margins, and into oak parkland in the far west. The most important game animal in the Northeast is the deer, but the region also supports bear, rabbits, squirrels, beavers, many varieties of fish, shellfish, crawfish, snakes, turtles, waterfowl, and numerous other birds (e.g., turkeys).

The Northeast has a generally temperate climate, with abundant precipitation. The winters are usually quite cold, with considerable snowfall. Depending on location, between 140 and 210 frost-free days occur per year, and agriculture can be practiced everywhere except in the farthest northern portion of the region. Summer temperatures are warm to hot, often reaching a humid 100°F along the coast and 90°F in the interior.

A Basic Prehistory of the Northeast

The prehistory of the Northeast is very complex, and considerable research has been conducted there. The following very brief summary was compiled from Brose (1978), Fitting (1978), Fowler and Hall (1978), Funk (1978), Griffin (1978), Snow (1978, 1980, 1981), Tuck (1978a, 1978b), Mason (1981), Muller (1986), Dent (1995), Fagan (2000), and Bragdon (2001).

The Paleoindian Period (ca. 15,000 to 10,000 B.P.)

At the height of the last glacial episode, ice sheets extended well into what is now the United States, including the northern portion of the Northeast. A tundra-like spruce parkland environment existed just to the south of the ice sheets, with a zone of deciduous forest to the south of the tundra. As the ice retreated at the end of the Pleistocene, the tundra and deciduous forest moved north and formed the two major environments present during Paleoindian times. Mammoths apparently did not live in the east in large numbers, but mastodon remains are relatively common. Some researchers have argued that people who lived in the tundra at this time depended heavily on caribou for food and other materials, while the forest adaptation was based on the hunting of a wider range of animals (e.g., Meltzer 1988).

The earliest known archaeological site in the Northeast is Meadowcroft Rock-shelter, located in Pennsylvania. It has been argued that this site has been continuously occupied for at least 19,000 years. However, considerable controversy exists regarding the accuracy of the early dates, and most researchers will accept only the more accurately dated initial occupation beginning about 14,000 years ago. A number of other Paleoindian sites have been well documented and accepted as authentic, and some contain the fluted points so typical of such sites. One of the better known is the Debert site in Nova Scotia, dating to about 10,000 years ago. People at the Debert site exploited caribou and perhaps sea mammals, and they probably lived in simple wood or skin-covered structures.

The Archaic Period (ca. 10,000 to 3,000 B.P.)

During the Early Archaic period (10,000 to 8,000 B.P.), there is more evidence of human occupation of the Northeast, mostly of small, highly mobile groups. The Koster site in Illinois (see Struever and Holton 1979) contains a record of human occupation that spans the entire Holocene, with the earliest occupation dated to about 9,500 B.P. Evidence of an Early Archaic camp dating to about 8,500 B.P., the occupants of which had a broad diet, was also discovered at Koster.

During the Middle Archaic period (ca. 8,000 to 5,000 B.P.), it appears that people were congregating in larger numbers and beginning to reside in larger and more permanent settlements. At Koster there is evidence of a substantial, but seasonal, settlement, with houses dating to about 7,500 B.P. Remains of a later permanent village (ca. 5,900 to 4,800 B.P.) also exist at Koster. By 6,000 B.P., cemeteries began to appear in association with permanent settlements; fixed territories and political organization were also developing.

At the beginning of the Late Archaic period (ca. 5,000 to 3,000 B.P.), population growth is evident, as well as the development of more complex political and social organizations. People likely began experimenting with the cultivation and/or domestication of some native plants, such as gourds, sunflowers, and sump-weed. The Old Copper Culture, known for its cold-hammered copper artifacts and dating between 5,000 and 4,500 B.P., became widespread in the western Northeast. The Archaic period lasted until historical times in the northern part of the Northeast, where agriculture was never adopted.

The Woodland Period (ca. 3,000 B.P. to Contact)

The Woodland period is defined by the presence of complex cultures and some agriculture. The convergence of three innovations marks the beginning of the Woodland period: (1) the manufacture of pottery, perhaps as early as 4,500 B.P.; (2) the cultivation of native plants, also occurring fairly early; and (3) the use of burial mounds.

In the central Ohio Valley, a cultural tradition known as the Adena Complex developed by about 3,000 B.P. Adena was not a single culture, but a number of related Early Woodland cultures in the same general region that shared general similarities. Most Adena sites consist of burial mounds with small occupation sites on top. Early and Middle Adena burials were relatively simple; however, a new mortuary pattern had developed by Late Adena (ca. 2,200 B.P.), with much more elaborate mounds and some burials in log tombs. This change in burial patterns is thought to reflect an increase in sociocultural complexity.

By the Middle Woodland (ca. 2,200 to 1,700 B.P.), a new and more elaborate cultural tradition, called Hopewell, had appeared in the Ohio River Valley. Like Adena, it did not consist of a single culture but a number of related Middle Woodland cultures located in the same general region. Hopewell entailed a considerable elaboration of Adena; it featured much larger mounds and occupation sites and was much more widespread. Hopewell sites are very complex, with impressive mounds and earthworks built within enclosures, called forts by Europeans. Several mound groups in Ohio were connected by "Great Hopewell Roads," wide lanes (about 150 feet) bordered by high (8- to 10-foot) parallel earthen walls. One such road was estimated to have been sixteen miles long and another is thought to have been about sixty miles long. These roads were probably part of the far-flung exchange system that characterized Hopewell.

Hopewell social and political systems were very complex, with a class structure and at least a tribal level of political organization, perhaps even a chiefdom level. It appears that "commoners" were cremated while the elite were buried in graves with lavish offerings. The burial rituals were elaborate. Individuals were placed in a special wooden chamber (a "house") and allowed to decompose; then the house containing the individual was burned and an earthen mound erected over the ashes. Because most research on Hopewell has so far been focused on burial mounds, relatively little is known about Hopewell subsistence.

By the Late Woodland (ca. 1,700 B.P. to contact), maize had spread across much of eastern North America; it had become the primary crop by about 1,200 B.P. At this time, the Hopewell tradition began to decline, perhaps due to overpopulation, climatic changes, the introduction of the bow and arrow (increasing hunting efficiency and resulting in the decimation of game), an increase in warfare, or other factors.

Most cultures in the Northeast developed a pattern of corn agriculture, hunting, warfare, large permanent towns, and complex political organizations. This pattern lasted until contact. To the south, however, the tradition known as Hopewell developed into the spectacular Mississippian cultures of the Southeast (see Chapter 12).

The Contact Period

European fishermen and fur traders began to exploit resources in the northern Northeast very soon after Columbus arrived in the New World in 1492, and it is even possible that the Basque fished the Grand Banks of Nova Scotia prior to 1492 (Quinn 1974). The fishermen would arrive in the summer, establish a temporary processing camp on shore, and then return to Europe in the fall with their catch. This contact probably had minimal impact on the local Indians. By the early sixteenth century, however, large numbers of European fishermen traveled to Newfoundland every summer, and whalers were operating off northeastern North America by 1536.

By the early sixteenth century, the Dutch, French, English, Portuguese, and Spanish were competing for the fur trade (see Chapter 2) in the Northeast, though the Portuguese and Spanish had dropped out by midcentury. The English established their first colony at Roanoke, Virginia, in 1585 and a second one at Jamestown, Virginia, in 1607. Additional colonies were subsequently established, including a Pilgrim colony in Plymouth, Massachusetts, in 1620, followed by a large Puritan colony at Boston in 1630. The French established a colony in southern Canada in 1608, and by the early seventeenth century the French had become allied with the Huron and northern Algonquians in the northern Northeast, while the English were allied with the Iroquois farther to the south.

Also in the early seventeenth century the Dutch established an installation, Fort New Amsterdam, on Manhattan Island, and another at what is now Albany. The Dutch intended to trade furs with the Indians of the region, but they later established colonies for farmers from Holland as the fur trade declined. The Dutch remained in control of the trade in the New York area until 1664, when the English conquered the Dutch New Netherland colony and renamed it New York. In 1673, a Dutch fleet reconquered New York and renamed it New Holland. After fifteen months, the Dutch traded the colony to the English—who again changed the name to New York—for an island in the Caribbean (see Rink 1986 for a history of the Dutch in New York). After that time, the Dutch had little influence in North America.

As the European colonies began to expand, they came into direct conflict with the Indians over land. The colonists instigated a series of small wars in an attempt to eliminate the Indian populations and take their land. In the Pequot War of 1637, the English massacred most of the Pequot tribe and claimed Connecticut. The last of these wars was King Philip's War (1675–1676), during which an Algonquian leader named Metacom (given the name King Philip by the English) led a defense of Indian lands. With the defeat of King Philip, Algonquian power was broken in the Northeast.

In 1641 the Iroquois began a concerted effort to defeat their enemy to the north, the Huron, driving them eastward. Over the next forty years, the Iroquois succeeded in defeating most of the groups in the central Northeast (the Erie, Shawnee, Miami, Illinois, Neutral, and others). By 1687, remnants of the defeated groups had joined the French and were attacking the Iroquois. The Iroquois were forced to withdraw from much of the territory they had conquered, but they still dominated the Northeast until the American Revolution.

The competition between the British and the French, along with their Indian allies, culminated with the French and Indian War (1754–1763, part of a larger Anglo-French conflict). The French were defeated, ceding Canada and the area south of the Great Lakes to the British. Many of the affected Indian groups were angry that the French had ceded territory that had not belonged to them, and when the British began to exercise control of the territory, they met with increasing hostility from the Indians.

The British occupied former French forts and established new ones across the Great Lakes region, attempting to subject the Indians to British rule. In response, a loosely organized alliance of Great Lakes area Indians, led in part by the Ottawa chief Pontiac, initiated a major war in 1763 to expel the British from the Great Lakes region and to restore Indian diplomatic power. Though the Indians lost a few battles, they defeated the British army on a number of occasions and finally forced the British to acknowledge Indian political power and to become trading partners. Peace was restored in 1766 (see Parmenter 1997).

Over the years, many native groups had moved west to the Ohio Valley to escape the colonists. After the American Revolution, however, settlers flooded the Ohio Valley, setting off a number of small conflicts between the United States and the Indians. In 1795, the Indians were forced to cede most of the Ohio Valley. Continued pressure from settlers started another war in 1811, during which the Shawnee chief Tecumseh led the resistance. Tecumseh had experienced a vision— all things European were to be rejected—and thereafter led the Shawnee and allied groups against the whites. The Indians were defeated by General (later President) Tyler at the Battle of Tippecanoe. In 1812, Tecumseh allied his forces with the British, who were again at war with the United States. The Indians were finally defeated by the Americans in 1813 at the Battle of the Thames in southern Ontario, and Tecumseh was killed, ending the Indian revolt.

After the Indian Removal Act of 1830, many Northeastern Indian groups were forced to move to Indian Territory, and many still have reservations there today. However, some groups, such as the Iroquois and the Ottawa, were fairly successful in resisting removal and still live in their original territories.

The Impact of European Contact

The impact of European diseases, genocide, and warfare on the native populations of the Northeast was massive, with a mortality rate of about 50 percent and occasionally as much as 95 percent (see Snow and Lanphear 1988; Stannard 1992). Many groups along the Atlantic coast were decimated before any written record of them was made. The Iroquois suffered from these maladies but were able to take advantage of the situation, becoming the major native political and military power in the region.

The first major epidemic (of an unknown disease) in the Northeast occured in 1616, before many Indians had even seen a European. In 1633, a major smallpox epidemic swept through the region and wiped out entire groups in the first widespread population decline. Although the surviving groups increased their numbers subsequent to this event, they endured many other epidemics up until the 1870s. Along with great population losses, these diseases led to an increase in warfare to even old scores, to obtain plunder, and to acquire captives. Many settlers viewed the epidemics among the Indians as an act of God to depopulate the region in order to make room for the colonies.

A Brief History of Ethnographic Research

Historical records of the Indians of the Northeast extend back almost 500 years (see Tooker 1978a). These include the writings of early explorers, missionaries, trading companies, newspapers and magazines, and government records. Although they contain biased language, such documents provide invaluable information on the early Indians of the Northeast. Scientific interest in the native peoples of the

Northeast began to emerge after the American Revolution; some of the most significant early work was done by Thomas Jefferson. In the 1840s, Lewis H. Morgan began to conduct research on Iroquois culture, and in 1851 he published *League of the Ho-dé-no-sau-nee, Iroquois*, the first ethnography ever published in anthropology. As a result, the Iroquois became well known, and since that time considerable research has been conducted on Iroquois culture.

Beginning in the late nineteenth century, significant efforts were made to assemble basic ethnographic data on Northeastern groups, although information on some was very limited. Subsequent to the 1950s, research shifted to specific issues such as ecological adaptations, kinship systems, and psychological characteristics. Most recently, anthropologists have been studying Indian land-claims cases, development, and gaming.

A considerable amount of information is available on many Northeastern groups. The Northeastern volume (Vol. 15) of the *Handbook of North American Indians* (Trigger 1978), written mostly in the mid-1970s, contains chapters on many specific groups, as well as a wide variety of topics. A more recent guide to native peoples of the Northeast was provided by Bragdon (2001). The groups discussed below are described as they were in the early nineteenth century.

A Broad Portrait of Northeastern Groups

One hallmark of the Northeast is the variety and complexity of its native cultures. Most groups relied both on farming and hunting and gathering, and most had relatively large populations with complex political organizations. Since the Iroquois nations of northern New York are probably the best-known groups, there has been a tendency to apply their traits to the other groups, masking the specific characteristics that distinguish each one.

Political Organization

Three main types of political organizations characterized the Northeast: bands, tribes, and confederacies. In general, leaders at any level were called sachems, or sagamores. A few hunter-gatherer groups along the northern extent of the Northeast were organized as bands; families coalesced in the fall and winter to form a band and dispersed in the spring and summer. The other groups in the Northeast were organized as tribes (often called nations). A number of towns would join to form a tribe; each town was governed by a council made up of leaders of the lineages in the town. Each town would then send representatives to a tribal council.

Many tribes were further organized into confederacies. A confederacy was governed by a council consisting of the leaders from each of the member tribes; the most influential leader would in effect lead the alliance. The largest and most successful confederacy was the League of the Iroquois, an organization that influenced the politics of the region for several hundred years. The league had a relatively large population and a strong military tradition, enabling its members to survive the onslaught of the French and the British. The league maintained significant

Highly romanticized drawing of Pocahontas, daughter of Powhatan, undated engraving. (CORBIS)

political influence over many groups and even held some regions as protectorates, including much of Ohio.

Another major alliance, the Powhatan Confederation (named after its leader, Powhatan), was formed in the Chesapeake Bay region. The Powhatan Confederation reached its height in the early seventeenth century and had a population of perhaps as many as 15,000 people. The English colony of Jamestown was founded in 1607 in Powhatan territory, leading to the destruction of the Powhatan by 1700 (see Rountree 1989, 1990; Rountree and Davidson 1997; Gleach 1997; also see this chapter's VIP Profile on Pocahontas). Other well-known confederations included the Wabanaki in Maine and southeastern Canada, the Delaware Confederation in the Delaware Valley (see Goddard 1978), the Huron, the Neutral, and the Erie.

Warfare

Warfare was a common, important aspect of Northeastern culture. Most warfare was conducted to avenge the deaths of people killed in earlier incidents, a practice that essentially ensured the continuation of warfare. It was also the vehicle by which men gained prestige and power. Although revenge and adventure were primary motives for most warfare, defense of territory became very important after European contact. In addition, the competition between groups that resulted from the fur trade precipitated major wars of conquest, with the intent of eliminating competitors.

Raiders usually set out to kill the enemy, take trophies (scalping may have been introduced by the French), and obtain captives, without suffering casualties. If the attackers lost any men, the loss would be announced to the town before the raiders returned. Enemy men would be beheaded and the heads brought back as trophies. Scalps would sometimes be taken instead of heads. These trophies would be displayed in the attackers' town. Male war captives would either be tortured to death or adopted by women who had lost sons or husbands in war.

The torture of captives was typically brutal, often directed by women who had lost loved ones to the enemy, and it could last for days. Captives were usually tied spread-eagle to wooden frames, their appendages would be burned or cut off, red-hot pokers would be thrust into any orifice, they would be forced to eat their own flesh, and finally they would be burned alive. After the death of a captive, the torturers might consume some of the flesh. One goal of torture was to break the spirit

VIP Profile

POCAHONTAS

Pocahontas, the "Indian Princess" well known to most Americans, was a real and remarkable woman. Her given name was Amonute (or Matoaka); she was called Pocahontas by her people as a nickname. It meant something like "mischievous" or "spoiled child." She was born in about 1596, one of the many daughters of Powhatan (whose real name was Wahunsunacock), the leader of the powerful Powhatan confederation in south coastal Virginia.

In 1607, the English established the Jamestown Colony—without the permission of Powhatan, in whose territory the colony was located. Relations between the colonists and the Indians rapidly became hostile, but the Indians retained a desire to trade with the English. Some of the Indians, including the young Pocahontas, visited the colony and became friends with a few of the colonists, including John Smith. Pocahontas and some of the other Indians provided food to the struggling colony; if they had not, it would have failed in its first year.

When the English did not leave as promised, hostilities began. John Smith was captured by the Indians and was taken before Powhatan. Smith was ordered to be killed, but Pocahontas threw herself on top of him to prevent the execution. Many now believe that this was a staged event, part of a ceremony intended to honor Smith as a guest. Smith was then interrogated, at which time he told Powhatan that the English were leaving soon; however, Powhatan soon realized that the English had no intention of departing. Powhatan continued to trade with the English to obtain arms. Pocahontas then began to serve as an ambassador between her father and the English.

In 1609, with the colony starving, John Smith went to Powhatan and asked for food. Powhatan, now knowing that the English had no intention of leaving Jamestown, was determined to kill Smith

as the opening shot in an effort to remove the colony. But Pocahontas, then only about thirteen years old, warned Smith of the impending assassination. Smith eventually left Jamestown and Pocahontas was told he had died.

The English had begun expanding the Jamestown Colony and were constructing new colonies. Powhatan was angry about this expansion and suspended all trade with the English, much to the detriment of the English, who needed food from the Indians. To ensure that trade continued, the English kidnaped Pocahontas. She was forced to adopt English customs and dress and to convert to Christianity. She was renamed Rebecca.

Meanwhile, a colonist named John Rolfe, a widower who started tobacco farming in Virginia (see Sidelight in Chapter 2), fell in love with Rebecca and married her on April 5, 1614. Thus, Pocahontas became Rebecca Rolfe. The Rolfes had a son, Thomas, in 1615. In her role as ambassador, Pocahontas (with her husband and child) sailed to England in 1616, where she and her family were presented to Queen Anne in London. Much to her shock, Pocahontas was visited in London by John Smith. In 1617, just as she was about to return to Virginia, she died of an unknown disease at the age of twenty-two. Her son, Thomas Rolfe, eventually did return to Virginia, where the descendants of the family still live.

The figure of Pocahontas has evolved into the romanticized "Indian Princess" of Western oral tradition (not to mention the Disney movie). She is usually portrayed as rejecting native culture and values, entering European culture, and becoming a "good" Indian (that is, a non-Indian; see Green 1975). This portrait of the savage seeing the light of civilization and thus being "rescued" may seem familiar and benign to many non-Indians, but it is offensive to many Indians. In reality, the story of Pocahontas represents the tragedy of a woman caught in the initial stages of the struggle for North America.

of the captive so he would cry and beg for mercy—in which case he would be ridiculed and tortured more. A few brave prisoners would endure without complaint, singing their death songs. If they were able to maintain this macho stance, they would be held in high esteem, and sometimes were even spared (see Knowles 1940 for a discussion of torture). Trigger (1990) suggested that torture and sacrifice of prisoners may have been related to world renewal and the maintenance of cosmic order through ceremony.

Social Organization

The basic social units in all Northeastern groups were the extended family and lineage, with the lineage owning the farmland. Most groups also had clans and some had moieties. The groups that primarily depended on farming (which were the majority) were matrilineal, and the few groups that depended mostly on hunting were patrilineal.

Women generally did the farming, but men helped clear the fields for planting. During menstruation and childbirth, women were isolated from the rest of the society. Women shared political power in many Northeastern groups, the best example being the Iroquois (see Bilharz 1995).

Economics

The hunter-gatherers along the eastern Canadian coast subsisted mainly by fishing, gathering shellfish, and hunting sea mammals, large and small land animals, and birds (they also gathered their eggs). In addition, a number of plants formed part of the diet.

Most Northeastern groups practiced an economy that included both agriculture and hunting and gathering. The agricultural system employed a slash-and-burn technique in which underbrush would be cut, dried, and burned, trees and large stones were left in place, decreasing the labor required to prepare a field. Crops were then planted between the trees and rocks. Corn was planted first, and after the stalks had grown to a sufficient height, beans were planted around the corn so that the vines could grow up the cornstalks. Other crops would be planted around the corn and beans, resulting in a very efficient use of the fields. Men cleared the fields; women did the planting, weeding, and harvesting; and children guarded the crops from pests. After several crops had been planted and harvested, the field would be abandoned and the native vegetation allowed to regrow. The same area could be used for crops again in a decade or so. The system required large tracts of land, as most had to lie fallow at any one time, but it generally destroyed less soil and animal habitat than did the European system of complete field clearance, plowing, permanent fields, and fencing.

Many different animals were hunted for meat and/or skins. Large and small mammals were very important, including deer, elk, bear, rabbits, porcupines, foxes, wolves, and muskrats. Bison were hunted in the western part of the Northeast and sea mammals along the northern Atlantic coast. Other game included a variety of birds (e.g., turkeys, geese, grouse, and waterfowl) and amphibians (e.g., turtles and frogs), as well as lobster, oysters, mussels, and clams along the seacoast. Fish were important everywhere, and a large variety of freshwater and saltwater fish were taken, such as salmon, trout, walleye, sturgeon, pike, bullhead, and eels from the rivers and lakes, and cod from the ocean.

Individual men did most of the hunting, using bows and arrows (and later guns), although deer would be hunted communally in the fall. Other animals would be captured in deadfall and pit traps, as well as snares. Fishing was often a communal activity, especially when harvesting species that migrated at certain times of the year.

Wild plants, including various berries, acorns, hickory nuts, plums, cherries, and greens, also formed significant food resources. Maple sap was used as a sweetener and candy. Wild rice, important in the Great Lakes region, was collected by knocking the rice grains into a canoe with a paddle. Some grains would be broadcast back into the marsh to grow the next year's crop. As in many native cultures, tobacco was also a critical resource.

Indians in the Northeast had used shells as a medium of exchange for many centuries. However, after the seventeenth century, the English and the Dutch began to make tubular white and purple beads from marine shells. These beads, known as wampum, were used as currency by these Europeans in transactions with some groups all across the Northeast, particularly the Iroquois, who assembled the beads into belts or strings and used them to record important events or agreements. Distinctive patterns of beads would document specific agreements—identical wampum belts were made for each occasion so that each party had a "copy" of the agreement—or to serve as emblems of title.

Material Culture and Technology

Houses varied by region and season. For most of the year, many Northeastern people lived in large communal houses, often referred to by their Iroquoian name, longhouses. A large house could be 150 feet long and 20 feet wide. A number of families lived in apartment-like chambers along the perimeter of the house, with communal cooking and meeting areas in the center. Food belonging to individual families was stored in special rooms at each end of the house, while clan food reserves were stored outside, sometimes above ground and sometimes in pits. At times when a family was away from the main town, they would live in small, conical (tepee-like) structures made from poles and covered with bark. These structures usually housed a single family, but some were large enough for several families. Others lived in small, dome-shaped, mat-covered structures.

All Northeastern people used canoes. Two main types were manufactured: dugouts and bark canoes. Dugout canoes could be quite large and were very sturdy. Bark canoes were generally used on rivers and lakes, though the Micmac made oceangoing bark canoes. These canoes were relatively fragile but were fast, highly maneuverable, and easy to move overland. Exceedingly fine birchbark canoes were manufactured by some groups living along the Great Lakes.

Most clothing was made from deerskin. Children generally wore little clothing, while men wore loincloths, women wore skirts, and everyone dressed in robes or blankets and moccasins in the winter. Animal fat was applied to the body for protection against insects. Face and body painting was common, and hair was often worn in elaborate styles. Many people also wore jewelry, such as earrings, necklaces, and pendants, all made from stone, shell, and native copper (and later of other metals and glass).

Tools were manufactured from a variety of materials. Mortars, pestles, bowls, dishes, and spoons were made from stone and wood. Hoes for the cornfields had handles of wood and blades of deer scapulae or thick ocean shell. Needles and other small tools were made of bone. Pottery, fine basketry, and textiles were also manufactured. Northeastern groups used bark to make containers, housing, and canoes. The primary weapons were the bow and arrow, wooden clubs, and a hatchetlike weapon, the tomahawk. After contact, European goods rapidly replaced some native items, with guns being particularly coveted. The native people came to depend on Europeans for gunpowder and bullets.

Religion

Northeastern people believed that the world was populated by spirits that inhabited all things, including humans, animals, rocks, water, and so on. These spirits had a status equal to that of humans and were treated with respect. It was necessary to keep the spirits happy, and much religious activity was oriented toward that goal. The other major (and related) goal of religion was world renewal.

The native peoples of the Northeast conducted many ceremonies, including those intended for curing, renewal, thanks, or celebration. The Green Corn Ceremony, which was widespread among people speaking Northern Iroquoian languages, was an annual renewal and thanksgiving ceremony held at the beginning of the corn harvest. Shamans took part in all ceremonies and were central figures in the curing ceremonies. Dreams were important in many Northeastern groups and took place when the spirit (or soul) of the dreamer tried to communicate with the mortal presence of that person. Many people acted on their dreams; it was important to fulfill them in order to avoid angering the spirits.

All Northeastern groups believed that the dead journeyed to an afterlife. Typically, a ceremony would be held when a person was buried, and the soul of the deceased would be assisted to the afterlife with prayer and offerings. The Neutral and Huron held a Feast of the Dead every few years to mourn all those who had died since the last such ceremony; some groups disinterred the bones of the recently dead and reburied them in a common grave during the ceremony.

Northeastern Indians Today

A number of Northeastern Indian groups did not survive into the twentieth century. Some coastal groups were completely destroyed hundreds of years ago. Other groups, such as the Delaware and Shawnee, fled to the west or were forced to move onto reservations in Oklahoma. A few groups managed to retain some of their original lands, and several dozen small reservations, some federal and some state, were established; for example, the Powhatan live on five small state reservations in

Virginia. Many Indians remained in the Northeast as individuals, without belonging to any formal tribal organization.

This situation is changing. Some tribes are reorganizing, seeking to recover members who had lost their identity and petitioning the government for formal recognition as tribes. One major issue facing native peoples in the Northeast is the reestablishment of tribal land bases. Many original tribes had never been formally recognized by the federal government and so have no federal reservations or land bases. In addition, a number of the Northeastern groups signed treaties with individual states, such as New York, rather than with the federal government, and there have been attempts to pursue land-claims cases in the state courts, but with little success. Interestingly, any treaty signed by a state after the U.S. Constitution was adopted is not valid. Thus, land claims have to be pursued in federal court.

Nevertheless, the situation of a number of groups is improving. Some are receiving assistance from the government. In one instance, in 1980, Congress passed the Maine Indian Settlement Act, by which the federal government purchased 300,000 acres for several Maine tribes and provided $27 million for economic development.

Other groups are helping themselves. Several tribes operate casinos and use the profits to establish health, police, fire, and educational services, as well as to purchase land within their traditional boundaries. One such casino is the Foxwoods Casino in eastern Connecticut, owned and operated by the Mashantucket Pequot tribe and one of the largest casinos in the world. The Oneida and Mohegans also have opened casinos.

Indians are beginning to win court cases as well. In 1987 a decision was rendered upholding the Chippewa (Ojibwa) right to hunt and gather resources within their traditional territory without regard to state regulations, as guaranteed by an old treaty with the federal government. This very significant ruling was opposed by many non-Indians, and it has opened the door for similar cases.

The future for most Northeastern groups seems bright. They are beginning the long process of regaining lands; revitalizing their languages, religions, and cultures; and developing their economic bases. It will not be an easy task, but progress is being made.

Learn More About Contemporary Northeastern Peoples

The discussion above provides only a very brief description of Northeastern people today. What else can you discover? Go to the library (see Bragdon 2001 for many good sources), and look on the Internet to learn more about Northeastern groups today. Topics you can explore include the following:

1. Chose a particular group or two, and investigate how they have adjusted to European conquest. Look at their tribal land base (e.g., whether they have a reservation), their tribal economy, and the general well-being of the tribal members.

2. What major differences exist between Northeastern groups living in the United States and those living in Canada? What sort of interaction takes place between the groups and their governments? What are the major issues in tribal/government relations?
3. What traditional practices have been retained by Northeastern groups? What roles do traditional religion, economics, and politics play in Northeastern groups today?
4. What has been the result of the Maine Indian Settlement Act? Have the tribes really benefited? What is the role of gaming in the Northeast?
5. A number of groups have used their gaming monies to buy back land. How is this effort proceeding? How will it affect relations between Indians and whites?

The Iroquois: A Northeastern Case Study

One of the best-known Native American groups is the Iroquois, who inhabited northern New York, a region often referred to as Iroquoia (Fig. 11.2). The Iroquois are not a single nation but a group of five original allied nations, the Seneca, Cayuga, Onondaga, Oneida, and Mohawk, organized into a confederacy called the League of the Iroquois. A sixth nation, the Tuscarora, joined the league later. The term *Iroquois* originated from the French use of a Basque word meaning "killer people." The members of the league referred to themselves by a term that meant "people of the longhouse," the Seneca word being *Haudenosaunee*.

In the early seventeenth century the Iroquois population stood at about 22,000 (Snow 1994: Table 5.1) but had declined to about 7,500 by 1770 (Snow 1994: Table 7.1). The Iroquois exercised great political power in the Northeast and even influenced events on the world stage. They had a considerable and justified reputation for being proficient in war and were greatly feared by Europeans and other

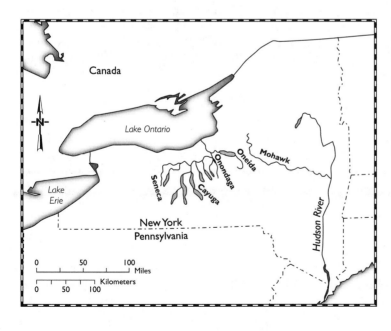

FIGURE 11.2 Location and core territories of the five Iroquois nations in northern New York in about 1700
Adapted from E. Tooker, "History of Research" in *Handbook of North American Indians, Vol. 15, Northeast,* B. E. Trigger, ed., Fig. 1; copyright © 1978 by the Smithsonian Institution. Reprinted by permission of the publisher.

Indians alike. This case study of the Iroquois generally describes all six nations as they were in about 1750.

While early records contain significant information on the Iroquois (see Snow et al. 1994), most anthropological information on the Iroquois was obtained by Lewis H. Morgan in the early-to-mid ninteenth century, J. N. B. Hewitt (himself an Iroquois) and W. M. Beauchamp in the late nineteenth and early twentieth centuries, A. C. Parker in the early twentieth century (see Parker 1919), and William Fenton since the 1930s. The classic work of Morgan (1851), which is still in print, remains a standard reference on the Iroquois. The most recent summaries on the six individual Iroquois nations are available in the *Handbook of North American Indians, Volume 15, Northeast* (Trigger 1978). Other important general syntheses on Iroquois culture are presented by Wallace (1969), Fenton (1978, 1998), Graymont (1988), Richter (1992), Snow (1994), and Tooker (1994). The information on the Iroquois below is summerized from these sources.

The Natural Environment

The Iroquois lived in northern New York, just south of Lake Ontario, and in eastern New York to the Hudson River. Most rivers in Iroquoia run north to Lake Ontario and the St. Lawrence River, and a series of long lakes are present in many of the north/south-trending river valleys. The winters are cold, with considerable snow. The summers are pleasant but humid, and in the fall the trees radiate spectacular colors.

Iroquoia encompasses several extensive forests. In northern Iroquoia, maple and beech predominate, while to the south a deciduous forest of oak, chestnut, and poplar extends into the Ohio River drainage. Walnut, hickory, elm, and white pine are present throughout.

An extensive variety of animals inhabit Iroquoia, many of which were important to the Indians. Many large mammals, including deer and bear, as well as many small mammals, are found in the region. Beaver, once present in large numbers, were decimated by the fur trade. Among the many available birds are pigeons, turkeys, waterfowl, and partridge. A broad diversity of freshwater fish inhabits the many streams, rivers, and lakes.

Language

The Iroquoian language family is divided into northern and southern parts. Each of the six Iroquois nations spoke a separate but closely related language of the Northern Iroquoian language family. A number of other nearby groups also spoke Northern Iroquoian languages, including the neighboring Neutral and Huron. The only extant Southern Iroquoian language is Cherokee, located in the Southeast culture area (see Chapter 12).

A Brief History

Archaeological data suggest that the various Iroquoian groups have lived in the region for at least a thousand years and that the specific Iroquois nations were established by at least 500 years ago. The five nations, from east to west, were the Mohawk, Oneida, Onondaga, Cayuga, and Seneca. While these groups recognized a general relatedness among themselves, considerable warfare apparently took place among them.

To put a stop to internal feuding and establish a common defense, two men, Deganawida (now called the Peacemaker; he may have been a Huron who joined the Mohawk) and Haion'hwa'tha' (or Hiawatha; see VIP Profile), founded the League of the Iroquois in the mid–fifteenth century. After much debate and compromise, the five nations accepted the "Great Law of Peace" and agreed to hold council meetings in Onondaga territory, the geographical center of the league (see Tooker 1978b). The Tuscarora, a Northern Iroquoian group that had moved south to Virginia and North Carolina long before, moved to Iroquoia in about 1712, and around 1722 joined the league as its sixth nation, although they were granted no seats on the league council.

The first Europeans to contact the Iroquois were the French, who in 1534 tried to establish a colony in northern Iroquois territory. The colony failed, as did a second one in the same location in 1541. In 1608, Samuel de Champlain, a French explorer, established a successful colony in the same location. By the early

---

///

VIP Profile

HIAWATHA

The individual known to most people as Hiawatha was long viewed as a mythical person involved in some romantic aspect of Indian life, a fabled Cree culture hero. *The Song of Hiawatha,* a poem written by Longfellow, cemented this image. However, it has recently been realized that Hiawatha was a real person, an Onondaga Iroquois named Haion'hwa'tha' who was intimately involved in creating the great League of the Iroquois.

The League of the Iroquois was founded in the mid–fifteenth century by Deganawida and Hiawatha. Their goal was to stop the constant internal feuding and warfare of the five Iroquois nations and to establish a common defense. Deganawida originated the idea for the league but had a difficult time communicating his views. By

contrast, Hiawatha was an effective communicator, and he convinced the leaders of the five tribes to join the league.

Hiawatha first induced the Mohawk to agree, then was able to persuade the Oneida and Cayuga to join. Representatives of the three groups then went to the Onondaga, whose leader resisted the plan. He was finally convinced, and the group then approached the Seneca, the westernmost of the tribes. The league was then formed and the capital was established in Onondaga territory, in the middle of the five tribes. Nevertheless, most of the credit for the formation of the league is given to Deganawida, whose name is the title of the Peacemaker Sachem position. Additional information on Hiawatha can be found in Bonvillain (1992).

///

seventeenth century European diseases had killed about 75 percent of the Iroquois population before it began to recover.

For many years the Iroquois had been involved in hostilities with the neighboring Huron, and this problem worsened after the French supported the Huron in this conflict. In the early seventeenth century the Iroquois were suppressed by the French and their Indian allies, but by 1650 the league had defeated the Huron and established themselves as the major power in the northern Northeast. In 1701 the Iroquois and the French reached an agreement, known as the Grand Settlement, whereby the Iroquois secured their northern frontier. With the defeat of the Huron, the Iroquois became heavily involved in the fur trade with the French. Beaver was the primary animal hunted for fur, and as the Iroquois depleted the local beaver populations, they were forced to expand their hunting territories. This expansion sparked a number of wars with their neighbors, wars that the Iroquois usually won.

The league established a complex of alliances, often referred to as the Covenant Chain, with other Indians and the British in the late seventeenth century. The role of the Iroquois as leaders of the chain thrust the league into a preeminent role in the politics of northeastern North America, and even of the world. As they were still angry with the French for earlier conflicts, the league generally sided with the British in the French and Indian War (1756–1763).

The league viewed the American Revolution (1775–1783) as a matter not of their concern and attempted to remain neutral. However, the British expected assistance from the league, and many individual Iroquois supported the British, while others supported the Americans. Due to this internal conflict, the league ceased to function and was ultimately disbanded. With the British defeat, the Iroquois were forced to seek a separate peace with the Americans, who contended that since the Iroquois were on the losing side they forfeited any rights to their lands.

The late eighteenth century was very difficult for the Iroquois. Most of their land was confiscated, populations had declined, and morale had deteriorated; as a result, alcoholism and other social problems were common. In 1794 the British granted the Iroquois a reserve in western Ontario (the Six Nations Reserve). The Americans established other reservations for the various Iroquois groups in New York, but the sizes of these reservations were steadily reduced. The political organization of the League of the Iroquois was reconstituted in two separate places after 1783, one at the Six Nations Reserve in Canada and one at the Buffalo Creek Reservation in New York.

In 1799, after being visited by several spirits while in a trance, an Iroquois prophet named Handsome Lake attempted to "revitalize" Iroquois society, urging individuals to give up alcohol and to be more responsible and productive. He subsequently formed the Longhouse Religion of the Iroquois, a revitalization movement that is still practiced and has preserved Iroquois spiritual beliefs and practices (see Deardorff 1951; Wallace 1978).

The various Iroquois nations signed a number of treaties with the United States from the late eighteenth to the mid–nineteenth century. With the treaty of 1838, the Iroquois lost most of their land in western New York State, although some lands were restored in the Compromise Treaty of 1842. The Mohawk, the easternmost of the league groups, had left their land and moved north into Canada during the American Revolution, exposing the Oneida to the colonists. As a result, most of the Oneida were moved to Wisconsin by 1846. Some individuals from the remaining groups (Onondaga, Cayuga, and Seneca) were moved to Indian Territory, while others stayed on small reservations in New York. In 1848, most of the Seneca remaining in New York established the Seneca Nation. The Mohawk began working in construction in the late nineteenth century and became famous as high-rise steelworkers.

Cosmology

Most Northern Iroquoian people believed that the world rested on the back of a turtle swimming in an ocean. The Iroquois origin tale is quite complex and embodies the many themes of Iroquois life (see Fenton 1998:34–50 for a detailed discussion). A summary (condensed from Snow 1994:3–4) is presented below.

A long time ago, people lived in the sky and the world was covered with water. A great tree grew in the sky world, and when the Great Chief became ill, he dreamed that he would be cured if the tree were uprooted. When this task was accomplished, the Chief told his pregnant daughter, Sky Woman, to descend to the watery world below, create land, and populate it. She descended to the water and, with the help of some animals, obtained mud from the bottom of the ocean to form the land. Sky Woman gave birth to a daughter, who grew up and was visited by a man who caused her to become pregnant. The daughter had twin boys, one named Sapling, who was good and handsome, and one named Flint, who was ugly and evil. Everything good that Sapling made was put into disarray by Flint. Sapling made the sun and Flint created darkness; Sapling made straight mountains and rivers, and Flint made them jagged and crooked; Sapling made humans and planted corn, and Flint created monsters, weeds, and vermin. Sapling finally drove Flint into an underground cave. Good and evil still exist in the world.

Soon after creation, the Great Creator sent the Iroquois the Four Sacred Rituals (see below) and, later, the Great Law of Peace (the basis of the league). After the Europeans disrupted Iroquois society, the Great Creator sent the Iroquois people the Code of Handsome Lake.

Politics and External Relations

The political organization of the Iroquois was very complex. They lived in large permanent towns containing as many as fifty houses organized in rows. These towns would usually be protected from attack by palisades. The settlements would be moved every ten to fifteen years as the firewood and agricultural soil became exhausted and game had been overexploited. It would require about ten years for a former town location to regain its fertility and firewood supply. The members of some settlements would relocate to smaller villages for the winter, to be near important resources or to spend the winter in warmer areas. In the spring, these small groups would reassemble near agricultural fields or good fishing areas and reoccupy their summer villages.

The Iroquois were (and still are) politically organized into four basic levels. The first level was based on kinship and residence—that of the family, lineage, and clan. Each clan within a town had a clan council to govern itself. The second level was that of the town; each town was largely independent and governed by a town council consisting of the senior clan leaders, along with other prominent men. At the third level, a number of towns would combine to form a nation (e.g., the Seneca or Mohawk); each sent representatives to the national council. Finally, each of the Five Nations (and later six) belonged to a larger organization called the League of the Iroquois. The league was divided into two halves (cf. moieties), with the Seneca, Onondaga, and Mohawk making up one half and the Oneida, Cayuga, and (later) Tuscarora the other half.

The league was a confederacy, a system in which the individual nations had more power than the overall government (a system admired and adopted by the newly independent United States). The league followed the Great Law of Peace, a constitution outlining laws, regulations, and the rights and duties of the league, the sachems (see below), and individual members. The Great Law was retained through oral tradition. The league council met in Onondaga territory, its geographic center. The Onondaga also kept the league wampum belts, reminders of decisions and actions. Only those agreements commemorated by wampum belts were considered binding; verbal agreements were not.

The league council consisted of fifty sachem positions, numbering eight to fourteen from each of the five nations; the Tuscarora, who joined late, were not represented. A sachem was a named office, and the person who occupied it took on its name. The original sachem position was that of Peacemaker (Deganawida), named for one of the two founders of the league, whose position was "retired" and never refilled. Thus, there were actually only forty-nine functioning sachems in the league. Sachems were selected from specific matrilineages by the women, who could also remove them. Thus, women were well represented in Iroquois politics, and they also owned all the land.

The league's decision-making process was complex. Issues originated with the Mohawk, who arrived at a decision and then passed the matter to the Seneca. If the Seneca agreed with the Mohawk, the issue was then sent to the Oneida and Cayuga. Any changes were passed back to the Mohawk and Seneca until all four groups agreed. The issue was then sent to the Onondaga for approval. This process entailed extensive consideration of any matter, and once agreement was reached, it was essentially unanimous.

In considering any matter, usually the youngest sachems spoke first, then the older ones, then the eldest. This allowed the eldest and most respected sachems to incorporate everyone's opinions into a coherent final argument. If agreement could not be reached on an issue, it was withdrawn. Individual nations were free to follow their own decisions as long as they entailed no harm to the league (this did not always work well). If a particular faction was dissatisfied, they were permitted to leave and form a new town or group.

In addition to sachems, other leaders included War Chiefs and Pine Tree Chiefs (prominent leaders who could not be sachems). Each position had a title, and the person holding it took the title as his name. When a vacancy occurred, a person in the same family (e.g., the son) would be nominated to fill the position, to be "raised up" into the title.

Warfare was the major passion for men, and they expended a considerable amount of energy and time in its pursuit. If a nation wanted to go to war, the council would authorize the action. The call to arms went out, and the war expedition was sent on its way in a public ceremony. The return of the fighters, with trophy heads and/or prisoners, was publicly celebrated. Both male and female captives were taken back to the attackers' town. Female captives were not raped, as sex and violence were separate concepts. The captives would be beaten and cut as they entered the town through a gauntlet of people armed with clubs and knives. Some male captives (usually the young ones) were adopted or kept as slaves by women who had lost husbands, brothers, or sons, and many female captives were either adopted or kept as slaves by various families. A disabling injury, such as the severing of a hamstring, might be administered to slaves to prevent them from escaping. Most male captives were tortured to death.

One of the councils would usually sanction the activities of war expeditions, but military societies or a particular war chief could raise a military expedition and act without council permission. Individuals desiring glory or revenge could engage in a "little war," uncontrolled by the council. The traditional enemies of the Iroquois were the Huron to the northwest, the Mahicans living just to the east, and the Catawba to the south in the Carolinas. The Iroquois defeated the Huron and Mahicans, and peace was finally made with the Catawba in the 1730s.

Prior to the adoption of the gun, Iroquois warfare was conducted with large groups of men in a formal and disciplined manner. Once guns were introduced, warfare tactics changed to a guerrilla style of fighting, involving small groups of individuals. The constant warfare resulted in the loss of many men.

Social Organization

The primary Iroquois social unit was the matrilineage, with descent and power emanating from the mother's side of the family, although there was some responsibility on the father's side. A group of related nuclear families lived together in a longhouse. The matrilineage was led by the eldest female, and the women owned the land and controlled the distribution of resources. The town (except the council house) and its fields were the domain of the women; the forest was the domain of the men. The matrilineages were further organized into clans and either moieties or phratries. Kinship played a vital role in the functioning of Iroquois society; sachems came from certain powerful matrilineages and were nominated and removed by women.

The Iroquois had a class structure related to the standing of the lineages. Sachems, other chiefs, clan leaders (often women), and powerful lineages formed an upper class. Most people were of the middle class, but it was possible for certain individuals who had distinguished themselves, such as those who had performed exceptionally in war, to move into the upper class. The lower class consisted of captives and slaves. In addition to classes, age-grade distinctions were also important. The dead formed the highest grade, followed by old people, the middle-aged, the young (including infants), and the unborn. Infants and the unborn were barely distinguished, as infants had not yet been integrated into society. A cycle of birth, ascent through the age grades, and reincarnation formed part of the Iroquois belief system.

The Iroquois followed a division of labor based primarily on sex. Women collected wild plant foods, tanned all the deer hides, cooked, and maintained the household. Cooking was almost constant, as meals were taken from a communal pot and people ate whenever they wished. All adults helped in the construction of houses and in the clearing, planting, and harvesting of crops. Men cleared land, hunted and fished, and conducted war.

The importance and status of women in Iroquois society were quite high (see Beauchamp 1900). Women owned almost everything, generally controlled the political system (through nomination and removal of sachems), and decided the fate of war captives. European females captured by the Iroquois generally enjoyed a higher status than in their own culture, and some chose to remain even when they had the opportunity to return home. Iroquois women served as a model for the early women's rights movement in the United States (see Wagner 1992).

The Iroquois organized a number of sodalities; the most important was the Medicine Societies, and the largest was the False Face Society (see Fenton 1941, 1987). Members of the Medicine Societies conducted ceremonies to cure illness and keep evil spirits away, and many of the members wore masks. Society members were men, although women might participate in some of the activities. Men would join a society if they dreamed they should and also left it if they dreamed they should.

Life Cycle

Women gave birth by kneeling on a deerskin and holding a post, possibly with the help of a female relative. The ideal number of children was three, spaced several years apart so that women could continue their agricultural duties; children born too close together required too much care. Infanticide was occasionally practiced if the child was unwanted for some reason. When twins were born, the second-born would be killed, as it was considered evil (as in the origin story). However, most children were much desired and loved. Infants were kept on cradleboards for their first several years of life but afterward were free to do what they wanted. Children were rarely subject to corporal punishment.

Girls tended to interact socially within their matrilineage, but boys made life-long friendships with boys from different lineages, friendships that carried mutual obligations, including dream fulfillment. Adolescents were given formal names that were the property of clans. When someone adopted a name, that person became the reincarnation of the individual who last held it. A person's name could change again if he or she assumed an office that had a name.

Puberty was an important event for both girls and boys. Menstruation was considered unclean, and upon first menses, girls would be isolated from the rest of the town. This practice would continue for the women until menopause. Males were also isolated at puberty. Under the supervision of a shaman, the young men would fast and dream, with the goal of obtaining spiritually based power.

Most marriages had little to do with romance; rather, they were arranged and approved by the senior women in a household. Husbands generally came from other towns, and the newly married couple lived in the wife's matrilineage longhouse. A marriage was confirmed by an exchange of gifts between the two families. The Iroquois practiced the sororate to maintain established matrilineal relations. Divorce was not uncommon.

Iroquois men, as well as other Northeast Indian males, were required to exercise rigid self-control; they could not show fear, anger, or other emotions. They were expected to be strong and "masculine" at all times. Men who displayed any emotion were subjected to considerable ridicule from their comrades. In fact, one goal of the torture of war captives was to break them down so they would cry and beg for mercy—a terrible loss of dignity for a man.

This rigid self-control placed considerable pressure on males, which seems to have found an outlet in dreams. Dreams were expected to be fulfilled, so every reasonable effort was made by a man's friends or family members to help him fulfill them. A man was not responsible for his dreams, so was not subject to ridicule for actions taken to fulfill them. He could act out fantasies, fears, or repressed desires if so dictated in a dream. If a man dreamed he was to lead a raid, he was allowed to do so. If he dreamed he should not join a raid, he did not.

When individuals died, they were dressed in their best clothing and buried in circular graves, along with tools and food to help them in the next world. Members of the opposite moiety arranged for the burial and related events. After death, the soul of the person was believed to remain in the town until the tenth day after burial. At that time a feast was held, during which the deceased's favorite food would be served. After being fed, the soul would then travel along the Milky Way to the afterlife.

Economics

Agriculture and hunting were the two major economic pursuits of the Iroquois. While some fresh food was available all year, most was obtained at specific times and stored for later use. Thus, the various social, political, and ceremonial cycles had to be planned around the agricultural and hunting cycles.

The primary crops were the "three sisters," corn, beans, and squash, with corn being the most important of the three. Agricultural fields were cleared of low brush, trees were either killed or removed, and the cleared vegetation was dried and burned. Tree stumps were left in the ground. Once a field was cleared, the corn was planted in small holes made with a digging stick. Beans and squash were later planted among the growing cornstalks. After harvest, as much food as possible was stored for the winter. Corn was parched so the seeds would not sprout and was stored in bark-lined pits.

Men hunted mammals and birds and fished all year long. The major game animals were deer, bear, and small mammals, usually hunted by individuals or small groups of men using bows and arrows (and later guns). Dogs assisted in bear hunting. After the fall harvest, large communal hunting parties would travel great distances to obtain deer. They brought the meat and skins of the deer to the towns, where the meat was dried and the skins processed. Several birds were also important food sources. Young pigeons were collected from their nests, and turkeys, waterfowl, and partridges were hunted. Hunters used spears, arrows, nets, and snares to capture birds.

The many rivers, streams, and lakes in Iroquoia yielded many kinds of fish. Iroquois fishermen used hooks and lines, nets, traps, weirs, and spears to catch them. Surplus fish were dried and taken back to the town for later consumption. Others were used as fertilizer in the planting of corn.

A wide variety of wild plants was gathered for food and manufacturing material. Various roots, berries (e.g., strawberries, blackberries, and raspberries), nuts (e.g., hickory, butternuts, acorns, and chestnuts), small seeds, and greens were collected. Maple sap was used as a sweetener.

Material Culture and Technology

The Iroquois lived in large permanent towns built on hills or ridges and surrounded by palisades for protection. Each town contained a few to dozens of longhouses and as many as 2,000 people. Drinking water was always available near the town, and a major waterway would be nearby. Longhouses averaged about twenty feet in width and a hundred feet in length and were built with a frame of poles covered with elm bark. The typical longhouse contained a number of apartments on either side of a long central corridor with a few fireplaces, each shared by the two families on either side of the fire. The layout of the Iroquois longhouse symbolically represented league geography, with the families on each side and the fire in the center. Six to ten families (a matrilineage) of five to six people each would usually live in a longhouse; a large structure could hold more than a hundred people. Most of the daily activities were performed on raised platforms, which were built to avoid cold, moisture, and fleas. A bed consisted of a mat, blankets of skin, and a wooden block or bundle of important objects as a pillow. People slept with their feet toward the fire.

The Iroquois usually traveled by foot. Unlike many other Northeastern groups, the Iroquois did not depend a great deal on canoes. Those they did use had to suit the relatively rough waters of the rivers and streams of Iroquoia, and so were rather sturdy and ungraceful.

Much of Iroquois technology was manufactured from wood and bark. The frames of houses, canoes, snowshoes, and backpacks were made of wood, steamed into the proper shape. Mortars, pestles, bowls, and the famous Iroquois Medicine Society masks were also made from wood. Bark covered houses and canoes, lined storage pits, and was used to make trays and containers. Some pottery was also used, primarily for cooking. Basketry served a variety of purposes, and cord and rope were made from plant fibers. As gun became available, they rapidly replaced the bow and arrow as the principal weapon, but clubs, blowguns, and tomahawks were also used.

Almost all clothing was made from deer hides that were dyed black. Children wore no clothing until puberty. Men dressed in shirts, leggings, loincloths, and moccasins. Women wore skirts, shirts, and leggings. Much of the clothing was decorated with porcupine quills and moose hair. The Iroquois also made slippers from corn husks and wore them in the summer.

In addition to decorated clothing, some people wore shell ornaments as earrings or strung into necklaces. Some men wore their hair long, but others would shave the sides of their heads, leaving a central ridge of hair, the so-called Mohawk style. Women wore their hair long. Men commonly painted their faces, blue for goodness, black for war or mourning, and red for ambiguous situations. Men also had many tattoos, sometimes all over their bodies. All people applied animal fat to their hair and bodies to protect themselves against insects.

Religion and Medicine

Most Iroquois ceremonies were held to give thanks or to combat evil. Ceremonies were variously conducted by members of longhouses, towns, and nations, but not by the league as a whole. The Iroquois were obsessed with luck, health, and doom, believing that misfortune served as punishment for bad behavior or neglect of the ceremonial cycle.

The yearly ceremonial cycle consisted of many events, including two major public functions, the Green Corn and Midwinter ceremonies; both gave thanks for the bounty of food. The Green Corn Ceremony was an annual celebration of thanksgiving held in the fall at the beginning of the corn harvest. The Midwinter Ceremony was held in January or February as a celebration of the New Year. During this event, people cleaned their homes, visited their neighbors, and stirred the ashes of each other's fires as a symbol of renewal. The guessing of other people's dreams was a major part of the ceremony. The Four Sacred Rituals—the Feather Dance, the Thanksgiving Dance, the Personal Chant, and the Bowl Game—were the principal rites performed at these ceremonies. In addition, Our Life Supporter Dances were conducted to celebrate the harvest of specific resources (e.g., the Maple Sap Dance and the Strawberry Dance). A third major ceremony was the Condolence Council, held after the death of a sachem. Its purposes were to elevate the new sachem to his position and to renew the ties and obligations of the league.

Many other ceremonies were designed for curing or for mitigating evil. Through songs, shamans could communicate with animal helpers and were highly skilled in the use of plant remedies for illness and injury (see Herrick 1995). They also used magic, the sucking cure, and sweat baths. Curing ceremonies were usually conducted by one or more shamans associated with one of the Medicine Societies, including the False Face and Little Water Medicine Societies. Members of some of these societies used masks, not as disguises but as representations of power. Tobacco (the old native species, not the imported one; see Sidelight in Chapter 2) was commonly used in ceremonies and meetings.

The animals that had allowed themselves to be killed for food were ritually thanked, and hunters tried to be respectful to game animals (e.g., by not throwing their bones to the dogs), in hopes of gaining the continued cooperation of the game. Ironically, the Iroquois were largely responsible for the near extinction of beavers in the region.

Art, Expression, and Recreation

Art was manifested in many aspects of Iroquois society, including clothing, orna-mentation, masks, and music. Songs were very important and were often sung for specific purposes, such as curing, mourning, or anticipation of death, rather than for entertainment. Musical instruments included drums and rattles made of turtle shells or gourds and flutes made of wood. Besides providing entertainment, oral tradition was an important source of information and the transmittal of values and history. Iroquois oral tradition was extensive, including many long, complex sto-ries. Some people specialized in remembering the stories, which were usually told in the winter.

Many games were played, usually outdoors (see Beauchamp 1896). Lacrosse was especially popular, played by teams of six to eight, usually representing op-posite moieties. Towns would sometimes challenge other towns to compete, and there were even national teams. Other popular games included footraces, hoop-and-pole (throwing a javelin at a rolling ring, the winner keeping the loser's javelin), deer-button and peach-stone games (both variations of "heads or tails"), and the Snowsnake game. In Snowsnake, a long stick was used to create a track in the snow and ice. Sticks shaped like snakes would be thrown underhand down the track so that they slid as far as possible. The player whose snake slid the farthest won the game and took possession of the other snakes. The Iroquois gambled on the outcomes of most games and competitions.

The Iroquois Today

The Iroquois have survived but are now geographically split, living in a number of regions (see Hauptman 1986). They live on several reservations in New York and six reserves in Ontario and Quebec, Canada. In addition, there is a Seneca and Cayuga reservation in Oklahoma and an Oneida reservation in Wisconsin. Most groups are now required by the government to have separate political organizations. A few groups, including the Six Nations Reserve in Canada, have retained the league struc-ture, although the sachems are now elected by all voters rather than appointed by the women. Today there are about 60,000 Iroquois, about 50,000 living in the United States and another 10,000 in Canada. The Longhouse Religion is still very active and influential and the Medicine Societies are still important.

Beginning in the late eighteenth century, the Iroquois were guaranteed reser-vations and lands by a number of treaties, few of which were honored. In the past few decades the Iroquois have been able to successfully pursue land claims, and they have a number of cases now progressing through the state courts (see Hauptman 1986; Vecsey and Starna 1988). A good example of the controversy and conflict arising from these claims is the case of the city of Salamanca in New York. The land upon which the city was built is completely within the Allegheny Reservation and was leased from the Seneca in 1892 at a ridiculously low rate. By the 1930s, many leaseholders had stopped making their lease payments and the Seneca took them to court. The Indians won the case in 1942, and by 1944, many of the leases had been renegotiated and renewed but have since expired. The

Seneca want to negotiate new leases at fair market value, but the white residents of the city are afraid that the Indians will force them to move. This issue has yet to be resolved.

Gambling has long been an Iroquois tradition, and some Iroquois have become involved in gaming on their reservations. The Oneida in Wisconsin opened a casino and bingo parlor and have made a fair amount of money, which they have used to improve their lives. The Mohawk on the Akwesasne Reservation in upstate New York had been operating a number of bingo parlors, but a faction of Mohawk wanted to open casinos. This action was not approved by the Mohawk Council, but the pro-gambling group opened eight casinos anyway. An anti-gambling faction of Mohawk protested, eventually leading to violent confrontations between the two groups. The state of New York initially stayed out of the dispute but then decided to shut down all the casinos. It later decided to allow one casino to remain open as long as the state got a share of the profit.

The Mohawk, following their traditional role in the decision-making process in the league, are now taking the lead in Iroquois resurgence (see Landsman 1988; Ciborski 1990). They are working to rebuild the league and seeking recognition by international organizations, including the United Nations. They have issued their own passports for use in travel between the United States and Canada, a right set forth in a 1794 treaty between the United States and Britain.

The Iroquois say that one must look to and respect the wisdom of the preceding seven generations and then use that wisdom to guide the next seven generations. The current generation has taken that advice to heart and is revitalizing Iroquois tradition and culture. For further information on the Iroquois, visit *www.sixnations.org.*

The Ottawa: A Northeastern Case Study

The Ottawa were farmers and hunters who lived in the northwestern upper Great Lakes region of the United States and Canada (Fig. 11.3). *Ottawa* is an Algonquian word meaning "to trade," as the people were active traders. The name Ottawa is commonly used in the United States, but those living in Canada prefer Odawa. In the early seventeenth century the Ottawa lived along the northern and western shores of Lake Huron. By mid century the Iroquois had pushed the Ottawa west to the west-central portion of the Michigan peninsula, along the eastern shore of Lake Michigan, where many Ottawa still reside (see Fig. 11.3). The Ottawa Indians never lived

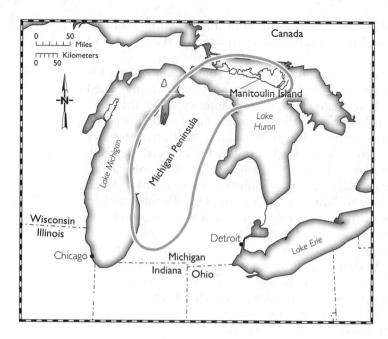

FIGURE 11.3 Location and territory of the Ottawa in the Great Lakes region of the Northeast in about 1800 Adapted from J. E. Feest and C. F. Feest, "Ottawa" in *Handbook of North American Indians, Vol. 15, Northeast,* B. E. Trigger, ed., Figs. 1 and 5; copyright © 1978 by the Smithsonian Institution. Reprinted by permission of the publisher.

in the Ottawa Valley of western Canada, although it bears their name (as does the capital city of Canada). This case study of the Ottawa describes them as they were in about 1700.

Relatively little information on the Ottawa is available. To make matters worse, few of the available data on the Ottawa have been published, so their culture is poorly understood by anthropologists. Important syntheses on Ottawa culture are present in the work of Blackbird (1887), Cash and Wolff (1976), Feest and Feest (1978), and McClurken (1986). The information on the Ottawa summarized below is from these sources.

The Natural Environment

Ottawa territory along the northern and western shores of Lake Huron generally extends east and west. The region contains thick forests, as well as many rivers, lakes, and islands, sharing a mostly similar climate. However, the territory later occupied by the Ottawa on the Michigan peninsula runs north and south, with fairly significant differences in climate between its southern and northern edges. While it also contains many rivers, lakes, and islands, the northern portion of Ottawa territory includes a coniferous forest, gradually turning into a hardwood forest to the south. The southern forest contains many types of trees, including birch, oak, maple, and beech. Thus, as a group, the Ottawa exploited the resources of both forests.

The climate of Ottawa territory varies, depending on latitude. In the north, of course, it is colder, while in the south it is warmer with more frost-free days. Corn can easily be grown in the south but is a gamble in the north; early winter can ruin the crop. Winters are cold and considerable snow is the rule. Summers are warm and humid.

A great variety of animals live in Ottawa territory, such as moose, deer, bear, rabbit, beaver, and otter. Many birds, including large numbers of migrating waterfowl, are also present. Of major importance to the Ottawa were the large number and variety of fish in the various watercourses and lakes.

Language

The Ottawa spoke an Algonquian language related to many of the other groups in the eastern Subarctic. The Ottawa language is actually a dialect of the very closely related Ojibwa, a group living just north of Lake Huron. Today, the Ottawa language is becoming lost as a result of acculturation.

A Brief History

Little is known of the Ottawa before about 1600. They were first contacted by the French in 1615, at which time they comprised at least four loosely related clans without a collective political organization. In the early seventeenth century the Ottawa became involved in wars with the Iroquois to the east, and by mid century the Iroquois had pushed the Ottawa to the west, some as far as Minnesota. Most Ottawa settled along the eastern shore of Lake Michigan, on lands obtained from the Potawatomi, with whom they had good relations.

After about 1650 the Ottawa became directly and heavily involved with the French in the fur trade. The Ottawa controlled the major water routes of the northern Great Lakes and charged a fee for their use. This arrangement not only allowed the Ottawa to profit greatly, but it also made it difficult for others to trade directly with the French. By 1700 the Ottawa had emerged as the major trading force in the Great Lakes region, and the French were treating them as a single political entity.

The Ottawa generally had good relations with the French, who treated them as equal trading partners. They were allied with the French during the French and Indian War, a conflict won by the British in 1763. After the war, the British took possession of the French forts in the Great Lakes region and began to treat the Indians as ungrateful subjects of the British Crown. This immediately provoked a revolt, led by the great Ottawa leader Pontiac. He won a series of impressive military victories against the British and succeeded in restoring Indian power to the Great Lakes region.

Knowing that the Indians needed good trading relations with the British—the Indians had become dependent on European blankets, some foods, and especially gunpowder—Pontiac agreed to cease hostilities. With peace, Pontiac was able to induce the British to trade with the Indians on an equal basis, as the French had done, and the British honored Pontiac as if he led a great Indian confederation, although such a confederation had never really existed. Pontiac developed an inflated sense of personal power and was murdered by another Indian in 1769 (see Bland 1995).

The Ottawa generally remained neutral during the American Revolution. After the war, when the Michigan region came under American jurisdiction in 1783, the Indians, including the Ottawa, disputed the legality of the British transfer of lands to the Americans—lands that the British had in fact never owned. The U.S. government ignored this and took control of the region, while the British allowed the Ottawa to keep their lands on Manitoulin Island in Canada.

The Ottawa were made to sign a number of treaties that forced them to cede title to lands. Under the treaty of 1795, they lost title to lands in Ohio; under the treaty of 1821, they lost lands in southern Michigan. The Indian Removal Act of 1830, threatened forced removal to areas west of the Mississippi, but the Ottawa resisted the move. They began buying land (to hold legal title under white law) in Michigan. In 1831, some of the southern Ottawa signed a treaty, and between 1832 and 1839 they were moved to a reservation in Kansas. In addition, missionaries entered the Ottawa region in 1823 and attempted to convert the Ottawa to Catholicism and "civilize" them.

The Ottawa lost more land under the treaty of 1836 but were granted some fishing rights and were given several small reservations, but only for five years. After that, they were expected to move elsewhere. During this time the Ottawa continued to buy land, and many managed to stay. In 1850 Michigan agreed to grant citizenship to those Ottawa who renounced their tribal affiliation.

A treaty signed in 1855 granted the Ottawa some 500,000 acres. However, the 1855 treaty recognized the Ottawa only as individuals, not as a tribe, and benefits were offered only to individuals. As a result, the tribe received little land. However, the federal government did take responsibility for building and running Indian schools, establishing a fine educational system. The school system was later dismantled by the government and the education of Ottawa children suffered as a result, as few were able to attend the public schools.

The Ottawa who had moved to Kansas in the 1830s were moved again to a new reservation in Oklahoma in 1869 and 1870. The reservation land had been seized from the Cherokee Reservation after the Civil War, partly as punishment of the Cherokee for their support of the Confederacy. Some lands given to the Ottawa in Oklahoma were then lost after the Allotment Act of 1887.

The impact of European diseases on the Ottawa is not well understood. It seems likely that they were affected before historical records were kept and that their population had recovered prior to 1700. However, smallpox did hit the Ottawa in 1835; the death rate may have been as high as 35 percent.

Cosmology

Several versions of the Ottawa creation story exist, and some details differ significantly; some discribe different numbers of earths being created and destroyed. The following version was adapted from Pflüg (1998:89–91).

Before the earth, there was only water. On the water was a great raft carrying all the animals, led by Great Hare (sometimes the culture hero Nanabozho is credited with this role). Unable to locate land, the animals dove to the bottom of the ocean and brought up mud to make the land. Once the task was completed, the animals inhabited the earth. When some of the animals died, Great Hare created people from their bodies, whose spirits were called Ododem. Thus, all people are related (e.g., through clan totems) to the animals that had died.

Politics and External Relations

Prior to about 1650 at least four separate Ottawa groups (sometimes referred to as bands or villages) existed; each was a separate, autonomous political entity. However, villages would sometimes form alliances and recognized relatedness among their people. After about 1700 the Ottawa developed a single tribal identity, mostly due to interactions with the French. Nevertheless, actual power generally remained at the village level.

In the villages, each family elected a representative who participated in a council. The council would then elect a leader, and that person would represent the village in its relations with other villages. Council decisions had to be unanimous. Major council leaders, called Ogema, were usually older men with experience, skills, and wisdom, although leadership was not restricted to older men.

In the summer, a number of families would live in communal houses in a single village of perhaps 500 people. These large villages would be protected from surprise attack by a stockade. In the winter, most people split into smaller units and moved south, living in smaller villages. Only the old and ill remained in the summer village during the winter. In the spring, the families would reassemble at the larger villages. Families owned hunting and fishing areas, which were often located at some distance from the village.

The Ottawa established extensive trade relations with other groups, dominating trade in the northern Great Lakes region. The Ottawa maintained excellent relations with the Potawatomi (referred to as Younger Brothers) to the south and the Chippewa/Ojibwa (referred to as Older Brothers) to the north. These relationships reflected similarity in language and culture and recognition of a common heritage.

Warfare was common; the Iroquois to the east were the major enemy. Following the basic warfare pattern of most Northeastern groups, the Ottawa raided, took scalps, adopted some prisoners, and tortured others to death. The principal war weapons were the bow and arrow (later replaced by rifles), clubs, and tomahawks.

Social Organization

The primary social unit among the Ottawa was the extended family, the group that lived together in communal houses. Descent was generally matrilineal, but Ottawa social organization was quite flexible and could change as needed. Clans were recognized and named after the animals from whose bodies humans had been created (see above).

The basic values of the Ottawa were respect for the individual and the importance of giving and sharing. Wealth was determined by what people shared, rather than what they retained. The Ottawa would adopt outsiders into their society—a common practice in eastern North America—as long as they behaved properly.

People who disrupted society could be exiled, and severe offenders (such as murderers) could be executed.

The division of labor among the Ottawa was based on both sex and age. Men hunted, fished, conducted war, and traded. Males were taught to hunt at a young age; learning to track different animals was central to hunting education. Both men and women participated in constucting and repairing canoes and houses. Women, assisted by old men, did most of the farming, including field preparation, planting, weeding, harvesting, and preparing and storing the crops. Women were also responsible for gathering wild plants and for manufacturing clothing, containers, and matting. In addition, women prepared food daily. Children helped the adults where possible. Everyone assisted in communal fishing.

Life Cycle

Newborns were washed and then placed in a cradleboard, where they spent their first few years. Children received formal names at about one year of age. A formal naming ceremony and feast were held at that time, during which the ears and sometimes the nose of the child were pierced. Names could be changed later in life based on a change in status. Children were subject to little formal discipline, and the young were taught adult skills as soon as possible. Adolescent boys would go on their first military expedition as the camp helper and learn the skills needed to succeed in war. Boys would later become full members of the expedition.

At about the time of puberty, all individuals (male and female) would seek a spirit-helper, a *manitou*, to help and guide them. The manitou was sought during a vision quest, in which the person would fast and pray until it appeared. A manitou could take a number of forms, although it generally appeared as an animal, and it would become a lifelong partner of the person. Individuals would carry a symbol of the manitou in order to call upon it for help in times of need. Some people were assisted by particularly powerful manitous, and those people could become shamans. Females would be isolated from the rest of the group at their first menses and during all subsequent menstrual periods.

Many marriages were arranged, usually by the family of the male. Males could select their own wives, and most courting was done in the summer when the whole village was together. When a suitable mate was found, the male's family would offer presents to the female's parents. If both the girl and her parents agreed, the gifts were accepted and the couple was considered married. A man could have more than one wife if he could both support and satisfy more than one; however, few men were up to the task. Adultery was not common and was very difficult to keep secret. Marriages were relatively stable, and though divorce was allowed, it was discouraged, especially if children were involved. If divorce was desired, the dissatisfied mate simply moved out and sought another partner.

The dead were buried in a shallow grave and a funeral ceremony was held. The souls of the dead would travel to a pleasant place to live, a journey that took ten days. Thus, the body was buried with materials necessary for the trip (e.g., an ax and tobacco), and food was placed on the grave for ten days so that the soul could eat during its journey. Every three years the Feast of the Dead was held, during which the bones of the dead were disinterred and reburied in a common grave. Men killed in battle away from Ottawa territory were stripped of their clothing, given a weapon (such as a gun) for their journey to the afterlife, and left in the woods to be cared for by the spirits.

Economics

The Ottawa practiced some agriculture but depended more on hunting and gathering. Crops grown included corn, beans, squash, and peas. Agriculture could not be practiced in the northern fringes of Ottawa territory, and many families moved south for the spring and summer to plant crops. However, even in the south the weather could sometimes prevent corn from growing.

Crops were raised in small fields prepared by women, with the assistance of old men and children. Native vegetation was cleared and burned, and the crops were then planted. Fields were used once or twice and then abandoned for at least ten years. The crops were harvested, processed, and stored. Peas and beans were shelled and dried, and squash was cut up and dried. Much of the agricultural produce was stored in pits. Corn could be eaten fresh, stored on the ear, or made into hominy, which was consumed with beans and bear fat.

Hunting was always a major activity. Moose, which were hunted mostly in the winter, were the most important terrestrial game animal. Moose were usually hunted by one or two men, often wearing moose disguises. Many other animals were also hunted, including deer, beavers, porcupines, muskrats, rabbits, and squirrels. Bear were sometimes hunted for skins and oil; whenever a bear was killed, a special ceremony would be held to thank its spirit. A number of birds, including ducks and geese, were also hunted. The primary hunting weapon was the bow and arrow, but clubs and various traps were also used.

Fish were very important to the Ottawa economy, and fishing was conducted all year long. Most fish were captured in nets. A long net would be set across a lake, and one end was gradually pulled around to form a U, trapping the fish in a small area. People of all ages and both sexes would participate in fishing. Other fishing methods made use of harpoons, poison, and hooks and lines.

Wild plant foods formed an important component of the diet. Wild rice grew in the many shallow lakes and marshes of the region and was a significant food source (and is still a major product of the region). The rice was collected in canoes by men and women, who would pull the ripe stalks into the canoe and beat them with sticks until the grains fell off. The rice would then be dried, threshed, winnowed, placed in containers, and stored in pits for later consumption. In addition, strawberries, blueberries, raspberries, and various nuts were collected and eaten.

Maple candy formed an indispensable food resource for the Ottawa. The candy was made from sap collected by cutting into the bark of a maple tree. The sap was cooked with hot stones until it thickened. When it cooled, it became solid, crystallized sugar. The candy served as a treat and as seasoning in many dishes. Each family owned a stand of maple trees from which they collected sap.

Material Culture and Technology

In the summer, a number of families would live in a communal longhouse similar to that of the Iroquois, some as large as 20 feet wide and 100 feet long. In the winter, families split up and lived in smaller houses, called wigwams. These generally circular structures, approximately 15 feet in diameter, had tepee-like frames covered with matting or strips of birchbark sewn together into large strips. Small conical tents were used when traveling or hunting.

Some travel was by foot, on snowshoes during the winter. Otherwise, the Ottawa traveled in their excellent birchbark canoes, a signature of the group. The canoes were expertly built, durable, and easy to transport over land. To make a canoe, builders would first make a cedar frame. Then, bark would be removed from three birch trees, producing three long strips. One strip was used for the keel and the others for the sides. They were sewn together and attached to the frame. Then the bark was allowed to dry, and any cracks were sealed with resin. Both men and women helped construct canoes.

Children wore no clothing in warm weather but donned moccasins and an outer garment in cold weather. In the summer, most men wore a loincloth and women wore a skirt or sleeveless dress tied at the waist. In the winter, this clothing would be augmented by a coat or blanket. Most summer clothing was made of deerskin, and moose hide was commonly used for winter coats. Blankets were made from bear skins. Most clothing was decorated with porcupine quills. Women usually wore their hair long; men wore their hair short and sticking up in the front, with feathers often fastened to it. Many people had pierced ears and noses and wore ornaments of stone, bone, and shell in the holes.

Weapons consisted of bows and arrows, round leather shields, stone axes, clubs, and thrusting spears. Wood was used to manufacture implements such as bowls. Birchbark covered canoes and some housing structures. Containers were made from birchbark as well, often decorated with porcupine quills; some could even be used for cooking by placing hot stones inside. European goods such as axes, knives, firearms, and traps eventually replaced many native items.

Religion and Medicine

Most religious beliefs were tied to nature. Every being had both a body and a spirit, the latter called the manitou (also the "spirit-helper"). A supreme manitou (*kičči-manito'*) and several other very powerful spirits, including Great Hare, existed (see above). The body and the manitou were separate, and the manitou could transform itself into animals or people as it desired. Many manitous inhabited the world, influencing events and people. Manitous could be good or bad, and some were more powerful than others. The Sun deity held the power of warmth and crop success, and Lightning could bring rain or destruction. Deer and other animals could change form or refuse to allow themselves to be killed for food. All beings were treated with respect and even referred to by family terms, such as mother or father.

The Ottawa held a series of ceremonies designed to renew the world, to celebrate changing seasons, as well as hunting and harvesting, and to appease and honor manitous. Other ceremonies were held during vision quests, funerals, marriages, the working of cures for illnesses, and other occasions.

Typically, shamans obtained the help of powerful spirits during vision quests. At least three types of shamans existed: Jessakids, Wabanos, and Midewiwins. Jessakids could summon and communicate with spirits to determine the source of problems that people faced. Wabanos could handle fire, influence spirits, cure illness, and cast hunting and love spells. Midewiwins were formally organized into a society, a sort of priesthood, and had the power to combat evil and renew the world. The Midewiwin Society conducted most major Ottawa ceremonies and helped unify Ottawa culture.

Art and Recreation

Music was important to Ottawa culture and was played on many occasions, including ceremonial events. Drums and rattles were the main instruments, and singing was also popular. Craftworkers artistically decorated many items with paint, porcupine quills, and ornaments.

Many games were played, the most popular being lacrosse. Though individuals could organize games, each village fielded a team that competed with teams from other villages. Races, including canoe races and footraces, were also favorites. Other games included the Snowsnake game, guessing games, and dice. Gambling on the outcome of events was also common.

The Ottawa Today

In 2000 it was estimated that there were some 6,500 Ottawa (census data). Many still live in Michigan and some still reside on Manitoulin Island in Canada. Over the past 150 years, the Ottawa survived on their own but lost most of their lands and land use rights. However, in 1980, the U.S. government officially recognized the Ottawa in Michigan, and a movement is under way to revitalize Ottawa society and regain its sovereignty (see Pflüg 1998). Ottawa fishing rights, guaranteed under the 1836 treaty, were finally restored in 1985 when the Ottawa, along with the Chippewa/Ojibwa, signed an agreement with the United States and the state of Michigan (see Doherty 1990). Nevertheless, conflicts with non-Indian fishermen continue. Traditional Ottawa rituals continue to be important (Pflüg 1996).

The Ottawa who moved west to Indian Territory in the 1830s still reside in Oklahoma. The Oklahoma Ottawa became an organized and chartered tribe in 1939, and though their tribal status was terminated by the government in 1956, it was reinstated in the 1970s. In 1965 the Ottawa in Oklahoma joined seven other tribes to form the Inter-Tribal Council. This organization received a number of grants to encourage native life. Few Oklahoma Ottawa still speak their native language, but they are making every effort to preserve their culture.

12 Native Peoples of the Southeast

In the Southeast extraordinarily large, complex cultures inhabited the woodlands that run in an arc from Virginia south and west to Texas (a boundary similar to that of the Confederate States of America, minus Texas, see Fig. 12.1). Spanish explorers called the entire Southeast La Florida. Most Southeastern cultures are characterized by agriculture and complex political and social organizations—several are the most complex in North America—and large, sedentary populations; as many as 1,250,000 people lived in the Southeast in the year 1500 (Hudson 1997:425). Not all Southeast groups practiced agriculture, however. The Calusa in southern Florida, for example, were hunters and gatherers, obtaining most of their food from the ocean. Nevertheless, their culture was also quite large and complex and, like many groups in the Southeast, had a chiefdom-level organization.

In spite of the size and complexity of many Southeast groups, they remain poorly known. By the time Europeans took an interest in recording information about these groups, many had ceased to exist and others had changed significantly. The Spanish entered the Southeast in the early sixteenth century, at which time European diseases began to wreak havoc on the populations of the region. As a result, many groups were utterly destroyed before anything was known about them. By 1750, some surviving groups had absorbed the remnants of destroyed tribes and merged into large confederacies distinctly different in character from the groups that had nearly disappeared.

Geography and Environment

The Southeast comprises three environmental zones (see Hudson 1976): the Coastal Plain, the Piedmont, and the southern Appalachian Mountains. The Coastal Plain

FIGURE 12.1 The Southeast culture area, showing the location of the various native groups
Adapted from *Handbook of North American Indians, Vol. 4, History of Indian-White Relations*, W. E. Washburn, ed., 1988, p. ix; and *The Southeastern Indians* by Charles Hudson, 1976, Knoxville: University of Tennessee Press, Map 1. Reprinted by permission.

extends the entire length of the coast of the Southeast, along the Atlantic Ocean from Virginia south to Florida, and along the coast of the Gulf of Mexico west into northern Mexico. The plain is dominated by an extensive pine forest with slow-moving rivers, bayous, and swamps, particularly along the coasts and in southern Florida. Mosquitoes have always been a nuisance in these areas. The Mississippi River, the largest river in North America, meanders through this broad plain, creating extensive alluvial floodplains ideal for flood-irrigated agriculture, although periodic large-scale flooding caused hardships. Plants commonly found on the Coastal Plain and utilized by the Indians included cypress and live oak trees, cane, various berries, grapes, roots, and Spanish moss. People exploited many animals living on the plain, including deer—the most important game animal in the Southeast—bear, opossums, rabbits, raccoons, squirrels, otters, beavers, fish (e.g., catfish and sturgeon), shellfish, crawfish, snakes, turtles, waterfowl, and many other birds, including turkeys.

The Piedmont encompasses the rolling hills below the Appalachian Mountains. The region contains a broad hardwood forest, dominated by oak and hickory, but also including pine, poplar, and sycamore trees. The Piedmont is transected by many rivers that enter the Coastal Plain from the Appalachians. Most animals that live on the Coastal Plain also inhabit the Piedmont. The combination of forested hills and fertile valleys offered an extensive array of resources to the native people, including some of the best and most productive fishing areas.

The Appalachian Mountains begin in the northern Southeast and extend north into southern Canada. The Appalachians are old and somewhat rugged mountains that are well eroded and fairly low. The numerous narrow alluvial valleys can be difficult to farm. A vast forest of poplar, chestnut, hickory, walnut, and pine covers the low mountains. Deer, bear, turkeys, and many other animals are found in the Appalachians. One particularly important animal, the eagle, was widely sought for its feathers, for ritual and decorative purposes. A variety of stone for toolmaking was also available in the mountain region (and lacking on the plains).

The Southeast has a generally mild climate; winters are usually mild and snowfall is rare. Depending on location, there are between 210 and 270 frost-free days per year, which is ideal for agriculture. Summer temperatures are moderate, averaging a humid 80° to 90°F on the plain to only 70°F in the mountains. Rainfall is abundant, with more than forty-eight inches a year on the Coastal Plain, about forty inches a year on the Piedmont, and over sixty-four inches a year in the Appalachians.

A Basic Prehistory of the Southeast

The prehistory of the Southeast is very complex but poorly understood. General summaries of Southeastern prehistory are available in Jennings (1989) and Fagan (2000), and detailed treatments are available in Smith (1986), Bense (1994), and Sassaman and Anderson (1996) (also see Toshingham et al. 2002).

The Paleoindian Period (to ca. 10,000 B.P.)

New evidence seems to indicate the existence of a Paleoindian occupation in the Southeast. Several recently discovered sites suggest Clovis, and even earlier, occupations. The Cactus Hill site in Virginia contains Clovis projectile points, with some deeper materials dated to about 15,000 B.P., suggesting a "pre-Clovis" occupation. In South Carolina, the Topper site has just been dated to about 12,000 B.P. These sites, coupled with the apparent concentration of fluted points east of the Mississippi River (Anderson and Faught 1998), could suggest that Clovis originated in the Southeast.

The Archaic Period (ca. 10,000 to 3,000 B.P.)

The Southeast was occupied by human populations by at least the Early Archaic period (ca. 10,000 to 8,000 B.P.), and by about 9,500 B.P. some of these people lived in relatively large villages, such as the Icehouse Bottom site in Tennessee (Chapman 1994), while exploiting a variety of food resources: mammals, fish, shellfish, and many plants, including hickory nuts. Genetic (DNA) studies on the preserved brain of a 7,300-year-old individual found in a peat bog at the Windover site in Florida suggest that the Windover people were related to current South American populations, an intriguing puzzle concerning early Archaic population origins. Analysis of food remains removed from the stomach of this individual indicates that the Windover people exploited river-dwelling animals and terrestrial plants, rather than land or marine mammals.

By the beginning of the Middle Archaic period (ca. 8,000 to 6,000 B.P.), the range of foods eaten seems to have narrowed, with a major increase in the use of riverine resources. By 6,000 B.P., cemeteries were common, suggesting that some form of sedentary settlement had begun, marked by fixed territories and more complex political and social organizations. Population appears to have expanded after 6,000 B.P.

In the Late Archaic period (ca. 6,000 to 3,000 B.P.), agriculture diffused into the region, although people continued a hunting-and-gathering lifestyle as well. Large earthen mounds appeared at some village sites (such as the Poverty Point site), the diversity of trade items increased, and Mesoamerican influences became prominent. In addition to the diffusion of corn agriculture into the region, people began to experiment with the cultivation and domestication of native plants, such as gourds, sunflowers, and sumpweed.

The Woodland Period (ca. 3,000 to 1,000 B.P.)

The Woodland period is characterized by increased use of locally domesticated plants, the development of pottery, the diffusion of corn into the region, and the appearance of elaborate burials in cemetery mounds. Good evidence points to considerable long-distance trade networks. The development of mounds and extensive trade, known as the Adena Complex, suggests a dramatic increase in sociocultural complexity. Adena does not refer to a single culture, but to a level of complexity in a region encompassing a number of related cultures.

At about 2,000 B.P. in the Southeast, Adena became more complex and developed into what is known as Hopewell. Like Adena, Hopewell denotes a number of related cultures in the same general region (see Muller 1986). Hopewell was more widespread than Adena, involving much larger sites and complexes of earthen mounds. Social stratification was complex; for example, commoners were cremated while the elite were buried in ostentatious graves topped with mounds. Another distinctive feature of Hopewell was the construction of a series of roads linking a number of large mound sites. Hopewell also included a far-flung trade system. Little is known about Hopewell subsistence, as most investigations have focused on the burial mounds.

By around 1,700 B.P., Hopewell began to decline. A number of hypotheses propose to explain this decline, including overpopulation, climate change, an increase in warfare, and/or an increase in hunting efficiency (and thus the decimation of game) due to the introduction of the bow and arrow. By 1,000 B.P., corn had spread across all of eastern North America and had become the primary resource in many cultures.

The Mississippian Period (ca. 1,000 to 500 B.P.)

Beginning about 1,000 B.P., exceedingly complex cultures began to emerge, primarily along the "American Bottom," the valley of the Mississippi River. Again, Mississippian refers not to a specific culture, but to a number of related cultures (see Scarry 1996). Corn agriculture provided the major food crop, and beans were introduced by about 1,000 B.P. Hunting and gathering remained important but secondary. Villages (or towns) grew in size and included earthen platform mounds arranged around plazas. This coincided with a considerable increase in agriculture, and farmers expanded their cultivated lands into previously unoccupied river valleys (flooding was always a risk, and remains so today). There is clear evidence of ranked social organization and specialization of labor, and political organization appears to have been at the chiefdom level. A system of warfare, ancestor worship, and fertility, called the Southeast Ceremonial Complex, developed at this time.

Some Mississippian centers were truly impressive. For example, the Mississippian site at Cahokia (Milner 1998), near St. Louis, contains a 200-acre walled enclosure and some hundred mounds spread out over five square miles, including Monk's Mound, the largest single mound in North America. The estimated population of Cahokia is about 30,000, and it has been argued that Cahokia was the capital of a state-level organization (O'Brien 1989). Another example is the Moundville site in Alabama, covering some 300 acres and containing more than twenty large mounds built around a plaza.

The Contact Period

When Columbus landed in the Caribbean, most Mississippian cultures seem to have been at their height, with large populations and very complex social and political systems. These vibrant cultures were severely impacted by European diseases in the early sixteenth century, and some had virtually ceased to exist by the time Europeans revisited the region in the mid–sixteenth century.

The earliest Europeans in the Southeast were Spaniards. Juan Ponce de León landed in southern Florida in 1513 and Spanish slavers landed in South Carolina in 1521. In 1526 a small Spanish colony was established somewhere along the coast of South Carolina or Georgia, and in 1528 another was founded in northern Florida. Although both colonies failed, their members may have introduced major diseases into the region at that time, resulting in the catastrophic epidemics that swept the region before 1540.

Hernando de Soto entered the Southeast in 1539 with a small army in an attempt to find a rich empire to conquer for Spain (see Hudson 1994, 1997; Galloway 1997). De Soto moved from town to town demanding tribute and women, destroying the economic base of many groups, fighting battles with the Indians, and inadvertently spreading famine and disease across the Southeast (de Soto himself died of disease in the Southeast in 1542). This Spanish expedition was followed by several others, resulting in a severe population collapse and the destruction of many groups (see Larsen et al. 1992; Powell 1992; Thornton et al. 1992). By the latter part of the seventeenth century, when other Europeans entered the region, many native towns had been abandoned and many cultures had become extinct (Smith 1994).

In 1565, the Spanish founded St. Augustine in Florida and set out to establish a series of 130 missions in northern Florida and along coastal Georgia, perhaps even as far north as Virginia (see Thomas 1990; Milanich 1994; Larsen et al. 2001; see Chapter 2). There were revolts against this oppression, the largest occurring in 1597, but each was ruthlessly repressed by the Spanish and their Indian allies. The Spanish missionization and occupation of what is now Florida effectively destroyed the major Indian groups in that region (see Worth 1998), particularly the Calusa, leaving much of Florida largely unoccupied until a number of Indian refugees fled into the area and reconstituted themselves into the Seminole (see chapter Sidelight).

The English began to encroach into La Florida from Carolina beginning in the late seventeenth century. In 1702 a war broke out between England and Spain. The English invaded La Florida in 1704 and destroyed the Spanish mission system in the north. The Spanish ceded all of La Florida to the British in 1763, but it reverted back to the Spanish in 1783 (as part of the Treaty of Paris that ended the American Revolution) and was later transferred to the United States in 1821.

The French initiated exploration of the Mississippi River in 1673, and in 1682 the explorer Sieur de La Salle claimed the region for France. By the time the French arrived there, most native cultures had already been severely impacted by disease and largely destroyed. In 1682 the French encountered the Natchez, an apparently surviving Mississippian culture, but by 1731 they had also been destroyed (see this chapter's Case Study on the Natchez).

An extensive trade in Indian slaves flourished in the Southeast. In native cultures, war captives were commonly kept as slaves by the victorious native group. After contact, these prisoners were also sold to the Europeans as slaves. The English commonly purchased slaves from the Indians, and as the demand grew, native warfare in the Southeast increased to obtain slaves for sale to the English. Interestingly, many Southeastern groups held black slaves prior to 1865.

By the early eighteenth century, the British controlled most of the Southeast, which was flooded by colonists. Conflicts between the Indians and the growing numbers of settlers inevitably arose and sparked several wars, the most important being the Yamasee War of 1715–1717, during which a number of groups revolted against the English traders and colonists. An uneasy peace was restored and the British imposed limits on colonization, but Indian power was in decline. After 1783 the United States controlled the region, eventually obtaining the Louisiana Territory from France in 1803 and Florida from Spain in 1821. The British restraint on colonization was removed.

Even greater trouble for native peoples was forthcoming. In 1830 the United States enacted the Indian Removal Act, declaring that the Indians of the Southeast must be removed to the newly created Indian Territory (in what is now Oklahoma).

Sidelight

THE DEVELOPMENT OF THE SEMINOLE

In 1704 an English army with its Indian allies invaded La Florida from South Carolina, destroying the Spanish missions and attacking many local native groups, including the Lower (southern) Creeks. Some Creeks tried to accommodate the invaders, while many others fled south into northern Florida as refugees. Once there, the Creek refugees organized themselves along traditional lines and began to absorb some of the survivors of local native groups that had been virtually destroyed by the Spanish. This new culture became the Seminole, a mispronunciation of a Creek word meaning "runaway." The Seminole even took in runaway black slaves, who also became Seminoles, and a mixed ethnic/racial group was formed in northern Spanish Florida (Katz 1997). The Seminole quickly established themselves as a powerful and independent group (see Hudson 1976, Wright 1986, and Covington 1993 for further discussions of the Seminole).

By the early nineteenth century, many Upper (northern) Creeks were being pressured to leave their homes by American settlers, so they moved south to join the Seminole in northern Florida, constituting the second migration of Seminole. American troops and allied Indians continued to raid the Seminole in northern Florida, and the First Seminole War was fought in 1817 and 1818.

When the United States acquired Florida from the Spanish in 1821, the government wanted to remove the Seminole from northern Florida to make room for white settlers. The Seminole tried to accommodate the Americans for a number of years, but the Second Seminole War broke out in 1835 when the United States attempted to remove all of the Seminole to Indian Territory, along with all Indians east of the Mississippi. The Seminole fought a seven-year war to remain free, costing the lives of more than 1,500 U.S. troops, an unknown number of Seminole, and more than $30 million. After finally being defeated in 1842, most Seminole were removed to the Creek reservation in Indian Territory, Oklahoma, where they became one of the Five Civilized Tribes. Nonetheless, perhaps as many as 500 Seminole remained in central Florida, hidden in the swamps. By the mid–nineteenth century, some Seminole, along with a number of escaped black slaves, fled to northern Mexico and served the Mexican government as border guards. Some later joined the U.S. Army (see Mulroy 1993).

The presence of runaway black slaves among the Seminole was a problem for the United States, which tried to force the Seminole to relinquish these runaways or to adopt slaveholding themselves in the hopes of reducing the flow of escaped slaves. The Seminole resisted this effort, increasing the American determination to completely remove them from Florida. A third war was fought from 1855 to 1858. Though most of the remaining Seminole were defeated and removed to Oklahoma in 1858, some families again managed to elude capture and continued to live in the swamp. Thus, a small Seminole population remained in central Florida, which later justified the establishment of several Seminole reservations there in the early twentieth century.

The Seminole in Florida established the formal Seminole Tribe of Florida in 1957. This group does not include many Seminole whose descendants had been moved to Oklahoma in the early nineteenth century. In 2000 some 12,400 people identified themselves as Seminole (census data), many living on four reservations in southern Florida. Hunting and fishing are still important, with seasonal labor from farmwork and sales of native crafts bringing in some revenue. One can visit the Oklahoma Seminole at *http://www.seminolenation.com*.

In 1830, the Choctaw were the first to move. Then followed the Creeks in 1837, although some had already fled to Florida and become the Seminole (see Sidelight). While the Creeks were being moved, the Chickasaw took matters into their own hands and, for the most part, moved themselves, avoiding many problems in dealing directly with the government. In 1838, most Cherokee were also forcibly moved (see this chapter's Case Study on the Cherokee). Finally, the newly formed Seminole were moved in 1842.

Each removal could be described as a Trail of Tears, although the Cherokee event is the most famous and probably the worst in terms of mistreatment and population loss (see Perdue and Green 2001:72–99). People were rounded up and allowed to take only what they could carry, put into camps, then moved to Indian Territory. Much of the money set aside to do the job ($5 million for the Choctaw alone, a huge sum in 1830) was siphoned off by corrupt officials, leaving very little money for supplies. As a result, many people died from malnutrition, disease, and exposure, as well as mistreatment.

After their removal and reestablishment in Indian Territory, the Cherokee, Creeks, Choctaw, Chickasaw, and Seminole became known as the Five Civilized Tribes, partly because they adopted many European-style practices (e.g., in farming, types of towns and government, dress) and partly because they were in the midst of the "wild" tribes on the Plains. Given the circumstances, the groups that were moved to Indian Territory functioned reasonably well.

During the Civil War, Indian Territory was surrounded by the Confederacy and many groups in Indian Territory signed treaties with the Confederate government. Since they lived in the South and owned black slaves, some Indians fought for the South, although some fought for the Union (see Hauptman 1995). After the war, the United States exacted revenge against the Southeastern Indians for siding with the South—including the Creeks, who had sent a contingent to fight with the Union—reversing agreements, denying benefits, and confiscating land. The relative independence of the Indians in Indian Territory ended in 1907 when Oklahoma was admitted to the Union.

Many individual Southeastern Indians continue to live in their former homelands across the Southeast; however, only a few, such as the Eastern Cherokee and the Seminole, have reservations in the region. The remainder of the groups have formal land bases in Oklahoma.

The Impact of European Contact

When the de Soto expedition made its way through the Southeast between 1539 and 1543, it made immediate impacts (see Worth 1998). First, the Spanish used military force to subdue some groups, whereas others that did not encounter the Spanish remained relatively unaffected. After the Spanish left the Southeast, groups that had been militarily weakened fell prey to their unaffected, and therefore stronger, enemies. An overall increase in native warfare resulted, bringing with it the destruction of some groups by their Indian enemies and a realignment of regional politics.

The second major impact was the introduction of European diseases, which had a much greater demographic impact than warfare, including many more deaths and the virtual destruction of many chiefdoms. For example, in 1542, de Soto encountered the Caddo in what is now Louisiana and eastern Texas; he noted that they comprised a large and complex chiefdom. The next Europeans in the Caddo region found it largely abandoned, its inhabitants apparently eradicated by disease (see Swanton 1942; Carter 1995; Smith 1995). Thus, we know very little of that vigorous culture (but see La Vere 1998). The Calusa in southern Florida were also virtually wiped out by disease and conflict with the Spanish. The Calusa culture included some 30,000 people in 1500, but few survived beyond 1600. Calusa territory was reoccupied by the Seminole in the early nineteenth century.

A Brief History of Ethnographic Research

As most Southeastern groups were destroyed before about 1800, relatively little information is available on them. Thus, the records of the various early expeditions, including those of the Spanish explorers de Soto in 1539 and Pardo in 1566, and the French explorer La Salle in 1682 (when the cultures still existed), are very important. In addition, the records of a number of other explorers, adventurers, missionaries, administrators, and soldiers (most notably Du Pratz 1758; also see Hudson 1976:11–12) add considerable information to the meager database.

Relatively little formal anthropological work has been undertaken in the Southeast, with some notable exceptions, such as the work of James Mooney, who worked with the Cherokee, and John Swanton, who conducted fieldwork in the Southeast in the early twentieth century (see Mooney 1900; Swanton 1911, 1942, 1946). The Southeast volume of the *Handbook of North American Indians* has not yet been published, so the best available references on the Indians of the Southeast are Hudson (1976), McEwan (2000), and Perdue and Green (2001). The discussion of Southeastern cultures presented below was summarized from these sources and describes the groups as they were in about the early nineteenth century.

A Broad Portrait of Southeastern Groups

Many native groups inhabited the Southeast at the time of contact. Several groups were large and powerful, while others were relatively small. Many small groups were completely destroyed early on; thus, our view of Southeastern Indians is biased by a partial understanding of a few of the larger groups.

The linguistic diversity of the Southeast is impressive, with languages from four major language families spoken there; there may have been others, but many languages are now extinct and their relationships with extant languages unknown. The four families are Muskogean, Southern Iroquoian, Siouan, and Caddoan (see Hudson 1976:22–27; Nicklas 1994). The Muskogean language family is the largest and most widespread, and one of its languages was (and still is) spoken by the Creeks,

Choctaw, Seminole, and Chickasaw. The Cherokee spoke Cherokee, the only remaining language of the Southern Iroquoian family. A number of groups along the gulf coast of present-day Louisiana and Mississippi spoke Siouan languages (related to languages spoken on the Plains). Lastly, Southeastern groups in what are now Louisiana and Arkansas, and a number of Plains groups, including the Pawnees, spoke Caddoan languages (see Chapter 10).

Political Organization

Prior to contact, most Southeastern groups were organized into chiefdoms of varying size and complexity. After 1500 disease and war shattered these groups. Many were destroyed, others broken up, and still others reorganized into new groups. As a result, probably fewer and larger political entities existed in the Southeast after about 1750. Each group had at least one town, which might be quite large, covering hundreds of acres and containing thousands of people. Towns were organized with planned streets, residential areas, and public areas (sometimes a central plaza), and they were protected with palisades. Houses were generally large and owned by matrilineages. Confederations of towns were common, with a number of smaller towns allied to larger ones. Some confederacies, such as that of the Creeks, were quite large and complex.

Towns were semi-independent but were usually allied to other towns or belonged to a confederation of towns. Each household had a leader and each town had a council composed of the most influential household leaders. Each town would send representatives to the council of its allies and/or to the confederation council. Leaders at every level, from the household to the small town to the large town, were responsible to the leader or council at the next level.

Elite, wealthy families and clans, from which most chiefs were selected, held most of the political power. Chiefs were almost always men, although a few town chiefs were women. Women could sit on councils as observers. People of lesser rank had to pay tribute to the chiefs. This wealth was usually redistributed to the populace in public events or to the needy. Chiefs maintained power by being generous.

Power was generally divided between two opposite political units, White and Red. The White Council was composed of men over fifty years of age who had experienced war but now favored peace. White leaders were often shamans and conducted many routine governmental duties. The Red Council was comprised of younger men, anxious to prove themselves in war. The two councils maintained a sort of checks-and-balances political system. During peaceful times the White Council held power, but in times of war the Red Council directed the government. A ritual beverage was consumed at all council meetings. The Indians called this beverage the White Drink, as it symbolized purity, although the Europeans called it the Black Drink in reference to its color (Hudson 1976:226). The drink was made from the leaves of a holly plant and brewed much like tea. The stimulant caffeine was the main ingredient.

Warfare was extensive and continuous but mostly entailed small-scale raiding conducted for revenge and/or honor. Few men were involved at one time, and there were relatively few casualties, although large-scale battles occasionally took place.

Scalping was fairly common, as was the taking of heads. War captives were either tortured to death (see Knowles 1940) or kept as slaves.

Social Organization

Most Southeastern groups were matrilineal. The primary social unit was the extended family, with the lineage, clan, and town forming the subsequent levels of organization. Lineages owned land and the various leaders came from particular clans; political leaders were from "Clan X," war chiefs from "Clan Y," shamans from "Clan Z," etc.

Kinship defined who people were and how they were to be treated. The kinship system consisted of two categories of people, family and enemy. Most groups used generational terms to refer to relatives. The mother's brother served as the father figure to the male children. Sexual activity before marriage was common and accepted, but after marriage, spouses were expected to be faithful.

Once a male had chosen a marriage partner, he usually sent his mother's sister to the mother's sister of the prospective bride to inquire if there was an interest in marriage. If the family expressed an interest, the girl also had to agree, as marriages were not forced. If the marriage was deemed acceptable, gifts were given to the bride's lineage. The male would then build a house, raise a corn crop, and kill a deer to demonstrate his manhood. The female would cook the corn to show that she was no longer a girl but was now a woman, and the couple were then married. The house and fields then became the property of the woman. If the marriage had proved unsatisfactory by the time of the next Green Corn Ceremony (see below), it was dissolved.

Polygyny was permitted but was not very common; only a wealthy man could afford more than one wife, and the second wife was often a sister of the first. Adultery was not usually legal, but a man could "purchase" a sexual partner with the permission of his wife. Widows were required to observe a long grieving period (sometimes as long as four years) but could then remarry.

Most Southeastern cultures maintained an intricate and rigid system of classification. As long as all things were properly ordered, purity and harmony were maintained. If categories were violated, if things were out of order, the result could only be bad. A number of binary oppositions were culturally encoded, including fire and water, which were never mixed in life (water was never used to extinguish a fire); white (peace) and red (war), as seen in political organizations; male and female; and birds and four-footed animals. Things that crossed these boundaries, such as menstruating women (blood outside the body) and bats (four-footed beasts that fly) were somehow contaminated, believed to have special power, and were both respected and feared.

The major life events were birth, marriage, and death. Puberty was not considered particularly significant, although a girl's first menses was meaningful, not because it signaled puberty, but because the girl was entering a different category, that of a menstruating woman. Menstruating women were isolated from the group, both to avoid contamination and to prevent some women's accompanying "mood changes" from disrupting social harmony.

Games were important both to individuals as well as to larger social units. Lineages, clans, and even towns competed in team sports. Footraces were very common and popular, as were guessing games. Most towns maintained fields where ball games were played, including games similar to field hockey, football, and soccer. Gambling on the outcomes was a popular pastime.

An important team ball game, sometimes involving several hundred people, took place on a field hundreds of yards long. The purpose was to throw a small, stuffed deerskin ball toward a goal made of two upright sticks set in the ground several yards apart. The ball was thrown using two sticks with small nets on the ends, and a point was scored when the ball either struck a goalpost or passed between the posts. Between twelve and twenty points were needed to win. Towns and sometimes clans would often challenge each other to contests. This game, now called lacrosse, was adopted by Western culture, although it is currently played using only one stick.

Another popular game was chunkey, a variation of the hoop-and-pole game. In chunkey, two participants would alternately roll a small, flat, circular stone down a field. Just as it was about to fall over, each player would throw a long stick toward the place where they thought the stone would come to rest. The player whose stick was closest to the stone won and rolled the stone next. Many towns had chunkey fields, and chunkey stones were owned by clans or towns.

Economics

Agriculture was the primary economic pursuit in the Southeast, with hunting an important second. The major crops were corn, beans, and squash. The slash-and-burn method was used to prepare many fields; the fields were cleared (slashed) and the debris burned to provide fertilizer. Other fields were created in alluvial floodplains. In some small fields, corn was planted along with beans and squash. In other small fields, corn was planted by itself as early as possible in the growing season, perhaps as early as March, and then harvested as soon as possible, after which the people planted a second crop of corn. In larger fields, a single crop of corn was planted late in the summer and harvested in late September or early October. Thus, corn crops became ripe at several different times of the year, decreasing the chances of crop failure or shortages. After one or two crops were harvested, the fields were abandoned, to be reused in about ten years. Men provided the bulk of the agricultural labor in most groups (but this was different with the Cherokee; see Case Study).

As the corn grew, soil was heaped on the roots, forming a small hill that protected it from drowning. Crops had to be weeded and safeguarded against pests, especially crows and blackbirds. The Indians would place hollow gourds on sticks to provide nesting sites for purple martins (a species of swallow). These birds protected the crops by eating insects and scaring away crows and blackbirds.

Hunting was a critical source of food and materials. Deer were the primary game animal, providing meat, skins, hooves, and bone for many uses. They were hunted by individuals wearing decoys made from deer heads and skins. These decoys could be so convincing that other hunters would sometimes shoot at them by mistake. Large groups of men would also hunt deer by setting fire in a circle as large as five miles across to drive the deer (as well as other animals) into a small area where they could be shot. Dogs sometimes assisted in hunting deer. Other animal resources included bear (for meat and fat rendered into oil), opossums, squirrels, rabbits, turkeys, waterfowl, turtles, alligators, insects, crabs, crawfish, shellfish, and fish (which were not very important in most of the Southeast). Snakes were generally avoided, as they represented the Under World (see below), but they were eaten in times of famine.

Women and children usually gathered wild plant foods and materials. Southeastern people utilized many species of nuts (e.g., chestnuts, walnuts, hickory nuts, and acorns), grapes, persimmons, a variety of berries (e.g., blackberries, mulberries, gooseberries, raspberries, and strawberries), some roots such as "swamp potatoes," seeds, and other vegetables and fruits. Honey was collected and a sweet syrup was made from tree sap.

Foods were stored for use throughout the year. Some corn was eaten fresh, but most was dried and stored in granaries; well-stored corn could keep for over a year. Other plant foods were also dried and eaten later. Corn was prepared in several ways, including whole roasted, boiled, hominy, and cornbread. Most nuts stayed fresh for many months, and hickory nut oil was a favorite for cooking. A common method of preparing meat was to cut it into strips, remove the fat, and either dry it or smoke it. Smoked meat could last up to a year. Other meat preparation techniques included boiling, broiling, and roasting. Small animals were usually cooked whole over a fire. Bear oil was used as a condiment and cooking oil. Soups and stews made from leftovers were also common.

No true money was used for exchange purposes; instead, barter and redistribution undergirded Southeastern economies. Deerskins were a common trade item, and after contact, Europeans became heavily involved in the deerskin trade, increasing the procurement of deerskins and the labor required for deerskin processing, most of which was done by women. The demand for deerskins became so great that deer grew scarce, creating instability in the food supply.

Material Culture and Technology

Most houses in the Southeast were either square or rectangular in shape and were built with gabled roofs; round houses were rare. Some houses of important people were built on earthen mounds, although this practice declined beginning in the seventeenth century. Some groups lived in a single house year-round, while others used light summer houses and more substantial winter houses to accommodate the seasonal changes in climate. Some houses had two stories, with storage on the ground floor and living space on the second floor.

The principal weapon in hunting and war was the bow and arrow. For warfare, heavy wooden clubs and body armor were also used. Arrow points were usually made of wood or bone. Southeastern peoples also used atlatls, and blowguns with unpoisoned darts were employed to kill small game. Weirs, nets, hooks and lines, and fish poison were used to catch fish.

Most essential items were manufactured from wood or cane, materials that were very abundant. Southeastern groups made generally good basketry and very fine pottery, both manufactured by women. Travel was primarily on foot, and a vast network of trails existed all across the Southeast. To cross rivers and bayous, small rafts or boats were quickly constructed and then abandoned. Some groups made more extensive use of rivers and bayous by building dugout canoes made from already fallen poplar and cypress trees (cypress wood is resistant to rot).

Religion

Southeastern Indians generally held the view that the earth, called "This World," was a large, flat island on an ocean, and the sky was a vault of rock that rose and fell to allow the passage of the Sun and Moon. An Upper World above the sky vault existed, as did an Under World below This World. The Upper World was grand and pure, and the deities lived there. The beings living in the Upper World were larger than humans but organized in the same basic manner, with towns, chiefs, and councils. The Under World embodied disorder and opposition, and the monsters who lived there sometimes came up to This World to harass people. The Sun was a major deity of the Upper World; some groups thought of the Sun as female, but others saw it as male. The Sun was the source of warmth, light, and life. The Moon, also a deity of the Upper World, was associated with rain and fertility. The four cardinal directions (north, south, east, and west) held great significance as well, as the earth was suspended from the Upper World by great ropes in each of these locations. The various worlds were inhabited by many spirits, and spirits were common in This World. Most spirits did not interfere with people but had to be treated with respect. If the spirits were offended, they could cause harm.

The primary goal of religious belief and practice was the maintenance of purity and harmony, ensuring that everything was in its place. Most towns kept an eternal sacred fire burning in a temple, symbolizing continuity and harmony. Evil manifested itself in the violation of harmony, doing things improperly, being impure, and crossing boundaries of classification. A heavy price was paid by those who did not follow the rules. Bad situations could be mitigated through proper ritual, and any situation could be altered by witchcraft, such as making evil people prosper and good people ill.

People had both souls and ghosts. After death the soul journeyed to the afterlife and the living were obligated to respect the soul and its wishes. Ghosts tended to stay around the town and had to be driven away by shouting. People were usually buried; their bones would later be removed and placed in ossuaries. Proper mortuary ceremonies were very important and those whose bodies could not be properly buried (e.g., those who died far away, in battle, or lost in the forest) were mourned to a greater extent.

The major ceremony of the Southeastern Indians was the Green Corn Ceremony, a three-day event held in late summer to celebrate the harvest and renew purity and harmony. Virtually everyone in a town attended, and numerous people, even entire chiefdoms, would gather. The ceremony was usually held in a large town, such as the capital of the chiefdom. As the ceremony began, people would eat a meal and then fast until the end of the event. On the first day, the men refurbished public buildings and the women cleaned the town. On the second day, outstanding issues, such as disputes, divorces, crimes, and arguments, were settled.

On the third day, a feast was held in the morning, and in the afternoon, the sacred fire (along with purity and harmony) was renewed. This latter event constituted the most important aspect of the ceremony.

Southeastern Indians Today

In 1500 many different groups were living in the Southeast. Many did not survive into the nineteenth century; most of those that did were forced to relocate to Indian Territory in the 1830s, where a number of groups have reservations today. Only a few groups managed to remain in the Southeast. Most Indians still residing there do not live on reservations but are integrated into the dominant culture.

Today, the Eastern Cherokee live on a federal reservation in western North Carolina, the Choctaw have retained a small federal reservation in Mississippi, and the Seminole have several state and federal reservations in southern Florida. In addition, numerous small state reservations exist across the Southeast. Other groups exist as communities but without trust lands.

Tourism is a major source of income for the Eastern Cherokee in the Great Smokey Mountains and the Seminole in the Everglades. There is some demand for native crafts, and Indians operate a number of casinos.

Increasingly, Southeastern tribes are beginning to reconstitute themselves, acquiring land and establishing industrial zones. By 1999, at least six tribes had opened casinos (see Perdue and Green 2001:125–149). A number of groups have been federally recognized, and many other have begun the application process.

Learn More About Contemporary Southeastern Peoples

The discussion above provides only a very brief description of Southeastern people today. What else can you discover? Go to the library (see Perdue and Green 2001 for many good sources) and look on the Internet to learn more about Southeastern groups today. Topics you can explore include the following:

1. Chose a particular group or two, and investigate how they have adjusted to European conquest. Look at their tribal land base (e.g., whether they have a reservation), their tribal economy, and the general well-being of the tribal members.
2. How do the Eastern and Western Cherokee cooperate and coordinate their governments?
3. What traditional practices have been retained by Southeastern groups? What are the roles of traditional religion, economics, and politics in Southeastern groups today?
4. What issues and problems have arisen in tribal industrial development in the Southeast?
5. Most Southeastern Indians seemingly blended into the majority culture over the past several hundred years. What problems exist in reconstituting tribal entities, concerning both people and land bases?

The Cherokee: A Southeastern Case Study

Before the arrival of Columbus, the Cherokee inhabited a large portion of the eastern United States, living mainly in the fertile valleys of the southern Appalachian Mountains (Fig. 12.2). They called themselves Ani'-Yun'wiya, the Real or Principal People. The term *Cherokee* seems to have resulted from a series of mistranslations (Portuguese to French to English) of the name of one of their villages. In 1540 there were perhaps as many as 50,000 Cherokee.

By about 1800 the Cherokee lived in some sixty towns distributed across parts of Alabama, Georgia, Tennessee, and North Carolina. Some left their homeland and moved west in the early nineteenth century, but most were forcibly removed to a reservation in Indian Territory in Oklahoma in 1838, subsequently becoming known as the Western Cherokee. A few managed to evade removal, surviving in North Carolina and eventually becoming the Eastern Cherokee (see Finger 1984, 1991; French 1998). This case study of the Cherokee describes them as they were in about 1800.

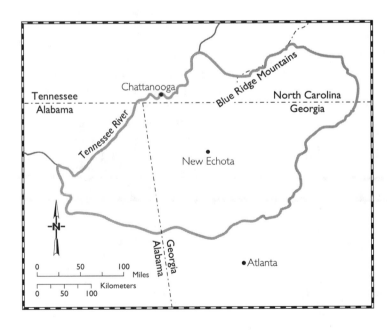

FIGURE 12.2 Location and territory of the Cherokee
Adapted from *Cherokees of the Old South* by Henry T. Malone. Copyright © 1956 by the University of Georgia Press. Reprinted by permission.

Much information on traditional Cherokee life was obtained by James Mooney, who worked with the Cherokee from 1887 to 1890 (see Mooney 1900). A Cherokee elder named Swimmer was Mooney's primary consultant, and Mooney learned a great deal from him. Important syntheses of Cherokee culture are present in Hudson (1976), Fogelson (1978), Perdue (1989, 1998), Mails (1992), and French (1998). The information on the Cherokee summarized below is from these sources.

The Natural Environment

The Cherokee occupied portions of the Piedmont and southern Appalachian Mountains. The rolling hills of the Piedmont contain a broad hardwood forest dominated by oak and hickory and are crossed by numerous rivers and streams. The Appalachians are covered with a thick forest and contain many narrow alluvial valleys suitable to small farms. The mixture of forested hills and fertile valleys creates an ideal habitat for a variety of animals, including deer, bear, and turkeys, as well as excellent fishing areas.

The climate of Cherokee country generally consists of mild winters and warm, humid summers. There are about 240 frost-free days per years, so growing crops was (and still is) not difficult. Rainfall averages between 40 and 64 inches a year. The sky is often cloudy and there is less sunshine than in areas to the south.

Cherokee leader, Sequoyah, from lithograph made between 1838 and 1844.
(CORBIS)

Language

The Cherokee speak Cherokee, a Southern Iroquoian language related to those spoken in the Northeast culture area. At least three dialects of Cherokee were spoken in the nineteenth century. In 1819, a Cherokee named Sequoyah invented an alphabet for the Cherokee language (see the VIP Profile). This was a very difficult task, given the complexity of the language and dialects, but eventually Sequoyah succeeded in creating an alphabet of eighty-six letters. By 1827, most adults could read and write Cherokee.

A Brief History

The Cherokee were first contacted by the Spanish in 1540 when de Soto traveled through their terri-

VIP Profile

SEQUOYAH: CHEROKEE LEADER

In the early nineteenth century, a Cherokee named Sequoyah realized that the Cherokee must become literate in order to survive in a world increasingly dominated by whites. So he created a system by which the Cherokee language could be written and read. It took years to perfect and initially provoked hostility from his family and other Cherokee, but the final result was very important to the Cherokee Nation and represents a remarkable achievement in its own right.

Sequoyah was born in about 1775 and raised in a traditional manner. He never attended a formal school and did not speak or write English. He joined the militia during the War of 1812, when the Cherokee were allied with the United States. He was known as George Guess (or George Gist) in government records. In 1817 Sequoyah moved west to Arkansas with those Cherokee who were dissatisfied with the injustices inflicted upon them by the whites. He then realized that having a written language would elevate the Cherokee in the eyes of the whites and could be a powerful tool in dealing with them.

Sequoyah undertook the monumental task of inventing a Cherokee alphabet. From his own speech, and from listening to other Cherokee, he charted the various sounds of the Cherokee language and its dialects. Not understanding his goal, his wife and others began to worry about his behavior. He behaved so oddly that he became an outcast and was even accused of witchcraft.

He eventually isolated some 200 different sounds, which by 1819 he had consolidated to an alphabet consisting of eighty-six letters (later reduced to eighty-five). In 1821 Sequoyah presented the alphabet to the elders and proved that it would work. Sequoyah began to travel about, teaching people how to read and write Cherokee, and most adults learned to do so. In 1828 the Cherokee established a Cherokee-language newspaper, the *Cherokee Phoenix*, published in their capital at New Echota. The newspaper continued until 1833, when it was essentially shut down by the government. In 1844 a new newspaper, the *Cherokee Advocate*, began publication in Indian Territory.

For his accomplishments and contribution to the Cherokee, Sequoyah was awarded a medal by the legislative council of the Cherokee Nation in 1824. In 1841 he was given a pension by the Cherokee Nation, and the money was subsequently paid to his widow. Sequoyah lived out his life teaching the language and died in 1843. The Cherokee Nation honored him by giving his name to many schools, counties, and other places of interest.

---

tory. In 1566, an expedition under the Spaniard Pardo passed through the area. The English entered the region beginning in 1673, and the French expedition led by La Salle contacted the Cherokee in 1682. All of these contacts greatly impacted the Cherokee through disease and warfare.

By 1700 the English were trading with the Cherokee, and permanent trading posts had been established by 1720. The Cherokee generally sided with the British in their conflicts against the Spanish, French, and other Indians, as well as the American rebels. A smallpox epidemic in 1738 resulted in the deaths of about half of the Cherokee population and shook the foundations of their government and society.

After the American Revolution, the Cherokee suddenly found themselves within the territory of the newly formed United States, and in 1791 they signed a treaty with the new government. Central to the treaty was a program to "civilize" the Cherokee. As part of that process, the United States was to provide the Cherokee with tools so that they could practice agriculture, despite the fact that the Cherokee had been agriculturalists for over 1,000 years. The Cherokee eventually ceded some land and converted some communal land to private ownership, a move the U.S. government considered a hallmark of civilization. The Cherokee generally complied with the government in order to avoid removal.

However, some Cherokee, unhappy about ceding land to the whites, moved to the central Prairies and established new towns; by 1817, a fairly large number of Cherokee were living west of the Mississippi River. By 1819, pressure from American settlers prompted these Cherokee to move south into Texas, then controlled by Spain. There the Cherokee later signed treaties with the newly independent Texas but were expelled in 1839.

The Cherokee who stayed in the east established a capital named New Echota (near Atlanta) in 1817. They elected to adopt Western ways and integrate themselves into American culture, although many Cherokee protested the "Americanization" of their culture. They established a written language and a free press, the *Cherokee Phoenix*, which was published in New Echota. Thus, they became a literate people (probably more so than the American settlers), were slaveholders, and lived in much the same manner as their white neighbors. In 1827, the Cherokee formed a republic called the Cherokee Nation, adopted a written constitution modeled after that of the United States, elected public officials, and codified their laws.

Neither the federal nor state governments wanted to recognize an independent Indian nation. Georgia abolished the Cherokee Nation, and the Cherokee sued Georgia in federal court. The case reached the Supreme Court, which ruled in 1831 that the Cherokee (and other Indians) were dependent and not sovereign nations—in essence, "wards of the government" (see Sherrow 1997). While this was happening, the federal government passed the Indian Removal Act and began to move Southeastern tribes to Indian Territory. The Cherokee filed another suit, which reached the Supreme Court in 1832. In that decision, Cherokee sovereignty was upheld, but the federal and state governments simply ignored the ruling.

Although some Cherokee had moved west of the Mississippi River in the early nineteenth century, most remained in their homeland. In 1835 a few Cherokee signed the New Echota Treaty, giving up all their lands and agreeing to move to Indian Territory. Then the government extended the agreement to apply to all Cherokee. In 1838 U.S. troops rounded up the Cherokee living east of the Mississippi River family by family, allowed to take only what they could carry, and forced them out of their homes at bayonet point. The Indians were then assembled in camps and subsequently marched hundreds of miles to Indian Territory. The government confiscated the houses and farms of the expelled Cherokee and sold them to whites. During the long march west, some 4,000 of the 12,000 people died (McLoughlin 1993); thus, it became known as the Trail of Tears. The next year, the

Texas Cherokee were expelled from Texas and forced to move into Indian Territory. Collectively these Cherokee became known as the Western Cherokee.

Some 1,000 Cherokee escaped the roundup in the east, and with the help of a few sympathetic whites, hid out in the hills of western North Carolina. These Cherokee, known as the Eastern Cherokee, lived on land purchased for them by white friends, as it was illegal for Indians to own land in North Carolina. In 1889, both the state and federal governments recognized the Eastern Cherokee as a separate tribe and established a reservation for them (see Finger 1984).

Meanwhile, in Indian Territory, the Western Cherokee had reorganized themselves as the Cherokee Nation, established a new capital, and set about rebuilding their society. Then came the Civil War, which created a dilemma for the Cherokee as to which side to support. The Union government had never been honest with them and they were living in Confederate territory. Thus, many sided with the Confederacy while others remained loyal to the Union. Feelings ran so deep that the Cherokee Nation almost split into two factions. After the Union victory, the Cherokee lost territory in Oklahoma as punishment because some of them had supported the Confederacy.

The Cherokee Nation was effectively abolished in 1891, at which time they had 19,500,000 acres in Oklahoma. By the time the nation was reestablished in 1971, Cherokee lands had been reduced to less than 150,000 acres, a loss of over 90 percent (see McLoughlin 1993 for a history of the Cherokee in Oklahoma and their struggle for sovereignty).

Cosmology

The Cherokee universe, typical of cosmologies of other peoples in the Southeast, consisted of three basic levels: the Under World (a place of chaos), This World (the earth, where people lived), and the Upper World (a place of order and harmony). Deities lived in the Upper World, where the dead went. Before This World was formed, the Upper and Under worlds existed. The Upper World was in the sky and was made of solid rock. But it was crowded and the beings there desired more space. Looking down, the Upper World beings saw an ocean. Water-beetle descended to the ocean, dove to the bottom, and scooped up the mud that eventually became This World (the earth). While the land was still wet, Great Buzzard flew over the land, creating valleys and mountains where his wings touched. The sun was made to pass over This World once a day. Beings from the Upper and Under Worlds inhabited This World but eventually returned to their worlds, leaving behind their images, which would become the people, animals, and plants of This World (summarized from Mooney 1900:239–240 and Hudson 1976:128).

Corn and game animals originated later. The first Cherokee were Kana'ti, his wife Selu, and their two sons. Kana'ti provided meat from animals he kept in a cave. The sons accidentally let the animals escape and now people must hunt them in the forest. Selu gave birth to corn (and so is the mother of corn) and grew it—along with beans—overnight, a skill only she possessed. Her sons thought she was a witch and killed her. Corn and beans sprouted from her blood, and now people have to work and wait to grow them (summarized from Mooney 1900:242–249).

Politics and External Relations

Prior to about 1800, the Cherokee were organized into at least four "districts," each of which operated as a separate and essentially independent chiefdom. Each chiefdom had a central political authority of White (peace) and Red (war) leaders and councils, members of which headed the various lineages and clans. Each council had a primary chief, who served as leader. Council meetings might last a long time, even many days, since anyone could speak. Power was maintained through consensus and not coercion. Women held considerable political power and had a voice in council meetings. Cherokee society was matrilineal; thus, hereditary offices were passed from the officeholder to a sister's son. Women also owned the fields, houses, and furniture.

Each town had White and Red leaders; however, if a town was very small, such leaders may have been scarce, so they were occasionally "borrowed" from other towns to conduct important business. Towns were organized around a central plaza, and council meetings were held in a large, circular building—sometimes constructed on an earthen mound—located in the plaza. Private houses were built away from the plaza.

In the early nineteenth century the Cherokee established a united, centralized state-level government to deal with the United States and resist removal. After the smallpox epidemic of 1738, the Cherokee began resisting efforts by white religious leaders to acculturate and they realized they had to unite to deal effectively with the U.S. government. Like many groups in eastern North America, the Cherokee recorded agreements on a wampum belt.

Justice was dispensed at the clan level rather than by a centralized authority, and the primary judicial philosophy was "an eye for an eye." The responsible person was not deemed guilty, nor was there a cry for justice. The offender was merely held legally liable for a disruption of harmony. If someone was killed, even if it was an accident, the wrongdoer must be killed to restore balance; if someone was injured, the perpetrator received the same injury. Euthanasia was practiced and was considered an act of compassion.

Warfare was incessant but not conducted for territorial or economic reasons. Most wars took place between clans to exact revenge for an earlier war death or to maintain balance. The Cherokee occasionally conducted warfare with other cultures, although this too usually involved revenge. Most warfare consisted of small-scale raiding, conducted primarily from spring to fall. Fame and honor were gained through war, and surprise attacks by groups of twenty to forty warriors were typical. The principal war weapons were bows and arrows and clubs. Enemy men were killed or taken captive; women and children were taken captive as well. Dead enemies might be scalped or beheaded and the trophies displayed in the village.

Most adult male captives were tortured to death to exact revenge for lost loved ones. Women participated in the torture but might also occasionally spare captives, choosing to adopt them into their clans, either as slaves or to replace lost husbands or sons. The Cherokee would cut the leg tendons of adopted captives so they could not run away. Captured women and children were sold into slavery.

A few women and/or berdaches might accompany a war expedition to cook and collect firewood, sometimes even participating in battle. Those that distinguished themselves in war were called "war women" and had the power to decide the fate of captives. Men isolated themselves for several days prior to going to war to purify themselves and ensure success. Similar rituals were conducted upon the return of a war expedition.

Social Organization

The basic social unit among the Cherokee was the extended family, but clans were also important. There were seven clans—perhaps more prior to contact—and descent was matrilineal. The Cherokee used generational kinship terms; all people of about the same age were considered brother or sister, those of the parents' general age were called mother and father, and so on.

The Cherokee believed that dichotomies such as war/peace, winter/summer, good/bad, male/female, and so on, formed the basis for the harmonious organization of the universe. Maintaining these separate categories ensured harmony. Disruptions to this system were considered unsettling, unclean, dangerous, and sometimes very powerful.

The division of labor was fairly strict in order to properly maintain the boundaries between the sexes. Men hunted and practiced warfare, although women would sometimes accompany war expeditions, preparing meals and doing other chores. Men also cleared the fields, helped plant the crops, and assisted in the harvest. Women were the primary farmers; corn was the main crop and was considered "female," as corn originated from Selu (see above). Women also did the cooking, provided firewood and water for the household, gathered wild plants, and built furniture. There were no formal meals; food was prepared and set out, and people ate whenever they were hungry.

Men did not dominate or control women, and women did have influence over the political process (see Sattler 1995; Perdue 1998). Women controlled their own sexuality, and premarital sex was common. Adultery was common as well, but if a married man was caught straying, his wife would frequently attack the other woman, causing considerable disharmony in the community. Male transvestites and homosexuals existed in Cherokee society, but it is not really clear how they were regarded. It seems they were frowned upon for crossing classifications. However, the few women who participated in warfare attained a high status in Cherokee society; unlike the men, these women crossed categories and gained power from it.

Life Cycle

During pregnancy, women became less active and observed a number of taboos regarding activities and foods. Husbands also restricted their activities to avoid adversely affecting the baby. When the baby was ready to be born, the mother was helped by one or more midwives, and perhaps other women as well. The baby was delivered while the mother was standing, sitting, or kneeling, but never lying down. The mother remained secluded for seven days after the birth, after which she cleansed herself and returned to the town. Children were put in cradleboards for their first few years, a practice that flattened the back of the skull, a trait that was considered desirable.

The Cherokee were indulgent parents. Children were allowed to nurse as long as they wanted or until the mother became pregnant again. Corporal punishment was rare; instead, children were "shamed" into conformity. Girls played domestic games and boys played at hunting and war and had contests to see who could tolerate the most pain. A boy's mentor was his mother's brother (a member of the same clan, to which the father did not belong). Some children were prepared from birth to be shamans; serious training began at about age ten.

At first menses, girls joined the older females in observing the rules of menstruating women. Such women were considered dangerous but not unclean; menstrual blood violated categories as it was not inside the body where it belonged. Menstruating women were isolated in special houses located at some distance from the main house, and they were careful not to contaminate materials such as men's hunting gear. Postmenopausal women were highly regarded—they were called beloved women—since they had attained purity by no longer menstruating and thus had ceased to violate categories.

One was required to marry someone from a different clan. When a man found a woman he wanted to marry, he had to obtain the permission of her relatives, especially her parents. Once permission was granted, and if the woman agreed, the couple would be married by a shaman in a brief ceremony held in the council house. Men could have more than one wife, although this practice was not common. After marriage, the couple lived with the girl's family (matrilocality).

Divorces were not unusual and were simple to accomplish. If a couple wanted to divorce, they were expected to wait until the Green Corn Ceremony in late summer, at which time the divorce was recognized. Afterward, the woman would stay in her family's house, the man would return to his mother's house, and the children would stay with their mother. When a spouse died, the survivor usually married a close relative of the deceased.

Death was a major ceremonial event. One's soul continued after the death of the body, and the living were expected to respect its wishes. People were usually buried in permanent graves, but some high-ranking people were buried for a few months, then disinterred and their bones placed in an ossuary.

Economics

Farming was the primary economic pursuit and the main crop was corn. A portion of the crop was given to the principal chief of the town, who was responsible for redistributing food and hosting feasts.

Two types of corn were grown, a multicolored "hominy" corn and a white corn used to make flour. Beans were planted between the corn plants so that their vines could grow up the cornstalks. A variety of other crops, including pumpkins, squash, watermelons, peas, and sunflowers, were grown in different fields. Corn and beans were allowed to dry and were then stored in granaries for the winter. Bread was baked by preparing the dough, placing the loaf in a bed of hot coals, and heaping up the coals to cover the loaf.

Deer were the most essential game animal, especially preferred for their meat and skin. Bear were also hunted for their meat, fat (a delicacy), and hides. These large animals were usually killed with the bow and arrow, but pit traps were occasionally used. Smaller game, such as birds and rabbits, was either trapped or killed with blowguns. Also important were fish, which were taken using hooks and lines, nets, and weirs. On occasion, streams were dammed and the resulting pool poisoned. The stunned fish could then simply be collected. Most meats were cooked in barbecue fashion. Men hunted throughout the year, and fresh meat was usually available. However, some venison was dried and stored for later use.

Women would gather wild plant foods, including grapes, persimmons, many types of berries, a variety of nuts (walnuts, hickory nuts, and acorns), seeds, roots, and other kinds of fruit. Women also collected honey and made a syrup from tree sap.

Material Culture and Technology

A family's residence might contain several structures, consisting of summer and winter houses, storage structures, and other buildings. The size of a house depended on the size of the family living in it. Summer houses were rectangular, with gabled roofs, wooden sides, and ventilation. They were often two stories high; the lower rooms were used for storage and the upper rooms for social activities. Winter houses were round, windowless, and covered with dried mud for insulation.

Most transportation was by foot, and the Cherokee used and maintained a vast network of trails. Small dugout canoes were sometimes used for fishing but rarely for traveling. People crossed rivers in small rafts or boats made on the spot and then abandoned.

The Cherokee wore relatively little clothing. Children wore nothing until they approached puberty, when they adopted the dress of adults. In warm weather, men dressed in loincloths, a belt, and perhaps leggings and moccasins. Men also wore a small pouch in which they carried personal items. Women wore a skirt from waist to knee, but no top. In cold weather, adults of both sexes donned cloaks made of bison skin. If bison skins were not available, other animal skins would be substituted. People of high status, such as chiefs or shamans, might wear more elaborate clothing, including garments that were feathered or painted in bright colors. People generally did not cover their heads, but dignitaries would wear elaborate headdresses for important occasions.

Adults wore jewelry of shell and bone as well as bear claws, which were usually made into necklaces. Sometimes copper was traded from the north and used in jewelry. Both sexes pierced their ears and sometimes wore large circular ornaments of shell in the earlobes, which were cut and stretched to accommodate them. Some men wore nose rings in perforated nasal septa. Both sexes adorned themselves with tattoos, but men involved in warfare had special tattoos applied to their cheeks.

Many important men, such as chiefs and shamans, wore their hair loose and long. Most other men shaved the tops of their heads, leaving a long tuft of hair on the crown. The hair on the sides would be cut fairly short. Women kept their hair long, wearing it either straight or tied up on the top of the head; they commonly applied bear fat to make their hair lustrous.

The Cherokee had greater access to stone than many other Southeastern Indians and used a number of stone tools, including knives, arrow points, pipes, pestles, and axes. Wood was utilized to manufacture mortars for grinding corn, bows and arrows, canoes, houses, and masks. Blowguns were fashioned from hollowed-out canes, some as long as twelve feet. Some types of arrow points, needles, and ornaments were made of bone. Containers were manufactured from gourds, basketry, and pottery.

Religion and Medicine

The Cherokee belief system combined the physical and spiritual worlds into a single harmonious whole. The Sun was a major deity, the source of warmth, light, and life. The Cherokee viewed the Sun as female; the Moon was Sun's brother, associated with rain and fertility. There were seven categories of spirits, including Great Spirits who lived in the Upper World and rarely had any impact on the everyday lives of the Cherokee (with the exception of the Immortals who occasionally intervened to protect the Cherokee), Little People (similar to European trolls) who were mischievous and could cause great harm, and the ghosts of the dead.

Most ceremonies were related to agriculture; there were no hunting ceremonies. In keeping with the dichotomy between the sexes, most ceremonies were conducted separately by men and women. The most important was the Green Corn Ceremony, held in late summer when the corn ripened. The corn could not be eaten until this ceremony was completed, as it was conducted to regenerate nature and society; debts and grievances were forgiven at that time. Women were active and central in the Green Corn Ceremony, presenting the new corn to the culture as Selu had done in the past.

The concept of evil and sin involved crossing or blurring the boundaries that existed between categories. The source of death, illness, and misfortune was disharmony caused by crossing boundaries or offending spirits, including those of animals killed for food. Much daily ritual was concerned with purification, which cured and prevented disease. Medicines were consumed to deal with both physical and spiritual problems.

Shamans were the religious specialists, and they sought the intervention of the Upper World spirits to cure illness. Shamans were also herbalists and knew a great deal about medicinal plants and their applications. Elderly people of either sex were often believed to be witches. People experienced anxiety regarding who might be a witch and what such a person's intentions might be. Therefore, older people were both respected and feared.

Art, Expression, and Recreation

Cherokee art took many forms. Although sculptures of stone, wood, and shell were common, the most typical form of artistic expression involved decorating useful and ceremonial objects, such as appliqués on pottery, carved ceremonial masks made of wood, shell incised with complex designs, stone flaked into elaborate shapes, sculpted and incised stone disks, and engraving on imported native copper. The human body was also decorated in a variety of ways, such as with jewelry, paint, and tattoos.

Music was important to Cherokee culture. Musical instruments consisted of drums, deer-hoof rattles, and flutes of bone or cane. Songs and dances were integral as well (see Speck and Broom 1983 for a discussion of Cherokee dance). The

Cherokee played numerous games, including chunkey (see above) and footraces. The ball game known today as lacrosse was probably the most popular form of entertainment. Among the Cherokee, the ball game "season" lasted from midsummer until the onset of cold weather. Any group, from families to clans to towns, could field a team and play the game. On the night before a big game, opposing groups would each hold a ball game dance to purify the players and summon the spirits to support the team.

The Cherokee Today

Today the Cherokee are the largest Indian tribe in the United States, claiming some 232,000 members as of 1980 (Kehoe 1992:206) and 281,000 members in 2000 (census data). They are still divided into two geographically distinct groups, the Western and Eastern Cherokee, a legacy of their forced removal west in the 1830s.

The Western Cherokee continue to reside in Oklahoma and are organized as the Cherokee Nation; most Cherokee are affiliated with the western organization. In 1985 the Western Cherokee elected the first female primary chief, Wilma Mankiller (see Mankiller and Wallis 1993). The Cherokee Nation belongs to the Intertribal Council of the Five Tribes (Cherokee, Choctaw, Chickasaw, Creeks, and Seminole) in Oklahoma.

Today there are some 10,000 Eastern Cherokee, descendants of the people who escaped the mass deportation of 1838. Many live on the 56,000-acre Qualla Reservation in western North Carolina, next to the Great Smokey Mountains National Park. Living at the entrance of the most visited park in the United States, the Eastern Cherokee make a living from the tourists traveling through the region (see Finger 1991). In 1995 the Eastern Cherokee also elected a female chief, Joyce Dugan. More information on the Cherokee can be obtained on the Web at *http://www.cherokee.org*.

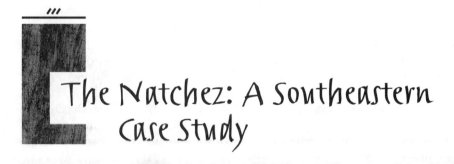

The Natchez: A Southeastern Case Study

The Natchez are one of the most complex native North American groups known, although many other groups in the Southeast may have been at least as complex (or perhaps more so) prior to contact. They lived along the Mississippi River in present-day Louisiana and Mississippi (Fig. 12.3). Aspects of Natchez culture (and the cultures of other Southeastern groups) may have diffused from Mesoamerica, including a Sun deity, skull deformation, complex social and political structures, and human sacrifice. The term *Natchez* is French, possibly derived from a native

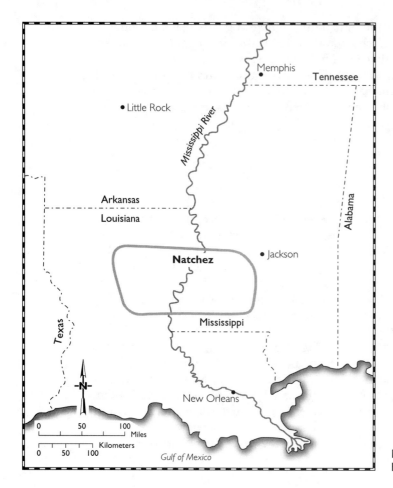

FIGURE 12.3 General location of the Natchez

town name; however, the Natchez called themselves Thelöel. In 1700 there were probably about 4,000 Natchez. The culture was ultimately destroyed by the French by 1731. This case study of the Natchez describes them as they were in about 1725.

Most knowledge of the Natchez was obtained in the early eighteenth century by the French; the best account is that of Du Pratz (1758). This information provides the basis for our limited understanding of the Natchez. Other syntheses of Natchez culture are available in the works of Swanton (1911), MacLeod (1924), Albrecht (1946), Hudson (1976), Spencer and Jennings (1977:414–424), and Lorenz (2000). The information summarized below is from these sources.

The Natural Environment

The Natchez lived on the Coastal Plain along the Mississippi River and its tributaries. Most of the rivers, bayous, and streams are slow-moving, and low-lying areas contain numerous swamps. Annual flooding inundates much of the Mississippi River Valley, depositing fresh alluvium and making agricultural fields wet and fertile (although periodic large-scale flooding presents problems). Extensive forests of oak, gum, and cypress trees dominate the lower Mississippi River Valley.

Moderate temperatures characterize the climate of Natchez territory, averaging 90°F in the summer and 55°F in the winter. Rainfall averages between forty-eight and sixty-four inches a year. The growing season is quite long, approximately 270 days, which is long enough to sustain two crops of corn annually.

Language

The Natchez language was part of the Natchezan language group spoken in the lower Mississippi River region. It was related to the Muskogean language family so widely represented across the Southeast, but is considered somewhat of an isolate. The Natchez language is now extinct.

A Brief History

The Natchez were probably first encountered by the de Soto expedition in 1542, but specific records are lacking. In 1682 a French expedition led by La Salle entered the region and established friendly relations with the Natchez and other groups. French traders and missionaries followed in 1700, but their activities were not very welcome. The French established a trading post at the current city of Natchez, Mississippi, in 1713, and began competing in trade with the English to the east. The Natchez destroyed the trading post in 1715, an action that resulted in the formation of pro-French and anti-French Natchez groups. In 1716, the French built a fort at Natchez to protect French farmers from the hostile Natchez, and by 1718 the French had encroached on Natchez farmlands to the point of open hostility.

Beginning in 1725, a series of events created political instability among the Natchez. In 1725 the Natchez war chief Tattooed Serpent died. He was the younger brother of the Great Sun (see below), who died in 1728. A new and inexperienced Great Sun took over, and the French seized this opportunity to take over all Natchez lands, an action that prompted a war beginning in 1729. The French enlisted Choctaw allies and defeated the Natchez in 1731. The Great Sun and many of his followers were sold into slavery and the few remaining Natchez left the area, later joining the Creeks and Cherokee.

Cosmology

A man and his wife from the Upper World entered an existing town. They were so bright in appearance that they were thought to have come from the Sun, the man being the younger brother of the Sun. The man told of the Great Spirit and said that the people should not drink, lie, steal, or commit adultery. He commanded the people to build a temple to communicate with the Great Spirit. This man became the first Great Sun.

A Native American chief, probably a Natchez Sun, being carried on a litter. From a 1758 drawing. (CORBIS)

Politics and External Relations

The leader of the Natchez was the Great Sun, a man who held the dual offices of "king" and "high priest" (something like an Egyptian pharaoh). The Great Sun was a theocratic ruler who traced his ancestry back to the sun itself. He had total power and could have people executed if they displeased him. To mitigate this power, the Natchez ruler was assisted by a council of advisers consisting of Sun-class men (see below), whom the Great Sun could not have executed. The Great Sun's mother, White Woman, also had considerable influence over him. People bowed in the presence of the Great Sun; he and his close relatives were carried on litters. As the Natchez were matrilineal, when a Great Sun died, his sister's son became the next Great Sun.

The Great Sun resided at the Natchez capital, now known as the Fatherland Site, located just a few miles southeast of the current city of Natchez, Mississippi. The Fatherland Site is believed to have served as the Natchez capital for at least 500 years prior to the French intrusion. It occupied hundreds of acres and contained a large central plaza for public ceremonies. The Great Sun lived in a house built on a platform mound on the northern side of the plaza. On the southern side, directly across from the Great Sun's residence, stood the large main temple, built on another mound. The primary religious activities were carried out at the temple, and an eternal flame was kept there. The war chief (the Great Sun's brother) lived in another house on the plaza; houses of ordinary citizens were located away from the plaza. The Natchez also founded many smaller towns, each organized in a manner similar to the capital (a plaza, temples, houses of chiefs, etc.). Each town was protected from attack by a palisade.

Because war was such an important activity, the second most important leader of the Natchez was the war chief, known as Tattooed Serpent. War was usually waged against neighboring tribes. Members of a military expedition would gather at the war chief's house, conduct ceremonies that would ensure success, travel to the enemy town, and then mount a surprise attack at dawn. If the warriors were discovered en route, they would usually retreat. The goals of an expedition were to kill or capture enemy men, capture women and children for slaves, and escape without casualties—the war chief was required to pay compensation to the families of men killed in raids. Scalps were taken and captured men were usually tortured to death, although they might be claimed by a Natchez widow to replace a husband lost in battle.

Social Organization

The social organization of the Natchez was quite complex, consisting of four major classes of people: Sun, Noble, Honored, and Commoner (or Stinkard). The Sun class, at the top of the social pyramid, had few members. There were a few more Nobles and still more Honored, but most Natchez people were Commoners. Some social mobility was possible, however; for example, by accomplishing some outstanding deed in war or peace or by offering one's children to be sacrificed at a major ceremonial event (e.g., the burial of the Great Sun), an individual might be elevated to a higher class.

Persons of the Sun class were required to marry Commoners. The class of the spouse did not change, but the class of the children might, depending on the situation. Descent was matrilineal, so the children retained the class of the mother if her class was higher than that of the father. If the father's class was higher, the children would become members of the next lowest class, rather than the class of the mother (see Table 12.1). If a Commoner man was married to a Sun woman, he was required to respect her status as if he were any other Commoner. He could not eat with her, had to behave as a servant in her presence, was required to remain faithful to her (although she had no such restrictions), and was expected to be sacrificed at her death. On the plus side, he did not have to work.

The basic Natchez social unit was the extended family. The eldest male was the primary leader. It is possible that Natchez clans and moieties existed, but little is known about them. The division of labor was straightforward. Men waged war, hunted, cleared the fields for

TABLE 12.1. Class of marriage partners and class of children among the Natchez

Class of Mother	Class of Father	Class of Child
Sun	Commoner	Sun
Noble	Noble	Noble
Noble	Honored	Noble
Honored	Noble	Honored
Honored	Noble	Honored
Honored	Commoner	Commoner
Commoner	Commoner	Commoner
Commoner	Sun	Noble
Commoner	Noble	Honored
Commoner	Honored	Commoner

planting, and built the houses. Women did most of the weeding in the fields, prepared meals, performed general domestic chores, and manufactured basketry, pottery, and nets. Women owned the meat obtained from hunting. Everyone helped with the planting and harvesting of the crops, as well as the construction of mounds in the towns.

Berdaches, though rare, were present in Natchez society. They would perform female duties, including tending fields, conducting domestic activities, and even assuming the female role in sexual activity. Records also indicate that some Natchez women who preferred to remain single, but their status within the society is not clear. Both berdaches and unmarried women were viewed as mixing opposing male and female categories; thus, they were both respected and feared.

Life Cycle

At birth, children were immediately placed into cradleboards, with their heads strapped to the board to flatten the back of the skull, a trait that was considered desirable. Children remained in the cradleboard, wearing diapers of Spanish moss, until ready to walk. The child was allowed to nurse until the mother became pregnant again. Children were taught to swim by the age of three. The education of boys was the responsibility of an older man (perhaps the grandfather), while girls learned from the mother. When the boy who would become the next Great Sun was born, other infants were offered as his servants, workers, guards, and so on. Those chosen were raised to fulfill such roles.

A girl was allowed to be free with her sexual favors until marriage. If she developed a reputation of being a great sexual partner, she might receive offers of marriage from higher-status men (this was to her advantage). However, children born out of wedlock were not very welcome, and infanticide was sometimes practiced by unmarried mothers. Such an act was not considered a crime.

Males usually married by about twenty-five years of age and females by twenty-two or twenty-three. The prospective groom requested the girl's hand from the male head of her family and presented her family with a bride-price, the amount of which depended on her status (including her sexual value) and the status of the prospective groom. Marriage consisted of a ceremony and feast involving the two families. The newly married couple then moved in with the husband's family (patrilocal residence). Polygyny was permitted but was not very common. Adultery was not permitted after marriage, although if the husband belonged to a higher class, he could "lend" the sexual favors of his wife to others. Divorce was rare.

When most individuals died, their bodies were placed on elevated platforms to decompose. Offerings of food were made to the deceased at that time. After the flesh had decayed, the bones were removed, placed in a basket, and stored in an ossuary. However, when a person of the Sun class died, the ceremony was much more elaborate and spectacular, especially the funeral of the Great Sun. The body of a Sun would lie in state for several days and was then buried near a temple in a large public ceremony. At the ceremony, close relatives (e.g., spouses and siblings), servants, and/or volunteers—who either wanted to accompany the deceased to the afterlife or who wished to gain status for their families—would be sacrificed, usually by being strangled by close kin after taking tobacco pills to render them unconscious. After several months, the bones of the high-status individual would be exhumed and stored in a temple.

Economics

As with most other Southeastern groups, agriculture was the primary economic pursuit, the most important crops being corn, beans, pumpkins, and tobacco. Most available farmland contained rich and very productive soil, and the long growing season meant that two crops of corn could be grown annually. Fields were prepared for planting by the slash-and-burn method, after which the crops were planted and raised to maturity, and the harvested crops stored in granaries for future use. Corn was processed and prepared as gruel, bread, and other foodstuffs.

Meat was obtained by hunting, and as in most of the Southeast, deer were the primary game animal. Individuals or pairs of men did most of the hunting, but some hunts were communal affairs. In a communal hunt, deer were driven toward hidden hunters or encircled and run to exhaustion, then taken back alive to the town, where they were killed and butchered. In the fall, large groups of men and women would travel west to the Plains to hunt bison. Waterfowl were taken by groups of hunters. After the hunts, women distributed or sold the meat.

Trained dogs chased turkeys into trees, where they were shot with arrows; dogs were also sometimes eaten. The Natchez did some fishing too. Harpoon-tipped arrows were used to catch large fish (e.g., carp and catfish) and nets for smaller fish. Men in canoes caught large sturgeon by roping their tails as they passed by, then held on until the fish tired and could be pulled to shore. Catfish were abundant in the rivers and bayous.

The gathering of wild plants formed a relatively small but important aspect of the economy. Plants such as grapes, persimmons, many types of berries, nuts, and seeds were used for food. Other plants were gathered for manufacturing purposes, such as those used in making basketry, houses, and canoes.

Material Culture and Technology

Natchez towns contained many public and private buildings and were occupied all year. The size and location of private houses within the town depended on the rank of the owner. Major public buildings, including the houses of the leaders, stood on mounds around the main plaza. The houses of Commoners were located away from the plaza. Most houses were square in floor plan and had domed roofs. Furniture was sparse, even in the Great Sun's house, consisting mostly of small chairs and a platform bed with bison-skin blankets and a wooden pillow.

The Natchez traveled by rivers and bayous as much as possible. Dugout canoes were used on rivers; some were as long as forty feet and could carry as many as eighty people. For short trips, a makeshift raft of cane would be quickly made, used, and abandoned. Other travel was on foot, and most men could traverse great distances with remarkable speed. The Great Sun did not travel on foot; he was carried on a litter by six or eight men.

Most people wore minimal clothing. Small children wore none at all, but by about the age of eight, girls began to wear an apron, adopting long skirts when they began to have sexual relations. Boys dressed in a loincloth by about the age of thirteen. The color of the loincloth varied, depending on status. In the summer, men wore little and women wore only long skirts. In the winter, everyone wore a deerskin shirt or blanket.

Both sexes wore tattoos on their noses to depict rank and status. The tattoos were augmented as a person gained honors and might eventually cover the entire body. Some people also painted their faces. All adorned themselves with jewelry, including shell earrings and necklaces. Men and women plucked all but their head hair. Men wore their hair in a variety of ways, perhaps depending on status; women kept theirs straight and long. Women also blackened their teeth with ash and tobacco.

The Mississippi Valley had little stone for the manufacture of tools, so the stone needed to make axes and pipes had to be imported. Most other tools were made from wood, including mortars, digging sticks, some containers, bows and arrows (arrow tips were made of fire-hardened wood), and clubs. Cane was used to make many things, including rafts, structures, knives (very sharp but not very durable), and basketry, which was often dyed in ways that produced intricate designs. Feathers and porcupine quills decorated baskets. Pottery was made in a variety of forms and served many purposes.

Religion and Medicine

The Natchez religion was basically similar to most others in the Southeast but was much more elaborate. The Sun was the major deity, and maintaining of harmony was a primary goal. The Great Sun was the high priest as well as the ruler, and he presided over the various agricultural, world renewal, and hunting ceremonies. A number of lesser full-time priests performed other functions, such as maintaining the eternal flame in the main temple. This temple was a rectangular structure located on a large mound on the northern side of the capital plaza. Other than priests, few people could actually enter it.

Major ceremonies were held during each of the thirteen new moons, to thank the supreme being for bounty and harmony. One of these, the Great Corn Ceremony, which corresponded to the Green Corn Ceremony elsewhere in the Southeast, was usually held in the month of the Great Corn (in late summer). Another important event, the Deer Festival, was held in March to inaugurate the beginning of the Natchez year.

Shamanism was integral to Natchez religion. Shamans had multiple functions, including controlling the weather by producing rain when necessary and driving it away when it was not wanted. An ineffective weather shaman risked death by execution but could accumulate considerable wealth if successful. Shamans also cured illness with a variety of techniques, such as the removal of foreign objects from the body (the sucking cure) and the use of various herbs and plant medicines. Shamans were usually men, but women (especially older women) could sometimes become shamans.

Art, Expression, and Recreation

Little is known about Natchez art. Sculptures, engravings, decorations on pottery, and some descriptions of other art are known, but they are difficult to interpret. Music, song, and dance were important, but few details are known.

A number of games were played. Boys and girls played catch with a small ball. Young men played and wagered heavily on chunkey. Footracing was popular. Women played a game with three split-cane "dice" thrown on the ground, earning a point if two of the three dice landed with their flat sides up; however, the women did not bet on the outcome.

The Natchez Today

The Natchez did not survive as a culture into the twenty-first century. Some individual Natchez did survive by joining other groups, notably the Creeks and the Chickasaw. Thus, the Natchez have joined an unknown number of other Southeastern cultures driven to extinction, many of which are known only from archaeology.

///

13 Contemporary Issues

Native North Americans have survived despite the impacts of Euroamerican contact. From a population low of less than 375,000 in 1900, North American Indians now number almost 2.5 million people, and that number is projected to increase to 4.4 million by 2050. The late twentieth century has witnessed a reassertion and popularization of native culture, undertaken both by native people themselves and by others who promote or emulate Indians.

Nevertheless, many stereotypical views of Indian life and culture remain. Many non-Indians still regard native North Americans as people of a romantic past, rather than as individuals and cultures that exist today. One popular sentiment presumes that Indians led an idyllic life in harmony with nature, a view that has some merit but cannot be universally applied. Also, some individuals and groups, especially by governmental agencies, perceive Indians as childlike people of nature who are incapable of making their own decisions and thus must be guided to civilization. Coupled with this ethnocentric view is the general belief that native thought and science are inferior.

There has been considerable research on contemporary native cultures (see Hirschfelder and de Montaño 1993; Reddy 1995; Thompson 1996; Champagne 1997; Iverson 1998; Thornton 1998; Johnson 1999). Native people today suffer from discrimination, poverty, and high rates of alcoholism, suicide, and murder. In 1990, some 23 percent of Indian households fell below the poverty line. In 1989, the unemployment rate among Indians living on reservations was approximately 40 percent, a rate that had been increasing steadily since 1970 (Snipp 1989: Table 7.10). These and other problems have frustrated reservation Indians and have prompted a movement to the cities, where communities of Indian people have taken root.

In 2000, some two-thirds of the Indians in the United States lived in cities (Fixico 2000), where they experienced problems of ethnocentrism, poor health care, unemployment, and loss of identity. Poor housing (e.g., no electricity, heating, or plumbing) also remains a problem, but the situation has generally improved since 1970 (Snipp 1989). Many native groups in the United States are adopting English as their standard language, and the number of Indians finishing high school is increasing, as is the number attending college. Patriotism among native peoples has always been high, and Indians have fought with distinction for the United States in all of its wars.

A Revival of Native Culture

For centuries, Euroamericans viewed Indians as inferior, second-class citizens with a dispensable culture. The past few decades, however, have witnessed a resurgence of pride in being Indian, and the perspective of most Americans has shifted to acceptance and admiration. Through rising political power, Indians are reasserting their sovereignty and regaining some rights related to land, water, hunting and fishing, mineral resources, and religion. There is an increasing presence of Native American views in the literature and of Native American literature itself (e.g., Crozier-Hogle and Wilson 1997).

Indians have focused much recent political activity on the plight of native peoples as a whole, rather than problems of specific tribes. This has helped form a Pan-Indian identity; both the non-Indian public and some Indians themselves, particularly those living in cities, have often adopted this view of Indians as essentially one large group, combining diverse heritages. One byproduct of this phenomenon is the idea of a "generic Indian," as seen in the stereotypical Plains Indian costume featured at many events, in the blending of ceremonies, dances, and songs from different traditions, and in the adoption of these generic traits by non-Indians. Yet at the same time, tribes are retaining their individual identity. In fact, many groups have revitalized their identities, have begun teaching traditional language and knowledge, have opened cultural centers, and are attempting to gain control of their own lives.

Some members of the 1960s counterculture adopted "Indian ideals," viewing native peoples as the original ecologists, at peace and living in harmony. This ideal was very attractive to some in the turmoil of the Vietnam era. This general trend continues today with the adoption of Indian ideals and views by "New Age" enthusiasts.

However, the New Age movement can be seen as a further exploitation of Indians by people who want to take but do not want to give back—people interested in Indian ceremonies and crafts but not so much in the Indians themselves (see P. Deloria 1998; Aldred 2000)—and many Indians are unhappy about non-Indians attempting to be Indians. It is interesting that beginning in 1960, when the census allowed people to declare their ethnicity, Indian populations greatly increased, perhaps partly due to "wannabe" whites declaring themselves to be Indians (e.g., Deloria 1995).

Sidelight

VISITING NATIVE NORTH AMERICA

There are a great many native places for the public to visit and appreciate in North America. These include reservations and visitor centers, casinos, cultural centers, archaeological sites, museums, and parks. Many native groups open traditional ceremonies, powwows, craft shows and exhibitions, and rodeos to the public. Native American heritage is rich and varied and is largely accessible if you find out where and when to go.

A number of guidebooks (mostly for U.S. sites) provide information about native places and events. A good source is *Indian America: A Traveler's Companion,* by Eagle/Walking Turtle. This guide provides information arranged both by state and by event. It also offers some guidelines for etiquette while visiting Indian locales. Tiller (1996) has complied a comprehensive list, description, and profile of Indian reservations in the United States. Guides to Native American landmarks include *North American Indian Landmarks: A Traveler's Guide* (Cantor 1993) and *Exploring Ancient Native America* (Thomas 1994).

Native American Politics

Throughout most of their history of interaction with Western culture, native peoples have been forced into a subordinate political role. Much of their political activity took place in reaction to the various mandates and policies of the government. More recently, tribes have taken a much more active role in asserting their legal rights. They are working to regain lands or to be compensated for their loss, to have treaties honored, to reassert sovereignty over their lands and people, and to make the government agencies responsible for Indian affairs more attentive to Indian needs. Great progress has been made, although much work remains. A history of Native American political resurgence is available in Cornell (1988) and a number of contemporary political issues were discussed by Johnson (1999).

The American Indian Movement

In 1968 a small group of Indians formed an organization, the American Indian Movement (AIM), to promote Indian rights (see Kelly 1990; Smith and Warrior 1996). While Indians had always been involved in the political process, they were rarely effective participants. The mission of AIM was to force the dominant U.S. culture to listen and to act on Indian rights, and the organization felt that only militant action, which would attract media coverage, could effectively communicate their message.

Among their first actions was the seizure and occupation of Alcatraz in San Francisco Bay, beginning in October 1969 and lasting nineteen months (see John-

With the Golden Gate Bridge in the background, a man stands outside a tepee set up on Alcatraz during the occupation of the island from 1969 to 1971 by members of the American Indian Movement. (CORBIS/Bettmann)

son et al. 1997 for perspectives on the Alcatraz occupation). Alcatraz was claimed for the Indians, an action designed to publicize the loss of Indian lands. The event was widely reported and raised awareness among the non-Indian public. Every Thanksgiving Day, AIM holds a ceremony on Alcatraz to commemorate the 1969 occupation and symbolize the loss of Indian lands.

In 1972, members of AIM seized the headquarters of the Bureau of Indian Affairs in Washington, D.C., for seven days to publicize the mismanagement of Indian lands by the BIA. Then, in early 1973, some 200 armed AIM members occupied Wounded Knee Creek, the site of the massacre of several hundred Sioux by the U.S. Army in 1890. The FBI surrounded Wounded Knee. A tense standoff lasted seventy-one days and led to the deaths of several people; a number of AIM members were sent to prison. The occupation accomplished little change at the time but resulted in considerable publicity for the Indian cause. After Wounded Knee, AIM lost its momentum—partly due to disagreements among the leadership and partly because several leaders were imprisoned—and is no longer a major force in Indian politics. Beginning in the mid-1990s, efforts have been initiated to revitalize AIM. Visit the AIM website at *http://www.aimovement.org.*

Sovereignty

Prior to contact, Indian nations had always been independent political entities. Upon European entrance into North America in the early sixteenth century, many Indian nations established government-to-government relations with the foreign powers. In the United States, the Indian groups' independent status quickly changed to that of dependent nations. Although Indian governments were reorganized and reformulated beginning in the 1930s, the BIA remained in control of Indian lands, resources, and lives. Any action by the Indians required approval of the BIA, which influenced all aspects of Indian life.

Today, many groups want to reclaim their sovereignty and abolish the BIA. At a minimum, they want the authority to act on their own lands and on their own behalf. On their reservations, they have legal jurisdiction over most matters, including tribal police forces and court systems, but the jurisdictional system is complicated.

However, the situation is improving. In 1994 President Clinton issued an Executive Memorandum directing government agencies to cooperate on a government-to-government basis with federally recognized tribes. Nevertheless, elements of the sovereignty issue remain problematic, including control of lands, resources, and the past.

Land Claims

A major political issue has always been the loss of Indian lands (see Sutton 1985; Vecsey and Starna 1988). Much land was ceded by treaty early on, although many treaties were obtained through questionable methods; however, vast tracts were taken through other means, many of which were illegal. If the Indians resisted militarily, they were forcibly removed. Other Indians fought the actions in court, but found little equity in the judicial system of the times. As the years went by, non-Indian ownership of Indian land became so entrenched that the Indians had very little hope of getting it back.

In 1946 the federal government formed the Indian Claims Commission to consider land claims against the federal government. The commission refused to consider claims against the original thirteen states, which had made separate treaties with Indian groups in the late eighteenth and early nineteenth centuries; it was decided that such claims should be handled in state courts. However, any treaties signed by states after the adoption of the U.S. Constitution were deemed invalid and claims originating from those treaties had to be heard in federal court.

The Indian Claims Commission has heard many cases and has decided in favor of the Indians in numerous instances. In 1971 the U. S. government reached a comprehensive settlement with native groups in Alaska, called the Alaska Native Claims Settlement Act (ANCSA), in which 44,000,000 acres were returned to native groups, along with a cash payment of $962 million, and a royalty of $500 million on mineral rights.

The Canadian government is also attempting to settle native claims. The Eskimo in the Northwest Territory agreed to a settlement that has created a new province, Nunavat, controlled by the Eskimo. Other settlements and agreements have been made as well. The Cree signed the James Bay Settlement in 1975 (see Niezen 1998), and in mid-1998, the Nisga (Nishga) tribe, a western Diné group in British Columbia, signed a treaty with the Canadian government, opening the way for future treaties with other groups, such as the one signed with the Nuu-chah-nulth of British Columbia in 2001.

In other instances, problems have not worked out so well. In the late 1970s the government of Alberta proceeded with the construction of an all-weather road through the territory of the Lubicon Lake Cree, an isolated band of Western Woods Cree (see Smith 1987; Goddard 1991). Upon completion of the road in 1978—which the Cree were not allowed to use—the government claimed ownership of Cree lands, threatened the Cree with eviction, and leased portions of the land for oil exploration and logging. The road and lease activities destroyed registered Lubicon Lake Cree traplines and impacted their ability to make a living. A suit to allow the Lubicon Lake Cree to block the leases was filed in 1982. The Cree lost and were ordered to pay the oil company's legal expenses. Loggers began clear-cutting timber and the Cree resisted, setting up roadblocks and burning a logging camp. The government responded by sending in police to protect the loggers.

The Lubicon Lake Cree gained the support of the United Nations Committee on Human Rights and organized a boycott of the 1988 Winter Olympics in Calgary. The government subsequently attempted to assign a reserve to the Lubicon Lake Band but refused to recognize all the members of the band. The government managed to split the band into four separate bands or factions and signed treaties with three of them, cutting off the Lubicon Lake Band and leaving them without a reserve. In spite of the billions of dollars in timber and oil removed from the Lake Lubicon area, the Indians have received no royalties and are forced to subsist on welfare.

Associated with land claims is the use of acknowledged Indian lands for commercial purposes such as mining. For example, many Indian lands are held in trust by the federal government, and it was often the government, not the tribes, that negotiated leases with the mining companies. In many cases the leases were exceedingly favorable to the companies, with very small royalties paid to the tribes (see examples in Grinde and Johansen 1995).

This type of inequity is beginning to be corrected. Many tribes have hired and/or trained their own legal staffs and are fighting exploitation in court. In 1975 twenty-five tribes with coal, oil, or gas reserves (including groups from the Plains, Southwest, Northwest, and Great Basin) formed the Council of Energy Resource Tribes (CERT) to better control the exploitation of resources on the reservations.

Another issue is non-Indian disapproval of the way Indians use their lands. For example, some non-Indians have protested the construction of casinos near their properties. In another instance, when a non-Indian community in the San Diego area of California protested the development of a landfill in a rural area, the project was abandoned until the local Indians offered to put the landfill on their lands, sparking a renewed protest over the presence of the facility.

In other cases, the Indians own the land that non-Indians live on. In one example, the entire city of Salamanca in western New York was built on lands leased from the Iroquois in the late nineteenth century. The leases were for ninety-nine years, at very low rates. Frequently, the lease payments were never made, and the land was bought and sold without consideration of the leases. Many people bought houses unaware that the land was leased. When the leases began to expire, residents feared that the Indians would expel them. However, the Indians preferred to renegotiate the leases at fair market value, although this angered many residents as well. Much of Palm Springs in California was also leased from the Indians, who are now poised to make a nice profit.

Other Rights

In addition to land, in many of the treaties signed with the government, Indians negotiated and retained rights to fishing, hunting, and gathering. In many instances these rights have been ignored and are now being reclaimed. For example, Indian fishing rights in Washington were reaffirmed in the 1974 *Boldt* decision and upheld by the U.S. Supreme Court in 1979 (see Cohen 1986); the decision is currently being implemented over the protests of non-Indians.

In 1987 the Chippewa won a court decision granting them the right to hunt and gather any resource within their territory without regard to state regulations. This had been affirmed by treaty in the nineteenth century but was subsequently ignored by the state government. This ruling, opposed by many non-Indians, set a precedent for other such suits.

The federal government, along with some state governments, is beginning to become more sensitive to Indian needs and wishes. For example, the U.S. Forest Service and U.S. Park Service have granted special permission to some native groups to gather traditional materials from areas normally closed to such activities. In addition, standard practices have been changed to accommodate native lifeways, such as halting the poisoning of Pandora moths so that the Owens Valley Paiute can continue to collect the caterpillars.

Control of the Past

It has been argued that Western science interprets the native past in a Western way and that Indians have little input, and this is generally true. Few anthropologists are Indians (although this is changing), and most interpretations of the past do not consider native views. To some, this is a colonial attitude designed to control the past. Partly in response to this issue, many tribal groups have established their own archaeological management programs (Stapp and Burney 2002) and museums, both to exercise sovereignty over the material remains of their past and to present their own interpretations of it.

In 1990, Congress enacted the Native American Graves Protection and Repatriation Act (NAGPRA). This law requires that institutions (e.g., museums and universities) holding Native American skeletal remains and associated objects identify the most likely descendants of such remains and provide the opportunity for that group to reclaim them. While the law provides for the study of such materials prior to their repatriation, many researchers resist returning these remains, arguing that they are important to science. To many native peoples, the issues are religion (reclaiming their dead), politics (the return of their heritage), and empowerment (ownership and interpretation of the past) (see Bordewich 1996:162–184). Repatriation remains a thorny issue to some but for the most part seems to be progressing smoothly. For additional information on the various issues involved with NAGPRA, see Svingen (1992), Swidler et al. (1997), Peregory (1999), and Mihesuah (2000).

Gaming

Tribal gaming is now a huge industry on many reservations (see McCulloch 1994; Bordewich 1996:107–110; Anders 1999). The trend in Indian gaming began in 1979 with the establishment of a high-stakes bingo parlor by the Seminole in Florida. Other groups followed suit. Congress then passed the Indian Gaming Regulatory Act of 1988 to encourage tribal self-sufficiency, as well as to give tribes exclusive rights to regulate gaming on their lands. The National Indian Gaming Commission was established as the federal agency responsible for the regulation of Indian gaming.

Federal law permits bingo and a few other games on Indian reservations. However, if an Indian casino wishes to feature card games or slot machines, an agreement must be made between the tribe and the state. Establishing such agreements has been somewhat difficult, partly due to a perceived moral issue and partly due to resistance by non-Indian casinos in Nevada and Atlantic City to the spread of Indian gaming.

In 2001, at least 200 tribes operated some 320 gaming facilities in 29 states. These institutions gross some $13 billion annually, only a small percentage of the total monies legally gambled. Many casinos are very profitable, while others are less so, and a few have failed. Gaming employs many Indians and non-Indians, and the federal government and various states collect considerable monies in taxes.

One of the largest casinos in the world is the Foxwoods Casino in eastern Connecticut, owned and operated by the Mashantucket Pequot tribe. It grosses more than one billion dollars a year and has allowed the tribe to establish health, police, fire, and educational services, as well as to buy back some of their traditional lands. The state of Connecticut originally objected to the establishment of the casino, but finally acquiesced when it was agreed that the state would be given a share of the gross (about $75 million a year).

Some tribes are not interested in gaming. One example is the Navajo Tribal Council, which approved a resolution to allow gambling and to build a casino; however, the council president vetoed it. The issue was

The sign for the Cities of Gold casino on the Pojoaque Pueblo in New Mexico, 1997.
(CORBIS/Miguel Gandert)

sent to the voters in 1994, who rejected gambling by a narrow margin (see Henderson and Russell 1997). However, in 2001, the Navajo amended the Navajo Nation Code to allow gaming and there are now plans to build at least one casino. (See *http://www.indiangaming.org* and *http://www.pechanga.net* for more information on Indian gaming.)

Native American Religion

For many years the U.S. government had a policy to control, restrict, and eliminate native religious practices and freedom. This was reinforced by missionaries who attempted to convert Indians to other religions, mostly Christianity. In the nineteenth and early twentieth centuries, Indians in white schools and on reservations were actively discouraged from practicing traditional religious rites; sometimes those involved were murdered. After the early twentieth century, government restrictions became less severe but continued to hamper the practice of native religions.

Within the past few decades, Congress has passed several acts, including the American Indian Religious Freedom Act of 1978 and the Religious Freedom Restoration Act of 1994, to ensure that Native Americans could freely practice their religions. These acts have not halted prejudice and discrimination, or the continuation of missionary work among Indians, but they at least prevent the federal government from interfering with native religions.

The Peyote Religion

In the late nineteenth century, some native peoples in the Southwest, the Plains, and the Great Basin began to use peyote, a small cactus that grows in Mexico. Peyote is a mild hallucinogen but is not narcotic. Use of this substance spread quickly as a means of communicating with the supernatural world. A number of states eventually banned peyote, and in response the Native American Church (NAC) was established in 1925; ingestion of peyote is a central practice of this faith (see Stewart 1987).

By the 1940s most state laws dealing with peyote had been repealed. Nevertheless, government officials often broke up peyote ceremonies as illegal drug parties, even arresting some participants. In 1959 California banned peyote, and in 1962 three Indians using it were arrested. These men were convicted, but the California Supreme Court overturned the conviction in 1964 on the basis of religious freedom. Federal drug laws subsequently exempted peyote use by members of the NAC, a right upheld by the U.S. Supreme Court in 1990. However, to legally use peyote, one has to be a member of the NAC, and membership is strictly regulated by the church to prevent abuse. Today the NAC has some 250,000 members (see Smith and Snake 1997) from many different tribes.

Other Issues

A number of other issues remain important to Native American people. The availability of health care is a continuing problem, as many Indian communities do not have health facilities and few doctors choose to work on Indian reservations. In addition, many Indians have major health problems such as diabetes (see Sievers and Fisher 1981).

Alcohol probably constitutes the greatest health problem facing Native Americans (see May 1999). After Prohibition was repealed in 1933, alcohol was still banned on reservations. After 1953 it became legal to sell alcohol on reservations, but most still do not permit it. Nonetheless, alcohol is heavily consumed; a great many Indians have an alcohol problem and pay a heavy price for it. Alcohol-related crime and death rates among Indians are much higher than those of the general population. Indian infants are more likely to be affected by fetal alcohol syndrome than non-Indian babies, treatment of alcohol-related illness consumes some 70 percent of the BIA health budget, and the emotional health and cultural productivity of Indian people are greatly impacted. It seems that a major cause of alcoholism is despair rooted in the experience of discrimination, lack of economic opportunity, and loss of culture.

The availability of education remains a concern as well. Historically, Indians have had a very high dropout rate; the rate of completion of high school is much lower than that of the rest of the U.S. population. However, some progress is being made and a great effort is being made to increase the number of Indians attending four-year universities. Part of that effort is making education more accessible, and within the past several decades, some twenty-six two-year Indian community colleges have been established on reservations along with a number of accredited Indian colleges (e.g., D-Q University in California). Increased availability of scholarships is allowing more Indians to attend other colleges and universities as well.

Many Indians have objected to the use of Native American images and icons in the dominant culture. Many sports teams, both professional (e.g., football's Redskins and Chiefs; baseball's Indians and Braves; hockey's Blackhawks) and amateur (e.g., many schools), use Indian images as icons or mascots. Some have argued that the use of such mascots further exploits Native Americans and that, as many other mascots are animals, the use of Indians as mascots equates them with animals (Deloria 1995). Considerable debate and protest have ensued, and many schools have dropped the use of Indian mascots (see Deloria 1995). A bill to require California schools to drop Indian names was defeated in 2002. On the other hand, others have argued that the use of Indian names conveys a healthy spirit of competitiveness. In that vein, the U.S. military continues to name many of its weapons after Indian groups or individuals, partly to convey a "warrior image" (e.g., Cheyenne, Kiowa, Apache, and Blackhawk helicopters and tomahawk missiles). In addition, the military continues to refer to enemy-occupied territory as "Indian Country."

Many Indian names are also used in commercial endeavors, such as the Jeep Cherokee, the Pontiac automobile, and the Winnebago recreational vehicle.

Further, hundreds of places, including twenty-eight states (e.g., North Dakota, South Dakota, Kansas, Missouri, Alabama, Delaware, Illinois), many cities (e.g., Wichita, Miami, Ottawa, Detroit, Seattle), and numerous other localities, are named for Native American names, locations, icons, and persons. The heritage of Native America is all around us.

Internet Resources for Materials on Native Americans

These are but a few of the general resource lists available on the Internet for topics related to Native Americans.

> **http://www.afn.org/~native/index.html**
> *Native American Information Resource Server.* Links to organizations, tribes, and many other resources.
> **http://www.hanksville.org/NAresources**
> *Index of Native American Resources on the Internet.* Includes many categories of information and has links to many sites.
> **www.wsu.edu:8080/~dee/NAINRES.HTM**
> *Internet Resources on Native Americans.* Links to research sites, information, and tribes.
> **http://historyoftheworld.com/soquel/native.htm**
> *Another Native American Links Page*
> **http://www.kstrom.net/isk/mainmenu.htm**
> *Native American Indian Resources.* Links to assorted sites, including tribes.

Glossary

aboriginal In Native American studies, referring to something of native origin or to a time before European contact.

achieved status Status gained by an individual through the person's own actions (e.g., the status of a soldier).

active resource management Physical management or control of resources to maintain and/or increase productivity.

Adena Complex A group of related Early Woodland cultures in east-central North America existing from about 3,000 to 2,200 B.P.

agriculture The cultivation and/or raising and use of domesticated plants and animals.

anadromous fish Those species of fish that are hatched in fresh water, migrate to and mature in the ocean, and return to their place of origin to spawn.

animism The concept of spirits or souls

Ancestral Puebloans (Anasazi) One of the four main prehistoric agricultural cultures that occupied the Southwest between 2,000 and 500 years ago (also see *Mogollon, Patayan,* and *Hohokam*). The Anasazi are the ancestors of the contemporary Pueblo groups living in the region today.

anthropology The study of humans' biological, social, and cultural development; broad in scope, the field includes study of language, group and individual behavior, material culture, and past, present, and future.

Archaic A generalized hunting-and-gathering economy and lifestyle, without agriculture.

ascribed status Status given to a person based on the person's family (e.g., royalty).

atlatl A spear thrower, used to increase the range, accuracy, and efficiency of a thrown spear, generally called a dart.

B.P. Before present (technically, before A.D. 1950); essentially "years ago."

band A small-scale society without formal leaders, in which the family is the primary sociopolitical and economic unit.

berdache A person of one sex who assumes the gender role of the other sex.

Beringia The land bridge between Asia and North America that existed during the Pleistocene.

bilateral descent Descent figured on both sides of the family; father's relatives and mother's relatives have the same basic status.

breechcloth A small apronlike piece of clothing, tied around the waist and hanging down over the groin and buttocks.

calumet A ceremonial stone pipe of the Plains, used in the Calumet Ceremonial; only sometimes used to actually smoke tobacco. It was usually made from catlinite, a soft red stone quarried in southwestern Minnesota and traded widely.

chief A major political leader in either a tribe or chiefdom.

chiefdom A society with a relatively large population, permanent settlements, some central authority, and a stratified social structure.

chunkey A variation of the hoop-and-pole game played by two participants rolling a circular stone and guessing where the stone would fall.

clan A group of lineages that share a common ancestor, which may or may not be human or real (in the Western sense of *real*); e.g., Bear.

class A layer of society usually linked to wealth, such as the middle class in American society. One can change classes if one's wealth changes.

Clovis The first well-documented occupation of North America, dating from about 12,000 B.P.

collector A classification of hunter-gatherers implying relatively large and sedentary groups.

cosmology The explanation of the origin of the universe and those things contained in it.

coup A brave and daring deed, usually performed in war, such as touching or striking a live enemy; counting coup is the recital of one's accomplishments in battle.

cradleboard A small backpack-like apparatus used to hold and carry infants.

culture In general, learned and shared behavior in humans that is passed from generation to generation.

a **culture** A group of humans who share a common set of traits and identify themselves as a group separate from other groups.

culture area A geographic region in which cultures are generally similar.

domestication A process by which organisms and/or landscapes are "controlled"; in agriculture, domestication means that the genetic makeup of an organism has been purposely altered by humans to their advantage.

drypainting A colored image produced by the Navajo using different colored sand (sometimes called sandpainting) representing events involving Holy People. Once finished, the drypainting had completed its function and was destroyed.

ecology The study of the relationships between an organism and its environment.

emic An insider's view of his or her own culture; the "folk perspective" (*also see* etic).

endogamy A rule that requires a person to marry someone from within a designated social unit.

environmental manipulation Large-scale alteration of the environment to the advantage of the culture.

ethnocentrism The view that one's own group is superior to another group.

ethnographic data Information on a particular group at a particular time.

ethnographic present A description of a group written as if it still existed the way it did in the past.

ethnography A comprehensive study of a particular group at a particular time.

ethnology The comparative study of culture.

etic An outsider's view of a different culture; the "scientific perspective" (*also see* emic).

exogamy A rule that requires a person to marry someone from outside the designated social unit.

extended family Three or more generations of one or more families living together.

family Broadly, a network of close relatives.

forager A classification of hunter-gatherers implying small, very mobile groups.

Folsom A Paleoindian culture often associated with giant bison remains.

Formative An economy that specializes in food production, i.e., agriculture.

Fremont Agriculturalists that occupied the eastern Great Basin between about 1,600 and 700 B.P.

garden A small agricultural plot, tilled by hand.

gender The behavioral role one plays in society irrespective of biological sex.

Ghost Dance A world renewal movement adopted by many Indians; some to better themselves and others in the hope of returning to a time before Euroamerican impacts. Major episodes of the Ghost Dance occurred in 1869 and 1890. A few groups continue the Ghost Dance today.

hand game A common game in which a game piece (stick, bead, etc.) was hidden in one person's hand; others tried to guess which hand held the piece. Often played by teams while others gambled on the outcome.

hogan The six or eight-sided log structures used by the Navajo for houses or ceremonies. Hogans always faced east, had earth-covered roofs, dirt floors, a blanket as a door, and little interior furniture.

Hohokam One of the four main prehistoric agricultural cultures that occupied the Southwest between 2,000 and 500 years ago (also see *Ancestral Puebloans, Patayan,* and *Mogollon*).

Holocene The most recent geologic period, after the Pleistocene, from about 10,000 years ago to the present.

hoop-and-pole game Common game in which a small hoop was rolled along the ground and someone attempted to throw a pole through it.

Hopewell culture A group of related Middle Woodland cultures in east-central North America existing from about 2,200 to 1,700 B.P. Hopewell was an elaboration of the Adena Complex and Hopewell groups had very complex social and political systems.

horticulture Low-intensity agriculture involving relatively small-scale fields, plots, and gardens; food raised primarily for personal consumption rather than for trade or a central authority.

hunter-gatherers Groups that make their primary living from the exploitation of wild foods.

igloo Any Eskimo dwelling; most non-Eskimo use the term to refer only to a snow house.

intensive agriculture Large-scale agriculture often involving the use of irrigation.

kachina Supernatural beings (often ancestors) that manifest themselves in human form to perform vital ceremonies and link Pueblo people to the supernatural world as messengers and mediators.

kinship The way people figure their relationships with, and responsibilities to, other people.

kiva The ceremonial structure used by the Indians of the Southwest, often built underground and circular in shape.

levirate A flexible marriage rule that obligates a widow to marry her dead husband's brother.

lineage A descent group that can trace itself to a known common ancestor, figured either through the male (patrilineal) or female (matrilineal) line.

longhouse A large, communal house used by people in the Northeast. A number of families lived in apartment-like chambers arranged along the perimeter of the house, with communal cooking and meeting areas in the center.

manitou A spirit helper sought by Ottawa individuals during their vision quest. Manitous generally took animal form and would become a lifelong partner of the person.

mano A hand-held stone used to grind materials on a metate (grinding stone).

matrilineal descent Unilineal descent figured through the female line.

matrilocality Practiced by which a newly married couple establishes residence with the bride's family.

memory culture Cultural practices and traditions that are understood through old stories rather than direct experience.

mestizo A term that originated in Mexico to denote a person of mixed ancestry or culture, usually European and Native American.

metate A large stone upon which materials were ground using a mano.

Mogollon One of the four main prehistoric agricultural cultures that occupied the Southwest between 2,000 and 500 years ago (also see *Ancestral Puebloans, Patayan,* and *Hohokam*).

moiety One of two groups of clans.

neolocality Practice by which a newly married couple establishes residence in a new location, away from either family.

nuclear family Parents and children (two generations) living together.

Old Copper culture A Late Aechaic (ca. 5,000 to 4,500 B.P.) culture in the western Northeast known for its cold-hammered copper artifacts.

oral tradition The verbally transmitted history, beliefs, and traditions of a culture.

Paleoindians The earliest occupants of the New World (during the Pleistocene).

passive resource management Nonphysical (e.g., ritual) management or control of resources to maintain and/or increase productivity.

pastoralism The herding, breeding, consumption, and use of managed or domesticated animals.

Patayan One of the four main prehistoric agricultural cultures that occupied the Southwest between 2,000 and 500 years ago (also see *Mogollon, Ancestral Puebloans,* and *Hohokam*).

patrilineal descent Unilineal descent figured through the male line.

patrilocality Practice by which a newly married couple establishes residence with the groom's family.

pemmican A mixture of dried meat, fat, and berries pounded together to form a long-lasting, nutritious food that could be carried as a "trail mix."

peyote A root with hallucinogenic properties taken by individuals both to symbolize and communicate with the supernatural. Today, peyote is used by the Native American Church in ceremonies.

pharmacology The use of plant and/or animal products for medical purposes.

phratry One of three or more groups of clans.

Pleistocene The geologic period lasting from about 2 million years to about 10,000 years ago; the "ice ages."

polyandry The practice by which a woman has more than one husband at the same time.

polygamy The practice by which a person has more than one spouse at the same time.

polygyny The practice by which a man has more than one wife at the same time.

potlatch A Northwest Coast ceremony of great social and political importance in which an individual or group marked important events or validated their rank, thereby demonstrating to their guests that they were worthy of possessing that rank.

rank Formal status that includes a title, rights, and responsibilities.

resource management The small-scale alteration of specific resources to the advantage of the culture (see *active resource management* and *passive resource management*).

sachem The title applied to a leader of any kind by the people of the Northeast. The Iroquois had 50 formal sachems in their national government.

sacred bundle (or Medicine Bundle) A group or sacred items kept together in a bag or other wrapping. Some of the items in a bundle were gifts from supernatural deities, others symbolized fertility, others represented war, and all were sacred to the group. Sacred bundles were kept by most groups on the Plains.

seasonal transhumance A system of movement of people based on the seasonal availability of resources and their geographic location.

secular Pertaining to functions that are not religious, such as those of a civil government.

sedentary Living in one place all the time.

shaman An individual in a society who controls supernatural power and whose responsibilities might include curing the sick, controlling evil, consulting and invoking supernatural forces, and conducting ceremonies. Some shamans controlled and used evil power and were feared.

shinny A team game similar to field hockey, in which a wooden or buckskin ball is struck with a stick (or feet, but never hands) and propelled into the opponents' goal. The game is usually played by women, but men, or men and women, played it in some groups. Most groups in North America played shinny.

sinew Animal connective tissue, e.g., tendons. Sinew was very strong and was used for a variety of purposes, including making bowstrings, attaching points to arrows, and creating elastic reinforcement for bows.

slash-and-burn method Agricultural technique that involves removing vegetation from a small plot, burning it, and planting crop in its place. The plot quickly loses its agricultural productivity and another plot must be processed (see *swidden*).

sodality An organization whose membership (usually voluntary) is not based on kinship but on some common interest or pursuit.

sororate A flexible marriage rule that obligates a widower to marry his dead wife's sister.

state A society with a large population, complex social and political structures, central authority, complex record keeping, urban centers (cities), and monumental architecture.

status The place a person holds in society.

subsistence strategy The basic way in which a group makes a living; its economy, e.g., farming or hunting and gathering.

sucking cure A technique used by shamans to remove sickness from a patient. If a foreign object was causing a sickness, the shaman would suck it from the body with the aid of supernatural power. Some would argue that the shaman hid the object in his mouth and just pretended to suck it from the body of the patient.

Sun Dance (or Medicine Lodge) A world renewal ceremony undertaken by an individual male who either wanted to contribute to the welfare of his tribe or to thank the supernatural for some past "favor." Self-sacrifice for the good of the group was the common theme of the ceremony, and it was calm and cheerful. Some groups still hold Sun Dances.

sweatlodge A structure, generally small and often earth-covered, in which individuals would ceremonially cleanse themselves. A fire would be built in the structure, rocks heated and splashed with water to create steam and cause people inside to sweat.

swidden Rotation of fields to accommodate slash-and-burn agriculture.

tepee A conical shelter made of a frame of wooden poles and covered with skins. The classic tepee of the Plains was large and typically covered with bison skins. Other groups used smaller tepees.

totem pole A large, carved, wooden pole depicting family and clan symbols (totems) of animals and supernatural beings. The poles told stories of family history, assumptions of rank, exploits, origin stories, memorials to individuals, or other events.

travois A sled pulled by an animal. Parallel poles were strapped to the animal; on the poles' trailing ends a platform was built for transporting goods. A travois pulled by a horse had a much larger capacity than one pulled by a dog.

tribe A society with a relatively large population, a number of villages, and leaders (chiefs) with some actual power.

umiak A large, open, walrus-shin boat used in the Arctic for transportation and whale hunting. Umiaks are often called "women's boats" because the women usually rowed them.

unilineal descent A descent system in which kinship is figured either through the male or female line.

vision quest A personal journey undertaken by an individual to seek guidance. A vision quest would often entail isolation and fasting until the person had some vision of power or was visited by a spirit-helper to assist the person in directing their life.

wampum Small tubular white and purple beads made from marine shells and assembled into belts or strings to serve both as money and as symbols of agreements. Used by groups in the Northeast.

References and Suggested Readings

Aberle, David F. 1983a. Peyote Religion Among the Navajo. In: *Handbook of North American Indians, Vol. 10, Southwest*, Alfonso Ortiz, ed., pp. 558–569. Washington: Smithsonian Institution.

———. 1983b. Navajo Economic Development. In: *Handbook of North American Indians, Vol. 10, Southwest*, Alfonso Ortiz, ed., pp. 641–658. Washington: Smithsonian Institution.

Ackerman, Lillian A. 1995. Complementary But Equal: Gender Status in the Plateau. In: *Women and Power in Native North America*, Laura F. Klein and Lillian A. Ackerman, eds., pp. 75–100. Norman: University of Oklahoma Press.

———. 1998. Kinship, Family, and Gender Roles. In: *Handbook of North American Indians, Vol. 12, Plateau*, Deward E. Walker, Jr., ed., pp. 515–524. Washington: Smithsonian Institution.

Acuna-Soto, Rodolfo, Leticia Calderon Romero, and James H. Maguire. 2000. Large Epidemics of Hemorrhagic Fevers in Mexico, 1545–1815. *The American Journal of Tropical Medicine and Hygiene* 62(6):733–739.

Adams, Alexander B. 1971. *Geronimo: A Biography.* New York: G. P. Putnam's Sons.

Adams, E. Charles. 1991. *The Origin and Development of the Pueblo Katsina Cult.* Tucson: University of Arizona Press.

Albrecht, Andrew C. 1946. Indian–French Relations at Natchez. *American Anthropologist* 48(3):321–354.

Aldred, Lisa. 2000. Plastic Shamans and Astroturf Sundances: New Age Commercialization of Native American Spirituality. *American Indian Quarterly* 24(3):329–352.

Allen, John Logan, ed. 1997. *North American Exploration* (3 vols.). Lincoln: University of Nebraska Press.

Alley, John R., Jr. 1986. Tribal Historical Projects. In: *Handbook of North American Indians, Vol. 11, Great Basin*, Warren L. d'Azevedo, ed., pp. 601–607. Washington: Smithsonian Institution.

Ames, Kenneth M. 1994. The Northwest Coast: Complex Hunter-Gatherers, Ecology, and Social Evolution. *Annual Reviews of Anthropology* 23:209–229.

Ames, Kenneth M., and Herbert D. G. Maschner. 1999. *Peoples of the Northwest Coast: Their Archaeology and Prehistory.* London: Thames and Hudson.

Ames, Kenneth M., Don E. Dumond, Jerry R. Galm, and Rick Minor. 1998. Prehistory of the Southern Plateau. In: *Handbook of North American Indians, Vol. 12, Plateau*, Deward E. Walker, Jr., ed., pp. 103–119. Washington: Smithsonian Institution.

Amsden, Charles A. 1934. *Navaho Weaving: Its Technic and History.* Santa Ana: The Fine Arts Press. Reprinted 1949. Glorieta, NM: Rio Grande Press.

Anastasio, Angelo. 1972. The Southern Plateau: An Ecological Analysis of Intergroups Relations. *Northwest Anthropological Research Notes* 6(2):109–229.

Anders, Gary C. 1999. Indian Gaming: Financial and Regulatory Issues. In: *Contemporary Native American Political Issues*, Troy R. Johnson, ed., pp. 163–173. Walnut Creek, CA: AltaMira Press.

Anderson, David G., and Michael K. Faught. 1998. The Distribution of Fluted Paleoindian Projectile Points: Update 1998. *Archaeology of Eastern North America* 26:163–187.

Applegate, Richard B. 1975. The Datura Cult Among the Chumash. *The Journal of California Anthropology* 2(1):6–17.

Archambault, JoAllyn. 2001. Sun Dance. In: *Handbook of North American Indians, Vol. 13, Plains*, Raymond J. DeMallie, ed., pp. 983–995. Washington: Smithsonian Institution.

Arkush, Brooke S. 1995. *The Archaeology of CA-MNO-2122: A Study of Pre-Contact and Post-Contact Lifeways Among the Mono Basin Paiute.* University of California Anthropological Records Vol. 31.

Axtell, Horace P., and Margo Aragon. 1997. *A Little Bit of Wisdom: Conversations with a Nez Perce Elder.* Lewiston, ID: Confluence Press.

Axtell, James. 2001. *Natives and Newcomers: The Cultural Origins of North America.* Oxford: Oxford University Press.

Baker, Brenda J., and Lisa Kealhoffer (eds.). 1996. *Bioarchaeology of Native American Adaptation in the Spanish Borderlands.* Gainesville: University of Florida Press.

Bamforth, Douglas B. 1994. Indigenous People, Indigenous Violence: Precontact Warfare on the North American Great Plains. *Man* 29(1):95–115.

Bataille, Gretchen M., and Laurie Lisa. 2001. *Native American Women: A Biographical Dictionary* (2nd ed.). New York: Routledge.

Bates, Craig D., and Martha J. Lee. 1993. Chukchansi Yokuts/Southern Miwok: Weavers of Yosemite National Park. *American Indian Art Magazine* 18(3):44–51.

Beal, Bob, and Rod Macleod. 1984. *Prairie Fire: The 1885 North-West Rebellion.* Edmonton: Hurtig Publishers.

Beauchamp, W. M. 1896. Iroquois Games. *Journal of American Folklore* 9(35):269–277.

———. 1900. Iroquois Women. *Journal of American Folklore* 13(49):81–91.

Beck, Charlotte, and George T. Jones. 1997. The Terminal Pleistocene/Early Holocene Archaeology of the Great Basin. *Journal of World Prehistory* 11(2):161–236.

Benedek, Emily. 1992. *The Wind Won't Know Me: A History of the Navajo–Hopi Land Dispute.* New York: Alfred A. Knopf.

Bennett, Wendell C., and Robert M. Zingg. 1935. *The Tarahumara: An Indian Tribe in Northern Mexico.* Chicago: University of Chicago Press. Reprinted 1976. Glorieta, NM: Rio Grande Press.

Bense, Judith A. 1994. *Archaeology of the Southeastern United States: Paleoindian to World War I*. San Diego: Academic Press.

Bergman, Robert L. 1983. Navajo Health Services and Projects. In: *Handbook of North American Indians, Vol. 10, Southwest*, Alfonso Ortiz, ed., pp. 672–678. Washington: Smithsonian Institution.

Bernotas, Bob. 1992. *Sitting Bull: Chief of the Sioux*. New York: Chelsea House Publishers.

Berryhill, Peggy. 1998. Hopi Potskwaniat: The Hopi Way to the Future. *Native Americas* 15(1):31–39.

Berthrong, Donald J. 1963. *The Southern Cheyennes*. Norman: University of Oklahoma Press.

———. 1976. *The Cheyenne and Arapaho Ordeal: Reservation and Agency Life in the Indian Territory, 1875–1907*. Norman: University of Oklahoma Press.

Bibby, Brian. 1996. *The Fine Art of California Indian Basketry*. Berkeley: Heyday Books.

Bierwert, Crisca. 1998. Remembering Chief Seattle: Reversing Cultural Studies of a Vanishing Native American. *American Indian Quarterly* 22(3):280–304.

Bilharz, Joy. 1995. First Among Equals? The Changing Status of Seneca Women. In: *Women and Power in Native North America*, Laura F. Klein and Lillian A. Ackerman, eds., pp. 101–112. Norman: University of Oklahoma Press.

Biolsi, Thomas, and Larry J. Zimmerman (eds.). 1997. *Indians and Anthropologists: Vine Deloria, Jr., and the Critique of Anthropology*. Tucson: University of Arizona Press.

Birket-Smith, Kaj. 1936. *The Eskimos*. London: Methuen & Co. Ltd. (a revised and enlarged edition was published by Methuen in 1959).

Bishop, Charles A. 1981. Territorial Groups Before 1821: Cree and Ojibwa. In: *Handbook of North American Indians, Vol. 6, Subarctic*, June Helm, ed., pp. 158–160. Washington: Smithsonian Institution.

Black, Lydia T. 1980. The Aleutians: The Early History. *Alaska Geographic* 7(3):82–89.

———. 1982. *Aleut Art: Unangam Aguqaadangin Unangan of the Aleutian Archipelago*. Anchorage: Aleutian/Pribilof Islands Association.

———. 1987. Whaling in the Aleutians. *Etudes/Inuit Studies* 11(2):7–50.

———. 1988. The Story of Russian America. In: *Crossroads of Continents: Cultures of Siberia and Alaska*, William W. Fitzhugh and Aron Crowell, eds., pp. 70–82. Washington: Smithsonian Institution Press.

———. 1991. *Glory Remembered: Wooden Headgear of Alaska Sea Hunters*. Juneau: Friends of the Alaska State Museums.

———. 1996. *Orthodoxy in Alaska, Christianization of Alaska, Veniaminov's Stewardship, and Orthodoxy in Alaska after 1867*. The Patriarch Athenagoras Orthodox Institute Distinguished Lectures No. 6. Berkeley: The Patriarch Athenagoras Orthodox Institute.

Black, Lydia T., and R. G. Liapunova. 1988. Aleut: Islanders of the North Pacific. In: *Crossroads of Continents: Cultures of Siberia and Alaska*, William W. Fitzhugh and Aron Crowell, eds., pp. 52–57. Washington: Smithsonian Institution Press.

Blackbird, Andrew J. 1887. *History of the Ottawa and Chippewa Indians of Michigan*. Ypsilanti, MI: Ypsilanti Job Printing House.

Blackman, Margaret B., and Edwin S. Hall, Jr. 1988. Alaska Native Arts in the Twentieth Century. In: *Crossroads of Continents: Cultures of Siberia and Alaska*, William W. Fitzhugh and Aron Crowell, eds., pp. 326–340. Washington: Smithsonian Institution Press.

Blackwood, Evelyn. 1984. Sexuality and Gender in Certain Native American Tribes: The Case of Cross-Gender Females. *Signs* 10:27–42.

Blaine, Martha Royce. 1983. The Pawnee Sacred Bundles: Their Present Use and Significance. *Papers in Anthropology* 24:145–155.

———. 1990. *Pawnee Passage, 1870–1875*. Norman: University of Oklahoma Press.

———. 1997. *Some Things Are Not Forgotten: A Pawnee Family Remembers*. Lincoln: University of Nebraska Press.

Bland, Celia. 1995. *Pontiac: Ottawa Rebel*. New York: Chelsea House Publishers.

Boas, Franz. 1897. The Social Organization and the Secret Societies of the Kwakiutl Indians. In: *Report of the U.S. National Museum for 1895*, pp. 311–737. Washington: Government Printing Office. Reprinted 1970. Johnson Reprint Corporation.

———. 1909. The Kwakiutl of Vancouver Island. In: *The Jesup North Pacific Expedition, Vol. 5*, Franz Boas, ed., pp. 301–522. New York: Memoir of the American Museum of Natural History.

———. 1921. Ethnology of the Kwakiutl [2 parts]. *Annual Report of the Bureau of American Ethnology for the Years 1913–1914*, pp. 43–1481. Washington: Government Printing Office.

Boas, Franz, and Helen Codere. 1966. *Kwakiutl Ethnography*. Chicago: University of Chicago Press.

Bol, Marsha C. 1998. *Stars Above, Earth Below: American Indians and Nature*. Niwot, CO: Roberts Reinhart Publishers.

Bonar, Eulalie H. (ed.). 1997. *Woven by the Grandmothers: Nineteenth-Century Navajo Textiles from the National Museum of the American Indian*. Washington: Smithsonian Institution Press.

Bone, Robert M. 1992. *The Geography of the Canadian North: Issues and Challenges*. Toronto: Oxford University Press.

Bonvillain, Nancy. 1992. *Hiawatha: Founder of the Iroquois Confederacy*. New York: Chelsea House Publishers.

———. 2001. *Native Nations: Cultures and Histories of Native North America*. Upper Saddle River, NJ: Prentice Hall.

Bordewich, Fergus M. 1996. *Killing the White Man's Indian: Reinventing Native Americans at the End of the Twentieth Century*. New York: Doubleday.

Boxberger, Daniel L. (ed.). 1990. *Native North Americans: An Ethnohistorical Approach*. Dubuque, IA: Kendall Hunt.

Boyd, Robert T. 1990. Demographic History, 1774–1874. In: *Handbook of North American Indians, Vol. 7, Northwest Coast*, Wayne Suttles, ed., pp. 135–148. Washington: Smithsonian Institution.

———. 1998. Demographic History Until 1900. In: *Handbook of North American Indians, Vol. 12, Plateau*,

Deward E. Walker, Jr., ed., pp. 467–483. Washington: Smithsonian Institution.

Boyer, Ruth McDonald, and Narcissus Duffy Gayton. 1992. *Apache Mothers and Daughters: Four Generations of a Family.* Norman: University of Oklahoma Press.

Brace, C. L., and Ashly Montagu. 1977. *Human Evolution.* New York: Macmillan Publishing Company.

Bradfield, Richard Maitland. 1995. *An Interpretation of Hopi Culture.* Derby, England: Privately printed.

Bragdon, Kathleen J. 2001. *The Columbia Guide to American Indians of the Northeast.* New York: Columbia University Press.

Brew, J. O. 1979. Hopi Prehistory and History to 1850. In: *Handbook of North American Indians, Vol. 9, Southwest,* Alfonso Ortiz, ed., pp. 514–523. Washington: Smithsonian Institution.

Brightman, Robert A. 1993. *Grateful Prey: Rock Cree Human–Animal Relationships.* Berkeley: University of California Press.

Brinkley-Rogers, Paul. 1990. Anglo "Tribe" Dances Controversial Steps. *Arizona Republic* (newspaper), August 5, pp. A1–A2.

Brose, David S. 1978. Late Prehistory of the Upper Great Lakes Region. In: *Handbook of North American Indians, Vol. 15, Northeast,* Bruce Trigger, ed., pp. 569–582. Washington: Smithsonian Institution.

Brown, Dee. 1970. *Bury My Heart at Wounded Knee: An Indian History of the American West.* New York: Henry Holt & Company.

Brown, Lester B. (ed.). 1997. *Two Spirit People: American Indian, Lesbian Women, and Gay Men.* New York: Haworth Press.

Brown, Steven C. 1998. *Native Visions: Evolution in Northwest Coast Art from the Eighteenth through the Twentieth Century.* Seattle: Seattle Art Museum.

Brugge, David M. 1983. Navajo Prehistory and History to 1850. In: *Handbook of North American Indians, Vol. 10, Southwest,* Alfonso Ortiz, ed., pp. 489–501. Washington: Smithsonian Institution.

———. 1994. *The Navajo–Hopi Land Dispute: An American Tragedy.* Albuquerque: University of New Mexico Press.

Brugge, Doug, Timothy Benally, and Esther Yazzie-Lewis. 2001. Uranium Mining on Navajo Indian Lands. *Cultural Survival Quarterly* 25(1):18–21.

Burch, Ernest S., Jr. 1979. The Ethnography of Northern North America: A Guide to Recent Research. *Arctic Anthropology* 16(1):62–146.

———. 1984. The Land Claims Era in Alaska. In: *Handbook of North American Indians, Vol. 5, Arctic,* David Damas, ed., pp. 657–661. Washington: Smithsonian Institution.

———. 1998. *The Iñupiaq Eskimo Nations of Northwest Alaska.* Fairbanks: University of Alaska Press.

Busby, Colin I., John M. Findlay, and James C. Bard. 1979. *A Cultural Resource Overview of the Bureau of Land Management Coleville, Bodie, Benton, and Owens Valley Planning Units, California.* Bakersfield: Bureau of Land Management Cultural Resource Publications, Anthropology–History.

Canfield, Gae Whitney. 1983. *Sarah Winnemucca of the Northern Paiutes.* Norman: University of Oklahoma Press.

Cantor, George. 1993. *North American Indian Landmarks: A Traveler's Guide.* Detroit: Gale Research Inc.

Carlson, Paul H. 1998. *The Plains Indians.* College Station: Texas A&M University Press.

Carlson, Roy L. (ed.). 1983. *Indian Art Traditions of the Northwest Coast.* Burnaby, B.C.: Archaeology Press, Simon Fraser University.

Carter, Cecile Elkins. 1995. *Caddo Indians: Where We Come From.* Norman: University of Oklahoma Press.

Cash, Joseph H., and Gerald W. Wolff. 1976. *The Ottawa People.* Phoenix: Indian Tribal Series.

Castaneda, Carlos. 1968. *The Teachings of Don Juan: A Yaqui Way of Knowledge.* New York: Ballantine.

———. 1993. *The Art of Dreaming.* New York: Harper Collins.

Castillo, Edward D. 1978. The Impact of Euro-American Exploration and Settlement. In: *Handbook of North American Indians, Vol. 8, California,* Robert F. Heizer, ed., pp. 99–127. Washington: Smithsonian Institution.

Catlin, George. 1844. *Letters and Notes on the Manners, Customs, and Condition of the North American Indians* (2 vols.). Reprinted 1973. Dover Publications.

Chalfant, W. A. 1933. *The Story of Inyo* (revised edition). Privately printed. Reprinted 1975. Bishop, CA: Chalfant Press.

Chamberlain, Von Del. 1982. *When Stars Came Down to Earth: Cosmology of the Skidi Pawnee Indians of North America.* Los Altos, CA: Ballena Press Anthropological Papers No. 26.

———. 1992. The Chief and His Council: Unity and Authority from the Stars. In: *Earth and Sky: Visions of the Cosmos in Native American Folklore,* Ray A. Williamson and Claire R. Farmer, eds., pp. 221–235. Albuquerque: University of New Mexico Press.

Champagne, Duane (ed.). 1999. *Contemporary Native American Cultural Issues.* Walnut Creek, CA: AltaMira Press

Champion, Jean R. 1962. A Study in Culture Persistence: The Tarahumaras of Northwestern Mexico. Ph.D. dissertation, Columbia University.

Chapman, Jefferson. 1994. *Tellico Archaeology* (2nd ed.). Knoxville: University of Tennessee Press.

Chartkoff, Joseph L., and Kerry Kona Chartkoff. 1984. *The Archaeology of California.* Stanford: Stanford University Press.

Chatters, James C. 1997. Encounter with an Ancestor. *Anthropology Newsletter* 38(1):9–10.

———. 1998. Environment. In: *Handbook of North American Indians, Vol. 12, Plateau,* Deward E. Walker, Jr., ed., pp. 29–48. Washington: Smithsonian Institution.

Chatters, James C., and David L. Pokotylo. 1998. Prehistory: Introduction. In: *Handbook of North American Indians, Vol. 12, Plateau,* Deward E. Walker, Jr., ed., pp. 73–80. Washington: Smithsonian Institution.

Chester, Sharon, and James Oetzel. 1998. *The Arctic Guide.* San Mateo, CA: Wandering Albatross.

Chief Joseph. 1995. *That All People May Be One People, Send Rain to Wash the Face of the Earth*. Sitka, AK: Mountain Meadow Press.

Churchill, Ward. 1999. The Crucible of American Indian Identity: Native Tradition Versus Colonial Imposition in Postconquest North America. In: *Contemporary Native American Cultural Issues*, Duane Champagne, ed., pp. 39–67. Walnut Creek, CA: AltaMira Press.

Ciborski, Sara. 1990. Culture and Power: The Emergence and Politics of Akwesana Mohawk Traditionalism. Ph.D. dissertation, State University of New York, Albany.

Clark, Donald W. 1981. Prehistory of the Western Subarctic. In: *Handbook of North American Indians, Vol. 6, Subarctic*, June Helm, ed., pp. 107–129. Washington: Smithsonian Institution.

———. 1984. Pacific Eskimo: Historical Ethnography. In: *Handbook of North American Indians, Vol. 5, Arctic*, David Damas, ed., pp. 185–197. Washington: Smithsonian Institution.

Clemmer, Richard O. 1979. Hopi History, 1940–1974. In: *Handbook of North American Indians, Vol. 9, Southwest*, Alfonso Ortiz, ed., pp. 53–538. Washington: Smithsonian Institution.

———. 1986. Hopis, Western Shoshonis, and Southern Utes: Three Different Responses to the Indian Reorganization Act of 1934. *American Indian Culture and Research Journal* 10(2):15–40.

———. 1991. Crying for the Children of Sacred Ground: A Review Article on the Hopi–Navajo Land Dispute. *American Indian Quarterly* 15(2):225–230.

Clemmer, Richard O., and Omer C. Stewart. 1986. Treaties, Reservations, and Claims. In: *Handbook of North American Indians, Vol. 11, Great Basin*, Warren L. d'Azevedo, ed., pp. 525–557. Washington: Smithsonian Institution.

Cliff, Janet M. 1990. Navajo Games. *American Indian Cultural and Research Journal* 14(3):1–81.

Cockburn, T. Aidan. 1971. Infectious Diseases in Ancient Populations. *Current Anthropology* 12(1):45–62.

Codere, Helen. 1950. Fighting with Property: A Study of Kwakiutl Potlatching and Warfare, 1792–1930. *Monographs of the American Ethnological Society 18*. Seattle: University of Washington Press.

———. 1990. Kwakiutl: Traditional Culture. In: *Handbook of North American Indians, Vol. 7, Northwest Coast*, Wayne Suttles, ed., pp. 359–377. Washington: Smithsonian Institution.

Cohen, Fay G. 1986. *Treaties on Trial: The Continuing Controversy over Northwest Indian Fishing Rights*. Seattle: University of Washington Press.

Cole, Douglas. 1985. *Captured Heritage: The Scramble for Northwest Coast Artifacts*. Seattle: University of Washington Press.

Cole, Douglas, and David Darling. 1990. History of the Early Period. In: *Handbook of North American Indians, Vol. 7, Northwest Coast*, Wayne Suttles, ed., pp. 119–134. Washington: Smithsonian Institution.

Collins, Henry B., Jr. 1984. History of Research Before 1945. In: *Handbook of North American Indians, Vol. 5, Arctic*, David Damas, ed., pp. 8–16. Washington: Smithsonian Institution.

Collins, Henry B., Jr., Austin H. Clark, and Egbert H. Walker. 1945. *The Aleutian Islands: Their People and Natural History*. Washington: Smithsonian Institution War Background Studies No. 21.

Condon, Richard G., Julia Ogina, and Holman Elders. 1996. *The Northern Copper Inuit*. Norman: University of Oklahoma Press.

Connelly, John C. 1979. Hopi Social Organization. In: *Handbook of North American Indians, Vol. 9, Southwest*, Alfonso Ortiz, ed., pp. 539–553. Washington: Smithsonian Institution.

Cook, Noble David. 1998. *Born to Die: Disease and New World Conquest, 1492–1650*. Cambridge: Cambridge University Press.

Cook, Sherburne F. 1971. The Aboriginal Population of Upper California. In: *The California Indians: A Source Book*, Robert F. Heizer and M. A. Whipple, eds., pp. 66–72. Berkeley: University of California Press.

———. 1976. *The Population of California Indians 1769–1970*. Berkeley: University of California Press.

———. 1978. Historical Demography. In: *Handbook of North American Indians, Vol. 8, California*, Robert F. Heizer, ed., pp. 91–98. Washington: Smithsonian Institution.

Corbett, Helen D., and Susanne M. Swibold. 2000. The Aleuts of Pribilof Islands, Alaska. In: *Endangered Peoples of the Arctic: Struggles to Survive and Thrive*, Milton M. R. Freeman, ed., pp. 1–16. Westport, CT: Greenwood Press.

Cordell, Linda S. 1994. *Ancient Pueblo Peoples*. Washington: Smithsonian Books.

———. 1997. *Archaeology of the Southwest* (2nd ed.). Orlando: Academic Press.

Cornell, Stephen. 1988. *The Return of the Native: American Indian Political Resurgence*. Oxford: Oxford University Press.

Costa, Rupert, and Jeannette Henry Costa (eds.). 1987. *The Missions of California: A Legacy of Genocide*. San Francisco: The Indian Historian Press.

Costello, Julia G., and David Hornbeck. 1989. Alta California: An Overview. In: *Columbian Consequences, Vol. 1, Archaeological and Historical Perspectives on the Spanish Borderlands West*, David H. Thomas, ed., pp. 303–331. Washington: Smithsonian Institution Press.

Covington, James W. 1993. *The Seminoles of Florida*. Gainesville: University Press of Florida.

Crosby, Harry W. 1994. *Antigua California: Mission and Colony on the Peninsular Frontier, 1697–1768*. Albuquerque: University of New Mexico Press.

Crowe, Keith J. 1991. *A History of the Original Peoples of Northern Canada*. Montreal: McGill-Queen's University Press.

Crown, Patricia L. 1990. The Hohokam of the American Southwest. *Journal of World Prehistory* 4(2):223–255.

Crozier-Hogle, Lois, and Darryl Babe Wilson. 1997. *Surviving in Two Worlds: Contemporary Native American Voices*. Austin: University of Texas Press.

Curtis, Edward S. 1907. The Navaho. In: *The North American Indian, Vol. 1*, pp. 73–127. Published by Edward S. Curtis (reprinted by Johnson Reprint Corporation, 1970).

———. 1907–1930. *The North American Indian, Being a Series of Volumes Picturing and Describing the Indians of* the United States and Alaska (20 vols.). Published by Edward S. Curtis (reprinted by Johnson Reprint Corporation, 1970).

———. 1911a. The Nez Percés. In: *The North American Indian, Vol. 8*, pp. 1–77. Published by Edward S. Curtis (reprinted by Johnson Reprint Corporation, 1970).

———. 1911b. The Cheyenne. In: *The North American Indian, Vol. 6*, pp. 87–135. Published by Edward S. Curtis (reprinted by Johnson Reprint Corporation, 1970).

———. 1915. The Kwakiutl. In: *The North American Indian, Vol. 10*. Published by Edward S. Curtis (reprinted by Johnson Reprint Corporation, 1970).

———. 1922. The Hopi. In: *The North American Indian, Vol. 12*. Published by Edward S. Curtis (reprinted by Johnson Reprint Corporation, 1970).

———. 1928. The Western Woods Cree. In: *The North American Indian, Vol. 18*, pp. 55–87. Published by Edward S. Curtis (reprinted by Johnson Reprint Corporation, 1970).

———. 1930. The Southern Cheyenne. In: *The North American Indian, Vol. 19*, pp. 107–148. Published by Edward S. Curtis (reprinted by Johnson Reprint Corporation, 1970).

Cutler, Charles L. 1994. *O Brave New Words! Native American Loanwords in Current English*. Norman: University of Oklahoma Press.

Damas, David (ed.). 1984a. *Handbook of North American Indians, Vol. 5, Arctic*. Washington: Smithsonian Institution.

Damas, David. 1984b. Copper Eskimo. In: *Handbook of North American Indians, Vol. 5, Arctic*, David Damas, ed., pp. 397–414. Washington: Smithsonian Institution.

Davidson, Gordon C. 1967. *The North West Company*. New York: Russell & Russell (reissue of a 1918 book).

Davis, Britton. 1976. *The Truth About Geronimo*. Lincoln: University of Nebraska Press (reprint of 1929 original, with a new foreword).

Davis, Mary B. (ed.). 1994. *Native America in the Twentieth Century: An Encyclopedia*. New York: Garland Publishing.

Davis, Nancy Yaw. 1981. History of Research in Subarctic Alaska. In: *Handbook of North American Indians, Vol. 6, Subarctic*, June Helm, ed., pp. 43–48. Washington: Smithsonian Institution.

d'Azevedo, Warren L. 1986a. Introduction. In: *Handbook of North American Indians, Vol. 11, Great Basin*, Warren L. d'Azevedo, ed., pp. 1–14. Washington: Smithsonian Institution.

———. 1986c. Washoe. In: *Handbook of North American Indians, Vol. 11, Great Basin*, Warren L. d'Azevedo, ed., pp. 466–498. Washington: Smithsonian Institution.

d'Azevedo, Warren L. (ed.). 1986b. *Handbook of North American Indians, Vol. 11, Great Basin*. Washington: Smithsonian Institution.

Deardorff, Merle H. 1951. The Religion of Handsome Lake: Its Origin and Development. In: *Symposium on Local Diversity in Iroquois Culture*, William N. Fenton, ed., pp. 77–107. Bureau of American Ethnology Bulletin 149.

Debo, Angie. 1976. *Geronimo: The Man, His Time, His Place*. Norman: University of Oklahoma Press.

DeJong, David H. 1993. *Promises of the Past: A History of Indian Education in the United States*. Golden, CO: North American Press.

de Laguna, Frederica. 1988. Potlatch Ceremonialism on the Northwest Coast. In: *Crossroads of Continents: Cultures of Siberia and Alaska*, William W. Fitzhugh and Aron Crowell, eds., pp. 271–280. Washington: Smithsonian Institution Press.

Deloria, Philip J. 1998. *Playing Indian*. New Haven: Yale University Press.

Deloria, Vine, Jr. 1969. *Custer Died for Your Sins: An Indian Manifesto*. New York: Macmillan.

———. 1995. *Red Earth, White Lies: Native Americans and the Myth of Scientific Fact*. New York: Scribner.

———. 1997. Anthros, Indians, and Planetary Reality. In: *Indians and Anthropologists: Vine Deloria, Jr., and the Critique of Anthropology*, Thomas Biolsi and Larry J. Zimmerman, eds., pp. 209–221. Tucson: University of Arizona Press.

Deloria, Vine, Jr. (ed.). 1985. *American Indian Policy in the Twentieth Century*. Norman: University of Oklahoma Press.

DeMallie, Raymond J. (ed.). 2001. *Plains. Handbook of North American Indians, Vol. 13*, Raymond J. DeMallie, ed. Washington: Smithsonian Institution.

de Mille, Richard. 1976. *Castaneda's Journey: The Power and the Allegory*. Santa Barbara, CA: Capra Press.

de Mille, Richard (ed.). 1990. *The Don Juan Papers: Further Castaneda Controversies* (2nd ed.). Belmont, CA: Wadsworth Publishing Company.

Densmore, Frances. 1929. *Pawnee Music*. Bureau of American Ethnology Bulletin 93.

Dent, Richard J. 1995. *Chesapeake Prehistory: Old Traditions, New Directions*. New York: Plenum Press.

Diamond, Jared. 1992. The Arrow of Disease. *Discover 13* (October):64–73.

Diessner, Don. 1993. *There Are No Indians Left But Me: Sitting Bull's Story*. El Segundo, CA: Upton and Sons.

Dippie, Brian W. 1982. *The Vanishing American: White Attitudes and U.S. Indian Policy*. Middletown, CT: Wesleyan University Press.

Dobyns, Henry F. 1993. Disease Transfer at Contact. *Annual Review of Anthropology* 22:273–291.

Dockstader, Frederick J. 1979. Hopi History, 1850–1940. In: *Handbook of North American Indians, Vol. 9, Southwest*, Alfonso Ortiz, ed., pp. 524–532. Washington: Smithsonian Institution.

Doherty, Robert. 1990. *Disputed Waters: Native Americans and the Great Lakes Fishery*. Lexington: The University Press of Kentucky.

Dolittle, William F. 2000. *Cultivated Landscapes of Native North America*. Oxford: Oxford University Press.

Donald, Leland. 1997. *Aboriginal Slavery on the Northwest Coast of North America*. Berkeley: University of California Press.

Dorsey, George A. 1905. *The Cheyenne*. Field Columbian Museum, Anthropological Series, Vol. 9, Parts 1 and 2 (reprinted by the Rio Grande Press, 1971).

Downs, James F. 1972. *The Navajo*. New York: Holt, Rinehart and Winston (reprinted by Waveland Press, 1984).

Dozier, Edward P. 1966. *Hano: A Tewa Indian Community in Arizona*. New York: Holt, Rinehart and Winston.

———. 1970 *The Pueblo Indians of North America*. New York: Holt, Rinehart and Winston.

Driver, Harold E. 1937. Culture Element Distributions: IV, Southern Sierra Nevada. *University of California Anthropological Records* 1(2).

Drucker, Philip. 1955. *Indians of the Northwest Coast*. New York: American Museum of Natural History.

———. 1965. *Culture of the North Pacific Coast*. San Francisco: Chandler.

Drucker, Philip, and Robert F. Heizer. 1967. *To Make My Name Good*. Berkeley: University of California Press.

Du Bois, Cora A. 1939. The 1870 Ghost Dance. *University of California Anthropological Records* 3(1).

Dumond, Don. 1984. Prehistory: Summary. In: *Handbook of North American Indians, Vol. 5, Arctic*, David Damas, ed., pp. 72–79. Washington: Smithsonian Institution.

———. 1987. *The Eskimos and Aleuts* (2nd ed.). New York: Thames and Hudson.

Dunne, Peter M. 1948. *Early Jesuit Missions in Tarahumara*. Berkeley: University of California Press.

Du Pratz, M. Le Page. 1758. *Histoire de la Louisiane* (3 vols.). Paris. (Translated into English and published in London in 1776. Reprinted by Louisiana State University Press, 1975.)

Dutton, Bertha P. 1976. *Navahos and Apaches: The Athabascan Peoples*. Englewood Cliffs, NJ: Prentice-Hall, Inc.

Eargle, Doland H., Jr. 1986. *The Earth Is Our Mother: A Guide to the Indians of California, Their Locales and Historic Sites*. San Francisco: Trees Company Press.

———. 1992. *California Indian Country: The Land and the People*. San Francisco: Trees Company Press.

Echo-Hawk, Roger C. 1992. Pawnee Mortuary Traditions. *American Indian Culture and Research Journal* 16(2):77–99.

Eggan, Fred. 1950. *Social Organization of the Western Pueblos*. Chicago: University of Chicago Press.

Ellingson, Ter. 2001. *The Myth of the Noble Savage*. Berkeley: University of California Press.

Emerson, Gloria J. 1983. Navajo Education. In: *Handbook of North American Indians, Vol. 10, Southwest*, Alfonso Ortiz, ed., pp. 659–671. Washington: Smithsonian Institution.

Everett, Diana. 1990. *The Texas Cherokee: A People Between Two Fires, 1819–1840*. Norman: University of Oklahoma Press.

Fagan, Brian M. 2000. *Ancient North America* (3rd ed.). New York: Thames and Hudson.

Farris, Glenn J. 1989. The Russian Imprint on the Colonization of California. In: *Columbian Consequences, Vol. 1, Archaeological and Historical Perspectives on the Spanish Borderlands West*, David H. Thomas, ed., pp. 481–497. Washington: Smithsonian Institution Press.

Feest, Joanna E., and Christian F. Feest. 1978. Ottawa. In: *Handbook of North American Indians, Vol. 15, Northeast*, Bruce Trigger, ed., pp. 772–786. Washington: Smithsonian Institution.

Feher-Elston, Catherine. 1988. *Children of the Sacred Ground*. Flagstaff: Northland Press.

Feit, Harvey A. 2000. The Cree of James Bay, Quebec, Canada. In: *Endangered Peoples of the Arctic: Struggles to Survive and Thrive*, Milton M. R. Freeman, ed., pp. 39–57. Westport, CT: Greenwood Press.

Fenton, William N. 1941. Masked Medicine Societies of the Iroquois. In: *Annual Report of the Smithsonian Institution for the Year 1940*, pp. 397–429. Washington: Government Printing Office.

———. 1978. Northern Iroquoian Culture Patterns. In: *Handbook of North American Indians, Vol. 15, Northeast*, Bruce Trigger, ed., pp. 296–321. Washington: Smithsonian Institution.

———. 1987. *The False Faces of the Iroquois*. Norman: University of Oklahoma Press.

———. 1998. *The Great Law and the Longhouse*. Norman: University of Oklahoma Press.

Fewkes, Jesse W. 1903. Hopi Katcinas. In: *Twenty-First Annual Report of the Bureau of American Ethnology*, pp. 15–190. Washington: Government Printing Office. Reprinted 1969. Glorieta, NM: Rio Grande Press.

Fiedel, Stuart J. 1999. Older Than We Thought: Implications of Corrected Dates for Paleoindians. *American Antiquity* 64(1):95–115.

Fienup-Riordan, Ann. 1988. Eye of the Dance: Spiritual Life of the Bering Sea Eskimo. In: *Crossroads of Continents: Cultures of Siberia and Alaska*, William W. Fitzhugh and Aron Crowell, eds., pp. 256–270. Washington: Smithsonian Institution Press.

———. 1990. *Eskimo Essays: Yup'ik Lives and How We See Them*. New Brunswick: Rutgers University Press.

Finger, John R. 1984. *The Eastern Band of Cherokees, 1819–1900*. Knoxville: University of Tennessee Press.

———. 1991. *Cherokee Americans: The Eastern Band of Cherokees in the Twentieth Century*. Lincoln: University of Nebraska Press.

Fisher, A. D. 1969. The Cree of Canada: Some Ecological and Evolutionary Considerations. *Western Canadian Journal of Anthropology* 1(1):7–19.

Fitting, James E. 1978. Regional Cultural Development, 300 B.C. to A.D. 1000. In: *Handbook of North American Indians, Vol. 15, Northeast*, Bruce Trigger, ed., pp. 44–57. Washington: Smithsonian Institution.

Fitzhugh, William W. 1985. Early Contacts North of Newfoundland Before A.D. 1600: A Review. In: *Cultures in Contact: The Impact of European Contacts on Native American Cultural Institutions A.D. 1000–1800*, William W. Fitzhugh, ed., pp. 23–43. Washington: Smithsonian Institution Press.

———. 1988. Comparative Art on the North Pacific Rim. In: *Crossroads of Continents: Cultures of Siberia and Alaska*, William W. Fitzhugh and Aron Crowell, eds., pp. 294–312. Washington: Smithsonian Institution Press.

Fitzhugh, William W. (ed.). 1985. *Cultures in Contact: The Impact of European Contacts on Native American Cultural Institutions A.D. 1000–1800*. Washington: Smithsonian Institution Press.

Fitzhugh, William W., and Aron Crowell (eds.). 1988. *Crossroads of Continents: Cultures of Siberia and Alaska*. Washington: Smithsonian Institution Press.

Fixico, Donald L. 2000. *The Urban Indian Experience in America*. Albuquerque: University of New Mexico Press.

Flaherty, Robert J. 1924. *My Eskimo Friends: "Nanook of the North."* New York: Doubleday, Page & Company.

Flannery, Regina. 1995. *Ellen Smallboy: Glimpses of a Cree Woman's Life.* Montreal: McGill-Queen's University Press.

Fogelson, Raymond D. 1978. *The Cherokees: A Critical Bibliography.* Bloomington: Indiana University Press.

Fontana, Bernard L. 1979. *Tarahumara: Where Night Is the Day of the Moon.* Flagstaff: Northland Press [includes many excellent photographs].

Ford, Clellan S. 1941. *Smoke From Their Fires: The Life of a Kwakiutl Chief.* New Haven: Yale University Press (reprinted by Shoe String Press, 1968).

Forde, C. Daryll. 1931. Hopi Agriculture and Land Ownership. *Journal of the Royal Anthropological Institute of Great Britain and Ireland* 61:357–405.

Forrest, Earle R. 1961. *The Snake Dance of the Hopi Indians.* Los Angeles: Westernlore Press.

Foster, Michael K. 1996. Language and the Culture History of North America. In: *Handbook of North American Indians, Vol. 17, Languages,* Ives Goddard, ed., pp. 64–110. Washington: Smithsonian Institution.

Fowler, Catherine S. 1978. Sarah Winnemucca, Northern Paiute, 1844–1891. In: *American Indian Intellectuals,* Margot Liberty, ed., pp. 32–42, 1976 Proceedings of the American Ethnological Society. St. Paul: West Publishing Co.

———. 1986. Subsistence. In: *Handbook of North American Indians, Vol. 11, Great Basin,* Warren L. d'Azevedo, ed., pp. 64–97. Washington: Smithsonian Institution.

———. 1990. *Tule Technology: Northern Paiute Uses of Marsh Resources in Western Nevada.* Washington: Smithsonian Folklife Studies No. 6.

Fowler, Catherine S., and Lawrence E. Dawson. 1986. Ethnographic Basketry. In: *Handbook of North American Indians, Vol. 11, Great Basin,* Warren L. d'Azevedo, ed., pp. 705–737. Washington: Smithsonian Institution.

Fowler, Catherine S., and Nancy P. Walter. 1985. Harvesting Pandora Moth Larvae with the Owens Valley Paiute. *Journal of California and Great Basin Anthropology* 7(2):155–165.

Fowler, Don D. 1986. History of Research. In: *Handbook of North American Indians, Vol. 11, Great Basin,* Warren L. d'Azevedo, ed., pp. 15–30. Washington: Smithsonian Institution.

Fowler, Don D., and David Koch. 1982. The Great Basin. In: *Reference Handbook on the Deserts of North America,* Gordon L. Bender, ed., pp. 7–63. Westport: Greenwood Press.

Fowler, Melvin L, and Robert L. Hall. 1978. Late Prehistory of the Illinois Area. In: *Handbook of North American Indians, Vol. 15, Northeast,* Bruce Trigger, ed., pp. 560–568. Washington: Smithsonian Institution.

Fox, Richard Allen, Jr. 1993. *Archaeology, History, and Custer's Last Battle.* Norman: University of Oklahoma Press.

Freeman, Milton M. R. (ed.). 2000. *Endangered Peoples of the Arctic: Struggles to Survive and Thrive,* Milton M. R. Freeman, ed. Westport, CT: Greenwood Press.

Freeman, Milton M. R., Lyudmila Bogoslovskaya, Richard A. Caulfield, Ingmar Egede, Igor I. Krupnik, and Marc G. Stevenson. 1998. *Inuit, Whaling, and Sustainability.* Walnut Creek, CA: AltaMira Press.

French, Laurence Armand. 1998. *The Qualla Cherokee Surviving in Two Worlds.* Lewiston, NY: The Edwin Mellen Press.

Fried, Jacob. 1969. The Tarahumara. In: *Handbook of Middle American Indians, Vol. 8, Part 2,* Evon Z. Vogt, ed., pp. 846–870. Austin: University of Texas Press.

Frigout, Arlette. 1979. Hopi Ceremonial Organization. In: *Handbook of North American Indians, Vol. 9, Southwest,* Alfonso Ortiz, ed., pp. 564–576. Washington: Smithsonian Institution.

Frison, George C. 1978. *Prehistoric Hunters of the High Plains.* New York: Academic Press.

Fulkerson, Mary Lee. 1995. *Weavers of Tradition and Beauty: Basketmakers of the Great Basin.* Reno: University of Nevada Press.

Funk, Robert E. 1978. Post-Pleistocene Adaptations. In: *Handbook of North American Indians, Vol. 15, Northeast,* Bruce Trigger, ed., pp. 16–27. Washington: Smithsonian Institution.

Furtaw, Julia C. (ed.). 1993. *Native Americans Information Directory.* Detroit: Gale Research Inc.

Gagné, Marie-Anik. 1994. *A Nation Within a Nation: Dependency and the Cree.* Montréal: Black Rose Books.

Galloway, Patricia (ed.). 1999. *The Hernando de Soto Expedition: History, Historiography, and "Discovery" in the Southeast.* Lincoln: University of Nebraska Press.

Galois, Robert. 1994. *Kwakw_ak_a'wakw Settlements, 1775–1920: A Geographical Analysis and Gazetteer.* Vancouver: University of British Columbia Press.

Garbarino, Merwyn S., and Robert F. Sasso. 1994. *Native American Heritage* (3rd ed.). Prospect Heights, IL: Waveland Press.

Gardner, James S. 1981. General Environment. In: *Handbook of North American Indians, Vol. 6, Subarctic,* June Helm, ed., pp. 5–14. Washington: Smithsonian Institution.

Gayton, Anna H. 1948. Yokuts and Western Mono Ethnography, I: Foothill Yokuts. *University of California Anthropological Records* 10(1).

Geronimo. 1970. *Geronimo: His Own Story.* New York: Dutton.

Gibbs, George. 1854. Indian Tribes of Washington Territory. In: *Report of Exploration of a Route for the Pacific Railroad from St. Paul to Puget Sound,* by G. McClellan, pp. 419–465. Washington: House Executive Document No. 129, Serial No. 736, 33rd Congress, 1st Session.

Gibson, Robert O. 1991. *The Chumash.* New York: Chelsea House Publishers.

Gidley, M. 1979. *With One Sky Above Us: Life on an Indian Reservation at the Turn of the Century.* New York: G. P. Putnam's Sons.

Giglio, Virginia. 1994. *Southern Cheyenne Women's Songs.* Norman: University of Oklahoma Press.

Gill, Sam D. 1983. Navajo Views of Their Origins. In: *Handbook of North American Indians, Vol. 10, Southwest,* Alfonso Ortiz, ed., pp. 502–505. Washington: Smithsonian Institution.

Gillespie, Beryl C. 1981. Major Fauna in the Traditional Economy. In: *Handbook of North American Indians, Vol.*

6, *Subarctic,* June Helm, ed., pp. 15–18. Washington: Smithsonian Institution.

Glassow, Michael A. 1996. *Purisimeño Chumash Prehistory: Maritime Adaptations along the Southern California Coast.* Fort Worth: Harcourt Brace.

Gleach, Frederic W. 1997. *Powhatan's World and Colonial Virginia: A Conflict of Cultures.* Lincoln: University of Nebraska Press.

Goddard, Ives. 1978. Delaware. In: *Handbook of North American Indians, Vol. 15, Northeast,* Bruce Trigger, ed., pp. 213–239. Washington: Smithsonian Institution.

———. 1996b. Introduction. In: *Handbook of North American Indians, Vol. 17, Languages,* Ives Goddard, ed., pp. 1–16. Washington: Smithsonian Institution.

———. 1996c. The Classification of Native Languages of North America. In: *Handbook of North American Indians, Vol. 17, Languages,* Ives Goddard, ed., pp. 290–323. Washington: Smithsonian Institution.

Goddard, Ives (ed.). 1996a. *Handbook of North American Indians, Vol. 17, Languages.* Washington: Smithsonian Institution.

Goddard, John. 1991. *Last Stand of the Lubicon Cree.* Vancouver: Douglas & McIntyre.

Graburn, Nelson H. H. 1976. Eskimo Art: The Eastern Canadian Arctic. In: *Ethnic and Tourist Arts: Cultural Expressions from the Fourth World,* Nelson H. H. Graburn, ed., pp. 39–55. Berkeley: University of California Press.

———. 1978. Commercial Eskimo Art: A Vehicle for Economic Development. *Inter-Nord* 15:131–142.

Grant, Campbell. 1978a. Chumash: Introduction. In: *Handbook of North American Indians, Vol. 8, California,* Robert F. Heizer, ed., pp. 505–508. Washington: Smithsonian Institution.

———. 1978b. Eastern Coastal Chumash. In: *Handbook of North American Indians, Vol. 8, California,* Robert F. Heizer, ed., pp. 509–519. Washington: Smithsonian Institution.

———. 1978c. Interior Chumash. In: *Handbook of North American Indians, Vol. 8, California,* Robert F. Heizer, ed., pp. 530–534. Washington: Smithsonian Institution.

———. 1978d. Island Chumash. In: *Handbook of North American Indians, Vol. 8, California,* Robert F. Heizer, ed., pp. 524–529. Washington: Smithsonian Institution.

Gray, John S. 1991. *Custer's Last Campaign: Mitch Boyer and the Little Bighorn Reconstructed.* Lincoln: University of Nebraska Press.

Gray, Sharon A. 1996. *Health of Native People of North America.* London: The Scarecrow Press, Inc.

Graymont, Barbara. 1988. *The Iroquois.* New York: Chelsea House Publishers.

Grayson, Donald. 1993. *The Desert's Past.* Washington: Smithsonian Institution Press.

Green, Rayna. 1975. "Pocahontas Perplex." *Massachusetts Review* 16(Autumn):698–714.

———. 1992. *Women in American Indian Society.* New York: Chelsea House Publishers.

Green, Rayna, and Melanie Fernandez. 1999. *The British Museum Encyclopedia of Native North America.* Bloomington: Indiana University Press.

Green, Thomas J., Bruce Cochran, Todd W. Fenton, James C. Woods, Gene L. Titmus, Larry Tieszen, Mary Anne Davis, and Susanne J. Miller. 1998. The Buhl Burial: A Paleoindian Woman from Southern Idaho. *American Antiquity* 63(3):437–456.

Greenwald, Emily. 2002. *Reconfiguring the Reservation: The Nez Perce, Jicarilla Apaches, and the Dawes Act.* Albuquerque: University of New Mexico Press.

Greenwood, Roberta S. 1978. Obispeño and Purisimeño Chumash. In: *Handbook of North American Indians, Vol. 8, California,* Robert F. Heizer, ed., pp. 520–523. Washington: Smithsonian Institution.

Griffin, James B. 1978. Late Prehistory of the Ohio Valley. In: *Handbook of North American Indians, Vol. 15, Northeast,* Bruce Trigger, ed., pp. 547–559. Washington: Smithsonian Institution.

Griffin-Pierce, Trudy. 1992. *Earth Is My Mother, Sky Is My Father: Space, Time, and Astronomy in Navajo Sandpainting.* Albuquerque: University of New Mexico Press.

———. 2000. *Native Peoples of the Southwest.* Albuquerque: University of New Mexico Press.

Griffith, James Seavey. 1983. Kachinas and Masking. In: *Handbook of North American Indians, Vol. 10, Southwest,* Alfonso Ortiz, ed., pp. 764–777. Washington: Smithsonian Institution.

Grinde, Donald A., and Bruce E. Johansen. 1995. *Ecocide of Native America: Environmental Destruction of Indian Lands and Peoples.* Santa Fe: Clear Light Publishers.

Grinnell, George B. 1889. *Pawnee Hero Stories and Folk-Tales, with Notes on the Origin, Customs and Character of the Pawnee People.* New York: The Forest and Stream Publishing Company (reprinted by the University of Nebraska Press, 1961).

———. 1915. *The Fighting Cheyennes.* New York: Scribner and Sons (reprinted by the University of Oklahoma Press, 1956).

———. 1923. The Cheyenne Indians: *Their History and Ways of Life* (2 vols.). New Haven: Yale University Press (reprinted by Cooper Square Publishers, 1962).

Guemple, Lee. 1995. Gender in Inuit Society. In: *Women and Power in Native North America,* Laura F. Klein and Lillian A. Ackerman, eds., pp. 17–27. Norman: University of Oklahoma Press.

Guest, Francis F., O. F. M. 1979. An Examination of the Thesis of S. F. Cook on the Forced Conversion of Indians in the California Missions. *Southern California Quarterly* 61(1):1–77.

———. 1983. Cultural Perspectives on California Mission Life. *Southern California Quarterly* 65(1):1–65.

Gumerman, George J., and Emil W. Haury. 1979. Prehistory: Hohokam. In: *Handbook of North American Indians, Vol. 9, Southwest,* Alfonzo Ortiz, ed., pp. 75–90. Washington: Smithsonian Institution.

Gutiérrez, Ramón A., and Richard J. Orsi (eds.). 1998. *Contested Eden: California Before the Gold Rush.* Berkeley: University of California Press.

Hack, John T. 1942. The Changing Physical Environment of the Hopi Indians of Arizona. *Papers of the Peabody Museum of American Archaeology and Ethnology* 35(1).

Haines, Francis. 1938. The Northward Spread of Horses Among the Plains Indians. *American Anthropologist* 40(3):429–437.

———. 1955. The Nez Percés: Tribesmen of the Columbia Plateau. Norman: University of Oklahoma Press.

Halpin, Marjorie M., and Margaret Seguin. 1990. Tsimshian Peoples: Southern Tsimshian, coast Tsimshian, Nishga, and Gitksan. In: *Handbook of North American Indians, Vol. 7, Northwest Coast,* Wayne Suttles, ed., pp. 267–284. Washington: Smithsonian Institution.

Harper, Kimball T. 1986. Historical Environments. In: *Handbook of North American Indians, Vol. 11, Great Basin,* Warren L. d'Azevedo, ed., pp. 51–63. Washington: Smithsonian Institution.

Harrington, John P. 1942. Culture Element Distributions: XIX, Central California Coast. *University of California Anthropological Records* 7(1).

Harrod, Howard L. 2000. *The Animals Came Dancing: Native American Sacred Ecology and Animal Kinship.* Tucson: University of Arizona Press.

Hauptman, Laurence M. 1986. *The Iroquois Struggle for Survival: World War II to Red Power.* Syracuse: Syracuse University Press.

———. 1995. *Between Two Fires: American Indians in the Civil War.* New York: The Free Press.

Hawkes, E. W. 1916. *The Labrador Eskimo.* Ottawa: Canada Department of Mines, Geological Survey Memoir 91, Anthropological Series 14.

Hawthorn, Audrey. 1967. *Art of the Kwakiutl Indians and Other Northwest Coast Tribes.* Seattle: University of Washington Press.

Hayden, Brian. 1997. *The Pithouses of Keatley Creek: Complex Hunter-Gatherers of the Northwestern Plateau.* Fort Worth: Harcourt Brace College Publishers.

Hays, H. R. 1975. *Children of the Raven.* New York: McGraw-Hill.

Heizer, Robert F. (ed.). 1978a. *Handbook of North American Indians, Vol. 8, California.* Washington: Smithsonian Institution.

Heizer, Robert F. 1978b. History of Research. In: *Handbook of North American Indians, Vol. 8, California,* Robert F. Heizer, ed., pp. 6–15. Washington: Smithsonian Institution.

Heizer, Robert F., and Theodora Kroeber (eds.). 1979. *Ishi, the Last Yahi: A Documentary History.* Berkeley: University of California Press.

Heizer, Robert F., and M. A. Whipple (eds.) 1971. *The California Indians: A Source Book.* Berkeley: University of California Press.

Helm, June (ed.). 1981. *Handbook of North American Indians, Vol. 6, Subarctic.* Washington: Smithsonian Institution.

Helm, June, and Eleanor B. Leacock. 1971. The Hunting Tribes of Subarctic Canada. In: *North American Indians in Historical Perspective,* Eleanor B. Leacock and Nancy O. Lurie, eds., pp. 343–374. New York: Random House.

Henderson, Eric, and Scott Russell. 1997. The Navajo Gaming Referendum: Reservations about Casinos Lead to Popular Rejection of Legalized Gambling. *Human Organization* 56(3):294–301.

Herrick, James W. 1995. *Iroquois Medical Botany.* Syracuse: Syracuse University Press.

Hessel, Ingo. 1998. *Inuit Art: An Introduction.* New York: Harry N. Abrams.

Hewes, Gordon W. 1998. Fishing. In: *Handbook of North American Indians, Vol. 12, Plateau,* Deward E. Walker, Jr., ed., pp. 620–640. Washington: Smithsonian Institution.

Hieb, Louis A. 1979. Hopi World View. In: *Handbook of North American Indians, Vol. 9, Southwest,* Alfonso Ortiz, ed., pp. 577–580. Washington: Smithsonian Institution.

Hinton, Leanne. 1994. *Flutes of Fire: Essays on California Indian Languages.* Berkeley: Heyday Books.

Hirschfelder, Arlene, and Martha Kreipe de Montaño. 1993. *The Native American Almanac: A Portrait of Native America Today.* New York: Macmillan.

Hodge, Frederick W. 1907–1910. *Handbook of American Indians North of Mexico* (2 vols.). Bureau of American Ethnology Bulletin 30.

Hodge, William H. 1981. *The First Americans: Then and Now.* New York: Holt, Rinehart and Winston.

Hoebel, E. Adamson. 1960. *The Cheyennes: Indians of the Great Plains.* New York: Holt, Rinehart and Winston.

Hoig, Stan. 1989. *The Cheyenne.* New York: Chelsea House Publishers.

———. 1992. *People of the Sacred Arrows: The Southern Cheyenne Today.* Dutton, NY: Cobblehill Books.

Holm, Bill. 1990. Kwakiutl: Winter Ceremonies. In: *Handbook of North American Indians, Vol. 7, Northwest Coast,* Wayne Suttles, ed., pp. 378–386. Washington: Smithsonian Institution.

Holmes, Marie S., and John R. Johnson. 1998. *The Chumash and Their Predecessors: An Annotated Bibliography.* Santa Barbara Museum of Natural History, Contributions in Anthropology No. 1.

Honigmann, John J. 1981a. Expressive Aspects of Subarctic Indian Culture. In: *Handbook of North American Indians, Vol. 6, Subarctic,* June Helm, ed., pp. 718–738. Washington: Smithsonian Institution.

———. 1981b. Modern Subarctic Indians and Métis. In: *Handbook of North American Indians, Vol. 6, Subarctic,* June Helm, ed., pp. 712–717. Washington: Smithsonian Institution.

———. 1981c. West Main Cree. In: *Handbook of North American Indians, Vol. 6, Subarctic,* June Helm, ed., pp. 217–230. Washington: Smithsonian Institution.

Hopkins, Sarah Winnemucca. 1883. *Life Among the Piutes: Their Wrongs and Claims.* Boston: Cupples, Upham & Co. Reprinted 1969. Bishop, CA: Chalfant Press.

Horsman, Reginald. 1967. *Expansion and American Indian Policy 1783–1812.* East Lansing: Michigan State University Press.

Hosley, Edward H. 1981. Environment and Culture in the Alaska Plateau. In: *Handbook of North American Indians, Vol. 6, Subarctic,* June Helm, ed., pp. 533–545. Washington: Smithsonian Institution.

Howard, Helen A., and Dan L. McGrath. 1941. *War Chief Joseph.* Caldwell, ID: Caxton Printers (reprinted by the University of Nebraska Press, 1964).

Hoxie, Frederick E. (ed.). 1996. *Encyclopedia of North American Indians.* Boston: Houghton Mifflin.

Hrdlička, Aleš. 1945. *The Aleutian and Commander Islands and Their Inhabitants.* Philadelphia: The Wistar Institute of Anatomy and Biology.

Huckell, Bruce B. 1996. The Archaic Prehistory of the North American Southwest. *Journal of World Prehistory* 10(3):305–373.

Hu-DeHart, Evelyn. 1984. *Yaqui Resistance and Survival: The Struggle for Land and Autonomy, 1821–1910.* Madison: University of Wisconsin Press.

Hudson, Charles. 1976. *The Southeastern Indians.* Knoxville: University of Tennessee Press.

———. 1994. The Hernando de Soto Expedition, 1539–1543. In: *The Forgotten Centuries: Indians and Europeans in the American South, 1521–1704,* Charles Hudson and Carmen Chaves Tesser, eds., pp. 74–103. Athens: University of Georgia Press.

———. 1997. *Knights of Spain, Warriors of the Sun: Hernando de Soto and the South's Ancient Chiefdoms.* Athens: University of Georgia Press.

Hudson, Travis, and Thomas C. Blackburn. 1982. *The Material Culture of the Chumash Interaction Sphere: Vol. 1: Food Procurement and Transportation.* Los Altos: Ballena Press Anthropological Paper No. 25.

———. 1983. *The Material Culture of the Chumash Interaction Sphere: Vol. 2: Food Preparation and Shelter.* Los Altos: Ballena Press Anthropological Paper No. 27.

———. 1985. *The Material Culture of the Chumash Interaction Sphere: Vol. 3: Clothing, Ornamentation, and Grooming.* Menlo Park: Ballena Press Anthropological Paper No. 28.

———. 1986. *The Material Culture of the Chumash Interaction Sphere: Vol. 4: Ceremonial Paraphernalia, Games, and Amusements.* Menlo Park: Ballena Press Anthropological Paper No. 30.

———. 1987. *The Material Culture of the Chumash Interaction Sphere: Vol. 5: Manufacturing Processes, Metrology, and Trade.* Menlo Park: Ballena Press Anthropological Paper No. 31.

Hughes, Charles C. 1984. History of Ethnography After 1945. In: *Handbook of North American Indians, Vol. 5, Arctic,* David Damas, ed., pp. 23–26. Washington: Smithsonian Institution.

Hultkrantz, Åke. 1986. Mythology and Religious Concepts. In: *Handbook of North American Indians, Vol. 11, Great Basin,* Warren L. d'Azevedo, ed., pp. 630–640. Washington: Smithsonian Institution.

Hunn, Eugene S. 1990a. The Plateau Culture Area. In: *Native North Americans: An Ethnohistoric Approach,* Daniel L. Boxberger, ed., pp. 361–385. Dubuque, IA: Kendall Hunt Publishing Company.

———. 1990b. *Nch'i-Wána: "The Big River": Mid-Columbia Indians and Their Land.* Seattle: University of Washington Press.

Hunn, Eugene S., Nancy J. Turner, and David H. French. 1998. Ethnobiology and Subsistence. In: *Handbook of North American Indians, Vol. 12, Plateau,* Deward E. Walker, Jr., ed., pp. 525–545. Washington: Smithsonian Institution.

Hurtado, Albert L. 1988. *Indian Survival on the California Frontier.* New Haven: Yale University Press.

Hyde, George E. 1951. *The Pawnee Indians.* Denver: University of Denver Press. Reprinted 1974 and 1988. Civilization of the American Indian Series, Vol. 128. Norman: University of Oklahoma Press.

———. 1959. *Indians of the High Plains.* Norman: University of Oklahoma Press.

Ingstad, Helge, and Anne Stein Ingstad. 2001. *The Viking Discovery of America: The Excavation of a Norse Settlement in L'Anse aux Meadows, Newfoundland.* New York: Checkmark Books.

Inverarity, Robert B. 1967. *Art of the Northwest Coast Indians.* Berkeley: University of California Press.

Iverson, Peter. 1981. *The Navajo Nation.* Albuquerque: University of New Mexico Press.

———. 1983. The Emerging Navajo Nation. In: *Handbook of North American Indians, Vol. 10, Southwest,* Alfonso Ortiz, ed., pp. 636–640. Washington: Smithsonian Institution.

———. 1990. *The Navajos.* New York: Chelsea House Publishers.

———. 1998. *"We Are Still Here": American Indians in the Twentieth Century.* Wheeling, IL: Harlan Davidson, Inc.

Iverson, Peter (ed.). 1985. *The Plains Indians of the Twentieth Century.* Norman: University of Oklahoma Press.

Jacknis, Ira. 1991. Northwest Coast Indian Culture and the World's Columbian Exposition. In: *Columbian Consequences, Vol. 3, The Spanish Borderlands in Pan-American Perspective,* David H. Thomas, ed., pp. 91–118. Washington: Smithsonian Institution Press.

Jackson, Curtis E., and Marcia J. Galli. 1977. *A History of the Bureau of Indian Affairs and Its Activities Among Indians.* San Francisco: R & E Research Associates.

Jackson, Robert H. 1994. *Indian Population Decline: The Missions of Northwestern New Spain, 1687–1840.* Albuquerque: University of New Mexico Press.

———. 2000. *From Savages to Subjects: Missions in the History of the American Southwest.* Armonk, NY: M. E. Sharpe.

Jackson, Robert H., and Edward Castillo. 1995. *Indians, Franciscans, and Spanish Colonization: The Impact of the Mission System on California Indians.* Albuquerque: University of New Mexico Press.

Jacobs, Sue-Ellen, Wesley Thomas, and Sabine Lang (eds.). 1997. *Two-Spirit People: Native American Gender Identity, Sexuality, and Spirituality.* Urbana: University of Illinois Press.

Jaeger, E. C. 1965. *The California Deserts.* Stanford: Stanford University Press.

James, Harry C. 1974. *Pages from Hopi History.* Tucson: University of Arizona Press.

Jennings, Francis. 1993. *The Founders of America.* New York: W. W. Norton & Company.

Jennings, Jesse D. 1989. *Prehistory of North America.* Mountain View, CA: Mayfield.

Jochelson, Waldemar. 1933. *History, Ethnology and Anthropology of the Aleut.* Washington: Carnegie Institution of Washington, Publication No. 432.

Johnson, Edward C. 1986. Issues: The Indian Perspective. In: *Handbook of North American Indians, Vol. 11, Great Basin,* Warren L. d'Azevedo, ed., pp. 592–600. Washington: Smithsonian Institution.

Johnson, John R. 1988. Chumash Social Organization: An Ethnohistoric Perspective. Ph.D. dissertation, University of California, Santa Barbara.

———. 1989. The Chumash and the Missions. In: *Columbian Consequences, Vol. 1, Archaeological and Historical Perspectives on the Spanish Borderlands West,* David H. Thomas, ed., pp. 365–375. Washington: Smithsonian Institution Press.

———. 1993. The Chumash Indians After Secularization. In: *The Spanish Mission Heritage of the United States,*

Howard Benoist and Sr. María Carolina Flores, C. P., eds., pp. 143–164. Washington: National Park Service.

Johnson, Troy R. (ed.) 1999. *Contemporary Native American Political Issues.* Walnut Creek, CA: AltaMira Press.

Johnson, Troy R., Joane Nagel, and Duane Champagne (eds.). 1997. *American Indian Activism: Alcatraz to the Longest Walk.* Urbana: University of Illinois Press.

Jonaitis, Aldona (ed.). 1991. *Chiefly Feasts: The Enduring Kwakiutl Potlatch.* New York: American Museum of Natural History.

Jones, Dorothy. 1976. *Aleuts in Transition: A Comparison of Two Villages.* Seattle: University of Washington Press.

———. 1980. *A Century of Servitude: Pribilof Aleuts Under U.S. Rule.* Washington, D.C.: University Press of America.

Jorgensen, Joseph G. 1986. Ghost Dance, Bear Dance, and Sun Dance. In: *Handbook of North American Indians, Vol. 11, Great Basin,* Warren L. d'Azevedo, ed., pp. 660–672. Washington: Smithsonian Institution.

Josephy, Alvin M. 1965. *The Nez Perce Indians and the Opening of the Northwest.* New Haven: Yale University Press.

Judd, Neil M. 1967. *The Bureau of American Ethnology: A Partial History.* Norman: University of Oklahoma Press.

Kammer, Jerry. 1980. *The Second Long Walk: The Navajo–Hopi Land Dispute.* Albuquerque: University of New Mexico Press.

Katz, William Loren. 1997. *Black Indians: A Hidden Heritage.* New York: Aladdin Paperbacks.

Kaufman, Alice, and Christopher Selser. 1985. *The Navajo Weaving Tradition: 1650 to the Present.* New York: E. P. Dutton, Inc.

Kehoe, Alice B. 1989. *The Ghost Dance: Ethnohistory and Revitalization.* New York: Holt, Rinehart and Winston.

———. 1992. *North American Indians: A Comprehensive Account.* Englewood Cliffs, NJ: Prentice-Hall.

———. 1995. Blackfoot Persons. In: *Women and Power in Native North America,* Laura F. Klein and Lillian A. Ackerman, eds., pp. 113–125. Norman: University of Oklahoma Press.

Kelly, Lawrence C. 1990. *Federal Indian Policy.* New York: Chelsea House Publishers.

Kelly, Robert L. 1997. Late Holocene Great Basin Prehistory. *Journal of World Prehistory* 11(1):1–49.

Kennard, Edward A. 1979. Hopi Economy and Subsistence. In: *Handbook of North American Indians, Vol. 9, Southwest,* Alfonso Ortiz, ed., pp. 554–563. Washington: Smithsonian Institution.

Kennedy, John G. 1978. *Tarahumara of the Sierra Madre: Beer, Ecology, and Social Organization.* Arlington Heights, IL: AHM Publishing Corporation.

———. 1990. *The Tarahumara.* New York: Chelsea House Publishers.

Kessell, John L. 1979. *Kiva, Cross, and Crown: The Pecos Indians and New Mexico.* Washington: National Park Service.

King, Chester D. 1990. *Evolution of Chumash Society: A Comparative Study of Artifacts Used for Social System Maintenance in the Santa Barbara Channel Region Before A.D. 1804.* New York: Garland.

King, J. C. H. 1999. *First Peoples, First Contact: Native Peoples of North America.* Cambridge: Harvard University Press.

Kinkade, M. Dale, William W. Elmendorf, Bruce Rigsby, and Haruo Aoki. 1998. Languages. In: *Handbook of North American Indians, Vol. 12, Plateau,* Deward E. Walker, Jr., ed., pp. 49–72. Washington: Smithsonian Institution.

Kirk, Ruth. 1986. *Tradition & Change on the Northwest Coast.* Seattle: University of Washington Press.

Klein, Barry. 2000. *Reference Encyclopedia of the American Indian* (9th ed.). West Nyack, NY: Todd Publications.

Klein, Laura F. 1995. Mother as Clanwoman: Rank and Gender in Tlingit Society. In: *Women and Power in Native North America,* Laura F. Klein and Lillian A. Ackerman, eds., pp. 28–45. Norman: University of Oklahoma Press.

Klein, Laura F., and Lillian A. Ackerman (eds.). 1995. *Women and Power in Native North America.* Norman: University of Oklahoma Press.

Kluckhohn, Clyde. 1944. Navaho Witchcraft. *Papers of the Peabody Museum of American Archaeology and Ethnology* 22(2). Reprinted 1967. Boston: Beacon Press.

Kluckhohn, Clyde, and Dorothea Leighton. 1946. *The Navaho.* Cambridge: Harvard University Press (a revised edition was published in 1974).

Knack, Martha C. 1986. Indian Economies, 1950–1980. In: *Handbook of North American Indians, Vol. 11, Great Basin,* Warren L. d'Azevedo, ed., pp. 573–591. Washington: Smithsonian Institution.

———. 1995. The Dynamics of Southern Paiute Women's Roles. In: *Women and Power in Native North America,* Laura F. Klein and Lillian A. Ackerman, eds., pp. 146–158. Norman: University of Oklahoma Press.

Knack, Martha, and Omer C. Stewart. 1984. *As Long as the River Shall Run: An Ethnohistory of Pyramid Lake Indian Reservation.* Berkeley: University of California Press.

Knaut, Andrew L. 1995. *The Pueblo Revolt of 1680: Conquest and Resistance in Seventeenth-Century New Mexico.* Norman: University of Oklahoma Press.

Knowles, Nathaniel. 1940. The Torture of Captives by the Indians of Eastern North America. *Proceedings of the American Philosophical Society* 82(2):151–225.

Krauss, Michael E. 1988. Many Tongues—Ancient Tales. In: *Crossroads of Continents: Cultures of Siberia and Alaska,* William W. Fitzhugh and Aron Crowell, eds., pp. 145–150. Washington: Smithsonian Institution Press.

Krauss, Michael E., and Victor K. Golla. 1981. Northern Athapaskan Languages. In: *Handbook of North American Indians, Vol. 6, Subarctic,* June Helm, ed., pp. 67–85. Washington: Smithsonian Institution.

Krech, Shepard (ed.). 1981. *Indians, Animals, and the Fur Trade.* Athens: University of Georgia Press.

———. 1984. *The Subarctic Fur Trade: Native Social and Economic Adaptations.* Vancouver: University of British Columbia Press.

———. 1999. *The Ecological Indian: Myth and History.* New York: W. W. Norton & Company.

Kroeber, Alfred L. 1925. *Handbook of the Indians of California.* Bureau of American Ethnology Bulletin 78.

Kroeber, Theodora 1971. *Ishi in Two Worlds.* Berkeley: University of California Press.

Kubler, George. 1940. *The Religious Architecture of New Mexico in the Colonial Period and Since the American Occupation*. Colorado Springs, CO: The Taylor Museum.

Kupferer, Harriet J. 1988. *Ancient Drums, Other Moccasins: Native North American Cultural Adaptation*. Englewood Cliffs, NJ: Prentice-Hall.

Lacerenza, Deborah. 1988. An Historical Overview of the Navajo Relocation. *Cultural Survival Quarterly* 12(3):3–6.

Lacey, Theresa Jensen. 1996. *The Pawnee*. New York: Chelsea House Publishers.

Lahren, Sylvester L., Jr. 1998. Reservations and Reserves. In: *Handbook of North American Indians, Vol. 12, Plateau*, Deward E. Walker, Jr., ed., pp. 484–498. Washington: Smithsonian Institution.

Laird, W. David. 1977. *Hopi Bibliography*. Tucson: University of Arizona Press.

Lamphere, Louise. 1989. Historical and Regional Variability in Navajo Women's Roles. *Journal of Anthropological Research* 45(4):431–456.

Landberg, Lief C. W. 1965. *The Chumash of Southern California*. Los Angeles: Southwest Museum Papers No. 19.

Landsman, Gail H. 1988. *Sovereignty and Symbol: Indian-White Conflict at Ganienkeh*. Albuquerque: University of New Mexico Press.

Lang, Sabine. 1998. *Men as Women, Women as Men: Changing Gender in Native American Cultures*. Austin: University of Texas Press.

Laniel-le-François, M. E. 1989. The Evolution of Hopi Kachina Doll Sculpture. *European Review of Native American Studies* 3(1):11–12.

Lantis, Margaret. 1984. Aleut. In: *Handbook of North American Indians, Vol. 5, Arctic*, David Damas, ed., pp. 161–184. Washington: Smithsonian Institution.

Larsen, Clark Spencer, Mark C. Griffin, Dale L. Huchinson, Vivian E. Nobel, Lynette Noor, Robert F. Pastor, Christopher B. Ruff, Katherine F. Russell, Margaret J. Schoeninger, Michael Schultz, Scott W. Simpson, and Mark F. Teaford. 2001. Frontiers of Contact: Bioarchaeology of Spanish Florida. *Journal of World Prehistory* 15(1):69–123.

Larsen, Clark Spencer, and George R. Milner (eds.). 1994. *In the Wake of Contact: Biological Responses to Conquest*. New York: Wiley-Liss.

Larsen, Clark Spencer, Christopher B. Ruff, Margaret J. Schoeninger, and Dale L. Hutchinson. 1992. Population Decline and Extinction in La Florida. In: *Disease and Demography in the Americas*, John W. Verano and Douglas H. Ubelaker, eds., pp. 25–39. Washington: Smithsonian Institution Press.

Larson, Daniel O., John R. Johnson, and Joel C. Michaelsen. 1994. Missionization Among the Coastal Chumash of Central California: A Study of Risk Minimization Strategies. *American Anthropologist* 96(2):263–299.

Latta, Frank F. 1977. *Handbook of Yokuts Indians*. Santa Cruz: Bear State Books.

Laughlin, William S. 1980. *Aleuts: Survivors of the Bering Land Bridge*. New York: Holt, Rinehart and Winston.

La Vere, David. 1998. *The Caddo Chiefdoms: Caddo Economics and Politics, 700–1835*. Lincoln: University of Nebraska Press.

Lawton, Harry W., Philip J. Wilke, Mary DeDecker, and William M. Mason. 1976. Agriculture Among the Paiute of Owens Valley. *The Journal of California Anthropology* 3(1):13–50.

Layton, Thomas N. 1981. Traders and Raiders: Aspects of Trans-Basin and California-Plateau Commerce, 1800–1830. *Journal of California and Great Basin Anthropology* 3(1):127–137.

Leacock, Eleanor B., and Nancy O. Lurie (eds.). 1971. *North American Indians in Historical Perspective*. New York: Random House.

Lee, Gaylen D. 1998. *Walking Where We Lived: Memoirs of a Mono Indian Family*. Norman: University of Oklahoma Press.

Leighton, Anna L. 1985. *Wild Plant Use by the Woods Cree (Nihithawak) of East-Central Saskatchewan*. National Museum of Canada, Canadian Ethnology Service, Paper No. 101.

Leland, Joy. 1986. Population. In: *Handbook of North American Indians, Vol. 11, Great Basin*, Warren L. d'Azevedo, ed., pp. 608–619. Washington: Smithsonian Institution.

Leroux, Odette, Marion E. Jackson, and Minnie A. Freeman (eds.). 1996. *Inuit Women Artists: Voices from Cape Dorset*. San Francisco: Chronicle Books.

Lesser, Alexander. 1933. *The Pawnee Ghost Dance Hand Game: A Study of Cultural Change*. Columbia University Contributions to Anthropology Volume 16 (reprinted by AMS Press, 1969).

Liberty, Margot. 1980. The Sun Dance. In: *Anthropology on the Great Plains*, W. Raymond Wood and Margot Liberty, eds., pp. 164–178. Lincoln: University of Nebraska Press.

Lieder, Michael, and Jake Page. 1997. *Wild Justice: The People of Geronimo vs. the United States*. New York: Random House.

Lightfoot, Kent G., and William S. Simmons. 1998. Culture Contact in Protohistoric California: Social Contexts of Native and European Encounters. *Journal of California and Great Basin Anthropology* 20(2):138–170

Liljeblad, Sven, and Catherine S. Fowler. 1986. Owens Valley Paiute. In: *Handbook of North American Indians, Vol. 11, Great Basin*, Warren L. d'Azevedo, ed., pp. 412–434. Washington: Smithsonian Institution.

Little Coyote, Bertha, and Virginia Giglo. 1997. *Leaving Everything Behind: The Songs and Memories of a Cheyenne Woman*. Norman: University of Oklahoma Press.

Llewellyn, K. N., and E. Adamson Hoebel. 1941. *The Cheyenne Way: Conflict and Case Law in Primitive Jurisprudence*. Norman: University of Oklahoma Press.

Lohse, E. S., and Roderick Sprague. 1998. History of Research. In: *Handbook of North American Indians, Vol. 12, Plateau*, Deward E. Walker, Jr., ed., pp. 8–28. Washington: Smithsonian Institution.

Lohse, E. S., and Frances Sundt. 1990. History of Research: Museum Collections. In: *Handbook of North American Indians, Vol. 7, Northwest Coast*, Wayne Suttles, ed., pp. 88–97. Washington: Smithsonian Institution.

Lorenz, Karl G. 2000. The Natchez of Southwest Mississippi. In: *Indians of the Greater Southeast: Historical Archaeology and Ethnohistory*, Bonnie G. McEwan, ed., pp. 142–177. Gainesville: University Press of Florida.

Lowenstein, Tom. 1993. *Ancient Land, Sacred Whale: The Inuit Hunt and Its Rituals*. New York: Farrar, Straus and Giroux.

Lowie, Robert H. 1935. *The Crow Indians*. New York: Holt, Rinehart and Winston.

———. 1954. *Indians of the Plains*. New York: McGraw-Hill.

Lumholtz, Carl. 1902. *Unknown Mexico* (2 vols.). New York: Charles Scribner's Sons. Reprinted 1973. Glorieta, NM: Rio Grande Press.

Mackie, Richard S. 1997. *Trading Beyond the Mountains*. Vancouver: UBC Press.

MacLeod, William C. 1924. Natchez Political Evolution. *American Anthropologist* 26(2):201–229.

Madden, Ryan. 1992. The Forgotten People: The Relocation and Interment of Aleuts During World War II. *American Indian Culture and Research Journal* 16(4):55–76.

Madsen, David B., and David Rhode (eds.). 1994. *Across the West: Human Population Movement and the Expansion of the Numa*. Salt Lake City: University of Utah Press.

Madsen, David B., and Steven R. Simms. 1998. The Fremont Complex: A Behavioral Perspective. *Journal of World Prehistory* 12(3):255–336.

Mails, Thomas E. 1992. *The Cherokee People: The Story of the Cherokees from Earliest Origins to Contemporary Times*. Tulsa: Council Oak Books.

Malinowski, Sharon, and Anna Sheets (eds.). 1998. *The Gale Encyclopedia of Native American Tribes* (4 vols.). Detroit: Gale Research.

Malone, Henry T. 1956. *Cherokees of the Old South: A People in Transition*. Athens: University of Georgia Press.

Malouf, Carling I., and John Findlay. 1986. Euro-American Impact Before 1870. In: *Handbook of North American Indians, Vol. 11, Great Basin*, Warren L. d'Azevedo, ed., pp. 499–516. Washington: Smithsonian Institution.

Maltz, Daniel, and JoAllyn Archambault. 1995. Gender and Power in Native North America: Concluding Remarks. In: *Women and Power in Native North America*, Laura F. Klein and Lillian A. Ackerman, eds., pp. 230–249. Norman: University of Oklahoma Press.

Mancall, Peter C., and James H. Merrell (eds.). 2000. *American Encounters: Natives and Newcomers from European Contact to Indian Removal, 1500–1850*. New York: Routledge.

Mandelbaum, David. 1940. *The Plains Cree*. New York: American Museum of Natural History Anthropological Papers 37(2).

Mankiller, Wilma, and Michael Wallis. 1993. *Mankiller: A Chief and Her People*. New York: St. Martin's Press.

Marriott, Alice Lee. 1977. *Dance Around the Sun: The Life of Mary Little Bear Inkanish, Cheyenne*. New York: Ty Crowell Co.

Marsden, Michael T., and Jack G. Nachbar. 1988. The Indian in the Movies. In: *Handbook of North American Indians, Vol. 4, History of Indian-White Relations*, Wilcomb E. Washburn, ed., pp. 607–616. Washington: Smithsonian Institution.

Marshall, Yvonne. 1998. By Way of Introduction from the Pacific Northwest Coast. *World Archaeology* 29(3):311–316.

Martijn, Charles A. 1964. Canadian Eskimo Carving in Historical Perspective. *Anthropos* 59(3–4):546–596.

Martin, Glen. 1996. Keepers of the Oaks. *Discover Magazine*, August:44–50.

Martin, Paul S. 1979. Prehistory: Mogollon. In: *Handbook of North American Indians, Vol. 9, Southwest*, Alfonzo Ortiz, ed., pp. 61–74. Washington: Smithsonian Institution.

Mason, Otis. 1894. Technogeography, or the Relation of the Earth to the Industries of Mankind. *American Anthropologist* 7(2):137–161.

Mason, Ronald J. 1981. *Great Lakes Archaeology*. New York: Academic Press.

Massey, William C. 1966. Archaeology and Ethnohistory of Lower California. In: *Handbook of Middle American Indians, Vol. 4, Archaeological Frontiers and External Connections*, Gordon F. Ekholm and Gordon R. Willey, eds., pp. 38–58. Austin: University of Texas Press.

Mathes, W. Michael. 1989. Baja California: A Special Area of Contact and Colonization, 1535–1697. In: *Columbian Consequences, Vol. 1, Archaeological and Historical Perspectives on the Spanish Borderlands West*, David H. Thomas, ed., pp. 407–422. Washington: Smithsonian Institution Press.

Matson, R. G., and Gary Coupland. 1995. *The Prehistory of the Northwest Coast*. New York: Academic Press.

Maxwell, Moreau S. 1985. *Prehistory of the Eastern Arctic*. Orlando: Academic Press.

May, Philip A. 1999. The Epidemiology of Alcohol Abuse Among American Indians: The Mythical and Real Properties. In: *Contemporary Native American Cultural Issues*, Duane Champagne, ed., pp. 227–244. Walnut Creek, CA: AltaMira Press.

McAllester, David P., and Douglas F. Mitchell. 1983. Navajo Music. In: *Handbook of North American Indians, Vol. 10, Southwest*, Alfonso Ortiz, ed., pp. 605–623. Washington: Smithsonian Institution.

McClellan, Catharine. 1981. History of Research in the Subarctic Cordillera. In: *Handbook of North American Indians, Vol. 6, Subarctic*, June Helm, ed., pp. 35–42. Washington: Smithsonian Institution.

McClellan, Catharine, and Glenda Denniston. 1981. Environment and Culture in the Cordillera. In: *Handbook of North American Indians, Vol. 6, Subarctic*, June Helm, ed., pp. 372–386. Washington: Smithsonian Institution.

McClurken, James M. 1986. Ottawa. In: *People of the Three Fires: The Ottawa, Potawatomi, and Ojibway of Michigan*, by James A. Clifton, George L. Cornell, and James M. McClurken, pp. 1–38. Grand Rapids: The Michigan Indian Press, Grand Rapids Inter-Tribal Council.

McCulloch, Merline. 1994. The Politics of Indian Gaming: Tribe/State Relations and American Federalism. *Publius* 24(3):99–112.

McCutcheon, Sean. 1991. *Electric Rivers: The Story of the James Bay Project*. Montreal: Black Rose Books.

McEwan, Bonnie G. (ed.). 2000. *Indians of the Greater Southeast: Historical Archaeology and Ethnohistory*. Gainesville: University Press of Florida.

McFeat, Tom (ed.). 1966. *Indians of the North Pacific Coast*. Toronto: McClelland and Stewart.

McGhee, Robert. 1984. Contact Between Native North Americans and the Medieval Norse: A Review of the Evidence. *American Antiquity* 49(1):4–26.

———. 1996. *Ancient People of the Arctic.* Vancouver: University of British Columbia Press.

McGuire, Randall H., and Michael B. Schiffer (eds.). 1982. *Hohokam and Patayan: Prehistory of Southwestern Arizona.* New York: Academic Press.

McLoughlin, William G. 1993. After the Trail of Tears: *The Cherokee's Struggle for Sovereignty, 1839–1880.* Chapel Hill: University of North Carolina Press.

McNeill, William H. 1976. *Plagues and Peoples.* New York: Anchor Press.

McWhorter, Lucullus V. 1952. *Hear Me, My Chiefs! Nez Perce History and Legend.* Caldwell, ID: Caxton Printers, Ltd.

———. 1983. *Yellow Wolf: His Own Story.* Caldwell, ID: Caxton Printers, Ltd. (the 1983 version is a revised and enlarged edition of the 1940 original).

Mehringer, Peter J., Jr. 1986. Prehistoric Environments. In: *Handbook of North American Indians, Vol. 11, Great Basin,* Warren L. d'Azevedo, ed., pp. 31–50. Washington: Smithsonian Institution.

Mehringer, Peter J., Jr., and F. F. Foit, Jr. 1990. Volcanic Ash Dating of the Clovis Cache at East Wenatchee, Washington. *National Geographic Research* 6:495–503.

Meltzer, David J. 1988. Late Pleistocene Human Adaptations in Eastern North America. *Journal of World Prehistory* 2(1):1–52.

Merrill, William L. 1983. Tarahumara Social Organization, Political Organization, and Religion. In: *Handbook of North American Indians, Vol. 10, Southwest,* Alfonso Ortiz, ed., pp. 290–305. Washington: Smithsonian Institution.

———. 1988. *Rarámuri Souls: Knowledge and Social Process in Northern Mexico.* Washington: Smithsonian Institution Press.

Meyer, Carter Jones, and Diana Royer (eds.). 2001. *Selling the Indian: Commercializing and Appropriating American Indian Cultures.* Tucson: University of Arizona Press.

Michelson, T. 1932. *The Narrative of a Southern Cheyenne Woman.* Washington: Smithsonian Miscellaneous Collections 87(5).

Michno, Gregory F. 1997. *Lakota Noon: The Indian Narrative of Custer's Defeat.* Missoula, MT: Mountain Press Publishing Company.

Mihesuah, Devon A. 1999. American Indian Identities: Issues of Individual Choices and Development. In: *Contemporary Native American Cultural Issues,* Duane Champagne, ed., pp. 13–38. Walnut Creek, CA: AltaMira Press.

Mihesuah, Devon A. (ed.). 2000. *Repatriation Reader: Who Owns American Indian Remains?* Lincoln: University of Nebraska Press.

Milanich, Jerald T. 1994. Franciscan Missions and Native Peoples in Spanish Florida. In: *The Forgotten Centuries: Indians and Europeans in the American South, 1521–1704,* Charles Hudson and Carmen Chaves Tesser, eds., pp. 276–303. Athens: University of Georgia Press.

Miller, Wick R. 1986. Numic Languages. In: *Handbook of North American Indians, Vol. 11, Great Basin,* Warren L. d'Azevedo, ed., pp. 98–106. Washington: Smithsonian Institution.

Milner, George R. 1998. *The Cahokia Chiefdom: The Archaeology of a Mississippian Society.* Washington: Smithsonian Institution Press.

Mooney, James. 1900. *Myths of the Cherokee.* Washington: Nineteenth Annual Report of the Bureau of American Ethnology, Part 1:3–548.

———. 1907. The Cheyenne Indians. *Memoirs of the American Anthropological Association* 1(6).

Moore, John H. 1987. *The Cheyenne Nation: A Social and Demographic History.* Lincoln: University of Nebraska Press.

———. 1996. *The Cheyenne.* Cambridge, MA: Blackwell Publishers.

Moore, John H., Margot P. Liberty, and A. Terry Straus. 2001. Cheyenne. In: *Handbook of North American Indians, Vol. 13, Plains,* Raymond J. DeMallie, ed., pp. 863–885. Washington: Smithsonian Institution.

Moratto, Michael J. 1984. *California Archaeology.* Orlando: Academic Press.

Morgan, Lewis H. 1851. *League of the Ho-dé-no-sau-nee, Iroquois.* Rochester, NY: Sage & Brother, Publishers. (This classic book, often called *League of the Iroquois,* has been reprinted many times and is still available.)

Morrison, David, and Georges-Hébert Germain. 1995. *Inuit: Glimpses of an Arctic Past.* Quebec: Canadian Museum of Civilization.

Morrison, Dorothy Nafus. 1990. *Chief Sarah: Sarah Winnemucca's Fight for Indian Rights* (2nd ed.). Portland: Oregon Historical Society Press.

Moss, Madonna L., and Jon M. Erlandson. 1992. Forts, Refuge Rocks, and Defensive Sites: The Antiquity of Warfare Along the North Pacific Coast of North America. *Arctic Anthropology* 29(2):73–90.

———. 1995. Reflections on North American Pacific Coast Prehistory. *Journal of World Prehistory* 9(1):1–45.

Muller, Jon. 1986. *Archaeology of the Lower Ohio River Valley.* Orlando: Academic Press.

Mulroy, Kevin. 1993. *Freedom on the Border: The Seminole Maroons in Florida, the Indian Territory, Chahuila, and Texas.* Lubbock: Texas Tech University Press.

Murie, James R. 1914. *Pawnee Indian Societies.* New York: American Museum of Natural History Anthropological Papers 9(7).

———. 1989. *Ceremonies of the Pawnee.* Lincoln: University of Nebraska Press (originally published as Smithsonian Contributions to Anthropology No. 27, 1981).

Nelson, Richard K. 1973. *Hunters of the Northern Forest.* Chicago: University of Chicago Press.

Newman, Peter C. 1989. *Empire of the Bay.* Toronto: Viking Studio Books.

Nichols, Roger L. (ed.). 1999. *The American Indian: Past and Present* (5th ed.). New York: McGraw-Hill.

Nicklas, T. Dale. 1994. Linguistic Provinces of the Southeast at the Time of Columbus. In: *Perspectives on the Southeast: Linguistics, Archaeology, and Ethnohistory,* Patricia B. Kwachka, ed., pp. 1–13. Athens: University of Georgia Press.

Niezen, Ronald. 1998. *Defending the Land: Sovereignty and Forest Life in James Bay Cree Society.* Boston: Allyn and Bacon.

Noble, William C. 1981. Prehistory of the Great Slave Lake and Great Bear Lake Region. In: *Handbook of North*

American Indians, Vol. 6, Subarctic, June Helm, ed., pp. 97–106. Washington: Smithsonian Institution.

O'Brien, Patricia J. 1989. Cahokia: The Political Capital of the "Ramey" State? *North American Archaeologist* 10(4):275–292.

Okada, Hiroaki. 1997. Changes in Aleut Culture During the Russian Period. *Bulletin of the Hokkaido Museum of Northern Peoples* 6:1–7 (in Japanese, summary in English).

Olsen, James S., and Raymond Wilson. 1984. *Native Americans in the Twentieth Century*. Provo: Brigham Young University Press.

Opler, Morris E. 1983. Chiricahua Apache. In: *Handbook of North American Indians, Vol. 10, Southwest*, Alfonso Ortiz, ed., pp. 401–418. Washington: Smithsonian Institution.

Ortiz, Alfonso (ed.). 1979. *Handbook of North American Indians, Vol. 9, Southwest*. Washington: Smithsonian Institution.

———. 1983. *Handbook of North American Indians, Vol. 10, Southwest*. Washington: Smithsonian Institution.

Oswalt, Wendell H. 1999. *Eskimos and Explorers*. (2nd ed.). Lincoln: University of Nebraska Press.

Oswalt, Wendell H., and Sharlotte Neely. 2002. *This Land Was Theirs: A Study of Native Americans* (7th ed.). Boston: McGraw-Hill Mayfield.

Page, Suzanne, and Jake Page. 1994. *Hopi* (2nd ed.). New York: Harry N. Abrams, Inc.

Parezo, Nancy J. 1983. *Navajo Sandpainting: From Religious Act to Commercial Art*. Tucson: University of Arizona Press.

———. 1996a. The Hopis: Hopivotskwani, the Hopi Path of Life. In: *Paths of Life: American Indians of the Southwest and Northern Mexico*, Thomas E. Sheridan and Nancy J. Parezo, eds., pp. 237–266. Tucson: University of Arizona Press.

———. 1996b. The Diné (Navajos): Sheep is Life. In: *Paths of Life: American Indians of the Southwest and Northern Mexico*, Thomas E. Sheridan and Nancy J. Parezo, eds., pp. 3–33. Tucson: University of Arizona Press.

Parker, Arthur C. 1919. *The Life of General Ely S. Parker: Last Grand Sachem of the Iroquois and General Grant's Military Secretary*. Buffalo: Buffalo Historical Society. Reprinted 1985. New York: AMS Press.

Parks, Douglas R. 1978. James R. Murie, Pawnee, 1862–1921. In: *American Indian Intellectuals*, Margot Liberty, ed., pp. 74–89. Proceedings of the American Ethnological Society. St. Paul: West Publishing Co.

———. 2001. Pawnee. In: *Handbook of North American Indians, Vol. 13, Plains*, Raymond J. DeMallie, ed., pp. 515–547. Washington: Smithsonian Institution.

Parlowe, Anita. 1988. *Cry, Sacred Ground*. Washington, D.C.: Christic Institute.

Parman, Donald L. 1984. Inconstant Advocacy: The Erosion of Indian Fishing Rights in the Pacific Northwest, 1933–1956. *Pacific Historical Review* 53:163–189.

Parmenter, Jon William. 1997. Pontiac's War: Forging New Links in the Anglo-Iroquois Covenant Chain, 1758–1766. *Ethnohistory* 44(4):617–654.

Passin, Herbert. 1942. Sorcery as a Phase of Tarahumara Economic Relations. *Man* 42(1):11–15.

Payment, Diane Paulette. 2001. Plains Métis. In: *Handbook of North American Indians, Vol. 13, Plains*, Raymond J. DeMallie, ed., pp. 661–676. Washington: Smithsonian Institution.

Pego, Christina M., Robert F. Hill, Glenn W. Solomon, Robert M. Chisholm, and Suzanne E. Ivey. 1999. Tobacco, Culture, and Health Among American Indians: A Historical Review. In: *Contemporary Native American Cultural Issues*, Duane Champagne, ed., pp. 245–262. Walnut Creek, CA: AltaMira Press.

Pennington, Campbell W. 1963. *The Tarahumara of Mexico: Their Environment and Material Culture*. Salt Lake City: University of Utah Press.

———. 1983. Tarahumara. In: *Handbook of North American Indians, Vol. 10, Southwest*, Alfonso Ortiz, ed., pp. 276–289. Washington: Smithsonian Institution.

Perdue, Theda. 1989. *The Cherokee*. New York: Chelsea House Publishers.

———. 1998. *Cherokee Women: Gender and Culture Change, 1700–1835*. Lincoln: University of Nebraska Press.

———. 1997. Writing the Ethnohistory of Native Women. In: *Rethinking American Indian History*, Donald L. Fixico, ed., pp. 73–86. Albuquerque: University of New Mexico Press.

Perdue, Theda, and Michael D. Green. 2001. *The Columbia Guide to American Indians of the Southeast*. New York: Columbia University Press.

Peregoy, Robert M. 1999. Nebraska's Landmark Repatriation Law: A Study of Cross-Cultural Conflict and Resolution. In: *Contemporary Native American Political Issues*, Troy R. Johnson, ed., pp. 229–274. Walnut Creek, CA: AltaMira Press.

Perttula, Timothy K. 1991. European Contact and Its Effects on Aboriginal Caddoan Populations Between A.D. 1520 and A.D. 1680. In: *Columbian Consequences, Vol. 3, The Spanish Borderlands in Pan-American Perspective*, David H. Thomas, ed., pp. 501–518. Washington: Smithsonian Institution Press.

Peters, Virginia Bergman. 2000. *Women of the Earth Lodges: Tribal Life on the Plains*. Norman: University of Oklahoma Press.

Pevar, Stephen L. 1997. *The Rights of American Indians and Their Tribes: American Civil Liberties Union, Handbooks for Young Americans*. New York: Puffin Books.

Pflüg, Melissa A. 1996. Pimadaziwin: Contemporary Rituals in Odawa Community. *American Indian Quarterly* 20(4):489–513.

———. 1998. *Ritual and Myth in Odawa Revitalization: Reclaiming a Sovereign Place*. Norman: University of Oklahoma Press.

Phillips, David A., Jr. 1989. Prehistory of Chihuahua and Sonora, Mexico. *Journal of World Prehistory* 3(4):373–401.

Phillips, George Harwood. 1993. *Indians and Intruders in Central California 1769–1849*. Norman: University of Oklahoma Press.

Philp, Kenneth R. 1977. *John Collier's Crusade for Indian Reform 1920–1954*. Tucson: University of Arizona Press.

Plog, Fred. 1979. Prehistory: Western Anasazi. In: *Handbook of North American Indians, Vol. 9, Southwest*, Alfonzo Ortiz, ed., pp. 108–130. Washington: Smithsonian Institution.

Plog, Stephen. 1997. *Ancient Peoples of the American Southwest*. London: Thames and Hudson.

Pokotylo, David L., and Donald Mitchell. 1998. Prehistory of the Northern Plateau. In: *Handbook of North American Indians, Vol. 12, Plateau*, Deward E. Walker, Jr., ed., pp. 81–102. Washington: Smithsonian Institution.

Polzer, Charles W. 1976. *Rules and Precepts of the Jesuit Missions of Northwestern New Spain*. Tucson: University of Arizona Press.

Polzer, Charles W., Thomas H. Naylor, Thomas E. Sheridan, and Diana Hadley (eds.). 1991. *The Jesuit Missions of Northern Mexico*. New York: Garland Publishing.

Porter, Frank W., III. 1988. *The Bureau of Indian Affairs*. New York: Chelsea House Publishers.

——. 1990. Indians of North America: Conflict and Survival. In: *Federal Indian Policy*, by Lawrence C. Kelly, pp. 7–11. New York: Chelsea House Publishers.

Powell, Mary Lucas. 1992. Health and Disease in the Late Prehistoric Southeast. In: *Disease and Demography in the Americas*, John W. Verano and Douglas H. Ubelaker, eds., pp. 41–53. Washington: Smithsonian Institution Press.

Powell, Peter J. 1980. *The Cheyennes, Ma?heo?o s 'eo↓ple: a çritical вibliography*. вloomington: ɪndiɬana ᴜniversity 'ress.

Powers, Stephen. 1877. *Tribes of California*. Berkeley: University of California Press.

Preston, Richard J. 1981. East Main Cree. In: *Handbook of North American Indians, Vol. 6, Subarctic*, June Helm, ed., pp. 196–207. Washington: Smithsonian Institution.

Preston, William L. 2002. Portents of Plague from California's Protohistoric Past. *Ethnohistory* 49(1):69–121.

Pritzker, Barry M. 1998. *Native Americans: An Encyclopedia of History, Culture, and Peoples* (2 vols.). Santa Barbara: ABC-CLIO.

Prucha, Francis Paul. 1984. *The Great Father: The United States Government and the American Indians* (2 vols.). Lincoln: University of Nebraska Press.

——. 1994. *American Indian Treaties: The History of a Political Anomaly*. Berkeley: University of California Press.

Quinn, Arthur. 1997. *Hell with the Fire Out: A History of the Modoc War*. Boston: Faber and Faber, Inc.

Quinn, David B. 1974. *England and the Discovery of America, 1481–1620*. New York: Alfred A. Knopf.

Raat, W. Dirk, and George R. Janecᵛek. 1996. *Mexico's Sierra Tarahumara: A Photohistory of the People of the Edge*. Norman: University of Oklahoma Press.

Ramenofsky, Ann F. 1987. *Vectors of Death: The Archaeology of European Contact*. Albuquerque: University of New Mexico Press.

Ray, Arthur J. 1974. *Indians in the Fur Trade: Their Role as Trappers, Hunters, and Middlemen in the Lands Southwest of Hudson Bay, 1660–1870*. Toronto: University of Toronto Press.

Ray, Dorothy Jean. 1996. *A Legacy of Arctic Art*. Seattle: University of Washington Press.

Ray, Verne F. 1938. Tribal Distributions in Eastern Oregon and Adjacent Regions. *American Anthropologist* 40(3):384–415.

——. 1939. *Cultural Relations in the Plateau of Northwestern America*. Los Angeles: Southwest Museum, Frederick W. Hodge Anniversary Fund, Vol. 3.

——. 1942. Culture Element Distributions: The Plateau. *University of California Anthropological Records* 8(2).

——. 1963. *Primitive Pragmatists: The Modoc Indians of Northern California*. Washington: American Ethnological Society Monograph No. 38.

Reddy, Marlita A. (ed.). 1995. *Statistical Record of Native North Americans* (2nd ed.). Detroit: Gale Research Inc.

Reichard, Gladys A. 1928. *Social Life of the Navajo Indians*. New York: Columbia University Contributions to Anthropology 7.

——. 1934. *Spider Woman: A Story of Navajo Weavers and Chanters*. New York: Macmillan. Reprinted 1997. Albuquerque: University of New Mexico Press.

——. 1950. *Navaho Religion: A Study of Symbolism* (2 vols.). New York: Pantheon Books (reprinted in one volume by Princeton University Press, 1970).

Reid, Jefferson, and Stephanie Whittlesey. 1997. *The Archaeology of Ancient Arizona*. Tucson: University of Arizona Press.

Rhodes, Richard A., and Evelyn M. Todd. 1981. Subarctic Algonquian Languages. In: *Handbook of North American Indians, Vol. 6, Subarctic*, June Helm, ed., pp. 52–66. Washington: Smithsonian Institution.

Richter, Daniel K. 1992. *The Ordeal of the Longhouse: The Peoples of the Iroquois League in the Era of European Colonization*. Chapel Hill: University of North Carolina Press.

Rigby, Bruce, John MacDonald, and Leah Otak. 2000. The Inuit of Nunavut, Canada. In: *Endangered Peoples of the Arctic: Struggles to Survive and Thrive*, Milton M. R. Freeman, ed., pp. 93–112. Westport, CT: Greenwood Press.

Riley, Carroll L. 1999. *The Kachina and the Cross: Indians and Spaniards in the Early Southwest*. Salt Lake City: University of Utah Press.

Riley, Glenda. 1997. The Historiography of American Indian and Other Western Women. In: *Rethinking American Indian History*, Donald L. Fixico, ed., pp. 43–70. Albuquerque: University of New Mexico Press.

Rink, Oliver A. 1986. *Holland on the Hudson: An Economic and Social History of Dutch New York*. Ithaca: Cornell University Press.

Roca, Paul M. 1979. *Spanish Jesuit Churches in Mexico's Tarahumara*. Tucson: University of Arizona Press.

Roessel, Robert A., Jr. 1983. Navajo History, 1850–1923. In: *Handbook of North American Indians, Vol. 10, Southwest*, Alfonso Ortiz, ed., pp. 506–523. Washington: Smithsonian Institution.

Roessel, Ruth. 1983. Navajo Arts and Crafts. In: *Handbook of North American Indians, Vol. 10, Southwest*, Alfonso Ortiz, ed., pp. 592–604. Washington: Smithsonian Institution.

Rogers, Edward S. 1981. History of Ethnological Research in the Subarctic Shield and Mackenzie Borderlands. In: *Handbook of North American Indians, Vol. 6, Subarctic*, June Helm, ed., pp. 30–34. Washington: Smithsonian Institution.

Rogers, Edward S., and Eleanor Leacock. 1981. Montagnais-Naskapi. In: *Handbook of North American Indians, Vol. 6, Subarctic*, June Helm, ed., pp. 169–189. Washington: Smithsonian Institution.

Rogers, Edward S., and James G. E. Smith. 1981. Environment and Culture in the Shield and Mackenzie Borderlands. In: *Handbook of North American Indians, Vol. 6, Subarctic,* June Helm, ed., pp. 130–145. Washington: Smithsonian Institution.

Rogers, Edward S., and J. Garth Taylor. 1981. Northern Ojibwa. In: *Handbook of North American Indians, Vol. 6, Subarctic,* June Helm, ed., pp. 231–243. Washington: Smithsonian Institution.

Rohner, Ronald P., and Evelyn C. Bettauer. 1986. *The Kwakiutl: Indians of British Columbia.* Prospect Heights, IL: Waveland Press.

Roll, Tom E., and Steven Hackenberger. 1998. Prehistory of the Eastern Plateau. In: *Handbook of North American Indians, Vol. 12, Plateau,* Deward E. Walker, Jr., ed., pp. 120–137. Washington: Smithsonian Institution.

Roscoe, Will. 1998. *Changing Ones: Third and Fourth Genders in Native North America.* New York: St. Martin's Press.

Rountree, Helen C. 1989. *The Powhatan Indians of Virginia: Their Traditional Culture.* Norman: University of Oklahoma Press.

———. 1990. *Pocahontas's People: The Powhatan Indians of Virginia Through Four Centuries.* Norman: University of Oklahoma Press.

Rountree, Helen C., and Thomas C. Davidson. 1997. *Eastern Shore Indians of Virginia and Maryland.* Charlottesville: University Press of Virginia.

Rowlands, Peter, Hyrum Johnson, Eric Ritter, and Albert Endo. 1982. The Mojave Desert. In: *Reference Handbook on the Deserts of North America,* Gordon L. Bender, ed., pp. 103–162. Westport, CT: Greenwood Press.

Rusco, Elmer R., and Mary K. Rusco 1986. Tribal Politics. In: *Handbook of North American Indians, Vol. 11, Great Basin,* Warren L. d'Azevedo, ed., pp. 558–572. Washington: Smithsonian Institution.

Rushforth, Scott, and Steadman Upham. 1992. *A Hopi Social History: Anthropological Perspectives on Sociocultural Persistence and Change.* Austin: University of Texas Press.

Saladin d'Anglure, Bernard. 1984a. Inuit of Quebec. In: *Handbook of North American Indians, Vol. 5, Arctic,* David Damas, ed., pp. 476–507. Washington: Smithsonian Institution.

———. 1984b Contemporary Inuit of Quebec. In: *Handbook of North American Indians, Vol. 5, Arctic,* David Damas, ed., pp. 683–688. Washington: Smithsonian Institution.

Salisbury, Richard F. 1986. *A Homeland for the Cree: Regional Development in James Bay 1971–1981.* Kingston: McGill-Queen's University Press.

Samuels, Stephan R. (ed.). 1991. *Ozette Archaeological Project Research Reports, Vol. 1, House Structure and Floor Midden.* Pullman: Washington State University, Department of Anthropology Reports of Investigations 63.

Sando, Joe S. 1979. The Pueblo Revolt. In: *Handbook of North American Indians, Vol. 9, Southwest,* Alfonso Ortiz, ed., pp. 194–197. Washington: Smithsonian Institution.

Sandoz, Mari. 1953. *Cheyenne Autumn.* New York: McGraw-Hill.

Sassaman, Kenneth E., and David G. Anderson (eds.). 1996. *Archaeology of the Mid-Holocene Southeast.* Gainesville: University Press of Florida.

Sattler, Richard A. 1995. Women's Status Among the Muskogee and Cherokee. In: *Women and Power in Native North America,* Laura F. Klein and Lillian A. Ackerman, eds., pp. 214–229. Norman: University of Oklahoma Press.

Scarry, John F. (ed.). 1996. *Political Structure and Change in the Prehistoric Southeastern United States.* Gainesville: University Press of Florida.

Schaafsma, Polly (ed.). 1994. *Kachinas in the Pueblo World.* Albuquerque: University of New Mexico Press.

Schiffer, Nancy N. 1991. *Navajo Weaving Today.* West Chester, PA: Schiffer Publishing.

Schroeder, Albert H. 1979. Prehistory: Hakataya. In: *Handbook of North American Indians, Vol. 9, Southwest,* Alfonzo Ortiz, ed., pp. 100–107. Washington: Smithsonian Institution.

Schwartz, Warren E. 1989. *The Last Contrary: The Story of Wesley Whiteman (Black Bear).* Sioux Falls: Center for Western Studies.

Schwarz, Maureen Trudelle. 1997. Unraveling the Anchoring Cord: Navajo Relocation, 1974 to 1996. *American Anthropologist* 99(1):43–55.

Scott, Douglas D., P. Willey, and Melissa A. Connor. 1998. *They Died with Custer: Soldier's Bones of the Little Bighorn.* Norman: University of Oklahoma Press.

Scott, Robert A. 1993. *Chief Joseph and the Nez Percés.* New York: Facts on File.

Secoy, Frank R. 1953. *Changing Military Patterns on the Great Plains.* Monographs of the American Ethnological Society No. 21.

Settipane, Guy A. (ed.). 1995. *Columbus and the New World: Medical Implications.* Providence, RI: OceanSide Publications.

Shepardson, Mary. 1963. *Najavo Ways in Government: A Study in Political Process.* American Anthropological Association Memoir 96.

———. 1982. The Status of Navajo Women. *American Indian Quarterly* 6(1–2):149–169.

———. 1983. Development of Navajo Tribal Government. In: *Handbook of North American Indians, Vol. 10, Southwest,* Alfonso Ortiz, ed., pp. 624–635. Washington: Smithsonian Institution.

———. 1995. The Gender Status of Navajo Women. In: *Women and Power in Native North America,* Laura F. Klein and Lillian A. Ackerman, eds., pp. 159–176. Norman: University of Oklahoma Press.

Sheridan, Thomas E. 1996. The Rarámuri (Tarahumaras). When We Walk in Circles. In: *Paths of Life: American Indians of the Southwest and Northern Mexico,* Thomas E. Sheridan and Nancy J. Parezo, eds., pp. 141–161. Tucson: University of Arizona Press.

Sheridan, Thomas E., and Thomas H. Naylor (eds.). 1979. *Rarámuri: A Tarahumara Colonial Chronicle 1607–1791.* Flagstaff: Northland Press.

Sheridan, Thomas E., and Nancy J. Parezo (eds.). 1996. *Paths of Life: American Indians of the Southwest and Northern Mexico.* Tucson: University of Arizona Press.

Sheridan, Thomas E., Charles W. Polzer, Thomas H. Naylor, and Diana Hadley (eds.). 1991. *The Franciscan Missions of Northern Mexico*. New York: Garland Publishing.

Sherrow, Victoria. 1997. *Cherokee Nation v. Georgia*. Springfield, NJ: Enslow Publishers, Inc.

Shimkin, Demitri B. 1986. Introduction of the Horse. In: *Handbook of North American Indians, Vol. 11, Great Basin*, Warren L. d'Azevedo, ed., pp. 517–524. Washington: Smithsonian Institution.

Shipley, William F. 1978. Native Languages of California. In: *Handbook of North American Indians, Vol. 8, California*, Robert F. Heizer, ed., pp. 80–90. Washington: Smithsonian Institution.

Sievers, Maurice L., and Jeffrey R. Fisher. 1981. Diseases of North American Indians. In: *Biocultural Aspects of Disease*, Henry Rothschild, ed., pp. 191–252. New York: Academic Press.

Sigler, William F., and John W. Sigler. 1987. *Fishes of the Great Basin: A Natural History*. Reno: University of Nevada Press.

Sills, Marc. 1986. Relocation Reconsidered: Competing Explanations of the Navajo–Hopi Land Settlement Act of 1974. *Journal of Ethnic Studies* 14(3):53–83.

Silverstein, Michael. 1978. Yokuts: Introduction. In: *Handbook of North American Indians, Vol. 8, California*, Robert F. Heizer, ed., pp. 446–447. Washington: Smithsonian Institution.

Slickpoo, Allen P., Jr., and Deward E. Walker, Jr. 1973. *Noon Nee-Me-Poo (We, the Nez Perces): Culture and History of the Nez Perces, Vol. 1*. Lapwai, ID: The Nez Perce Tribe of Idaho.

Slobodin, Richard. 1981. Subarctic Métis. In: *Handbook of North American Indians, Vol. 6, Subarctic*, June Helm, ed., pp. 361–371. Washington: Smithsonian Institution.

Smith, Bruce D. 1986. The Archaeology of the Southeastern United States: From Dalton to de Soto, 10,500–500 B.P. In: *Advances in World Archaeology, Vol. 5*, Fred Wendorf and Angela E. Close, eds., pp. 1–92. Orlando: Academic Press.

Smith, D. Z. 1852. Description of the Manners and Customs of the Pawnee Indians. In: *Moravian Church Miscellany*, pp. 86–94. Bethlehem, PA: Church of the United Brethren.

Smith, F. Todd. 1995. *The Caddo Indians: Tribes at the Convergence of Empires, 1542–1854*. College Station: Texas A & M University Press.

Smith, Huston, and Reuben Snake (eds.). 1997. *One Nation Under God: The Triumph of the Native American Church*. Santa Fe, NM: Clear Light Publishers.

Smith, James G. E. 1981. Western Woods Cree. In: *Handbook of North American Indians, Vol. 6, Subarctic*, June Helm, ed., pp. 256–270. Washington: Smithsonian Institution.

———. 1987 Canada—The Lubicon Lake Cree. *Cultural Survival Quarterly* 11(3):61–62.

Smith, Marvin T. 1994. Aboriginal Depopulation in the Postcontact Southeast. In: *The Forgotten Centuries: Indians and Europeans in the American South, 1521–1704*, Charles Hudson and Carmen Chaves Tesser, eds., pp. 257–275. Athens: University of Georgia Press.

Smith, Paul Chaat, and Robert Allen Warrior. 1996. *Like A Hurricane: The American Indian Movement from Alcatraz to Wounded Knee*. New York: The New Press.

Snipp, C. Matthew. 1989. *American Indians: The First of This Land*. New York: Russell Sage Foundation.

Snow, Dean R. 1978. Late Prehistory of the East Coast. In: *Handbook of North American Indians, Vol. 15, Northeast*, Bruce Trigger, ed., pp. 58–69. Washington: Smithsonian Institution.

———. 1980. *The Archaeology of New England*. New York: Academic Press.

———. 1994. *The Iroquois*. Oxford: Blackwell.

Snow, Dean R. (ed.). 1981. *Foundations of Northeastern Archaeology*. New York: Academic Press.

Snow, Dean R., and Kim M. Lanphear. 1988. European Contact and Indian Depopulation in the Northeast: The Timing of the First Epidemics. *Ethnohistory* 35(1):15–33.

Snow, Dean R., Charles T. Gehring, and William A. Starna (eds.). 1994. In *Mohawk Country: Early Narratives about a Native People*. Syracuse: Syracuse University Press.

Snow, Jeanne H. 1981. Ingalik. In: *Handbook of North American Indians, Vol. 6, Subarctic*, June Helm, ed., pp. 602–617. Washington: Smithsonian Institution.

Soleri, Daniela, and David A. Cleveland. 1993. Hopi Crop Diversity and Change. *Journal of Ethnobiology* 13(2):203–231.

Sonneborn, Liz. 1998. *A to Z of Native American Women*. New York: Facts on File.

Speck, Frank G., and Leonard Broom. 1983. *Cherokee Dance and Drama*. Norman: University of Oklahoma Press.

Spencer, Robert F., and Jesse D. Jennings. 1977. *The Native Americans* (2nd ed.). New York: Harper & Row.

Spicer, Edward H. 1962. *Cycles of Conquest: The Impact of Spain, Mexico, and the United States on the Indians of the Southwest, 1533–1960*. Tucson: University of Arizona Press.

———. 1980. *The Yaquis: A Cultural History*. Tucson: University of Arizona Press.

Spier, Robert F. G. 1978. Foothill Yokuts. In: *Handbook of North American Indians, Vol. 8, California*, Robert F. Heizer, ed., pp. 471–484. Washington: Smithsonian Institution.

Spinden, Herbert J. 1908. The Nez Percé Indians. *Memoirs of the American Anthropological Association* No. 2:165–274.

Spradley, James P. (ed.). 1972. *Guests Never Leave Hungry: The Autobiography of James Sewid, a Kwakiutl Indian*. Montreal: McGill-Queen's University Press.

Stands in Timber, John, and Margot Liberty. 1998. *Cheyenne Memories* (2nd ed.). New Haven: Yale University Press.

Stanislawski, Michael B. 1979. Hopi-Tewa. In: *Handbook of North American Indians, Vol. 9, Southwest*, Alfonso Ortiz, ed., pp. 587–602. Washington: Smithsonian Institution.

Stannard, David E. 1992. *American Holocaust: Columbus and the Conquest of the New World*. Oxford: Oxford University Press.

Stapp, Darby C., and Michael S. Burney. 2002. *Tribal Cultural Resource Management: The Full Circle to Stewardship*. Walnut Creek: AltaMira Press.

Stephen, Alexander M. 1936. Hopi Journal of Alexander M. Stephen, 2 parts, Elsie C. Parsons, ed. Columbia University Contributions to Anthropology Vol. 23.

Steward, Julian H. 1933. Ethnography of the Owens Valley Paiute. *University of California Publications in American Archaeology and Ethnology 33*(3).

———. 1936. Myths of the Owens Valley Paiute. *University of California Publications in American Archaeology and Ethnology 34*(5).

———. 1938. *Basin-Plateau Aboriginal Sociopolitical Groups.* Bureau of American Ethnology Bulletin 120.

Stewart, Hilary. 1993. *Looking at Totem Poles.* Seattle: University of Washington Press.

Stewart, Omer C. 1980. The Ghost Dance. In: *Anthropology on the Great Plains,* W. Raymond Wood and Margot Liberty, eds., pp. 179–187. Lincoln: University of Nebraska Press.

———. 1986. The Peyote Religion. In: *Handbook of North American Indians, Vol. 11, Great Basin,* Warren L. d'Azevedo, ed., pp. 673–681. Washington: Smithsonian Institution.

———. 1987. *Peyote Religion: A History.* Norman: University of Oklahoma Press.

Stodder, Ann L. W., and Debra L. Martin. 1992. Health and Disease in the Southwest Before and After Spanish Contact. In: *Disease and Demography in the Americas,* John W. Verano and Douglas H. Ubelaker, eds., pp. 55–73. Washington: Smithsonian Institution Press.

Struever, Stuart, and Felicia Antonelli Holton. 1979. *Koster: Americans in Search of their Prehistoric Past.* Garden City, NY: Anchor Press.

Surtees, Robert J. 1980. *Canadian Indian Policies: A Critical Bibliography.* Bloomington: Indiana University Press.

Suttles, Wayne. 1990a. Introduction. In: *Handbook of North American Indians, Vol. 7, Northwest Coast,* Wayne Suttles, ed., pp. 1–15. Washington: Smithsonian Institution.

———. 1990b. Environment. In: *Handbook of North American Indians, Vol. 7, Northwest Coast,* Wayne Suttles, ed., pp. 16–29. Washington: Smithsonian Institution.

———. 1990c. History of Research: Early Sources. In: *Handbook of North American Indians, Vol. 7, Northwest Coast,* Wayne Suttles, ed., pp. 70–72. Washington: Smithsonian Institution.

Suttles, Wayne (ed.). 1990. *Handbook of North American Indians, Vol. 7, Northwest Coast.* Washington: Smithsonian Institution.

Suttles, Wayne, and Aldona Jonaitis. 1990. History of Research in Ethnology. In: *Handbook of North American Indians, Vol. 7, Northwest Coast,* Wayne Suttles, ed., pp. 73–87. Washington: Smithsonian Institution.

Sutton, Imre (ed.). 1985. *Irredeemable America: The Indians' Estate and Land Claims.* Albuquerque: University of New Mexico Press.

Sutton, Mark Q. 1988. *Insects as Food: Aboriginal Entomophagy in the Great Basin.* Menlo Park, CA: Ballena Press Anthropological Papers No. 33.

Svingen, Orlan J. 1992. The Bounties of Nebraska Twice Removed. *American Indian Culture and Research Journal 16*(2):121–137.

———. 1993. *The Northern Cheyenne Indian Reservation 1877–1900.* Niwot, CO: University Press of Colorado.

Swanton, John R. 1911. *Indian Tribes of the Lower Mississippi Valley and Adjacent Coast of the Gulf of Mexico.* Bureau of American Ethnology Bulletin 43.

———. 1942. *Source Material on the History and Ethnology of the Caddo Indians.* Bureau of American Ethnology Bulletin 132 (reprinted by the University of Oklahoma Press, 1996).

———. 1946. *The Indians of the Southeastern United States.* Bureau of American Ethnology Bulletin 137.

———. 1953. *The Indian Tribes of North America.* Bureau of American Ethnology Bulletin 145.

Swidler, Nina, Kurt E. Dongoske, Roger Anyon, and Alan S. Downer (eds.). 1997. *Native Americans and Archaeologists: Stepping Stones to Common Ground.* Walnut Creek: AltaMira Press.

Swinton, George. 1992. *Sculpture of the Inuit* (revised ed.). Toronto: McClelland and Stewart, Inc.

Szathmary, Emöke J. E. 1984. Human Biology of the Arctic. In: *Handbook of North American Indians, Vol. 5, Arctic,* David Damas, ed., pp. 64–71. Washington: Smithsonian Institution.

Taylor, Colin F. 1994. *The Plains Indians: A Cultural and Historical View of the North American Plains Tribes of the Pre-Reservation Period.* London: Salamander Books.

Taylor, Marian W. 1993. *Chief Joseph: Nez Perce Leader.* New York: Chelsea House Publishers.

Teit, J. A. 1930. The Salishan Tribes of the Western Plateau. *Annual Report of the Bureau of American Ethnology 45:295–396.*

Teiwes, Helga. 1989. Contemporary Development in Hopi Kachina Doll Carving. *American Indian Art Magazine 14:40–51.*

Thomas, David Hurst. 1983. The Archaeology of Monitor Valley 1: Epistemology. *American Museum of Natural History Anthropological Papers 58*(1).

———. 1990. The Spanish Missions of La Florida: An Overview. In: *Columbian Consequences, Vol. 2, Archaeological and Historical Perspectives on the Spanish Borderlands East,* David Hurst Thomas, ed., pp. 357–397. Washington: Smithsonian Institution Press.

———. 1991. Harvesting Ramona's Garden: Life in California's Mythical Mission Past. In: *Columbian Consequences, Vol. 3, The Spanish Borderlands in Pan-American Perspective,* David H. Thomas, ed., pp. 119–157. Washington: Smithsonian Institution Press.

———. 1994. *Exploring Ancient Native America.* New York: Macmillan.

Thomas, David Hurst (ed.). 1989. *Columbian Consequences, Vol. 1, Archaeological and Historical Perspectives on the Spanish Borderlands West.* Washington: Smithsonian Institution Press.

Thomas, David Hurst, Lorann S. A. Pendleton, and Stephen C. Cappannari. 1986. Western Shoshone. In: *Handbook of North American Indians, Vol. 11, Great Basin,* Warren L. d'Azevedo, ed., pp. 262–283. Washington: Smithsonian Institution.

Thompson, Laura, and Alice Joseph. 1944. *The Hopi Way.* Lawrence, KS: The Haskell Institute. Reprinted 1947. Chicago: University of Chicago Press.

Thompson, Laurence C., and M. Dale Kinkade. 1990. Languages. In: *Handbook of North American Indians,*

Vol. 7, Northwest Coast, Wayne Suttles, ed., pp. 30–51. Washington: Smithsonian Institution.

Thompson, William N. 1996. *Native American Issues: A Reference Handbook.* Santa Barbara: ABC-CLIO.

Thornton, Russell. 1987. *American Indian Holocaust and Survival: A Population History Since 1492.* Norman: University of Oklahoma Press.

———. 1997. Aboriginal North American Population and Rates of Decline, ca. A.D. 1500–1900. *Current Anthropology* 38(2):310–315.

———. 2000. Population History of Native North Americans. In: *A Population History of North America,* Michael R. Haines and Richard H. Steckel, eds., pp. 9–50. Cambridge, UK: Cambridge University Press.

Thornton, Russell (ed.). 1998. *Studying Native America: Problems and Prospects.* Madison: University of Wisconsin Press.

Thornton, Russell, Jonathan Warren, and Tim Miller. 1992. Depopulation in the Southeast after 1492. In: *Disease and Demography in the Americas,* John W. Verano and Douglas H. Ubelaker, eds., pp. 187–195. Washington: Smithsonian Institution Press.

Thwaites, Reuben Gold (ed.). 1904. *Original Journals of the Lewis and Clark Expedition, 1804–1806.* New York: Antiquarian Press.

Tiller, Veronica E. Velarde. 1996. *Tiller's Guide to Indian Country: Economic Profiles of American Indian Reservations.* Albuquerque: BowArrow Publishing Company.

Timbrook, Jan, John R. Johnson, and David D. Earle. 1982. Vegetation Burning by the Chumash. *Journal of California and Great Basin Anthropology* 4(2):163–186.

Tinker, George E. 1993. *Missionary Conquest: The Gospel and Native American Cultural Genocide.* Minneapolis: Fortress Press.

Titiev, Mischa. 1944. Old Oraibi: A Study of the Hopi Indians of Third Mesa. *Papers of the Peabody Museum of American Archaeology and Ethnology* 22(1).

Tome, Marshall. 1983. The Navajo Nation Today. In: *Handbook of North American Indians, Vol. 10, Southwest,* Alfonso Ortiz, ed., pp. 679–683. Washington: Smithsonian Institution.

Tooker, Elisabeth. 1978a. History of Research. In: *Handbook of North American Indians, Vol. 15, Northeast,* Bruce Trigger, ed., pp. 4–15. Washington: Smithsonian Institution.

———. 1978b. The League of the Iroquois: Its History, Politics, and Ritual. In: *Handbook of North American Indians, Vol. 15, Northeast,* Bruce Trigger, ed., pp. 418–441. Washington: Smithsonian Institution.

———. 1994. *Lewis H. Morgan on Iroquois Material Culture.* Tucson: University of Arizona Press.

Trafzer, Clifford E. 1992. *The Nez Perce.* New York: Chelsea House Publishers.

Trigger, Bruce G. 1985. *Natives and Newcomers: Canada's "Heroic Age" Reconsidered.* Kingston: McGill-Queen's University Press.

———. 1990. *The Huron: Farmers of the North* (2nd ed.). Fort Worth: Holt, Reinhart and Winston.

Trigger, Bruce G. (ed.). 1978. *Handbook of North American Indians, Vol. 15, Northeast.* Washington: Smithsonian Institution.

Trigger, Bruce G., and Wilcomb E. Washburn (eds.). 1996. *The Cambridge History of the Native Peoples of the Americas, Vol. 1, North America* (Parts 1 and 2). Cambridge: Cambridge University Press.

Trimble, Michael K. 1992. The 1832 Inoculation Program on the Missouri River. In: *Disease and Demography in the Americas,* John W. Verano and Douglas H. Ubelaker, eds., pp. 257–264. Washington: Smithsonian Institution Press.

Tuck, James A. 1978a. Regional Cultural Development, 300 B.C. to A.D. 1000. In: *Handbook of North American Indians, Vol. 15, Northeast,* Bruce Trigger, ed., pp. 28–43. Washington: Smithsonian Institution.

———. 1978b. Northern Iroquoian Prehistory. In: *Handbook of North American Indians, Vol. 15, Northeast,* Bruce Trigger, ed., pp. 322–333. Washington: Smithsonian Institution.

Turner, Lucien M. 1888. On the Indians and Eskimos of the Ungava District. *Proceedings and Transactions of the Royal Society of Canada for the Year 1887, Vol. 5,* pp. 99–119. Montreal: Dawson Brothers Publishers.

———. 1894. Ethnology of the Ungava District, Hudson Bay Territory. *Eleventh Annual Report of the Bureau of Ethnology, 1889–90,* pp. 159–350. Washington: Government Printing Office.

Tushingham, Shannon, Jane Hill, and Charles H. McNutt (eds.). 2002. *Histories of Southeastern Archaeology.* Tuscaloosa: University of Alabama Press.

Ubelaker, Douglas H. 1992. North American Indian Population Size: Changing Perspectives. In: *Disease and Demography in the Americas,* John W. Verano and Douglas H. Ubelaker, eds., pp. 169–176. Washington: Smithsonian Institution Press.

Underhill, Ruth M. 1956. *The Navajos.* Norman: University of Oklahoma Press.

———. 1991. *Life in the Pueblos.* Santa Fe, NM: Ancient City Press.

United States Commission on Wartime Relocation and Internment of Civilians. 1982. *Personal Justice Denied* (2 vols.). *Report of the United States Commission on Wartime Relocation and Internment of Civilians.* Washington D.C.: Government Printing Office. Republished 1997. Seattle: University of Washington Press.

Upham, Steadman. 1992. Population and Spanish Contact in the Southwest. In: *Disease and Demography in the Americas,* John W. Verano and Douglas H. Ubelaker, eds., pp. 223–236. Washington: Smithsonian Institution Press.

Utley, Robert M. 1967. *Frontiersmen in Blue: The United States Army and the Indian 1848–1865.* New York: Macmillan.

———. 1973. *Frontier Regulars: The United States Army and the Indian 1866–1891.* New York: Macmillan.

Vane, Sylvia Brakke, and Lowell John Bean. 1990. *California Indians: Primary Resources: A Guide to Manuscripts, Artifacts, Documents, Serials, Music and Illustrations.* Menlo Park, CA: Ballena Press Anthropological Papers No. 36.

VanStone, James W. 1974. *Athapaskan Adaptations: Hunters and Fishermen of the Subarctic Forests.* Chicago: Aldine Publishing Company.

Vaughan, Thomas, and Bill Holm. 1990. *Soft Gold: The Fur Trade & Cultural Exchange on the Northwest Coast of America* (2nd edition). Portland: Oregon Historical Society Press.

Vecsey, Christopher, and William A. Starna (eds.). 1988. *Iroquois Land Claims*. Syracuse: Syracuse University Press.

Veniaminov, I. 1840. Zapiski ob ostrovakh Unalaskinskago otdiela. 3 vols. St. Petersburg: Russian-American Company.

Viola, Herman J. (ed.). 1999. *Little Bighorn Remembered: The Untold Indian Story of Custer's Last Stand*. New York: Times Books.

Voegelin, C. F., F. M. Voegelin, and Laverne Masayesva Jeanne. 1979. Hopi Semantics. In: *Handbook of North American Indians, Vol. 9, Southwest*, Alfonso Ortiz, ed., pp. 581–586. Washington: Smithsonian Institution.

Voth, H. R. 1905. *Traditions of the Hopi*. Chicago: Field Museum of Natural History Publication 96, Anthropological Series, Vol. 8.

Wagner, Sally R. 1992. The Iroquois Influence on Women's Rights. *Akwe:kon Journal* 9(1):4–15.

Waldman, Carl. 2000. *Atlas of the North American Indians*. New York: Facts on File Publications.

———. 2001. *Biographical Dictionary of American Indian History to 1900*. New York: Facts on File.

Walens, Stanley. 1981. *Feasting with Cannibals: An Essay on Kwakiutl Cosmology*. Princeton: Princeton University Press.

———. 1992. *The Kwakiutl*. New York: Chelsea House Publications.

Walker, Deward E., Jr. 1998a. Introduction. In: *Handbook of North American Indians, Vol. 12, Plateau*, Deward E. Walker, Jr., ed., pp. 1–7. Washington: Smithsonian Institution.

———. 1998c. Nez Perce. In: *Handbook of North American Indians, Vol. 12, Plateau*, Deward E. Walker, Jr., ed., pp. 420–438. Washington: Smithsonian Institution.

Walker, Deward E., Jr. (ed.). 1998b. *Handbook of North American Indians, Vol. 12, Plateau*. Washington: Smithsonian Institution.

Walker, Deward E., Jr., and Helen H. Schuster. 1998. Religious Movements. In: *Handbook of North American Indians, Vol. 12, Plateau*, Deward E. Walker, Jr., ed., pp. 499–514. Washington: Smithsonian Institution.

Walker, Phillip L., and John R. Johnson. 1992. Effects of Contact on the Chumash Indians. In: *Disease and Demography in the Americas*, John W. Verano and Douglas H. Ubelaker, eds., pp. 127–139. Washington: Smithsonian Institution Press.

Walker, Phillip L., Patricia Lambert, and Michael J. DeNiro. 1989. The Effects of European Contact on the Health of Alta California Indians. In: *Columbian Consequences, Vol. 1, Archaeological and Historical Perspectives on the Spanish Borderlands West*, David H. Thomas, ed., pp. 303–331. Washington: Smithsonian Institution Press.

Walking Turtle, Eagle. 1989. *Indian America: A Traveler's Companion*. Santa Fe, NM: John Muir.

Wallace, Anthony F. C. 1969. *The Death and Rebirth of the Seneca*. New York: Vintage Books.

———. 1978. Origins of the Longhouse Religion. In: *Handbook of North American Indians, Vol. 15, Northeast*, Bruce Trigger, ed., pp. 442–448. Washington: Smithsonian Institution.

Wallace, Ernest, and E. Adamson Hoebel. 1952. *The Comanches: Lords of the South Plains*. Norman: University of Oklahoma Press.

Wallace, William J. 1978a. Southern Valley Yokuts. In: *Handbook of North American Indians, Vol. 8, California*, Robert F. Heizer, ed., pp. 448–461. Washington: Smithsonian Institution.

———. 1978b. Northern Valley Yokuts. In: *Handbook of North American Indians, Vol. 8, California*, Robert F. Heizer, ed., pp. 462–470. Washington: Smithsonian Institution.

Warhus, Mark. 1997. *Another America: Native American Maps and the History of Our Land*. New York: St. Martin's Press.

Washburn, Wilcomb E. 1973. *The American Indian and the United States: A Documentary History* (4 vols.). New York: Random House.

Washburn, Wilcomb E. (ed.) 1988. *Handbook of North American Indians, Vol. 4, History of Indian-White Relations*. Washington: Smithsonian Institution.

Weatherford, Jack. 1988. *Indian Givers: How the Indians of the Americas Transformed the World*. New York: Crown Publishers.

———. 1991. *Native Roots: How the Indians Enriched America*. New York: Fawcett Columbine.

Weaver, Hilary N. 2001. Indigenous Identity: What Is It, and Who *Really* Has It? *American Indian Quarterly* 25(2):240–255.

Webster, Gloria Cranmer. 1990. Kwakiutl Since 1980. In: *Handbook of North American Indians, Vol. 7, Northwest Coast*, Wayne Suttles, ed., pp. 387–390. Washington: Smithsonian Institution.

Wedel, Waldo R. 1961. *Prehistoric Man on the Great Plains*. Norman: University of Oklahoma Press.

Wedel, Waldo R., and George C. Frison. 2001. Environment and Subsistence. In: *Handbook of North American Indians, Vol. 13, Plains*, Raymond J. DeMallie, ed., pp. 44–60. Washington: Smithsonian Institution.

Weeks, Philip. 1990. *Farewell My Nation: The American Indian and the United States, 1820–1890*. Arlington Heights, IL: Harlan Davidson, Inc.

Weist, Katherine M. 1980. Plains Indian Women: An Assessment. In: *Anthropology on the Great Plains*, W. Raymond Wood and Margot Liberty, eds., pp. 255–271. Lincoln: University of Nebraska Press.

Weist, Katherine M. (ed.). 1979. *Belle Highwalking: The Narrative of a Northern Cheyenne Woman*. Billings, MT: Montana Council for Indian Education.

Weltfish, Gene. 1965. *The Lost Universe*. New York: Basic Books.

Werner, Oswald, Allen Manning, and Kenneth Y. Begishe. 1983. A Taxonomic View of the Traditional Navajo Universe. In: *Handbook of North American Indians, Vol. 10, Southwest*, Alfonso Ortiz, ed., pp. 579–591. Washington: Smithsonian Institution.

West, Frederick Hadleigh (ed.). 1996. *American Beginnings: The Prehistory and Paleoecology of Beringia*. Chicago: University of Chicago Press.

West, Robert C., and John P. Augelli. 1989. *Middle America: Its Land and Peoples* (3rd ed.). Englewood Cliffs, NJ: Prentice-Hall.

Weston, May Ann. 1996. *Native Americans in the News: Images of Indians in the Twentieth Century Press.* Westport, CT: Greenwood Press.

Weyer, Edward M. 1932. *The Eskimos: Their Environment and Folkways.* New Haven: Yale University Press. Reprinted 1969. Hamdon, CT: Archon Books.

Wheat, Margaret M. 1967. *Survival Arts of the Primitive Paiutes.* Reno: University of Nevada Press.

White, Richard. 1997. Indian People and the Natural World: Asking the Right Questions. In: *Rethinking American Indian History,* Donald L. Fixico, ed., pp. 87–100. Albuquerque: University of New Mexico Press.

Whiteley, Peter M. 1988. *Deliberate Acts: Changing Hopi Culture Through the Oraibi Split.* Tucson: University of Arizona Press.

———. 1997. The End of Anthropology (at Hopi)? In: *Indians and Anthropologists: Vine Deloria, Jr., and the Critique of Anthropology,* Thomas Biolsi and Larry J. Zimmerman, eds., pp. 177–207. Tucson: University of Arizona Press.

———. 1998. *Rethinking Hopi Ethnography.* Washington: Smithsonian Institution Press.

Whiting, Alfred F. 1939. *Ethnobotany of the Hopi.* Flagstaff: Museum of Northern Arizona Bulletin No. 15. Reprinted 1966. Flagstaff, AZ: Northland Press.

Wilke, Philip J. 1988. Bow Staves Harvested from Juniper Trees by Indians of Nevada. *Journal of California and Great Basin Anthropology* 10(1):3–31.

Wilke, Philip J., and Harry W. Lawton. 1976. *The Expedition of Capt. J. W. Davidson from Fort Tejon to the Owens Valley in 1859.* Menlo Park, CA: Ballena Press Publications in Archaeology, Ethnology, and History No. 8.

Wilkins, David E. 1997. *American Indian Sovereignty and the U.S. Supreme Court: The Making of Justice.* Austin: University of Texas Press.

Williams, Kitty. 1994. Return of the Tarahumara. *Native Peoples* 7(3):20–27.

Williams, Walter L. 1986. *The Spirit and the Flesh: Sexual Diversity in American Indian Culture.* Boston: Beacon Press.

Wilson, James. 1998. *The Earth Shall Weep: A History of Native America.* New York: Atlantic Monthly Press.

Wishart, David J. 1979a. *The Fur Trade of the American West: A Geographical Synthesis.* Lincoln: University of Nebraska Press (reprinted in 1992).

———. 1979b. The Dispossession of the Pawnee. *Annals of the Association of American Geographers* 69(3):382–401.

Wissler, Clark. 1948. *North American Indians of the Plains* (3rd ed.). New York: American Museum of Natural History, Handbook Series No. 1.

Witherspoon, Gary. 1981. *Navajo Kinship and Marriage.* Chicago: University of Chicago Press.

———. 1983. Navajo Social Organization. In: *Handbook of North American Indians, Vol. 10, Southwest,* Alfonso Ortiz, ed., pp. 524–535. Washington: Smithsonian Institution.

Wolcott, Harry F. 1967. *A Kwakiutl Village and School.* New York: Holt, Rinehart and Winston.

———. 1996. Perpheral Participation and the Kwakiutl Potlatch. *Anthropology & Education Quarterly* 27(4):467–492.

Wood, John J. 1985. Navajo Livestock Reduction. *Nomadic Peoples* 9:21–31.

Wood, W. Raymond (ed.). 1998. *Archaeology on the Great Plains.* Lawrence: University of Kansas Press.

Woodbury, Anthony C. 1984. Eskimo and Aleut Languages. In: *Handbook of North American Indians, Vol. 5, Arctic,* David Damas, ed., pp. 49–63. Washington: Smithsonian Institution.

Woodcock, George. 1977. *People of the Coast: Indians of the Northwest Coast.* Bloomington: Indiana University Press.

Worth, John E. 1998. *The Timucuan Chiefdoms of Spanish Florida: Volume 1: Assimilation.* Gainesville: University Press of Florida.

Wright, J. Leicht, Jr. 1986. *Creeks and Seminoles: The Destruction and Regeneration of the Muscogulge People.* Lincoln: University of Nebraska Press.

Wright, James V. 1981. Prehistory of the Canadian Shield. In: *Handbook of North American Indians, Vol. 6, Subarctic,* June Helm, ed., pp. 86–96. Washington: Smithsonian Institution.

Wyman, Leland C. 1983. Navajo Ceremonial System. In: *Handbook of North American Indians, Vol. 10, Southwest,* Alfonso Ortiz, ed., pp. 536–557. Washington: Smithsonian Institution.

Yellow Bird, Michael. 1999. What We Want to be Called: Indigenous Peoples' Perspectives on Racial and Ethnic Identity Labels. *American Indian Quarterly* 23(2):1–21.

Zolbrod, Paul G. 1984. *Diné bahane': The Navajo Creation Story.* Albuquerque: University of New Mexico Press.

Index